THE SADDAM TAPES

The Inner Workings of a Tyrant

MW00609037

During the 2003 war that ended Sad(
thousands of hours of secret recordi..g.. -- --
Originally prepared by the Institute for Defense Analyses for the Office of the Undersecretary of Defense for Policy, this study presents annotated transcripts of Iraqi
audio recordings of meetings between Saddam Hussein and his inner circle. *The
Saddam Tapes*, along with the much larger digital collection of captured records at
the National Defense University's Conflict Records Research Center, will provide
researchers with important insights into the inner workings of the regime and, it is
hoped, the nature of authoritarian regimes more generally.

The collection has implications for a range of historical questions. How did
Saddam react to the pressures of his wars? How did he manage the Machiavellian
world he created? How did he react to the signals and actions of the international
community on matters of war and peace? Was there a difference between the public
and the private Saddam on critical matters of state? A close examination of this
material in the context of events and other available evidence will address these and
other questions.

Kevin M. Woods is a member of the research staff of the Institute for Defense Analyses. His studies on Iraq have been published in *Foreign Affairs*, *Journal of Strategic
Studies*, and *Intelligence and National Security*, among others. He has authored and
coauthored numerous studies, including *Iraqi Perspective Report: Saddam's Senior
Leadership on Operation Iraqi Freedom* (2006) and *The Mother of All Battles:
Saddam Hussein's Strategic Plans for the Persian Gulf War* (2008). Woods is a
retired U.S. Army officer with operational experience in Iraq during the 1991 and
2003 wars. Woods was the recipient of the 1997 J. William Middendorf II Award
for Research at the Naval War College and the 2007 Andrew J. Goodpaster Award
for Excellence in Research at the Institute for Defense Analyses.

David D. Palkki is the deputy director and senior researcher at the National Defense
University's Conflict Records Research Center. He has authored and coauthored
articles and chapters on Iraq for *International Security*, *Diplomatic History*, and the
Center for Strategic and International Studies. Palkki is a Ph.D. candidate in political
science at the University of California, Los Angeles. His dissertation, "Deterring
Saddam's Iraq: Theory and Practice," draws heavily on the captured Iraqi records.
He previously worked as a contractor at the Institute for Defense Analyses. He
is a recipient of the Institute on Global Conflict and Cooperation's Herbert York
Fellowship and a National Science Foundation fellowship.

Mark E. Stout is a lecturer at Johns Hopkins University's Krieger School of Arts
and Sciences, where he teaches courses in intelligence and strategic studies. He is
also the historian at the International Spy Museum in Washington, DC. He was
previously a research staff member at the Institute for Defense Analyses, and he has
worked for the Department of the Army, the Department of State, and the Central
Intelligence Agency. He is the coauthor of three books, including *Iraqi Perspective
Report: Saddam's Senior Leadership on Operation Iraqi Freedom* (2006), *First to the
Rhine: The 6th Army Group in World War II* (2007), and *The Terrorist Perspectives
Project: Strategic and Operational Views of Al Qaida and Associated Movements*
(2008). He has published articles in *Intelligence and National Security*, *Studies in
Intelligence*, *Journal of Strategic Studies*, and *Studies in Conflict and Terrorism*.

The Saddam Tapes

THE INNER WORKINGS OF A
TYRANT'S REGIME, 1978–2001

Kevin M. Woods

Institute for Defense Analyses

David D. Palkki

National Defense University

Mark E. Stout

Johns Hopkins University

CAMBRIDGE
UNIVERSITY PRESS

CAMBRIDGE UNIVERSITY PRESS
Cambridge, New York, Melbourne, Madrid, Cape Town,
Singapore, São Paulo, Delhi, Tokyo, Mexico City

Cambridge University Press
32 Avenue of the Americas, New York, NY 10013-2473, USA

www.cambridge.org
Information on this title: www.cambridge.org/9781107693487

First published 2011

Printed in the United States of America

A catalog record for this publication is available from the British Library.

Library of Congress Cataloging in Publication data

Woods, Kevin M.
The Saddam tapes : the inner workings of a tyrant's regime, 1978–2001 / Kevin M. Woods,
David D. Palkki, Mark E. Stout.
   p.   cm.
Includes bibliographical references and index.
ISBN 978-1-107-01685-9 (hardback) – ISBN 978-1-107-69348-7 (paperback)
1. Iraq – Politics and government – 1979–1991 – Sources.   2. Iraq – Politics and
government – 1991–2003 – Sources.   3. Hussein, Saddam, 1937–2006 – Archives.
4. Hussein, Saddam, 1937–2006 – Friends and associates.   5. Hussein, Saddam,
1937–2006 – Political and social views.   6. Authoritarianism – Iraq – History –
20th century – Sources.   I. Palkki, David D., 1974–   II. Stout, Mark, 1964–   III. Title.
DS79.7.W66   2011
956.7044092–dc23   2011026512

ISBN 978-1-107-01685-9 Hardback
ISBN 978-1-107-69348-7 Paperback

This work was conducted under contract DASW01-04-C-0003, Task AJ-8-2826, "Adversary
Document Research," for the Office of the Secretary Defense. The publication of this IDA
document does not indicate endorsement by the Department of Defense, nor should the
contents be construed as reflecting the official position of the sponsoring agency.

© 2010, Institute for Defense Analyses, 4850 Mark Center Drive, Alexandria, Virginia
22311-1882 ● (703) 845-2000.

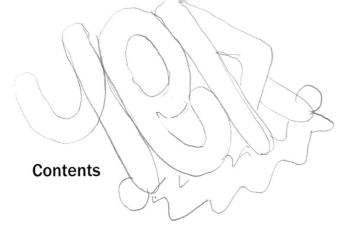

Contents

Figures

Foreword

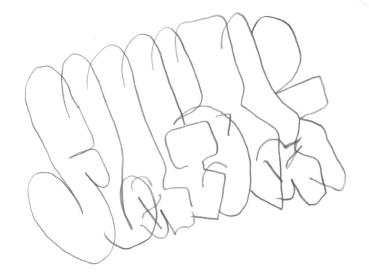

The Institute for Defense Analyses prepared the original version of this book for the Office of the Undersecretary of Defense for Policy, under task order AJ-8-2826, the Conflict Records Research Center. The study addresses the task objective of drawing lessons from captured Iraqi records and making information in the captured materials available to the scholarly community. The original study, and the larger body of captured recordings on which it rests, was designed to provide researchers with important insights into the inner workings of the regime of Saddam Hussein and, it is hoped, the nature of authoritarian regimes more generally.

Analysts will benefit for years to come from reviewing copies of the captured records at the Conflict Records Research Center (CRRC), which recently opened its doors at the National Defense University's Institute for National Strategic Studies, in Washington, DC. Saddam's regime is gone forever, yet important insights will emerge, and understandings evolve, as a new generation of students and scholars cuts its teeth on these fascinating records. Lessons derived from the captured records will also be of considerable import to policymakers, because conventional understandings about how Saddam's regime operated continue to influence expectations about events in and outside of Iraq. As William Faulkner once observed, "The past is never dead. It's not even past."

Saddam emerges from these transcripts as a highly intelligent yet frequently deluded man. As the editors point out, his worldview consisted of a "curious mix of shrewdness and nonsense." He was a tyrant who foolishly and ruthlessly invaded his neighbors and repressed his people, yet he was also a pragmatist whose perspicuity at times exceeded that of his generals and advisors. He ordered his lieutenants to restrict UN inspectors' access to suspected WMD sites, to bribe inspectors, and to refuse to deliver information on Iraq's foreign suppliers of WMD-related materials. Despite such obstructionism, the recordings are consistent with other evidence indicating that Iraq had divested itself of prohibited nuclear, chemical, and biological weapon stockpiles and activities prior to the 2003 invasion. As Saddam emphasized to his inner circle, "We have nothing; not even one screw."

The editors provide context to the transcripts and highlight key observations, yet emphasize that the book was intended more to introduce the recordings to scholars, and to enable them to ask their own questions and to reach their own conclusions, than to compile a list of definitive findings. The National Defense University is pleased to invite scholars to visit the CRRC to conduct this important research.

Dr. Hans Binnendijk

Vice President for Research and Applied
Learning, National Defense University

Acknowledgments

The editors wish to thank the Office of the Undersecretary of Defense for Policy for generously sponsoring this project. The Joint Advanced Warfighting Division, which is responsible for the development and publication of this study, is a division at the Institute for Defense Analyses. Related works were cosponsored by the Undersecretary of Defense for Acquisition, Technology, and Logistics; the Undersecretary of Defense for Policy; the vice chairman of the Joint Chiefs of Staff; and the Commander of U.S. Joint Forces Command.

The editors owe a debt of gratitude to a number of individuals. Significant contributions by Jessica M. Huckabey and Elizabeth A. Nathan on early drafts of several chapters were invaluable. Research support from Hal Brands, Jon Grinspan, Kristen Sproat, and Ana Venegas was critical in managing the scope of this project. Mike Pease played a key role in locating and categorizing candidate recordings for translation. Laila Sabara spent countless hours summarizing recordings, translating, and correcting others' translations. Carolyn Leonard provided expert editing assistance. The Conflict Records Research Center staff, especially Joseph Simons, assisted in creating CRRC citations. Robert Jervis, Marcus Jones, James Kurtz, Peter (Pooch) Picucci, Judith Yaphe, and four anonymous Cambridge University Press reviewers read the entire manuscript and offered invaluable comments and suggestions. Despite all of the help, any mistakes in this study are the sole responsibility of the editors.

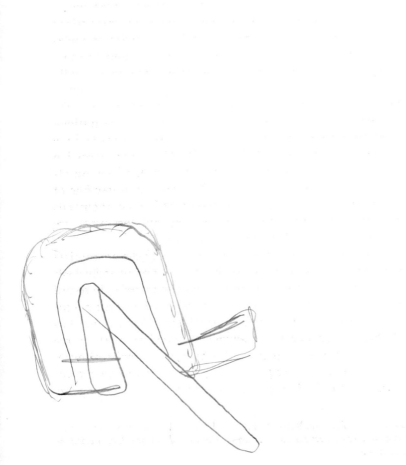

Note to Readers

In preparing this volume, the editors worked through a vast amount of material, most of it fascinating. Unfortunately, space constraints required painful trade-offs, and the material here represents only a small portion of the available Saddam tapes. Furthermore, none of the transcripts here is complete. In theory, the less excised from a transcript, the better the reader can understand the context of the conversation. In practice, many of the translations contain rambling, tangential discussions or otherwise distracting and relatively unimportant material. Therefore, in many places, the editors deleted material they considered to be less important to cover more ground, fully aware that these represented decisions with which others might disagree. In an effort to provide researchers the opportunity to explore the material to decide for themselves, the editors and their colleagues at the Institute for Defense Analyses have worked with the staff of the National Defense University's Conflict Records Research Center (CRRC) under sponsorship from the U.S. Department of Defense to open digital copies of the records to the general scholarly community at the CRRC. The full transcripts of conversations presented here, as well as digital copies of tens of thousands of pages of other Iraqi state records and Al Qaeda related documents, are or will shortly become available to scholars at the CRRC.

The editors of this study are aware of concerns about the appropriate use of captured records and potential for harm to innocent individuals that could occur through careless disclosure of sensitive material. In regard to the first concern, the editors find that analyzing captured state records for historical purposes is consistent with international law and has a lengthy history of precedents in state behavior. Although debates exist as to the future definition of records, archives, and cultural property, the copies of material accessed for this research clearly fall into the category of state records seized during armed conflict.[1] The clearest precedent was the capture,

---

[1] See Douglas Cox, "Archives and Records in Armed Conflict: International Law and the Current Debate over Iraqi Records and Archives," *Catholic University Law Review* 59 (July 2010): 1001–56.

copy, and research into the records of the former Axis powers at the close of World War II. The Allies treated these records, in accordance with international law, as "public moveable property seized during hostilities pursuant to military necessity."[2] Title to these state records, as distinguished from cultural property, passed to the capturing power. The United States eventually returned (technically "donated") the vast majority of the original records to the postwar governments in both West Germany and Japan. It did, however, retain copies of certain state records, which it subsequently made available to scholars. The "emancipation" of these records made an important contribution to historical scholarship of the shared history between former adversaries.

The second concern is equally important. In any dissemination of original records or copies thereof, whether to Iraqis, Americans, or others, great care must be taken to minimize risk of harm to innocent individuals. Guided by such concerns, in one transcript the editors redacted the names of Iraqi citizens who were not senior government officials acting in their official capacities. Such considerations are central to the ethical use of any such records and a major consideration in both the preparation of this work and ongoing research at the Conflict Records Research Center. These same considerations should, and almost certainly will, influence the timing and manner in which the original records may eventually be returned.

Several devices occur throughout to indicate where sections have been deleted from the transcripts, or to clarify meaning. Ellipses and centered section dividers indicate deleted text. When the words of only one speaker have been deleted, ellipses are found within the text. When words from multiple speakers have been deleted, centered section dividers replace the excised passages. A dash indicates when a speaker has trailed off or been interrupted; "[interrupting]" will often appear to distinguish between the two. When one word or words was incomprehensible to the translator, this has been marked as "[inaudible]." Laughter, discontinuities in the recording, and other such disruptions are similarly indicated with an italicized comment inside square brackets. In a few places, the editors added unitalicized words in square brackets to the dialogue to summarize excised text or to otherwise enhance clarity.

Insofar as possible, the editors have tried to present these transcripts from an Iraqi perspective. Because individuals in Arabic generally go by their first names, speakers are identified by their first rather than last names. Where Iraqi names for events differ from their English counterparts, these terms have been translated directly. For instance, Iraq's war with the international coalition in 1991 was the Mother of All Battles, Iraq's primary enemy to its

[2] Such records are treated as "Spoils of War" in accordance with U.S. law (50 USC sec. 2204) and international law (specifically, but not limited to, the 1907 Hague Regulations).

west was the Zionist Entity, and so forth. Throughout the study, the editors have sought to use the most common English transliterations of Arabic names.

Identifying the speakers in each recording has been difficult, as they did not always address one another by name. Most of the recordings are audio files without an index to contents, and the translators had to identify individuals by recognizing voices and other cues. This was particularly challenging because the recordings are often of poor sound quality and frequently contain extraneous noises such as clinking dishes or even, in a few cases, street sounds. A few conversations were videotaped, and these, of course, provide additional clues. Despite our efforts, many speakers remain unidentified. Electronic enhancement of the recordings might, in the future, improve the audio quality, thus enabling better speaker identification and improved translations. Unidentified speakers are enumerated as Male 1, Male 2, and so on (as it happens, all the voices in the transcripts here are male); however, Male 1 in one conversation is not necessarily the same Male 1 in another. When different parts of the same recording are used in different places, though, the numbering of unidentified males remains constant. In the few cases where their other names are unknown, speakers are identified only by their "Abu" names, an informal naming convention in the Arab world: Abu X means "father of X."

Beyond identifying the speakers, identifying those present in meetings was, for this study, generally infeasible. Most of the tapes lack lists of meeting participants. Although it is often possible to confirm the presence of speakers by their voices, voice recognition cannot identify individuals who might have remained silent. Even when we know the type of meeting (e.g., cabinet, RCC), this is no guarantee that all members were present. Nor does knowledge of the meeting type necessarily tell us who else might have been invited to temporarily take a seat at the table. Perhaps ongoing translation efforts will reveal master lists of meetings and meeting participants. Alternatively, interviews with identified participants could help establish who was in the room during given meetings. In the meantime, interested readers might benefit from reviewing lists of Iraqi officials already in the public sphere.[3]

This project was fortunate to have the services of Ms. Laila Sabara, a native Arabic speaker with substantial experience translating Iraqi documents. In addition to her work as the project's lead translator, she reviewed translations repurposed from U.S. government military operations, intelligence efforts (notably the Iraq Survey Group), and legal investigations.

---

[3] For instance, see Edmund A. Ghareeb, with Beth Dougherty, *Historical Dictionary of Iraq: Historical Dictionaries of Asia, Oceania, and the Middle East*, No. 44 (Lanham, MD: Scarecrow Press, 2004).

The full transcripts of conversations excerpted here, as well as digital copies of tens of thousands of pages of other Iraqi state records and Al Qaeda–related documents are or will shortly become available to scholars at the CRRC. Notwithstanding Ms. Sabara's considerable expertise, visiting researchers at the CRRC will almost certainly discover translation errors in this study. The editors encourage researchers to visit the CRRC to read the full transcripts, to listen to the audio files, and to explore other captured records from Iraq and Afghanistan not referenced in this book. Approximately two-thirds of the records cited in this study, along with full English translations, were available in the CRRC when *The Saddam Tapes* manuscript went to press. Asterisk marks preceding certain CRRC citations indicate that these records are not yet available at the CRRC. The CRRC record numbers reveal whether the records are audio, video, or document files.[4] The CRRC provides transcripts and audio files of three records from the 1991 Gulf War on its Web site and is preparing dozens of records from the Iran-Iraq War for release to the Internet.[5]

---

[4] All CRRC records cited in this book began with an "SH," indicating that they belong to the "Saddam Hussein Regime" portion of the CRRC's collection. The next series of letters is tied to the originating Iraqi agency of the specific record. For instance, the special category "Saddam Tapes" is marked *SHTP*. An *A* for audio, *V* for video, or *D* for document follows the abbreviation of the originating agency. The remaining numbers merely indicate the order in which the records were added to the database.

[5] The CRRC posts a list of all CRRC records on its Web site, which it will update as it adds new records to the collection. The center currently houses roughly 1,200 records, constituting some thirty-four thousand pages. Of those records, 138 are audio files involving conversations with Saddam (see www.ndu.edu/inss/index.cfm?secID=101&pageID=4& type=section).

Dramatis Personae

Name	Biographical Details
Abd al-Ghani al-Ghafur	Iraqi Regional Command member (1982–2001), cabinet minister without portfolio (1982–91)
Abdul Halim Khaddam	Syrian foreign minister (1970–1984) and vice president (1984–2000)
Abid Hamid Mahmud al-Tikriti	Iraqi military officer, later Hussein's personal secretary (1990s)
Ahmed Hassan al-Bakr	President of Iraq (1968–79)
Ahmed Hussein Khudayr al-Samarrai	Iraq's minister of foreign affairs (1991–1993), prime minister (1993–1994), finance minister (1994–2001)
Ahmed Yassin al-Samarrai	Iraq's head of the presidential cabinet during the Gulf War (1991)
Alain Juppe	French foreign minister (1993–1995) and prime minister (1995–1997)
Alexey Kosygin	Premier of Soviet Union (1964–1980)
Ali Akbar Hashemi Rafsanjani	President of Iran (1989–1997)
Ali Hassan al-Majid, aka Chemical Ali	Iraq's military governor of Kuwait (1990), defense minister (1991–1995), interior minister (1991), and member of the Revolutionary Command Council (1991–2003)
Amir Hamudi Hassan al-Sa'di	Iraqi presidential science adviser
Amir Muhammad Rashid al-Ubaydi	Iraq's minister of oil (1996–2003), head of the Organization of Military Industrialization (early 1990s)
Andrei Kozyrev	Russian foreign minister (1990–1996)
Anthony (Tony) Lake	U.S. national security adviser (1993–1997)
Anwar Sadat	President of Egypt (1970–1981)

(continued)

(continued)

Name	Biographical Details
Boutros Boutros-Ghali	UN secretary-general (1992–1997)
Colin Powell	Chairman of the U.S. Joint Chiefs of Staff during the Gulf War (1991)
Elias Farah	Syrian Ba'athist intellectual
Fahd Ahmad Al-Fahd	Kuwaiti director of state security during the Gulf War (1991)
Fahd bin Abdul Aziz Al Saud	Ruler of Saudi Arabia (1982–1995)
Gamal abd Nasser	President of Egypt (1956–1970)
George Habash, aka al-Hakim	Founder of the Popular Front for the Liberation of Palestine
George Herbert Walker Bush	U.S. president (1989–1993)
George Schultz	U.S. secretary of state (1982–1989)
Haitham Rashid Wihaib	Iraq's minister of protocol (1980–1993)
Hamid Hammadi	Saddam's secretary and president's office director (1982–?), Iraq's information minister (1991–2001), and culture minister (1992–2003)
Hazim Ali	Senior official in Iraq's biological weapons program
Hazim Ayubi	Lieutenant general who commanded Iraqi Scud forces during the Gulf War (1991)
Hikmat Mizban Ibrahim al-Azzawi	Iraq's minister of finance (1995–2003)
Hosni Mubarak	President of Egypt (1981–2011)
Houari Boumedienne	Ruler of Algeria (1965–1978)
Husam Muhammad al-Yasin, aka Husam Muhammad Amin	Iraqi Head of National Monitoring Directorate (liaison between UN inspectors and Iraqi officials)
Hussein Kamil al Majid	Saddam's son-in-law, head of Special Security Organization (1983–1989), head of Military Industrial Commission (1987–1995)
Hussein Rashid Muhammad al-Tikriti	Commander of the Republican Guard (1980–1987), Iraqi Army chief of staff (1990–1991)
Igor Ivanov	Russian first deputy minister of foreign affairs (1994–1998) and foreign minister (1998–2004)
Iyad Khali Zakil	Iraqi major general, commander, IV Corps during Gulf War (1991)
Izzat Ibrahim al-Duri	Iraqi vice chairman of the Revolutionary Command Council (1982–2001)
Jaber al-Ahmed al-Jaber al-Sabah	Emir of Kuwait (1977–2006)
Jalal al-Talabani	Kurdish separatist leader and founder of the Patriotic Union of Kurdistan
James Baker	U.S. secretary of state (1989–1992)
Jimmy Carter	U.S. president (1977–1981)

Name	Biographical Details
John Major	British prime minister (1990–1997)
Khidir Hamza, aka Hazem	Iraqi nuclear physicist who defected in 1994
King Hussein bin Talal	King of Jordan (1952–1999)
Latif Jasim	Iraq's minister of culture and information (1979–1991), member of Regional Command (1982–91), minister of labor and social affairs (1993–1996), member of Revolutionary Command Council (1994–2001)
Leonid Brezhnev	Head of state, Soviet Union (1964–1982)
Madeleine Albright	U.S. secretary of state (1997–2001)
Mahdi Obeidi	Nuclear scientist who headed Iraq's centrifuge enrichment program (1987–1991), director of Ministry of Industry and Military Industrialization (2000–2003)
Mahmud Fayzi Muhammad al-Hazza	Head of Jihad Operations Command during the Gulf War (1991)
Margaret Thatcher	British prime minister (1979–1990)
Mazban Khader Hadi	Iraqi member of Revolutionary Command Council and Republican Guard commander
Menachim Begin	Israeli prime minister (1977–1983)
Mikhael Gorbachev	Head of state, Soviet Union (1985–1991)
Mizban Khadr al-Hadi	Iraqi member of Revolutionary Command Council (1991–2001)
Muammar al-Gaddafi	Leader of Libya (1969–present)
Muhammad Hamzah al-Zubaydi	Iraq's deputy prime minister (1991, 1994–2001), prime minister (1991–1993), member of Revolutionary Command Council (1991–2001), Regional Command member (1982–1991)
Muhammad Nuri al-Shammari	Iraq's director of Civil Defense Department (1990s–2003)
Muhammad Reza Pahlavi	Shah of Iran (1941–1979)
Muhammad Saeed al-Sahhaf, aka Baghdad Bob	Iraqi foreign minister (1992–2001) and information minister (2001–2003)
Na'im Haddad	Speaker of Iraqi National Assembly (1980–1984), member of Revolutionary Command Council (1977–1986)
Nizar al-Khazraji	Head of the Iraqi army's First Corps (1984–1988), Iraqi Army chief of staff (1988–1990), fled Iraq in 1996
Nizar Hamdun	Iraq's ambassador to the United States (1984–1987), deputy foreign minister (1988–1992), ambassador to the United Nations (1992–98), and secretary of the Foreign Ministry (1999–2001)

(continued)

(continued)

Name	Biographical Details
Norman Schwarzkopf	Commander of coalition forces during the Gulf War (1991)
Omid Medhat Mubarak, aka Ahmeed Medhat	Iraqi health minister (1993–2003), Iraqi labor and social affairs minister (1989–1993)
Oscar Wyatt	American businessman implicated in the UN oil-for-food scandal
Peter de la Billiere	Commander of British forces during the Gulf War (1991)
Qaboos Bin Sa'id Bin Taimour al-Sa-id	Ruler of Oman (1970–present)
Qays (possibly Qais Abd al-Mu'nim al-Zawawi)	Omani foreign minister
Qusay Hussein	Saddam's son, head of Special Security Organization (1995–2003)
Ra'ad al-Hamdani	Republican Guard officer (1980s–2003)
Richard (Dick) Cheney	U.S. secretary of defense (1989–1993) and vice president (2001–2009)
Richard Holbrooke	U.S. ambassador to Germany (1993–1994), envoy to Bosnia (1995–1996), and ambassador to the United Nations (1999–2001)
Robert (Bob) Dole	U.S. senator (R-KS) (1969–1996)
Rolf Ekeus	Swedish diplomat and head of the UN Special Commission (1991–1997)
Ronald Reagan	U.S. president (1981–1989)
Ruhollah Khomeini	Supreme Leader of Iran (1979–1989)
Saddam Hussein Abd al-Majid al-Tikriti	President of Iraq (1979–2003)
Sa'dun Hammadi	Iraqi foreign minister (1974–1983), member of the Revolutionary Command Council (1986–91), and prime minister (March–September 1991), oil minister (1969–1974), speaker of the National Assembly (1984–2003)
Saman Abdul Majid	Saddam's interpreter (1987–2003)
Samir Vincent	Iraqi American businessman convicted in 2008 on fraud charges related to the UN oil-for-food program
Samuel Berger	U.S. national security adviser (1997–2001)
Suleyman Demirel	Turkish prime minister (1975–1980, 1991–1993) and president (1993–2000)
Taha Muhyi al-Din Ma'ruf	Revolutionary Command Council member (1982–1994) and vice president of Iraq (1975–2003)
Taha Yasin Ramadan, aka Taha al-Jazrawi	Vice president of Iraq (1991–2003) and member of the Revolutionary Command Council (1969–2001)

Name	Biographical Details
Tariq Aziz, aka Abu-Ziyad	Iraq's foreign minister (1983–1991) and deputy prime minister (1979–2003)
Uday Hussein	Saddam's son
Viktor Posuvalyuk	Russian deputy foreign minister, envoy to the Middle East (1992–1999)
William (Bill) Clinton	U.S. president (1993–2001)
William (Bill) Cohen	U.S. secretary of defense (1997–2001)
William (Bill) Richardson	U.S. congressman (D-NM) (1983–1997), U.S. secretary of energy (1998–2001), ambassador to the United Nations (1997–1998), and governor of New Mexico (2003–present)
Yasir Arafat, aka Abu-'Ammar	Chairman of the Palestinian Liberation Organization and head of Fatah (1959–2004)
Zaid bin Sultan al-Nahayan	President of United Arab Emirates (1971–2004)

Map of Iraq

Source: Iraq, no. 3835 Rev. 5 March 2011, United Nations.

Introduction

Having a whole generation of Iraqi and Americans grow up without understanding each other [can have] negative implications and could lead to mix-ups.[1]

– Saddam Hussein, 1983

Why do you think we trusted the Prophets? It is because they recorded every incident.[2]

– Saddam Hussein, circa 1991

OVERVIEW

Sir Michael Howard, the great British military historian, once warned that "the past is a foreign country; there is very little we can say about it until we have learned the language and understood its assumptions."[3] A recurring insight when reviewing transcripts of discussions between Saddam and members of his inner circle is the extent to which the West's failure to

---

[1] This quote is from a 21 December 1983 cable from the U.S. embassy in London to the secretary of state. Interestingly, Saddam borrows this language from a statement delivered by Donald Rumsfeld during his discussion with the Iraqi foreign minister in Baghdad the previous day. See "Rumsfeld Mission: December 20 Meeting with Iraqi President Saddam Hussein," London 27572, accessed 6 June 2009 at www.gwu.edu/~nsarchiv/NSAEBB/NSAEBB82/iraq31.pdf.

[2] *SH-SHTP-A-001-203, "Saddam and His Senior Advisers Discussing UN Security Council Efforts to Create a Ceasefire in the Iran-Iraq War," undated (1987). Asterisk marks preceding CRRC citations indicate that these records are not yet available at the CRRC. Approximately two-thirds of the records cited in this study, along with full English translations, were available in the CRRC when *The Saddam Tapes* manuscript went to press. Efforts are under way at the CRRC to make the remainder available.

[3] Michael Howard, "The Lessons of History," *History Teacher*, 15 August 1982, 494. Howard is paraphrasing Leslie Hartley, who wrote, "The past is a foreign country: they do things differently there." Hartley, *The Go-Between* (New York: New York Review Book, 1953), 1.

Saddam in a meeting with Barzan Ibrahim al-Tikriti. The date of the picture is unknown, but the picture appears to have been taken in the late 1980s or 1990. An electronic device, apparently an audio recorder, is on the table between the two men. (*Source*: *SH-MISC-D-001-271, "Collection of Saddam's Personal and Family Pictures Including Uday's Wedding," undated).

understand this opaque regime were as much a failure of Westerners to understand their own assumptions as they were a deficit of fact.[4] Extrapolating from Howard's quote, one could say that to Western policy makers, totalitarian regimes may be the most exotic of all foreign countries. The inglorious demise of Saddam Hussein's totalitarian regime might provide insights to the kind of thinking that emerges from the innermost regions of totalitarianism and a guidebook to improving assumptions of the "other." Saddam recorded many important meetings with his generals, Iraq's

---

[4] The Senate Select Committee on Intelligence noted that many faulty estimates of Iraq's WMD programs stemmed more from analysts' assumptions than from specific evidence or reports. See Robert Jervis, "Bridges, Barriers, and Gaps: Research and Policy," *Political Psychology* 29, no. 4 (2008): 585.

political leaders, and foreign dignitaries. These tapes, on which the present volume rests, promise to become a resource that academic and governmental researchers will draw on for decades.

The rapid collapse of the Ba'ath regime in 2003 resulted in the U.S. government's capture of an extensive collection of "state records" comprising media files and documents.[5] A tiny percentage of these have already been made public in whole or in part.[6] A handful of studies, based on captured documents, are also available.[7] New reports, drawing on captured documents and, in one case, interviews with former Iraqi officials, are also under way. These new studies will provide additional context for several of the chapters in this book.[8]

Collecting, analyzing, and publicly releasing documents from previously closed regimes occurred at the end of World War II and more recently the collapse of communist regimes at the end of the Cold War.[9] Although this is not unusual at the end of wars or revolutions, unedited recordings of people at the heart of power remain rare. Only eleven minutes of audio recording exist of Adolf Hitler in private meetings.[10] A handful of brief,

[5] See Trudy Peterson, "Archives in Service to the State: The Law of War and Records Seizure," in *Political Pressure and the Archival Record*, ed. Margaret Procter et al. (Society of American Archivists, 2006; rpt. in *Lligall* in 2004), accessed 12 June 2009 at www.trudypeterson.com/publications.html.

[6] The director of National Intelligence released a collection of approximately eleven thousand records to the Internet in 2006. In November 2006, the U.S. government removed the collection from the Internet following concerns that some of the documents contained scientific data relating to nuclear research. In 2008, the Department of Defense released a five-volume collection of terrorism-related documents. For the terrorism documents, see Kevin M. Woods with James Lacey, *Iraqi Perspectives Project – Primary Source Materials for Saddam and Terrorism: Emerging Insights from Captured Iraqi Documents*, vols. 1–5, accessed 9 February 2009 at www.jfcom.mil/newslink/storyarchive/2008/pa032008.html.

[7] Kevin M. Woods and Mark E. Stout, "Saddam's Perceptions and Misperceptions: The Case of Desert Storm," *Journal of Strategic Studies* 33, no. 1 (February 2010): 5–41; Kevin M. Woods, *The Mother of All Battles: Saddam Hussein's Strategic Plan for the Persian Gulf War* (Annapolis, MD: Naval Institute Press, 2008); Kevin M. Woods et al., *Iraqi Perspectives Project: A View of Operation Iraqi Freedom from Saddam's Senior Leadership* (Washington, D.C.: Joint Center for Operational Analyses, 2006), accessed 2 February 2009 at www.jfcom.mil/newslink/storyarchive/2006/ipp.pdf; Central Intelligence Agency, *Comprehensive Report of the Special Advisor to the DCI on Iraq's WMD*, 30 September 2004, vols. 1–3, referred to hereafter as the *Duelfer Report*.

[8] Studies are under way at IDA on Iraq's nonuse of chemical and biological weapons during the Gulf War, Iraq's tribes under Saddam, the Iran-Iraq War, Saddam's perceptions of Irangate, and how Saddam's image of the United States affected his decision to invade Kuwait.

[9] Robert Wolfe, ed., *Captured German and Related Records: A National Archives Conference* (Athens: Ohio University Press, 1974); Woodrow Wilson International Center for Scholars, Cold War International History Project.

[10] Matti Huuhtanen, "Historic, Secret Recording of Hitler's 1942 Visit to Finland Aired on Radio," *Associated Press*, 18 October 2004. Unlike Saddam's recordings, Hitler was unaware this conversation was being taped.

clandestinely taped conversations with Kim Jong Il and Kim Il Sung of North Korea have also entered the public sphere.[11] By contrast, several thousand hours of audio and video recordings of Saddam meeting with members of his inner circle have emerged from Iraq. These recordings uniquely illuminate the regime's decisions, decision-making processes, perspectives, and personalities.

The present volume provides a brief introduction to the vast collection of audio (and a few video) recordings of Saddam Hussein from formal and informal meetings.[12] The U.S. military captured the original tapes, along with other Iraqi state records, from government buildings and associated facilities in and around Baghdad during the early phases of Operation Iraqi Freedom. To create this volume, the editors screened written summaries and digital copies of the original recordings for material that provides a sense of the wider collection. The focus of this screen was to identify broad national security topics.

The collection has implications for a range of historical questions. How did Saddam react to the pressures of his wars? How did he manage the Machiavellian world he created? How did he react to the signals and actions of the international community on matters of war and peace? Was there a difference between the public and the private Saddam on critical matters of state? A close examination of this material in the context of events and other available evidence will go a long way to address these and other questions.

Beyond their utility for the historian and policy maker, these recordings provide a wealth of material for other disciplines. Fields such as international relations, political psychology, and Middle Eastern studies seem particularly likely to benefit. The editors hope that such historical evidence, previously unavailable, will fuel new studies and reassessments of existing theories and historical understandings. Before reviewing the content of this volume, however, it is worth considering the collection's inherent strengths and limitations.

---

[11] Kongdan Oh and Ralph C. Hassig, *North Korea through the Looking Glass* (Washington, D.C.: Brookings Institution, 2000), 77, 92.

[12] This study was derived from a summary review of more than 2,300 hours of conversations in which Saddam was a participant. Selections from eighty-seven recordings are included in the text, and another forty recordings are cited as additional references in the footnotes. The closest parallel to the material here is probably available only in the most sensitive communications intercepts by intelligence agencies (rarely made available to the public). In terms of capturing unguarded comments from a totalitarian leader, the musings of Hitler, recorded by two stenographers during World War II, are also noteworthy. First published in German just after the war, several English editions date to the early 1950s – most recently H. R. Trevor-Roper's *Hitler's Table Talk 1941–1944: Secret Conversations* (New York: Enigma Books, 2007).

BACKGROUND: RECORDING THE "TABLE TALK" OF SENIOR LEADERS

For most historians, the opportunity to listen in on the unguarded speech of senior political leaders on policy or in reaction to unfolding events is the equivalent of a unicorn sighting. Compared with materials on which historians normally depend – official documents, contemporary news accounts, letters, diaries, and memoirs – tapes provide an unparalleled window into the past. As Ernest R. May and Philip D. Zelikow, editors of *The Kennedy Tapes*, have noted, such recordings have the virtue of "being almost totally unfiltered" and "give eavesdroppers the experience of high-level decision making probably not obtainable by other means."[13] In the American experience this unicorn has made an occasional appearance. In addition to the small collections from the Roosevelt, Eisenhower, and Kennedy administrations, there are substantial holdings of President Lyndon Johnson's secret tapes, and perhaps most famously, President Richard Nixon's – the so-called Watergate Tapes.[14] The Nixon tapes not only helped to end a presidency but also in all likelihood ended the practice of American presidential recordings.

The very existence of such tapes has always been a point of fascination and dread. Arthur Schlesinger Jr., upon learning that President Johnson was routinely taping his Oval Office phone conversations, recorded in his diary that such tapes would be "a treasure trove for the historian!" but then went on to add that such recordings would also become "a threat to the rational and uninhibited conduct of government!"[15] That is, the very access the recordings would give future historians to Oval Office discussions would one day discourage officials from engaging in the private deliberations necessary for good policy making. Of course, Schlesinger was speaking of the reactions of men and women in an open society who at some level must have suspected that their actions would eventually be made known. How might secret or even routine recording of government deliberations affect a totalitarian leader and his inner circle?

It is unclear whether the participants in Saddam's meetings knew he was recording them, although given the nature of the regime they almost certainly

---

[13] Ernest R. May and Philip D. Zelikow, "White House Tapes: Extraordinary Treasures for Historical Research," *Chronicle of Higher Education*, 28 November 1997.

[14] Major works in this area include the following: Ernest R. May and Philip D. Zelikow, *The Kennedy Tapes: Inside the White House during the Cuban Missile Crisis* (New York: Harvard University Press, 1997); Michael R. Beschloss, ed., *Taking Charge: The Johnson White House Tapes, 1963–1964* (New York: Touchstone, 1997); Stanley I. Kutler, *Abuse of Power: The Nixon Tapes* (New York: Free Press, 1997). Transcripts of some of the more than five thousand hours of released presidential tapes can be reviewed at the University of Virginia, Miller Center of Public Affairs, Presidential Recordings Program, at http://tapes .millercenter.virginia.edu/.

[15] Arthur M. Schlesinger Jr., diary entry for 25 March 1964, cited on the Miller Center's Presidential Recordings Program Web site, at http://tapes.millercenter.virginia.edu/.

would have been surprised if he were not.[16] Interviews with senior members of the Ba'ath regime make clear that eavesdropping was the norm. There may have been many reasons for his advisers to withhold their "rational and uninhibited" advice, fear of arbitrary execution no doubt among them, but secret recordings were probably not high on that list. At the least, the sensitive and candid nature of many of the conversations contained in this study suggests that the participants, including Saddam, did not expect the raw tapes or unedited transcripts to become part of a non-Ba'ath controlled historical record.

All of this leaves unresolved the question of why Saddam made these tapes. A simple or single answer does not emerge from this volume, but there are at least three plausible explanations. The reality is likely a combination of all of them to varying degrees. On the one hand, Saddam governed an authoritarian state in which, to protect themselves against charges of disloyalty, officials meticulously documented every piece of bureaucratic minutia. Fear of making mistakes, well justified in a culture of suspicion, provided a strong incentive to record (the ultimate documentation) as much as possible. Recording events also provided a measure of insurance, and a weapon, against one's peers.[17]

Routine recordings may have also been the surest way for the presidential staff to track decisions and manage requests for further information. Saddam and his personal staff oversaw a stunning array of issues ranging from grand strategy to the collar style on new uniforms for the Republican Guard. Accurate records and recordings would clearly enhance the tracking of such an idiosyncratic decision-making process. Saddam used the recordings to track the vast amount of information he needed to master. Toward the end of a long and often confusing series of telephone calls with commanders and intervening discussions with his general staff on 7 January 1981, Saddam instructed his staff, "From now on let us record all telephone

---

[16] For evidence that Saddam's subordinates and even foreign diplomats were aware that he recorded his meetings with them, see Charles Cullimore interview of Sir Terence Clark, 8 November 2002, British Diplomatic Oral History Programme, p. 30, accessed 6 June 2009 at www.chu.cam.ac.uk/archives/collections/BDOHP/Clark.pdf; "Reaction to King Husayn's Speech: Husayn Kamil Says Atmosphere in Saddam Husayn's Family Is 'Troubled,'" Radio Monte Carlo – Middle East, Paris (in Arabic), 25 August 1995, in BBC Summary of World Broadcasts, 28 August 1995; Saïd K. Aburish, Saddam Hussein: The Politics of Revenge (London: Bloomsbury, 2000), 327.

[17] In several instances, Iraqi leaders apparently used recordings to undermine domestic rivals. According to Barzan al-Tikriti, Hussein Kamil taped a 1988 phone call in which Uday Hussein, a key rival and Saddam's son, told the U.S. embassy in Switzerland that he wished to defect. Hussein Kamil reportedly shared this tape with Saddam, which led to Uday's arrest. Years later, in an attempt to discredit Hussein Kamil after he had defected, Saddam released a recording in which Hussein Kamil appears to call on Iraq to invade Kuwait. See *SH-MISC-D-001-204, "Diary of Barzan al-Tikriti," undated (circa 2000); "Reaction to King Husayn's Speech," 25 August 1995.

conversations."[18] Although this guidance clearly does not account for all of the Iraqi recordings, the volume of tapes, especially on military topics, does take off from this point forward. It is possible that once Saddam issued this directive, recording phone calls and meetings became a standard operating procedure.

Finally, Saddam may have wanted these recordings to help document his greatness and thereby secure his legacy well into the future. Although not as permanent as Saddam's order to have his initials inscribed into the bricks used to rebuild the ruins of Babylon, a detailed documentary record was the intellectual equivalent. For Saddam, history was nothing if not instrumental – his purpose was to "affirm the facts of the past and the linear trajectory of the future."[19] Using the royal *we*, Saddam addressed army officers on the eve of the Iran-Iraq War and reminded them that "it is essential that we wrest the historical opportunity [to play] the historical role performed by our grandfathers in the service of the nation and humanity."[20]

Of course, just playing the role was no guarantee of good reviews. The only way Saddam could guarantee his historical role was to become one of Iraq's greatest historians. In 1979, while vice president of Iraq (but de facto ruler), Saddam led a Ba'ath Party effort called the Project for the Rewriting of History, in which he argued that any Iraqi analysis of historical events must "apply our specifically Ba'athist perspective in building the Arab nation."[21] Much like Churchill's famous quip about assuring himself a favorable judgment of history by writing it, Saddam understood that some legacies are earned, some are myth, but truly great legacies are a mix of both.

On the eve of his 2006 execution, Saddam declared that he was prepared to be judged "after our current situation becomes a glorious history" and that his role provided "the foundation upon which the success of the future phases of history can be built."[22] These tapes may in fact leave an important historical legacy for Saddam, although not necessarily the one he envisioned.

---

[18] See SH-AFGC-D-000-393, "Transcript of a Meeting of the General Command of the Armed Forces during the Iran-Iraq War and Telephone Conversations," 7 January 1981.

[19] Eric Davis, *Memories of State: Politics, History, and Collective Identity in Modern Iraq* (Berkeley: University of California Press, 2005), 148, 172. The project resulted in a book credited to Saddam titled *On the Rewriting of History*.

[20] Quoted in Jerry M. Long, *Saddam's War of Words: Politics, Religion, and the Iraqi Invasion of Kuwait* (Austin: University of Texas Press, 2004), 74.

[21] Quoted in Davis, *Memories of State*, 148. For an overview of government efforts to remove perceived colonial influences by rewriting history in six Arab states (Iraq, Algeria, Libya, Egypt, Syria, and Kuwait), see Ulrike Freitag, "Writing Arab History: The Search for the Nation," *British Journal of Middle Eastern Studies* 21, no. 1 (1994): 19–37.

[22] Translation of a letter released by Saddam's legal team printed in the *Daily Telegraph*, 30 December 2006.

THE PAST IS PROLOGUE

The transcripts in this volume come from a large collection of state records captured in Iraq during the early phases of Operation Iraqi Freedom. The original tapes, primarily audio cassettes, were subsequently copied as digital media files as a part of a U.S. Department of Defense postwar documentation project. This project and related efforts are similar to the post–World War II efforts to understand events from the enemy's perspective.[23]

In 1945, captured document exploitation operations in both the European and Pacific theaters transitioned from focusing primarily on intelligence to a broad range of research and public documentation activities. The most notable efforts included the U.S. Army's use of the German perspective in its official histories ("Green Books") of the war; the chilling documents revealed in the Nuremberg War Crimes Tribunals; and the publication of the Department of State's "Nazi-Soviet Relations, 1939–1941" collection of documents, an early salvo in the battle of ideas during the Cold War.

After a few years of extensive government research, private scholars began exploring a deeper set of political, military, and cultural questions. Notable efforts include Columbia University's War Documentation Project; the American Historical Association's American Committee for the Study of War Documents; and Harvard University's Russian Research Center, where Merle Fainsod produced his seminal work, *Smolensk under Soviet Rule*. Although it remains to be seen if this latest generation of captured records contains the potential to expand our knowledge as much as those from World War II, it is hard to argue that the need to better understand the closed regimes of the Middle East is any less acute than that which drove these earlier efforts.

CHALLENGES

The majority of transcripts included in this volume appear to have been recorded during meetings of the Revolutionary Command Council (officially Iraq's senior decision-making body), the Council of Ministers (Iraq's cabinet), or one of several national security–related working groups. Still others appear to have been made in relatively informal gatherings of Saddam's inner circle or, on occasion, in meetings with less senior members of the regime, including various military officers.

---

[23] See Robert Wolfe, ed., *Captured German and Related Records*; Donald M. Goldstein and Katherine V. Dillon, *The Pacific War Papers: Japanese Documents of World War II* (Washington, D.C.: Potomac Books, 2006); Kevin M. Woods, "Captured Records – Lessons from the Civil War through World War II," paper presented at the International Studies Association Annual Convention, San Francisco, 29 March 2008.

Some of the conversations begin and end within the confines of a single recording. Often, however, the recordings are incomplete. Reasons for this vary. Some recordings capture only part of what were clearly longer conversations on the same topic, or they capture single parts of wider ranging conversations. For this reason, analysts should be wary of drawing definitive conclusions about any topic based on this material.

Much about the recording procedures remains unclear. However, on the basis of a review of related presidential material, a few characteristics of the program are inferable. The Iraqi Intelligence Services provided at least some of the recording equipment for cabinet meetings and meetings involving foreign officials, after testing it for explosives; bugs; and chemical, biological, and radiological contaminants. We know that the Iraqis prepared transcripts based on some of the recordings, thus revealing at least a minimal level of staff knowledge of, and involvement in, the recording process. Saddam's press secretary was responsible for the transcripts of Iraq's cabinet meetings and Saddam's meetings with foreign dignitaries. The presidential secretary appears to have overseen the press secretary's transcriptions.[24] Saddam's phone clearly included a recording device, although it is unclear where else the recording machinery was located. The mechanics of the recording process remain obscure, yet at least one tape indicates that Saddam wanted some conversations to remain strictly private. When a conversation with senior advisers ventured into the subject of "the missing Iraqis, Saudis, and Kuwaitis" from the 1991 war, Saddam ordered his staff to "turn off the recording" before he told them something that was not "for the report."[25]

A second challenge – how to account for the totality of recordings made compared to the number now on hand – is more difficult to overcome. There will probably never be a clear accounting; the editors have not found an Iraqi government index or catalog of presidential recordings, desk calendars, or a schedule of meetings that provide a sense of what was and was not recorded. Coalition troops acquired these recordings during or immediately following combat operations. Collecting and processing captured documents is a standard but inexact battlefield activity. The procedures used do not necessarily preserve the kind of archival details that researchers might want and expect for such a collection. Regime records were found in conditions ranging from pristine (in their original place) to trashed (rooms piled with

---

[24] Additional background and anlysis of the recording program is found in United Kingdom, House of Commons, Committee on Standards and Privileges, Annex of the Sixth Report, "Combined Media Processing Centre-Qatar/UK CI Report: Authenticity of Harmony File ISGP-2003-00014623," 17 July 2007, accessed 19 January 2010 at www.parliament.the-stationery-office.co.uk.

[25] *SH-SHTP-A-001-269, "Saddam and His Advisors Discuss Iraq's Compliance with UN Inspectors, UN Sanctions on Iraq, Iraqi Tribes, and Other Issues," undated (circa 1991–1992). The recording resumed after a few minutes and did not return to the missing-persons subject.

material awaiting destruction) to hidden (bags of documents buried in a garden). Although documentation is abundant on many issues, the regime's efforts to destroy records dealing with sensitive topics, such as weapons of mass destruction (WMD) and ethnic cleansing in the Kurdish north, have in all likelihood left major gaps.[26] Fortunately, most of the records do come with some information about the date and general location of their capture. On the basis of this data, the editors conclude that most of the materials quoted in this volume were captured in and around facilities associated with the office of the presidency or the presidential secretary's office.[27]

Third, it is reasonable to assume that not all surviving records are equally reliable. On occasion, Saddam's regime appears to have distributed heavily edited transcripts, even recordings, of private conversations. According to Richard Butler, a former head of the UN Special Commission (UNSCOM) inspectors in Iraq, Baghdad provided international media outlets with heavily edited video recordings of meetings with him and other inspectors in an attempt to cast them in a poor light.[28] Hussein Kamil, after defecting to Jordan, accused Iraqi television of doctoring a recording to give a false impression that he wanted Iraq to invade Kuwait and Saudi Arabia.[29] Documents and recordings that the regime publicly released, or intended for public release, are certainly among the least trustworthy. Only a miniscule portion of the recordings in the collection appear to fit this category.

Despite the occasionally spotty provenance of the original recordings, one can gain a sense of the authenticity of the recordings from the voices and conversations themselves. With minor exceptions, the Ba'ath leadership maintained a degree of formality in their conversations. Deference to Saddam by use of an honorific title is a consistent attribute. Saddam often responded in kind before reverting to a more informal style. Except on rare, formal occasions, he spoke in the colloquial. His tone changed when he was angry, yet Saddam seldom raised his voice. Almost invariably, his voice and word choice evinced determination. Iraqi textual records as well as other reporting and analyses developed over the course of Operation Iraqi Freedom also

---

[26] A few weeks before the U.S. invasion, Saddam's government reportedly ordered the destruction of all documents related to its ethnic-cleansing program. Outside the municipal building in Kirkuk, an enormous bonfire of these documents burned for nearly twenty-four hours. See George Packer, "The Next Iraqi War: What Kirkuk's Struggle to Reverse Saddam's Ethnic Cleansing Signals for the Future of Iraq," *New Yorker*, 4 October 2004.

[27] For a detailed description of the Presidential Diwan and supporting offices, see *Comprehensive Report of the Special Advisor to the DCI on Iraq's WMD*, vol. 1, December 2004.

[28] Richard Butler and James Charles Roy, *The Greatest Threat: Iraq, Weapons of Mass Destruction, and the Crisis of Global Security* (Cambridge: Public Affairs, 2000), 113; Cameron Stewart, "Butler Smeared in Iraqi Talks Video," *Weekend Australian*, 15 August 1998.

[29] "Reaction to King Husayn's Speech," 25 August 1995.

helped the editors authenticate recordings, some of which are footnoted at relevant points throughout the present volume.[30]

Fourth, determining the veracity of information in a given tape is a far greater challenge than confirming the tape's authenticity; that is, that it is not a fabrication. As one student of the Arab world predicted many years ago, if certain Arab states opened their archives, the information therein "would consist of a hodgepodge of account, conjecture, rumour, suspicion and vilification."[31] When reading the transcripts in this study, it is important to keep in mind that just because Saddam or his advisers make a claim does not necessarily mean that it is true, or even that they believe it to be correct. At times, advisers apparently misled Saddam because they feared he would punish messengers of unwanted news, to conceal information from bureaucratic rivals, or because they themselves were confused or misinformed.

Although some of the information in the tapes is clearly false, inadequate data prevented the editors from refuting every suspected inaccuracy. Whether Saddam and his advisers' statements were accurate, and whether they believed them to be so, are of necessity sometimes left to future researchers. Readers should not assume that the lack of a rebuttal to information in the transcripts implies acceptance of Iraqi claims. It goes without saying that the editors do not believe that the United States was behind the Iranian Revolution or that the *Protocols of the Elders of Zion* provides useful insights regarding Jews or Israel, both of which Saddam and his advisers asserted and apparently believed.[32] It is easy to discount these claims, yet at times the veracity of information in the transcripts is more difficult to ascertain. For instance, whether UN Secretary-General Boutros Boutros-Ghali encouraged Tariq Aziz to bribe UN inspectors, as Tariq told Saddam, remains unclear.[33] It is possible that the secretary-general mentioned attempts to influence UN Security Council members through foreign aid, which Tariq then interpreted for Saddam as bribery.[34] Alternatively,

---

[30] For an insightful authentication of a captured Iraqi document, see United Kingdom, House of Commons, Committee on Standards and Privileges, Sixth Report, Annex.

[31] Eliezer Be'eri, *Army Officers in Arab Politics and Society* (Jerusalem: Israel Universities Press, 1969), viii.

[32] See section "Saddam, meeting with senior advisors, says that the United States orchestrated the overthrow of the Shah of Iran," in Chapter 1; section "Saddam discusses the importance of *The Protocols of the Elders of Zion*," in Chapter 2.

[33] See section "Tariq Aziz informs Saddam that UN Secretary-General," in Chapter 7. The Iraqis' comments about Boutros Boutros-Ghali are quite interesting. On the one hand, they complained that he picked on Iraq. On the other hand, they also described him as highly critical of U.S. officials. An unidentified Iraqi official told Saddam that whenever he and Tariq Aziz met with Boutros Boutros-Ghali, the secretary-general would "curse" about the Americans. See, SH-SHTP-A-001-010, "Saddam and Senior Ba'ath Party Officials Discussing UN Sanctions on Iraq," 15 April 1995.

[34] One study finds that U.S. aid for a country increases by 59 percent, and UN aid by 8 percent, when it becomes a rotating member of the UN Security Council. See Ilyana Kuziemko and

Tariq might have lied to tell his boss what he thought he wanted to hear. On this issue, as with others in this study, the editors raise questions about an Iraqi claim without taking a stance on the veracity of the information.

The fifth challenge was deciding what to include. The Saddam tapes cover the period from late 1976 to 2003. The chronological distribution is uneven, with very few tapes from 1976–1977 or 2002–2003.[35] The highest volume of tapes occurred between 1983 and 1996.[36] For the purposes of this volume, the irregular nature of the collection is not a serious problem. However, for some specific topics there are obvious gaps. Often these gaps are manifest in the conversations themselves. In some cases Saddam and his advisers refer to a prior meeting on the same subject. Finding that specific tape in the captured collection or even determining whether that particular conversation has survived or was ever recorded was, for this volume, an unreachable goal. We fully expect that many more years of work will be necessary before the entire collection – of which this volume is, after all, but a small sample – can be fully understood.

The editors used two simple screening methods in selecting transcripts. The first was to review summaries of more than seven thousand audio files to narrow them down to those in which Saddam was a primary or significant participant in the conversation. This general search reduced the field to approximately 2,300 tapes. The editors then reviewed these for topics related to Iraqi national security. What constitutes national security is, of course, subjective, and the editors' determinations may not align with Saddam's or the reader's. This second criterion resulted in approximately nine hundred candidate tapes. The topics addressed in these tapes sorted themselves roughly into the subject outline of this volume. The transcripts presented here capture portions of conversations among senior members of the Ba'ath regime across the following topics: the United States; the Arab world; Israel or the "Zionist Entity"; the Iran-Iraq War, or Qadisiyyah Saddam; the 1991 Gulf War, or the Mother of All Battles; weapons of

Eric Werker, "How Much Is a Seat on the Security Council Worth? Foreign Aid and Bribery at the United Nations," *Journal of Political Economy* 114, no. 5 (2006): 905–30.

[35] Although the editors reviewed recordings from 1976 to 2003, Saddam played too little a role in the tapes from 1976–1977 and 2002–2003 to merit inclusion in this study.

[36] The decreasing volume of recordings is likely attributable to Saddam's growing concern about his personal security. According to Saddam's presidential secretary, Saddam thought UN weapon inspectors had placed listening devices in his presidential palaces. Therefore, he increasingly met with his advisers outside and in private (rather than in the meeting rooms that might have been bugged). According to Lieutenant General Raad Hamdani, whereas Saddam spent 90 percent of his time before the August 1995 defection of Hussein Kamil in Baghdad, afterward he spent only 20 percent of his time in the capital. It is possible that many of Saddam's residences outside of the capital were unequipped with recording devices. See Charles Duelfer, *Hide and Seek: The Search for Truth in Iraq* (New York: Public Affairs, 2009), 375; Woods interview of General Raad Hamdani, Aqaba, Jordan, 15–17 May 2007.

mass destruction, or special munitions; the UN embargo and the UN Special Commission; and the defection of Hussein Kamil. A more detailed review of a translation's status, clarity of discussion, and relevance to other tapes rounded out the selection process. Another editorial board using the same criteria would certainly have chosen differently.[37] Readers are cautioned that any selection criteria used against a collection such as this may result in an unintended narrative. This leads to a final issue.

As with the fifth, the sixth challenge is related to the selection criteria for the material covered in the recordings. Saddam recorded thousands of conversations covering a variety of topics over several decades. Researchers can best use recordings to understand how leaders interact with their sub-ordinates or manage a particular issue by following a complete series of conversations on a single topic across a short period of time, such as that found in *The Kennedy Tapes*.[38] Readers of this volume will undoubtedly find themselves frustrated by the lack of such continuity and focus. The nature of the original collection means that many topics are incomplete or not covered at all. In some cases, recordings probably once existed but have not been located or identified. In other cases, such as the discussions that led up to the violent death of Hussein Kamil, they may never have existed. It appears that a few of the most sensitive discussions about Iraq's WMD programs took place as one-on-one conversations between Saddam and advisers such as Hussein Kamil rather than in more formal, recorded meetings.[39] Saddam almost certainly would have also highly compartmentalized any discussion that might have taken place about the alleged Iraqi assassination attempt on former President George H. W. Bush in 1993 or other such sensitive topics. One must therefore be cautious when drawing conclusions from such gaps

---

[37] A chapter on Saddam's views and behavior regarding Iraq's Kurds is notably absent from this study, although numerous recordings and documents exist on the subject. The editors decided against including a chapter on the Kurds because many relevant documents and transcripts of recordings have already entered the public sphere. For instance, the University of Colorado at Boulder houses a digital collection of 5.5 million documents that Kurdish forces captured in northern Iraq during the uprisings of 1991. Much information also became publicly available during Saddam's trials. See "International Projects: Iraqi Secret Police Files Seized by the Kurds during the 1991 Gulf War," accessed 5 February 2010 at http://ucblibraries.colorado.edu/archives/collections/international.htm; Case Western Reserve University School of Law, "Iraqi High Tribunal Trials," *Grotian Moment: The International War Crimes Trial Blog*, accessed 4 February 2010 at http://law.case.edu/saddamtrial/index.asp?t=1.

[38] *The Kennedy Tapes* covers a series of twenty-one meetings between the period 16 October and 29 October 1961. But even in this case, relevant conversations were not all recorded.

[39] In a 2 May 1995 meeting of Saddam and his most trusted advisers, Hussein Kamil commented that he "did not want to talk and be this open" in the meeting about the status of Iraq's prohibited weapon programs but would speak frankly because Saddam initiated the discussion and people in the room were confused on the topic. See section "Three months before Hussein Kamil defected," in Chapter 7.

in the recordings; the absence of evidence does not necessarily equate to evidence of absence. Researchers should use the full range of other sources from the regime, such as captured written materials and interviews with principals for the former Iraqi regime, before drawing conclusions on a given issue.

TOWARD AN UNDERSTANDING OF AUTHORITARIAN REGIMES

For many members of the regime's inner circle, understanding Saddam was not a parlor game or an academic exercise but rather a matter of personal survival. Proximity to Saddam did not necessarily bring with it understanding or safety. One need only recall the occasional mysterious deaths of senior ministers or incidents like the bizarre defection-forgiveness-murder of Hussein Kamil to appreciate that proximity often failed to assure either. However, as these tapes underline, for a small group of trusted advisers – men like Tariq Aziz, Ali Hasan Majid, Taha Ramadan, and Izzat al Duri – surviving and even thriving was possible in this environment. What these tapes cannot tell us, of course, is the effect that being so close to Saddam for so many years had on the psyche of these advisers.

It is said that insight into an enemy's intent is the rarest of all strategic intelligence. Modern collection methods have substantially reduced, though not eliminated, the potential for being surprised by an enemy's capabilities. Although technology has in many instances allowed intelligence analysts and policy makers to read the other side's mail, enemy intent remains frustratingly opaque because "reading a man's mail is not the same thing as reading his mind."[40] Often the best analysts can hope for are historical examples and case studies to help craft critical questions that will guide their analysis of present-day mysteries. More often than not the best leadership studies, owing to access to primary materials, are likely to be on leaders within one's own political or cultural context.

Totalitarian regimes provide few opportunities to develop understanding of their leaders. As a result, intelligence agencies have attempted to create profiles through which some predictive analysis might flow. Jerrold Post, the founding director of the Central Intelligence Agency's Center for the Analysis of Personality and Political Behavior, did pioneering work in this regard. Such analysis, however useful, did not always engender confidence among policy makers.[41] Secretary of Defense Robert Gates once lamented

---

[40] Peter Calvocoressi cited in Charles E. Lathrop, *The Literary Spy: The Ultimate Source for Quotations on Espionage and Intelligence* (New Haven, CT: Yale University Press, 2004), 217.

[41] In one report, Post found that Saddam was "psychologically in touch with reality" but "often politically out of touch with reality." An earlier Defense Intelligence Agency profile concluded, however, that Saddam was "irrational." It is unclear why the analyses differed,

that "trying to diagnose somebody from 5,000 miles away who you've never seen does not fill me with confidence."[42] The Saddam tapes will not solve the lack of access to the decision-making process of some future tyrant, but they can improve analysts' ability to appreciate unfamiliar decision-making processes and, as well, the limits of their own judgments about the other side's intent.

Notwithstanding all the caveats, cautions, and limitations mentioned in this introduction, these tapes offer a glimpse into a world where regime insiders once trod carefully and where outsiders were clearly never meant to go. The thousands of hours of recorded conversations have the potential to strip from Saddam Hussein's legacy his "monopoly of knowledge." Ironically, one of the most opaque regimes of the late twentieth century may, because of these tapes, become one of the most transparent.

but one can appreciate the limited confidence such variations might engender among policy makers. See Jerrold M. Post, "Explaining Saddam Hussein: A Psychological Profile," presented to the House Armed Services Committee, December 1990; Tom Mathews, "The Road to War," *Newsweek*, 28 January 1991; Eric D. Shaw, "Saddam Hussein: Political Psychological Profiling Results Relevant to His Possession, Use, and Possible Transfer of Weapons of Mass Destruction (WMD) to Terrorist Groups," *Studies in Conflict and Terrorism* 26 (2003): 347–64; Thomas Omestad, "Psychology and the CIA: Leaders on the Couch," *Foreign Policy* 95 (Summer 1994).

[42] Omestad, "Psychology and the CIA," 114.

ONE

The United States

> Your Excellency...knows that we were raised hating the Americans.
> – Letter from Hussein Kamil, 19 February 1996[1]

> Saddam did not consider the United States a natural adversary.
> – *Duelfer Report*, Central Intelligence Agency[2]

Throughout the 1980s and 1990s, the world looked radically different to decision makers in Baghdad than to their counterparts in Washington, D.C. Saddam Hussein, trying to understand the baffling aspects of U.S. domestic politics, spent countless hours discussing America with his advisers. As he told visiting U.S. senators in April 1990, politicians in America and Iraq "need to know the history of the two countries as to the basic factors related to social, cultural, and political life, because this knowledge is indispensable if one wants to draw the proper conclusions."[3] For Saddam, America was a "complicated country" with confusing political processes.[4] Despite his efforts to learn, Saddam's beliefs about the United States were frequently grossly inaccurate.

Saddam clearly never understood the role that American domestic politics played in U.S. policies and actions against Iraq. During the 1990 midterm elections, Saddam and his advisers discussed how constrained President George H. W. Bush would be given the Democratic control of Congress and Bush's desire to help his own party by taking military action against

---

[1] *SH-SHTP-A-001-205, "Saddam and His Inner Circle Discussing a Letter from Hussein Kamil," 19 February 1996.

[2] *Duelfer Report*, "Regime Strategic Intent," vol. 1, 31. Here the Duelfer Report is citing Tariq Aziz and Abed Hamid Mahmud.

[3] Foreign Broadcast Information Service (FBIS), "Saddam Husayn Addresses Visiting U.S. Senators," *Baghdad Domestic Service in Arabic*, 17 April 1990.

[4] SH-SHTP-A-000-670, "Saddam and His Senior Advisers Discussing Iraq's Foreign Relations and the Policies of Various Countries," 11 October 1990.

Revolutionary Command Council meeting discussing military industrialization. Persons with their backs to the camera on the left of the image are unknown, with the exception of Saddam's son Qusay, seated immediately to Saddam's right. To Saddam's left sit Deputy Prime Minister and Minister of Military Industrial Commission Abd Al-Tawab Mullah Huwaysh, Saddam's son Uday, and an unidentified individual. This picture is dated sometime during or after 1991. (*Source*: *SH-MISC-D-001-272, "Photos of Saddam on Different Occasions," November 2002).

Iraq.[5] Saddam later expressed satisfaction that Bush lost the 1992 election and pleasure with the role Iraq played in "Bush's fall."[6] In contrast, Saddam felt that a war, or any hostile action against Iraq, would benefit the party in power in Washington and that the accompanying rhetoric would fuel American patriotism. Saddam again wondered "whether the American president needs a war before the elections" in November 1995.[7]

In the decades before Iraq invaded Kuwait, American support for Baghdad's primary enemies, the "Zionist Entity" (Israel), Iran, and domestic opposition groups had already vexed Saddam. In 1967, Iraq cut off diplomatic relations with the United States, as did other Arab states, after Israeli

[5] SH-SHTP-A-000-670, "Saddam and His Senior Advisers Discussing Iraq's Foreign Relations and the Policies of Various Countries," 11 October 1990.

[6] SH-SHTP-A-000-838, "Saddam and Senior Ba'ath Party Members Discussing the Transition from Bush to Clinton," undated (circa 4 November 1992).

[7] *SH-SHTP-A-001-206, "Saddam and His Inner Circle Discussing UN Inspections, Elections in the United States and Russia, and Other Issues," 22 November 1995.

strikes on Iraqi airfields and U.S. support for Israel during the Six-Day War. In May 1972, the United States solidified its friendship with Iran when President Richard Nixon and Secretary of State Henry Kissinger visited Shah Muhammad Reza Pahlavi in Tehran.[8] Also in 1972, then vice president Saddam Hussein signed the fifteen-year Treaty of Friendship and Cooperation with the Soviet Union, America's arch rival. Iraq's relations with the Soviets suffered during Saddam's persecution of Iraqi communists, yet Saddam's correct belief that America, Israel, and Iran were arming and financing Kurdish rebels in northern Iraq prevented U.S.-Iraq relations from faring better than those between Baghdad and Moscow.[9] In the late 1970s, Iraq reportedly conducted limited internal discussions about improving relations with the United States, but the war with Iran put such thoughts on hold.[10] Saddam's belief that the United States had supported the Iranian Revolution, including the removal of the Shah, might also have limited his willingness to pursue improved relations.[11]

In Saddam's view, the United States tried to use not only Israel but also Iran as strategic weapons against Iraq. The United States, he thought, wanted to perpetuate the mutually destructive Iran-Iraq War as long as possible to weaken Iraq vis-à-vis Israel.[12] As Foreign Minister Tariq Aziz explained, the Iraqi leadership considered former Secretary of State Henry Kissinger's statement that the United States wanted both parties to lose to be "a frank and clear description of the real American position."[13] America and Iraq restored diplomatic relations in 1984, and the United States provided Baghdad with dual-use materials and equipment, agricultural credits, and intelligence on the Iranians, but Saddam's view of the United States as treacherous and conspiratorial persisted.

---

[8] Gary Sick, "The United States in the Persian Gulf," in *The Middle East and the United States: A Historical and Political Reassessment*, ed. David W. Lesch (Boulder, CO: Westview Press, 2003), 292.

[9] Efraim Karsh and Inari Rautsi, *Saddam Hussein: A Political Biography* (New York: Grove Press, 1991), 75, 96–98; FBIS, "Text of President's Speech to National Assembly," *Baghdad Domestic Service in Arabic*, 18 September 1980; "Memorandum from the President's Assistant for National Security Affairs (Kissinger) to President Nixon," 5 October 1972, accessed 5 December 2009 at www.state.gov/r/pa/ho/frus/nixon/e4/c17628.htm.

[10] PBS *Frontline* interview with Tariq Aziz, original broadcast 25 January 2000, accessed 25 May 2006 at www.pbs.org/wgbh/pages/frontline/shows/saddam/interviews/aziz.html.

[11] See section "Saddam, meeting with senior advisers, says that the United States orchestrated the overthrow of the Shah of Iran," in this chapter. On the broader strategic relationship, see also Hal Brands, "Inside the Iraqi State Records: Saddam Hussein, 'Irangate,' and the United States," *Journal of Strategic Studies*, 34 (February 2011): 95–118; Hal Brands and David Palkki, "'Conspiring Bastards': Saddam Hussein's Strategic View of the United States," *Diplomatic History*, forthcoming (2012).

[12] FBIS, "Turkish Paper *Hurriyet* Interviews Saddam: Third Installment," *Hurriyet* (in Turkish), 13 February 1992.

[13] PBS *Frontline* interview with Tariq Aziz, original broadcast 25 January 2000.

Saddam and his advisers suspected that America was helping Iran in many of the same ways as it was helping Iraq. Indeed, throughout the early 1980s, they believed the United States was arming the Persians. Israeli arms shipments to Iran, widely reported in the media, created a general impression throughout the Middle East that the United States was indirectly supporting Iran.[14] Saddam also claimed that America's North American Treaty Organization (NATO) allies, "prompted by the United States," were supplying Iran with arms.[15] U.S. officials' repeated denials further undermined American credibility while solidifying Saddam's distrust of the United States and faith in his conspiratorial Weltanschauung, when Iran-Contra revelations eventually came to light. U.S. assistance to Iran, Saddam complained to his advisers, was a "stab in the back."[16]

As Saddam suspected, the United States also shared intelligence with the Iranians, including an instance in 1986 that might have helped the latter capture the Al-Fao Peninsula.[17] Surprised by the offensive, Saddam's advisers publicly blamed the United States for deceiving Iraq with faulty intelligence to prolong the Iran-Iraq War.[18] The reliability of U.S. intelligence varied considerably, Saddam privately noted, and "was sometimes accurate, and sometimes vague, and sometimes partial, and sometimes expanded."[19] Saddam explained to his subordinates that as Iraq's power grew in relation to Iran's, American conspiracies against Baghdad would increase. His conclusion – not "subject to error" – was that the United States and Britain had helped Iran achieve military victories over Iraq. He emphasized after Iraq's

[14] Briefing Memorandum, from: Howe, Jonathan T. Veliotes, Nicholas A., To: Haig, Alexander M., Jr., "Your Meeting with Israeli Defense Minister Ariel Sharon, 4:00–5:00 p.m., Tuesday, May 25" [pp. 1–2, 8, 11 only], declassified (formerly secret), 21 May 1982, 4 pp., Digital National Security Archive IG00071. Origin: United States, Department of State, Bureau of Near Eastern and South Asian Affairs; United States, Department of State, Bureau of Politico-Military Affairs.

[15] "25 Aug Solarz Interview with Saddam Husayn," JN021914 Baghdad INA (in Arabic), 25 August 1982, Digital National Security Archive IG00075.

[16] SH-SHTP-D-000-609, "Saddam and His Inner Circle Discussing the Iran-Contra Affair," undated (circa late 1986 or early 1987).

[17] Kenneth Pollack writes that U.S. intelligence facilitated this Iranian battlefield victory, although Robert Gates, Oliver North, and George Cave claim that the information the United States shared was not particularly useful. See Kenneth M. Pollack, *The Persian Puzzle: The Conflict between Iran and America* (New York: Random House, 2004), 213, 219; conference transcript of "Towards an International History of the Iran-Iraq War, 1980–1988," *A Critical Oral History Workshop*, Woodrow Wilson Center, 25–26 July 2005, 67–70; Senate Select Committee on Intelligence, "Nomination of Robert M. Gates to Be Director of Central Intelligence," Report together with Additional Reviews, 102nd Congress, 1st sess., 1992, Exec. Rept. 102-19, 49–51.

[18] Karsh and Rautsi, *Saddam Hussein*, 161.

[19] See "Transcript of a Meeting between Saddam, Vice President of the RCC Izzat Ibrahim al-Tikriti, Minister of Defense Adnan Khairallah, and Army Chief of Staff Abd al-Jawad Zinun," 31 July 1986, in SH-SHTP-D-000-607, in SH-PDWN-D-000-607, "Transcripts of Meetings between Saddam and Senior Advisers," 25 February 1985–31 July 1986.

recapture of the Al-Fao Peninsula in April 1988 that enhanced deception, secrecy, and other measures were necessary to stymie growing U.S. intelligence collection efforts against Iraq. He told his commanders, "We have to be aware of America more than the Iranians" because "they are now the police for Iran, they will turn anything they find over to Iran."[20] While Saddam recognized and appreciated the U.S. escort of Kuwaiti oil tankers and skirmishes with Iranian vessels in the Persian Gulf, he believed that America's decision to leave part of its fleet in the Gulf manifested hostile intentions toward Iraq.[21]

U.S. policy from October 1989 through the invasion of Kuwait was to engage Iraq with the hope of improving its behavior while simultaneously defending America's friends in the Gulf and deterring against external threats.[22] U.S. deterrent efforts led Iraqi officials to complain, on numerous occasions in 1989 and 1990, that the United States sought to establish an anti-Iraq coalition in the Gulf.[23] In the months before and after the invasion, Saddam and his senior advisers discussed how American domestic politics, culture, and other factors might affect the likelihood of U.S. military action against Iraq. Unfortunately, the editors found no mention in the tapes of Saddam's famous prewar meeting with April Glaspie, the U.S. ambassador. After the war had ended, Saddam boasted to his advisers that Iraq achieved

[20] See SH-PDWN-D-000-730, "Transcript of an Armed Forces General Command Meeting," 26 May 1988. The document states that a committee of ten retired and active duty military officials prepared the transcript, basing it on three audio recordings, and presented it for approval to an unidentified audience on 7 September 1994; SH-SHTP-V-000-612, "Saddam and Senior Military Officials Discussing Efforts to Retake the Majnun Area," undated (circa summer 1988); SH-SHTP-A-000-813, "Saddam and Senior Military Officials Discussing Various Military Operations, including Re-capturing the al-Fao Peninsula," undated (circa 1992).

[21] "Iraqi President Addresses ACC Summit Issue of Soviet Jews and US Presence in Gulf," BBC Summary of World Broadcasts, 26 February 1990; Duelfer Report, vol. 1, "Regime Strategic Intent," 31.

[22] The U.S. engagement policy was laid out in National Security Directive-26 (NSD-26). See NSD-26, "US Policy toward the Persian Gulf," 2 October 1989, accessed 30 March 2009 at http://bushlibrary.tamu.edu/research/nsd.php. U.S. policy to deter and defend against threats in the Gulf, originally aimed at the Soviet Union, was first articulated by President Jimmy Carter in his 23 January 1980 State of the Union address. U.S. officials affirmed this policy and gave Iraq deterrent warnings on multiple occasions in the months before it invaded Kuwait. Sick, "The United States in the Persian Gulf," 294; Patrick E. Tyler, "US Finds Persian Gulf Threat Ebbs; a 'Strategic Shift' over Iran's Oil," Washington Post, 7 February 1990; State 046070, "Reaffirmation of Persian Gulf Policy," 02/11/90, Bush Presidential Records, National Security Council, Richard N. Haass Files, Iraq Pre 8/2/90 [1]; Donald Oberdorfer, "Missed Signals in the Middle East," Washington Post, 17 March 1991; "Iraqi Letter to Arab League Threatening Kuwait," declassified cable (formerly confidential), State 235637, 19 July 1990, Digital National Security Archive IG01465.

[23] See "Secretary's October 6 Meeting with Iraqi Foreign Minister Tariq Aziz," State 327801, 13 October 1989, accessed 3 April 2008 at http://foia.state.gov; "Wall Street Journal Interviews Saddam," FBIS-NES-90-128, 3 July 1990, JN0107095890, Baghdad INA (in Arabic), 1 July 1990, 25.

a great "victory" over the United States in the "Mother of all Battles" because it had forced the United States to request a unilateral cease-fire. Furthermore, he explained, the American people voted Bush out of power because he failed to fulfill his promise to replace the Ba'athist regime.

American-backed sanctions and weapons inspections, calls for regime change, threats of military strikes, and those carried out led to countless discussions between Saddam and his advisers about the United States. On occasion, circumstances arose that led the Iraqis to consider improving relations with the United States. President Bill Clinton's election and a Jordanian mediation effort in 1995 are two examples.[24] Between 1994 and 1998, senior Iraqis repeatedly told Charles Duelfer and Rolf Ekeus, the most senior UN Special Commission weapon inspectors, that they wanted to enter into a dialogue with the United States and were prepared to be the United States' "best friend in the region bar none." Saddam's secretary informed Duelfer that Iraq was prepared to help resolve the Israel-Palestine conflict and to sign oil deals and enter into security arrangements with the United States. The United States, however, was reportedly uninterested.[25]

Mutual misunderstandings continued until the end. The United States invaded Iraq in 2003 in part because U.S. policy makers thought Baghdad possessed prohibited weapons and weapon programs and aided and abetted terrorists (including members of Al Qaeda).[26] Although Iraq was guilty on some counts, several key U.S. assessments were later found to be inaccurate.[27] When it was clear to everyone outside of Iraq that the United States was poised to invade and that Saddam's days were numbered, Saddam was "very confident" that the United States would not attack. If it did, he reasoned, Iraq would not lose.[28] Despite efforts on the part of both countries to understand each other, US-Iraq relations were fatally marred by misperceptions.[29]

---

[24] For Saddam's reaction to the Jordanian mediation effort, see section "Saddam and the National Command speculate that King Hussein is using Kamil to provoke a confrontation with Iraq," in Chapter 8.

[25] Duelfer Report, vol. 1, "Regime Strategic Intent," 31–32; Charles Duelfer, *Hide and Seek: The Search for Truth in Iraq* (New York: Public Affairs, 2009), 150–51.

[26] "Bush's State of the Union Speech," 29 January 2003, accessed 1 March 2010 at www.cnn.com; "Bush State of the Union Address," 29 January 2002, accessed 1 March 2010 at www.cnn.com.

[27] Iraq appears to have possessed neither weapons of mass destruction (WMD) nor active WMD programs, and it seems that no close ties or operational relationship existed between Iraq and Al Qaeda. However, Iraq did possess prohibited rockets and rocket programs, obstructed UN inspections, and supported a variety of terrorists and terrorist organizations.

[28] Kevin M. Woods, with Michael R. Pease, Mark E. Stout, Williamson Murray, and James G. Lacey, *The Iraqi Perspectives Project: A View of Operation Iraqi Freedom from Saddam's Senior Leadership* (2006) 28–32 (http://www.dtic.mil/dtic/tr/fulltext/u2/a446305.pdf).

[29] Although Saddam recognized the importance of understanding the United States, he found America's difficulties in making sense of his own thinking to be comical. As he told his

AMERICAN CONSPIRACIES WITH THE PERSIAN ENEMY

Saddam's private discussions reveal his deep distrust of the United States and his conspiratorial worldview. Although some analysts have discounted the more conspiratorial and anti-American elements of his public rhetoric as merely intended to garner domestic or regional support, and deemed them unreflective of his true thinking,[30] the Iraqi leader's private comments on the topic suggest otherwise. The following recordings, on the Iranian Revolution and the Iran-Contra Affair, provide excellent examples.

Saddam, Meeting with Senior Advisers, Says that the United States Orchestrated the Overthrow of the Shah of Iran (between 4 and 20 November 1979)[31]

Saddam: They [the Americans] are involved in the events of Iran, including the removal of the shah [Muhammad Reza Pahlavi], which is completely an American decision.[32] The will of the Iranian people is true. Nations cannot be [*inaudible*]; it is impossible. But there are some existing technical circles that, when a connection exists between achieving the technical will and the people's rising, will play their role in accelerating things. They will raise the Hormuz issue so that the American fleet will come and do, I do not know what, to Iraq. They will come to an agreement with the Iranians in order to scare the Gulf people so that they can have a presence and arrange the situation in the region, and then turn to Iraq and say that the Gulf people fear us and that we do not help them [the Gulf people]. That is why they [the Gulf people] were forced to bring the Americans for protection.

They became very nervous. They wanted to arrange the Iranian situation according to their plan, and they also want to arrange the Gulf situation according to their plan that depicts the role of Iranian events. Fine, but every time they do something we go and get involved in it. They said these were international forces. Well, as long as they

advisers, "Saddam Hussein's mind is like any person's mind," and he and his leadership thought exactly "like any Iraqi citizen who cares about his country." SH-SHTP-A-001-041, "Saddam and His Cabinet Discussing Sanctions, the United States, Egypt, Turkey, and Other Issues," 6 October 1996; SH-SHTP-A-001-207, "Saddam and Senior Ba'ath Party Members Discussing Iraqi Laws, Pardons, and Various Other Issues," 22 July 1995.

[30] For instance, see Bruce W. Jentleson, *With Friends Like These: Reagan, Bush, and Saddam, 1982–1990* (New York: W. W. Norton & Company, 1994), 203–6.

[31] SH-SHTP-D-000-559, "Saddam and His Inner Circle Discussing Relations with Various Arab States, Russia, China, and the United States," undated (circa 4-20 November 1979).

[32] Saddam was not alone in accusing the United States of backing the revolution. Shahpur Bakhtiar, who served as prime minister during the final few weeks of the shah's regime, the shah himself, and many others charged the United States with undermining the Shah's regime and supporting the revolution. Jahangir Amuzegar, *The Dynamics of the Iranian Revolution: The Pahlavis' Triumph and Tragedy* (Albany: State University of New York Press, 1991), 79–81; Shahpur Bakhtiar and Fred Halliday, "Shahpur Bakhtiar: 'The Americans Played a Disgusting Role,'" Middle East Research and Information Project Report No. 104, (March–April 1982), 13.

do this and they have international forces, you, Arabs of the Gulf, need to be afraid of them and take them into account in a way that you don't [*inaudible*] for them or international forces [*Saddam laughs*]. So, they came up with this new [*inaudible*], the Iranians hold American hostages. The Americans are citizens of a major power. And Iran warned America, "If you do not extradite the shah, we will continue to hold your American citizens."[33] Two days ago, they [the Americans] sent doctors to treat the shah. They are really caring and after two days they [the Iranians] captured the hostages.[34] All of this is a soap opera. We know all of this, but what bothers us more and within the same plan is that if the Arabs in Ahwaz [*inaudible*] or if they need weapons, money, media propaganda, films, they are willing to help.[35] But whether to revolt or not it is up to them [the Arabs in Ahwaz]. Even to disseminate these slogans, it is up to them, but as long as they come to us and they are looking for our support, we can tell them what we can offer. If they provoke the Kurds, we will still be in the middle. What a disaster, and at the end, they will still want to bargain about this situation. Well, we are one of the involved parties and we do not bargain. We do not belong to a major power and we do not object if someone wants to revolt. But they did not experience this. They have organized technical circles that can reach a certain extent so that they can adjust the political situation in Tehran afterward according to their plans, as well as their influence on the region according to their plans.

It is very likely that an American airdrop would happen in order to restore dignity to clerics whose influence has diminished. We are talking about the American occupation here. The Americans came, the Americans go, [*inaudible*], they want to embarrass the Iraqi position . . .

Saddam and the Revolutionary Command Council analyze American Involvement in the Iran-Contra Affair (13 November 1986)[36]

Tariq: Sir, we said that the president [Ronald Reagan] ignored in his speech on November 13 the role of Israel in the deal that took place with the renowned leaders of Tehran, and that the American administration has full knowledge that Israel's goals regarding the war Iran is carrying out against Iraq contradict the goals President Reagan announced in his speech.[37] The Zionist role in this operation is

---

[33] The Shah entered the United States on 22 October for medical treatment. On 24 October, doctors in New York removed his gall bladder and gallstones and performed exploratory cancer surgery. See Victor Cohn and Susan Okie, "Doctors Say Shah Could Leave U.S. in 4 Weeks," *Washington Post*, 15 November 1979; "When the Shah Needed the Best in Care," *U.S. News & World Report*, 5 November 1979.

[34] Iranian students stormed the U.S. embassy and seized the hostages on 4 November 1979.

[35] Saddam is referring to the Arab population of the southwestern Iranian province of Khuzestan (often referred to as Ahwaz or Arabistan). Some of these Arabs pushed for separation from the Persian-dominated nation, often with Saddam's help. The struggle for this diverse and oil-rich region was one of Saddam's motivations for the Iran-Iraq War.

[36] SH-SHTP-A-000-555, "Saddam and His Revolutionary Command Council Discussing Reagan's Speech to the Nation on Iran-Contra Revelations (part 2)," 15 November 1986.

[37] Ronald Reagan, "Address to the Nation on the Iran Arms and Contra Aid Controversy," 13 November 1986, accessed 8 August 2008 at www.reagan.utexas.edu/archives/speeches/1986/111386c.htm.

one of the reasons that not only allows, but strengthens doubt about the authenticity of the announced goals of the secret meetings with Tehran, unless there are clear steps for these types and [*inaudible*]. This is just a light expression that the Zionist role –

Saddam: [*Interrupting*] Yes, but we need to confirm our doubts regarding the overlapping of activities.

Tariq: Yes.

Saddam: Between Zionism, known for its hostility to Iraq and its personal goals, and the American behavior in this manner.

Tariq: Israel's goal regarding the war Iran is conducting against Iraq contradict what has been announced, because what he stated was to reach a quick conclusion.[38]

Saddam: Look into what the answer could be. Yes, Comrade Taha?

Taha Yasin Ramadan: Yes, actually, my evaluation of this issue has to do with the intentions and what is behind the actions. When we see them in detail, they don't seem to be of great significance, yet they are indicators of dangerous intentions. Before Reagan's statement and during the last meeting on Wednesday, I considered the issue a conspiracy and still do, and after listening to Reagan's statement I did not expect him to talk this way. Where some paragraphs were – in my opinion, in looking at the way the issue was disclosed, and even in the way of dealing with the issue until now – it serves us. I mean, it is more to our benefit than against us.[39] In my evaluation of the American behavior that comes immediately after restoring relations between us and them – I mean I distinguish it and would call it a conspiracy and a dirty one if this had taken place before relations were restored. But practically the first contact was after restoring relations.[40] So, this gives an intended goal to this conspiracy. There was a purpose where even restoring relations did not calm people down and become something normal.

––––––

Saddam: The significance of American action, Comrade Taha, is that for the last 12, 18 or 14 months – they just started at the president's level designing a plan on how to deliver weapons to America.

Taha: To Iran.

Saddam: To Iran. Therefore, how much time do they need to come close to achieving their goals, which Reagan announced, and achieve the desired influence?

[38] Whereas Reagan reiterated in his speech a U.S. desire to foster a cease-fire between Iran and Iraq, the Iraqis believed that Israel sought to perpetuate the war as long as possible to weaken Iraq and to keep Iraq's attention focused eastward.

[39] Saddam, however, claimed to view U.S. interference differently. Shortly after Iraq invaded Kuwait, an adviser reminded Saddam, "Entering the Iranian war, America and the rest of the world interfered, which had an impact on us and affected us tremendously." Saddam responded, "You are right. Such a battle injured us." SH-SHTP-A-000-674, "Saddam and His Inner Circle Discussing the United States, Leaders of Gulf States, the 1991 Gulf War, and Other Issues," undated (circa February–March 1991).

[40] The United States and Iraq reestablished formal diplomatic relations in November 1984.

Male 1: Yes, it continues.

Saddam: Therefore, according to U.S. desires, as long as weapons are the approach to the war – I forgot to mention the new relations we need to record and that Comrade Tariq needs to mention in his letter.[41] As long as the key to this new relationship is weapons, then it is our right to remain suspicious that the U.S. will always consider the weapons issue primarily to wield influence and get close to the regime that Reagan set forth in his speech. And since the need for weapons increases during wartime, we have the right to be suspicious of the U.S. call to stop the war.

Tariq: The speech you mean?

Saddam: No, I want it detailed. I want the letter to be this detailed – that we, now and in the future, will be suspicious of U.S. invitations and we will doubt them in a practical way. Reagan said, "We get closer to Iran through weapons." Iran needs weapons the most during the war; therefore, how many more years does Reagan need the war to continue so he can get closer to achieving the goals he has set, and for the influence he wants to get out of Iran? This is the dangerous point in the conspiracy. And if you are going to answer and say you don't need this during a state of war, then it is our right to be suspicious of the manner by which you aim to stop the war. This is connected to my old suspicion and I agree and discussed with Comrade Tariq how to be careful and pay attention even to the difference in expression between stopping the war and ending the war.

So you see, we are sensitive about this issue to that extent. The Americans are being watched. That is why I am telling you that I was not surprised. Though this level of bad and immoral behavior is a new thing, I, and I swear, I am not surprised, because I have noticed that even in the nations of the region, there is a Zionist desire that if the war stops outside of its wish, that the war will stop but will not end. And this is also connected to the desire of some people or nations in the region.

Taha: Yes.

Saddam: Because they want you to keep asking for their friendship as long as the war continues, and to continue dealing with them with some measure of flexibility. And they want Iraq to keep dealing with a measure of flexibility at the cost of principles, be it with the Western world or with neighboring countries. And they want some of the governments they want to create illegitimately in the area to remain standing and have influence and be effective, as long as Iran fears that Iraq would return to war and Iraq fears that Iran would return to war. And that is what the conspiracy is, to cease fire and negotiate in this conspiracy. Now our land is in the hand of Iran and

---

[41] This is probably a reference to Saddam's 18 November letter to Reagan. As Richard Murphy, the State Department's assistant secretary for Near Eastern affairs, summarized, the letter provided "a measure of the intense anger and sense of betrayal felt by the Iraqis... it is difficult to refute the Iraqis' underlying accusation – that the U.S. has armed Iran to kill Iraqis, and that the action may well have spurred others to sell to Tehran." See State Department Memorandum, Richard W. Murphy to Undersecretary Armacost, "U.S.-Iraqi Relations: Picking up the Pieces," declassified (formerly secret), 5 December 1986, available in "The Origins, Conduct, and Impact of the Iran-Iraq War, 1980-1988," a Cold War International History Project–National Security Archive documentary reader, accessed 30 March 2009 at www.wilsoncenter.org.

we keep negotiating, and our lands remain with Iran while the U.S. keeps creating fear in the Iranians. And after that, the weapons would be the main ingredient that would give Reagan the desired influence and bring him closer to the decided-upon degree [of influence], as long as the war stops without ending. But the situation of the war either continuing or stopping without ending is the only state in which Reagan thinks he can reach, according to his speech, the desired influence in Iran. And in all cases, this cannot happen, except at Iraq's expense and as a form of conspiracy against Iraq, because a conspiracy is nothing but a continuation of the war and the high death toll. That is a conspiracy, while stopping the war while maintaining a state of war is also a conspiracy.

———

Saddam: I mean, the president's speech talks about two militarily warring parties. As far as scandal, it is true that the issue is not related to both of them, but as far as circumstances, they both engaged in a war against each other. So, when it [the United States] considers one party [more] important, this means it is possible to act at the cost of the other party. It is obvious because this is –

Male 2: Because they are not friends of Iran. They were not friends, originally.

Saddam: Because when he talks about an ongoing war and two disputing parties, the issue becomes one of weapons reaching the other party. He also gave it a strategic analysis to highlight the importance of the other party to American interests. So, this is clear and he did not discuss the importance of the other party – not in the region, not regarding security and balance or any other thing. It means it would not have been so bad had he not talked about the war at all, but about this aspect only. But he came and said, "We will stop the war, this and that and so forth." Well, when he leaves out the other party and its significance when talking about the war between two parties, this means he might accept a sacrifice from the other party in order to please the party he is talking about.

Adnan: This is understood. I did cover the money issue that Your Excellency mentioned and I am not going to talk about it since it is clear, because it created an effect and had an impact, and therefore, [inaudible] they are going to learn some secrets and interfere with them, which means that the armament process for the next step, Mr. President, is going to be [inaudible].

Saddam: Of course.

Adnan: And he is trying to cover up. Iraq, Mr. President, has been present on the national territories for four years, and Iran also has a presence on the Iraqi national territories. Iran spent the last four and-a-half years attacking while Iraq was on the defensive. Iraq responded to all peace calls while Iran remained stubborn.

Izzat: He says [inaudible] the defense as if –

Adnan: When are they going to be on the defensive side in order to get defensive weapons?

Saddam: We are more deserving of these defensive weapons.

Izzat: We are.

Adnan: [Inaudible] the statements of the American president.

Saddam: True. [*Tariq Aziz laughs in the background.*] He who talks this way should give to his brothers, I mean he needs to give to his defending brothers instead of his attacking brothers! [*Saddam laughs.*]

Taha: Because Iran says it is going to be attacking instead of defending!

Saddam: But, brothers, Iran is the original one.

Tariq: He said the one who [*inaudible*] is one of their folks. He asked that person, "Do you give weapons?"

Adnan: So, as far as the political relations, Mr. President, first, they are related to the embassy and hostages issue, and they are still hostages. We have had a good relationship with them [the Americans] for about two years now.

Saddam: Zionism, Abu Ali, Zionism; Zionism, all of the propaganda talk that you know. You know where it reaches and where it pours and you know who represents the real danger to you.

Male 2: True.

———

Abd al-Ghani: The issue of Al-Fao during this period concerning [*inaudible*], Your Excellency pointed out precisely in a previous analysis the participation of Americans in concealment and the intent of deception that took place [*inaudible*] – the Al-Fao matter [*inaudible*], Sir.[42] There is an indication when talking about the source of the American decision – in my opinion, it was not a big mistake to determine the source of the American decision to be the president and some ministers. The American intelligence is a primary source for an American decision since the decision source was [*inaudible*]. And this is why I am quoting what Comrade Tariq said after he left the United Nations and following his meeting with some American officials – I say, Sir, that all American officials who are related to the source of the decision contributed to this matter [*inaudible*] Iraq and standing by Iran, without taking [into account] American intelligence and the Secretary of State as the source of one decision, where the influence of Zionism on it is obvious and certain in this direction.

———

Abd al-Ghani: What I wanted to say, sir, is that the source of the American decision is one – one source with a Zionist influence. As for the Arab situation, I believe that

---

[42] Iran attacked and overran the Al-Fao Peninsula in February 1986. Although Iraqi commanders on the ground reportedly observed Iran's preparations to attack the peninsula, Baghdad insisted that the attack would come further north. The attack at Al-Fao took the command by complete surprise, and Iraq was unable to repulse the Iranians or retake the peninsula until two years later. Saddam appears to have believed that the United States shared intentionally misleading intelligence with Iraq to help Iran achieve the battlefield victory. Later, he and his advisers attributed their April 1988 retaking of the peninsula to their care in deceiving the United States about Iraq's military plans. See SH-SHTP-V-000-612, "Saddam and Senior Military Officials Discussing Efforts to Retake the Majnun Area," undated (circa summer 1988); Karsh and Rautsi, *Saddam Hussein*, 161; Kevin M. Woods, Williamson Murray, Thomas Holaday, Mounir Elkhamri, *Saddam's War: An Iraqi Military Perspective of the Iran-Iraq War*, McNair Paper No. 70 (Washington, D.C.: National Defense University Press, 2009), 70.

the Arab Gulf countries are going to react to Reagan's speech. Therefore, they need our support, as Your Excellency has mentioned. At the European level, I believe the speech indicates that Reagan acquitted Iran from being involved in terrorist operations.

Saddam: [*Inaudible.*] The news agencies say that an official statement on Iraq regarding the American stance toward the new relations will be issued today in the afternoon, I mean so that the news agencies will be psychologically prepared.

Abd al-Ghani: At the European level, sir, Reagan acquitted Iran of being involved –

Saddam: [*Interrupting, talking to another unidentified male.*] You can leave the meeting, go and let them know and then come back.

Male 3: Yes, Sir.

Saddam: [*Inaudible.*] The news agencies. Yes, Comrade Abd al-Ghani.

Abd al-Ghani: The American president absolves Iran of its involvement in terrorist operations while all European countries issued successive statements saying that Iran is an obvious source of terror in the world. I believe this is an important issue we need to mention. [*Inaudible.*] As for the internal situation, I think, Sir, it is important for us not to magnify the matter internally in the direction that the-American-weapons-this and the-American-weapons-that.[43] We should focus on building our nation and reinforcing the infrastructure and mobilizing and continuing this mobilization in this [*inaudible*].

Saddam: When the US weapons were at their strongest in Iran, we damaged them and turned them to scrap. Even now, thank God, with our aerial power a third or quarter of its previous size, and thank God we turned them all to scrap metal.[44] So what is going to happen to the American weapons now?

––––––––

Hasan: Sir, I pointed out in the last meeting that America's stance is conspiratorial and that the conspiracy is continuous whether it is from the Iranian attack or supplying Iran with weapons from different sources or America's latest stance, which is the last part of conspiracy before the war ends. I also mentioned that the fact that countries supply Iran with weapons means the war will continue, and this is part of the conspiracy. Therefore, if we want the war to stop, the countries should stop providing Iran with weapons. Sir, through reading Reagan's letter, there is a quite complete and obvious bias toward Iran. Also, it appears that Reagan's announcement of this letter, in addition to his being under American pressure and public opinion, I think the letter shows his desire to continue this dialogue. When he says, "Our goals were and still are to restore our relationship with Iran," and what they offered in terms of weapons is the start of a political bribe to Iran in order to get inside Iran. Therefore, Sir, I also think this letter is a form of terrorism toward the region – especially the Gulf countries. Maybe once these countries become familiar

43 Abd might be referring to the TOW and Hawk missiles that the United States delivered to Iran. These weapons helped Iran's light infantry resist Iraq's attempts to retake the Al-Fao Peninsula. Pollack, *The Persian Puzzle*, 219.

44 Throughout this volume, we translated "Allah" as "God" rather than leaving it in the original Arabic.

with America's stance, their [own] stance might look concerned, reluctant or passive toward Iraq. Therefore, I believe we need to rush to activate the – we need quick diplomatic action so that we can stop this situation at a certain point, make Iraq's stance clear to these Gulf countries, and continue to expose America's stance.

_____

Saddam: As for me, I was not convinced, not for a single day, that America does not provide Iran with weapons. Not for one day, meaning never, because here in front of us are the Iranian weapons and they are working, which means I am not convinced with what Rafsanjani said, that he is manufacturing missiles and I don't know what. [*Inaudible*], we have been dealing with each other for the last seven years and these things are known, the same way it is impossible for Iran to be convinced that the Soviets do not provide Iraq with weapons.

Tariq: And you were never convinced of the information we received.

Saddam: Never!

Tariq: You used to doubt it.

Saddam: I mean always –

Tariq: You were the person who most doubted it, and many times I used to say, "You are a bit skeptical" and would ask why [*inaudible*].

Saddam: Why do you think I used to doubt the American side? I mean in the last three or four years – meaning when the war, of course, just started. I mean my doubt was not that great at the beginning of the war, but grew more and more six months after the war had started, and that is because there were some clear statements and what we did not see from them, we used to see in the general situation of the area before us. Therefore, comrades, the Americans used to supply Iran with weapons in the past.

. . . He [Reagan], as the head of the White House, interfered in the transaction for the following general reasons: first, Iran was in a weak position and not a strong position, as Comrade Taha mentioned; second, because Khomeini will soon pass away. I mean Khomeini will not live for one thousand years. He is 87 years old now plus three, this means it is getting close to the end.[45] Close to dying, he is 90 – which means that Khomeini is practically not a factor in the decision. Meaning he is really outside the decision – meaning who makes the decision today from Khomeini's vital side now and daily practical implementation is his son Ahmad and not Khomeini.

_____

Saddam: Therefore, the "after Khomeini" period is coming upon us. We have taken that period into account. The Soviets focus on it and so do the Americans; as a superpower they have to focus on it and take it into account. What happened was no surprise then, while the way it took place was, meaning the manner was surprising. The fear is that Americans in particular and their supporters conspire at a cost to Iraq, meaning giving in to the Iranian stubbornness at a price to Iraq's sovereignty

---

45 Khomeini was born in 1902; thus, at the time of this conversation, he was eighty-four.

is something, you know, that has never been out of my mind for one day since the war started to this very day. Never, and we have been very careful in this regard, even the details, even the Islamic committee.[46] Maybe Comrade Tariq noticed how extra sensitive I was toward it and I told him at that point, and I told him, "Cease the committee's activities, because it was a conspiratorial committee and in the end it will conspire against us. And in order to stop the war it will give something to Iran at our expense. Kill it, because the Americans are in it."

Male 2: They are in it and with significance.

Saddam: It had been a while, not today, for over a year, a year-and-a-half ago –

Tariq: I have done it before –

Saddam: He [Tariq] killed it at the Fez meeting, but once again we were taken by surprise with these absurd decisions that we know are conspiratorial.[47]

Tariq: This is the last meeting, sir, a meeting before –

Saddam: Meaning, there is nothing new and let us not be stubborn. It is true that the Gulf countries are friends with America as far as sharing the same ideas, a mutual space of modern perspectives exists between them and America, but do not think that the Gulf countries are not cautious of America and don't get this impression. Don't get the impression that the Gulf countries can't make independent decisions, to a certain extent, without fearing that America will hurt them. To the contrary, they have the ability to think and analyze [independently]. In any case, the Gulf countries are not willing to ignore the fact that Iraq is equal [in weight] to Iran and Syria, Syria is equal to Iraq, just as Iran is equal to Iraq. They are not willing to ignore these facts, from Dubai to Saudi Arabia, they all face this matter. So, they will always have this equation before their eyes. I mean no American behavior can erase this equation, but it can partly affect this equation to the degree we mentioned, where Iranian stubbornness receives compensation at the expense of our sovereignty, or our interests, or both, I mean to some degree.

Besides, this is the Americans' policy: they will enter and their president said the way they entered was through the position of [providing] weapons, while we are at war with Iran. Okay? But do you think the collapse of Iraq would bring the Americans closer to the location where a strike might take place and leave an impact? As analysts, as people on the outside, do you think a weak Iraq would make Americans stronger and their weapons more valuable in their relationship with Iran, or would it be if Iraq were strong? I say that Iraq somewhat strong is better than a weak Iraq, and I say this from a perspective as if I were in the Americans' place, when using the weapons card as a foray into restructuring the Iranian government, with an eye on

---

[46] This may be a reference to the Islamic Peace Committee, a component of the Organization of the Islamic Conference.

[47] In November 1981, the Arab League held its twelfth summit meeting in Fez, Morocco. At the meeting, Crown Prince Fahd of Saudi Arabia presented an eight-point peace proposal (the "Fahd Plan"), which recognized Israel's de facto right to exist, as an alternative to the Camp David process. Saddam refused to attend the conference, as did leaders of seven other Arab states. The summit ended in acrimonious disagreement, suspended until the following year. See Johanna McGeary, George Russell, and William Stewart, "Failure in Fez," *Time*, 7 December 1981.

the future in the relationship between Iran and the US. That is how I see things as an analyst.

So, the sure thing is that we must ask ourselves how much the Soviets believe that extending the war would give them influence inside Iran or inside Iraq. How much do the Americans believe that extending the war will give them influence inside Iraq or inside Iran? This question has been on my mind and it is not new to us.

––––––––

Saddam: I told him [the Kuwaiti Minister of Finance] that I was confused as to why the US refuses to give the Kuwaitis weapons.

Tariq: But they can –

Saddam: At that time, I gave him the name of the weapon. I told him, "I didn't like the American behavior. Did that mean the Americans intend for Kuwait to be weak before the Iranian threats and Iranian danger? Did they want to put Kuwait in the corner facing the danger from Iran so that it would give more facilities to the U.S.?" So, as you see, I am not just sitting there; my mind is mulling over even the little things and taking them into account...

So, yes, they want more facilities than what we have given them in the Gulf, and they believe that putting pressure on Kuwait is required in this regard, but not to the extent that I went to in my suspicions, but less than that, and yet the man said – No, his analysis, I mean the man had some logic, but he said, "I am going to talk to your brother, Sheik Jaber [Al-Ahmed al-Jaber al-Sabah] about this issue" –

Male 4: I am sure he didn't say anything –

Saddam: But I am going to express my personal opinion. So, we have been watching the Americans for a long time. They want to scare the Gulf countries so that they can get privileges, and since the Al-Fao issue happened, I was convinced there was something going on. And I told [Kuwaiti Finance Minister] al-Atiqi, I told him, "The Al-Fao issue and the deceptive role played by the Americans was striking." So, what was the purpose? The purpose was that the danger would come closer to the Gulf countries so they could push them more, in addition to the issue of Iraq and the marginal issue we discussed, where they believe and not only they, but the Japanese also believe, and so do the Soviets and Arabs, meaning putting pressure on this stubborn party must be [*end of recording*].

Saddam and His Inner Circle Discuss Why America Has Supported Iran (15 November 1986)[48]

Saddam: [*Tape begins midsentence.*] That is what I wanted to say, because this is not unusual; [however,] it is new as far as the lack of ethics and the low level of morals of Americans and their president, in particular. And what is new is that it allowed us – outside the conclusions – to confirm a few of our conclusions, but they are clearer as far as the balance they [the Americans] want to set for Iran and as a result, they might agree to take sides at Iraq's expense once they give this significance

––––––––

[48] SH-SHTP-A-000-556, "Saddam and His Inner Circle Discussing Iran-Contra Revelations," 15 November 1986.

to Iran. We are aware of this in our conclusions, but they admit it now – I mean through their president and not through a journalist or some low-rank individual. This is no surprise to us and therefore, don't elaborate much on it. This is truly what it is. But if you want to be more enthusiastic and so forth, that is what the results are going to be at the end and nothing more.

The Americans have supplied them [the Iranians] with weapons before, favored them before as Comrade Tariq Aziz previously stated, and they previously preferred them to us along with the rest of the big nations, not because they are better looking than we are or because they are better than us, but because it is more possible to control them than us, which means it is possible to influence them. Why would they come to us? What for? We welcome them. Have not our relations with the Americans been ongoing for nearly two years?

Tariq: Yes, since 1984.

Saddam: Then what?

Tariq: Exactly two years.

Saddam: I am trying to understand exactly what happened here and why we are being punished because of our position toward Zimbabwe, the Palestinian issue, or something else. I do not understand what illegal thing the Americans hold against us.

Tariq: Sir, we modified Puerto Rico's issue; we used to demand the independence of Puerto Rico.

Saddam: Yes.

Tariq: Now we vote for Puerto Rico, but [*inaudible*] and Puerto Rico is considered a part of America [*laughter*].[49] You know, Sir, this is an internal matter and it does not make sense to vote for one part of the United States. It is not more than politics, Sir, and we must not let anyone extort our external politics and if we want to embrace a new situation –

Saddam: We must do it gradually.

Tariq: [*Voices overlap.*] To Turkey. I told him in Turkey I can act in a way that will not harm US interests, but –

Saddam: What is the significance whether or not we voted for Puerto Rico's independence? The Puerto Rico issue should not have a major effect on the basic politics of a country or on the Iraqi economy and national politics... Of course, they care about Iran. America wants to use Iran since it is one of the Soviet Union's neighbors. It has one common border with the Soviets and another one with the Gulf and oil

---

49 On 14 October 1986, Iraq voted in the UN Special Committee on Decolonization to "decolonize" Puerto Rico and to "reaffirm the inalienable right of the people of Puerto Rico" to "self-determination and independence." It had cast similar votes on the issue in previous years. See Ivan Zverina, "U.N. Committee Votes to 'Decolonize' Puerto Rico," *United Press International*, 14 August 1986; "U.N. Committee Reaffirms Right of Puerto Ricans to Independence," *Associated Press*, 15 August 1985; "General Assembly renews call for free Puerto Rico," *United Press International*, 4 August 1982.

countries. That is what is going to happen. They will enter the Gulf and Syria, attack both of them, and enter Iraq. That is exactly their strategy...

Tariq: Sir, I would like to comment on a topic we already discussed at the Command meeting.

Saddam: I just want to remind all of you that the Americans' stance was very bad, but the Gulf countries helped us. We should not believe that once the Americans act tactically with regard to their own strategy, it will automatically affect the position of the Gulf countries.

Male 1: No, actually, I believe it is the opposite; this is going to anger America.

Saddam: As I stated in the beginning of this meeting, they could attack our country in order to invade Iran...

————

Tariq: In fact, I am convinced because they [Iran] exceeded their limits by attacking our capital...I suggest we should strike them back one for one. If they strike Baghdad, we strike their city...

Saddam: Because of the American story yesterday, I did not want public opinion to take the [inaudible] direction, otherwise, I would have told them, "Go ahead and [inaudible]," since I don't see any more reason for us not to strike. But I thought about it myself and wondered why we are diverting the public Iranian [opinion], Iraqi [opinion], and the region's opinion from this issue. Let us be quiet regarding this issue and wait for the proper time for it. But for them to strike Basra but we don't [retaliate] or to strike Baghdad but we don't [retaliate], the issue is no longer –

————

Latif: Sir, I have something simple to say. I believe the Americans – belief means concluding and sometimes feeling, and one should thank God because one's feeling was sometimes accurate. What Your Excellency said is like someone who had a dream that came true. We used to say what Reagan said and we used to say what the Iranians said. If you read between the lines you will realize that, apparently, the Americans promised the Iranians more than this, a lot more than weapons and issues related to Iraq. We should keep looking closely at this until it reaches, some day, the position they agreed or disagreed on. The proof of this is the speech Rafsanjani gave and I will go back to its text and send it to Your Excellency. Rafsanjani stated, "We have no objection if the Americans want to change the regime in Iraq, but then the new government would give us our right."[50] This speech of Rafsanjani is taped, so who inspired Rafsanjani to give such a speech and how can America change the regime in Iraq? We need to go back to this.

Male 2: Especially to his third speech and today's [speech].

Latif: What did you say? No, his speech just two months ago. That talk occurred two months ago. Who suggested that to him? We are not afraid of such a statement, thank God; however, we must clarify it with others.

————

[50] Iranian Speaker of the Parliament, Ali Akbar Hashemi Rafsanjani, spoke before the Iranian Parliament on 4 November 1986, the seventh anniversary of the U.S. embassy seizure.

Saddam: That is very true.

Latif: We must investigate the motives of others and on what basis they made such a statement. If they are opposed to our regime – that means if they ever invaded an area – they might claim it was based on their agreement of dividing our country among them. They might have agreed previously on sharing the lands of Iraq as soon as the war stops; therefore, we will be stubborn and refuse to cease fire until all parties withdraw. It is absurd to imagine them splitting our country. I believe some groups have been promised – Iran has been hallucinating based on America's promises. We shall seek the truth regarding this matter, as I mentioned to you, Sir.

Saddam: Yes, we need to investigate such a matter thoroughly. It is very easy for Iraqi aircraft to strike Iranian aircraft and in return, the Iranian aircraft will strike us, followed by another aircraft that will intentionally strike the iron and steel factory, followed by another aircraft striking the Ministry of Foreign Affairs, God forbid, followed by [thirty seconds blank in the recording]. No matter how independent I am or what kind of principles I have, even if I stop the war, this infrastructure – the wise one will probably say, "Why should I negotiate with a party who promises me nothing in return, when another party offers me everything?" Let us talk about the Iranian mentality, I mean the bad shape they are going to end up in and the losses they will suffer. Their infrastructure and what was built during the last ten years is going to be destroyed. Why doesn't America ask Iran to negotiate with us?[51]

Latif: We should ask them.

Saddam: It does not have to be [inaudible], just a true and existing need and not created. The need of the Iranians for the Americans is not created and neither is the need of Americans for the Iranians. Their objective facts are clear and evident. So, it does not have to be the Iranians' illusions that makes them get closer to the Americans; it does not have to be just the [influence of] Zionism that makes the Americans get closer to the Iranians. There are facts, but additional known factors play a role expressing these facts. So, as long as the Iranians wish the war to continue, they should resort to the Americans or the Soviets, but they will need to pay a price for it.

Saddam, Meeting with Senior Officials, Discusses How Lessons from the Iran-Contra Affair Affected Iraq's Decision to Invade Kuwait (15 December 1990)[52]

Saddam: Do you remember when they [the Americans] were preparing Israel to attack us? And we said clearly, "If Israel attacks us, we will attack back, and if it [Israel] attempts or thinks that possessing the nuclear bomb would be enough [to scare us, they are wrong], because we are capable of burning half of Israel."[53]

---

[51] Saddam and Latif appear to be suggesting that U.S. encouragement and unspecified promises to Iran, most likely possession of Iraq's predominantly southern Shi'a region, have dissuaded the Iranians from making peace with Iraq.

[52] SH-SHTP-D-000-557, "Saddam and His Senior Advisers Discussing Iraq's Historical Rights to Kuwait and the US Position," 15 December 1990.

[53] Saddam exclaimed in a 2 April 1990 speech, "If an aggression is committed against an Arab and that Arab seeks our assistance from afar, we will not fail to come to his assistance. [The United States and England] will be deluded if they imagine that they can give Israel

This happened last April, right before the events. The war was launched on us long before all of this. It officially started in the 1986 meeting, and was exposed under the title "Irangate," which included Iran, Israel, and America, supported by some regional countries. All this documentation was released. Then the situation developed to where it is now.[54] August the second was an attack and a defense both at the same time, because we were unable to keep a base taken from Iraq and yet we accepted this face, hoping they [Kuwaitis] would be our virtuous brothers while it [Kuwait] turned into a base for villainous people to conspire against us.

THE UNITED STATES IN THE MOTHER OF ALL BATTLES

Saddam and his advisers paid close attention to U.S. signals and domestic politics in the months before Operation Desert Storm (January–February 1991). Saddam himself was the ultimate analyst, instructing his intelligence services to provide raw news on America but not analysis. Nevertheless, his understanding of the United States lacked depth. He discussed with his foreign minister whether President Bush would attack Iraq even if both branches of Congress opposed, whether he would attack days before an election in the hope of securing Republican congressional victories, or whether he might postpone elections if he thought his party would lose. In the second recording that follows, Saddam says the United States would have been unable to fight Iraq were it not for others' financial support. America lost in Vietnam because, unlike the war with Iraq, corporations were unwilling to finance the war. Rulers in America and the rest of the West, Saddam said, are merely representatives of corporations.

Saddam and His Inner Circle Analyze U.S. Domestic Politics, American Warnings, and the Likelihood of U.S. Military Action Against Iraq (circa late October 1990)[55]

Saddam: On the same day, I sent for Comrades Tariq and Latif and told them my analysis now is – it seems to me that things are 50/50, or let's say on the edge; neither war, nor – both possibilities exist and they might be to the same degree. The first consists of choosing the diplomatic way and long, drawn-out negotiations, but then things will settle however they will settle. While the other one is the decisive

---

a cover in order to come and strike at some industrial metalworks. By God, we will make fire eat up half of Israel if it tried against Iraq." "President Warns Israel, Criticizes U.S.," FBIS-NES-90-064, 3 April 1990, from Baghdad Domestic Service (in Arabic), 2 April 1990.

54 While in U.S. custody, Tariq Aziz reported that Iran-Contra disclosures reinforced Saddam's image of America as untrustworthy and "out to get him personally." Tariq claimed that this mindset contributed to Saddam's decision to invade Kuwait. See *Duelfer Report*, vol. 1, "Regime Strategic Intent," 31. The quotes are from the *Duelfer Report*'s summary of Tariq's statement.

55 SH-SHTP-A-000-670, "Saddam and His Senior Advisers Discussing Iraq's Foreign Relations and the Policies of Various Countries," 11 October 1990.

way, resorting to the military option. What we have here is a complicated country, meaning that decision making is complicated in this country, to make the decision and identify it. When we want to gather information about America, it is not a country like Iran where we can easily gather information. The decision is also not Saudi so we can gather intelligence on Saudi [Arabia]. The decision is American and requires being alert as politicians even before the intelligence community. Actually, I forbade the intelligence outfits from deducing from press [reports] and political analysis. I told them this was not their specialty, because these organizations, when they are unable to find hard facts, they start deducing from newspapers, which is what I already know. I said I don't want either intelligence organization to give me analysis; that is my specialty. I told them they should only give me news so that they don't get distracted and cover their failure with news they don't understand.[56]

We also understand our political role in finding the connection. So, I brought together both comrades [Latif Jasim and Tariq Aziz] and told them, one of you will be assigned to the Ministry of Information and the other to the Ministry of Foreign Affairs, which are the two most important sources in politics. I want you to pay attention to how things are leaning, toward war or peace, so that we may have enough time to give our troops, our organizations, and our people the signal to be ready, and not let them be caught unaware, because constant pushing makes them indifferent and no pushing makes them indifferent, both ways. We have arrived at the same conclusion that the way things are going now, we can't say [whether] they are going toward peace or a state of war. We agreed to continue on that basis of analysis, which is what I used with the Iranians, some of it out of deduction and some of it through intuition and making connections between issues all without having hard evidence.[57]

———

Tariq: The Secretary of Defense said that they needed a hundred thousand soldiers.[58] The number, a hundred thousand soldiers, is either to con us – if it is a bluff, then so be it – it means the strike is near. But if the timeframe of the expected military strike passes, he cannot continue bluffing. He has to come out and say he is not going to send a hundred thousand soldiers. Then he is going to be asked and required

[56] Saddam is not alone in concluding that political leaders are more qualified to assess their counterparts than intelligence community analysts. According to Kenneth Lieberthal, "Presidents and many other senior policymakers are experts at 'reading' other political leaders – a skill most IC analysts understandably do not share. If such insights are routinely shared they may improve the quality of intelligence analysis, especially as regards elite politics." Kenneth Lieberthal, "The U.S. Intelligence Community and Foreign Policy: Getting Analysis Right," Brookings Institution Foreign Policy Paper Series No. 17, September 2009, xiv, 56–57.

[57] A few weeks earlier, Saddam instructed his advisers to concentrate on Iraqi deductions rather than on what Bush chose to emphasize. *SH-SHTP-A-001-209, "Saddam and Senior Ba'ath Party Officials Discussing Iraq's Occupation of Kuwait," September 1990.

[58] Dick Cheney actually said that the United States would send 100,000 more soldiers (in addition to the 210,000 U.S. troops already there) to the Gulf region. The purpose of this additional deployment was to give the United States an offensive capability against Iraq and to increase the pressure on Saddam to withdraw from Kuwait. Michael Gordon, "US Decides to Add as Many as 100,000 to Its Gulf Forces," *New York Times*, 26 October 1990; John King, "Cheney: Administration Plans to Continue Gulf Buildup," *Associated Press*, 25 October 1990.

to answer why he is not sending a hundred thousand soldiers. If he is planning on sending –

Saddam: [*Interrupting.*] In their latest statements, they have been pulling back from discussing details. They are making general statements.

Tariq: Yes, but Sir, he has to respond. These Americans are daily under questioning, God help them, even the Americans. Sometimes I see them being chased by the journalists, almost cornering a person – he has to give a response. Cheney yesterday was on TV and was asked, "When you send [troops] how many are you going to send?" He said that there was no limit to the number of soldiers that are going to be sent. So they, if they don't –

Saddam: So he generalized instead of being specific.

Tariq: If he doesn't carry out the operation tomorrow or the day after, they will wait until they have the hundred thousand sitting in Saudi Arabia.

Saddam: So he evaded responding to the last question?

Tariq: Yes, he evaded. What is even more than that, yes –

Saddam: Yes, he evaded giving a number, even from saying a hundred.

Tariq: Yesterday, the British commander of the Desert Rats said he would be ready for a strike on November 15 – [59]

Saddam: So, he gave a specific date, meaning there is danger before the 15th.

Tariq: Yes, he said he would be ready on November 15, and therefore, if he is not going to strike soon since he is not ready by November 15, he has to be committed to his word because he is going to be held accountable...

Saddam: Holidays – we postponed a strike on Iran because of the holidays.

Tariq: Yes, the holiday season is here, leave for the holidays. Christmas and New Years are not something they are willing to compromise on. They are times for family gatherings and entertainment, and the president who brings corpses to his country at Christmas time will be skinned alive in the US. Because if a war happens, they know it would not end between November 15 and December 15. It would not end in one month and they know it, which would mean New Year's and Christmas would come with the tragic results of the war obvious to them. He will not risk it; therefore, in my estimate we can start calculating from –

Saddam: Then how will they do it now?

Tariq: Now, now, it is still a while away.

Saddam: Hmm, only two steps away?

Tariq: Sir, allow me. I told you the reason, the reason is the elections. Bush has a problem running his country. He is a Republican president, and both houses are

---

[59] This reference is to the British Seventh Armoured Brigade, which would become part of Britain's 1st Armoured Division when additional units of the British Army arrived. See Patrick Cordingley, *In the Eye of the Storm: Commanding the Desert Rats in the Gulf War* (London: Hodder and Stoughton, 1996), 13.

Democratic. Reagan ruled for a long time with a Democratic Congress, but his senate was a Republican majority and they were supporting him. Now the majority of the house is Democratic as usual, and the senate is also Democratic, and they are giving him a very hard time. For the budget they gave him a hard time; thus, for this reason he may consider war to gain a Republican majority, which would strengthen his chances of ruling the US and of staying for another term. That is the only reason. As I explained to you, Sir, I have no other reason. He is now on the campaign trail in support of the Republicans in the elections. He is visiting the states and giving speeches, which is common for American presidents to do. Meaning, he goes to speak on behalf of the candidates from his party generally and for the –

Saddam: [*Interrupting.*] But in that case, if he can't reach an agreement with the opposing party, would the president be able to make a monumental decision, if both parts of the house were from the opposing party?

Tariq: Sir, they –

Saddam: [*Interrupting.*] They are going to stand there and tell him they are not going to take responsibility and that he would have to do it and bear full responsibility on his own. Would he be able to do that?

Tariq: Well, he met with the leaders of the Congress the day before yesterday, and they came out and said they support the president in his current policies. But they also said they advised him to be a little more patient. One of them even said that when the president said he has lost patience, he responded that losing patience should not necessarily lead to war.

———

Taha: Yasin Ramadan I believe that the US and its allies know that the war will not end in five or ten days, so why would they strike 15 days before the elections? So you hit and lose, and let the other party win the elections?

Tariq: The elections are on the sixth of the month, and the idea is that they can announce the war three to four days before the elections, because at the beginning of any war the people always feel more patriotic, so that could help win the election [*inaudible*].

Saddam: But if he sees the other party, would he say, "Let's postpone the elections"?

Tariq: [*Inaudible.*]

Taha: I am not entirely convinced that announcing the war by the American president now that he is a nominee during the election period, after three months have gone by, is going to improve his popularity and enable him to win.[60] That is a little – not very [*inaudible*]. The Congress [*inaudible*]. Second, when he says, and we heard him say that on the 20th he will be visiting Saudi Arabia. So, how could he go to war before then?

Saddam: It could be to trick us.

---

[60] Bush was not a nominee in October 1990, when this meeting was recorded. The United States was having midterm congressional elections, not presidential elections, at the time. As this makes clear, Taha fundamentally misunderstood basic U.S. political processes.

Saddam Discusses the Role of Capitalism in America's Involvement in the Mother of All Battles (circa 19–21 August 1991)[61]

Saddam: Some people thought that when you are a Westerner, all the treasures of the world open up before you. They forgot that the ruler in the West has become the representative of the corporations. The whole policy of corporations is built on the basis of profits and losses. And their representative cannot make any risky decision and cannot make any decision with dignity. There is no more dignity in the West.

Tariq: It has never existed.

Saddam: Well, it has never existed, but even –

Tariq: [*Inaudible.*]

Saddam: Even the way it existed in the '40s and '50s, this way doesn't exist anymore today. It doesn't exist. So, the – the change has many advantages to the – the world, the Arabs and Iraq. We should know how to behave with regard to what happened. Every – every situation has an indicator that could be measured up to the day and the hour. It is true that they understand our situation, but at the same time, it is clear to us and clear to the whole world that this is a victory for us, one way or the other.

———

Saddam: America, comrades, America is not an easy country. But I am telling you that America disclosed its weakness when it launched its military operations against us in the same way it unveiled its strength. I previously told you, "Let's theoretically suppose that Saudi territory and Saudi wealth did not exist. Would America have been able to undertake a military campaign with this magnitude against Iraq?"

Male 1: No, no, impossible.

Saddam: If all the Arab wealth and all the Arab territories did not exist, would America and the West have been able to undertake the campaign they launched against Iraq?

Abu Khair:[62] It is very unlikely.

Saddam: If the Soviet Union had not been in the condition it was, would America have been able to continue with the military campaign the way it did?[63]

Male 1: No.

Saddam: Three factors. Well, if any one of these three factors did not exist, the Western campaign would not have been, at least we could say, would not have been able to continue all this long time . . .

Male 1: No. That's correct.

---

[61] *SH-SHTP-A-001-210, "Saddam and His Inner Circle Discussing Upheaval and the Communist Coup Attempt in the Soviet Union," undated (circa 19–21 August 1991).

[62] The editors were unable to identify this individual, other than with the informal "Abu name" provided here.

[63] Earlier in the recording, Saddam and his advisers were discussing the communist coup attempt in the Soviet Union. The coup, which began 19 August 1991, was defeated two days later.

Saddam: Well, with regard to Vietnam, they couldn't find people who would fund a military campaign. So, in fact, the West is very strong but at the same time it is very weak. As we said, those who are now powerful in the West are those who are governing in the name of the corporations. They cannot fund a large campaign, because corporations are not ready to pay, and we saw the results. One of the reasons in Vietnam and in other places was due to the factor we indicated. The voter said he would not pay taxes anymore [*clears his throat*]. To continue their campaign, the taxpayer would pay them small amounts, little by little. They would not pay 100 all at once, or I don't know how many billion, 50 billion in one lump sum. Who in the world would fund a military campaign for 50 billion?

Male 2: 100 billion.

Male 1: Everything has an end.

AMERICA DURING THE CLINTON YEARS: POTENTIAL FOR RAPPROCHEMENT?

After Bill Clinton's 1992 electoral victory, Iraqi leaders met to consider the possibility of rapprochement with the new administration and agreed to take a softer tone toward America in the hope of improving relations.[64] Saddam commented that U.S. support for Israel and its desire for cheap oil would hinder rapprochement, but he described the new administration as pragmatic, recognized the new administration's softer rhetoric toward Iraq, and believed that America would need to limit its foreign military adventures if it wished to improve its economy. In a recording from mid-1995, Saddam discusses his frustrations with American unwillingness to abide by agreements reached during the visit of Congressman William (Bill) Richardson, who had come to Iraq to secure the release of two American prisoners. In the future, Saddam commented, communications would go only through Iraq's ambassador in Washington.

In recordings from November 1995 and February 1998, Saddam and Tariq Aziz discuss how U.S. electoral politics affect America's policies toward Baghdad. In one, the Iraqis wonder whether Clinton will attack Iraq to help him win reelection. In the second, they conclude that Republican calls for regime change were intended to weaken Clinton without prematurely replacing him, and that Democrats and Republicans alike recognized that America was unable to unseat Saddam. The chapter ends with Saddam and his cabinet discussing the need to link newly elected President George W. Bush's interests with those of oil companies.

---

[64] On 19 January 1993, Iraq announced a cease-fire in the no-fly zones as a "goodwill gesture to the new US President." See "Iraqi Cease-Fire Offer and Comment: RCC Declares Unilateral Cease-Fire, Calls for 'Constructive Dialogue' with US," BBC *Summary of World Broadcasts*, 21 January 1993, from *Republic of Iraq Radio*, 19 January 1993.

Saddam and Top-Level Ba'ath Officials Discuss the Causes and Consequences of Clinton's Electoral Victory and the Potential for Improved Relations (Circa 4 November 1992)[65]

Saddam: Good morning, good morning. Good morning, everybody. The [people] of al-Anbar did well with [cheering] "Bush, Bush, listen well."[66] [*Laughter.*]

Male 1: The group of comrade [*inaudible*].

Saddam: When they first started it. [*Pause.*] I don't have an urgent thing, but I thought maybe the comrades have ideas concerning the – the – the transition of authority from our friend the –

Male 2: The bitter.

Saddam: The bitter [*laughing*] to the new person especially in the media perhaps they need a stand or a [*inaudible*]. So, let us hear if the comrades have any comment. Yes, Comrade Tariq.

Tariq: Mr. President, as a formal stand, in my opinion, we shouldn't take a formal stand on what has occurred in the American elections. We have previously discussed this in the National Command, and there was an agreement. In the media, a new president has been elected now. This president has not taken a specific stand toward us. He took – he made some negative comments, not very severe, even though [the comments] were of a negative nature, as I said. But the election campaign is one thing and the politics practiced is something else.

Thus, I recommend that we don't have words with this man. In other words, we should not show Clinton a negative stand, but we should also be very clear that we don't let our people live in illusions, [thinking] this change is in its favor or in the Arab Nation's favor. That is to say, this should be clear in the analysis, because Your Excellency used to, more than once, advise – advise us that one doesn't necessarily need to express his opinion through direct speech, but rather through analysis that leads to this conclusion. Let us watch where his policies will settle.

––––––––

Saddam: We were able to assess the situation, which I believe is still true. There are proven facts in the American policy that we shouldn't ignore. Among these facts are interests that meet with – in part – keeping the Zionist entity strong at the expense of the Arabs. And with such a basis, we'll find ourselves clashing with it [the United States] in one way or another, and so will every genuine Arab who's ardent for his nation, even if he is not a Ba'athist, because keeping the Zionist entity strong and effective at the expense of the Arabs merely strengthens the extortion and constitutes a continuous insult to Arab sovereignty and to Arab rights, including the harm done to the future that's supposed to, or must, or ought to be open for the Arabs as a nation, which has the right to live and has the right to make progress according to its capabilities and circumstances.

––––––––

[65] SH-SHTP-A-000-838, "Saddam and Senior Ba'ath Party Members Discussing the Transition from Bush to Clinton," undated (circa 4 November 1992).

[66] Al-Anbar is a large, majority-Sunni province in western Iraq.

But does – doesn't Bush's fall reflect one side of Iraq's role in his fall? In other words, hasn't the Mother of All Battles been a basic reason for overthrowing Bush?... Comrade Dr. Elias's expression is true indeed.[67] That it is true that Clinton fell –

Male 3: [*Inaudible*] Bush.

Saddam: Bush fell – pardon, Clinton won in America, but Bush's fall has its reasons... We say that Bush depended basically on the saying that he saved the world and saved the West. Or rather he saved the West, if we concentrate, thus he saved the West from the regime in Iraq. His foes were answering him, saying, "You did not save us from the regime in Iraq." In other words, even in the subject of his success, he postulated that he couldn't achieve successes inside American society. But so he could say he understands foreign policy, and to express his understanding, that in foreign policy, [he said] there was a severe danger for the West. This danger was coming from Iraq, and he confronted it. They answered him saying: "You raised the topic of overthrowing the regime. Even in this, where you say you succeeded, you failed."

_____

Saddam: Let them [the Iraqi and Arab people] enjoy this part, but we just need to tell them, "This is the part of your rejoicing that cannot be a permanent state of rejoicing, except for one condition that exists in the same part of your joy; why did Bush fall?"

_____

Saddam: But through our subsequent analyses, we should remind [you] of the established facts that meet with the Zionist policy and lead the American ruler to imperial thinking regarding the Arab nations on two points: wherever the American policy meets the Zionist policy, it becomes hostile; and wherever the American policy supposes it must obtain its interests at the expense of the Arabs, it is imperialistic. And wherever there is oil, of course in the second possibility we mentioned, wherever oil is brought up as one of the reasons it is because the Americans must get it for the lowest price possible and in the quantities they want, and at the Arabs' expense, they project their prices. I would not say the lowest price, but we should notice that even the right substitutes have prices that suit them, regardless of what harm that might inflict on the Arabs, and in the quantity they want, regardless of anything that pertains to the interests of the Arabs, we will then find ourselves clashing with American policy. Thus, as a matter of fact, what happened in the Mother of All Battles, and not in the symbol of Kuwait, is that we clashed with the West, and the West – and the West clashed with us...

Bush's failure to achieve his goal was a basic reason for his fall. In other words, he put himself in – in the position that it's either him or Iraq. That is, within this – this – this concept. So when that was not achieved, his competitors used it against him, to weaken him, I mean. We can say nothing, namely, political, and won't lose a thing. And we can say things and won't lose a thing. But sometimes in circumstances of this kind, results occur without a word, under the title of politics in its traditional

[67] Earlier in the meeting, Dr. Elias had stated that although Clinton won the election in America, on the international scene, Saddam was the victor.

meaning. [For example,] "An official so-and-so speaker stated such-and-such, and [*inaudible*] such and such," I believe. But we can say all this speech also without losing a thing. Not toward the new ruler, or toward anyone else. In other words, we say that we are against the bad stands and bad intentions and not against persons and –

Male 4: We would then have delivered an opinion.

Saddam: Yes, we would then have delivered an opinion.

Male 4: Yes.

Saddam: ... All the world is now saying, "Man, why are we then afraid so much?" Bush fell and Iraq lasted. That is, definitely, there are people who [*inaudible*] say [*inaudible*] people that he changed. Besides, there are some people who [*inaudible*] who's changed. Namely, when different results come out from one, people are afraid, etc., and shaking. Besides, look at – look at his nestlings he hatched since he was an intelligence manager in the Arab homeland. Look at how they're doing now. In this region, his nestlings are many. Half the Arab rulers who are ruling now are his nestlings since he was an intelligence manager. The one in Turkey is also among his nestlings.[68]

Tariq: I want to alert you to one aspect: this man was elected as a president of the – of the American state. Perhaps he doesn't intend to say bad words about us, and about you personally. That is, perhaps, it's – it's – it's not his aim to do so, it's not on his mind.

Male 5: [*Inaudible.*] We prepare.

Tariq: If there is any imbalanced behavior, the Jews will extort him. That is to say, let's not forget the Jewish factor.

Saddam: The Jews will take advantage of it.

Tariq: Yes.

Saddam: They're going to say the same day, "Bush offered us this" –

Tariq: No...

Saddam: "What do you have to offer us?"

Tariq: ... No, no, they are going to extort him. I meant that some vicious Jews are going to extort him and say, "Look –"

Male 6: To provoke him.

Tariq: "You are weak, the Iraqis say you are weak. Look at Bush and how they used to fear him and so forth while they make light of you." In return, he is going to say something bad. As a result, the possibility to give and take will become slim if not missed. Hence, all that I am asking is for the comrades to notice this aspect, which is that we should not give the Jewish viciousness the chance to play –

---

[68] Saddam appears to be referring to Bush's tenure as director of Central Intelligence and of the Central Intelligence Agency (1976–1977).

Saddam: I have one last point, so that I don't forget it. It is not – not important for this meeting, but for the future. The Westerners are going to maliciously extort us once again along with the inspection committees. Now, this is Clinton, I don't know what to do in order not to ruin our relationship with him. What is [*inaudible*].

I will actually no longer accept extortion, because we have nothing left. Let everyone stay where he is. If they lift the siege, we can reach an understanding, but if they don't lift [it], we will have no more hope of reaching an understanding. We have nothing. Whatever happens, we're not going to knock at their door. But we don't accept that every day someone comes knocking at our door, [saying], "Actually, don't let Clinton get upset," and "Don't let what's his name, the new British Prime Minister, get upset, or this one, [John] Major, or the other one." That is the limit. This talk, I mean, is not the basis of our policy. That is, we reached this limit. Namely, if Bush is staying, that's the limit we've reached. And the memorandum we sent them is clear in its language, and its vocabulary, and in –

They're going to come to us. Bush has four months left. There are two months. Two months. "Don't get that one, Clinton, upset with you." "Don't let so-and-so." And we tell them, "We actually – it is Clinton who is supposed to be willing to carefully handle the relationship between us in a way where *we* don't get upset with him." Why is it only he who gets upset with us? Why doesn't he carefully handle his demeanor that is legitimate in all standards? To have his demeanor balanced toward us? Why should we be careful in handling our demeanor toward him? He is a state – a part of a state that assaulted us and is still assaulting us.

In other words, if we accept peace with him, just because he says, "Hi" and we say "Hi" back, this, in itself, is a big improvement. But on the level of diplomacy, [if] so-and-so tells him a story, he tells him, "Hey buddy, Clinton, you don't want to take an action that forces us to take an action in return toward you and show a relationship of a kind that we don't want." That is to say, I think all such talk is supposed to be this way.

Saddam and Senior Advisers Discuss Clinton's Desire for Talks With Iraq and Impediments to Improved Relations (13 January 1993)[69]

Saddam: What I want to arrive at, although I have elaborated a little bit and given you comparisons, what I want to arrive at is that the new American president should review the . . . policy. Well, who considers it useless and sometimes dangerous? It's the one who reaches something – something he didn't take into account and something not in his interest. [*Inaudible.*] Well, all this animosity toward the United States and all its interests in the Middle East are due to – are due to an international and Arab imbalance. It means two imbalances. If an Arab regime were to suddenly change – let's suppose they said in the morning that the regime in Egypt or Saudi Arabia changed.

Usama:[70] Yes, every [*Inaudible*].

Saddam: Well, what would happen to the US interests in the presence of such animosity toward Iraq? Okay, let's suppose we were told in the morning that a

---

[69] SH-SHTP-A-000-872, "Saddam and Advisers Discussing the US Airstrikes on Iraq, the Election of Clinton, and Sanctions on Iraq," 13 January 1993.
[70] Usama Abd al-Razzaq Hammadi al-Hiti, minister of oil (1991–1993).

revolution occurred in Russia and the young men are hungry and, I mean, agitated and filled with anger against the – against the – against the – against the old regime because it placed a great country at the service of the US State Department's staff. What would happen? Nothing would happen. It's impossible that any reasonable person would stand up and say, "Let me forget about it." [*Inaudible*]. With the existence of such animosity, the killing of children and women and the shortage of – of – of medicines, well, it's not possible.

For this reason, I believe that during this man's reign, a change will occur. I could detect in today's recent statements after the operation what he was obliged to say because he is American and the President of the United States.[71] Besides, this man – this Bush is being asked on a daily basis about behaviors, stories, and questions. So, he [Clinton] should say something related to this atmosphere that is [*inaudible*] and pertaining to the official president before he assumes power. Despite that, he is still patient, he didn't try to push things. And he told a story where part of it, for sure, is related to – to the core of the subject. He [Clinton] said that if he [Saddam] had spent the time he has been spending on the maneuver of SAM [surface-to-air] missiles on the well-being of his people instead, he would have become a great figure, or something like this.[72]

Male 1: Yes, Sir.

Saddam: He started to talk.

Usama: It means he was unconvinced.

Saddam: What's this SAM maneuver? Do they think we are going to maneuver while their planes are on top of us all day? Stop your planes. The – all this indicates is that after he assumes power and after the development, expected in France in March, there will be changes.[73] At what level will the changes be and to what extent? I don't – I mean, I don't want to anticipate because we mainly rely on God, and then we rely on – we did not go anywhere. We are still standing on our feet and our feet are steady on the ground and we cannot say that the coming US president could review his policy after saying he will modify the image of [it], which objects to our existence. This is the logic. These are the political and economic reasons we should look at. They always want to prepare something so that when this thing becomes allowed [*inaudible*] Ozal, Demirel and others for personal political and economic reasons.[74] They want to say that they were negotiating before this thing happened, but don't expect them to take a step if they don't feel there is a change in the US administration. Of course, they hear more through their channels from the Americans than we do, because we have no relations with the Americans [*inaudible*], their experience, their

---

[71] The "operation" refers to U.S. bombing of Iraqi antiaircraft missile batteries in southern Iraq on 13 January 1993.

[72] President-elect Clinton said the following: "You know, if he spent just a half, maybe even a third of the time worrying about the welfare of his people that he spends worrying about where he positions his SAM missiles and whether he can aggravate Bush by violating the cease-fire agreement ... I think he'd be a stronger leader and be in a lot better shape over the long run." See "The New Presidency: Excerpts from an Interview with Clinton after the Air Strikes," *New York Times*, 14 January 1993.

[73] Saddam might be referring to France's March 1993 legislative elections.

[74] Turgut Ozal, president of Turkey; Suleyman Demirel, Turkish prime minister.

age, and the fact that they had relations with the Americans before us. Since '84, Bush has messed the relations up.[75] Well, that's what happened. So, when they tell you they are going to speak with Clinton and so on, they might, in fact, speak with him.

Male 1: They won't get along with each other.

Saddam: Well, they will talk and their talk is useful . . . All those are subordinates, I mean, the Middle East governments are all subordinates and followers of the West, or at least when they see that the West has a viewpoint, each of them swallows his viewpoint. That's the subordination. Their move is useful, but don't put too much hope in it because it is separate from the transformation that will take place in Europe and the United States. Yes?

Usama: Your Excellency, I would like to add a word to what you have said. Clinton, today, despite the fact that he wants to support Bush in his measure, has said at the end of the – the sentence you mentioned –

Saddam: The issue of the assassination – [76]

Usama: Sir, this is one thing.

Saddam: Well, he is happy about it!

Usama: He said, let's open a new page for Iraq to comply with the UN resolutions.

Saddam: This is addressed to me, I mean.[77]

Usama: But three days ago, if I remember well, he said, "What do we want from Iraq? What we want is its return to the international circle."

Saddam: Yes.

Usama: Well, the truth is that his words were full of optimism.

Saddam: The news agencies and the political commentators said that what Iraq did delayed – delayed lifting the economic embargo from us. It's possible. Who are you to speak about the economic embargo? What are you claiming now – that we

---

[75] The United States reestablished normal diplomatic relations with Iraq in November 1984 and did not withdraw its ambassador until Iraq invaded Kuwait in 1990. The official policy of the Bush administration, as summarized in National Security Directive 26, was to engage Iraq in the hope of moderating its behavior. See NSD 26, "US Policy Toward the Persian Gulf," 2 October 1989, accessed 30 March 2009 at http://bushlibrary.tamu.edu/research/nsd.php.

[76] In Clinton's 13 January 1992 interview with the New York Times, which the Iraqis are discussing, the president-elect said that "the people of Iraq would be better off if they had a different leader. But my job is not to pick their rulers for them. I always tell everybody, 'I'm a Baptist; I believe in deathbed conversions.'" Saddam and Usama appear to be referring to this statement. "The New Presidency: Excerpts from an Interview with Clinton after the Air Strikes," New York Times, 14 January 1993.

[77] Clinton said, "If you [Saddam] want a different relationship with me, you could begin by upholding the UN requirements to change your behavior. You know, I'm not obsessed with the man, but I am obsessed with the standards of conduct embodied in those UN accords." "The New Presidency: Excerpts from an Interview with Clinton after the Air Strikes," New York Times, 14 January 1993.

impacted the lifting of the economic embargo! This indicated that the main issues have begun moving in the back of their mind. All of this falls within our analysis, since the division of our Iraq into lines during the Bush regime did not cause a storm, it would perplex the man when we raise the issue with him.[78] In other words, these are "pragmatic" [*in English*] people. It means they are not – they are not – they are not ruled by some viewpoints which, although we noticed that he [*inaudible*], that's Bush. It means that he did not use any objectivity and – you would say he belongs to one of the underdeveloped third world countries.

Usama: [*Laughs.*]

Male 1: Sir, if you allow me, we have a connection, Your Excellency.

Saddam: I meant to say that all the man's [Clinton] statements will show all the tricks they tried with him and how much they wanted to involve him, and the only thing he said was "I support Bush's measures to have Iraq implement the UN resolutions." Many UN resolutions have nothing to do with the UN Charter. Many of the resolutions that have been approved have nothing to do even with the United Nations. For example, what do the lines have to do with the United Nations?

Male 1: Not one resolution of the United Nations.

Saddam: I mean they have nothing to do with it. And the call to protect the –

[*End of tape.*]

Saddam and His Advisers Discuss the Decline of the United States and the Possibility of Rapprochement with the Incoming Clinton Administration (Circa 14 January 1993)[79]

Male 1: [*Recording begins midsentence.*] He provided us with information along with – what is his name, Samir Vincent?[80]

Male 2: Yes, his name is Samir along with that other individual. I do not remember his name. I mean that man, the oilman.

Saddam: His name is Oscar.[81]

---

[78] Saddam's comment about the division of Iraq into lines apparently refers to the U.S., British, and French imposition of no-fly zones to protect Kurds and humanitarian operations north of the thirty-sixth parallel, and Shi'a Muslims south of the thirty-second parallel. See David M. Malone, *The International Struggle over Iraq: Politics in the UN Security Council, 1980–2005* (New York: Oxford University Press, 2006), 97–99.

[79] SH-SHTP-A-000-753, "Saddam and Senior Advisers Discussing Bill Clinton's Administration and Its Attitudes toward Iraq," undated (circa 14 January 1993).

[80] Samir Vincent, an Iraqi American businessman, pleaded guilty in January 2005 to illegally helping Iraq evade the economic sanctions for millions of dollars in oil profits. For a number of years, he acted as an unofficial envoy between Iraqi, U.S., and UN officials. See Paul A. Volcker, Richard J. Goldstone, and Mark Pieth, *Independent Inquiry into the United Nations Oil-for-Food Programme* (New York: United Nations, 2005), vol. 2, 72–96, accessed 3 April 2009 at www.iic-offp.org/documents/Sept05/Mgmt_V2.pdf; Department of State, Bureau of International Information Programs, "Justice Department Secures Guilty Plea in Oil for Food Scandal" (19 January 2005).

[81] This is a reference to Oscar Wyatt, the founder of Houston's Coastal Corporation. Wyatt acted as an unofficial intermediary between the United States and Iraq and in later years

Male 2: Yes, his name is Oscar. However, Sir, the inclination of the Clinton Administration staff members, as Mr. Tariq Aziz noticed during the meeting, had, in fact, a
positive aspect. I mean, Clinton had other alternatives along with some negative elements toward us to the extent that the head of the National Security Group, Admiral
Kraus [Crowe], who is known for his inclination to support Iraq.[82] But, there are
some positive influencing factors. Also, the US Department of State is working on
some elements and is going to say, as Your Excellency recalls, they are working on
this staff in a way that the Zionist organization in addition to Bush's hostile elements
want to pave the way in the Clinton administration for stances where it would be
difficult for him to get out of them later on. Therefore, they want the British to say
–

Saddam: Such politics still abided, according to his [Clinton's] saying, because they
say that they [the United Nations] comply with Bush's decisions and that is of course
a strong message to Saddam Hussein since he refers to the UN resolutions in every
matter. He is very much aware and knowledgeable of the UN resolutions. If anyone
comes back and asks him, "Did you say that?" he will reply, "Yes, I said that.
However, I did not issue the UN resolutions." He will probably say, "I was forced
to say that for America's sake and according to my position as a president."

Male 1: There is a story, Sir, about that man you are familiar with: Oscar.

Saddam: Who is that?

Male 1: His name is Oscar, Sir, the oilman.

Male 3: That is an old story.

Male 1: Yes, he has good relations with us and Samir. We made the connection so
that we don't take time from Your Excellency – we connected him with Mr. Tariq.
He is going to carry letters to the new administration. We are not going to write
anything to Your Excellency because as soon as he arrives here with Samir Vincent,
we will send them over to Mr. Tariq and hear what they want to say. We shall follow
your instructions about the way to talk, in a surprising way to them and make them
wonder whether or not Iraq is capable of such discussion. But we are going to focus
on the unity of Iraq and noninterference, as well as other issues.[83]

---

paid illegal kickbacks to Saddam's government for oil sales though the UN oil-for-food
program. See Press Release, U.S. Attorney, Southern District of New York "Texas Oilman
Enters Mid-Trial Guilty Plea to Charges of Conspiring to Make Illegal Payments to the
Former Government of Iraq" (1 October 2007), accessed 23 March 2009 at http://newyork.
fbi.gov/dojpressrel/pressrel07/illegal%20payment100107.htm.

[82] Although Saddam pronounces an *s* at the end of the name, this is a reference to Admiral
William Crowe, chairman of the Joint Chiefs of Staff under Reagan and George H. W.
Bush. Saddam might have viewed Crowe as inclined to support Iraq because Crowe turned
down Bush's offer to serve a third term after his second expired in September 1989; testified
before Congress that a ground war with Iraq would result in six thousand to thirty-six
thousand American casualties; and endorsed Bush's rival, Clinton, for president during the
1992 election campaign.

[83] According to Samir Vincent, Wyatt provided Iraq with telecommunications equipment,
global positioning systems for army helicopters, and medical supplies. See David Ivanovich,
"Defense for Iraqi Notes Emerges; Wyatt's Lawyers Say Oilman Relayed Messages in Bid
to Avert War," *Houston Chronicle*, 7 September 2007.

Male 4: Sir, after the meeting between the minister and Mr. Tariq Aziz, there were the same inclinations that he wrote about and summarized [*inaudible*] memorandum [*inaudible*]. When he showed it to some influential elements of Clinton's administration, they could not believe the fact that the [Iraqi] officials can write in this manner and the distorted picture representing us [*laughter*]. He said, "They want to hide your picture from the new administration. Even, Sir, Mr. Nizar Hamdun, when he presented our memorandum four or five days ago to the four representatives, it contained about four or five issues which Nizar said he had heard differently.[84]

I called Nizar Hamdun to inform him of what I heard. He stated that it was not what we presented and he requested a copy from me to send to his people who work for the new Secretary of State.[85]

It was not at all how we presented them through Nizar. We do not deserve that. It did not present the current Iraqi situation at all, Sir. We do not want the world to ask, "What did the Iraqis say?" And they will think we are being stubborn, arrogant, and so forth. Therefore, we need to provide them with the main points in order for our enemies to be aware of our issues. Samir and Oscar are very optimistic. Moreover, Oscar sent letters informing us of his arrival around the 20th. God willing, we will receive positive news and –

Male 1: As the saying goes, "Bringing us his money." [*Laughter.*]

Male 4: Yes Sir, he is right, "Bringing us his money." Then Jesus may punish me later. [*Laughter.*] No, honestly he is a very practical individual and loveable.

Male 1: He is excellent, Sir, very honest and not a sneaky person by any means because he is an old man.

Male 4: He donated $5 million to Clinton's campaign.[86]

Male 1: He said we made him lose it. [*Laughter.*] He is a friend of the new Minister of Finance [Secretary of the Treasury].[87]

---

[84] On 14 and 15 January 1993, Nizar met with the U.S., British, French, and Russian ambassadors to the United Nations to discuss resumption of UN weapon inspection flights. The identity of the minister with whom Tariq met is unclear. Although the reference to the "memorandum" is also unclear, Nizar delivered an Iraqi letter to the president of the UN Security Council on 13 January that noted that "the United States gave the Council incomplete information" and exaggerated Iraqi objectives in prohibiting UN Special Commission flights. The prohibition, Iraq's letter claimed, was merely "a temporary request." See John Wright, "Iraq Told to Allow U.N. Flights to Resume . . . or Else," *Associated Press*, 15 January 1993; "Iraq and Kuwait: Iraqi Foreign Minister's Letter to President of UN Security Council," *BBC Summary of World Broadcasts*, 14 January 1993, from *Iraqi News Agency*, 13 January 1993.

[85] This is apparently a reference to Warren Christopher, who became secretary of state on 20 January 1993.

[86] According to Federal Election Commission records, Wyatt did not donate any money to Clinton's 1992 election campaign. He gave $1,500 to the Democratic National Committee in January 1991, but this is a far cry from what Saddam's adviser is describing.

[87] Apparently a reference to Senator Lloyd Bentsen, whom press reports indicated as early as 9 December 1992 would become secretary of the treasury. It is unclear why Saddam's adviser described Wyatt and Bentsen as friends, though the two shared various acquaintances among Texan elites.

Saddam: They are unbeatable and known for being good negotiators. I mean they are experts in negotiations.

Male 4: They are lawyers.

Male 1: As far as the Secretary of Defense, it is too late.[88]

Saddam: Do you mean too late to work with him?

Male 1: Yes.

———

Male 4: Today he [likely Clinton] had to present a statement that explained everything. He was forced to do so and had no choice.

Saddam: Well, he realized that the first one was not enough and unsuitable, therefore, he had to strengthen it.[89]

Male 1: They did not agree with him at all.

Saddam: It definitely did a major damage to America. Similar to Mikhail Gorbachev when he destroyed the Soviet Union, he will eventually destroy America, bit by bit.

Male 1: Yes Sir, you are right.

Saddam: I mean that they are not about to use an obviously harsh approach, they will gradually and smoothly destroy America. America must adapt to the new international situation, where the populations will recognize Somalia. They will face difficulties in Somalia.[90]

Male 1: They are already facing obstacles in Somalia.

Saddam: I already told you that you just wait and see what is going to happen to them in Somalia. They will probably face obstacles and problems before they even arrive there.

Male 1: It is going to be a slaughterhouse.

[88] Apparently Les Aspin, secretary of defense (21 January 1993–3 February 1994). Saddam's adviser might have considered it too late to work with Aspin because of Aspin's support for the 1991 Gulf War.

[89] The first statement apparently refers to Clinton's 13 January *New York Times* interview, in which the president-elect emphasized interest in behavior change rather than regime change in Iraq. The second statement seems to refer to a 14 January press conference, in which Clinton, on the defensive, accused the *New York Times* of misinterpreting his words and stressed that "no difference" existed between his policy toward Saddam and that of his predecessor. See Thomas L. Friedman, "Clinton Affirms U.S. Policy on Iraq," *New York Times*, 15 January 1993; "Clinton Has 'No Difference' with Bush on Iraq Policy," *United Press International*, 14 January 1993.

[90] President George H. W. Bush ordered U.S. forces to Somalia as part of Operation Restore Hope in December 1992. In support of UN Resolution 794, the United States was to lead the transitional United Task Force (UNITAF) to ensure humanitarian aid until the establishment of the UN Operation in Somalia II (UNOSOM II) later in 1993. The first Marines landed in early December. Saddam and his advisers, reflecting on the continued U.S. military buildup and involvement of the incoming Clinton administration, apparently viewed this operation as an attack on a defenseless country rather than a relief effort.

Saddam: The method used in attacking Somalia was unfair, since they had no government or stability. If you were fighting an average country, you could strike its factories or its buildings. What could you do to starving, naked people, fighting with their AK-47s? They have no government you could send tanks to attack, and that they could send their tanks to defend. The Somalis did not even own one plane to fly in order for America to strike it. They were only carrying their AK-47s and fighting.

The Somalis were desperately fighting the Americans to obtain their shirts off their backs. The Americans involved themselves in a major chaos and unnecessary financial debts. The Somalis were fighting with stones, so to speak, and they gave hell to the Americans and to the Israeli soldiers. On the Egyptian TV, they used to present the Israelis as heroes until they were finally exposed and the Somalis gave them hell.[91]

If the Americans continue such politics, they are going to face major troubles. Why would anyone want to elect an American? What did he say to him to influence him? He will probably say to him that he promises to improve the economic situation. How could he improve the economic situation with American soldiers spread all over the world?

Their economy will never improve with the expenses they spent in the Gulf and in Europe. They spent [$]68 billion in the Gulf, and in Europe, they spent [$]128 billion. If America does not withdraw its troops from all over the world, its economy could never improve. America is not in its youth phase. America is at the edge of elderliness and at the beginning phase of old age. This is nature, once you reach [inaudible]. The man might delay the deterioration; however, I cannot imagine the deterioration continuing. I mean it is impossible to give up its role of interference and influencing, and the latest foolishness made people apprehend it more and forced the blocks to move faster than before.

If America implemented a good policy, made a political difference in the world, emphasized improving the economy, etc., America would earn more respect from the rest of the world; however, it is not afraid at all. This means it is not aware of the consequences. That might result in close relations with China, the Soviet Union and India, Japan with Asia. Germany will develop to be an industrial threat and France will overspread the world markets. It will cause a major chaos all over the world.

Male 1: Sir, yesterday, as Your Excellency knows, the American president stated that the first thing he needs to do is allocate funds for the American troops overseas, [inaudible]. He made such a statement yesterday at the conference.

Saddam: It is impossible for him to do that in order to improve his economy. He could save a billion dollars from here, a million dollars from somewhere else, another two million from another place that could be useful, but it would not heal his wound that is so deep it cannot be healed unless he turns to the military budget.

Male 1: Reduction means withdrawal, Sir.

Male 4: Sir, he made a statement very similar to yours, Sir, I don't recall the exact day, but lately –

Saddam: I meant he is trying to make a connection with our issue.

[91] The meaning of this comment is unclear.

Male 4: He said, "We will not accept anything conditional if we want to adopt "policing," [*said in English*] meaning "control" if you do not want [*inaudible*].

Saddam: Now, the issue is ours. I mean opening the wound this way, missiles striking and aircraft flying and so forth does not agree with their policy. So, the first thing he is going to do is to reach an agreement with us, saying, "Okay, now we have withdrawn, please give us a break." Fine, we do not want to kill the thief; we want him to leave by the garden's back door.

[*A pause of one minute, forty-nine seconds in conversation.*]

Saddam: Did you hear what he [apparently Clinton] is saying? He said the 88,000 tons did not accomplish anything.[92] How about one ton [*inaudible*] that they hit?

Male 1: He also said, Sir, that the United Nations became a policeman serving the United States of America.

Saddam: All countries are going to be against the United Nations.

Iraqis Discuss Communications with the Clinton Administration Concerning Two Americans in Iraqi Custody (22 July 1995)[93]

Saddam: Read it to the comrades.

Tariq: Through one of his deputies, [Bill] Richardson has informed us today about his letter to Congress since he is supposed to come to New York next week to meet with me, saying that he met with President Clinton last night, I mean on the 18th, upon his arrival in Washington for one hour, in addition to other meetings with the president's assistants. He presented a report about his visit and particularly about his meeting with Mr. President, the Commander [Saddam]. Clinton's reaction was to confirm the possibility of communicating with the Iraqis and dealing with them.[94] There were hundreds of questions from President Clinton about the meeting with Mr. President the Commander, which indicates President Clinton's interest. Mr. Richardson wants to reiterate his statement to [the Iraqi] Mr. Vice President, "Stay cool," I mean for him to calm down. I will phone him tomorrow, and I will remind him that their side did not abide by the agreement that required confirmation

---

[92] The 88,000 tons appears to refer to the approximately 88,500 tons of bombs dropped on Iraq during Operation Desert Storm.

[93] SH-SHTP-A-001-207, "Saddam and Senior Ba'ath Party Members Discussing Iraqi laws, Pardons, and Various Other Issues," 22 July 1995. In March 1995, two American aerospace workers in Kuwait crossed the border into Iraq. They were detained by the authorities, charged as spies, and sentenced to eight years in prison. A 16 July 1995 meeting in Baghdad between Saddam and Congressman Bill Richardson led to the release of the prisoners. Peter Grier, "Iraq's Hussein Raises Eyebrows by Freeing American Hostages," *Christian Science Monitor*, 17 July 1995; David Wallis, "The Way We Live Now: 1-26-03: Questions for Bill Richardson; Negotiator at Large," *New York Times*, 26 January 2003; "UCLA: Gov Richardson Recounts His Deals with Hussein, Castro," 11 March 2008, accessed 28 July 2009 at www.youtube.com/watch?v=trqEqll6-iE.

[94] The Iraqis apparently also believed that Clinton sought to communicate with them through Wyatt. Three days after this meeting was recorded, Clinton called Wyatt to discuss issues involving Iraq. Later in the week, Vincent briefed Nizar Hamdun on Wyatt's conversation with the president. Ivanovich, "Defense for Iraqi Notes Converges."

from the White House, because the member of Congress was to carry a letter from President Clinton and also to express gratitude for the Iraqi position.[95]

Saddam: This made me doubt his intention. Perhaps next time he will want to discuss certain issues. As for me, perhaps next time I will not be able to meet with him, because not only is it unnecessary that I see him, but also what he told us was not implemented. As for us, all that we told him we carried out completely, but as for him, all the matters he talked about, none of them materialized. I mean everything. Okay, fine. How am I supposed to ensure his credibility, that he is coming to negotiate on behalf of the American government, as dispatched by his president or as instructed by his president? There is nothing here.

Male 1: Your Excellency, he presented the [*inaudible*] [*laughter in the background*]. It is scary. [*Inaudible*] on television, I believe, Mr. President, there is no need to [*inaudible*]. He immediately [*inaudible*].

Saddam: Maybe this is related to slaves, the American slaves.

Tariq: They regard this as a traditional saying, just as if someone is invited to a setting and he brings food with him, then he would start eating the food that he brought.

Ali:[96] [*Inaudible.*] That is in the event that it amounts to something.

Saddam: They will give him an antidote. They know what the cure is.

Taha: Mr. President, based on the developments and even the statements, you can deduce that it is easy for him to leave. It is obvious he is coming [*inaudible*].

Saddam: No, no, they needed to come, so that they can release the [prisoners].

Taha: Yes, but, their good preparation and this statement released to us were done according to an agreement with him. The correspondents went and asked him about the statement. They asked, "Did the Iraqis do this?" He said, "No." They asked, "Did the Iraqis do that?" He said, "No, fine." [*Inaudible.*] I mean he did not see this issued statement. Well, he did not deliver a letter.

Saddam: "Stay cool." That's what he said, or what? "Stay cool," just like what they say.

Taha: As for him being the representative, this is a known fact.[97]

---

95 Although the Iraqi media reported that Richardson delivered a direct plea from Clinton and the U.S. Congress, U.S. officials insisted that he visited only as a private citizen, delivered no letter or other type of document, and lacked authority to negotiate any deals. Grier, "Iraq's Hussein."

96 Ali Hassan al-Majid ("Chemical Ali") served as minister of defense (1991–1995) and member of the Revolutionary Command Council (1991–2003). On 16 July 1995, approximately one week before this recording, Saddam replaced Ali as defense minister and made him party head of the Baghdad-al Karakh region.

97 According to Richardson, the Clinton administration favored his mission as an unofficial envoy but did not want to be blamed if it failed. He later recalled, "The Clinton administration basically said, 'You're not a member of the administration, but if you succeed in getting the two out we want some credit. If you don't succeed, nice meeting you.'" See "UCLA: Gov Richardson Recounts His Deals with Hussein, Castro," 2:08–2:21.

Saddam: Don't be upset because of those people, this is how they deal. As for us, we already agreed, in the future, let them deal with the ambassador over there and wonder now who lacks credibility, they or we.

Tariq: He said you.

Male 1: Mr. President, I expect some kind of relief. This is the first time an American would come, despite all these announcements.[98]

Saddam: They needed that, and they were willing to take other steps if we wanted it. [*Voices overlapping.*] The visit was positive. No, no, positive. Once they go to America, despite all this animosity, and appear on TV and talk about torturing people, then what they say will no longer be considered credible, at least about the torture and terrorism. They will ask him, "Did you see Saddam Hussein? Is he like normal people? Does he speak nicely like normal people? Does he sip tea? Did you see him? What is this?" He will answer, "Oh brother, this is the first time we have seen things like that! He is a cordial man, he converses, and we found him as a normal person." And this imbecile, their Secretary of State, when asked, "Are they going to release them? Did Saddam Hussein release them" – do they mean that Saddam Hussein is a difficult person to deal with? They did not say that verbatim, but that was what they meant. He said he was tired of figuring out the difficult mind of Saddam Hussein.[99] I don't know why he is tired. Is this a chemical equation? Don't you know that Saddam Hussein's mind is like any person's mind? How are we supposed to deal with this, I mean?[100]

Saddam and His Advisers Question Whether U.S. Presidential Candidates Seek War with Iraq for Domestic Political Gain (22 November 1995)[101]

Saddam: Our battle is not over yet; it is still ongoing. Comrade Tariq, what I want for you and for the Minister of Foreign Affairs to focus on during this period is

---

[98] This is incorrect. In November 1993, Senator David L. Boren met with Tariq Aziz in Baghdad to secure the release of an American who had also, according to press reports, accidentally crossed the border into Iraq. Mark Fineman, "Iraq Frees American Jailed for 205 Days," *Houston Chronicle*, 16 November 1993.

[99] On 16 July 1995, Christopher publicly claimed he did not know why Iraq had freed the two Americans. "It's very hard to probe the mind of Saddam Hussein," he declared. A year previously, Christopher said in a CNN interview, "It is very difficult for me to get inside his [Saddam's] mind. He has a very warped mind." Peter Grier, "Iraq's Hussein Raises Eyebrows by Freeing American Hostages," *Christian Science Monitor*, 17 July 1995; "Hussein Must Not Be Allowed to Provoke Future Crises: Christopher," *Agence France-Presse*, 12 October 1994.

[100] A few weeks after this meeting took place, Hussein Kamil defected. The director of Iraq's Intelligence Service assessed that Richardson's visit, along with other indicators, made it "evident" that "the American administration attempted to comfort the Iraqi regime that there are good American intentions in easing sanctions or opening a secret channel for dialogue." However, he continued, "It appears that all of this was nothing but a cover to evade their true, seditious intentions." SH-IISX-D-000-407, "Report by the Director of Iraq's Intelligence Service on the Defection of Hussein Kamil," 29 August 1995.

[101] *SH-SHTP-A-001-206, "Saddam and His Inner Circle Discussing UN Inspections, Elections in the United States and Russia, and Other Issues," 22 November 1995.

whether the American president needs a war before the elections, or a war like the Iraqi war, in which he does not guarantee its results since he did not guarantee the results of the attack that happened before. Is he going to push it off and try to avoid it? Because if he tries to avoid it, its idea will put him in a critical situation. Making any type of reference to it would make him face the fear of embarrassment when matters come to this point. If he wanted it, then I do not think the opposite will happen...

Tariq: Sir, whether the president needs a war cannot be predicted before May or June. It will be hard for an analyst in November to say when, and the battle has not started yet. Until now, it is not known who is going to be his Republican opponent. It is true they have [Senator Robert] Dole, but there are ten from the Republican Party. From the Republican Party, ten entered the race. Will his party enter the race or not?[102] It has not yet been decided, but sometimes it happens. Because in the previous election there were other candidates against George Bush from the Republican Party but –

Saddam: They withdrew.

Tariq: They withdrew. Will his popularity rise, so that he will be in a comfortable situation in the election? Or will he be in a very critical situation and consequently the gang will start, the White House gang, which usually decides the election by looking for outside scenarios to support this candidate? In '92, it was clear that Bush wanted a war with us.[103] He wanted a war, but does he need it now? Now it is hard, I think it is difficult before the campaign begins, which will officially start in February. Also, Sir, as far as [Rolf] Ekeus, the papers and the reports issue, we still need some time to mitigate the turmoil that happened. The turmoil is less now than in August, but it did not disappear.[104]

From the tactical side, we are prepared to do a good job, I mean, preparing papers and answering questions. I mean the technical work is much better than before because entering the war with the United States will be fully understood at the political level when the technical side is strong and it will remain obvious that America, for a political and not for a legal reason, is the one hindering lifting the sanctions. Sir, the battle has a political nature and America has been unjust in this regard, and subsequently, this helps create support for our position, not necessarily from the Western countries, but from the other countries in the world. But following the technical and legal matter the atmosphere is still –

---

[102] Tariq is saying that it is too early to say if a Democrat would challenge President Clinton for the 1996 Democratic Party nomination.

[103] Tariq is apparently referring to the crisis during 6–29 July 1992, which followed Iraq's refusal to allow UN Special Commission inspectors access to Iraq's Ministry of Agriculture. In a meeting with his cabinet in July 1992, Saddam similarly shared his "high probability analysis" that Iraq's enemies "fabricated the Ministry of Agriculture matter" because "they intended military action." In the view of most Western observers, by contrast, Bush clearly did not want war. See Tim Trevan, *Saddam's Secrets: The Hunt for Iraq's Hidden Weapons* (London: HarperCollins, 1999), 185; section "Saddam orders Iraqis to resist and intimidate UN inspectors," in Chapter 7.

[104] In August, Hussein Kamil, the director of Iraq's Military Industrialization Commission, created a crisis for Saddam by defecting to Jordan and providing UN inspectors and Western intelligence agencies with information on Iraq's prohibited WMD programs. See Chapter 8.

Saddam: No, no, I do not think we will disagree on this matter, but the follow-up on the other side is important.

Tariq: Of course, we will follow-up.

Saddam: Because if it is not clear to him yet what will benefit him before next June, this means any war before next June will put him in a situation whose results will be unknown to him, because the nation's image became clearer to him after the referendum regardless of anything. The nation's image is clearer to him now than it was in the past.

At the same time he has his colleague's [opponent's] experience where he entered with a known weight, but did not get any result, a decisive result that would count for his side in the elections. He also has an experience when he engaged in a strike where someone launched his bombs outside the target. I mean when he bombarded the Intelligence and bombarded al-Nidaa.[105]

Saddam Discusses the Role of American Domestic Politics on U.S. Calls for Regime Change in Iraq (9 February 1998)[106]

Saddam: America uses the north and uses any kind of traitor under colorful covers in the south; however, it will not allow the creation of a state that would be under Iranian influence at the present time. This is the discussion going on right now. America wants and hopes, but a disagreement in slogans emerged between senators and Democrats.[107] The senators suggested that operations should have ousted the regime to make it difficult for Clinton, and so that they say they know best, since they have the experience. And so that they can tell him he failed in achieving the goal, if the regime is not ousted. And if he does not strike militarily, they will embarrass him. Clinton proposed instead, since he knows their intentions and they know each others' intentions, and said, "No, we want a military strike to stop Iraq from producing weapons of mass destruction; we don't aim to oust the regime."[108] This way he can say he achieves the goal wherever he reaches. Our analysis says that

[105] Saddam is apparently conflating two U.S. attacks: the cruise missile attacks launched at the headquarters of the Iraqi Intelligence Service by President Clinton in retaliation for an alleged Iraqi attempt to assassinate former President George H. W. Bush in 1993 and a similar attack Bush launched against Iraqi industrial targets on 17 January 1993, just before he left office.

[106] SH-SHTP-A-000-756, "Saddam and Senior Advisers Discussing a Potential Military Conflict with the United States," 9 February 1998.

[107] Saddam is apparently contrasting senators and Democrats, as the U.S. Senate at the time was controlled by Republicans.

[108] On 5 February 1998, Clinton said, "Our interest is preventing Saddam Hussein from building biological, chemical, nuclear weapons capability and the missiles to deliver such weapons." Regarding regime change, he noted, "That is not what the United Nations has authorized us to do. That is not what our immediate interest is about." Senate Majority Leader Trent Lott, Speaker of the House Newt Gingrich, and a host of other conservatives, however, called on the administration to replace the Iraqi regime. At the time of the recording, the United States had mobilized three aircraft carriers, twenty-four thousand troops, and hundreds of warplanes in the Persian Gulf to punish Iraq for failing to comply with its disarmament obligations. See Robin Wright, "News Analysis; Pressure to Remove Saddam Hussein Builds; Persian Gulf: Calls to Eliminate Iraqi Leader Come from Many Corners. All Strategies Are Fraught with Difficulties," *Los Angeles Times*, 6 February 1998; Steven Lee Myers, "Standoff with Iraq: The Overview; The President and the G.O.P. Diverge on

of course Zionism is in agreement with the idea of ousting the regime and will not feel comfortable unless the regime is ousted, despite all they say about destruction, because they witnessed an event experience with their own eyes. They witnessed how the re-building took place after the destruction of Iraq and watched when Iraq possessed weapons and said it would hit Tel Aviv if Baghdad were hit.[109] Therefore, he [apparently Clinton] carried out this plan.

But under the American planning, those in power know very well they are unable to oust the regime. Therefore, they have to identify a target within their power, which is destroying all the capabilities they can.[110] Also, the Republicans know, of course, that the regime cannot be ousted, and because they are aware of this fact they raise the slogan of ousting the regime since they know that Clinton is not going to oust the regime. As a result, they will use it against him and the mind will weaken. The Republicans want to see Clinton weak [but] they don't want him to fall. They want him to be weak because if he falls, Al Gore would take over.[111] And once Al Gore takes over, he might have the chance in two years to run for president again. In this case, it is possible for the Democratic Party to continue ruling for six more years. They want the Democratic Party's representative to be very weak so that they can create problems for him to the point that he weakens without falling, yet allow him to continue until the last day of the two years, giving them the chance once again to return to power. These are the existing cases.

We are sure that Europe, except for Britain, does not want Iraq. As for Germany, not everything it says is true; it did not wish for everything it said, but it had no other choice. What we know to be true according to our analysis that the French and Italians are talking about it, is that all of Europe does not want a weak Iraq, because they have started to make the connection between their interests to have America control the oil region by itself, or a weaker America.

Saddam and His Senior Advisers Discuss the Environment with the New Bush Administration (29 December 2000–6 January 2001)[112]

Saddam: Now, we have to make it clear that a connection exists between the new American president and the interests of the entities, the oil companies, regarding increasing or decreasing prices.

Iraq," *New York Times*, 5 February 1998; Peter Jennings and Forrest Sawyer, "Showdown with Saddam," *ABC News Saturday Night: Peter Jennings Reporting*, 7 February 1998.

[109] This might refer to Saddam's 26 December 1990 threat that Iraq would immediately strike Tel Aviv if Baghdad were attacked. See "Saddam Husayn's Interview for Spanish Television," *BBC Summary of World Broadcasts*, 29 December 1990, from *Republic of Iraq Radio*, 26 December 1990.

[110] William Cohen, the U.S. secretary of defense, warned that a U.S. military strike on Iraq would be "substantial in size and...impact." He added, however, "I think we should not raise expectations unreasonably high. What we would hope to accomplish...is to curtail, as best we can, Saddam Hussein's capacity to regenerate his weapons of mass-destruction capability." Susanne M. Schafer, "Cohen Dampens Expectations about Military Strike Capabilities," *Associated Press*, 1 February 1998.

[111] On 6 February, President Clinton had faced questions in a press conference as to whether he would resign in the face of the Monica Lewinsky scandal.

[112] SH-SHTP-A-001-197, "Saddam and Senior Advisers Discussing Ties between a Variety of Countries, including Iraq-Egypt and Iraq-US Relations," undated (between 29 December 2000 and 6 January 2001).

Male 1: [*Inaudible.*] I wanted to elaborate on Your Excellency's question.[113] There seems to be an intersection between the position of the Gulf States and the American position. [Bill] Richardson, the Secretary of Energy, has decided to meet with the Secretary General of the OPEC Organization, for the purpose of not reducing production, and at the time, the Gulf Cooperation Council for within their group framework, had an opinion[114] –

Saddam: Is this the new or the old?

Multiple Unidentified Males: The old.

Saddam: This is the old one. This is from another and we have to see the new one because they lean more toward Bush's family, especially the Saudis.

Male 1: This is what I believe they are going to [*inaudible*] him about the new direction.

Saddam: Why do you think I say let us see what is [*inaudible*].

Male 1: Correct.

Saddam: Because this is way beyond the capacity at which they used to work. Therefore, this means there is a green light from the new president. So –

Tariq: The Republican Party and the Bush family are closer to the oil companies that [*inaudible, overlapping voices.*] It is very necessary that you pay attention to the oil market study.

---

[113] Earlier in the recording, Saddam discussed a fluctuation in oil prices and instructed his staff to analyze a Gulf Cooperation Council statement on the subject. The reference to Saddam's "question" appears to refer to that request.

[114] Richardson met with Ali Rodriguez, the new Organization of Petroleum-Exporting Countries secretary-general, on 6 January 2001.

TWO

The "Zionist Entity"

We should reflect on all that we were able to learn from The Protocols of the Elders of Zion, and reflect on the nature of discussions that took place. We should identify the methods adopted by these hostile Zionist forces; we already know their objectives. I do not believe that there was any falsification with regard to those Zionist objectives.

– Saddam Hussein[1]

There is little disagreement today that anti-Semitism is widespread, though certainly not universal, among Arab publics.[2] The Pew Research Center reported in 2006 that "Anti-Jewish sentiment remains overwhelming in predominantly Muslim countries." These feelings were particularly pronounced in Egypt and Jordan, where Pew found only 2 percent and 1 percent of the populations, respectively, holding positive opinions of Jews.[3] Anecdotal evidence suggests that anti-Semitic feelings are widespread among Arab elites, not just the general population. For instance, Saudi King Faisal ibn Abdul Aziz al-Saud reportedly used to present copies of *The Protocols of the Elders of Zion*, an anti-Semitic tract plagiarized by the tsarist Russian security service from an earlier French document (which did not refer to Jews at all),

---

[1] *SH-SHTP-A-001-211, "Saddam and Ba'ath Party Members Discussing Issues Involving Oil, the United States, Terrorism, and Other Topics," 1 March 2001.

[2] The debate that remains is over the origins of these anti-Semitic feelings. Some scholars claim that it is a recent phenomenon, caused by the trauma resulting from the creation of Israel in 1948 and Israel's crushing victory in the 1967 War, and sustained by the subsequent miseries of the Palestinian people and anti-Semitic themes imported from Europe. Other scholars maintain that, though the 1967 War played a role, the roots of Arab anti-Semitism are deeper, nourished by a mixture of local and theological issues, and that importation of European forms of hostility to Jews has been constant throughout the twentieth century. The 1967 War played a greater role than the war in 1973 because the Arabs' defeat in the former was more pronounced. For a useful and wide-ranging review of this debate, see Gudrun Kramer, "Anti-Semitism in the Muslim World: A Critical Review," *Die Welt des Islam* 46 (November 2006): 243–76.

[3] Pew Global Attitudes Project, "Europe's Muslims More Moderate: The Great Divide: How Westerners and Muslims View Each Other," 22 June 2006, 4, 12, 19.

To Saddam's right, on the bottom row, stand Major General Faisal Hamid and Staff General Yehya Taha. On the bottom, to Saddam's left, stand Deputy Prime Minister and Minister of Military Industrialization Abd al-Tawab Mullah Huwaysh and Major General Dr. Ra'ad Ismail. In the back row, from right to left, are Head of Engineers Abd Al-Karim Abbas, Major Majid Sarar, and Brigadier General Nizar Abd Al-Rasul. The picture is dated 29 May 2002. *SH-MISC-D-001-273, "Photos of Saddam with High Ranking Military Officers and Government Officials," (May 2002–February 2003).

to visiting diplomats, even Henry Kissinger.[4] According to Saddam, every time the Saudi king met with a visitor he brought up the dangers of Zionism, communism, and Masonry, which he considered one and the same threat.[5]

Saddam's public utterances put him firmly within this stream of anti-Semitic discourse.[6] For instance, he publicly made the expansive comment that "anyone who insists on causing harm to people cannot but be linked to Zionism, regardless of where he comes from."[7] Nor was that an isolated

[4] Richard Webster, "Saddam, Arafat and the Saudis Hate the Jews and Want to See Them Destroyed," *New Statesman*, 2 December 2002.

[5] *SH-SHTP-A-001-212, "Saddam and Ba'ath Party Members Discussing a Variety of Issues, Including the Overthrow of Qassem and 'The Protocols of the Elders of Zion,'" undated.

[6] Ofra Bengio, *Saddam's Word: Political Discourse in Iraq* (New York: Oxford University Press, 1998), 134–39.

[7] Quoted in Daniel Pipes, *The Hidden Hand: Middle East Fears of Conspiracy* (New York: St. Martin's Press, 1998), 104.

sentiment. Saddam has been publicly quoted as seeing the manipulative hand of Jews as far back as the thirteenth century. In that period, the Mongol king Hulagu, a grandson of Genghis Khan, conquered much of southwest Asia, including Baghdad, which was the center of Islamic power at the time. In a phrasing that conflates Jews, Zionists, and Americans, Saddam told Iraqis in early 2003:

> History tells us that Western peoples and circles had played, for their own reasons, a role in directing Hulagu to the east, indeed to the Arab world in particular. The Jews and their supporters played a remarkably malicious role against Baghdad in the past and this conspiratorial, aggressive and wicked role is today reverting to them, to the Zionist Jews and to the Zionists who are not of Jewish origin, particularly those who are in the U.S. administration and around who stood in opposite front of our nation and Iraq. The force in America proved itself to be incapable of educating itself. It was not able to change itself into a capability, so that its impact would be humanitarian and instructive. Zionism and prejudicial people had pushed it to search for a role through a devastating brutal instinct instead of ascending to a position of responsible ability and to its civic, cultural role which suits this age and suits the role of balanced nations and their construction role in the collective milieu and work.[8]

Some observers, however, have come to Saddam's defense on the question of anti-Semitism, suggesting that Westerners, particularly Americans, have consistently taken Saddam's provocative utterances about Zionists, Israel, and Jews out of context, overinterpreting them and even charging Saddam with anti-Semitism because of his mere association with people who held (allegedly) anti-Semitic views. For instance, the fact that Saddam's father-in-law proposed in a pamphlet written in the early 1970s that three things God should not have created were Persians, Jews, and flies is sometimes used to paint Saddam with the brush of guilt by association.[9] More broadly, one might argue that Saddam's undeniable opposition to Israel can too easily be mistaken for anti-Semitism. One might even argue that Saddam supported public executions of Jews and use of anti-Israeli and anti-Semitic tropes only cynically, as tools to direct the population's anger outward, not toward him.

The captured Iraqi recordings do not support such contentions; their contents confirm that Saddam's anti-Semitism was deep and abiding. Nor do they indicate that Saddam and his inner circle deployed anti-Semitic and

---

[8] "Full Text: Saddam Hussein's speech," *Guardian*, 17 January 2003, accessed 2 October 2008 at www.guardian.co.uk/world/2003/jan/17/iraq2.

[9] Saddam's father-in-law was also his uncle, Khair Allah Talfah, a former major who lost his rank and position, and went to jail, for his involvement in a 1941 coup attempt. As a boy, Saddam left his home to live with his uncle; as president of Iraq, he had his uncle's pamphlet published and distributed. For claims that emphasizing Saddam's relationship with his uncle constitute attempts to prove guilt by association, see Najib Ghadban, "Some Remarks on the Distorting Literature about Saddam Hussein," *Political Psychology* 13 (December 1992): 783–89. For a similar assessment of Saddam's views of Jews, see "Aljazeera – Saddam and Jews," accessed 2 February 2008 at www.youtube.com/watch?v=G9z7aWRAy5U.

anti-Zionist rhetoric only as tools to control the population. It is clear that Saddam was subject to the same sort of prejudices and conspiracy theories that circulate throughout the Arab world.

Perhaps this should not be surprising. Although Saddam and his inner circle had enormous government bureaucracies constantly feeding them information, it seems likely that the bureaucracies validated and reinforced anti-Semitic notions rather than serving as sources for alternative perspectives. In 2001, for instance, the General Security Directorate reported to Saddam that *Pokémon* meant "I am Jewish" in Hebrew and that the popularity of Pokémon among Iraqi youths represented a dangerous inroad of Zionism into the country.[10] A lecture at the Special Security Institute taught students that "spying, sabotage, and treachery are an old Jewish craft because the Jewish character has all the attributes of a spy." These purportedly included being "sneaky, conniving," avaricious, and lacking in moral restraint.[11] The tapes also reveal that one of Saddam's advisers observed in his presence that New York was a Jewish city, hinting that UN official Javier Pérez de Cuéllar, who lived there, would, of course, fall under American and Jewish influence.[12]

Saddam was certainly many things besides merely an anti-Semite. Indeed, he had respect for his adversary: "the Jews are usually smart," he once commented in private.[13] Nonetheless, if Saddam truly believed that Jews had a remarkable unity of purpose and a near-supernatural ability to influence world affairs, this must have influenced the way he deployed Iraq's resources. A full understanding of the man and his acts would seem to require some recognition of the anti-Semitic aspect of his belief system.

SADDAM'S VIEWS TOWARD ZIONISM AND JEWS

In Saddam's opinion, Zionists were everywhere.[14] It is clear from the discussions that Saddam believed *The Protocols* was a reliable guide to understanding Zionist actions. Zionism, he thought, was unalterably opposed to "progressive movements throughout the world" and fought the notion of

---

[10] See *SH-IDGS-D-001-213, "General Security Directorate Memorandum on the Dangers of the Cartoon Character Pokémon," 2001.

[11] See *SH-SSOX-D-001-214, "Lecture by the Director of the Special Security Institute on Zionist Intelligence Guidelines and Duties," 11 September 2002.

[12] SH-SHTP-A-000-561, "Saddam and His Inner Circle Discussing the Iran-Iraq War and UN Security Council Resolutions Related to the War," undated (circa 1981).

[13] SH-SHTP-A-000-561, "Saddam and His Inner Circle Discussing the Iran-Iraq War and UN Security Council Resolutions Related to the War," undated (circa 1981).

[14] Zionism is an international political movement that believes that Jews should have a homeland in Palestine.

Arab unity by seeking to revive earlier cultures: Pharaoanic Egypt, Phoeni-
cia, and so forth. The audacity and rudeness of the Zionists, Saddam said
to his friends, was such that the "Arab mentality" had a hard time grasping
it. This made it all the more important to educate the Iraqi masses about
the threat and to confront it. Saddam grasped Israel's audacity and rudeness
and thus was more upset, by his own admission, about its 1985 raid on
the Palestinian Liberation Organization (PLO) headquarters than he was
about all the losses to date of the Iran-Iraq War. Of course, the Americans
(and assorted others, such as UN Secretary-General Boutros Boutros-Ghali)
supported the Zionists to the hilt. Nevertheless, Saddam and his colleagues
were willing to consider the possibility that the "Zionist lobby" was behind
the 1993 terrorist attack on the World Trade Center in New York City.[15]

Then there were the Jews. Saddam's words suggest that he thought the
difference between Jews and Zionists was at best nuanced and subtle. He
would sometimes slip back and forth between the two, as when he said:
"the Zionists are greedy, I mean the Jews are greedy. Whenever any issue
relates to the economy, their greed is very high."[16] This identification among
Jews, Zionists, and Israel is evident elsewhere, as in Saddam's hypothesis
that the Jews spread around the world were a resource that enabled the
Israeli intelligence service to punch above its weight. Similarly, it seemed
important to him to determine whether Boutros Boutros-Ghali's wife and
mother were Jewish, a question whose import is hard to explain without
reference to conspiratorial feelings toward Jews as such. Moreover, *The
Protocols*, the most famous anti-Semitic text ever written, played a role in
the Iraqi leadership's discussions that is hard to explain away.

Saddam's treatment of Jews in his literary endeavors, a private sanctuary
into which he retreated during his last days in power, is consistent with
his views from the tapes. As the 2003 Iraq War approached, Saddam was
putting the finishing touches on a novel, titled *Be Gone, Demons!* The novel
was an allegory set in an ancient time but with a contemporary lesson. In
this work, an Arab warrior leads his people to triumph over a force representing Americans on dates coinciding with those of Operation Desert
Storm. The triumph culminates with the destruction of two towers belong-
ing to the Americans. There is, however, an additional strand to the plot.
The novel also features a character named Ibrahim, whose three sons represent Judaism, Christianity, and Islam. Although the Christian and Muslim
characters are portrayed in a positive light, the son representing Judaism,
who is named Ezekiel, tells his father that the only important thing in life is

---

[15] See Saddam Hussein and his inner circle discuss the then-recent attack on the World Trade
Center, circa 1993. A full transcript of this recording is available in Kevin M. Woods, *Iraqi
Perspectives Project – Primary Source Materials*, vol. 4, 63–83.

[16] For an identification of Zionists and Jews, see Saman Abdul Majid, *Les années Saddam:
Révélations exclusives* (Paris: Fayard, 2003), 134.

money. Expelled from the household, he becomes a usurer. Subsequently, he becomes a weapons producer and uses his influence to stir up confrontations among the tribes so that he can sell more swords. When he falls in love with a woman and finds himself spurned, he attempts to rape her. In the end, he gets his just deserts alongside the characters representing America.[17]

Saddam Discusses the Importance of *The Protocols of the Elders of Zion* (circa mid-1990s)[18]

Saddam: As for Zionism and its role in attacking the progressive movements throughout the world, I applaud the words stated by Comrade Qasim that we have to read *The Protocols of the Elders of Zion*.[19] And after that, we will study this matter. Comrade Qasim, why don't you bring some books for us, books about *The Protocols of the Elders of Zion*.

Taha [Yasin Ramadan]: [*Inaudible*] at the Ministry of Media.

Male 1 [*possibly Qasim*]: It is available at the bookstores.

Saddam: It is available at the bookstores, I think I have a copy of it.

Taha: We need some copies.

Male 1: We want a number of issues so that we can circulate them around [*inaudible*] for further study.

Taha: [*Inaudible*] we are among those who promote criticism.[20]

Saddam: I feel great about the State Command meetings, perhaps more so than any other meetings.

Izzat: Your Excellency, because these are more than just meetings.

Saddam: Because of what they discuss, as they do not bring up daily issues –

Izzat: That depress people.

Saddam: Yes, but because these meetings discuss thoughts and strategy and this is a very important matter, as it renews the vitality of the intellectual and political thinking in a person.

---

[17] Majid, *Les années Saddam*, 131–33. See also Jo Tatchell, "Saddam the Romancier," *Prospect Magazine* 100 (July 2004), accessed 18 June 2011 at www.prospect-magazine .co.uk/article_details.php?id=6171; Ofra Bengio, "Saddam Husayn's Novel of Fear," *Middle East Quarterly* 9 (Winter 2002), www.meforum.org/article/125.

[18] See *SH-SHTP-A-001-215, "Saddam and His Inner Circle Discuss Zionism and 'The Protocols of the Elders of Zion,'" undated (circa mid-1990s).

[19] Saddam might be referring to Marwan Qasim, the chief of the Royal Court in Jordan. If so, this is ironic because Marwan Qasim reportedly suggested that Saddam improve relations with Israel to end economic sanctions on Iraq. See section "Saddam and the National Command speculate that King Hussein is using Kamil to provoke a confrontation with Iraq," in Chapter 8.

[20] Taha is unquestionably referring to criticism of Jews and Israel, as opposed to criticism of *The Protocols*.

Saddam's Inner Circle Discusses the Greedy and Aggressive Nature of Zionism and Ways in Which the Ba'ath Cadre could be Educated about This Topic (circa mid-1990s)[21]

Saddam: What steps are we going to take after this discussion about Zionism? I believe we need further analysis of the information and discussion, then to produce an announcement, or produce a booklet from the Cultural Office, but this has to be done after the comrades have reviewed their presentations and briefs. They will have to develop those briefs, because this is the first time we have conducted such discussion about Zionism at the State Command. At minimum, we should produce an analysis of the information that was presented at the meeting. I believe that the comrades have gained knowledge that will help them when they discuss a subject matter like this one. We are constantly facing Zionism as Arabs, whether in Iraq or everywhere throughout the Arab nation. Yes, Comrade Taha?

Taha: Comrade [*inaudible*], the secretary-general, I believe in the importance and uniqueness of this matter, it is true.

Saddam: [*To an aide.*] Bring us cigars.

Taha: That is one of the main subjects we have discussed after the conference, and I find this subject to be a section of the conference, the conference's political report includes a section about the Gulf phenomena, it contained analysis and validation. It contained analysis of the religious phenomena, an analysis that benefited from the two consecutive state conferences, from Your Excellency's writings, and discussions carried out by you. There was an analysis about the communist camp, and its collapse.[22] I mean, there were manifestations, like the non-aligned movement.

As for Zionism, Your Excellency, Mr. President, I mean, this subject matter was embedded within all subjects of discussion. However, it was not discussed as a subject on its own. The Party has rendered its point of view and analysis with regard to this matter. Your Excellency, Mr. President, I believe that the Cultural Office should prepare for this subject, so that we can learn and benefit from the study of *The Protocols of the Elders of Zion* with all its constants and ramifications. This way, the subject of Zionism would become comprehensive because this is one of the conference's recommendations, to study this subject of Zionism. It was one of the agendas of the national conference. This is a subject that deserves follow-up, and anything that will be published as a result of such follow-up could be addressed to leadership ranks only, or perhaps leaflets will be issued to the lower ranks, but we aspire to achieve a level of a national conference decision. I mean, we have to give it such stature.

I personally [*inaudible*], have started to reflect on many of the issues the comrades discussed. I started to think about the subject of Zionism and its dangers, because in the past, we used to use words like colonialism. We have really made progress with regard to the subject of Zionism; this was due to the discussions we had, in addition to reading two complete books. This will require more time to consolidate our thoughts, I mean this requires time to relate our understanding with our leadership structures,

---

[21] *SH-SHTP-A-001-211, "Saddam and Ba'ath Party Members Discussing Issues Involving Oil, the United States, Terrorism, and Other Topics," 1 March 2001.

[22] Taha is apparently referring to the fall of communist states in Eastern Europe and Russia.

and we have to enhance awareness at the lower ranks, increase the general awareness about Zionism. Your Excellency, Mr. President, the Zionist will overcome a simple media attack. There is no true understanding of the dangers of Zionism, with its ramifications, its material influences, and such understanding does not exist. In the past, Ba'athists had a backward thinking. We could not sit down with them, but when Your Excellency convened the eighth state conference, and before the publication of this manual about heritage and religion, a discussion took place about what the party leadership published.[23] The Cultural Office started to research this subject [Zionism], and by then, it had formed a solid foundation upon which it will build its research. Not only general remarks, like we used to say simple remarks like, "the Zionists are backward [and] they are linked with the English."

Zionism now needs to be fully understood, its true dangers need to be compre-hended, as its dangers are linked with its history. This is because we are witnessing reconciliation with Zionism. Why do you think we started to study and read about Zionism? Many authors whom we used to say had nationalistic backgrounds are somewhat acknowledging the word *Zionism*, and it will be banned from usage. In the same manner [as at the] Baghdad Summit Conference – whose anniversary is today – we were requested not to use the term *American imperialism*.[24] I mean, this was part of the Conference's recommendations. So one day, even in the context of the Arab League, there will be talk about reconciliation, and that there is no need to be harsh on the word *Zionism*.[25] That is why, Your Excellency, we should con-centrate on this subject of Zionism. It should be one of the chapters of the twelfth national conference, to be the foundation of the next conference, this subject must gain priority with regard to the political report. This subject should be published in booklets and distributed to the main leadership; perhaps the National Cultural Office will be given the authority to publish books from this report for the lower ranks, to the level of Command members. Thank you.

Saddam: If we need to research the subject of Zionism to the extent that it is incorporated within the Conference agenda, I think the research we talked about is insufficient. I mean, we have to branch out to other topics, because we should not adopt a title like "a view about Zionism," but we should adopt a title of "how we should confront Zionist plans," then we could incorporate that into our conference. We have to adopt an Arab revolutionary movement that will encompass the entire Arab World, whose future will be the future of the entire Arab Nation. We have to say "how will the Arabs confront Zionism," or a point of view "on how to confront Zionism." After that, we should reflect on all that we were able to learn from *The*

[23] Saddam's forty-five-page *On History, Heritage, and Religion* was published in 1981.

[24] The "Baghdad Summit Conference" appears to refer to a 28–30 May 1990 Arab League summit, held in Baghdad, aimed to prevent emigration of Soviet Jews to Israel. Before the meeting, the United States had sent a memorandum to Arab League states that, Sad-dam complained, indicated "that we should not use the word imperialism." "Arab Sum-mit Opening Speech by President Saddam Husayn," BBC *Summary of World Broadcasts*, 30 May 1990.

[25] On 16 December 1991, the UN General Assembly revoked UN Resolution 3379, which had "determine[d] that Zionism is a form of racism and racial discrimination." An Arab League resolution from the May 1990 Baghdad summit, backed by Iraq, had called for "vigorous opposition" to U.S. efforts to repeal the UN resolution. Ben Lynfield, "Rhetoric for Iraq, a Respite for Egypt," *Jerusalem Post*, 1 June 1990.

Protocols of the Elders of Zion, and to reflect on the nature of discussions that took place. We should identify the methods adopted by these hostile Zionist forces; we already know their objectives. I do not believe that there was any falsification with regard to those Zionist objectives, specifically with regard to the Zionist desire to usurp – usurping the economies of people . . . This is in general terms.

Zionism, after it has chosen among the choices that it has discussed, has realized that the promising opportunity at the moment is to build its foundation on Palestinian land. From that time onward, it has transformed into an imperialistic claw used against the Arab nation. Zionism has partnered with imperialism and participated in its economic and political plans. Moreover, it relies on its unfounded, imaginary historical belief for the purpose of destroying the Arab nation . . . destroying here may not be sufficiently understood. This means maintaining the weak state of the Arab nation and gradually reinforcing and transforming the feeling that it is incapable of forming an Arab nation, because the belief and the feeling that it is an Arab nation will be a permanent impetus for its unity.

Zionism regards unity of Arabs as contradictory to its existence. Therefore, Zionism's line of defense is based on the principle that the Arab nation must be broken. And to reinforce the feeling of non-commitment to the concept of Arab nationalism, in other words, the Arabs are not one nation, but they are peoples and countries. Following that, it is necessary for Zionism to revive all the old historical frictions that took place in the path of nationhood, so it can use them as the foundation, as a first phase, to break up the fabric of Arab nations. By this, Zionism strives to revive Pharaonic [civilization] in Egypt, revive Phoenician [civilization] in another, it revives Berber [civilization]. It is as if Zionism is opposing Arabism, and it revives and revives, etc.

If we notice that one of the items that Zionism does not revive or does not desire to talk about is the history of Iraq. I mean, Zionism does not say, you [Iraqis] are originally Babylon, nor does Zionism say that you are Assyrians. It does not say that you are Sumerians. I mean, this is because Zionism regards this history as a threat. So Zionism will avoid talking about any part that it considers strong for a nation's progress. However, Zionism will talk. For example, it will raise the issue that Iraq is not a united nation; it is not a people that has formed historically and in a mature manner. It would say that the Iraqis are people who have formed recently, and this is what the Western media is saying about Iraq. How did Iraq form recently? It formed recently because there are Kurds, and the Kurds have [*inaudible*] element, and the Arabs are divided into Shi'a and Sunni, and there is a certain percentage of Christians, and that some Arabs do not know their original roots, whether they have an Indian origin in the south or whether they have peninsula roots. In other words, were they from the Arabian Peninsula? Or are they so and so? It is true that there are new theories about some aspects of these issues; they all originate from Western thinking.

However, Zionism talks about Sudan. It would talk about the Arab minority that settled there and originally came in from the Arabian Peninsula, etc., and then talks about the true inhabitants and then talks about religions and so forth. As for the economy, the first phase, we said that Zionism has partnered with Imperialism with regard to usurping the Arab national fortunes. This was manifested through direct colonization. However, as the era developed, direct colonization became impossible. Then the indirect colonization theory emerged, also the type of colonization that is expressed within Imperialism, this term that the American rulers attempted to delete from the Arab political dictionary at the Arab summit held in Baghdad.[26] So how will Zionism react, especially when it will have means for dealing politically and economically with the Arab world, means that are different from the ones used at its old fortified trenches? Will Zionism be satisfied only by partnering with Western colonialism through its companies, through its institutions to fulfill its ransacking of Arab fortunes? Or will Zionism gradually form the mentality of independence, in other words, solely controlling Arab fortunes?

The occupied Arab land is supported by Zionism everywhere in the world that Zionism has established its presence. I believe such a development will take place; however, the Zionists, I mean, they will face two phenomena. The first is that greed sometimes gives impetus to premature action, and the Zionists are greedy – I mean the Jews are greedy. Whenever any issue relates to the economy, their greed is very high. The other aspect is the Zionists' feeling that they are in need of the West, that when they provoke Western national companies in a rude, provocative manner, I mean this is an analysis of an Arab mind, however, we see that Zionist provocation is rude. I mean, the Arab mentality, regardless, even with the enemy, it projects a bit of its own character. In other words, the Arab mentality does not think that the enemy could reach that level of rudeness or belligerence or the extremes. This is because the spirit of the [Arab] nation, even its [dealings] with its enemies, is different.

But look, I would say that we were not surprised. I mean, sometimes the enemies go to the extreme, more so than what we envisioned; likewise with the Zionists. When you observe the Zionists, you will find them to be very rude. They are rude; they speak very rudely in America about the Zionist entity's interests, even if it appears to the American viewer that such talk contradicts his own national interests. Likewise, they do the same thing in England, France, Russia, and other countries. Despite that, we would say that greed is in a haste, and economic requirements necessitate that they [the Zionists] should not provoke Western national institutions at an early stage – that is in terms of economic interests – unless they assess that they have realized that they are incapable of establishing influence in the Arab World, and secure a reasonable portion of their interest without observing this aspect with the West.

After that, and I do not mean after that in terms of timing, but this trend of Western division of ransacked Arab fortunes will be parallel to an independent Zionist line [trend] in ransacking the largest possible portion of national fortunes, and to work according to its approach in destroying the psyche of the sons of the Arab nation, through its economic interest, interests that are not necessarily agreed upon by the West, or at least not accepted by the Western phased political plans. After that, they will start talking about how to usurp trade. However, upon reading, one would not know how they will usurp trade and industry. But in light of what comrade Dr. Elias has presented, it became clear to me that trade tactics are pretty old.[27] I mean, it is the core nerve of inherited economic activities. However, from the time humanity was capable of forging contacts outside their stated countries, within human presence, extend bridges with humanity outside the countries' borders, international trade was established. However, industry is the trait of the era.

So how will they [Zionists] use trade and industry? They will persuade some weak Arabs, or those who are working on weakening the Arabs, to fall prey in their arms,

---

[26] See *supra* note 24.
[27] Probably Elias Farah, a Ba'athist intellectual.

for the purpose of creating a trend of mutual interests between them and other circles within each and every Arab country. And they will select the weak to promote such a call. Given Zionist greed, its first phase planning necessitates the establishment of beneficial interests – I mean small interests – and handing it to those who will be tasked to carry out promotion activities for these plans. Despite that, and I say this from an Arab mind, because it was proven in reality that Zionism – do they really like to abuse, usurp money, and act unilaterally? To the extent that they are not ready to, I mean, even the people that they could use, they give them any form of persuasive participation in Arab world fortune. This is taking place in Jordan during such a short time. This is happening in Egypt. I mean no one came to us and said that the Zionists are spending billions of dollars to streamline their political activities, etc. These, in my assessment, are the tactics of big countries that have a stable economy and have large resources, just like America's methods at one stage, British methods at one stage. I mean even if they give out crumbs, even though the British are very stingy, they are not like Americans.

But I would say, there are problems, sometimes, when one speaks about them. They are worse than one that would speak about them, I mean in terms of economic matters, and in terms of envy and chicanery that is manifested in their policies, when they control the Arab nation. Therefore, if we argued along these lines, we would ask ourselves how to confront this, how to confront these plans. And after that we have to penetrate outside the context of just talking about political and historical concepts of Zionist actions; we should start talking about a view of culture, a view on economic issues, specifically financial issues, funds institutions, trade, then talk about industry and how it is fortified, and how to resist Zionism, etc., and other details. I mean, when we say that such a topic should be included in the Conference agenda, it has to be presented with a political plan in mind. I mean, this plan requires diagnosis of all pros and cons. I mean, confrontation, after that, we will realize that whatever we covered in our last meeting is insufficient to cover all the aspects pertaining to this matter.

SADDAM'S VIEW OF THE THREAT ISRAEL POSED

Saddam's views of Israel were conditioned by his view of Zionists and of Jews, the majority population in Israel. That said, whatever Saddam thought of Israelis as people, the two countries were objectively antagonistic to each other. Saddam also felt that Israel was a threat to the entire Arab nation, which he saw as (or at least wished to be) a unified entity. Israel might also have been a threat to him personally. The General Military Intelligence Directorate reported to Saddam in 1990 that Israel might attempt to assassinate him because of his prominent role in leading the Arab world and because they recognized that Iraq's "scientific accomplishments" in the military realm were only possible because of his leadership.[28]

---

[28] See SH-PDWN-D-000-546, "General Military Intelligence Directorate Assessment of Israeli Intentions toward Iraq," 22 May 1990. Saddam often used the phrase "scientific accomplishments" to refer to Iraq's nuclear program.

Saddam and his partners perceived an expansionist threat from Israel. They saw a small state, certainly, but one with a powerful military and a highly capable intelligence service. Israel's hard power, in their view, was comparable even to that of the United States. For instance, when considering the 1991 air campaign the United States and its coalition partners launched in Operation Desert Storm, Saddam's point of comparison was the Israeli air campaign during the 1967 War.[29] Israel's soft power was also seen as substantial, as evidenced by a 1981 discussion of the cultural threat from Israel and the Pokémon issue reported to him in 2001.

Thus, Saddam felt locked in a potentially deadly confrontation with Israel, "the Zionist entity." Although the war might not be hot at any given moment, Saddam thought that Israel was an intrinsically expansionist, aggressive state ready to use military aggression or subversion. At the same time, while not necessarily desiring war with Israel at any particular instant, he longed for a world in which there would be no Israel, and he envisioned himself as just the historic leader to bring this about. Nevertheless, it is far from clear that he thought he had a realistic chance of doing so. Whether this calculation would have changed once he had nuclear weapons will probably never be known.

After the Israeli Air Strike on the Palestine Liberation Organization Headquarters in Tunis, Saddam Explains Israel's Threat to the Arabs (5 October 1985)[30]

Saddam: Now the operation that we are discussing is a new technique worldwide. I mean it never happened before, worldwide, where Israel or a country other than Israel would carry out such an operation and have a superpower nation support it and have had prior coordination with it. I mean the American position is not one of support, it is rather an American attitude, and the action is a joint American-Zionist effort and not a mere Zionist act. Fine, we agree that the Zionists, by God, strike. They would launch a strike and an explosion, they would send a booby-trapped car, they conduct piracy at sea, but they would not go to attack a country just because it hosts the headquarters of an organization! A country [Tunisia] the West considers moderate, and one that, for two or three decades, faced Arab criticism for its position over the issue of division. All of this gets thrown up against the wall and it goes to Tunisia and strikes the [Palestinian Liberation] Organization with planes.

Better yet, and what is more difficult in the new international relations, is that a superpower like the United States declares its complete support. Furthermore, it justifies its support by stating that the Zionists' act is a legitimate act of self-defense. This certainly confirms what we have read between the lines a long time ago, that Zionism and the Arabs cannot live together. Even if it achieved security in the manner

---

[29] Kevin M. Woods, *The Mother of All Battles: Saddam Hussein's Strategic Plan for the Persian Gulf War*, (Annapolis: Naval Institute Press, 2008), 271.

[30] SH-SHTP-V-000-567, "Saddam and Yasser Arafat Discussing the Israeli Attack on the Palestinian Liberation Organization's Headquarters," 5 October 1985.

that we now see – meaning geographic security – the social and political security will absolutely never be achieved between Israel and the Arabs. Because, tomorrow Israel would say, "Iraq, you have elected a president with a history of anti-Zionism. On such a date and at such a time he gave a speech against us, 30 years ago. Replace him. And if you do not replace him we will come and demolish your palaces over your heads. And, so-and-so employee in his industrialized policy encourages aggressive Iraqi acts. So, you must remove him from arms manufacturing and from heavy civilian industries. Also, we believe that so-and-so's project is a preparation for a future field of operation, which means that you have aggressive intentions towards Israel and you must change that course."

I have discussed this subject years ago. This issue between the Arabs and Israel will never be resolved. It is either Israel or the Arabs. I mean, there is no solution! Things will range between two situations, a flexible action here, and another flexible action there, either by Israel or by the Arabs. This is considered an in-between situation; that is the indecisive situation. The decisive situation would be either this way or that way. Either the Arabs are slaves to Israel and Israel controls their destinies, or the Arabs can be their own masters and Israel is like Formosa's location to China, at best. Without that rule, it is not possible to ease the issue between the Arabs and Israel.

So, how long have we been? I mean we have been at war [with Iran] and we have paid with thousands upon thousands of martyrs, yet I have never been so upset over an issue, before or during the war, as much as I am over this one. I mean it suggests carelessness and humiliation to every human being, not only to every Arab. Toward every human being, toward every human being of the modern age and a violation of all human laws, a violation of the simplest meanings of international conduct, and a disrespect for humans' worth. In other words, "Arabs! Who are you? You are nothing." Up until now, the reactions from the Arab world do not exist. I mean, I called Comrade Tariq Aziz in New York and he issued a statement. I called [Saudi] King Fahd and I told him that this issue is big and dangerous, and that he must act because before the American statement was issued and before we learned that the Americans support the action – I told him that he must at least present [trails off]. I told him, "What else do we have but to talk? Isn't that right? Talk is all that we have left. Or is it only hand signals now? At a minimum, a strong statement should be issued by the [UN] Security Council. And no doubt, the Americans will use the veto. And so, you must work on it and that's it."

[Possibly Na'im]: They did not use it. The resolution was issued and the Americans did not vote.

Saddam: They did not vote! God damn them.

[Possibly Na'im]: Their representative issued a resolution; I mean a statement, condemning the aggression without specifying the concerned side. The American representative to the United Nations [pause] – but they abstained from voting. [Inaudible.]

Saddam: Who was it among them, who declared their support for the aggression in the beginning?

[Possibly Na'im]: The American president, Reagan.

Saddam: Himself?

[Possibly Na'im]: Himself, himself. He said like this: it is a legitimate act and it is self defense and that it agrees with the American policy.[31]

[*Inaudible background conversations.*]

Saddam: Let's go on, Na'im! Just let's finish this issue, brother. But, I mean there is no justice left, by God. I mean at least, that's it? By God, do we remain silent? I mean, at least from a national standpoint and a political standpoint, we should do something. Something that would make humans feel, make the world feel, make the universe feel, that we tell them, "Hey people, the Arabs reject this." I swear by God if we weren't tied up, we would have attacked Tel Aviv, by God. I mean we won't wait for Tunisia or the resistance or the universe to get us going.

So I thought of putting this issue forth and seeing what the comrades think. There are two suggestions on my mind. The first one is to rally people all over Iraq at the same time and in every city and every place and divide up the cities. Divide up Baghdad into places, I mean places where people can mass, because it is difficult to transport them from one place to another. I mean, they can stand there and chant against the three; against America, against Israel, and against the Khomeini aggression considering the connection is one and that it is from one side. I mean, they will put together an activity so the Iraqi press can broadcast it. Or see if it can be a massing of people in a central area, a courtyard, the great festivals square and one of the comrades would deliver a powerful speech regarding this subject. I mean, that's one. The other one is to be an official Arab response. Since the Arab foreign ministers are there, meeting, we can make it count. Maybe we should call the kings and presidents by phone so they can study the rhetoric of a single unified letter signed by all Arab leaders. I mean a single copy or multiple copies if it is an administrative difficulty as far as timing is concerned. This same copy can be sent to the Americans and to all the countries of the world and to all of the international organizations, containing an Arab objection to this criminal act and considering it an unprecedented dangerous act in international diplomacy.

The other action – since the Americans remained quiet and made such a statement, I mean, they are still tyrants. The Americans are still conspiring bastards and this thing is their doing. The Arabs all together should at least pull their ambassadors for a period of one month as an objection to the American policy in supporting the Zionist entity. The weaponry is American, the American president himself supported the act and the conniving has been happening before then, and this is a country they call "moderate" and they consider Yasser Arafat among "the moderate mainstream." I mean any suggestion from you comrades, the first thing, by God, what are the things that you would accept and what are the things that you would reject from this? But by God, I'm not going to come and go, like that, one doesn't know what to do.

---

[31] The UN Security Council voted 14–0, with the United States abstaining, to condemn Israel for the attack. U.S. Secretary of State George Shultz claimed the United States supported the raid as a legitimate act of self-defense but did not veto the resolution, as doing so would likely lead to the overthrow of the pro-Western government in Tunisia. Reagan announced that every state has the right to retaliate for terrorist attacks "so long as they have the right people." Bernard Gwertzman, "U.S. Defends Action in U.N. on Raid," *New York Times*, 7 October 1985.

Saddam Attributes the Effectiveness of Israeli Intelligence to the Jewish Diaspora (30 December 1996)[32]

Saddam: The best technically able intelligence outfits in the world are the British, the ex-Soviet, and the Israeli. But the most technologically advanced are the British. Why? Because the Jews use Jews from all around the world to sympathize with the intelligence service.[33]

Tariq: The Israelis?

Saddam: Yes, the Israelis, they use the Jews from all around the world for intelligence matters. The Soviets use all the communist movements and what you would call the international peace movements, all the names you can think of for the sake of their intelligence services. But, technologically the British intelligence service is more advanced than any of them.

Saddam, in a Meeting with Military Officers during the Iran-Iraq War, Analyzes the Sources of Israeli Military Prowess (possibly late 1983 or early 1984)[34]

Saddam: Look at this Israeli general [name unclear], he is known for developing a famous military tactic.[35] He had the ability and background to develop the tactic from his experience fighting four years with the Allies in World War II. Therefore when he puts [together] war plans, it is a normal routine for him. He knows ahead of time what and how much it takes to have before he goes into battle. So their expectations and calculations are as close to reality as they can be. The military exercises and war games should resemble what is anticipated in the battlefield. In addition, directing the battlefield is like doing an exercise: the more you do it the better you get. And all know that the result of the battle depends on how the battle is directed.

In contrast to the Israelis, the Arabs lack warfare experience. Consequently, leaders in Israel are enraged and worried over the experience that our leaders, officers and army staff are gaining in this [Iran-Iraq] war. Israel is afraid that it would lose its edge over us in warfare experience. Therefore, Israel will do its best to remove from power all the leadership personnel and army personnel in our country; it would do

---

[32] *SH-SHTP-A-001-216, "Saddam and His Inner Circle Discussing Various Intelligence Services, Hamas, and Other Issues," 30 December 1996.

[33] In the intelligence business, this practice is known as ethnic targeting. Israel is one of several countries thought to use ethnic targeting in intelligence recruitment. F. W. Rustmann Jr., *CIA Inc.: Espionage and the Craft of Business Intelligence* (Washington, D.C.: Brassey's, 2002), 125; Duncan L. Clarke, "Israel's Economic Espionage in the United States," *Journal of Palestinian Studies* 27 (Summer 1998): 26–27.

[34] SH-SHTP-A-000-627, "Saddam and Senior Military Officials Discussing Arms Imports and Other Issues Related to the Iran-Iraq War," undated (circa late 1983 or early 1984). Other people in the meeting include a Major General Sa'di, a General Sami, and a man probably named Hamid. It is unclear which of these are quoted herein.

[35] Saddam is likely referring to the Israeli general and politician Moshe Dayan, who played a great role in the Israeli victories in the 1956 Suez campaign as commander of the Israeli Defense Forces and as minister of defense in the 1967 Six-Day War and the 1973 Yom Kippur conflict.

away with the experience we acquired fighting this war, so it would end up with a less experienced foe.

Male 2: Your Excellency, we cannot forget that the Iraqi people withstood in this war and learned a great deal from it. It prepared them to face and overcome any obstacle the war may bring in the next few years.

Saddam: Death and its effect on people is usually overwhelming, but by now the Iraqis have encountered death in the martyrs of this war and are accustomed to handling it properly. Human nature represented by the heart of the families and sisters of the Iraqi martyrs in their own weeping and mourning will always be felt; but the Iraqis are better prepared than ever to deal with it. If it ever happens that the Iraqi people were in a conflict with their Israeli enemy, then the Iraqis would be able to withstand three years of fighting in a war. However, the Israelis cannot withstand one year of fighting in a war.

Male 1: Sir, if you were fighting a war with Israel it would not have lasted for a year and you would have won by now. Just with the sheer size of our force we would win, regardless of how good their leadership is.

Tariq Aziz Discusses Israel's Strengths and Limitations (2 November, circa early 1990s)[36]

Tariq: Just as the discussion that took place the last time and previous times, the Arabs, throughout their conflict have either grossly underestimated Israeli strength or they are very much scared of it. Both approaches are wrong. I mean underestimating the enemy is wrong, and the excessive fear of the enemy is also wrong.

Saddam: The two phenomena are caused by ignorance.

Tariq: Ignorance, so we have to know our enemy, we have to know its points of strength, I mean the factors that led to its strength, and we need to know the factors that contribute to its weakness. The enemy's strength factors have enabled it to achieve the current state of success and we have to know its weakness factors so that we can counteract them, work on deepening such factors of weakness. The enemy – just as Your Excellency and the comrades stated – has studied the Arab nation, they have studied the current Arab realities, they saw the weak points in it, and they have deepened them. They did not create new weak points, just as I recall in the seventies, when we confronted the Kurdish issue and the colonialist intervention in the Kurdish issue. Your Excellency stated that Imperialism, colonialism, and Zionism did not create phenomena. They took advantage of existing phenomena. I mean there are phenomena, our society is a historical one. I mean the entire Arab society is a historical one. We are not an African nation that has developed recently, our age is thousands and thousands of years. We have religions, sects, ethnic groups that developed in the Arab world, we have problems and historical complications, we have conflicts among ourselves as Arabs, we have love and hatred, we have regional issues, we have national feelings as a natural phenomenon. Zionism is constantly studying this, and it continues to study these phenomena. It is not like it has studied and stopped. No, it continues its studies through research centers and Israeli universities. They are all interested in these phenomena and their development.

---

[36] *SH-SHTP-A-001-211, "Saddam and Ba'ath Party Members Discussing Issues Involving Oil, the United States, Terrorism, and Other Topics," 1 March 2001.

The Israeli government and the Israeli intelligence services as well as the Israeli diplomatic institution establish strategic and tactical plans to deepen those phenomena and use them to achieve their objective, which was stated by his Excellency, Mr. President, which is the weakening of the Arab nation. So we, on the other side, study the weakness factors that also exist in Zionism and the Zionist entity. It is not all factors of strength.

If we want to summarize, a few years ago, we used to ask about Israel and its capability. I have described Israel as an exceptionally poisonous snake; however, its ability to devour and digest is limited, and it is not a tiger or a lion that attacks its prey and eats it in one day or in hours like what happened with the grand colonial powers. I mean, if we take Britain as a big colonial country that had capabilities, it used to attack a region and capture it. It captured and ruled India for 300 years. India is 20 times the area of Britain, no, not in terms of area, in terms of population, and about four or five times the size, and beside India there were other countries as well. Why did this happen? It is because of the capability. Britain, in terms of size, it was not bad, its population at the time was big and consequently it was able to conscript a large number of [citizens], and its objective was colonialism and not settlement. France was able to colonize and settle for a very long time in various parts in Africa and the Arab Africa. Israel occupied the West Bank, Golan [Heights] and Sinai in six days in 1967. Just like the snake would bite its prey and paralyze it, either to kill it or paralyze it, paralyze the area that it has bitten, especially if the prey is large, so it bites it and paralyzes it. Until now, and Israel's objective is the West Bank, its objective is the West Bank, and the West Bank and Gaza do not exceed 5,700 square kilometers in terms of size. Until now, Israel has not been able to devour or digest the West Bank because it is a snake, its body is small, no matter how much it eats, its stomach is small, but its poisonous lethality is high. I mean its poison is very lethal to the extent that its prey either dies or is paralyzed, but Israel cannot easily eat up the prey.

Male 1: [*Inaudible.*]

Tariq: Yes, yes, the Arab nation is big; even the prey that is closer to it [Israel], which is the West Bank, it is very small, I mean the West Bank is the same size as [the Iraqi city of] al-Hillah. [*Laughs.*] It is like an Iraqi governorate, what is this? All these expeditions that took place throughout history, I mean the nations that conquer other nations, and defeat them militarily just like what happened in 1967, it takes the land and takes the people, the local citizens, it either expels them or brings large numbers of its own sons and consequently overwhelms the natives in terms of population, in addition to its occupation of the land. But it doesn't have [sufficient] people. All the Jews throughout the world are 14 to 15, let's say 20 million people. What is 20 million in a world of 6 billion people? And in an Arab world of 200 million people, this is all the Jews. I mean this includes the Jews from Japan, in Argentina, to the Jews who live in Israel.

Taha: They say 20 million.

Tariq: The –

Ahmed:[37] [*Interrupting.*] They say 20, and this is an exaggerated figure.

---

[37] Possibly Ahmed Hussein Khudayr al-Samarrai, who served as minister of foreign affairs (1991–1992) and acting finance minister and prime minister (1993–1994).

Tariq: Let us say 30, Comrade Ahmed. Those who live in Israel are 4 [million], I mean, these are accounted for. Now, and in the future, there are no large opportunities for Jewish immigration to Israel. I mean Israel, from the time of its inception, has absorbed the Arab Jews, all of them. They all immigrated, throughout 40 years, the Jews who live in America, in Latin America, those who wanted to go to Israel have gone already. There were some Falasha Jews, Ja'far al-Numayri has transported them to Israel and no more, I mean there are no more Falasha Jews in Africa.[38] There was a hope that Jews from the Soviet [Union] and Eastern European countries would emigrate to Israel in large numbers, and indeed they came in large numbers, and it is over, there is no anticipated intensive wave of Jewish immigration to Israel similar to the wave during that period. During that time, the Jew who wanted to travel [out of the Soviet Union] was not given permission. There was no democracy during that time, but now, there is democracy. There was no business during that time, now there is business.

Male 1: There was no free economy.

Tariq: Ha, so why would the Jew who lives in Hungary leave? He is living in Hungary, the ideological motives, the feeling of discomfort and poor economic reasons do not exist anymore. Consequently, it is not expected there will be large emigration to Israel. Therefore, Israel, Your Excellency, will maintain this description during the upcoming period. The description as a snake, that paralyzes here and paralyzes there, and it poisons more than it devours, and I believe this applies to the economy as well as the land. Because if we talk about the Israeli economy, there is a difference between the international Zionist economy and that of Israel. The Zionists and the Jews have, and the numbers of those who own large capital is not small, they integrate with many institutions, but they come through Britain, France, and America. They do not come through Israel; their masks are Western in nature. Israel, Your Excellency, just like we stated at the last meeting and following up on our points, Israel's economy is that of a state economy, more so than a business economy. There are no private companies in Israel owned by large numbers of people like General Motors, large oil companies, and the companies we know in Europe. Because Israel was founded on socialist principles, and the public ownership in it is more than the private one. Generally, Your Excellency, Mr. President, in Israel, I mean Israeli society, we consider it a part of the Middle East, it is the least Middle Eastern society in terms of numbers of millionaires. I mean, there are more millionaires in Lebanon than Israel. This is because Israel is a society that does not have much private ownership, because he who becomes a millionaire, how did he become a millionaire?

Saddam: This requires an environment that encourages the development of millionaires.

Tariq: The majority of Israeli industries and institutions are publicly owned, and if there is a private ownership within them, it is usually in the form of partnership, just like we have here – the mixed economy. Of course, we have to study that.

---

[38] *Falasha* refers to Jews from Ethiopia. In Ethiopia the term is pejorative. In Israel, where most of these Jews now reside, they are called Beta Israel. Between 1984 and 1991, three covert airlifts brought almost all the Ethiopian Jews to new homes in Israel.

I mean, I am talking here in general terms, a general culture, my presentation is not a specialized one. However, what I am saying is correct.

In the Wake of Israel's Air Strike on Iraq's Tamuz (Osirak) Nuclear Reactor, Saddam Discusses the Israeli Nuclear and Cultural Threat (probably mid-June 1981)[39]

Saddam: You will notice that [Israeli Prime Minister Menachem] Begin is concentrating on two issues. Unfortunately the international media did not cover this as they should. At the time, they talked about Iraqi nuclear power as if it is a dangerous project for the security of Israel. The media concentrated on an issue that seemed to be trivial, however, they have the right to cover it technically, but he [Begin] has no right to concentrate on it. In terms of humanity or socially, this matter is the treatment of children. He stated in his announcement, and I think you have paid attention to what was stated, I think this was published in the Iraqi media, but the international media did not cover it as necessary. He said, how do you expect me to be comforted by a regime, where the president of that regime [Saddam] asks the children, he tells them, "Who is your main enemy?" And he corrects their response telling them that your main enemy is Israel. Therefore, the Zionist entity and its allies are afraid of two main factors, which are included in one container, they are integrated together, they are the human in his pursuit of social development and the human in his pursuit of gaining new scientific knowledge within a clear political context and methodology. This will make Iraq very proud of its national experiment, will encourage Iraq to be eager to defend such pride, and to enhance such development, and will make such scientific advancement available for the benefit of the Arab nation as a whole. This is the case that made Begin suffer from insomnia for the last two years, as he stated, didn't he say two years?

Tariq: Yes.

Saddam: For two years, he suffered from insomnia because of the Iraqi situation. This is the case that caused him insomnia, and not his claim of Iraq's production of an atomic bomb, the same type that destroyed Hiroshima. All experts and officials of atomic bomb affairs, and the so-called Middle Eastern affairs admit that Israel currently possesses a number of atomic bombs. What if Israel said to the Arabs, if it has imposed conditions on the Arabs, that if they did not comply with, it will use atomic bomb against them, what will happen to the Arabs? But what will happen to humanity? What will happen to the Arabs in the shadow of such blackmail, and in the shadow of such a dangerous situation? I believe that despite the losses that have been inflicted on us as a result of this action Israel carried out, the Zionist entity, the one who raped our land, the despised entity, the historically rejected entity by the nation, the one rejected by humanity and by the nation, because Israel is a focal

---

[39] SH-SHTP-A-001-039, "Saddam and His Senior Advisers Discussing Israel's Attack on the Tamuz (Osirak) Reactor and Iraqi Civil Defenses," undated (circa mid- to late 1981). On 30 September 1980, two Iranian F-4 aircraft struck and damaged Iraq's Tamuz nuclear reactor at Osirak. On 7 June 1981, Israeli F-16 aircraft bombed the facility again to impede what Israel perceived as Saddam's march toward the acquisition of a nuclear weapon. The raid succeeded in destroying the reactor. For an account of the Israeli strike, see Rodger Claire, *Raid on the Sun: Inside Israel's Secret Campaign That Denied Saddam the Bomb* (New York: Broadway Books, 2004).

point of aggression and hostility, the Zionist entity in reality is not the same as their claimed intentions. They are nothing but a group of Jews who were subjected to Nazi persecution and are looking for a peaceful land, who aimed to stay away from any frictions with Nazi ideologies or fall under Nazi persecution like what happened in the past.

The Zionist entity now and in reality is the same as it was originally intended: They are a focal point of aggression and hostility and expansion, they are a focal point in which many parties are helping and enabling it for the purpose of subjugating the Arab Nation by the laws of this Zionist entity, and it is not a state that will live in peace, just as they originally envisioned before the year 1967. I believe that all of humanity free from corrupt influences has started to realize that the Zionist entity is not weak and oppressed. It is not an oppressed entity seeking peace. They realized that it is a hostile, arrogant entity that is imposed on the Middle East region and that the Zionist entity's main purpose is to prevent the Arab nation from developing, progress, and living a lifestyle worthy of it. It is our duty to clarify this point and to continue to clarify this point on a large scale, because the Zionist entity may come up with various interpretations about its previous aggression against the Arab nation. But this aggression, in my belief, they are not capable of giving a convincing interpretation to humanity. We have to turn this aggression to lessons learned, into a much deeper understanding that transcends the obvious loss of an important ring in our scientific and technological development.

The Arabs, as a whole, must realize that even if all the Arabs acknowledge what is called Israel, and with safe borders within the entire occupied Arab land, and even if the Arabs have honored on their part such a state, and even if they complied or, let us say, bowed to it, the Zionist entity will not accept such a situation. Not only because they are determined in their expansionist agenda on the land at the expense of Arab sovereignty, but the Zionist entity will even interfere in all aspects to include a request to change the path of a road that extends from a certain location in Saudi Arabia, as they will claim that such action threatens the Zionist entity, or on the basis that this is a military matter, or considering it a matter that is not acceptable to Israel. The Zionist entity will impose on the Arabs to change their educational curriculum in colleges, in high school. They will ban the teaching of chemistry, physics, math, and astronomy as these are the type of sciences that could lead to forming and accumulating human experience in a military field considered dangerous to its security. Israeli intervention will reach the level of interfering in changing princes, the direct-changing of princes, the requests of changing princes, and replacing them with others, and changing kings and replacing them with others, changing presidents and replacing them with others, changing the ministers and replacing them with others. And perhaps the Zionist entity's requests will reach the level of requesting the changing of the director of an elementary school because he is teaching the children in his school with nationalistic studies and social sciences. And they will even reach the point of asking the Arabs to amend their history and to rewrite it with a new direction, including the history of Prophet Muhammad, peace be upon him, and his struggle with Beni Qaynuqa and Beni Nadir in Medina.[40]

---

[40] The Beni Qaynuqa and Beni Nadir were Jewish tribes that Muhammad caused to be forcibly expelled from Medina.

ISRAEL AND ITS ALLIES

Saddam and his associates believed that Israel had a great number of allies. These included the United States, of course, although the Iraqis never seemed entirely clear about whether the United States controlled Israel or the other way around. Israel's allies also included Iran, the United Nations, and others. Sometimes the commonalities that held these strange bedfellows were clear (whether they were correct is another question): Israel and Iran's shared interest in keeping Iraq militarily weak, for example. Other times, it almost seemed as if the very exposure to Jews, for instance, in the heavily Jewish New York City, was osmotically subversive.

Saddam and His Colleagues Discuss the Array of Adversaries Facing Them: Iran, Israel, the United States, and the United Nations (probably 1981)[41]

Saddam: This is a fact, I mean you should not belittle this [Iranian enemy], and regard them as turbans.[42] No, they are not turbans, the Iranians are *satanic* turbans, and they know how to conspire and know how to plan a sedition, and they know how to communicate with the world, because they are not the ones doing the communication. Look, can we communicate with the world? Let us try to buy weapons now from the black market. Can we achieve that the same way the Iranians can? It is Zionism, it is Zionism that is guiding them [the Iranians]. Zionism is taking the Iranians by the hand and introducing them to each party, one by one, channel by channel. I mean Zionism – come on comrades – do I have to repeat that every time, I mean is this the time that we should end the Iraqi war, and in this manner?

––––––

Male 1: Your Excellency, Mr. President, with regard to the latest announcements of [then former prime minister of Israel] Yitzhak Rabin, [he] frankly wants the [Iran-Iraq] war to continue.

Saddam: Yitzhak Rabin is not important, the important thing is that we are convinced there is a conspiracy being prepared, and even the [UN] secretary-general is an accomplice in it.

Male 1: Oh yes, he is an accomplice.

Saddam: He is trying to present himself as if he were the lamb, but in fact, he is the Satan, and he coordinates [this conspiracy]. And I have said this from early on. I have told you that there is such coordination, I mean America has two faces, one face that it displays in front of us, but there is another face that aims to contain the Iranians, but it does not want the Iranians to be defeated.

––––––

[41] SH-SHTP-A-000-561, "Saddam and His Inner Circle Discussing the Iran-Iraq War and UN Security Council Resolutions Related to the War," undated (circa 1981).

[42] Although Saddam used the word *turban*, his choice of words would have conveyed a connotation of Shi'a clerics to his audience.

Tariq: Generally, the secretary-general of the United Nations [Kurt Waldheim] at the end, at the end, he is an American.[43] I mean, this is the position of the secretary-general of the United Nations, no matter what he tries or how hard he tries to reduce his compliance with American policies, this depends on the person.

Taha: The Americans can influence the weak ones.

Tariq: No, in reality, in the last 20 years, the United Nations was bought. Basically, after the Second World War, the United Nations has become an American institution.[44]

Male 1: A quarter of its budget.

Tariq: A quarter of its budget is supplied by the United States of America, and consequently, the American influence over the United Nations' authority is very strong. The secretary-general lives in New York, he lives there with his wife, and children, I mean.

Male 1: His residence.

Tariq: [Javier Pérez] de Cuéllar, the deputy secretary-general is an international employee.[45] Previously he was Peru's representative to the United Nations. In other words, he was an ambassador. I mean he was there for 20 years living there in New York. So at the end, at the end, he is American, an American who lives in New York, which is a Jewish city.

Shortly after Israel's Air Strike on Iraq's Tamuz (Osirak) Nuclear Reactor, Saddam Thinks He Sees Collusion between Israel and an "International Party" (circa mid-June 1981)[46]

Saddam: I also forgot to comment on something that came up in the statements of the Israeli officials, including [Menachem] Begin's. Which is that after the failure of their first attempt, which was spoken of in the Iraqi media and official statements and which took place at the beginning of the war that took place with the Persians, and after the failure of these strikes, the strikes of the Persian Air Force against the [Osirak reactor. And after they [the Israelis] concluded that the Air Force, the Persian Air Force, was demoralized and had lost a lot of its equipment, they decided to train their pilots for a long period to carry out this task. And they put in their schedule to train for several months, some said six months.

[Possibly Tariq]: [*Inaudible.*]

Saddam: No, they said six months, and if they deny that for a reason, then I will say it. What do they know of what all their targets were? I think they did not intend

---

[43] Although it is never explicitly stated, Saddam and his colleagues appear to suggest that UN Secretary-General Kurt Waldheim is a lackey not only of the United States but also of the Zionists. In 1985, four years after leaving the United Nations, Waldheim ran for the presidency of Austria. During the campaign, it was revealed that he had served as an intelligence officer in the Wehrmacht during World War II.

[44] The United Nations was founded after World War II.

[45] Javier Pérez de Cuéllar was undersecretary-general for special political affairs from April 1979 to December 1981, when he became secretary-general.

[46] SH-SHTP-A-000-571, "Saddam and His Inner Circle Discussing Israel's Attack on the Tamuz (Osirak) Reactor," undated (circa mid-June 1981).

to reveal the target at the beginning of the training, they intended to claim it as part of the war, but there were factors that made them realize that we knew this strike was from Israel.

The experience of the first strike was one of the lessons, and that other parties knew of the strike, whether before it occurred or during its execution. And that this matter was going to be revealed and so they were forced and also as a re-election factor for Begin, they were forced to reveal the strike. If they knew that the [Iran-Iraq] war was going to extend at least six more months, to allow them to go in under its cover and carry out this hit, which they trained for several months to carry out, and if they wanted to carry it out under the cover of war, then they must have been fully aware that the war was going to extend for an additional six months.

And that is not possible with just the information and the knowledge of the Mossad [Israeli foreign intelligence service]. There must have been another international party cooperating with them, not only on the strike and on information, but also on giving them information regarding how long the war was going to continue between Iraq and Iran. We don't know who this international party is, so we will at least leave all the excuses because the strike is directed toward us. So it must be in the Iranian nation. And through this and other factors you can guess why the war took place. Not only to direct a strike against the Iraqi atomic reactor, but also to stop Iraqi development. And you are also aware why the war continues.

Saddam Discusses Israel's Influence over the United States (circa 21 January 1988)[47]

Saddam: I always sensed that I have [encountered] suspicion from everybody, even those who say that they are our friends. No matter how bad the situation is with regard to the Soviets, I still suspect the Americans more than the Soviets, because the Soviets do not have a ready agenda that necessitates their hostility toward us. The Soviet nature is that they are a communist party, and the communist party throughout the world has started to shift from the Soviet affairs. Therefore, the Soviets, perhaps they are benefiting from serious friendships, that is, in terms of economic affairs and other matters, more so than benefiting from a particular matter that works against their intellect, even the communist methods. However, the integration between the Americans and the Zionist entity, I know ourselves, I know the extent to which the Zionist entity regards us as dangerous, and even our own realization that we represent danger to this Zionist entity, this is for your knowledge, I know myself, at least I know myself amidst my comrades.

Izzat: The Zionist entity knows you.

Saddam: And I also know my comrades to a great extent. So this integration, as long as it exists between America and Israel, this will constitute an instigating, annoying state between the Arabs and America. The Arabs should always aim for the reduction of this factor in American policy. Because America is a superpower, and that is a fact, America's influence is wide and extensive with regard to other matters, more so than the influence of the Soviets, that is in terms of influencing countries of the

---

47 *SH-SHTP-A-001-217, "Saddam and His Inner Circle Discussing the Iraqi Army's Performance in Northern Iraq, Relations with the United States and Russia, and UN Security Council Resolution 598," undated (circa 21 January 1988).

region, in the international economic aspect. And as an advanced country, as Arabs, we should always maintain relations with it [America] and to continue dealing with the variables that will benefit our country and our people. But this is a fact in terms of our relation with America, at least in the long run, this will continue. Every Arab national, a genuine nationalistic Arab, he has to always and continue to be alert about this factor, this integration [between America and Israel] and its ramifications.

Taha: We in Iraq, especially, we have to be suspicious and alert.

Saddam Suspects Israel and the "Zionist Lobby" in the 1993 World Trade Center Bombing (circa 1993)[48]

Saddam: There has obviously been a special technical arrangement in which the United States seems to have a hand. These dirty games are games that the American intelligence would play if it had a bigger purpose, which would be bigger than the losses and sacrifices it would have to suffer. But this issue concerns the American public – you would expect losses in the bombing of the World Trade Center. Losses. And they had losses; the media announced it and you remember it. So how could – would the American intelligence do such a thing even though they knew there would be American human losses?

Because this is not in the preparatory stage for us to claim that it is just a technical tactic intended for a certain party. It must be done by a party whose heart would not break over the loss of American lives and who would not suffer direct political consequences. Of course we immediately think of Israel. Israel, when it conducts such an operation is willing to suffer losses and it also has its methods by which even if some plans lead to it, it is able to cover the matter up and distract people from it. The Zionist Lobby is alive and effective in the United States. So this is one of the options.

Izzat: Sir, it is possible the Zionists played a major role in it.[49]

In the Context of a Discussion about the UN Sanctions, Saddam and His Advisers Discuss Whether the Egyptian Secretary-General of the United Nations, Boutros Boutros-Ghali, Is Jewish (15 April 1995)[50]

Male 1: All of us say that [Boutros] Boutros-Ghali is married to a Jewish female and he is a Zionist. How can we talk, discuss, and speak with him? And his mother is Jewish.[51] What can we say to him? How can he understand us, as well as his teacher [Egyptian president] Hosni Mubarak?

---

[48] See Saddam Hussein and his inner circle discuss the recent attack on the World Trade Center, circa 1993. On 26 February 1993, Ramzi Yousef, a terrorist associated with the Egyptian Islamic Group, detonated a truck bomb under the World Trade Center, killing six people. A more complete translation of this audio file is available in Woods, *Iraqi Perspectives Project – Primary Source Materials*, vol. 4, 63–83.

[49] Belief that Israel was responsible for the 1993 attack on the World Trade Center was widespread in the Arab world. For example, see Pipes, *The Hidden Hand*, 253, 261, 271.

[50] SH-SHTP-A-001-010, "Saddam and Senior Ba'ath Party Officials Discussing UN Sanctions on Iraq," 15 April 1995. Boutros-Ghali is, in fact, a Coptic Christian.

[51] Boutros-Ghali's mother is a Coptic Christian. His wife is Jewish. See Dilip Hiro, *The Essential Middle East: A Comprehensive Guide* (London: Carroll and Graf, 2003), 101. The reference to Boutros-Ghali as being a Zionist may be a reference to the fact that he was

Saddam: If his mother is Jewish, he must be a Jew because the son gains his mother's religion.

Male 2: His mother is married, Sir.

Saddam: I do not know.

[*Inaudible background talk.*]

Male 2: His mother is married.

Tariq: His wife is Jewish.

Male 3: In Judaism, if a Jewish man marries a Christian woman, the son will not be Jewish. But if a Jewish woman marries a Christian man, the son will be Jewish. The basis here is what comes from the mother and not from the father.

Saddam: It means if his mother is a Jew, he is a Jew, not a Christian. Is his mother Jewish?

Male 2: His wife is Jewish. His mother is Jewish and his wife is his cousin.[52]

Saddam: Anyway, there are people who are Arabs and their parents are also Arabs and Jewish. There are many ethnicities to which Arabs are not connected.

Saddam and His Advisers Discuss the Role of Jews in the Clinton Administration (late 1996 or early 1997)[53]

Male 1: Sir, another subject deals with the recent changes that Clinton has carried out in his government. Such changes confirm the extent of Zionist influence in his administration. [Madeleine] Albright became the secretary of state; and William Cohen, who is also a Jewish Republican, became secretary of defense; and Anthony Lake, who created the theory of "dual containment" [of Iraq and Iran], he, as well, is a Zionist, he became director of [Central] Intelligence; and another one named [Sandy] Berger who is also Jewish, he took Anthony Lake's position as secretary of the National Security Council.[54] What draws attention is that the Egyptian newspapers, the day before yesterday, the Egyptian media in general has vehemently attacked Albright, even the government's official newspaper . . .

———

Saddam: We do not attack anyone, because we regard Clinton or Cohen or Albright as all the same. This does not make any difference for us; we should not adopt the same path the Arabs are taking. They [the Americans] are obliged, whether they like it or not, to deal with us, and Iraq will be here, they have to put up with us, whether his name is Cohen or Clinton or whatever other name.

Anwar Sadat's foreign minister when Egypt and Israel made peace. Stanley Meisler, *United Nations: The First Fifty Years* (New York: Atlantic Monthly Press, 1997), 281.

[52] Boutros-Ghali's wife was not his cousin.

[53] SH-SHTP-A-001-218, "Saddam and His Senior Advisers Discussing Relations with Jordan and Changes in Clinton's National Security Team," undated (circa late 1996 or early 1997).

[54] Much of what this adviser is telling Saddam is inaccurate. Cohen's father was a Russian Jew, but Cohen is a Unitarian Christian. Although Clinton nominated Lake to become the director of the Central Intelligence Agency, the president withdrew the nomination in the face of Republican opposition.

The Arab World

There is no escape from the responsibility of leadership. It is not our choice to accept it or not. It is, rather, imposed on us . . . Iraq can make this nation rise and can be its center post of its big abode. There are smaller posts, but it must always be Iraq that feels the responsibility, and feels it is the central support post of the Arab nation. If Iraq falls, then the entire Arab nation will fall.
— Saddam Hussein, circa 1980–1981[1]

Saddam struggled to find a balance between the secular and religious aspects of political rule. In theory, Ba'athism was nonreligious and Iraq a secular state. During the 1970s, there were virtually no references to religion in the regime's public language. In fact, the regime emphasized language and symbols recalling the glories of pre-Islamic Mesopotamia. During this period, the state increasingly banned Shi'a religious observances, which led to Shi'a rioting in Najaf and Karbala in 1977. In his capacity as vice president, Saddam responded to this unrest by telling state officials that they should not use religious terms to have a "momentary encounter" (i.e., a temporary accommodation) with religious groups.[2] Years later, he expressed continuing distrust of individuals who used religion as a political tool: "By God, I do not like them, I do not like those who work politics under the guise of religion. My trust in them is not good."[3]

Saddam, however, was first and foremost a pragmatist in his dealings with Islamists; he had no problem accommodating religious groups or politicizing religion when expediency required. His modus operandi involved both punishment and accommodation. In an attempt to placate Iraqi Shi'a

[1] See section "Saddam claims that Iraq's history and scientific expertise uniquely qualify it to lead the Arab nation" in this chapter.
[2] Ofra Bengio, *Saddam's Word: Political Discourse in Iraq* (New York: Oxford University Press, 1998), 178.
[3] Saddam said this in January 2001 in response to an advisor's mention of Louis Farrakhan and his "million man" march. *SH-SHTP-A-001-219, "Saddam and Military Officials Discussing Reorganizing the Intelligence Service," 14 January 2001.

Saddam meeting with Yasser Arafat, chairman of the Palestine Liberation Organization and head of Fatah (1959–2004). The date of this meeting is unknown but probably around 1990. (*Source*: *SH-MISC-D-001-272, "Photos of Saddam on Different Occasions," November 2002.)

anger over the state's repressive intrusions into the religious realm, in 1979 Saddam spent up to $80.5 million on mosques, shrines, and other religious affairs; prayed at Shi'a shrines on national television; and made a fantastic claim to have descended from the prophet Muhammad.[4] In 1986, while fighting for survival against theocratic Iran, he explained to his advisers that if foreign Islamist groups would cease advocating theocracy and were not on the verge of taking power, then Iraq could work with them. Tariq Aziz added that fighting imperialists and Zionists were more important missions

[4] Bengio, *Saddam's Word*, 179; Sandra Mackey, *The Reckoning: Iraq and the Legacy of Saddam Hussein*, (New York: W. W. Norton & Co., 2002), 248–49. Saddam was prone to boastful hyperbole. For instance, after hearing a report that Khomeini's father lived until he was more than 100 years old, and that Khomeini's brother was in his 90s, Saddam exclaimed that his own uncle was able to ride a horse with a "very straight back" as a 120-year old and had lived to the age of 125 by smoking a pipe and eating lots of onions. *SH-SHTP-A-001-220, "Saddam Meeting with a Foreign Official," undated (circa 19 August 1987).

for Iraq than opposing Islamists.[5] Saddam's public use of Islamic rhetoric and symbols to garner increased foreign and domestic support reached its pinnacle just before Iraq fought the United States and launched Scud missiles at Israel during the "Mother of All Battles."[6] Later years saw additional public displays of Saddam's piety and support for state sanctioned Islamic undertakings.[7]

Saddam's public expressions of belief in Islam, however, might not have been purely tactical; the dictator's private conversations also include numerous references to his belief in God, Muhammad, and the Quran. Saddam attributed Iraq's victory in the Iran-Iraq War to Iraq's "dependence on God."[8] A week after conquering Kuwait, Saddam explained to his advisers that in deciding to invade, God "showed us the path . . . guided us . . . turned us . . . [and] blessed us."[9] According to Saddam, the uprisings following the war were partially attributable to a failure by Iraqis to "remember the mercy of God, and that God is stronger than any other power."[10] After the war, Saddam explained the need to execute rebels and cross-dressers by referencing a fatwa.[11] Saddam noted that even Muhammad had lost military encounters, and that because what happened in the Gulf War was God's will, Saddam would be grateful.[12] Saddam's expressions indicating a fatalistic reliance on God resurfaced while discussing relations with the incoming Clinton administration, negotiating with the international community the disarmament demands imposed on Iraq, and recognizing his descent from power while in U.S. captivity.[13]

[5] See section "Saddam and his advisers discuss their desire to find a modus vivendi with the Muslim Brotherhood" in this chapter.

[6] Bengio, *Saddam's Word*, 191.

[7] In 1994, Saddam fostered mosque building and banned alcohol to shore up his image as a faithful Muslim. According to Iraqi reports, Saddam donated twenty-eight liters of blood over a three-year period so that a Quran in a mosque memorializing the Mother of All Battles could be handwritten with his blood. Around 2000, Saddam further shifted Iraq's identity from a secular to a religious state. See Philip Smucker, "Iraq Builds 'Mother of All Battles' Mosque in Praise of Saddam," *Daily Telegraph*, 29 July 2001; Ajami, *The Foreigner's Gift*, 318.

[8] See section "Saddam recounts some of his favorite war stories during the last month of the conflict," in Chapter 4.

[9] See section "Saddam appraises American and international reactions to the invasion of Kuwait," in Chapter 5.

[10] See section "Hussein Kamil informs Saddam that his inner circle was too scared to tell him about the low morale," in Chapter 5.

[11] See section "Saddam meets with tribal leaders," in Chapter 5.

[12] See section "Saddam discusses how Iraq won the Gulf War," in Chapter 5.

[13] See sections "Saddam and senior advisers discuss Clinton's desire for talks," in Chapter 1; "Saddam discusses areas in which Iraq should continue refusing UN disarmament demands," in Chapter 7; George Piro Informal Conversation with Saddam, 11 June 2004, accessed 2 September 2009 at www.gwu.edu/~nsarchiv. All subsequent citations to Piro's interrogation reports and reports of informal conversations are also found at the National Security Archive Web site.

Ideology

It is difficult to determine the degree to which Saddam's religious beliefs motivated, as opposed to merely justified, his geopolitical ambitions.[14] By all accounts, Saddam aspired to expand Iraqi influence and lead the Arab world. A year before becoming president, Saddam told a group of military officials that he could not guarantee them a quiet life. Iraq had formerly reached China and southern Europe, he told them, and "We have the right to aspire to make the shape of the present reflect the splendor of the past."[15] Only Iraq, Saddam told his advisers, had the necessary historical experience, population density, and scientific and material capabilities to lead the Arab world. "There is no escape from the responsibility of leadership," he exclaimed.[16] Saddam viewed himself on par with such historical leaders as Nebuchadnezzar and Saladin. When encouraged to declare himself caliph (leader of all Muslims) during a 1990 meeting with the head of the Palestinian Islamic Jihad, Saddam did not renounce such ambition; instead, he responded, "It is too early for that."[17] Saddam's ambitions for Iraq apparently persisted even while he languished in U.S. captivity. As he explained to his Federal Bureau of Investigation interrogator, God had destined Iraq for greatness. Few countries had ever led the world, he noted, yet God had given Iraq a unique "gift" that enabled it to "go to the top" many times.[18]

Saddam's pursuit of regional leadership, which he considered Iraq's historical destiny, lay at the heart of much of his foreign policy. Anwar Sadat's decision to make peace with Israel provided Saddam with the opportunity of a lifetime to replace Egypt as the leader of the Arab world. Baghdad headed the states rejecting the Camp David Treaty by hosting Arab League conferences to discuss how to punish Egypt and by leading the charge in implementing the league's decisions.

A few years later, Iraq found itself in a war with Iran that Saddam framed in terms of defending the Arab world against an aggressive horde of Persian religious fanatics. In a September 1980 conversation on Iraq's war objectives with Iran, Saddam noted that Arab public opinion supported Iraq's military actions against Iran. Retaking the Shatt al-Arab, he claimed, would have a profound effect on the Arab psyche by showing Arabs that they could

---

[14] For an argument that Saddam used Islam solely instrumentally, and was not a sincere believer, see Jerry M. Long, *Saddam's War of Words: Politics, Religion, and the Iraqi Invasion of Kuwait* (Austin: University of Texas Press, 2004), 56–58. One of Saddam's interpreters, however, described him as "a practising Muslim who wanted to be a good man." See Philip Delves Broughton, "The Nice Side of Saddam," *Spectator*, 6 December 2003.

[15] Bengio, *Saddam's Word*, 166.

[16] See section "Saddam claims that Iraq's history and scientific expertise uniquely qualify it to lead the Arab nation" in this Chapter.

[17] See *SH-PDWN-D-001-221, "Minutes of the Meeting between Saddam and As'ad Bayud Al-Tamimi, the Chief of the Islamic Jihad Movement (Bait Al-Maqdis)," 30 September 1990.

[18] George Piro Interrogation of Saddam, session number 1, 7 February 2004.

⌐8 ₑe said that if the Arabs would provide him with a
ould use it to coerce Israel to cede control of the land
..ice 1967.[19]

..n's perspective, Zionists and the Western media were primar-
..ole for Arab divisions. They sought to enervate pan-Arab senti-
ı. ₑalleged, by reviving Pharaonic, Phoenician, and Berber civilizations
in c ₑ.rerent areas of the Arab world. Moreover, he observed, they undermined Iraqi unity by emphasizing Kurdish, Shi'a, and Sunni divisions.[20]
Saddam, by contrast, drew on pre-Islamic themes to unify Iraqis. He funded
festivals, museums, historians, and archaeologists to develop and draw attention to Iraq's "deep" pre-Islamic history. He also used themes from Shi'a
Islam in his efforts to create an Iraqi identity.[21] During his war with Iran
and conflict with the United States, Saddam increasingly turned to Islamic
rhetoric to inspire Iraqis to fight, yet he was careful to use religious language
only in ways that would unify Iraqis and garner support from the "Arab
street."[22]

Although Saddam drew on Shi'a symbols, one is hard-pressed to find
explicit references to Iraq's Shi'a population or "Sunni-Shi'a divide," even
during the war with Iran. The tapes reveal that the topic was as taboo in
Saddam's private meetings as in his party's public communications. This was
clearly intentional. In 1975 Saddam, as vice president, instructed educators:

We must speak of the Iraqi who comes from Sulaymaniyya [i.e., a Kurd] and he who
comes from Basra [i.e., a Shi'a, without pointing to his ethnic origins ... Let us delete
the words Arabs and Kurds and replace them with the term the Iraqi people.[23]

When the Ba'ath used the term *Shi'a* in public, it almost always referred
to non-Iraqi Shiites in Lebanon, Saudi Arabia, or elsewhere. According to
Ofra Bengio, "The regime had enacted a 'conspiracy of silence' around the
issue of the Shi'is, lest they might have to share power with them." The
Ba'ath used a variety of proxy terms to describe Iraq's Shi'a population. In
contrast to the lack of explicit references to Shiites or Shi'ism, Iraqi leaders'
comments on the Arab-Persian cleavage abound. In the transcripts reviewed
for this study, comments about Persians frequently refer to Iraqi Shiites of
suspect loyalty to the regime.[24]

[19] SH-SHTP-A-000-835, "Saddam and Military Officials Discussing the Iran-Iraq War," 16
September 1980.
[20] See section "Saddam's inner circle discusses the greedy and aggressive nature of Zionism,"
in Chapter 2.
[21] Long, *Saddam's War of Words*, 52, 66; Amatzia Baram, "Mesopotamian Identity in Ba'thi
Iraq," *Middle Eastern Studies* 19, no. 4 (October 1983): 426–55.
[22] Long, *Saddam's War of Words*, 66–73.
[23] Long, *Saddam's War of Words*, 50.
[24] Bengio, *Saddam's Word*, 99–102.

Although Saddam held Jewish and Zionists' malevolence responsible for Arab divisions, opposition to the "Zionist entity" proved useful in unifying Arabs behind his leadership. Iraq's anti-Israel and pro-Palestinian behavior and public rhetoric bolstered Baghdad's regional standing and garnered it support from the Arab street. Such behavior and rhetoric, though heartfelt, were also strategically useful. As one of Saddam's advisors observed, "Leadership belongs . . . to those who defend Palestine and those who cheer for it."[25] Saddam was a leading sponsor of Palestinian terrorists, though, as recordings quoted in this chapter demonstrate, his relationship with Arafat and other Palestinian leaders could be volatile.[26] Evidence of close ties or an operational relationship between Saddam's Iraq and Al Qaeda does not emerge from the recordings or captured documents.[27]

Because Saddam saw Iraq and therefore himself as the rightful leader of the Arab world, he was wary of any individual or movement seeking influence over his domain. Of course, this meant that his relationship with Hosni Mubarak, the leader of the largest Arab country, was likely to be strained. By the same token, it meant that he was deeply suspicious of the Muslim Brotherhood, and its far more radical offshoot, Al Qaeda. The Muslim Brotherhood, founded in 1928 by an Egyptian Hassan al-Banna under the slogan, "Islam is the solution," used tactics from terrorism to electoral politics to become a leading opposition force in Egypt and other countries. Its Iraqi branch spent most of the Ba'athist period underground. Saddam might have been willing to overlook the existence of groups such as the Brotherhood or Al Qaeda and its like-minded affiliates as long as they were a thorn in the side of his enemies or rivals. He did not, however, wish to see them become so powerful as to offer a realistic alternative to Ba'athism or his personal position.

ARAB STATE LEADERS

Saddam and the Egyptian president Hosni Mubarak spent many years vying for leadership of the Arab world. The Baghdad Summit, a meeting that brought together Arab leaders in Iraq in November 1978, came on the heels

---

[25] See section "Saddam and his advisers castigate Egyptian President Hosni Mubarak," in this chapter.

[26] On Iraq's support for Palestinian terrorists, see Woods et al., *Iraqi Perspectives Project: Saddam and Terrorism: Emerging Insights from Captured Iraqi Documents, Volumes 1–5*, IDA Paper No. P-4287 (Alexandria, VA: Institute for Defense Analyses, 2007); *SH-SHTP-A-001-222, "Saddam and His Senior Advisers Discussing the Second Palestinian Intifada," 6 December 2000; and see SH-PDWN-D-000-499, "Order from Saddam to Give $25,000 to the Families of Palestinian Suicide Bombers," 4 March 2002.

[27] Woods, et al., *Iraqi Perspectives Project: Saddam and Terrorism* (2007), especially vol. 1, ES-1.

of Egypt's peace treaty with Israel. Following this summit, Egypt, absent from the discussions in Baghdad, was expelled from the Arab League, not to be reinstated until 1989 under Mubarak.[28] In this section's first recording, from September 1990, the Iraqi leaders ridicule Mubarak's pan-Arab leadership aspirations. In the second, a retrospective 1992 conversation, they discuss the treachery of Egypt and Saudi Arabia in the Mother of All Battles. Saddam says that Mubarak was a plotter more evil than King Fahd, as Egypt had no reason to fear Iraq, and calls for assassination operations against the two leaders. In the third, from November 1990, Saddam and his advisers discuss a decline in Libya's support for the terrorist Abu Abbas and the conditions under which Iraq will sponsor terrorist operations against various targets.

Saddam and His Advisers Castigate Egyptian President Hosni Mubarak, Discuss Iraqi Scud Missiles in Sudan Aimed at Egypt's Aswan High Dam, and Joke about Arab Unity under Various Leaders (30 September 1990)[29]

Male 1: Have Mubarak's words reached you yet, Sir?

Saddam: What?

Male 1: Mubarak's.

Saddam: No.

Male 1: Okay, I will brief you with regard to what I have done.

Saddam: He does not mean anything! He does not mean anything anymore!

Male 1: No, [*inaudible*] talking!

Saddam: I mean his role [*pauses*] has no more value.

Male 1: Right now he is saying that the whole problem revolves around the idea that we want to take the leadership from him. [*Whispering in background.*] Yes, of course, I found his report.

Saddam: Does this brother really think he is a leader?

Male 1: Yes, that he is a leader. So he is saying –

Saddam: Oh, what kind of brains we Arabs have!

Male 1: Yes, of course!

Saddam: Wrong, wrong, wrong! That is enough. If Mubarak is imagining he is our leader, I swear to God nobody put it in his head other than us. Honest to God, he

---

[28] BBC News, "Timeline: Arab League," (17 September 2008), accessed 1 May 2009 at http://news.bbc.co.uk/1/hi/world/middle_east/country_profiles/1550977.stm.

[29] SH-SHTP-A-000-671, "Saddam and Senior Advisers Discussing the Iraqi Invasion of Kuwait," 30 September 1990.

is such a good speaker, I mean this extreme knowledge, some people are really not able to digest it.[30]

Male 2: We [*inaudible*] Mubarak's issue.

Sa'dun: [*Inaudible*] that he is generous.

Saddam: I know, he is not generous, but villainous.

Sa'dun: [*Inaudible.*]

Male 1: So he is saying that the problem is that we want to take a leadership role.

Saddam: Wrong.

Male 1: "But I will never give up leadership, period!" [*apparently quoting Mubarak*].

Saddam: No brother, he does not have to give it up. No, no, it is wrong, it is wrong. My friend, we will give it to him, count on God.[31]

Male 1: Yes, he also said, "They put me up in the [Gulf] Cooperation Council, but this is a conspiracy council. [*Saddam laughs.*] I have seen the way they talk about poverty, wealth, and oil, and I found out that this is –"

[*Laughter.*]

Saddam: [*Inaudible.*]

Male 1: I cannot talk about it anymore.

Male 2: [*Inaudible.*]

Male 1: "So this is how it is. These folks intend to take over everyone." [*Laughter.*] "This is truly a conspiracy council; I do not want to conspire" [*Apparently quoting Mubarak; laughter in background*]. With regard to the rockets that were supposedly set up against him in Sudan, "I will strike them, I will destroy them!" [*apparently quoting Mubarak*].[32]

Saddam: Where are these rockets in Sudan?

Male 1: "I will not joke about it!" [*apparently quoting Mubarak*].

Male 2: We set up rockets in Sudan?

Male 1: Yes, we have Scud missiles in the north of Sudan where we want to hit the [Aswan] High Dam.

---

[30] Saddam seems to be speaking sarcastically.

[31] Saddam seems to be speaking sarcastically.

[32] In response to demonstrations in Khartoum calling for attacks on Egypt's Aswan Dam and pyramids, and reports that Sudan had deployed Iraqi Scuds near its border with Egypt to attack the dam, Mubarak warned on 22 January 1991 that Saddam "cannot attack the High Dam, even if he has anything (such as Scud missiles in Sudan)...and even if he managed to get anything in Sudan, I wouldn't allow it to remain intact, and Sudan would pay a dear price." See Naguib Megally, "Mubarak Firmly Backing Coalition," *United Press International*, 22 January 1991; "Gadhafi Expected in Cairo to Restore Egypt-Sudan Links," *United Press International*, 1 July 1991.

Saddam: Okay, but somebody needs to respond to that! Do not let it slip!

Male 1: Sir, I told Your Excellency previously that the presidents are not my specialty.

Saddam: Yes.

Male 1: So, I sent you the speech, and please do not laugh at me! It is just fun.

Saddam: Where is it, where?

Male 1: I sent it to you a while ago.

Saddam: When did he give this statement? What month?

Male 1: No, it was just the day before yesterday, and yesterday I sent it to you printed on papers yesterday.

Male 2: If he was talking about the others, then it was addressed to the others, not to Mr. President.

Male 1: According to him, he said "The media is a little bit filled with insults, ridiculousness, etc. We are civilized ones" [*Interruption*] No, our media, our media. "I will not lower myself to the level of these insults. In regards to King Hussein, he is my brother and he is a good man, but his media buddies are not polite." [*Apparently quoting Mubarak*]

Saddam: Check this statement. How come he is a good man and a man of conspiracy at the same time?

Male 1: Yes, according to Mr. Taha, [*pauses*] according to what Mr. Taha, who is a [*inaudible*] representative with him, says. "He came to me and I told him that they needed to withdraw." [*Apparently quoting Mubarak*] Taha said, "We will never withdraw, period." "The Vice President of the Republic came to me" [*quoting Mubarak*]. He means Vice President of the Federation Council and [he] said, "What have you done with this statement of yours?" "I said to him, it is necessary that you withdraw" [*quoting Mubarak*]. "We will not withdraw." Let me give you the conclusion Sir – ! I emphasized to him under the name Sakhr Jasim.[33] What I am trying to explain is that Hosni Mubarak does not have any nerves left.

Saddam: He never did, the man is gone.

Male 1: What is up with this leadership? What is up with him trying to become involved with the leadership? Is it a building where we have a dispute about it? We said to him, we said to him, "Leadership belongs to its people, to those who defend Palestine and those who cheer for it from the eastern part of the Arabic homeland to the ocean to the gulf. Leadership does not belong to the people whom Bush calls friends and believers. Leadership does not belong to the people who devote themselves as servants of colonialism. And it looks like, Hosni, you are a midget inside this giant body! We presented it to him just like that! So the whole subject with Hosni is we are struggling with him and we want to strip him from the leadership. He said, "Today he had an entire country to himself." [*Laughter.*]

---

[33] Articles sometimes appeared in the Iraqi media under this name. For instance, see *al-Jumhuriyya*, 4 April 1990.

Saddam: [*Inaudible.*]

Male 1: And they want him to stay in the [Gulf] Cooperation Council. [*Mumbling in background.*]

———

Saddam: We need to look at the battle through the general creative and strategic lens. Yes. These are all of the chapters from the battle and each chapter where we achieve victory will be victorious, building up toward the strategic goal.

Male 3: The territories of 1967 have been liberated now without war. Once we confirm [*inaudible*], two or three years from now, Saddam Hussein from Baghdad – the 1967 territories –

Saddam: Not in two years; right now [French President François] Mitterrand is going to talk about it.[34]

Male 3: I mean the Soviets, China, [*inaudible*], the Italians. Right now the subject of poverty, the case of the Middle East, the case of Palestine, and the case of Lebanon, all of these things are considered to be our issue right now.

Saddam: These are our issues.

Male 3: This is what we wanted.

Saddam: Okay, we have to confirm this and come out with results from it.

Male 3: But –

Saddam: Otherwise, how could we leave it unsettled?

Male 2: [*Inaudible.*]

Saddam: Today I am against them with this; I am against them openly. If I do not do so, it will still be okay. I even crossed them off my list and said, "I am afraid you wanted [*inaudible*] against them so that we can remove them." Go ahead and read, Hamed.

Hamed:[35] This is what it says up until Monday, "The borders between the Arabic and Islamic states are illegal. It is a religious proclamation. The situation of Kuwait and its legitimate aspect is illegal."

Saddam: Well, we would remove our borders.

Male 3: Right?

Saddam: We have no borders. We would like to be integrated with Syria and Egypt and anyone who wants to take us in can do so [*pauses*] can take us. [*Laughing.*]

---

[34] Saddam is apparently referring to Mitterrand's 25 September speech at the United Nations in which the French president said that if Iraq would "declare its determination to withdraw from Kuwait and free the hostages," then "everything might be possible," including settlement of the conflict in Lebanon and a resolution of the Palestinian issue. See Paul Lewis, "Confrontation in the Gulf: Mitterrand Says Iraqi Withdrawal Could Help End Mideast Disputes," *New York Times*, 25 September 1990.

[35] Hamed's identity is unclear.

If the Saudis are okay with the idea, we can establish a union with them tomorrow. The King can stay King and we are his deputies.

Male 3: [*Inaudible*] the presidency of the republic.

Saddam: [*Inaudible. Everybody laughs.*]

[*Inaudible background talk.*]

Saddam: What is he going to ask us for?

Male 1: He even told them that he became a higher ranked leader in the armed forces. [*Inaudible. Laughing.*]

Saddam: May God forgive them.

Male 3: When Mubarak says his battle is going to take place in a year.

Saddam: He is crazy.

Male 3: [*Inaudible*] look Mr. President accused me of this [*laughter*]. I have not said this one [*inaudible*].

Saddam: Let him wait three months to see what is going to happen!

Male 3: And the [*inaudible*], how could Mr. President accuse me of such a thing! [*Another male laughs.*] [*Inaudible.*] He said he did not say it; he contacts [*inaudible*] and this one sends a telegram and [*inaudible*].

Saddam: It happens that if you limp and you are upset, your deformity will surface more when you are upset. I mean, we are very good human beings, we are polite and smooth, but if someone pushes us and tries to walk all over us, we will retaliate, that is all. We will line up all of his wrongdoings, one by one.

Male 4: Mr. President, I sent you two telegrams, which you received in the last six months [*inaudible*].

Saddam: No, it is clear.

Male 4: [*Inaudible.*]

Saddam: He is an actor and a liar. He wants to gather issues so that he can find a cover for his conspiracy against us. This is a conspirator; he appeared to be a conspirator, this villain!

[*Inaudible background talk.*]

Male 4: [*Inaudible*] but he said that you said a lot of things.

Saddam: I have not said that, but right now I am telling you that. [*Voices overlap.*]

Male 4: One, two, three, [*inaudible*].

Male 3: [*Inaudible*] why did King Hussein [of Jordan] [*inaudible*] Mubarak's behavior and the way he humiliated the presidents. I was delighted because his case was [*inaudible*].

Saddam: He is not a noble person, and it looks as though he has been humiliated a lot in his life. And he accepted the humiliation to the point that he does not behave nicely toward people.

Male 1: Unfortunately it is because he has no decent communication skills. His language is not –

Male 2: I mean, it hurt me to see Your Excellency [*inaudible*].

Male 1: I mean he did not give up the leadership, period. I mean that is the point.[36]

In a Retrospective Conversation, the Iraqi Leadership Discusses the Treachery of Mubarak and King Fahd during the Mother of All Battles; Saddam Expresses a Desire for Assassination Attempts on the Two Men. The Iraqis Also Talk about How to Strengthen Baghdad's Historical Claims to Kuwait (9 May 1992)[37]

Saddam: Sometimes, I hear a story from the comrades and I tell them I must see the original and see how it was written and expressed. We did not insult them. We simply said that the first responsible person was Hosni. We also said that [Saudi King] Fahd was the second responsible one, and Bush was the third.

Izzat: Fahd is the first one; the first responsible one was Fahd.

Saddam: Yes, but Hosni played a big role. First, he was the tool behind bungling any Arab solution.

Izzat: He was a saboteur.

Saddam: He was also the first to announce official Arab support before the world that the Arab Summit Council made the decision. That was very important. There were also the dirty intelligence games and curtailed information, which Westerners know are lies, but they depend on them. They say, "President Mubarak said such-and-such a thing, and Fahd said such-and-such a thing." It was important to use Egypt's moral power in a devious way. The reason I placed Fahd in this sequence is because he had the excuse of fear, so what was Hosni's excuse? This is what I need to understand.[38]

[36] Saddam had a long-standing rivalry with Mubarak for leadership of the Arab world. Although Iraq gained influence among Arab states at the expense of Egypt after Egypt made peace with Israel in 1979, Iraq's invasion of Kuwait and subsequent military defeat enabled Egypt to emerge from the war with the strongest Arab military. Moreover, unlike Iraq, it could plausibly claim to have helped protect the Gulf states. See Gregory L. Aftandilian, *Egypt's Bid for Arab Leadership: Implications for U.S. Policy* (New York: Council on Foreign Relations, 1993), 30–31.

[37] *SH-SHTP-A-001-223, "Saddam and Government Officials Discussing Ba'ath Party Issues, International Sanctions, and Other Political Concerns," 9 May 1992.

[38] In the days before Iraq invaded Kuwait, Mubarak and Fahd mediated between the two. After Iraq invaded, Mubarak publicly accused Saddam of dishonesty for telling him that Iraq would not invade. Moreover, Egypt was the primary author of a resolution, appearing under the name of the Gulf Cooperation Council, which condemned Iraq's invasion. The Arab League voted in favor of this resolution on 11 August 1990. Egypt also dispatched an armored division to Saudi Arabia to participate in the liberation of Kuwait. See "Egypt President Mubarak Comments on Gulf Crisis," *BBC Summary of World Broadcasts*, 10 August 1990; John Kifner, "Confrontation in the Gulf; Arab Vote to Send Troops to Help Saudis; Boycott of Iraqi Oil Is Reported Near 100%," *New York Times*, 11 August 1990. The Iraqi leadership castigated Saudi Arabia for providing financial assistance to states that sided against Iraq during the Gulf War. Without Saudi money, Saddam argued, the

Izzat: Hosni was an old plotter.

Saddam: And I explained it. Hosni sat with us to the end where we talked to him about the evils, the circumstances, the plotting against us. We were annoyed. He came without any justification. On the other hand, Fahd was next to Kuwait. He said whoever attacks Kuwait will attack us. This was possible. There is logic in what he said. But, why did Hosni volunteer from behind the borders?

Male 1: [*Inaudible.*]

Saddam: The main thing is, it was Mubarak and Fahd among the Arabs who brought these foreigners to attack us.

Male 1: [*Inaudible.*]

Saddam: These people – they are moving because whoever wants to stop at a certain point, that is it, it is over with Kuwait [*inaudible*]. True, they want to hurt us, but is it easy to antagonize us? Are we so simple that one can antagonize us and stay next to us, and continue to kill our children? Is it so easy?

Male 2: [*Inaudible.*]

Saddam: In this period, after we gave the Arabs all this opportunity to retreat, they still continued with their evil. One must strike the evil ones, Hosni and Fahd, and leave all the others; especially Hosni and Fahd, and leave the others, even the Saudi family.[39] Hosni and Fahd because they don't seem to have given up their evil. They have not given up their evil. Yes, comrade [*inaudible*].

Male 3: Excuse me, Sir. That is why the sense of guilt will remain and they will continue to feel it. They will always worry about everything in Iraq. Comrade Tariq's visit to Morocco was successful and good, but I think the visit must diplomatically be followed by a visit to the United Nations.[40] It might be better if he were there to explain the contents of the letter.[41]

Another point I wanted to talk about is that we should follow up on these issues with the Arab states that are either friendly or at least are neutral. It is important to move on the Arab level, in addition to what the comrades said, in terms of the friendly and neutral countries. Thank you, Sir.

United States and other countries would have been unwilling or unable to fight. See section "Saddam discusses the role of capitalism in America's involvement in the Mother of all Battles," in Chapter 1.

[39] In late 1990, Izzat al-Duri told Saddam that he expected to see assassination attempts on these two leaders for siding with the United States against Iraq. See *SH-SHTP-A-001-224, "Saddam and His Political Advisers Discussing the Possibility of a US Attack and Perceptions of other Arab Countries," undated (circa 1990–1991).

[40] Tariq Aziz visited Morocco in early May 1992 in search of Arab support to end the sanctions. On 4 May, he gave King Hassan a message from Saddam. See "King of Morocco Receives Iraqi Deputy Prime Minister," *BBC Summary of World Broadcasts: The Monitoring Report*, 6 May 1992; "Tareq Aziz Seeks Arab Support to End Sanctions on Iraq," *Agence France-Presse*, 4 May 1992.

[41] This might refer to the fifty-seven-page letter to the UN secretary-general in which Iraq's foreign minister described the UN demarcation of the Iraq-Kuwait border as "illegitimate." During this period Iraq, Kuwait, and the United Nations exchanged a number of letters regarding the work of the Iraq-Kuwait boundary demarcation commission. See "Iraq Balks at Border," *Newsday*, 2 June 1992.

Saddam: Therefore, by the grace of God, we will proceed and if something new and important crops up, we will revise our position. Concerning the other point on the international borders committee's decision, which has not been approved by the UN Security Council – am I right?[42] We have also realized it is logical to behave and express ourselves in the same way – even though we were not easy to deal with, even on the subject of the border, our memoranda have been essentially the same in terms of the contents.

But after all this time and after the issue became [*inaudible*], are we not required to present another paper for history? What is required is to present another paper for history, because it has been proven that papers and history continue to work. No one can get rid of them, especially on the subject of land and sovereignty, and history – I mean historical documents that speak.

It is clear that the strongest card is that we went, ruled, and sat [in Kuwait]. But it is also necessary because there might be some confusion about our approval of decision number such-and-such, being forced, so that no one can use the Iraqis as an excuse in the future. The weak always try to find an excuse to go inside. We want to set documents for the strong ones, to support them, whether in the ranks of the people or the authority. An endeavor was made within this limited committee to develop a document so that we can explain again the old historical background and how Kuwait was such-and-such throughout history. Despite all this, you [possibly referring to the United Nations] now come to make such a decision, when they themselves admit that there were Kuwaitis there. Even in the case of the oil wells, during the Saudi talks, they said that their money is not so much; that it was about $2 billion and plus. Even the Kuwaiti rulers agreed to that. They [Kuwaiti rulers] wanted more to take new oil wells and add them to the other ones.

This is injustice that completely conflicts with every historical and equitable situation. We must establish them. Some say, we will fight you until you say that Kuwait is – [*pause*]. No, it is over. It doesn't help. They [possibly the Kuwaitis] are annoyed and I do not know why. Let them get annoyed. But we must establish it as a document. There will come a day.

Even the Western newspapers are not satisfied with this decision. I read articles after I received the memorandum. Almost on the same day I received new articles other than the ones they cited. They [probably the Kuwaitis] cited these articles cleverly by referring to an article from here and there and referring to a statement from there. What are they doing? This means they are giving the Iraqis justification to continue this subject.

Izzat: They are strengthening their justification.

Saddam: The diligence reached this point. If the comrades have something to discuss about the idea, the discussion is open, and if they have something to discuss regarding the drafting, the discussion is also open. Is this not the essence of the subject, comrade Tariq? Comrades Tariq and Izzat were [*inaudible*]. Yes, Comrade Muhammad?

Muhammad:[43] If you allow me, Sir, in line with what Your Excellency said and the amendments, it is clear what Your Excellency means by them. On page 40, a

---

[42] On 26 August 1992, the UN Security Council expressed approval of the commission's demarcation of the Iraq-Kuwait border in UN Security Council Resolution 773.

[43] This is probably Muhammad Saeed al-Sahhaf, Iraqi minister of information.

paragraph says, "After sometime, Sa'd al-Abdallah visited Iraq."[44] In my opinion, it should be he visited Baghdad, from a historical point of view.

Saddam: Visited Baghdad, yes. Wherever Iraq is mentioned based on the meanings we changed, it should be replaced by Baghdad.[45]

Muhammad: Yes.

Saddam: You may notice that in some forms I used the name of Kuwait, etc., but in other forms related to our part and how we speak [inaudible]. The other ones remain as a cover, but the essence expresses it better.

Izzat: Kuwait is an area, [inaudible] a name of a state. You say Kuwait [inaudible] but we do not say the State of Kuwait. Kuwait is an area.

Saddam: Comrade Abd-al-Ghani[46] says a book has been published under the title of "The Gulf War: Who is Responsible?" The author is Dr. Awdah Butrus Awdah.[47] In this book, there are clarifications about the positions of Hosni and Fahd and their conspiring even before 2 August.

Izzat: Send us copies of the book.

Male 4: I will send a copy to Your Excellency.

Saddam: What?

Izzat: We want copies for all of us.

Saddam: All comrades should read it [inaudible].

Izzat: [Inaudible] valuable book. Sir, let us assign –

Saddam: [Interrupting] Yes, but I have not read it. Abd-al-Muhsin [inaudible] somebody expresses thanks to you, etc. Okay, but I have not read it.

Izzat: Let us ask the Ministry of Foreign Affairs.

Tariq: The book is good and it has a very good pan-Arab tendency.

Male 4: Dr. Awdah was a Ba'athist.

Saddam and the Revolutionary Command Council Discuss Libyan Leader Mu'amar Qadafi's (and Iraq's) Terrorist Affiliations and Potential Operations (1 November 1990)[48]

Male 1: I am not comfortable at all with the decision Mu'amar al-Qadafi made yesterday.

---

[44] Sa'd al-Abdallah al-Salim al-Sabah, Kuwait's prime minister and crown prince.

[45] This apparently is in keeping with the position that Baghdad is an historic Arab city, immovable and permanent. The borders of Iraq, like those of Kuwait, in this context, however, are not fixed.

[46] Abd al-Ghani was a member of Saddam's cabinet from 1982 to 1991.

[47] The Arabic title of the book is *Harb Khaliij min al-mas'ul?*

[48] *SH-SHTP-A-001-225, "Saddam and His Political Advisers Discussing Iraq's Foreign Policy, Security Council Decisions, and the Possibility of War with the United States," 1 November 1990.

Saddam: What did he decide?

Male 1: He closed AbuAbbas's offices.[49] This guy, Qadafi is such a malicious guy. Is he not Abu-al-'Abbas's friend? This means that he wants – I don't want to accuse Abu-al-'Abbas. I just met him one time – he only wants to prove to people –

Saddam: He is the type you can expect anything from.

Izzat: [*Inaudible.*]

Male 1: What?

Izzat: [*Inaudible*] from Abu-al-'Abbas.

Male 1: I have no objection –

Male 2: It is not because of the Americans, he just wants to stick his nose in –

Tariq: [*Inaudible*] Hosni Mubarak.

Male 1: My opinion is that, with his [*inaudible*] Qadafi feared there was something guaranteed and then he would say to his bosses, "Look, I don't have any, I kicked them out." This is from the Brothers.

Izzat: No, he figured he was going to be [targeted] next and decided to come out and be truthful with the Americans.

Male 1: They attack him for what?

Male 2: This is his opinion. They will not attack him[;] they will consult with him.

Male 1: By God, I can't believe Qadafi is scared.[50]

Izzat: I was sitting next to him in Cairo.

Male 1: Anyway, it's just an observation. I emphasize the observation Mr. President presented that we should monitor it, because once we get to next year – Sir, people –

Saddam: It will be its two-year mark.[51]

Male 1: The indications are something else. Every day in the world –

---

[49] Abu Abbas was the leader of the Palestine Liberation Front, a terrorist organization, and the mastermind of the 1985 hijacking of the cruise ship *Achille Lauro*. In early November 1990, Qadafi reportedly shut down Abu Abbas's four training camps in Libya and expelled the group. See Salah Nasrawi, "Leader of Radical PLO Unit Confirms Libya Closed his Camps," *Associated Press*, 5 November 1990. Also see Woods, et al., *Iraqi Perspectives Project: Saddam and Terrorism* (2007), especially vol. 1, 27–30, for more background on Abu Abbas.

[50] This disagreement between Saddam's advisers is an interesting foreshadowing to the debate that would take place after Operation Iraqi Freedom over the causes of Libya's nuclear reversal. In this recording, Saddam's advisers debate whether Qadafi decided to limit support for terrorists and to come clean with the Americans out of fear that the United States would punish him after it had dealt with Iraq. A similar debate ensued in the United States in 2003 over whether the U.S.-led regime change in Iraq caused Qadafi to accept verifiable weapons of mass destruction (WMD) disarmament for fear that he would be next.

[51] This might refer to Libyan-sponsored terrorists' 19 September 1989 bombing of France's UTA DC-10 airliner. The attack killed 170 persons, among them seven Americans.

Saddam: When it will be its two years['] mark –

Male 1: It will be two years –

Saddam: Psychologically, the year 1990.

Male 1: Yes.

Saddam: And we are in 1991. [*Inaudible group background talk.*] I mean, handling the situation on a public level is possible; I mean after six or seven months, it will be considered a year.

Izzat: They might carry out a fedayeen operation.[52]

Male 1: Huh?

Izzat: They might carry out a fedayeen operation and blame it on us.

Male 1: The Americans might even do it.

Izzat: [*Inaudible.*]

Saddam: The Israelis –

Male 1: It could be the Americans, the Israelis, etc. So, we should monitor the situation and deny anything of this sort.[53]

Saddam: If Qadafi has any dealings with the group and this work will still be ongoing, it will continue. But, he announced it officially that there will be a break.

Male 1: What is going to happen? Yes, obstruction.

Tariq: Sir, any work [*inaudible*]. They can't prove Iraq is responsible, only partly responsible.[54]

Izzat: [*Inaudible.*] And if we attack Saudi Arabia?

Saddam: What?

Izzat: From the point of view of responsibility, it is not going to go well if we attack Saudi Arabia?

[52] The term fedayeen (translated as "one who sacrifices") has several connotations, including high-risk military "commando" operations and terrorist operations. It can also refer to untrained fighters who risk their lives recklessly and are prepared to sacrifice themselves for a cause.

[53] In February 1993, when a terrorist associated with the Egyptian Islamic Group detonated a truck bomb under the World Trade Center, Saddam and his advisers immediately suspected the United States or Israel of carrying out the attack. See "Saddam suspects Israel and the 'Zionist lobby' in the 1993 World Trade Center bombing," in Chapter 2. A more complete translation is available in Woods, *Iraqi Perspectives Project – Primary Source Materials for Saddam and Terrorism: Emerging Insights from Captured Iraqi Documents*, vol. 4, 63–83, accessed 9 February 2009 at www.jfcom.mil/newslink/storyarchive/ 2008/pa032008.html.

[54] Years later, Tariq noted, "It has never been proven that Iraq participated in a terrorist operation." See SH-SHTP-D-000-760, "Saddam and Political Advisers Discussing the Production of Biological Materials in Iraq, the Iran-Iraq War, UN Inspections, and the Arab-Israeli Conflict," undated (circa 1996). A transcript of this recording is also found in Woods and Lacey, *Iraqi Perspectives Project – Primary Source Materials*, vol. 4.

Saddam: What time?

Izzat: Because we are ready now.

Saddam: No, all of this is insignificant, but we will discuss everything.

Izzat: Not at this time, Sir?

Saddam: We discuss everything. What do I want from this issue? I want us to win. I want time and everything else to work in our favor.

Male 1: Excellent.

Izzat: It took us two months to reach this point!

Saddam: It does not matter, but we have it guaranteed, right?

Izzat: Yes.

Saddam: Yes, in our hands.

Izzat: They went twice to the locations – they went to five or six locations.

Saddam: Very good. So, we stop. Up to now, we gained information, we trained, and we were there. Now we work on the role of collecting information and drawing plans.

Izzat: We don't carry out anything?

Saddam: I would rather not carry out anything at this time because time is going to work out fine. But, we won't wait for the strike.

Izzat: Yes.

Saddam: Meaning everything is permissible.

Male 3: In yesterday's meeting between Mitterrand and the Israelis, he stated –

Male 1: Mr. President, the individuals in the Egyptian arena – there will be an insurgency against us even if we prevent it –

Saddam: No, we don't prevent it, but we don't lead it.

Male 2: We are not Egypt or the Americans.

Tariq: [Inaudible.] Egypt is an arena.

Saddam: No, Egypt is not a field.

Male 2: Yes.

Saddam: And even the officials, we are – for example, when a gas explosion takes place in a such a location, it could kill about 20 [to] 40 Americans.

Male 2: No, no, not like this.

Tariq: Even in Egypt [inaudible].

Saddam: Whether here or abroad, anyway – we prepared specific operations, otherwise all of this will not constitute an excuse. On the other hand, some of them will indicate that Arab people are dissatisfied.

Male 1: This is what I wanted –

Tariq: Sir, if I understand you correctly, if something happens inside the country since they are concentrated on the border, if an American enters –

Saddam: Inside Iraq, yes.

Male 2: Yes.

Tariq: Yes, an attack might take place at an ambassador's house or embassy location, something like this.

Saddam: The only thing I am pursuing now is a sabotage explosion taking place in a sensitive place that will impact the Americans, or that they flee in masses and the [Republican] Guard opens fire and kills them all.[55]

Tariq: Yes.

Saddam: From a certain location. That is all and I think we can take care of it.

Male 2: God willing.

Tariq: Yes, and other than that [*inaudible*].

Male 3: Sir, on the contrary, I think this will serve us –

Izzat: [*Inaudible.*]

Tariq: [*Inaudible.*]

Saddam: Very much.

Tariq: Because [*inaudible.*]

Saddam: This is a quick summary if the comrade is finished with his opinion. We are not here to boost each other's morale, so I am not going to talk to you about morale now. There are things we all agree on, that we should pay attention to, and not take lightly. We did pay attention, we did it openly because our army and our people listen to us, I mean they get the news from us, and when Saddam announces news, it will not be just regular news.

Izzat: I personally and psychologically feel comfortable with what we heard from you.

Saddam: Everyone listens, and that is what happened. Therefore, we are required to take everything into account. There are no changes in our plan. When the enemy confronts us, we confront them with all our means and fight them [*inaudible*]. In essence, once we fight, we continue to fight.

Izzat: We defend ourselves.

Saddam: This is what we will continue to do. I don't believe we have any new development, but once we are attacked, we will strike Israel. I mean this was included in the old plan, I mean we will adhere to it.

[55] By Lawrence Freedman's count, roughly 160 instances of terrorism occurred during the Gulf War, about half against American targets. Most, however, were "freelance operations by local sympathizers." See Lawrence Freedman, *A Choice of Enemies: America Confronts the Middle East* (New York: Public Affairs, 2008), 245.

REGIONAL NONSTATE ACTORS

In the following recordings, Saddam discusses issues pertaining to nonstate groups in the Arab World: the Muslim Brotherhood, different Palestinian groups, and the Organization of the Islamic Conference. In the first conversation, Saddam criticizes Yasser Arafat and discusses the proper level of autonomy and freedom of action for Baghdad to allow different Iraq-supported Palestinian groups. Saddam's famous pragmatism is evident in the second discussion, in which he tells his advisers that Iraq will fight Islamist opposition groups in other countries if these groups attack Ba'ath cells, take control of the state or come close to doing so; otherwise, he emphasizes, party members should avoid conflict with such groups. The third recording documents an April 1990 meeting between Saddam and Arafat in which the two discuss the coming conflict with America and potential terrorist operations against Americans. In the fourth, recorded sometime around February 1991, Saddam and his advisers discuss how the Ba'ath Party has initiated suicide missions and inspired "freedom-fighting" activities in the Arab world.

Saddam, as Vice President, Discusses Various Palestinian Groups and Leaders and Criticizes Yasser Arafat (9 August 1978)[56]

Saddam: This Party is a genuine party that developed through a revolution. Therefore, we do not use the struggle or any other means as a tool or cover to carry out any operation, unless we are convinced it would serve the revolution or would help an Arab cause. Our leadership position from the beginning was always and still is against turning Arab contenders in Iraq into mobilization means, benefiting from Gamal Abdel Nasser's experiment that was condemned by all the Arab contenders in Egypt.[57] And during which Abdel Nasser made them negotiate with their respective government they were in opposition to because that was not in the adversary's interest. Consequently, Abdel Nasser lost the support of all the true Arab contenders during the last period of his rule. This is the basic point: is it possible to turn the Arab contender into a part of our apparatus or should we give him freedom of action? . . . He might make a mistake and he may regret it, but we should not make him a part of our apparatus, neither the Party nor the government.

In fact, we do conduct our communication through means of dialogue and understandings with the people and entities that reside on our soil. Abu Nidal did not deny the assassination of Hamami. Isn't the name of that one in London Hamami?[58]

Male 1: [*Inaudible*] Sa'd Hamami.

---

56 SH-SHTP-A-000-619, "Culture and Information Office Meeting in Which Saddam Talks about the Palestinian Issue and Yasser Arafat," 8 September 1978.

57 From the context, "Arab contenders" appears to refer to Arab political parties or activist groups.

58 Sa'd Hamami was Fatah's representative in London. He was assassinated there in December 1977. Abu-Nidal, based in Baghdad, claimed responsibility.

Saddam: Hamami has connections with Zionist components and so forth, which is a well-known fact within the Palestinian circles. While this is denied, we believe it was true because in many cases, we don't need to wait for anyone to come and tell us what to do or where to go, nor did our politics cause us to accept it from this man. But when we ask whether he [Abu Nidal] knew with whom such and such a person met, his answer will be [*inaudible*]. He insisted he had nothing to do with the issue of Abu-Yasin's office.[59] He also insisted that the assassin is someone from Abu-Ammar's [Yasser Arafat's] group. Mas'ad's group is centralized. So, when we accept it as an ally we should make it a part of our apparatus on the Arab arena, we will give it the freedom to be diligent, yet consistent with our strategy and its general objective and general guideline.

If we force those allies to accept, they would become weak and would become part of the Iraqi political apparatus or the Party apparatus. Sometimes those allies would have judgments that are, according to our point of view, mistakes, but according to their point of view, correct. If their points of view always agreed with ours, then they would become Ba'athists like us or we would become like them. Usually the differences in the political make-up or the system between different entities is acceptable and is expected. So is the difference in judgments or points of view, but there should be an agreement on the central issues relevant to the corresponding political stage. On this stage, the main issue is that planning and laying out policy must be centralized and that the Palestinian masses are in control to take the initiative, and guide their people in the right direction that they will decide. According to those principles, we find an ideological meeting point with Abu Nidal and George Habash and their organizations as well as any other group.[60] As long as we do not think they are taking advantage of our alliance with them, as they think they are doing us a favor whenever they unite with us, then we can go a long way with them. We are assuming that we are willing to offer them more than they are willing to offer us, as we are willing to defend them and defend the positions they would take, and so forth.

Additionally, if we would take a position supporting those allies, we have to bear in mind that it would cost us credibility and support in the Arab political arena. Our regime in Baghdad would directly pay the price it would cost to support those allies' positions. Outsiders would not pay it, because the regime became influential now and so did the Party . . . But now our party became and gained considerable weight in the Arab and international political arena, as well as [gained] leverage, not in the cheap talk or media propaganda. The leverage is what scares and not the media. I mean the leverage that is consistent with the general guidelines and expressed by the media, giving it its integrated dimension, is the one that scares. So, when you gain leverage, you need to take into account the [*inaudible*], how much you pay out of it and how much you keep to yourselves.

However, we are not going to talk or discuss this subject any further. Let us talk about another subject that involves our national revolution. We have mentioned previously that we would be faced with attacks from different entities like the ones we are facing now from the right wing of the Palestinian resistance, because the goal

---

[59] Probably a reference to the June 1978 assassination of Ali Yasin, the PLO's representative to Kuwait.
[60] George Habash founded the Popular Front for the Liberation of Palestine (PFLP) in 1967.

of those attacks is to keep this revolution inside Iraq and diminish its effect outside Iraq. Since they could not bring down the revolution inside Iraq, they will try to limit its influence outside Iraq, and they will not allow its influence to spread outside Iraq unless that influence is in line with an existing international policy. In that case, its influence will be serving the interest and goals of that international policy and will be independent to serve the national interest. However, if the revolution's influence outside Iraq was not serving anybody's interest like the Americans, the Soviet Union, the French, [or] the British, but would serve only the interest of the Arabs, then this is not allowed to take place.

So, if there were a tactical mistake – a big mistake we could have made – it would be the fact that we embraced the rejection wing, including Abu-Nidal.[61] However, it is a mistake to expect anything from a regime that has some appealing or favorable parts while the rest of its parts are disgraceful and shameful. We have issued only one order so far in that we asked the comrades at the embassy in Paris not to let the perpetrators escape alive and to kill them even if that meant killing them while in the custody of the French police. In fact, one of the comrades was shot dead by the French police as he tried to approach one of the perpetrators in the custody of the French police. Consequently, the rest of the comrades opened fire on the French police as they saw their comrade become a martyr. This is the only thing we did so far. Although we have Ba'athists everywhere and we could have reacted, we have not yet issued any other direction or order to kill or to carry out a reaction except the one that had to with the incident in Paris.[62]

Yasser Arafat is not a true representative of the Palestinian revolution; you can tell when he talks about the revolution that he is reluctant and not confident. Accordingly, let us distinguish between the Palestinian revolution and the revolution of the Palestinian people. There is a big difference between the Palestinian revolutionaries and others. The revolutionaries are true noble fighters and are willing to sacrifice their lives for Palestine: they die as martyrs. Others are willing to compromise Palestine's cause as they operate houses of prostitution and deal with drugs. Although our leadership is highly organized and efficient, we still need to conduct meetings at least at the higher level. That should bring us together; there should not be a controversy about whether or not we should meet. Furthermore, we should always make a point to talk about those meetings. Actually, we have illustrated what is called the Palestinian revolution, which does not pose a worry or threat to us, because we are not a regime like any other regime that can be overthrown or removed and is worried about its well-being. However, the enemies think of us as a regime, even though our

---

[61] After Arafat turned down an offer to join the Iraqi cabinet as Minister of Palestine Affairs, Saddam began supporting Arafat's competitors within the PLO and creating rival Palestinian groups. Abu Nidal, a terrorist who had previously belonged to Fatah, received Iraqi support. From 1976 to 1978, a conflict between Iraq and the PLO raged throughout the Middle East and Europe. See Said K. Aburish, *Saddam Hussein: The Politics of Revenge* (London: Bloomsbury, 2000), 115–16.

[62] On 2 August 1978, a group called the Rejectionist Front of Stateless Palestinian Arabs claimed responsibility for assassinating Izziddin Qalaq, a PLO representative, in Paris. When French police arrived on the scene, they coordinated the surrender of a Palestinian terrorist who was occupying the Iraqi embassy. As he was being taken away by the French police, several Iraqi embassy staffers opened fire, killing a French policeman and an Iraqi guard. Paul Chutkow, *Associated Press*, 3 August 1978.

leadership stated in the declaration released a month and a half ago that we are not a regime.

We can say, "Who the heck is Yasser Arafat?" but we do not want to put down anyone. However, when certain people mean to act against the revolution or mean to harm the revolution in any way, we would react. In fact, we will not hit the Palestinian people that carry a status similar to ours; but we will hit Yasser Arafat personally as he wears his headband.[63] If Arafat continues with his bad behavior, then let one of the brave Iraqis among the crowd draw a pistol and shoot Arafat in his chest and surrender himself afterward. Everything has its limit, but what Arafat is doing exceeds the limit. Behind that headband of Arafat there is an evil brain that has a plan for people in Iran, Saudi Arabia, Iraq, Syria, and everywhere else to execute his attacks against us. As the Syrian slaughtered hundreds of men and large masses of the innocent Palestinians, Arafat did not move a whisker and was not the least shaken. This shows people the treason of Yasser Arafat and [just] who are Arafat's people.[64]

At present, we are not to engage in battle. We have no plans to engage in battle nor do we intend to engage in battle. But when he insists on battle, we will know how to engage. Once we engage in battle with the [*inaudible, possibly Nizar the Palestinian*] they are very optimistic, although the report we received – no their spirit [*inaudible*] as it is in Paris, but they are very optimistic even on that one, I don't know what his name is [*inaudible background talk*]. However, if things change and we have to engage, then let nobody be misled, as we know very well how to handle such an engagement. Although the Arafat camp has conspired in every issue with which it was involved, there is no way we would engage in a battle with them or anyone that would harm the cause of Palestine. What happened in Paris left an emotional scar with us since Kupti the Palestinian, who was involved in the incident, was harmed.[65] We feel a deep sorrow for him not only because he is a Palestinian, but also as an Arab like any Iraqi is living in the street of Rashid [a famous street in Baghdad] or any other Iraqi living in Salaamed or any Iraqi that lives anywhere else. We are not going to let the Paris incident end with the small guy paying the price, but everybody who plays a role will be paying accordingly. We are not amateurs and we are not lightweight players; we know where the big guys in our opponent are and we know how to hit him hard.

Actually, we have no interest in engaging anybody nor do we care who should hit whom. However, if someone tries to cross us or attempts to hit us, we will hit him so hard and so deep, he will feel it in his bones. Furthermore, we are not going to be intimidated, nor are we going to stay put and not hit back if we are attacked,

---

[63] This is apparently a reference to Arafat's well-known keffiyeh, the traditional headdress worn by Arab men.

[64] This is a reference to the massacre of Palestinians at the Tel el-Zaatar refugee camp, in Beirut, by Israel's Lebanese Christian allies in 1976. Many observers shared Saddam's criticism that Arafat was unconcerned about the Palestinian casualties. As Robert Fisk wrote, Arafat was "a man who was prepared to watch his people massacred in the Tel el-Zaatar refugee camp . . . so that he could show the world the brutality of his enemies." Robert Fisk, "Vain Leader Playing a Dangerous Game That He Can't Afford to Lose," *Independent*, 14 October 2000.

[65] See *supra* note 62.

because that is not our nature – nor is it our party's nature, nor the nature of our regime, and we are not used to it. It is clear and understood by now that we have no intention of engaging in any battle with Arafat and his camp, but they are counting on the strength of the message in the speeches Arafat is going to deliver in the next few months. This message is aimed to agitate the feeling of the masses and turn those masses against the regime in Iraq. Consequently, those speeches will give excuses for any mob or any irresponsible party to commit crimes in Iraq. There is nobody that is more dishonorable or could have such a dishonorable make-up as Arafat. No creature could fit in such a dishonorable make up as him.

Saddam and His Advisers Discuss Their Desire to Find a Modus Vivendi with Islamists, in this Case the Muslim Brotherhood, and the Limits to Such Cooperation (24 July 1986)[66]

Saddam: ...I don't believe it would be wise to clash with the religious current in the Arab world when it is possible to avoid it. On the other hand, we would launch a big attack on them if they are close to taking power. One of the issues I understood from comrade Badr is that a truce would be in their favor to jump into power.[67] The reason I raised the issue now is because through the developments in Sudan, this issue no longer represents a permanent threat, but a possible and temporary threat. So, until it becomes a permanent danger, let's make them go through this stage, and after that, we will be stronger when we open fire on them once they become a permanent danger for the command. That's when it will be allowed in the political movements to open fire on them. Meaning to expose them, to attack them and so forth because taking power is against our Party in the strategic results at the Arab-world level. But weakening the ruler is not against our Party. Many governors in the Arab world, whether from the religious current or others, if it wants to weaken them, this will not be against our Party, I mean as a direct situation. So, why should we be the direct clash aspect of it?

The danger of the religious current in the Arab world now is that Khomeini would gain from it, because in the general politics we seem to be with the regimes since we have a regime and a state, while Khomeini in the general sense does not have it. If he did have a regime – it is obvious he is not against Syria and Libya, and Muslims are persecuted in both places, and there are persecuted religious, political, and Islamic movements also in both places and yet, he is the rulers' friend. It is true we recognize this situation, but we have to understand that when the religious current emerges in Saudi Arabia, with whom we are friends, it is psychologically closer to Iran than it is

---

[66] SH-SHTP-A-001-167, "Saddam and Ba'ath Party Members Discussing the Status of the Party in the Arab World and the Exploitation of the Muslim Brotherhood as an Ally," 24 July 1986. In April 1985, a military coup overthrew the president of Sudan, who had introduced elements of Sharia law. Parliamentary elections in April 1986 brought a broad-based coalition of Islamist parties to power. The National Islamic Front, the Muslim Brotherhood–affiliated party, gained seats to become the third largest block, with fifty-one seats. By contrast, the Ummah Party had one hundred seats and the Democratic Unionist Party sixty-three. After the election, the primary concern in Sudan was how the parties would share power, and the main debate involved the role of Islamic law. Peter Woodward, *The Horn of Africa: Politics and International Relations* (London: I. B. Tauris, 1996), 53.

[67] "Comrade Badr" likely refers to Badr al-Din Muddaththir, secretary of the Arab Socialist Ba'ath Party in Sudan, who appears to have been present at this meeting.

to Iraq. Therefore, if we engage in a battle with him, it will be a case of Iran against Iraq regardless of the other issues.

Badr: In the Maghreb, in Tunisia –

Saddam: In all these places. Therefore, there is an additional factor that requires us to handle these religious currents with flexibility so that our strategic enemy will not gain it, and upon which the future of one of us will be built as a result of the clash. Or, let's not say the future of one of us since his future is guaranteed, as well as the future of anyone who would follow in his footsteps, but it affects our Party's future strategically and not tactically. Let's put it this way. So, why don't we act with flexibility toward the political and religious movements whenever possible? We can do this without isolating or paving the way for it to become a permanent danger trying to take power. On the other hand, criticism will always be allowed, but criticism in a way – I mean it is known that non-contradictory political criticism is one thing and the criticism from two opposing positions – I mean as two political adversaries – is known, as well. It is enough for us to define the [type of] state that we believe it would be useful for Sudan to be; we also believe that the religious state does want [favor] Sudan for these considerations.

Badr: They might consider it a battle. [*Laughter.*]

Saddam: That's why we can initiate a dialogue with them stating that an attack is one thing, while expressing the doctrine is something completely different. We can also tell them, "You are our brothers and your talk about the religious state is an attack against us." When they ask why that is, we reply, "We establish a state not through religion; we establish a secular state, but believe in religion as rituals and a road for its associates, but do not interpret religion as a state formula. If you stop talking about the religious state we will stop criticizing the religious state. [If] you continue to talk about the religious state, we will criticize the religious state, but not the Muslim Brotherhoods [*inaudible*] in the past, Numairi was recently overthrown,[68] his shortcomings are known, people chose him – they brought 28 members from the Muslim Brotherhood to the Parliament –

[*Overlapping voices debating the number of members.*]

Saddam: Fine, 53. This means they have popular impact, otherwise they would not have been selected![69]

Badr: It could have been much more than this, Mr. President.

Saddam: True, true, Comrade Badr –

Badr: If it were not for –

Saddam: Of course, there are factors! Okay then, they are not in power now to be our target and neither are those in power now our target, and their opportunistic political situation became a part of Numairi's situation, so why don't we conclude a truce with them? The only difference between their technical danger and others' is that they came to power – I mean they were in power more recently than others. So, they

---

[68] Jafar Numairi, president of Sudan (1969–1985).

[69] Saddam is apparently referring to the number of National Islamic Front seats in Sudan's parliament. It controlled fifty-one seats. See *supra* note 66.

know people in the army that, some of them, belong to the old regime. Therefore, the Muslim Brotherhood are the closest people to them because the Muslim Brotherhood was a part of the old regime . . .

Badr: [*Inaudible.*]

Saddam: . . . we know that once we topple Khomeini, these [religious] currents are going to be very much affected. The enemies of religious currents, other than us, even the governors, after Khomeini is toppled and [*inaudible*] the religious currents, even the investigators with the lash and the executioners are going to say, "Where are you going, come and see what Khomeini did to Iran?" I mean they are going to benefit from this situation. But in our daily behavior, we should not let the religious political currents believe that the fall of Khomeini means their collapse. So, one of the factors that will alleviate this feeling is our good relations with them because this fatalistic condition is not good – not good for us as a Nationalist Socialist Party considering the nature of conflict between Khomeini and us. This is something brief and quick so that we can solve this issue.

Tariq: . . . The religious current now in Egypt is not going to fight an atheist government and the fact that we are supporters. It is going to fight a civilian and regular regime, which it wants to oust and [then] control the country – not even the Shah's surprised regime that was against the religion. We are talking about Mubarak, and his government consists of Muslim people. He fasts, prays, believes in Islam and his social behavior is good, but they want to oust it because it is a regular civilian government; they have the chance and they want to take advantage of it to the utmost. Well, if we were a big party now in Egypt, wouldn't we engage in the political and ideological battle? You know people are engaged in Egypt. I mean, there are writers and politicians, some of them from the delegation and some from the ruling party, and other figures engaged in the battle this far, I mean not against the religion, but against the religious groups' concept or the Islamist groups' concept of the state whether they are Brothers or others –

[*One minute, fifty-seven seconds are blank in the recording.*]

Tariq: I believe we must engage in this battle. We cannot do anything in Egypt but engage and participate, one way or the other! We engaged in it in Iraq. I mean, what comrade Saddam said in the '70s explained our position toward religion because it was brought up; we had a strong religious movement that struck us with bullets. I mean, we had armed demonstrations that launched bombs at us. Therefore, we had to face them with an ideological position in addition to the popular, and even repressive, measures that were necessary. So, Comrade Saddam spoke clearly and said, "We do not accept the religious state, but we are Muslims and believers."[70]

So, it depends on the situation we are facing. If we stop the ideological struggle against the Muslim Brotherhood in Sudan, are they going to stop their ideological struggle against the nationalistic concept? We have to find a way to reach an agreement, comrade Abu-Nadia [Taha Yassin Ramadan]. Comrade Badr did not create an

---

[70] For Shi'a demonstrations in Iraq during the 1970s, and the regime's responses, see Efraim Karsh and Inari Rautsi, *Saddam Hussein: A Political Biography* (New York: Grove Press, 1991), 138–46.

agenda for himself in Sudan to take power. He may compromise tactically, but Al-Turabi will not. He wants to take the power in Sudan, instead, and he is right. I would have thought the same thing if I were in his place! Is he going to abandon his ideological struggle and ideological mobilization for a plan, so that we can abandon our struggle? In this case, we would leave the arena in Sudan for them or for the weak people from the Al-Ummah Party and the Unionists who do not have the appropriate ideological weapon to face this current. We should take this into account as well. We cannot say the other party is willing to compromise so that we can do the same. Yes, if we can reach a compromise that guarantees they are not going to provoke the nationalistic ideology and within the state's nationalistic concept while we cannot provoke their concept, it – politics accept this, I mean. But for us to leave the ideological struggle while they stay and keep bringing in young men [i.e., fighters] and the public [opinion] is with the religious state, this means we are going to give up Sudan and even Egypt, but at least willingly! It is true we are not in control of everything, but we will be outside of this struggle.

The position toward Iran – the Islamist groups' position toward Iran – is internally contradictory and known to us. From one side, all Islamist groups, with few exceptions, look at the regime in Iran as a power and an example to follow. At least, what happened in Iran makes whomever believes in establishing the religious state that became possible even in the twentieth century – because as you know and as we assume, in the '50s, '60s, and '70s, those people used to say, "Yes, we are believers and we want to establish a religious state, but maybe the era does not allow us." But once the Islamic state is established in Iran, this experience may repeat what happened to communism. When communism was established in the Soviet Union, communism around the world supported it and said, "In this case, communism is possible!" The problem they are going to face is that [because] Iran is a Shi'ite [country] first, they did not wish for the first experience to be Shi'ite. They wanted the first experience to be Sunni instead. This is a fact from the sectarian point of view. They wished for this to happen in Egypt, Pakistan or somewhere, I mean [where] they could more easily blend with it ideologically. The other thing is that what happened in Iran clashed with Iraq and patriotism, which is a power and essence in Islam, as well as the Iranian acts that are hard to defend. All of this makes some of them hesitant to follow Iran, but sincerely, I sincerely believe, with some exceptions, that no one can believe in establishing the religious state unless he considers the Iranian experience an allied experience one way or another. Not fully an ally – not the ally wanted from the heart, the one he wishes for, but objectively it is an ally and we are going to witness it. This is a fact.

––––––––

Saddam: Comrade Tariq came late, so we agree with all the concepts he mentioned as a general direction. We wanted to talk about the phase in addition to the ideology background mentioned by Mr. [*inaudible*], the religious current in the Arab world is ruled [*pause*], it strives against the Arab governments, the Arab governments in their approach. We have Ba'athists striving against these governments – so, do we launch the battle against the religious current or do we launch the battle against the religious current when it has certain specifications? The answer is we launch the battle against the religious current with certain political or behavioral specifications. If it launches a battle against us, we will launch a battle against it and if it gains power or gets close to it, we would launch a battle against it. And if it gets closer to power alone, we would be forced to come closer. Through criticism we try to come closer and use the [public] exposure means – the exposure method, and if it reaches power it will launch a battle against us, for sure, wherever we are, whether as a party or a state. This is certain whether this was the Muslim Brotherhood in Sudan or Egypt or anywhere else. Unless [there are] exceptions, this would be a different story because we are general and so are they.

We aren't satisfied with preaching our theory at the state level that we reach only through power; rather, we make a model out of it that helps, one way or another, our comrades to strive in other regions...

Those who talk about the Arab Unity – those Nasserites do not understand those who do not talk about the Arab Unity in the first place. They do not understand the Islamic religion, otherwise, they would first build a base in the Arab world to be able afterward to spread Islam in other Islamic countries – the religious state! They are private, we are private, too. We want to build a state and they want to build a state, too, and therefore, clashing is inevitable in one area and over the issue of building the state and which one is right, the nationalistic socialist state or the Islamic state? This is expected. We don't wish it, they may not wish it, but this is one of the strongest and expected cases. But when they are in strife, we can prevent clashing with them if the chance to avoid clashing is available. It has not yet happened in Sudan. No, we are going to talk about Sudan. We are going to talk about Sudan and that's why this issue is interpretative since it is an existing political situation and a circumstantial situation that is different than Iraq's situation, Syria's situation. This is in Sudan and therefore, it allows their interpretation to set the parameters.

So, is it required to stop our ideological strife? The answer is no, because once we stop our ideological strife, we stop the polarization process toward our way of thinking, as well as the awakening process of our members and the capability to influence our surroundings. But the ideological strife always expresses itself in forms related to its circumstance. For sure, when it changes from general ideology to specific ideology, the phase is going to play a role here. So, when they talk, when they raise slogans that insinuate the possession of exclusive power in Sudan, we have no other choice but to face them. But to raise slogans to develop the power within a collective work, this would be a normal issue for them, for us and for others.

Badr: [*Inaudible.*] The first –

Saddam: I cannot go into details, Comrade Badr. I am going to discuss at the end what we are going to do, I mean the regional command in Sudan, in light of this talk... We talked before comrade Tariq started and asked why there was a resurgence in the religious current. I mean with regard to one aspect and not all of them, because there are many aspects we talked about before in two meetings of the National Command, including that nationalism was against the foreign state persecuting the Arabs, nationalism was placed face-to-face with the foreign religious state persecuting the Arabs.

Male 1: The Ottomans?

Saddam: The Ottomans, yes, against the Ottoman Empire that used the religious cover, but wanted to persecute the Arabs and carried out nationalistic persecution of the Arabs. Therefore, the slogan of Arab nationalism is a political weapon in addition to all its ideological and historic backgrounds in the face of the occupying foreign invader. I mean under different covers...This is one of the main reasons why Abd-al-Nasser emerged as the Arab Leader. If Abd-al-Nasser emerged now, he would have had a different chance than before. He would have had his chance and the chance of the big slogan of the nationalistic Arab state as a case in the face of the people whom the British brought in and the Ottoman Empire persecuting the nationalistic Arab and the Arabs, and even the Muslims; persecuting Muslims in the name of Islam and persecuting the nationalistic in the name of the Islamic state.

———

Tariq: I have a clarification, in fact, I may not have been able to express myself accurately, but I don't consider our main mission before or at present as striving against the religious current at all at the expense of other key missions. And I agree with what our comrade the President said about dealing with this issue within the tangible circumstances: if there is danger, we resist it, and if there is not, then we don't engage in an unnecessary ideological or political confrontation. But let us study our experience in Iraq with more depth and see whether this religious current is easy or not and consequently, can we reach an agreement with it?

As of the second half of the '70s, our main regime in Iraq was against the religious current, and we have been fighting against it and not against the Western state. If Iraq were a pure Western state like Turkey – not Muslim and had no religious inclination – the matter would have been different. People who carried out the revolution – some of them still resist us while others are a generation of this revolution itself. I mean, we have been in power for 18 years, and anyone who wants to resist us is 24, 26, 28, and 30, even 36 years grew up during the revolution's era.

We are not the Shah of Iran, but a national, pan-Arab, anti-imperialist regime, socialist, and working for social justice, and like Mr. President said, we even provided a living to the insane. We eliminated unemployment during our regime. During our regime, the worker whose wages were 300 fils a day, became three dinars. Our regime is not corrupt, we are not crooks, and we are people with good personal morals, unlike the Shah of Iran and his sisters, and the wives of people in power who were adulterers in Paris, London, and Switzerland, and yet we are facing people who want to slaughter us from ear to ear and in tens of thousands. We slaughtered tens of thousands of them here in Iraq. In the history of the national striving of Iraq, no narrow-minded people were slaughtered.

Saddam: [*Interrupting.*] No, there is no [*overlapping voices*].

Tariq: Huh? In the thousands. In the history of national striving – in the history of national striving, no narrow-minded, no communist and no others were slaughtered as much as those who, because of the way they acted, reached the highest level of national treason. When they used the aircraft and the missile as an amusement at the beginning of the war, they killed the Iraqi Arab Muslim who was their colleague at the air base as a favor to Iran, while they were Iraqis, too. Some of them might be of Iranian descent, but the other part was non-Iraqi because this ideology is not easy.[71] I mean let's think, yes, it is not our main task since we are still striving

———

[71] Tariq appears to be referring to sabotage activities by Iraqi Shi'a. During the Iran-Iraq War, members of the Dawa party, a Shi'ite opposition group, reportedly attempted to sabotage

against imperialism and Zionism, as well as striving for unity and socialism. Yes, but this is an easy ideology and we should deal with it diplomatically until we see the reason for that ogre [the religious current] that is going to emerge in the Arab world. One of the main reasons could be ideological tolerance toward it, being more courteous than resistant to it. Being more courteous than resistant to it would help the emergence of a ghoul in Egypt, Sudan, Tunisia, Morocco, and everywhere, but we are ideologically very strong, very strong as a regime, leader, and command. So, we don't underestimate this current and think it is easy to deal with it. The Muslim Brotherhood in Sudan, we need to study the situation in Sudan. They [the Brotherhood] did not assume power. They became like the communists during the era of Karim Qassem.[72] I mean they have a court that they control, but as far as police station or newspaper, look at what he did to people. Didn't we discuss here at the command what we are supposed to do regarding the trial of Ba'athist comrades? He wants to cut off their heads. You know that one, what was his name? [*Inaudible background talk.*] What? Yes, this is that governor with the strange name [from] Magashi.[73] He wanted to execute the Ba'athists as atheists while he had not yet assumed power; I mean the power was not his!

Male 2: Al-Numairi, Al-Numairi was against the Ba'athists [*inaudible*].

Tariq: So, the opposition they have in Sudan against the [Ba'ath] Party and others is not a regular and limited matter where we can be tolerant toward it. It constitutes a very dangerous opposition! [*Laughter.*]

Male 2: [*Inaudible.*]

Saddam: Well, this is something good.

Male 2: [*Inaudible.*]

Male 3: The issue of the Maghreb –

Male 2: [*Inaudible.*]

Saddam: It is just the [*pause*] so, we authorized our comrades in Sudan to act, because if the strategy does not take privacy into consideration, it will fail as far as implementation. I remember the analysis of the National Command and that we should prevent clashing with the communists the same way – but when it is time to implement it – had we implemented it before 1974, it would not have had a chance to succeed – I mean before 1972 – it would not have had a chance to succeed, but we would have led the operation at that time until we established a relation, but it was not successful![74] So, privacy is required and we leave to the field

---

Iraqi aircraft. See SH-PDWN-D-000-240, "Letters Authorizing the Execution of an Air Force Warrant Officer for Sabotaging a Plane Engine," April–May 1986.

[72] 'Abd-al-Karim Qassem was a Nasser-like military nationalist who seized power in Iraq in 1958 and ruled the country as prime minister until the Ba'ath coup of 1963.

[73] Magashi is the name of a village in northern Sudan.

[74] An "uneasy coexistence" with the communists existed in the early 1970s, apparently since Saddam needed domestic support and sought rapprochement with the Soviet Union. During these years, the communists were allowed increased freedom of expression and opportunities to organize. By late 1975, however, Baghdad had begun arresting and persecuting Iraqi communists. In May 1978, the regime executed twenty-one communists and began

command the freedom to act in this regard, so that we don't lose strategically or tactically.[75]

Saddam Meets with Yasser Arafat (aka Abu-Ammar) and a Palestinian Delegation to Discuss a Variety of Topics, Including Potential Terrorist Operations Against the United States (19 April 1990)[76]

Saddam: [*Recording starts in midsentence*] the Iraqi politics. They said they wanted to state that to Iraq before the American congressional delegation meets me, but, since the American congressional delegation met me and couldn't deliver these points to me, they want to deliver them now. One of these points that they wanted to tell me is, "Your deployed missiles threaten the American bases."[77] As you said when you prayed in Beirut and you said, "It is time to die, and now I can smell the breeze of heavens," it is the same for us. As long as the small players are gone, and it is time for America to play the game directly, we are ready for it. We are ready, we will fight America, and with God's help we will defeat it and kick it out of the whole region, because it is not about the fight itself. We know that America has larger aircraft than we do. America has more rockets than us. But I think that when the Arab people see the action of war is real, not only talk, they will do the same and fight America everywhere. So, in order to be fair, we have to get ready to fight America. We are ready to fight when they are. When they strike, we will strike. We will strike any American troops in the Arab Gulf with our air force, and then we will state it, saying that our air force has assaulted the American bases on that day.

Therefore, when the battle is on, you do not say, "How much did you lose?" and do not have expectations, or even have some expectations for the end of the battle. It is what happened for us during the war with Iran. We had a lot of expectations for that war ... but when the war occurred, we did not have expectations about how much we were going to lose, because it was inevitable. So be ready for this level of

ruthlessly stamping out the communist party as a force in Iraqi politics. Karsh and Rautsi, *Saddam Hussein: A Political Biography*, 96–98.

[75] Saddam's generals had recently persuaded him to grant them additional control over military operations. A July 1986 Ba'ath Party congress confirmed these changes. Phebe Marr, *The Modern History of Iraq*, 2nd ed. (Boulder, CO: Westview Press, 2004), 188.

[76] SH-SHTP-A-001-037, "Saddam Meeting with Iraqi officials, Yasser Arafat, and the Palestinian Delegation," 19 April 1990. While the Iraqis videotaped this meeting, the record at the Conflict Records Research Center is an audio file derived from the video format.

[77] Saddam is referring to a recent meeting he had in Baghdad with a U.S. Senate delegation. The U.S. ambassador to Iraq, April Glaspie, cabled Washington, "Senator Dole masterfully covered the points suggested to him by the Secretary [of State]" in his meeting with Saddam. She mentioned nothing in the cable about any omissions in the message the senators delivered. The Iraqis released a "full text" transcript of the meeting, although Glaspie's predecessor in Baghdad (David Newton), who accompanied the Senators to the meeting, claims that this Iraqi record "left out anything that was unpleasant to them [the Iraqis] and made the Senators look like a bunch of saps." See the following sources: Baghdad 02186, "Codel Dole: Meeting with Saddam Hussein," 12 April 1990, available through the Declassified Documents Reference System; FBIS-NES-90-074, 17 April 1990, "Saddam Husayn Addresses Visiting Senators," Baghdad Domestic Service (in Arabic), 16 April 1990; David Palkki telephone interview with Ambassador David Newton, 25 March 2008.

battle in your land. You don't have a state, you don't have oil or a factory to be struck, unlike us. We got out of eight years of war.

Frankly, let me tell you something. If America strikes us, we will hit back. We said that before, you know us. We are not that talkative type of people who holds the microphone to say things only. We do what we say. Maybe we cannot reach Washington, but we can send someone who has an explosive belt to reach Washington. Our missiles do not reach America, but I swear if they did I would strike it. We can't keep silent like this, while the Americans are hitting Arabs or Iraqis, and say we can do nothing. Yes we can: we can send a lot of people to Washington just like the old days.[78] For instance, the person with an explosive belt around him would throw himself on Bush's car.[79]

However, the American bases, which are all over the world, in Turkey, etc., we can sweep them. We have to be ready for that level... We know their conspiracies, those Americans and Israelis. Maybe we stop for 20 days, and then we hit back one time with rockets and air forces hitting Tel Aviv. We don't have to strike them daily. We will choose times so they will never know the meaning of sleeping. We are powerful and we may look nice and flexible, but once we grab someone who provokes hostility, we will not have mercy on him, we will not let him go unless he gets on his knees or crawls on the ground. We don't have something in the middle, we don't want to negotiate, we don't want any mediators. Right Abu-Ammar?

Yasser: Yes, 100 percent.

Saddam: Today, one of my Arab brothers stood by my side and said that if someone says "hi" to you, he is on your side. I told him, "Tell him 'hi' back and tell him that I know his attitude." We don't know the mediators. We don't know how to work with them. This war we had with the Iranians, we didn't know how to mediate with them.

Yasser: In spite of my efforts in the Islamic, non-alignment, and eastern countries.

Saddam: We don't know this way. You either have an enemy or a friend. You can't have something in the middle... So Sabawi[80] [*talking to one of the Iraqi delegation members*], get all of your old books, coordinate with the intelligence director and our Palestinian brothers to check every single place the Americans exist in the Middle East. Even if some American man came to Greece for trade, we have to know about him also. This is the battle. We have to be beasts in the battles, to remain beasts to the next –

Yasser: Yes, beasts.

[78] There is no evidence indicating that the PLO had ever sent individuals to Washington, D.C., to perform acts of terrorism. Saddam's mention of "the old days" likely refers to Iraq's sponsorship of PLO attacks in Lebanon and perhaps elsewhere in the Middle East.

[79] In June 1993, President Clinton announced that Saddam had sought to assassinate former President George H. W. Bush. One of the alleged Iraqi assassins was reportedly given a "bomb belt" and instructed to wear it, approach Bush, and blow both men up if earlier efforts to kill Bush with a car bomb were unsuccessful. David Von Drehle and R. Jeffrey Smith, "U.S. Strikes Iraq for Plot to Kill Bush," *Washington Post*, 27 June 1993.

[80] Possibly presidential adviser Sabawi Ibrahim Hassan Al-Tikriti.

Sheikh ʿAbd-al-Hamid Al-Saʾih:[81] We have to get ready for the battle.

Saddam: And the battle develops. For me – it may not be a bad idea to take the Ummah [the Islamic nation] into consideration – I do take the Ummah's capabilities into consideration, but I don't consider traditional considerations, such as how many cannons do we have, how many aircraft do we have? These are important, but what is more important than this is what we have seen in the war, I mean every case.

[*Tape pauses and then resumes midsentence.*]

Saddam: the information to Israel, they would get in and strike us, so we have to be ready for that level of war.

Yasser: Almost like what they have done in Panama.[82]

Saddam: No, not like Panama.

Yasser: I mean the way that they got in.

Saddam: I wish, [*inaudible*] evil, but maybe the USA needs some discipline. I wish America would bring its army and occupy Iraq. I wish they would do it so we can kill all Americans and sweep all of them – sweep all of them, by God.

Male 1: But as you know, Mr. President, this is an oil region and it will be burnt.

Saddam: No, what oil? I will give them guarantees that I am not going to burn the oil. Just let them bring their American army in and occupy Iraq. Let them start from Al-Fao borders and watch me demolish them all in Al-Mamlaha.

Male 1: But they won't risk that.

Saddam: Panama! Panama is nothing compared to us. I swear Abu-Ammar, we are something different. We will roast them and eat them. [*Pause in the tape and resuming midsentence*] these words are stronger than action. So, Abu-Ammar, when it comes to timing, if the matters of Arabs were fine and the matters of Palestinians fine, we would not have said what we are saying now or we would even be ashamed of saying it. But considering the way our matters are and that the enemy does not give us a chance – does not give a chance – seeing one missile made it so sure that Iraq has missiles that can reach Tel Aviv! Well, Tel Aviv has always had missiles that can reach all Arab capitals! Iraq has chemicals it used successfully on the Iranians, and Iraq will not hesitate to use them again on Tel Aviv. Well, instead of asking Tel Aviv, "Why would Iraq use it on you," you should [tell them to] give the Arabs back their Palestine and do not attack them. That is all, why would you worry about the chemicals after that? But it is okay if Israel has the atomic bomb, it has the right!

Yasser: And the germ bomb is okay.

Saddam: It has the right!

Yasser: And the chemical. The germ, chemical, and atomic, and it has been proven. It [Israel] has 240 nuclear warheads, 12 out of them for each Arab capital and yet this is not a threat to Arab security![83]

---

[81] ʿAbd-al-Hamid Al-Saʾih, president of the Palestine National Council.
[82] A reference to the December 1989 U.S. invasion of Panama.
[83] Arafat seems to be speaking sarcastically.

Saddam: I say this and I am very calm and wearing a civil suit [*everyone laughs*]. But I say this so that we can get ready at this level.

———

Saddam: We did not forget Palestine and our Palestinian brothers. They call us the invaders while Israel occupies Palestine, rapes the Palestinian women, and kills the kids daily. And they are not invaders! This is an old excuse, the diplomatic language. No one has talked about Palestine for a long time, and the Arab union, as if it is shameful to talk about it. It is like when someone is talking about the Arab union and Palestinian issue with his head down because of being ashamed of talking about that thing. Israel did it because no one talked about it and if someone talks about it he is not Palestinian, he is an invader. It is the same for us. Have you ever seen someone who has been in war for eight years and at last you call him an invader? Even if he is an invader from the start, is there any invader who can keep going in a war for eight years? So do you want to step on Arabs' dignity daily and everybody has to keep silent, so you did not call anyone invader? That's it, when we get mad, we get mad for a while, but we get really mad.

Yasser: Beware of the patient one's evil [*Arabic proverb*].

Saddam: Rely on God.

Yasser: Together until victory.

Saddam: With God's power, I can see the victory in front of my eyes.

Saddam Discusses the Role of the Ba'ath Party in Initiating Suicide Missions and Inspiring Freedom-Fighting Activities across the Arab World (circa February 1991)[84]

Saddam: You need not forget that the [Ba'ath] Party was the first to introduce the fedayeen experiment in the Arab world.

Izzat: In 1948.

Saddam: The Party was also the first to initiate militarized civilian suicide activities. This was not publicized at the national level due to the distortion to which it was subjected. As a result of the fighting for the sake of Palestine, however, the Party's experiment in Iraq was very clear.

Male 1: In Lebanon.

Saddam: No, there were large-scale fedayeen fighting activities in Lebanon, but in 1959, the party organized fedayeen activity against 'Abd-al-Karim Qasim. In 1963, the Party organized a fedayeen activity carried out by armed Ba'athists who took to the streets on the side of the Army in attacking the strongholds of 'Abd-al-Karim Qasim, and consequently, all these strongholds collapsed. As did the control of power, and after that, the fedayeen activities began in the Arab world.

Izzat: Sir, in 1968, we also organized a fedayeen activity group [*inaudible.*]

---

[84] *SH-SHTP-A-001-212, "Saddam and Ba'ath Party Members Discussing a Variety of Issues, Including the Overthrow of Qassem and 'The Protocols of the Elders of Zion,'" undated.

Taha: Your Excellency, Mr. President.

Saddam: Oh yes, in 1968, but 1963 was before it, 1959 was before it, in 1968; the Palestine Liberation Organization started in 1965. I mean, there could be some distortion in that regard, as the beginning was in 1965, the Palestine Liberation Organization.[85] However, in addition to the Party brigades that were formed, the fedayeen brigades formed in Syria, the Party's fedayeen work emerged with the highest ulterior motives and with its highest strength in terms of sacrifice and the Party as a Party and not as a resistance to imperialism like what took place in Algeria . . . but it was an organized Party, armed fedayeen activity. It began in 1959 and was crowned in 1963, and then it continued, I mean it has continued.

Taha: It was present also between 1959 and 1963.

Saddam: Yes, I said, it started in 1959 and was crowned in 1963, and then it continued.

ARAB UNITY

Saddam was committed to advancing himself, Iraq, and the Arab nation, devoting much energy and ample resources to shape the pan-Arab agenda. In the first recording he describes Egypt's recognition of Israel as a dangerous precedent and discusses how Iraq will punish Arab states that follow Cairo's lead. In the second, Saddam explains the factors that "imposed" leadership of the Arab world on Baghdad, "the central post." After 1985, he states, Iraq's enemies will no longer be able to harm Iraq or stem its progress. In the final tapes, from 1988 and 1989, Saddam and Tariq Aziz analyze the sources of disunity in the Arab world and the need for Arabs to follow the example of European states in taking unified military, economic, and political stands.

Saddam and His Advisers Discuss How to Punish Countries that Sided with Egypt after Anwar Sadat Made Peace with Israel (27 March 1979)[86]

Male 1: On the other hand, I do wish to direct a question to the Deputy.[87] The position we all heard and rejoiced over was when you said that any Arab regime that does not implement Baghdad's decisions, which are the least, and that anything less is treason and whoever does that would be considered a traitor. My question is,

---

[85] The PLO was, in fact, founded in May 1964.

[86] SH-SHTP-A-000-553, "Saddam and Senior Advisers Meeting after the Baghdad Conference," 27 March 1979.

[87] This is a reference to Saddam. Before becoming president on 16 July 1979, Saddam was the deputy chairman of the Revolutionary Command Council and insisted on being addressed as "Mr. Deputy." Although he was technically only second in command at the time of this recording, he was easily the most powerful man in Iraq. Karsh and Rautsi, *Saddam Hussein: A Political Biography*, 86.

do you have an idea of the course of action [to be taken] against these Arab nations that do not abide by the decisions?

Saddam: We have said it publicly and it was broadcast with our recorded voice and before the ministers conference took place. We stated that he [Sadat] is a traitor and we would deal with him on that basis, by instigating the people to give all they can to topple him as a traitor. We said it publicly and they heard it before they came here. We repeated it today, the same words. I fear that they think that those are just words for the public, but not that it is for them also. We stand by what we have said.

Male 1: I emphasize Mr. Deputy, it is clear as of today, that there are at least three Arab nations that refuse to abide by the Baghdad decisions and even refuse to attend the Foreign Affairs Ministers conference in Baghdad.[88] And to be honest, in my estimate there are other Arab countries that are candidates for the same position. So, taking these measures – binding the other Arab nations to these measures is a key and central matter in my opinion, in order to prevent other Arab countries from having positions of vacillation and non-commitment. This is a central matter...

The USA, Mr. Deputy, is threatening the Arab nations who refuse the treason deal, that it will take measures against them.[89] Therefore, we should form an Arab [inaudible] stance that refuses this surrender deal. This issue will also need an initiative. Without an initiative, we will be leaving every Arab nation to behave as it wishes in this specific issue...

Male 2: The point that comrade Saddam stated, in that Sadat did not arrive in Jerusalem by accident, is a very important and dangerous point, which we have discussed at length for many years!...We stated that a settlement would mean an end to our Palestinian cause. And we said that we if looked upon it from a national view and considered the struggle with the Zionist enemy as a struggle for our lives, and a struggle of civilizations, in which we either defeat and wipe out this Zionist enemy or are wiped out by him, this means we must not accept a settlement. And we must not educate the Arab and Palestinian populace with the ideology of settlement.

––––––

Saddam: As for the regimes that stoop, I mean that go below the minimum level in the joint relation, and, as we said, this is to the extent of the level of treason, which of course has no level. Maybe we can say that nationalism represents a level in expressing the national stance, but we cannot say that there are levels to treason. But we assumed this hypothetical assumption, in order to emphasize to those who support Sadat that they are traitors like him and to the same extent. What is our stance toward them? In fact, we did say what our stance toward them is. We stated it publicly with a live audio recording which was broadcast and distributed. But is

[88] This adviser's reference to "Baghdad's decisions" refers to decisions associated with a November 1978 summit meeting in Baghdad, in which Arab League states discussed how to punish Egypt for making peace with Israel. The Arab League's foreign ministers would meet in Baghdad on 28 March 1979 to continue the discussion of how to punish Egypt. Sudan, Oman, and Djibouti all refused to attend the March 1979 meeting. Thomas W. Lippman, "Arab Plan Moves to Counter Treaty: Arab Foreign Ministers Meet to Plan Retaliation for Pact," *Washington Post*, 27 March 1979.

[89] The "treason deal" apparently refers to the Camp David accords.

that a style for the governments or for the revolutionary work of the revolutionaries and the people?

Actually, the idea of holding those who supported or will support Sadat, holding them responsible for treason, is first of all the idea of – first and foremost – the populace and revolutionary organizations. At another level, as national organizations we must not give any importance to the stance of other governments. And imagine the possibility of any kind of agreement to punish the regimes that stoop to Sadat's level. We only want these regimes to adhere to the Baghdad Summit resolutions by boycotting Sadat; if they had expected him to sign, they probably would not have signed on to the Baghdad Summit resolutions.

But some of them thought the matter would go on for a long time and so some regimes fell into a sort of trap, thinking that Sadat really signed, and that they really signed these resolutions and they are now expected to adhere to them. This method is from us, the revolutionary fighters, and the revolutionary fighters have their own methods of dealing with traitors that are well known and that I don't want to explain. As for national regimes, the stance changed only from a general, preliminary, practical one to a public position, meaning a position where we don't feel ashamed at all to take a shipment of weapons and say it is coming from Iraq against the Sudanese regime. We will also state on the radio that, yes, we did send it to the fighters in Sudan, we state it out loud.

Because that does not mean a new position. Our relationship with the fighters of Sudan goes back much earlier than that with the backward regime. But now the situation has taken another position from this backward regime. It is excusable for us to say it officially and broadcast it that we consider such people to be traitors. And today, before we came here, it was possibly announced in the six o'clock news –

Tariq: Eight o'clock, there was no six o'clock news –

Saddam: [*Interrupting.*] Not the talk with the ministers, but the comment on the situation in Sudan, because the Sudanese position is no longer – their position is obvious where they officially said they will not attend. So, practically, they sided with Sadat, and therefore, we thought we should announce in all the newscasts the fact that Sudan will not attend and that the ruler of Sudan supported the traitor Sadat and thus became his partner in treason.[90] In the past we would not say that. But now we do. We state it officially, meaning as the position of the government. And not the position of the freedom fighters, meaning the position of the nation. So let us act on that basis.

There were two nations that officially expressed their displeasure at what was stated on the news, Saudi Arabia and Kuwait – to different degrees but with obvious displeasure. And we told the Ministry of Foreign Affairs to contact both ambassadors and to tell them that they should not imagine that what was announced was incorrect, but to tell them that it was the position of the Iraqi nation, and that we will apply

[90] The event that Sudan will not attend is apparently the March 1979 Arab League meeting of foreign and finance ministers, in which Egypt was kicked out of the league for making peace with Israel. Numairi was a close U.S. ally and backed Sadat after Sadat signed the Camp David accords. "Gaafar Numeiri: Sudan Leader Backed Camp David Accord," *Boston Globe*, 31 May 2009; Marr, *The Modern History of Iraq*, 168–69.

it to the letter. It was not a slip of the tongue or a mistake. But rather it is a policy of the Iraqi nation, stated with all its capabilities and political power, which we will apply and consider any ruler who does not adhere to the resolutions of the Baghdad Summit to be as much a traitor as Sadat. This definition of our position has created a new framework and new look.

Any national regime can work in the same framework, so we need to encourage it, but we must not expect the other governments to behave like those who are not national or not progressive or not national progressive. However, as freedom fighters you must not be silent. We must not expect that an official ruling regime we [*inaudible*] and instigate the people in an organized manner to plan to destroy the regime . . . You must express and state with [*inaudible*] that Numairi is a traitor, a traitor like Sadat.[91] Our people have asked that we revolt against him and we are required to demand of him like Sadat wherever we see him and not be embarrassed at all. And if one of you needs weapons and wants to kill Numairi that [*inaudible*] these weapons from our embassy in France. And if it is discovered that the weapon was sent through your embassy by diplomatic pouch, and is officially stated to be from Iraq, we will admit that it was sent from Iraq, for killing the traitor Numairi, who is as much of a criminal as Sadat, just as we would do with Sadat.

Saddam Claims that Iraq's History and Scientific Expertise Uniquely Qualify it to Lead the Arab Nation but Expresses Concern that Israel will Seek to Stem the Arabs' Ascent (between September 1980 and November 1981)[92]

Saddam: It is what we call in the military jargon *the local field*. This is what happened in Yemen. This is what happened with the Syrian unity. This is what happened in 1967. I mean if a regime is toppled in Syria it can be replaced by another one, but for some issues – Syria will have a weight and a big part to play to save the Arab Nation when it becomes part of Iraq.[93]

But it cannot do it on its own, even if a sincere ruler takes the helm and so on and so forth and with the cooperation of the others, it cannot be the central post of the Arab Nation. There are necessities that must be available for it to be the center post. In Saudi Arabia, the rulers will go and others will take their place. There is a great deal of money. Yes, in billions and without sweat, but the human being is missing. There is no density of population and no quality. The one who is going to raise the Arab Nation should be the one who is richer in scientific knowledge than the others. However, Algeria, because of its distant location and the limit in

---

[91] Jafar Numairi, president of Sudan (1969–1985).

[92] SH-SHTP-A-000-626, "Saddam Discussing Neighboring Countries and their Regimes," undated (circa 1980–1981).

[93] After Egypt signed the Camp David accords, Iraq and Syria temporarily set aside years of hostility to better cooperate against Egypt. Leaders in Baghdad and Damascus even proclaimed a common goal of politically unifying their countries. Although Saddam formally ended unification talks only after becoming president, they had been dead since early 1979 and were likely never entirely sincere in the first place. Thomas W. Lippman, "Iraq and Syria: Two Old Foes Move to End Their Hostility," *Washington Post*, 17 May 1979; Karsh and Rautsi, *Saddam Hussein*, 104–7; Malik Mufti, *Sovereign Creations: Pan-Arabism and Political Order in Syria and Iraq* (Ithaca, NY: Cornell University Press, 1996).

the depth of its national thinking, cannot assume the leadership. There is no escape from the responsibility of leadership. It is not our choice to accept it or not. It is, rather, imposed on us. The fact is that we say that we are the Nation, we must take this direction. It must be Iraq due to the fact that Iraq has everything going for it. It has the depth in its civilization, it has the depth in the population density, and has the various types of advanced sciences in comparison to the others and has the material capabilities as well as the historical events to support it. It has Baghdad and its recent role, as well as the historical role it played during the Islamic era in addition to Babylon and Nineveh before the Islamic era. Baghdad is all of this.

This is all necessary, so that when you tell someone these facts he will believe he is part of a great message. You will tell him he is part of those great people. Those people would not have been so great had it not been for these subjective capabilities. Who can carry out this role? It is no one else but Iraq. Iraq can make this Nation rise and can be its center post of its big abode. There are smaller posts, but it must always be Iraq that feels the responsibility, and feels it is the central support post of the Arab nation. If Iraq falls, then the entire Arab nation will fall. When the central post breaks, the whole house will collapse. You cannot build this house in an area of thunderstorms. It means you build it in a valley, because you cannot build the house on high ground. We will then continue charging our people with this feeling. I prefer to build our army on a sound scientific base, and I want to talk about this to the young and the old, to the soldier, the officer, and the atomic scientist, and the university professor. We should tell it to the woman so that she can play her role at home and at the work place. We should also tell it to the old man so that he can let his children benefit from his experience and so forth. Is Qassem coming?

Male 1: You will see him.

Saddam: If they are going to hit Iraq, they will hit it before 1985 with an atomic bomb. After that, they will not be able to hit it. That means all of its enemies. May God protect Iraq from the stumbling blocks placed in its path. May God protect Iraq from, what shall I say, the sons of the pure who are accompanying the people of Iraq in the principles. We shall remain, God willing, after '85 so that any weakening or as the Arabs say, *Zubair*, will not be able to harm Iraq. It will not be able to stand the momentum while Iraq is on the roll. He will be the knight and the ruler who will be concerned about Iraq and a patriot who will continue the forward march. However, before '85, it is not so. The building posts have been put in place, but the structure has not taken its final form.

Male 1: Sir, after '85, even the Iranians cannot do anything. You mean the Iranians?

Saddam: No. I mean all of the enemies of Iraq, including Iran.

Male 1: I mean even Iran was not able to do anything before '85.

Saddam: No, Iran cannot do anything without the help of the Zionist enemy.

Male 1: A Zionist attack, as Your Excellency mentioned, is something else.

Saddam: Only with the atomic bomb and this is a complicated operation and not easy.

Male 1: That means from now until '85 God will protect us.

Saddam: God willing in 1985 the structure will take its final form. I mean its relative form. Of course, the final shape will keep up with the pace of the advance. I do not mean the final structure.

Male 1: With God's protection you shall return.

Saddam: There are matters that need our attention after the war is over. We must put up a schedule. We must take advantage of the experience we gained to implement what we did not attend to before so that we finish the job.

Tariq Aziz Explains How Imperialists have Fostered Disunity in the Arab World (circa 1988)[94]

Tariq: I believe that the challenge we faced during the last eight or ten years and since the advent of this Iranian regime is the most dangerous we have faced since the fall of Egypt.[95] Because the challenge of imperialism – despite the fact that it is dangerous from the materialistic perspective and to a great extent from the spiritual perspective – Imperialism is strange – strange where some people became agents of the imperialist, but it could not be frozen in the society, as the writers express it and despite the imperialists' attempts to divide the Iraqi society and the Arab Nation. The reaction in the face of the imperialists was Arab unity. Likewise with the Israeli danger. It is very strong from the materialistic aspect. It was and still is a very real danger. However, it is unable to isolate the self-structuring and the social result of the Arab society. The danger that emanated from Iran – it came along with the tremendous material strength it possessed. Yes, it was backward, but nevertheless it was tremendous as we witnessed. At times, we used to receive tremendous attacks from the Iranians indicative of great strength and energy. It was, admittedly less strong than the forces the Israelis deployed in the 1967 War.

Saddam: Every attack by Iran had such an insistence and a great number of fighting forces and capabilities, that, if things were different, were much more than the capabilities imparted in 1973 for an entire year.

Tariq: It used to carry with it a tremendous amount of energy in addition to an energy we can figuratively call spiritual, but, in fact, it was backward and dark and was based on a superstitious insistence on destruction and venom, because the motto Khomeini raised from the beginning of his movement and before he was in authority was that if a person wished to reach martyrdom in order for him, as he called it, to "reach the goal," then he should kill. Killing, then, becomes a sacred duty as he calls it in his devious thinking. He represents forces that are dark, twisted, and bent on killing and insisting on destruction. It was trying to reach out and penetrate the Arab and Muslim masses claiming it belonged to the religion of the Nation. Its danger was, if left unchecked, to divide the Arab Nation into segments that would be difficult to reunite in our modern days.

We notice, based on our experience as Arabs and as Arab Ba'athists, how unhappy we were with the division of the Arab Nation affected by the British and the French in the

---

[94] SH-SHTP-A-000-631, "Saddam Discussing General Issues and Iraqi Military History," undated (circa 1988).

[95] This might refer to the 1979 peace treaty between Israel and Egypt.

Sykes-Picot agreement.[96] We tried to bypass it in the early years of our independence. Lebanon, which is the size of an Arab county, became a state. Imagine, Lebanon is an independent state. Qatar, which is a small, tiny municipality, is now spoken of as one with history, culture, and literature of its own. It is like someone comes and talks about the inhabitants of Mahmoodiyah.[97] One can then talk about the history, literature, and culture of Mahmoodiyah. Qatar is about the size of Mahmoodiyah as far as its population. Therefore, if we allow the Arab Nation to be divided a second and third time in a new form of Sykes-Picot on a sectarian basis, such a division will have the same result as that of Sykes-Picot.

These little countries will fight each other in political terms, in propaganda and other means of destruction. They did not need to enter a war. However, the Khomeini-type countries will enter into wars with each other for backward sectarian reasons. We will fight to divide the water resources among us, and the railroads, and the electricity stations, and the money in the central bank. Therefore, the country will be splintered. The Arab nation and especially the Eastern part of the Arab nations will be transformed to a number of small, scattered countries fighting among themselves and easy prey for anyone who wishes to control them. The structure of the Arab Nation as such would be finished as one Nation or even as the separate countries that exist now, which we do not like at all. This state, although bad, would become worse and we would start down the slope of the collapse of the Arab Nation as we have known it historically. Several nations throughout history would have collapsed and been wiped from the map had it not been for the Iraqis who played a great role in their stand to save the Arab Nation. The party had a great role in this and the leadership had a great role.

Saddam and His Advisers Discuss Economic and Political Unification Efforts in Europe, and the Need for Arab States to Similarly Unify to Expand Their Influence and Face Foreign Threats (January 1989)[98]

Saddam: The Arab League became – it has been confirmed in more than one conference that the summit meetings take place yearly, but actually you see that it's not taking place. Why doesn't it happen? Because once the country hosting the conference sees that the conference shouldn't happen this year, but in two years [it] will be sufficient to impede the interest of the entire Ummah. So we have to look for another base that can express the possibility of agreement in deeper and bigger ways. That's first, that's regarding the background of our thinking as Iraqis, but how the thoughts developed, I have already explained that to you.

The other side is related to Arab national security. Every threat to any Arab state should bind all Arabs to unite. But at the same time, it should bind a group of Arabs, if this group was in internal agreement and strong, it could influence the other group

---

[96] The Sykes-Picot agreement was a secret agreement between Great Britain and France, with Russian approval, to dismember the Ottoman Empire. Reached in May 1916, the agreement resulted in the division of Iraq, Syria, Lebanon, and Palestine into British- and French-administered areas. See Sykes-Picot Agreement, 15 and 16 May 1916, accessed 16 April 2009 at www.lib.byu.edu.

[97] Mahmoodiyah is an Iraqi city just south of Baghdad.

[98] SH-SHTP-A-001-226, "Saddam and His Advisers Discussing Pan-Arab Security Issues," undated (circa January 1989).

and force it to reach a unified position regarding Arab national security. It is not a simple matter for Iraq, Egypt, Jordan, and Yemen to meet in one organization and agree on joint steps in an effective and brotherly way.[99] Another thing [is that] the world around us, the world around us where the greater countries – the countries greater than Iraq, Egypt, Jordan, and Yemen – started looking for greater entities at the economic and political levels.

Let us look at Europe. For instance, the capabilities of France or England are not equal to the capabilities of Iraq or Egypt; they are greater and yet it [Iraq] started feeling that its existence is less than its national need, and in order to express itself better, it has to look for a greater tent. This did not happen randomly to mature countries. It did not happen under a feeling of military threat either, because they are members of the Atlantic Alliance [the North Atlantic Treaty Organization] and they consider it enough to face a situation initiated by the Soviet Union and Washington Alliance. But this feeling of looking for a greater tent, cooperation, opening windows, doors and channels within, this feeling was dictated by the social, cultural, and economic development of the world. And since the world today is no longer the world of the '40s or '50s, but the influence of one country on another became greater – whether it's a positive or negative influence – it became appropriate to take into consideration the development taking place in the world, in order to adopt it in our thoughts and steps at the national or patriotic levels. In this case, we realize – of course we were hoping that the Arab League developed to this level if not even better, the entire League step by step – but it looks like we must continue to strive within the Arab League until we reach the top. However, we discovered that establishing such a step doesn't conflict with striving within, and what I mean by striving here is bringing up thoughts, interacting with the neighboring countries, and enlightening them more and more with patience and readiness for sacrifices within the Arab League as far as our relation with our brotherly countries. We realized that this relation between the four countries is just a support that pushes the situation forward and not an alternative to the current situation.

[99] These four countries formed the Arab Cooperation Council in February 1989. The organization disbanded after Iraq's invasion of Kuwait.

FOUR

Qadisiyyah Saddam (The Iran-Iraq War)

Iran has planned animosity for us from the beginning, as if the change [Revolution] that took place in Iran was designed with the intention to be against the interest of Iraq... [W]e have treated them more kindly than they deserve.

– Saddam Hussein, November 1979[1]

On 22 September 1980, after months of border skirmishes, Saddam's army streamed into Iran. Though hoping for a quick victory, Saddam soon found himself mired in an ill-conceived conflict against a powerful and motivated opponent. For eight long years, hundreds of thousands of soldiers fought in the marshes, mountains, and deserts dividing the two countries. As the conflict wore on, Saddam's desperate military employed chemical weapons, bombarded Iranian cities, and brutalized ethnic minorities. Iran responded by sending human waves of teenage zealots storming across Iraqi minefields and targeting neutral shipping in the Gulf. By the time both sides accepted a UN cease-fire in August 1988, the fighting had led to nearly a million casualties, thousands more sat in prison camps, and the region was poorer by billions of dollars. Saddam's glib conversations in this chapter belie the terrible suffering his words inflicted.

These recordings correspond to the three basic phases of the war. They begin with the optimism of the initial invasion, displaying Saddam's geopolitical calculations and generally triumphant rhetoric (1979–1981). As Iran halted the invasion and pushed back onto Iraqi soil, Saddam's conversations reflect the slogging mess of trench warfare and contain his calls for gross violations of human rights (1982–1987). In the final section, Saddam struggles to turn his growing military successes into a viable cease-fire with Tehran (1987–1988). Together, the transcripts illuminate a war launched with unclear motivation, pursued with few concrete goals, and led by a man

---

[1] SH-SHTP-D-000-559, "Saddam and His Inner Circle Discussing Relations with Various Arab States, Russia, China, and the United States," undated (circa 4–20 November 1979).

Saddam meets with members of his General Staff; Ali Hassan Al-Majid (aka "Chemical Ali") is on Saddam's right. The date of this picture is unknown. (*Source*: *SH-MISC-D-001-275, "Pictures of Saddam and an Identity Card," undated)

who frequently exhibited an unwillingness to follow professional military advice or protect noncombatants.

There has been a great deal of speculation about why Saddam launched this war. Although publicly and privately he justified it with reference to his unhappiness with a 1975 border treaty with Iran and aggressive Persian behavior, Saddam also fought his war for larger, vaguer reasons. From Saddam's perspective, Iraq was destined to become a major regional power. By contrast, he saw Iran both as a vulnerable target weakened by the chaos of its recent Islamic Revolution and a usurper of Iraq's leadership of the Gulf states.[2] He spoke of a clash of civilizations, a reprise of the ancient Battle of Qadisiyyah, in which Arab armies routed the Persian Empire. "Saddam's

[2] Saddam's General Military Intelligence Directorate (GMID) reinforced these views. On 1 July 1980 it reported, "It is clear that, at present, Iran has no power to launch wide offensive operations against Iraq, or to defend on a large scale." On 29 July, it reported that ten thousand Iranian officers had been discharged or retired, that with every day Iran lost another hundred officers, and that the troops in Iran's 92nd Armored Division had received no tactical drilling since the fall of the shah. See Intelligence Report on Iran issued by the GMID, 1 July 1980, in SH-GMID-D-000-842, "General Military Intelligence

Qadisiyyah" was used by the Ba'ath regime as a rallying cry for Arabs – Sunni and Shi'a – to unite against a racially inferior and racist Persian foe.

International fear of revolutionary Iran provided Iraq with a widening pool of reluctant and often greedy backers, and Saddam benefited from their anxieties. He armed his forces with modern French, Soviet, and Chinese weapons (often paid for with Kuwaiti and Saudi money). He profited from the Reagan administration's willingness to share American military intelligence with Iraq, although he also appears to have believed that U.S. intelligence sharing with Iran led to important Iranian victories.[3] More than anything else, however, these tapes expose Saddam's almost obsessive focus on his nation's image despite sometimes less-than-impressive realities on the battlefield. Saddam also liked to speculate about Western militaries and ruminate on the predictive role of history.

For all his global interests, Saddam tried to manage much of the war personally, both in its larger and its smaller aspects. When employing chemical weapons against Kurdish villages, he reminded his commanders that "the chemical weapon cannot be used unless I give the order to use it!"[4] He was also not above reminding his soldiers how to emplace sandbags.[5] Because of this intimate role in even the most minor details, the Iran-Iraq War cannot be understood independent of Saddam Hussein.

OUR VICTORY WILL BE A HISTORIC ONE: FROM INVASION TO RETREAT (1979–1981)

In the lead-up to the war, Iraq was at the height of its power relative to its historical foe. The Iranian Revolution the previous year had left Iran's military weakened and vulnerable. In the first recording, Saddam worries about the Islamic Republic's efforts to alter the balance of power in the Gulf. During the following year, tensions between the two nations mounted as they tried to undermine each other and engaged in border skirmishes. On 4 September, Iran's shelling of Iraqi border cities caused many casualties.

Directorate (GMID) Intelligence Reports on Iran," January–July 1980; and see SH-GMID-D-001-227, "Intelligence Reports on Iranian Military Capabilities Including Artillery, Air Power, Ammunitions, and Bases," 29 July 1980.

[3] *SH-SHTP-A-001-220, "Saddam Meeting with a Foreign Official," undated (circa 19 August 1987); SH-PDWN-D-000-730, "Transcript of an Armed Forces General Command Meeting," 26 May 1988; SH-SHTP-V-000-612, "Saddam and Senior Military Officials Discussing Efforts to Retake the Majnun Area," undated (circa summer 1988); SH-SHTP-A-000-813, "Saddam and Senior Military Officials Discussing Various Military Operations, Including Re-capturing the al-Fao Peninsula," undated (circa 1992). For a discussion of U.S. intelligence sharing with Iran, see Chapter 1.

[4] SH-SHTP-A-001-023, "Saddam and Ba'ath Party Members Discussing the Iran-Iraq War," 6 March 1987.

[5] SH-SHTP-A-001-228, "Saddam Discussing Ba'ath Party Principles and History, Military Strategy, and General Administrative Issues," undated (circa February 1982).

Iran "waged war against us on the fourth of September when it attacked Iraqi cities," Saddam told his cabinet, "after it failed to achieve a full-scale military reaction from us, in relation to incidents at the border checkpoints."[6] These 4 September attacks marked, for Iraq, the official beginning of the war.[7] On 22 September Iraq invaded Iran.

In the second recording, from 16 September, Saddam and his advisers discuss recent attacks on Iranian border posts, Iraqi political and military objectives, and various worst-case scenarios for the conflict with Iran. Saddam expresses repeated desire to limit the conflict but recognizes that Iran might choose to expand the fighting. The third tape reveals Saddam buoyed by his initial successes, predicting a quick triumph. By the time of the fourth conversation, however, Iraqi forces were falling back and Saddam's attitude turned darker as he cast around for scapegoats, which included the international community and the psychology of Iraqis.

Saddam and His Advisers Discuss Iranian Diplomatic Efforts in the Gulf (November 1979)[8]

Saddam: People consider Iraq to be a leading country, and people are very proud of the friendly relations they enjoy with Iraq . . . The important fact is that we support [Arab nations] and we must regard them in our calculation [*inaudible*]. The Ba'ath party is an indicator of Iraq's independence and it is also a requirement for Arab unity. Arab unity will not be achieved through foreign will . . .

Latif: Mr. President, our relationships with the Gulf Countries have passed through two stages. The first stage is the beginning of the Iranian movement toward the Gulf. I believe that the recent Iranian announcements were more real than people thought, people who do not have a relation with the Iranian regime or do not have decision-making capability. The policy was real and it will remain that way toward the Gulf. The Gulf region became a scary one and we are not happy about this, a frightened region, seeking help through different forms of media or movements or any relation with the Revolution and with Iraq. It seems that Iran is discovering these points and believes Iraq is playing a role bigger than its size, the role of policeman, the protector, to –

Saddam: Describe this to the Syrian consultant.

Latif: He did not come to me.

Saddam: I mean Hafez al-Assad.[9]

Latif: This discovery, as it seems the Iranians have discovered, they realize that this new Iraqi phenomena will give Iraq a bigger strategic role in the Gulf region. There

---

[6] See section "Saddam and his senior advisers discuss Iraq's need for civil defenses," in Chapter 6.

[7] Ige F. Dekker and H. G. Post, eds., *The Gulf War of 1980–1988: The Iran-Iraq War in International Legal Perspective* (Boston: Martinus Nijhoff, 1992), 28n86.

[8] SH-SHTP-D-000-559, "Saddam and His Inner Circle Discussing Relations with Various Arab States, Russia, China, and the United States," undated (circa 4–20 November 1979).

[9] Hafez al-Assad, president of Syria (1970–2000).

has been much coordination, in addition to information I have received. Coordination took place following the Iranian deputy prime minister's visit to Lebanon and to Syria in a prior visit, and the Gulf tour that was designed to assure the Gulf States that there is no real or intrinsic threat from Iran toward Gulf States and the region, that it is not necessary to side with Iraq. The Iranians have lobbied hard so that they can hold a meeting in Taif [Saudi Arabia] without Iraq's presence. And this is a new phenomenon, a dangerous one if I may add, in Gulf politics. And we must be very attentive to this phenomenon – careful.

The Gulf people must be warned that the Iranian policy will remain that way whether their [Iran's] regime has changed quickly or whether it stayed another year, the Iranian policies will remain based on the above principle and doctrine ... I believe they seek to isolate Iraq. Second, they desire that Iraq would have limited political influence. Additionally, that the new Iranian policies aim to make the Arabs believe that Iran does not have any problems with them, and that Iran's problem is only with Iraq. And [regarding] the border issue, Iraq is seriously pursuing targets in Northern and Southern Iran and that Iraq has new issues with Iran. Adding to this is that Iraq – some Iranian media and some Western media started to talk about Iraq's attempt to acquire a leading role. And that Iraq is restless and is pursuing a role outside its boundaries, it pursues other political influence and to project its own policies in the region ...

We are facing issues where we must be proactive. We should not be complacent and let events die down. We should acknowledge the real dangers affecting the region. We should be observant of all political activities that affect us whether they relate to the Palestinian problem, the Lebanon problem, the Gulf problems and Iran's objectives in the region. All these events do not exist in isolation ... I support that the campaign against Iran should be at its fullest scale, and that could be achieved through instigation, in the official policies and the sharpest media announcements and arranging activities [*inaudible*] overseas. I mean overseas as Your Excellency has stated, we use all our resources for the betterment of Iraq. Now people who are influenced by their media imagine Iraq wants to play a leading role, that it wants to be a successor of Nasser's policies, and that Iraq is doing such and such.[10] All of this falls under the psychological factor, a psychological factor aimed at destroying rulers and breaking their unity and making them surrender, which is why our path and methodology must be stern and sharp. We should not be lenient with them [*inaudible*].

———

Saddam: It is not a shame for Iraqis to explore influences outside their borders, but it is a shame that they would rush the matter. Rushing is not correct and imagining the role without objective accurate calculations is not correct. We are not going to repeat the same mistakes that Nasser and Boumédienne have committed;[11] we are not going

[10] Gamal Abd al-Nasser (1918–1970) was president of Egypt from 1956 to 1970. He attempted to unite the Arab world behind his Arab nationalist banner, although Saddam Hussein came to view him as a cautionary example because of his defeat by Israel in 1967.

[11] Houari Boumédienne (1932–1978) ruled Algeria from 1965 to 1978. He aggressively supported radical anticolonialism and the Non-Aligned Movement but spent much of his reign feuding with Morocco.

to fall into the same trap, even though the conflict with Israel continues. The subject of our relation with Iran – Iran plans animosity for us from the beginning, as if the change that took place in Iran was designed with the intentions to be against the interest of Iraq.[12] We have to be patient, the slogans that we use [inaudible]. We are not bargaining with Iran, we have treated them more kindly than they deserve.[13] We have to include in our calculation a central point. If we want to bargain, tomorrow the Iranians will send their highest ranking official to Baghdad, [and] they will release news that we have come to an agreement. We do not bargain [inaudible]. We do not bargain unless we put our hand with the people of any nation. Now the Kurds fight in the North, and the Arabs fight in the south. This issue, these two issues, are not related to any possible bargaining. This issue, we will continue to support them, until self-rule is achieved in Arabistan and the self rule is achieved in Kurdistan.[14] [Inaudible] as if they, the people of Arabistan want to split from the rest in order to form a government, this is an expected matter, Kurdish people splitting from the rest and want to form whatever they want to achieve, this is an expected matter. We do not have any obligations you see until now, not for the Kurds and not for the Arabs...

The Arabs in the Gulf, the Gulf Arabs, they did not change. God help us, they are the Arabs of decay, the Arabs of shame, Arabs whose values contradict all the values known in heaven and on earth. We were the first ones to realize their decay. Khomeini will not give them a chance to survive. Slaughtering them is a sacrificial blessing, a great deed. Slaughtering them will prove beneficial. It is because of the corruption and decay, all the decay of earth and that all of you can imagine, it is found in the Gulf Arab States. But what we can do? We have all these challenges that the Ba'ath party faces.

I mean the Iraqi policies here, it states that we have to get rid of the ruler of Kuwait. But if one overthrows the ruler of Kuwait, he must be able at the same time to safeguard the interest of its people and to safeguard its Arab identity for its people. If we do not have these plans, then we are against anyone who wants to carry out the change.

These are the Iraqi political analyses, oh, Brothers! This is it. It is complicated, it is unique. That is why they want us to be with them [inaudible] only when an enemy attacks them. They cannot do without us, because this is the policy of balances, [Inaudible] all organizations in the Arab world, everyone has its weight, the variable and the fixed, [inaudible] it is not possible for them to isolate us, this is fixed ... Saudi

---

[12] Later in the meeting, Saddam asserts that the United States was behind the revolution in Iran. See section "Saddam, meeting with senior advisers, says that the United States orchestrated the overthrow of the Shah of Iran," in Chapter 1.

[13] Saddam had cautiously welcomed the new revolutionary regime in Iran and sought good relations with it through the end of summer 1979. Iran, however, had urged Iraqis to overthrow "the Saddamite regime" and incited assassination attempts against members of Saddam's inner circle. Karsh and Rautsi, *Saddam Hussein*, 137–39.

[14] Saddam is referring to the Arab population of the southwestern Iranian province of Khuzestan (alternatively referred to as Ahwaz or Arabistan). Some of these Arabs pushed for separation from the Persian-dominated nation, often with aid from Saddam Hussein. The struggle for this diverse and oil-rich region was one of the motivations for beginning the Iran-Iraq War. This support was also a violation of the 1975 Algiers Accords.

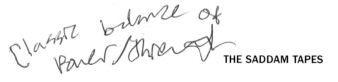

Arabia wants to balance us out with Iran, and balance us with Syria, and balance us with Jordan. And Jordan wants to balance us with Syria, and wants to balance us with Saudi Arabia, and wants to balance us – we are a priority weight balance over all... All of this is a soap opera. We know all of this and we are disturbed. The same plan took place with the Ahwaz Arabs, [*inaudible*] they have weapons, money, media propaganda, films.[15] But we are here. It is up to you [Arabs] whether you want to revolt or not. You disseminate these slogans. It is up to you...

Following Recent Border Skirmishes with Iran, Saddam Discusses His Political and Military Objectives in a Meeting with the Revolutionary Command Council and National Command (16 September 1980)[16]

Saddam: My comrades, in our previous meeting we reviewed the developing military situation and the decision to retake our land from Iran.[17] We explained to you the military position regarding getting back the areas of Zain al Qaws and Saif Saad.[18] There are a number of posts in harmony with the position we took, which is that the Iranians [*inaudible*] a little at a time so they will not go further than we want. We do not want them to take themselves and us to a situation that we do not want, especially when they learn that the whole situation regards returning the lands they extorted. We had a number of posts, I think six or five. Comrade 'Adnan [Khairallah]?

'Adnan: [*Inaudible*.]

Saddam: Maybe there are six that we postponed discussing until now. I think the comrades returned them today. There is one post for which they have a night operation planned. Is there anything else?

'Adnan: Nothing is left, Sir.

Saddam: They were all returned. Today we can say that all of the lands extorted by Iran are back under our sovereignty. We are at the international borders that are agreed on in all historical agreements.

_____

Saddam: Iran is angry about how we can kill its agents, close the borders, and stop supplies from arriving to [*inaudible*] its agents. It was supplying them directly... [L]egal excuses should be said to international public opinion as... weapons in our

[15] See *supra* note 14. Saddam provided Arab rebels in Khuzestan with arms and infiltrated Iraqi operatives into the area to sabotage Iranian oil facilities. He appears to have mistakenly believed that the Ahwaz Liberation Movement, which was based in Iraq, would rouse Khuzestan's Arabs to assist Iraqi invaders. See Kenneth M. Pollack, *The Persian Puzzle: The Conflict between Iran and America* (New York: Random House, 2005), 184; Saskia Gieling, *Religion and War in Revolutionary Iran* (London: I. B. Taurus and Co., 1999), 12–13.

[16] SH-SHTP-A-000-835, "Saddam and Military Officials Discussing the Iran-Iraq War," 16 September 1980.

[17] The editors found no record of this meeting.

[18] Iraq captured Zain al Qaws on 7 September, and Saif Saad on 10 September. See Bahman Baktiari, "International Law: Observations and Violations," in *The Iran-Iraq War: The Politics of Aggression*, ed. Farhang Rajaee (Gainesville: University Press of Florida, 1993), 161.

hands to face the international and the Arab situation. In reality, the Iranians gave us this weapon. This is before they came and announced that the agreement of 1975 is a colonization agreement [inaudible]. After they [the new Iranian regime] came in, they announced that they do not approve of the agreement of 1975, and lately one of the important officials announced this... [19] We will set aside all the legal excuses. There is an agreement between us [inaudible]. The extorted Iraqi lands are to come back peacefully. And the Iranian-American horse, Mullah Mustafa al-Barzani, is to be afflicted.[20] This is what Iran provided to Iraq. Iraq offered to Iran [inaudible] in the Shatt al-Arab. We gave Iran all this time to return the land, but the Iranians did not return it according to the agreement.[21] We have to gain it back with the blood of our soldiers and by force... When we have the ability to return what is our right, we will do it. No patriot would let go of his rights. Now we have the Shatt al-Arab... [T]here are facts that we must make the comrades remember. In 1975, we used almost all the artillery ammunition we had. Our situation was such that we only had three heavy bombs for the air force. We sent the staff commander to the Soviet Union where he signed an agreement. They told him they only had 1,200 artillery rounds.[22] At that time, 1,200 artillery rounds meant only [enough for] a day of fighting.

'Adnan: Using only one battery, Sir.

Saddam: Yes, using one battery. These are military facts. As for the political facts... we announced that we were ready to discuss peacefully resolving the issues between us and Iran... And we pulled our army from the front. We left the front without troops, at the same time as the Shah's army was mobilized in front of our army... This is what you gain from flexibility. Anyway, if we had ammunition, we

[19] Saddam is referring to the 6 March 1975 Algiers Accord, in which Iran and Iraq agreed to share the Shatt al-Arab waterway.

[20] Barzani was the leader of the Kurdish Democratic Party (KDP). His party's guerrilla campaign against the regime in the mid-1970s contributed to Iraq's decision to accept the unfavorable terms of the Algiers Accord, in exchange for Iran's agreement to quit supporting the insurgency. Barzani had received financial support and military supplies for his insurgency from Iran and the United States. See Karsh and Rautsi, *Saddam Hussein*, 75–80; "Memorandum from the President's Assistant for National Security Affairs," National Archives, Nixon Presidential Materials, NSC Files, box 138, Kissinger Office Files, Kissinger Country Files, Middle East, Kurdish Problem vol. 1, June '72–Oct. '73, formerly classified "Secret; Sensitive; Exclusively Eyes Only," accessed 20 October 2009 at www.state.gov/r/pa/ho/frus/nixon/e4/c17628.htm.

[21] On 6 September, Iraq threatened to take 115 to 145 miles of territory in the Qasr-e-Shirin region (including the cities Zian al Qaws and Saif Saad) if Iran did not cede it within a week. Iraq claimed that Iran had awarded it this territory in a secret clause of the Algiers Accord. On 8 September, Iraq attacked Qasr-e-Shirin with mortar and cannon fire. See Abdolrahman Alem, "War Responsibility: Governments or Individuals?" in Rajaee, *Iran-Iraq War*, 61; Dilip Hiro, *The Longest War: The Iran-Iraq Military Conflict* (New York: Routledge, 1991), 17, 39.

[22] Oles M. Smolansky and Bettie M. Smolansky provide an overview of Soviet military deliveries to Iraq in the mid-1970s. They conclude that in early 1975, "Russian military supplies were reaching Baghdad in unprecedented numbers and contributed to the 'solution' of the Kurdish question." Saddam, however, was reportedly unsatisfied. See Smolansky and Smolansky, *The USSR and Iraq: The Soviet Quest for Influence* (Durham, NC: Duke University Press, 1991), 25–33, 296n74.

have shown him any flexibility nor would we have given him the [*inaudible*] ,hatt al-Arab. If our political and military circumstance would have allowed different position, we wouldn't have been pushed into something we did not want... And with all of this, I was in pain. I came back in pain... Maybe someone will ask you why you kept quiet at the time of the shah. We signed it at the time of the shah, not at another time... If someone's father is killed, he can ask his son to avenge him. This is a fact. Sometimes a man cannot build a big palace as a heritage, so he asks those after him to build one. Many of our ancestors lost a military battle, and then they gathered themselves and they returned to win in another battle. Our highest guidance, Muhammad Ibn 'Abdullah, peace and prayers upon him, used to work this way...

'Adnan: [*Inaudible.*]

Saddam: Okay.

'Adnan: [*Inaudible.*]

Saddam: Okay. And therefore, the National Command's decision was to announce these facts to the public opinion and to do as we please with the Shatt al-Arab... Some will say, "Do you guarantee that the Soviet Union would continue to supply you with weapons if you were to go through the same condition that you went through in 1975?" The answer is that there is no one who will guarantee this. "Can you deny that Iran will confront you with a force and that Iran will escalate the work to a full-scale war?" There is no one who will give us [such] an assessment. The calculations we made for the Arab world, internationally, Iraq, and Iran tell us that this kind of decision is correct. And that it is possible to implement it with a commanding role and to mobilize the people and the enthusiasm of the army. The enthusiasm of the people is available... If you could let the Arab people make their own decision and if you could tell the Arab people that I have an extorted land, do not ask me how it was extorted, but it is extorted and it is part of Iraq, and I have the ability to get it back – should I get it back or not? All the Arab people will tell you to get it back... [*inaudible*] all the people who have an extorted land and they can get it back. This is a fact. Getting your land back will scare them, because it takes you to another level of ability and to another psychological effect on the Arab people and the national [i.e., pan-Arab] public opinion.[23] It is natural that regimes with a prejudiced opinion regarding your system and your party will not be relaxed. We are now discussing all of these matters in this joint meeting [to prepare] to give a speech in the National Assembly.[24]

———

Saddam: ... [Iraq conducted calculations] in case the Iranians do anything, even though their reaction up until now has been [only] a field reaction. However, this kind of a situation cannot be assessed according to what you see. You have to

[23] Saddam is probably referring primarily to the Israelis as the individuals who will become frightened when Iraq regains "Arab" land. As he explains in this meeting, Iraq's reincorporation of the Shatt al-Arab will show Arabs that they can retake other extorted lands (i.e., Palestine).

[24] In a speech to the National Assembly the next day, 17 September, Saddam announced his decision to abrogate the 1975 Algiers treaty and offered justifications to support his position. See Rajaee, *Iran-Iraq War*, 160–61.

calculate it according to the worst [possible] scenario. You would have to prepare yourselves to face the worst case scenario. At the same time, we did not want to pause for too long and lose the main idea. The army has been mobilizing on their [the Iranians'] border for the past ten days, or maybe even more, maybe 15 days. In the beginning it was a limited mobilization, but now we have whole divisions mobilizing on the borders. They [the Iranians] are probably thinking they [the Iraqis] took this small piece of land and several posts, why do they have all of these armed forces? What is the need? They might miscalculate and fall into an illusion that will lead themselves and us to a situation neither of us wants.

Saddam: After our forces get the land back, we will tell them. We will say that our forces on this date and at this time got back this land from you, now give us the remainder of the land or we will take it by force. If they do not give it to us, then we will grab it back. Militarily this will cost more. It was possible at Saif Saad and the other posts to cause them more losses, and we would have encountered fewer losses. However, in exchange, to understand us, and understand why we acted this way, and why [we engaged in] all of this mobilization, we chose to act this way . . . This is to return the Shatt al-Arab, so if they do not act as we wish, we will strike them just as we struck them at Zain al Qaws and Saif Saad, and in the other posts [*inaudible*] they are getting struck.

Male 1: This is our chance. This is a historical chance. It does not only mean to get back the Shatt al-Arab and we see the [*inaudible*], rather it means much more than this. It means that Iraq has moved from one stage to the other. In my opinion, we will have a positive effect in the Arab world and internationally. There is nothing like it, especially in the Arab world and for the Arab people, and the Arab regimes . . . If this procedure is completed, it will move Iraq into a big and dangerously effective position. Through this, in the future, Iraq can take big steps to accomplish its goals, whether they are within the country or national [i.e., pan-Arab]. Also, there are benefits for building a revolutionary, ideological army . . . the international circumstances and the Arab circumstances are the best they have ever been at this time. At any other time [*inaudible*] it might be harder to get back this part of the country, especially the Shatt al-Arab. I see that this is the best chance to get back the part under Iranian control in the Shatt al-Arab. What is needed is to calculate the possibilities Your Excellency mentioned, to calculate the worst case scenario. And it is that Iran might escalate, or its reaction might be vast. The Soviet Union might pressure us by using the ammunition [*inaudible*]. We should look for another source from which to import ammunition – other countries in the world. Let us rely on God and start based on the time we established. My belief is that Iran will not behave in a vast way. If they react in a big way, how far are they going to go and lose?

Saddam: In other words, do they have a mind to fight us while they are in this bad military condition?[25]

[25] Recent purges and executions in the Iranian military had severely weakened Iran. See Hiro, *Longest War*, 43, 47–48.

Abu Bashar: Getting the land back is a great move. The decision to get the Shatt al-Arab back is also something that makes us happy, and it is great. This is something that gives us self-confidence regarding the army, the people, and the command. However, I have some questions. You know my evaluation, and you must have taken it into consideration. There is no doubt that the international circumstance, presently, is in our favor to get the land back and to conduct operations internationally. In the future, the international circumstances might not stay as they are if things take a long time. So, is there anything that can be done to settle these matters so it will not take a long time? Because taking a long time means that we will drain our resources. There is a transit agreement between Iran and the Soviet Union.[26] The Iranians will allow the Soviet goods to pass through their land, and the Soviets in return will allow the Iranian goods to pass through their land. Also, the hostages' situation... they might find a solution for it if both parties would back down on some of the conditions. If these problems are solved, it is possible that both countries [the United States and the Soviet Union] would drain us and Iran at the same time. In particular, you cannot rely on the Arab rulers. The people, as you said [*inaudible*].

Saddam: If you do not want to calculate the possibilities of enmity, then do not calculate the possibilities of friendship.

Saddam: The command must not accept draining the resources. In other words, they [the Iranians] should not keep quiet after all of these steps. Iran should not stay quiet without a yes or a no answer. We have to stick its head in the mud and tell them to say the truth. This way we will quickly resolve this matter. If they continue without saying yes or no [*inaudible*] and if they keep bombarding us with artillery while our army is mobilized on the Iranian border, then this situation will not be accepted. The correct situation is that we have to put them in a political and military position so they will say yes. Or they would have to pull back their army and assume that the matter is over, and that we can do as we please. We cannot stay on the border forever. This is what we are thinking about in full. What you said is correct – that the international situation is in our favor; however, who is going to guarantee that the international situation will continue the same way forever? This is another good question. Expect that the situation will change in Iran. And therefore, it is important to settle and determine the matter and make it a fact of life that they have to live with. Or we have to make it legally done and over with.

Abu Bashar: [*Inaudible.*]

---

[26] In October 1962, Iran and the Soviet Union concluded a transit agreement that provided for Iran to send goods to Europe through the Soviet Union. Transit of Iranian goods through the Soviet Union increased during the Iranian hostage crisis and the two countries appear to have renewed the agreement in September 1980. See Tarun Chandra Bose, *The Super Powers and the Middle East* (New York: Asia Publishing House, 1972), 82; Cheryl Benard and Zalmay Khalilzad, *The Government of God: Iran's Islamic Republic* (New York: Columbia University Press, 1984), 175; Adam Terock, *The Superpowers' Involvement in the Iran-Iraq War* (Commack, NY: Nova Science Publishers, 1998), 44.

Saddam: Abu Bashar, we just accepted mediation. I told the comrades if anyone comes to you and asks to mediate, tell him that he is welcome to do so. That we would love for you to mediate.

———

Abu Hasan: What is painful is that the Arab reply, and it is the reply of the regimes, is negative. They are either spectators, rejoicing over the misfortune, or they are paid conspirers. I do not expect, as the president mentioned, that the Arab regimes will help us. As for the Arab people, it is certain that the situation is different and without the negative effect of the Arab regimes. The Arab people will come out happy if the result is a success. And at that time the Arab regimes will not have an effect. As you know, things are judged according to the final result. It is clear to all that the situation of the Shatt al-Arab is not like Zain al Qaws or Saif Saad. It is very complicated, and might lead to a full-scale war. This is my opinion. Especially since the Iranians have a better navy than we do. And they are marked by their many military bases spread over an 860-kilometer coast. Also, the outcome and its effect on the international navigation for oil in the Strait of Hormuz – all of these issues are supposed to be well-figured out.

There is one issue remaining that the comrades might not have digested, which is that the Iraqi borders end about five or seven kilometers before Muhammarah [Korromshar]. Right after this the Iranian borders start directly on this beach. In other words, there is no Iraqi land on the other side that we can move on to control safe and stable navigation. This situation has to be calculated very carefully. Iraq has land on both sides reaching 72 kilometers after Basra; thereafter, Iraq only has the western beach. The other side belongs to Arabistan; however, the sovereignty has been Persian since 1954.[27] So the Iraqi soldier cannot go to the other beach –

Saddam: [*Inaudible*] Abu Hasan?

Abu Hasan: Yes, here we [*inaudible*] have the oil issue.

Saddam: If they harm the navigation, then let us move the Iraqi soldier over there.

———

Saddam: We have to stick their noses in mud so we can impose our political will over them. This cannot take place except militarily.

Abu Hasan: Afterward, the oil establishments will be within reach.

Saddam: Both of ours might burn. This is war. You cannot say during a war that I have a guarantee that my oil establishments will not burn. When our establishments are on fire, theirs will be on fire too. That is, one situation is met by another. This is known all over the world, not just by us. This matter is controlled by one entity only. If it were controlled by us, then we would not want a full-scale war. We do not want the destruction of oil, and we do not want raids on the cities. We want to bombard the military targets. We want to twist their hands until they accept the legal fact. What is stopping us from taking Qasr [*inaudible*] militarily at any time?[28]

[27] See *supra* note 14.
[28] See *supra* note 21.

Comrade Minister of Defense, what is stopping us from taking Qasr [inaudible] any time we want? What is stopping us from moving forward on all axes and surrounding their armies and imprisoning them? Or doing as we please with some areas [inaudible]? Inside the [inaudible] land [inaudible]. No one is saying there would be no resistance; no one is saying there would be no losses or dead. The result of our calculations is that we can reach into the heartland of Iran. We want to get to our international borders [inaudible]. They might brush against us [i.e., skirmish with us]. A plane will come and we will down it. This current stage is different than the previous stage. We will give them enough time to kick some sand off. However, once a plane takes off and attacks Baghdad, that is it. It will be over and done with. Things are different now. If they accept with some pressure to preserve the dignity [inaudible], then there is no problem. But if they try to bombard oil establishments, then matters will escalate. There would be no more sitting down and discussions. We would retaliate immediately. It would take a single telephone call and a decision would reach them fast . . . You are saying that we can get back our lands with some losses. We have to accept the bad eventualities. Historically, what could we say? If we can get our land back, but we do not do anything, then what could we say historically? We cannot accept this.

Abu Hasan: If you would – the other thing is regarding the Soviet Union. I am sure you are following the situation more than I, and you know the Soviet intentions regarding us. In my opinion, the Soviets are more lenient toward us than before. However, I do not think they will provide good support to Iraq.

Saddam: They have not said anything up to now.

Abu Hasan: Yes, this is it. The matters do not depend only on Soviet calculations. I mean it is not only the Soviet relations with both Iran and Iraq. There are other calculations that pertain to Syria and other groups that do not want Iraq to have this position or this role. And therefore, in my estimation, the Soviet Union will be tight regarding the supply of ammunition. This is if the situation escalates. If it is a few days of war, then we do not need them. However, the Soviet Union will not supply [us] for a long period of time. Please calculate this in the decision. This is a very precise matter. The other thing on my mind is that there is no authority in Iran now that can make a decision except for Khomeini. He is a stubborn man . . .

Saddam Presides Over an Optimistic Meeting with Iraqi Military Officers Early in the Conflict (30 October 1980)[29]

Saddam: I do not envisage that the war will end. It could stretch for a year. It is possible that it will stretch for six months, [inaudible] some countries are purchasing and contracting [weapons] but we are in a state of war. Preparedness items and weapons we need should be part of the naval plan, so that we can assess our needs and acquire them. As for the question of ending the war, of course, these matters – let us say we can postpone these items until we end the war. But we are expected to use all our available equipment and preparations, use the weapons at our disposal . . .

[29] *SH-SHTP-A-001-229, "Saddam and Military Officials Discussing the Iran-Iraq War and Iraqi Military Capabilities," 30 October 1980.

If we want a basic item in wartime [from a superpower], we are obliged to compromise. We are told, "We will give you this but in return we expect this political position." They do not say this directly; they implicitly relay the message in a manner that we understand. That is why our Air Force is in good shape, thank God, but we want it to be in good shape until the war ends.[30] I also say the same thing about our artillery. It is in a good shape now and we want it to be in a good shape after the war. We have told you as well about our Navy. Try to economize in it.

[handwritten: possible refutation of Saddam's belief. I'll be...]

Saddam: All experts in military and political affairs said that Iraq is betting on a blitzkrieg war, therefore, all these military results will be [*inaudible*] after one or two weeks, and consequently, it is 40 days and we are fighting now, and military results are tilting for the benefit of Iraq. Every time they cross Karun, we control Karun, every time they attack Muhammarah [Korromshar], we control Muhammarah. We have made progress in many areas.[31]

[handwritten: to blitzkrieg war]

———

Saddam: God bless you. This is your country, and it deserves your sacrifices, and you work for the history of the nation in its entirety. This plan [*inaudible*] so that we rise, [*inaudible*] our victory will be an historical one, [a] victory that generations will be talking about a hundred years from now. You are playing a unique role. I cannot tell you in detail the importance of your role as I envision it, that is in terms of the Arab's dismal social situation. And your role will contribute to the development of the Arab nation and its civilization and human development.

[handwritten: ideology]

Saddam Prepares for the Arab League Summit as the Invasion Grinds to a Halt. He Discusses His International Alliances in Relation to the Faltering War Effort (3 October 1981)[32]

Saddam: For a long time I have noticed that our psychological outlook has been affecting us adversely in a manner that has influenced our clear judgment and changed our central convictions and judgments from day to day, from month to month, and from one year to the next. This has resulted in being confronted with surprises in our comrades' thinking that we are incapable of managing our foreign policy correctly...

I want to ask about the Iraqi people that die now in the hundreds and the thousands. They are sacrificed daily under the fire of the guns and cling to the land. What are they holding on to? It is the strength of our party's principles. It is the accomplishments of our party. It is the achievements of the revolution that our party is leading. They

---

[30] Saddam was concerned about the Iranian air force – particularly its American-made F-14s – and often chose to reserve his own air force rather than risk losing planes to superior Iranian equipment and pilots.

[31] In the first month of the invasion of Iran, Iraqi forces crossed the Karun River and captured the disputed border city of Muhammarah (also known as Korromshar). This victory, on 26 October 1980, marked the early high point in Saddam's war effort.

[32] SH-SHTP-A-000-711, "Saddam and Iraqi Officials Discussing the King Fahad Initiative, Relations with the USSR, and Perceptions of other Middle Eastern Countries," 3 October 1981.

are now fighting all of the big powers and all of the middle countries and the rest of the world.

The Soviet Union cannot comprehend the role the Iraqi Army has undertaken. I am confident that the Soviet Union could not hold on to the same area of ground we are holding. They have people from the Afghans on their side, but no one is with us from our neighbors.[33] Is it not because of our faith in our revolution? Then why don't we direct this radiation to the outside and influence people just like it influenced our people and made them patient and steadfast for one year and two months? Why can't we shift this radiance to Saudi Arabia so that we change the ten to five hundred cells and make the Saudi crown sway from within the country of Saudi Arabia?[34] I know very well and everything about this point, and I always hold on to the Iraqi people. The Iraqi people, for instance – America is against us and so is the Soviet Union – let us not talk about how strong our relations are and who supplies us with weapons... and what is expected from the Americans, Soviets and most Arab regimes, from many of the large and medium-sized countries. What were they able to do? Our people and party are the source of our power. It was those 14 years that made the tattered Iraqi who was backward and riddled with tribal divisions as well as the regional, local, sectarian, religious, nationalistic divisions, made him stand up as one nation and achieve this great miracle.[35] That was because of the leadership of the Ba'ath socialist Arab party. We could say to the Saudis, look, do not be afraid, for you could very well be like those Ba'athists...

When we have reached a point of adversity with the Soviets, in fact there is nothing that should lead us to this situation as long as we make things clear in our relationship with them and be forthright in an exchange of interests. It should involve exchange and improvement of relations. As long as we realize this has taken place, it is on its way to being cleared, and relations should return to normal and friendly...

However, siding with the Soviets is indicative of weakness. At the same time, opposing the Soviets is completely unacceptable. We don't want to be seen as dependent or regarded as being in the Soviet camp. And if we do not improve our relations with them it is as if we have severed our agreement with them. Never mind, there is room for improving the atmosphere and returning to good relations like they were before...

Na'im: There is no need at all to be enemies of the Soviets. This is not basically our job. Also, we cannot support and be bound to the Soviet's strategy in a way that was pointed out by the secretary-general...[36] The Soviets have their own information about the war and they have their intelligence about the region and they have their

[33] Saddam is referring to the Soviet war in Afghanistan (1978–1988) and the aid the Soviets received from the People's Democratic Party of Afghanistan. Although Saddam likely expected Iranian Arabs to provide a similar fifth column that would aid his invasion of Iran, most Arabs in Khuzestan remained cautiously distant from his war effort.

[34] This appears to be a reference to Iraq-sponsored Ba'ath Party cells in Saudi Arabia.

[35] Saddam is referring to the fourteen years of Ba'ath Party rule, beginning with a bloodless coup on 16 July 1968.

[36] This is apparently a reference to the secretary-general of the Arab League. Elsewhere in the tape, participants discuss the Arab League's secretary-general, but never secretaries-general of other organizations.

own strategy regarding the Palestinian issue and the Fahd Plan.[37] I have given this example to show the possibility of coming in to conflict with them. Therefore, I feel that quiet diplomacy, and not to even mention their cutting the supply of arms to us, and supplying the Persian enemy with arms is also not to be mentioned. As I said, their supplying Iran with weapons serves to improve their relations with Iran. What concerns us now is that we must have a relationship with them and move ahead quietly without indicating that we are forcibly prevented from breaking up this relationship.

PEOPLE USED TO DREAM ABOUT SUCH WONDERFUL IDEAS: SEVEN YEARS IN THE TRENCHES (1981–1987)

As Iranian troops settled down on Iraqi territory, the fighting fell into a dreary pattern. Drastically outnumbered but better equipped Iraqi forces built an elaborate defensive line and struggled to cope with massive offensives by poorly trained Iranian militia. Saddam focused on finding a technological edge, first by purchasing thousands of tanks and artillery pieces, and later by employing chemical weapons and surface-to-surface missiles. In the following conversations, he discusses arming his forces, punishing Iran, and attacking disloyal elements within Iraq.

Saddam Pontificates on Defensive Fortifications, the International Arms Market, and Learning from Past Military Experience (circa late 1983 or early 1984)[38]

Male 1: I think it [the defensive channel, i.e., moat] is a good obstacle in the face of the enemy and can be counted on to do the job of stopping and slowing down the enemy attack, but its capabilities are limited since it can do so well [only] against a certain number of enemy troops. If the enemy increases the number of troops of the attacking force, then it will not hold up . . . Certainly this channel's defensive line does not change or affect the strategies or formations of the main defensive line on the ground. The main defensive line is still intact. I mean, the man-made obstacles are still as-is, and the land mines are still as-is and of course will be there to stay.[39]

Saddam: Those main defenses could overlap with the areas that constitute the channel line defense.

---

[37] In 1981, Saudi Crown Prince Fahd proposed giving the Palestinians a state and implicitly recognizing Israel as part of a plan to end the Arab-Israeli conflict.

[38] SH-SHTP-A-000-627, "Saddam and Senior Military Officials Discussing Arms Imports and Other Issues Related to the Iran-Iraq War," undated (circa late 1983–early 1984).

[39] Saddam's army relied heavily on multiple lines of defense including channels, trenches, dug-in tanks, minefields, and deliberate flooding and draining systems to defend against the far larger Iranian army. Here, the Iraqis are discussing a channel (i.e., moat) along the border with Iran. We learn earlier in the recording that the channel was seven meters wide and at least two meters deep. For an overview of Iraq's use of moats and other fortifications in the Iran-Iraq War, see Hiro, *The Longest War*, 180–81; Kenneth M. Pollack, *Arabs at War: Military Effectiveness, 1948–1991* (Lincoln: University of Nebraska Press, 2002), 203–6.

Male 1: In the adjacent areas that could overlap, we have designed the in-between areas into triangular sections. I mean, I can cross from two points by breaking the barrier and crossing to them, so that in case we lose something, God forbid, it would be for hundreds of meters. I will bring the water until the end of the eighth sector. Additionally, they will not know or be able to detect the source of water we will use to flood the channel. We are in the process of –

Saddam: Did our comrades make it back? How about the civilians?

Male 1: No, Sir, they have not made it back yet. By the way, the train the enemy uses to supply and transport his equipment was hit the night before. As the train exploded, it went into many pieces. We have been trying to hit this train for a long time. We have used air reconnaissance on two different occasions to locate it as a target, but we missed both times. However, this time we caught the train while it was in the station and the hit was direct – they did a good job zeroing in on the target. Sir, the letters and messages are in and will be ready in a little while.

Saddam: To be stationary, fixed, and stay still and the same; in general I do not like fixed and stationary things. To be the same in your style is deadly in a long war. Using the same style of warfare will teach your enemy your style of fighting. Moreover the stationary target is an easy target to be hit; this is a basic rule.

––––––––

Saddam: I already tried to get those weapons from our Soviet friends with no luck. I also tried to find them in the open market, but I could not find any. I said there is nobody else left to go to but China, so I asked the Chinese ambassador to meet with me. In the meeting, the chief of staff of the armed forces was present. If my memory serves me right I think it was three months before the war started –

Male 1: Yes Sir, it was around that time.

Saddam: After five months, maybe. Sometimes things can take a strange turn of events. Even though we tried to plan and use the best available option at that time, nevertheless, the market did not cooperate. The market was not big and in return, we were limited in our choices and options. That and its implications on this area of the world, on our surroundings, and on the Arab world. I told the Chinese ambassador, "Don't we have the right to be independent, don't we have the right to grow up as you grew up?"

We have our friendly relations with the different countries of the world. Some of those countries are Western countries and others are communist countries. However, we must say that the great countries, because of their strategic competition, always favor partition because each part does not guarantee at one time what each part guarantees when they are united. Their inability to guarantee it [prevents] them all from battling against [the Great Powers], and afterward they split on the one hand here and on the other hand there. Frequently, the uncertainty over which direction the proposed new country will take tempts the superpowers to fight over it, each hoping it will fall under his sphere of its influence. As each camp tries to pull the proposed new country under its influence, the new country is pulled apart and the concept of unity usually dies in the process.

––––––––

Saddam: Furthermore we concluded through our strategic considerations that in our dealings with the Soviet Union, we need to allow a long period for it, to offer it and delay it, because they discovered their calculations about Iran were mistaken. I said to them, "You will discover that your calculations are wrong and you will come back to our side."

———

Saddam: The principal weapons in a long war are the tank and the cannon. Since we have destroyed their air force, now more than ever, the principal weapons are the cannon and the tank.

Male 1: Yes, they are to the highest degree the principal weapons.

Saddam: I put more emphasis on those two weapons. I tried to get as many cannons and tanks of the best quality that were available. Since we do not have many options, we did not have much room to pick and choose. Actually, we have purchased an excellent brand of artillery.[40] In addition, this artillery is superior to the artillery that the enemy possesses. However, the tanks we have will do for now.

Male 1: Sir, you have not come up short; you have done well. In contrast, the Iranians have bought worthless iron as tanks. After the war is over, they will be obsolete. Those tanks they are using now in their army, we turned them down in the sixties. In the sixties, the Iraqi army refused offers to purchase the M-47 and the M-48.[41] Meanwhile, the Iranians are desperate; they have agreed to purchase the T-62 and have agreed to deal with Americans according to the Americans' price tag.[42] Basically, the [T-]55 and [T-]54 Chinese tanks are still better than the Russian tanks.[43] Since we have used the Russian tank very well in the Iraqi Army and we are familiar with it, we will do well with its modified Chinese counterpart. Sir, the different brands we have acquired will complement the T-55. As the T-55 relatively considered –

Saddam: But the tank is a killer tank. I have seen in it in action.

Male 1: I have seen it too, Sir, but the Chinese equipment that was added to it changed [it] to a tank that is different from the original 55 we are used to.

Saddam: The changes made the tank an enhanced one.

Male 1: Nowadays, the 55 is considered to be in the same class as the enhanced M-60, not any less; as we know nowadays, everything is being modified and enhanced.[44]

[40] Saddam may be referring to the GHN-45, an Austrian-made towed 155mm howitzer that was designed by artillery genius Gerald Bull. Iraq acquired some 100 GHN-45s between 1981 and 1983. Bull went on to design the famous "Super-Gun" found in Iraq after Desert Storm. William Lowther, *Arms and the Man*, (New York: Ivy Books, 1991), 166–67.

[41] The M-47 and M-48 were American tanks primarily used in the 1950s and 1960s. Iran had 470 of them in 1980.

[42] The T-62 was a Soviet tank from the 1960s. This last reference is unclear. It may refer to the belief, expressed by Saddam and his advisers on various occasions, that the United States sold military equipment to Iran. For instance, see section "Saddam and the Revolutionary Command Council analyze American involvement in the Iran-Contra Affair," in Chapter 1.

[43] He is referring to the Type 59, a Chinese version of the Soviet 1950s-era T-54/55 tank.

[44] Iran purchased some 460 M60A1 tanks from the United States before 1977.

It is imperative to use all that you have. Others own the advanced 72 and still went and put the 34 back in use.[45]

Saddam: The Chinese expressed their regret that they could not fulfill the initial number of tanks we requested. Eventually we agreed to purchase only 2,700 tanks from them, one-thousand of which will be coming to us though the black market. Two-hundred fifty-five tanks from Poland. The Polish are in desperate financial condition, so we used the Palestinians to purchase those tanks for us. We have bought 100 tanks from Romania. The Egyptians offered us tanks, but after going back and forth so many times I think we finally ended up buying [only] 50 tanks from them. They offered initially 200 tanks but we chose 50, they were old and expensive. We bought each one for 4,500 dollars.

Male 1: Many were making fun of the army shortly before the war started, saying it had only as few as 2,400 or 2,500 tanks. In addition to that –

Male 2: Nobody can purchase as much as you did. The way that Your Excellency acquired the artillery was a bold move.

———

Saddam: The whole world knows Iraq will be in war for three or four years, and the arms that will be used in this war will be evaluated after the war ends. There will be a new evaluation of weapons. We will be careful not to give anyone feedback on how these weapons perform during war. Since those arms we are using can be used against us and the suppliers can raise the prices of the better weapons, it would be disadvantageous for us to tell anybody how those arms performed. When we are asked how the arms we used in war have performed, we should say that we fought very well with them as Iraqis. However, we should not tell them that this weapon or that one is a good weapon, only that our soldiers used them very well. There is nothing for us to gain by promoting those new weapons. As the reputation of these new weapons is raising their demand, it will increase their price. This will encourage the Chinese to come up with a new weapon superior to the one we have, which would have its own political implications.

———

Saddam: In all circumstances, no country can evaluate its arms or make any improvements to them unless it uses them in the war zone. Countries learn how to fight by fighting in actual wars. This is a fact I realized after I fought a war. Previously I was not aware of this fact. But war, in spite of its consequences, it brings with it many scientific advances.

Male 2: A great economical and scientific boom took place in Japan, Germany, and Italy after the war.

---

[45] At the time, the Soviet T-72 tank was top of the line; the T-34 was a Soviet tank from World War II. Saddam's advisers are grossly misinforming him about the relative quality of these armored vehicles, and he does not appear to know the difference. For U.S. officials' concerns about T-72 capabilities, see Michael Wines and Richard E. Meyer, "North Apparently Tried a Swap for Soviet Tank: Deal with Iran for Captured Vehicle Failed," *Washington Post*, 22 January 1987; Richard Halloran, "U.S. Has Acquired Soviet T-72 Tanks," *New York Times*, 13 March 1987.

Saddam: All scientific advances in the world occurred during and after World War I and World War II. The Western countries use war to their advantage. Conflict erodes the expertise that had been created for the war. It is expected to be devoured. [But] because we have a continuous regime, meaning a continuous heritage under the principles of the party, the experience they obtained is not eroded. Conflict also gives them the experience of a long war.

Male 1: Nevertheless, there is a possibility that the people leading the country now would not be there after the war is over.

Saddam: Yes, that is true. Look at the Iranians; they brought their retired generals back in service.[46] Those generals have been away too long from war games, warfare, and everything that has to do with war. Furthermore, those generals will resist any ideas that have to do with war as a humanitarian reaction [in order] to cover their feeling of weakness. Since this can be an asset for us, I took it into consideration for our war planning. In contrast to the Iranian army, our army, our generals and officers in the army, they have been involved in war and warfare since the war started and are a part of it. They would be enraged if somebody tried to think negatively about the war, because they have spent their blood, effort, and their lives on this war. They also see that they are making history and glory for their country as they fight this war.

The Jews are disturbed and in rage. Their rage is growing as the war goes on and they see no sign that our regime will be toppled and our officers and leaders will be replaced. The Jews are willing to pay any price to replace our regime. They see that the experience we are gaining from the war, as it goes on, will be intact after the war. And that will be a threat to them later. Recently, the Jews are using their influence on the Americans to put more pressure on us. The Americans are becoming more restrictive with us. However, our country and nation should consider everything and look at the big picture. Historical events like war may have a good outcome in the long run even though present consequences are harmful. As history would tell us now, if we did end the war earlier and did not fight to reach this stage, many of our judgments would have been based erroneously.

Male 1: We would have suffered severe harm.

———

Saddam: We were late using the infantry for five months during the war and before that, of course, we had to blame someone, because what we have in the north right now – the north now supports the other war cities with capabilities equal to one-sixth of the entire army there. Therefore, five-sixths of the force should have returned for training.

Male 1: Sir, frankly, training on the armored vehicles has been going very well within our army. Since we had to use the armored units primarily in our fighting, our soldiers have learned how to use those armored vehicles very well. However,

---

[46] The Iranian Revolution led to retirements, desertions, and purges of many of the military's top personnel. Political infighting during the next two years, and Khomeini's crackdown on foreign-trained commanders, dramatically weakened the Iranian military on the eve of war with Iraq.

armor cannot provide the only help in this war. Fortunately we have been fighting primarily with armor for more than two years with no problems.

Saddam: Now we can clearly see things. For a year, we have been depending primarily on the tank in our front defensive lines. All the defensive stands we have achieved, we achieved by using the tanks. For a whole year the tank was fighting by itself in the battlefield. In the second year of the war, we introduced some infantry units to the battlefield.

Saddam Expresses Concern That His Subordinates Fear Passing Negative News up the Chain of Command (7 July 1984)[47]

Saddam: Sometimes I believe when you task some people at a lower level to look into an investigative matter, they would want to come up with something and tell the air force commander they found such a thing, especially if Saddam Hussein assigned this task they have to come up with something.

Male 1: Yes, Sir, this is clear.

Saddam: And because of that I am not referring the intentions to anything in particular towards you, or Salem, or Hasan, but I take it back to the right interpretation, that they want to say to Saddam Hussein, "that we have investigated and we have found this particular reason."[48]

Male 1: Sir, but when –

Saddam: [*Interrupting.*] This could possibly happen. So, our role in the educational aspect is to warn, saying that what makes Saddam Hussein satisfied is the truth, even the painful one. You know sometimes even the brothers at the General Command, they used to keep things away from me. Like such-and-such things, we had such formation at that location, they used to keep things hush-hush and I would not hear about it from the brothers until noon. So what about Saddam Hussein! The front must report even the painful issues to me, so that I can evaluate the situation and know the factors that caused this pain and make a right decision! If you twist the painful truth you will get it to me with factors that are different than the major ones.[49]

Male 1: Sir.

Saddam: This is one of the reasons that made me check the front and the soldier. It never happened in the history of wars in the world to check on the soldiers sitting

---

47 SH-SHTP-A-001-035, "Saddam and Air Force Officers Discussing the Movements and Performance of the Iraqi Air Force during the Iran-Iraq War," 7 July 1984.

48 Identities of "Salem" and "Hasan" are unknown.

49 This was not the only occasion when Saddam recognized or was told that his subordinates might be too frightened to deliver bad news up the chain of command. According to a variety of sources, Saddam's tendency to punish the messenger led his aides to present him with more favorable news than circumstances warranted. SH-SHTP-A-000-614, "Saddam and Officials Discussing the Uprising in the South," undated (circa March 1991); Charles Duelfer, *Hide and Seek: The Search for Truth in Iraq* (New York: Public Affairs, 2009), 400; Woods et al., *Iraqi Perspectives Project: A View Of* (2006), 7–10.

with the commanders after each battle.[50] The soldier is sitting with his leader the division commander and the corps commander. I do not mean that I do not have confidence in the leaders, no, but I wanted [information] to come out of the soldier's mouth in a way that it can help me conclude something that the corps commander cannot conclude. When he says, "when they came to us at night and told us, 'they are coming to you'" – the word *coming* to us – I do not want it to be sent to me in a book by the corps commander stating that they told the soldiers they are coming and they went, I mean from what is behind it. I can evaluate the psychological status in that position. They told them that they are coming, fine but are they sitting there to come to you or not? Originally they exist there because they are coming to you. Why did they do that? It has to be a special psychological status. I mean that it is necessary to [*inaudible*] so the educational aspect in saying that what is required is the truth and not the opposite.

Male 1: Sir, if –

Saddam: So, when you say that "we found out that it is the right usage and that we have to search for another factor," I mean that this will satisfy me better than you saying that the usage is not right and let the other factor drop another aircraft of ours.

Male 1: Sir, when we report to Your Excellency incorrect words, the thing you find most unacceptable is for one to report something to you other than the truth.

Saddam: [*Inaudible*] especially [*inaudible*].

Male 1: And that is what really hurts! If it were said, for example, that an air force commander made a decision and this is the decision and the mistakes were blah, blah, blah. Yes, I am making the decision and I am taking responsibility, and none of them should be responsible at all, I am making the decision and I am going to make the decision in the future and I will be responsible for it. But when he says that there were technicians, operations, and intelligence, and we determined that this is not a good thing to do, while the air force commander says he insists on this type of work, the report would be false, Sir!

Male 2: Everyone was happy, Sir, and everyone said we took the initiative in this regard.

Male 1: I want everybody to come and say in front of his group, that "I am the air force commander" [*interruption – inaudible*].

Saddam: Even the leaders are not us, I don't know who he is but maybe a foreigner. He says –and I hope this does not apply to us – a part of this case, he says the defeat is what we are going to get and everyone attributes victory to him.

Male 1: They are all with it.

---

[50] During the Iran-Iraq War, Saddam frequently visited army units and asked pointed questions in pursuit of unfiltered, firsthand information. By the time of Operation Iraqi Freedom, he no longer made such visits. In the months preceding the 2003 invasion, Iraqi commanders' exaggerations of their ability to fight the United States led Saddam to overestimate Iraq's military prospects. *Duelfer Report*, vol. 1, "Strategic Intent," 5, 11.

Saddam: Everybody wants to refer to himself. So this is a human, international, psychological issue. The important thing is how do we reduce its impact. We had this, thank God, on the leader's level. Now if there is negligence from somebody he should say "I did it" if he did that, but if somebody else did it, he should say that "somebody else did it, but I think that the factors were such and such." So it was not an intentional, but an interpretative mistake. So they became [*inaudible*]. But things were not like this at the beginning.

At the beginning of the war, I needed to tell them to make the decision and I will take the responsibility for it, make the decision without presenting it to me, and I am responsible. This does not exist. Without me looking at it, but I will say I take the responsibility, you are not responsible until it formed. At the beginning, there was the general commander, of course, because he knew [*inaudible*]. All this will go away with the time.

Male 1: It will, God willing, Sir. [*Inaudible.*]

Male 3: But Sir, we want to clarify the truth since the situation that developed as a result of the feeling, Sir, [*inaudible*] I mean, it is the feeling that we have, I mean even the staff generals in the operations who work with us [*inaudible*] and we call the air cell. Even those, Your Honor, actually the deadly thing did not die, but the possibility of making a decision or multiple decisions will die, so as a result of this feeling we started to acknowledge [*inaudible*] the battle there.

Saddam and Military Advisers Debate the Appropriate Use of Chemical Weapons (6 March 1987)[51]

Muhammad: I recommend that our attacks be severe and intensified as well as continuous, as much as possible, even if there are international interventions or mediation, we should not cease such severe blows. We should not stop and give them another chance, this is my first observation.

The second observation that I have, Your Excellency – I see the Iranian arrogance and their continuous fighting and continuous blood letting. I suggest, and I say, the situation is ripe for us to choose an important city in Iran and attack it with a chemical strike, in a very violent and severe manner. I mean an intensified blow that would wipe it from existence, and whatever happens, happens.

I mean, I mean, what I see, I believe with regard to the chemical attack, we have the capability, even though I am not sure in that regard, because I do not have precise information. But what I see is that the conditions are ripe, that we choose an important city, not just any insignificant city, but we should choose an important city and we should mount a heavy chemical strike, equivalent to an atomic weapon, and totally annihilate that city, so that no living soul will survive.

---

[51] *SH-SHTP-A-000-896, "Saddam and Other Government Officials Discussing the State of the Country during the Iran-Iraq War and the Use of Chemical Weapons," 6 March 1987; SH-SHTP-A-001-023, "Saddam and Ba'ath Party Members Discussing the Iran-Iraq War," 6 March 1987. For a partial transcript of the second recording, see section "Saddam and Ba'ath Party members discuss using chemical weapons against Iranian soldiers and civilians," in Chapter 6.

And I believe that by taking such a measure we will really teach them a lesson, will make them behave, and will deter, and we are in front of God, in front of the whole world, in front of the world, in front of humanity. We have fulfilled our message, and they should bear responsibility for their reckless actions. It is true, the world and the United Nations and others [have been trying to resolve this conflict] but we have been fighting for seven years, and this United Nations and the world, what have they done? They are not intervening, just as Your Excellency has stated. We are confident that if the burden is not lifted by its people, it is impossible. All they do is denunciations, but seven years is more than enough. In my opinion, I believe that we should be very vicious and use all weapons and we should choose a city, an important city in Iran and attack it with chemical weapons. Thank you, Your Excellency.

Saddam: Comrade Muhammad, the matters that you have alerted me to in the document, frankly, they are in mind. But the reason that I have not assigned any of the comrades to provide you with a briefing is because the State General Secretariat does not attend. So from now on, the State General Secretariat must attend the meetings held at the State Command level. This matter was always introduced in meetings. Who has introduced it before? Oh yes, Na'im introduced it at one point, and a number of comrades at the Command level have introduced it. They presented this matter and it also crossed our mind that this is one type of weapon that we might need to use in our attacks. So I have asked the comrades in our previous meeting and told them, "This matter has always been proposed, so let us review it seriously." So we have reviewed this matter, I mean, this review has resulted in our belief that this weapon is strategic, and we should not rule out its use.[52]

However, we should be very careful in timing its use. The comrade's evaluation for the time of the review, and we are still in it, I mean our current situation is the same as at the time we did the assessment, and that the current situation does not call to use this weapon now. So if we are forced to use it, I mean if the enemy has bothered us, for example, at al-Basra, and the enemy's threat is more serious than the current state of affairs, then we at that time, we should not rule out using this weapon. So we have reached this conclusion, that we have the weapon within our hands, and now there is no urgency in using it, so we should not use it. Because this is the final evaluation, of course, more than half of the Command was enthusiastic to use this weapon, so at the end, and through discussion, this is what we have reached. Yes, Comrade Mizban.

Mizban: Your Excellency, what I would want to add to this announcement is the number of our martyrs who have lost their lives in our cities, so we prove that the number of martyrs is a result of the Iranians' blatant disrespect for the [cease-fire] announcement.[53]

---

[52] This conversation marks a shift from the use of chemical weapons as a tactical and defensive tool against Iranian offensives to a strategic weapon used against civilian centers.

[53] This probably refers to Iraq's acceptance of UN Security Council Resolution 588 (October 1986). This call for negotiations was rejected outright by Iran and used by Iraq in an attempt to regain the moral high ground following UN condemnations of its chemical weapon use earlier in the year.

Mizban: Oh yes, they attacked, but there has been no activity during the last few days. Perhaps they have attacked the Hartha area today. This is what I believe, our announcements are very clear, Your Excellency. We have the number of our martyrs. With regard to attacking cities, I mean, I believe, what I want to add, we have to concentrate on large cities, Your Excellency. I mean, for example, many people hear various locations, but when they hear [that we have attacked] Qum, it is like lifting the Iraqi morale.[54] They will hail the action, and say, "Let's hang them," and say, "We [have] started to defeat them."

Saddam: Of course, Qum is equivalent to their capital.

Mizban: Yes, I mean Qum is central and the main center.

Saddam: ...So, what we are adopting now is that we are concentrating on a severe blow, but we should leave for another city, so that the enemy will be forced to distribute its defenses in all Iranian cities. This way the enemy will be weaker in every Iranian city. I mean this is the policy that we are adopting, and at the same time, all the Iranians are feeling that every one of their cities is being targeted at any moment. And in any case, our capabilities are the same. They are the capabilities of Iraq. They are not unlimited. I mean, we have a limited number of aircraft. We cannot attack every city with five hundred aircraft, I mean, we do not have that capability. But this is the available capability that we have right now. Dr. Sa'dun, and after that Comrade Latif.

Sa'dun: ...I suggest that we resume bombing economic targets, and in a severe, vicious, intensive manner. If they bombed our cities, so now, and as Comrade Mizban has stated there are no bombings on Basra now. So if they bomb, we should respond proportionally. And if we want to increase our bombing, I mean, the increase should be concentrated on economic targets.

———

Sa'dun: I mean that our reaction, the increase in our reaction should not be targeted toward cities, but toward economic targets. On the subject matter of economic targets, Your Excellency, I have an opinion. Attacking cities, Your Excellency Mr. President, kills people. Also, the economic targets kill people also, I mean bombing them.

[Bombing] economic targets achieves two goals. It destroys an economic facility that generates revenue and kills the type of people that are more beneficial to us – in our opinion –compared to the people we are killing in the cities. Because these people whom we kill in economic targets are specialty labor, working in [oil] fields, factories, electric power plants. Those staff are better targets for us, in terms of military effort, than the people living in neighborhoods whom we are dropping bombs on in the night, and killing people of that type.

So, I believe that bombing the economic targets has dual purposes. It destroys an economic facility and at the same time, it achieves the horrific psychological effect and all that the bombing of cities achieves, will also be achieved by bombing the economic

---

[54] Qum, a city of more than 650,000 residents, is located ninety miles south of Tehran. It is the most important Shi'a center in Iran and the base of many key ayatollahs.

targets. Of course I have the same opinion, that within the economic targets we have to concentrate on oil targets. And within the oil targets, we have concentrate on the oil targets that are designated for exports. The ones that export overseas. I mean, the petroleum targets that have a relation with the interior, and even the refineries, they are not of the first priority. The first priority must be to facilities associated with exporting oil. With regard to chemical weapons, Your Excellency, I of course believe this weapon must be used against [military] sectors, and not against cities.

Saddam: We have discussed the chemical matter in our previous meeting and we have made a decision in that regard.

Sa'dun: Yes, I mean, because the comrades have spoken about it, so if we want to use this weapon, I believe that it should be used against [military] sectors. Also, I want to state an observation, Your Excellency, with regard to the current situation. Why, if we have a wide capability, are we saving our capabilities for a critical time? Let us be preemptive at this time if we have the ability. Now, if we have the ability to attack Iranian concentrations [of troops] and the Iranian military forces, the ones mounting their attacks on us, why don't we attack the enemy, if we can, before it comes to us? Why don't we do this, if we have the capability to launch a strike now, and at the late hour that Your Excellency has talked about, I mean, it is not necessary to wait for a disruption in our forces or a strategic breach, but if we can abort the enemy's attacks now, do the remaining Iranian forces –

Saddam: [*Interrupting.*] The discrepancy in our position is that we are attacking cities. It is not a matter of attacking sectors, we are attacking sectors all the time, whether they are deploying, whether they are attacking, and everywhere.

Sa'dun: Fine, Your Excellency, the situation requires that we affect the Iranian military effort to our favor, the one mounting the attacks on our sectors. Now, it is true that the time is not critical, it is true that our front is intact and strong, but for them, they believe that this is the final hour of the game, so why aren't we preemptive and, the weapon –

Saddam: [*Interrupting.*] Oh, Doctor, do you think we are not using our weapons?

Sa'dun: No, I am talking specifically about the chemical.

Saddam: And the chemical, the chemical is working, it has not stopped.

Sa'dun: We are not objecting to that, Your Excellency, Mr. President.

Saddam: We have not stopped using the chemical weapon, with regard to military formations, we have not decided to stop it; this is continuous.

Sa'dun: Your Excellency, Mr. President, I am under the impression that no, we are not using it.

Saddam: No, no, we are using it.

Sa'dun: I mean, that was the impression that I was under, so, I [do not agree to attack] the cities with chemical weapon at least during the current time, and all the efforts should be directed against Iranian military sectors because they are the most important ones.

Saddam: Okay. [*Laughing.*]

THIS BLOODY ROUTE HAS TAKEN EIGHT LONG YEARS:
ABORTING AL-QADISIYYAH (1987–1988)

The tapes from the final year of the war contain conversations in which
Saddam and his advisers discuss Iraqi military achievements and how to
bring the fighting to a close on favorable terms. Saddam and his subordinates
discuss why an Iraqi commander allegedly betrayed Iraq in the battle for the
Al-Fao Peninsula. Saddam revels in Iraq's capture of Al-Fao and explains
the different psychological effects this will have on the Iraqi and Persian
publics. In the final tape, he reminisces about his military genius during
the war.

Saddam and His Advisers Assess UN Security Council Resolution 598, Which Called for an Immediate Cease-fire between Iran and Iraq (19 July 1987)[55]

Tahir[56]: Mr. President, I want to give my opinion regarding the language of the articles. And as Comrade Tariq indicated, we hope it would be introduced by unanimous
agreement.

———

Tahir: If there were an observation I would like to point out, Mr. President, an
important issue is that the first half of the first clause is subject to interpretation
despite my belief, and my saying, that Iran was the reason for the aggression; it does
not imply who did [aggress].

Saddam: Absolutely.

Tahir: This is my personal opinion. I interpret it to my advantage, and this is –

Saddam: This is very clear. This is the aggression; we are convinced that Iran caused
the conflict.

Tahir: Indeed, Iran. And for us, to be fair, we can provide the documents.

Saddam: To succeed in that we need to present adequate documentation.

Tahir: Adequate, indeed. The second part of the first clause very clearly states who
contributed to prolonging the war. It is as clear as the sun. I mean, it is unacceptable.
I mean the other side can't exploit it to his advantage. However, the only clause,
if included, was the possibility of condemning the infiltration into Iraqi territories
especially during the previous aggression . . .

---

[55] SH-SHTP-A-000-733, "Saddam and His Advisers Discussing UN Security Council Resolutions and a Possible Ceasefire during the Iran-Iraq War," 19 July 1987. The UN Security
Council unanimously passed Resolution 598 on 20 July 1987. Iraq accepted this cease-fire –
on the condition that Iran would also – but Iran rejected it, because it lacked a clause blaming Iraq for starting the war. One year later, on 20 July 1988, Iran accepted Resolution
598, forming the basis for the end of the war on 20 August 1988.

[56] Possibly Tahir Jalil Habbush al-Tikriti, who later became director of the Mukhabarat (Iraqi
Intelligence Service).

However, once we state that we would approach this agreement from this perspective, where its clauses are correlated, there will probably be general decisions regarding the issue of complete withdrawal. Though [the resolution] could be phrased "without any delay," it would still lack the mechanism and accuracy. Yet, it was very clear. I mean there is a possibility that it would be passed immediately; I would say in two hours and without any delay.

––––––

Tahir: It was obvious that Comrade Tariq Aziz was aware of the general mood inside the United Nations. The nations sought in one form or another to pass an even-handed resolution that would be more pleasing to Iran than to Iraq. I mean, this resolution was initially passed to underscore the idea of dealing with the United Nations and United Nations resolutions. I mean, I personally lean toward the concept of no Iranian army currently present on Iraqi territories. Indeed, if there were no one present, then the resolution would be to our advantage. Thus, the Iranians would probably not welcome it because it would work for our benefit. However, now with the presence of the Iranian army, because the resolution will be issued on Monday, we could take advantage of another day, if there were a ten-hour time difference between us and the United States instead of, if the resolution passed when they were behind us ten, eight or nine hours in the United States during the Security Council meeting. We would probably have a full day. In this period we could execute a decisive action with our troops present.

––––––

Tahir: I truly believe that this resolution with its current language will be accepted immediately by the Iranians because most of its clauses are to their advantage. For example, when it comes to ceasing all aerial military activities, we have a complete supremacy in the air; by contrast, they do not hold any advantage in the air. In addition to other issues like stopping the navigation in the Gulf, it also worked to their advantage and not our benefit. I mean, accordingly, the articles are going to be a great benefit to them once the ceasefire takes place and the war ends.

––––––

Male 1: The resolution will not be balanced. We cannot say that only we were being attacked. I mean there are some issues; we attacked them with chemical weapons and they attacked us with chemical weapons.[57] There is no problem there. No problem, but there are some pending issues.

––––––

[57] Iran appears to have used chemical weapons rather sparingly, if at all. The GMID correspondence and memos claim that Iran used phosgene in 1987, mustard gas on several occasions in 1987, and CS (tear gas) in 1983, 1986, and 1987. The GMID concluded that Iran's production of chemical weapons remained limited, that Iran feared storing chemical munitions near its launchers for fear of Iraqi air power and artillery, and that Iran lacked effective, locally produced chemical weapons. Moreover, one report noted, Iran was desperately trying to produce chemical agents and would use them in response to Iraqi use or in the event that Iran was unable to deter Iraqi attacks. For instances of possible Iranian chemical weapon use against Iraq, see memos issued by the GMID discussing Iran's chemical weapons capability, 14 September 1988, in SH-GMID-D-000-898, "General Military Intelligence Directorate (GMID) Memos Discussing Iranian Chemical Weapons Capability,"

Saddam: Comrade Izzat.

_____

Izzat: Mr. President, I was actually taken by surprise by the resolution...Iran refuses over and over and still attacks. Iran follows the motto, "our motto is to defend our country, regain our land and its sovereignty." Iran declares that by all means it wants to occupy Iraq, overthrow the Iraqi regime, to change the system and the way of governance. Obviously, they are anxious to gain the land, people, Iraqi principles and even the mere presence of Iraq. This international community that has been listening and monitoring for six years, then issues such a balanced resolution via the Security Council where it tried to accommodate the Iranian concerns without any regard to the Iraqi position and its concerns. Even, the denunciation comes, even the denunciation was mentioned in general terms in the first article. With respect to occupying the land, we occupied land and they occupied land. They also added that we targeted ships, launched chemical attacks, and targeted civilian planes. They claim that we targeted them as if they never targeted us.

Saddam: And striking civilian areas.

Izzat: Excuse me, and bombing civilian areas, bombing the civilian population. They added six clauses in total, claiming we did that. Except only one clause we both have in common, which was the first clause [that] pertains to the occupation of land, in common. We occupy and they occupy. However, the next four clauses address us only. As if we did that, as if we targeted ships, launched attacks with chemical weapons, and bombed civilian populated areas.

_____

Izzat: We will also argue about the chemical attacks. We say that you [the Iranians] also attacked us. We can bring eyewitnesses and evidence to them. From our side, we can bring the wounded and the dead from the chemical attacks. I mean the matter should be kept between us only.

_____

Saddam: Comrades, it is clear that the whole world [i.e., all countries], including the superpowers, place their interests and responsibilities ahead of the world's interests during military conflicts. Under any circumstances, any type of resolution will affect other parties. For a long time, this issue was clearly reflected by the Iranians. Their decision in not dealing with international and regional agencies made these international and regional agencies lean toward appeasing them at our expense.

I did warn Comrade Tariq of this issue; I told him to be political but also clear and sharp in pursuing it. Otherwise, one day they will pass resolutions against our interests; notably these regional agencies and mediations that led us in the last Islamic conference to say, "Enough with these Islamic matters." As a result, they will deal with – there has to be a resolution after all this pressure. With regard to the issues between us and Iran, the Security Council will not bring us the peace. It is clear that this resolution will not bring us peace because it is not a resolution, recommendation

October 1987–September 1988; Anthony H. Cordesman, *Iraq and the War of Sanctions: Conventional Threats and Weapons of Mass Destruction* (Westport, CT: Praeger, 1999), 529–30.

or declaration. There is no obligation, no compulsion. Iran will seek peace only when it feels that the war is against its interests, especially if the [war] is hurting it more than the peace. And if they believed that the peace will be worse than war, then they will keep fighting. As long as they believe that the war helps them make gains, they will continue to fight.

Iran exploited the factor of surprise against us in terms of direction and timing. They came through the worst terrain, which was favorable to them and not to us. I mean, God willing, after we crush them in this battle, I would think that the battle militarily is almost concluded because it was accomplished through two important factors. Iran lost the third factor that comprised political and economic aspects, in addition to the psychological factor that comes immediately after their military defeat. Iran did not imagine surprising Iraq in the timing and location. Both – at the same location that was – the same location and the day where both were unfavorable to Iraq, Tarbiza, airport, salt marshes, Al-Fao, and others. They mobilized so far. Until yesterday, 14 divisions were crushed. If Iran will not realize its military demise, it will continue to fight. Do we all agree on that?

Multiple male voices: Yes. Yes.

Saddam: Well, that means that they do not want peace. However, one aspect we need to maintain, well, it is not only one aspect but three aspects that we need to maintain: The psychological status of the people, our people. We need not to be taken by surprise. The Security Council or the international organizations should not fool us by statements to deprive us from any rights; just like when the Arabs were fooled by the American arguments or the British arguments. Arab territories were lost due to American justifications. We will not allow ourselves to lose anything. And why should we lose anything anyway. Why? If they want war, then we will continue to fight. If they want peace, then we would resort to peace. But we will not allow anyone to deprive us of any rights. We will not succumb to unlawful negotiations. Is it not? We will not accept a solution that harms our people.

My last and third point is that we need to behave wisely at a level that accommodates the international community. Sometimes it's helpful to show firmness in the international arena. Thus, I believe we should not answer. We should not answer anyone. Indeed. Why should we not respond? We do not respond even if the resolution is passed. We can respond by saying the leadership is still formulating a response. The leadership is contemplating the issue. We do not respond until the Security Council realizes that it needs to take us seriously. And only then are they going to have to consider the Iraqi position and implement a mechanism that is in our interest.

[The Security Council] has to realize that there is that thing. That Iraq has limits and boundaries it cannot cross. Regarding this one, we, God willing, I mean, common sense suggests that if it was determined 99 percent then Iran will turn it down and 1 percent is left. Is it the same for us? Would we agree for 99 percent and turn down 1 percent? Shame on us. I mean shame on us, if this is the case, they will definitely steal from us. They will steal from us. Iran will then strengthen its foothold on the occupied Iraqi territories. It will decide at its leisure when to withdraw. Regarding our prisoners, they will decide when to exchange prisoners – whether it would be full or partial. If we swayed to this attitude by avoiding targeting civilian targets and infrastructure, avoiding using chemical weapons, and avoiding intercepting marine and air navigation, then we start to whine and panic. I am sure you know what I mean by whine? It is just like a little kid who is running after an adult . . . Try not to hold high hopes for any Arab country. Any one of them starts to panic once it comes under attack. We, for how long, we have agreed and yet we still fight the Iranians. We have abided by every resolution. But now it is unacceptable because Iran attacked us. Once we succeed in expelling the Iranians then we would compromise. This will strengthen us to keep struggling and fighting. We will not give them the chance to say that Iraq objected.

Saddam and His Advisers Rejoice after the Iraqi Army Reclaimed the Al-Fao Peninsula in Southern Iraq (18 April 1988)[58]

Tariq: Your Excellency, during the eight-year war with the Iranian enemy, there was a very deep feeling of self-confidence among the leadership and among the people, among the Iraqi Armed Forces. There is confidence in Iraq, the Iraqi people, [the] Iraqi Army and in the Leader. This confidence exists and it is, I mean, this confidence was the reason for our endurance, because the challenge we faced was indeed a large challenge. I mean, from all different perspectives, the challenge varied in terms of a moral and a physical one. There was the challenge of confronting the large mass of Iranian troops, the challenge of confronting the insanity and backwardness as well as Iranian fundamentalism.

———

Tariq: We had confidence that even if the war stretched, I mean, even if it stretched 20 years, we would be victorious. But we needed a clear and bright proof. I mean we needed bright proof that would express the Iraqi and Saddamiyyah sentiments, which is the return to the spirit of intrepidness which Comrade Izzat has described.[59] The spirit of the Iraqi Conqueror, whom, I mean, will give the enemy a lesson; not by elongating and stretching only, and patience as well as planning and firmness, but also by jolting and decisiveness of the sword.

———

Tariq: Your leadership decided to strike the head of the enemy, to give him a lesson, and tell him to stop. This is enough, Iraq is not a – it is true that Iraq is a peaceful nation. That is correct. Iraq wants good neighborly relations, this is correct. Iraq wants development, this is correct. Iraqis want to live and be happy, this is correct. But the Iraqis are not a humiliated people. The Iraqis, if need be, after a long [period of] patience, will strike the head of the enemy. We needed that, and thank God, today we have achieved that. Because one more time, we have made the Iranians feel that Iraq represents patience, planning and cool-headedness, diplomacy, astuteness,

---

[58] SH-SHTP-A-000-857, "Saddam and Iraqi Officials Discussing the Liberation of Al-Fao and Its Broader Implications," 18 April 1988.

[59] The Iraqi media coined the term *Saddamiyyah* (Saddamism), which embodied Saddam's unique leadership attributes and the deep love between the dictator and his people. Ofra Bengio, "Iraq," in *Middle East Contemporary Survey*, vol. 16, ed. Ami Ayalon (CD-ROM; Tel Aviv: Dayan Center for Middle Eastern and African Studies, Shiloah Institute, Tel Aviv University, 453, accessed 29 January 2009 at www.dayan.org/people/mecs_pdf/IQ1602. pdf.

good neighborly relations, etc. But Iraq is also a sword and a steel hammer. Iraq is decisive when it takes its decision . . .

Saddam: Thank you, I was blessed. Do you mean in terms of politics?

Tariq: No, no, not the politics, not the political aspect.

Saddam: The balance.

Tariq: No, today, today, the announcement that Your Excellency has written today, is an announcement of the wise Commander who has a long vision as well as the victorious. You are victorious today, but you have written an announcement. I mean one that manifests in Arab dreams. I mean it represents Arab dreams. When I hear it, this is the feeling that I get. The way I interpret this is that the Arabs have achieved victory, this is how Muhammad, this is how Umar was victorious.[60] This is how so and so became victorious, the Arabs became victorious . . .

And the equation is in front of the enemy. There is a very important vision for this war, Your Excellency, that is within the current situation the region is going through. The region now has gone through an atrocious conflict period of 20 years or more, to include the war between us and Iran.

There is an international trend toward settlements; this direction toward settlements is considered one of the most dangerous phases in the history of nations and peoples. It is possible that we [will] achieve peace, but the question here is under what circumstances, under what conditions, and under what type of psychological perimeter?

There is a difference between your achievement of peace when you are one, just as the saying goes, kneeling down, and between one who achieves peace when he is, I mean, his situation, he regards himself in front of the world as one who achieved the desired goal. This type of peace, especially in an area that has not been totally developed, and with sneaky [wicked or mean] people, I mean with sneaky enemies, who are the Jews and the Persians, they are mean, meaner than wars that took place.

In Europe between the Germans, the French, the Russians and others, all of them, unfortunately, were full of sectarian and ethnic faults through thousands of years. If peace is not founded on strong foundations, [it] will not be achieved, and even if it is achieved it will be very fragile, fragile. The Iranians will come sooner or later, as much as they want to prolong [the conflict]. Perhaps one year, six months, two years. This war, and if we maintain our spirit of victory will bring in the Iranians acquiescing to the fair and clean peace. I mean the clean peace that will remove all the illusions from the Iranian racism and the state of Khomeini backwardness.

And I am confident that this war will indirectly balance the scale. I mean it will indirectly balance the scale with regard to the Palestinian cause. Despite Iraq's military achievement over the past eight years, the war experience we gained, our armament capability and the great successes that we achieved in the military and missile industry, [the] Al-Fao battle has instituted an equation between us and Israel, and between the Arabs and the oppressed. These Jihadist people in Palestine, who are mounting Jihad against Israeli arrogance, want to eradicate from the minds of the Jews this

---

[60] Caliph Umar bin al-Khattab oversaw the Arab victory over the Persians at the Battle of Qadisiyyah.

idea that occupation of land is possible.[61] I mean that it is not possible for the land to remain occupied. And the occupier has to be expelled or has to withdraw. Do you follow me? This Al-Fao victory will help eradicate such an idea from the Jews' mind, and make them understand that the Arabs are capable of going through bold and assaulting battles to uproot the wicked enemy from the land it occupied and reinforced, no matter how long it takes, and to expel them from it.

So, now, frankly, I feel great optimism that reinforces our confidence. I mean, undoubtedly, there is no one day when our confidence was shaken, but the confidence now is reinforced with stable optimism, with a clear vision about the future of the conflict between us and Iran and the future of conflict between the Arab nation and its enemies. We, Your Excellency, you know how much we love you. And you are our leader. And we have chosen you, I mean, as our leader. I mean from our heart. I mean, through our struggled march, we do not cajole you or flatter you, but frankly, frankly, your leadership was a great guarantee to Iraq. And it has a great meaning for the Arab Nation. And your leadership was behind this victory, because we know how much you suffered to achieve this victory.

Frankly, I do not know all the details; our comrades, the military leadership knows. But we watch you and we see how much hard work you do, how much you suffer, how much you think, how frequently you stay up late, how much you plan. You have followed through the minutest details, and indeed, from the technical point of view, this battle enters history. All of its elements, whether personal or objective, the detailed elements as well as the general, they were all blessed and successful. And God bless you.

———

Saddam: Frankly, I was happy about the victory yesterday, not today. I mean, when the [battle] performance started to take shape, the one that I hoped for, I realized that victory was within reach. Victory is a state within me, I felt it, but I wanted the performance to be a grand one that suits the Iraqis, and the Iraqi Army. I mean, I wanted the performance to be so grand, not only to achieve our objective and regain Al-Fao, to liberate it, but I wanted the performance to make us reach the grand political, intellectual, and psychological euphoric state that we wanted to relay to our enemy, which is the core of choices, as to why Al-Fao and not any other objective, not Halabja. I mean, why this location, and not that one? And why now and for example after six months, when I saw that outstanding performance, I became happy yesterday...

I mean sometimes results may not make us happy, even if they are very excellent and make everyone else happy, if there are other factors we see that would truly make us happy. We could lose one city, two cities, three, four or five. I have spoken with the General Command and told them, I regard Halabja as an Iraqi city and regard it very dearly, and every single atom of dust is dear, but I get upset. I am upset because the manner in which we lost Halabja was totally outside the context. If this was a passing event, a state of semi-weakness, then there is no problem...[62]

---

[61] Tariq is referring to the Palestinian uprising in the West Bank. This 1987–1991 uprising came to be known as the First Intifada.

[62] Saddam is referring to the town of Halabja in Iraqi Kurdistan. In early 1988, Kurdish rebels supported by Iranian forces captured Halabja in a campaign against the regional capital

The whole world has started to talk about the new standards of the Iraqi Army. Countries are watching how the Iraqis are fighting. There are countries currently engaged in conflicts placing the spotlights on the Iraqi Army . . .

We need this stage. We need to deliver a message, an overt one that could not be camouflaged. We need to send it to the world, which has the keys in its hand, and jingles them. And a message to Iran, the Iranian people, and Iranian leadership, and to the Arabs, also to awaken them one more time. In a long war like this, it is inevitable that we lose a village here, a city there. This is not important. This is important, but what is more important [for the enemy] is defeating the will of the Iraqi people. The question of whether the Iraqi will is capable of enduring and regaining the lost village and the lost city.

And for what purpose? For the purpose of convincing everybody that the Iranians are not the only ones who want results. The message is that there is no other alternative except peace, and Iraqis, unlike all the other experiences that they been through, will not accept a limping peace. Iraqis have no ambitions in Iranian territories, and our victory will not harm them, to the extent that it will incubate Iranian ambition.

And at the same time, all the technical aspects will not make the Iraqis retreat from their own thinking, which is the pursuit of a right. And we have no ambition, and Iraqis will not tolerate anyone with ambition. Therefore, I was so keen that we appear in front of ourselves and in front of the world and in front of history because all these events are being recorded for me. I regard history as more important than anything else. I mean, we have to appear just as we are. Just as Comrade Tariq has expressed, we are a balanced people in all circumstances. I mean when we lose a city, we should remain balanced, and when we liberate a city, we should also remain balanced. We should not be imbalanced, and this is important. I mean, our enemy and friends know that very well.

———

Saddam: How many blows will they have to endure? How many blows to their head and face? I mean, it is difficult to estimate. I mean it is possible to say that the Iranians will be inflicted with heavy casualties and there is no doubt that this will constitute an awakening. By awakening, I mean the current events will demoralize the current regime in Iran. A new breed will emerge in Iran even among the Iranian leadership, one that is opposing the current regime. This new voice will say, "Oh brothers, every time we try to reorganize and reshuffle the cards, you are not using them reasonably. You will continue to be beaten by those who are superior [in battle]. Don't you think you would have been better off had you accepted the Security Council resolution? Before the Al-Fao events, don't you think you would have been better off?"

Rather than losing Al-Fao, I mean, additionally, what concerns me is the message to the minds of people who will form a trend that there is no hope. Not in terms of playing games. First, we are not the type of people to be fooled. And not in terms of gambling on the military approach, this is the Al-Fao, they have captured it since 1986. Until just now, the Iraqi has reclaimed it, what do they have? . . .

Sulaymaniyah. Iraqi forces retook the town using chemical weapons, killing thousands of Kurdish civilians in the process. This conversation, recorded one month after the fighting in Halabja, shows that Saddam is still upset about the temporary loss of the town.

I mean, the Iranian has taken Al-Fao after sacrificing 120,000 casualties, and non-stop fighting between the Iraqis and the Iranians that lasted a month-and-a-half. However, to extract Al-Fao from them, it took us only 35 hours. That is, after they roamed the territories in an unimaginable manner. We have confronted three channels, isn't that so Abu Ali?

Abu Ali:[63]   Yes, Your Excellency.

Saddam: Three channels, the width of each channel is 70 meters. And a depth, oh, you ought to go there and see it for yourselves, just to see it. Just to be able to see how difficult this mission was, to see the capability of this [Iraqi] soldier . . .

I want to bring the American, the Jew, the Zionist and whatever; Al-Fao was at the hands of the Iranians and they [the Americans] know all the details in that regard. I mean, there is no military secret here.[64] Bring them in, they are welcome. Everybody is welcome to come in and see Al-Fao for themselves. And we have to present it with all its photos and complete reports on the Iraqi television, and in front of the Iraqi people, and let them comment on it. Our role is to explain to them. For example, this barrier was like that, this sector was like that, all of these, [*inaudible*]. We should show them the channel, its length, its depth, its width, I mean like that.

There is no message more important than Al-Fao. And there is no event that will heal their wound [like Al-Fao] . . . Our people needed that, our people are confident of our endurance. However, not all our people were confident that we would be able to reclaim the land we lost, especially a territory like Al-Fao, a phenomenon like Al-Fao. I have told you about my wife. After the Al-Fao events, her mood has changed, as a human being. I mean her mood has changed. I mean, imagine the extent of the influence Al-Fao will have. I listen to her. I mean, she is exuberant following Al-Fao. I mean, this is proof of the Al-Fao effect. She is a citizen, she is not in the leadership, she is not a politician, except within a small margin. So this is really a story to be told, just as was told to them yesterday.

Saddam Discusses an Officer Who Panicked during the Battle on the Al-Fao Peninsula (18 April 1988)[65]

Male 1: We felt, in fact, that the 7th Corps was somehow slow and therefore, we went and visited the 7th Corps headquarters at –

Male 2: In the morning.

---

[63] The identity of Abu Ali ("the father of Ali") is unclear.

[64] Rick Francona, a Defense Intelligence Agency officer who toured the Al-Fao battlefield shortly after the fighting, concluded otherwise. He wrote that his observations provided the United States with valuable insights regarding Iraq's defensive doctrine, Iraqi morale, and the quality of Iran's armed forces. He also acquired evidence of Iraqi chemical weapon use and was able to inspect a captured artillery piece of North Korean origin, which at that time was the world's longest-range field gun. See Rick Francona, *Ally to Adversary: An Eyewitness Account of Iraq's Fall from Grace* (Annapolis. MD: Naval Institute Press, 1999), 23–27.

[65] *SH-SHTP-A-001-231, "Iraqi Officials Discussing the Iran-Iraq War and the Al-Fao Battle," 18 April 1988.

Male 1: In the morning, and in fact, we did not go to the corps headquarters, but to the 6th Division instead – the mobile headquarters of the 6th Division. The position that Nawfal talked about – the Infantry Brigades that were there – the position was difficult.[66] And the formation commander, who did not mention the numbers of these brigades, was talking to a staff officer at the 6th Division headquarters, but in a way that meant we were going to attack with the determination we wanted, although we launched an offensive. Yes, there might have been some difficulties! I recall the staff officer there, whose name I do not know but the comrades know, used to receive information from the brigade saying it was over for the brigade. This is an expression used by the army where some operations –

Saddam: It is not an appropriate expression.

Male 1: This expression is wrong. I said to him, "What do you mean by 'We are done?' You are attacking, the Republican Guard was achieving a tremendous success at that time, and the armored formation of the 6th Division was moving normally, which leaves only a confined area while you are launching an offensive; so how can you say you were done and it is over for the brigade?" Even when the Major General asked about the brigade, they said it was over with! I am not sure about the officer there, but I felt he was not such a –

Male 2: He was an officer, staff lieutenant colonel, but now he is with those low level people; the opposition.

Saddam: Huh, you see with the traitors!

Male 2: He had such an inappropriate demeanor.

Saddam: Could you believe that? What goes around comes around! As soon as he talked about the brigade, he was done, himself.

Male 1: He acted as if he were in the act!

Saddam: I mean he did not want to exert extra effort, otherwise how do you explain the fact that both his brigade and the other one were done? But when he realized we liberated Al-Fao, it was like an opportunity for him to betray. So, since then he betrayed. I mean this is the known result.

Male 2: Sir, if you allow me, please; in fact, both General Nizar and General Hussein said this was the al-Dawa Party based on his way of using the equipment for talking.[67] And I remember either General Nizar or General Hussein took the equipment from him and dismissed him. Now, he is supposedly the chief of staff of the Army with Adnan Muhammad al-Nuri[68] and [*inaudible*; *laughter*].

Saddam: We thank God. Thank God. Once one comrade said to me, "If those people were any good, they would never shave their beard and mustache." I replied, "People

---

[66] Possibly Staff Major Nawfal Isma'il Khudayyir, who helped Saddam retake the Al-Fao Peninsula as commander of Iraq's 3rd Armored Division.

[67] General Nizar is probably Nizar al-Khazraji, Army chief of staff. General Hussein is probably Brigadier General Hussein Kamil, head of the Ministry of Industry and Military Industrialization. For more on Hussein Kamil, see Chapter 8. The al-Dawa Party was a Shi'a party in Iraq that received backing from Tehran and supported Iran during Saddam's Qadisiyyah.

[68] Adnan Muhammad al-Nuri, a military leader of the Iraqi National Accord (INA). The INA was an Iraqi opposition group.

who are well groomed do not mix with such individuals. Be grateful to God for that because those individuals are low class." [*Laughter.*] Whoever imitates Americans, Zionists, and Europeans is low class; they shave their beard and mustaches, and what about that betrayer officer's family? They have been destroyed as well. Now do you see? Such is life.

Male 1: I really did not know the officer, but he kept repeating it was also over with the other brigade; he truly aggravated me where we wanted to attack with all that effort we had, but it was hard to believe that two brigades were finished in five minutes within the early hours of the morning! We launched an offensive and the armored formations of the 6th Brigade were moving in such an acceptable way despite the problems they encountered on the road and so forth. I was truly disturbed by him and we requested to –

Saddam: So, they made this traitor the chief of staff of the army, right? [*Laughter.*]

Saddam Recounts Some of His Favorite War Stories during the Last Month of the Conflict (between 18 July–20 August 1988)[69]

Saddam: The end was better than we had hoped. In the difficult battles that happened in Qadisiyyah, which are all of them, every battle must have difficulties and problems. Any way you put it, there will be human sacrifices and difficult situations that are hard to understand unless one knows the full details at some point. But the hardest situation I went through was when we feared that the Iranians would accept our ceasefire suggestion after Muhammarah.[70] We agreed to the decision of the Security Council on the 28th. Do you remember it? On September 28, 1980, we agreed to the Security Council decision after six days of a large scale deterrence battle. One of the clauses of the resolution was that both parties would agree to an immediate ceasefire and to hold negotiations.[71] We agreed, but the Iranians refused. My fear was that the Iranians would agree to this decision after the Muhammarah battle. Because that would put us in an awkward position in front of our people and the world since we had previously agreed. If we refused, we would not have had reasons for refusing that would convince our people and the world. Even though I know the Iranian mentality, I know they are very devious and are treacherous and play games, when they get a chance to mess things up, they will. So I was hoping that there would not be a ceasefire. For me, that was the image with which I thought our army should end this war. The appropriate image for our army is to end the war with the Iranians broken and our army strengthened by God, able to end this war with each of us retaining our permanent [*inaudible*] rights. What was accomplished was the highest of my hopes for this bloody route that has taken eight long years. And we have truly been able to be the victors in our dependence on God.

---

[69] SH-SHTP-V-000-589, "Saddam and Military Officials Discussing the Iran-Iraq War and the Al-Qadisiyyah Battle," undated (circa July–August 1988).

[70] In the first month of the invasion of Iran, Iraqi forces crossed the Karun River and captured the disputed border city of Muhammarah (also known as Korromshar).

[71] Saddam is referring to UN Security Council Resolution 479.

Abu Zaid:[72] Sir, I would like to point out at this point Your Excellency's directives during the liberation battles, which I personally received directly, to bomb as many vital enemy targets before the end of the battle, that you were expecting.

Also, another target that was postponed [*inaudible*]. Your Excellency, your directives were to prepare for the plan, practice and train [*inaudible*]. That target was very vital to Iraq, the atomic reactor.[73] It was very big and it was being prepared to be used at the end, meaning the war. They had started building it and a German team of experts had arrived and started on – one of the reactors was almost 85 percent ready and the other was almost 50 percent. So, you issued your order to hit the reactor, which, indeed, we destroyed completely.[74] The head of the German experts was killed as well as the head of the Iranian team who was at the reactor. We started bombing during the liberation battles, Sir, Bandar Khomeini oil compound, which was almost the largest compound ready for operation.

We also bombed the largest oil tanker in the world, which was at al-Aharat Island in the Arabian Sea. It was the British one of 550,000 tons and the Spanish one of 350,000 tons. This was the largest sea battle we had in terms of bombing tankers, where one of the commanders said that we should launch a battle like Pearl Harbor and surprise the Iranian oil tankers. So, it really was a decisive battle or hit against the enemy, and which also was the farthest point the Iraqi Air Force reached, while refueling twice. Previously we had carried out recon with a MiG-25, which landed in Abu Dhabi and was almost shot down. But we were able to get clear aerial photographs and were able to find out where they stored their oil, so that was the fatal stroke.

Saddam: So we didn't land by prearrangement?

Abu Zaid: Yes.

Saddam: Our comrades told us that they needed photographs, and if this plane flies, it would need to be refueled somewhere. I told them to go, shoot the photographs, and land in any of the nearby countries, and tell them that you were flying but that you ran out of fuel, and if they could possibly refuel you, and you would be on your way. Isn't that right?

Abu Zaid: Yes, Sir, yes, Sir, they were upset with the whole operation.

Saddam: They were upset where they said we caused them all kind of problems and asked why we were there? We told them we got lost and came to you. Please refuel us and we will be on our way. So they gave us fuel and let the plane go. But we accomplished –

Abu Zaid: Yes, we accomplished. And we continued destroying the refineries and fields during the liberation battles, especially the stations pumping to Tehran, Esfahan, and Shiraz refineries. We also destroyed main bridges, and communication stations, all of those. To the last day of operations we were savagely bombing the

---

[72] The nom de guerre Abu Zaid appears to refer to Hamid Shaaban, commander of Iraq's Air Force.

[73] He is referring to the Iranian nuclear reactors at Bushehr.

[74] Iraq attacked the Iranian Bushehr facility on several occasions beginning in early 1984. The strike referred to here was conducted on 17 November 1987.

enemy's vital targets. And victory was ours under your leadership, Sir. May God keep and preserve you to us. Thank you, Sir.

Saddam: Thank you, Abu Zaid. Let me tell you one of our war stories. It has some interesting points in terms of camouflage and "sound deception," as they call it, even though it is a little complicated. We were preparing to bomb Kharj Island. The Iranian F-14s were assigned to defend it as an alternative to anti-aircraft weapons. In that area the F-14s were known to be excellent in long-distance release in addition to their range and maneuverability. So we were watching out for it, because we knew it could hurt [our] airplanes in either the trip over or the trip back, which would ultimately hurt our pilots in either case. So I asked a certain party to go tell the political party in a certain Gulf nation that some Iranians are going to strike with F-14 aircrafts and land in your territories. Therefore, please once they are downed in your country – we agreed with them to seek asylum in Iraq – if you can facilitate the mission of those who will come to Iraq, and even if you send the aircrafts back this would be fine with us. This message was sent. I know these people and I knew that they would immediately tell the Iranians, which was my intent, as that would keep the airplanes from flying.

Male: They prevented them from flying.

Saddam: So, the planes stopped flying and this was our purpose. So they did actually go and inform the Iranians, and all the F-14 planes were grounded. [*Laughter*.]

Male: No one knew.

Saddam: So, our airplanes went and bombed their targets and came back without any interference on the Iranian part.

———

FIVE

The Mother of All Battles

This war [the Gulf War] . . . was beneficial for us.

– Saddam Hussein, 1993 [1]

The invasion of Kuwait in August 1990 by Saddam Hussein's Iraq set in motion a long conflict with the United States that ended only in 2003. For Saddam and the Ba'ath regime he had controlled since 1979, the invasion would ultimately prove fatal. It ensured that most Iraqis, who were still cherishing the recent end of the Iran-Iraq War, would suffer the deprivations of yet another long war, one that would lead to a third: a destructive civil war. As Saddam later noted, "Being at peace is not easy." [2]

Likewise, the victors of the 1991 campaign to eject Saddam from Kuwait did not achieve lasting political stability. The war, and subsequent UN sanctions and enforcement measures, increasingly placed the United States on the wrong side of Arab public opinion. This in turn further energized an already-growing global terrorist movement that today plagues much of the world. But in 1990 and 1991, all of that lay in the unknowable future.

This chapter captures glimpses of Saddam and his senior ministers as they made military and diplomatic decisions before, during, and just after the Gulf War. The first section presents a sample of discussions concerning the invasion of Kuwait and its immediate aftermath. The second provides insight into the regime's reaction to the coalition's air campaign that began in January 1991. Conversations in the third section provide the regime's initial reactions to the coalition's ground assault and the frantic diplomatic efforts that ensued. In the fourth, the Iraqis discuss the Shi'a and Kurdish uprisings. In the final section, Saddam and his inner circle discuss what they learned from "the Mother of All Battles."

---

[1] SH-SHTP-A-000-834, "Saddam and Political Officials Discussing How to Deal with the Republican Guard and Other Issues following the 1991 Gulf War," undated (circa 1992).
[2] Piro interview of Saddam, Session Number 3, 10 February 2004, 3.

Saddam Hussein meeting with air force officials in the air force and air defense headquarters on the morning of 17 January 1991. All identities in this photograph are unknown except for Saddam. (*Source*: SH-MISC-D-000-903, "Book on the Events of the 1991 Gulf War," 25 September 1992)

The historical context of the events leading up to the invasion of Kuwait is as complex as any in the Middle East. The seeds of the invasion predate Saddam. Factors such as the perceived "arrogance" of the small wealthy Gulf states in their relations to the larger Arab world, historical grievances dating to the Ottoman Empire and British establishment of Iraq and Kuwait, and the perpetual vulnerability of a small state lacking any meaningful natural or man-made defenses on the border of a militarized state were always a part of the equation. In the end, however, Saddam acted largely out of economic and political desperation.

In 1988, Iraq emerged from a devastating and fruitless eight-year war against Iran in desperate economic straits. It owed more than $80 billion to its Arab neighbors. Some, like Saudi Arabia, forgave or restructured Iraq's debt; Kuwait chose to use it as a bargaining chip to settle several long-standing issues. The late 1980s also saw a rise in oil production, particularly among the Gulf states, which caused oil prices to fall, allegedly costing Iraq $1 billion for every dollar's drop in the price of a barrel of oil. Saddam saw these events as a form of economic warfare. Unlike the Gulf states, Iraq could not increase its oil output because its infrastructure was in poor condition. Providing a metanarrative to all of these contemporary reasons, Saddam believed, as he had when he invaded Iran, that war and the righting of historic wrongs was the path to consolidating political and economic power in the Arab world. In Saddam's worldview, the pan-Arab dream could be achieved only when the center pole of the tent was firmly planted in Baghdad and protected by a heroic leader in the mold of Saladin, Nebuchadnezzar, or Hammurabi.

In this context, Saddam dispatched Iraqi forces to Kuwait's northern and western borders in late July 1990. The world watched the buildup of Iraqi forces with intense interest and some degree of unease. Diplomats shuttled from capital to capital to prevent what many believed – despite the sometimes heated rhetoric – was a war with a low probability of occurring.[3] Nevertheless, on 2 August, after Egypt and Saudi Arabia failed in a last-minute attempt to negotiate a settlement, Saddam ordered a Republican Guard force of six divisions to execute a lighting invasion of Kuwait.[4]

The national defenses of tiny Kuwait and the government of the ruling Sheikh Jaber al Ahmad al Sabah collapsed in a matter of hours. Iraqi forces quickly took control of Kuwait City and its infrastructure. For Iraq, the invasion was a triumphant military moment. After the long, bloody slugfest with Iran, the rapid and nearly bloodless seizure of Kuwait infused the regime with a shot of confidence.

The international community reacted swiftly. Spurred by the United States, the UN Security Council (UNSC) issued what would become a long line of resolutions condemning Iraq and its actions, and warning of the potential for international action. Iraq inflamed the situation further when it began to use its Western "guests" as hostages in a poorly orchestrated attempt to intimidate the coalition forming against it. At the same time, Iraq found it could no longer rely on its old allies in Moscow to counterbalance Washington's influence in the Security Council.

During the fall of 1990, Saddam's forces consolidated their positions and began establishing defenses along the Kuwait–Saudi Arabia border. Iraq prepared extensive earthworks and naval mines, and rigged Kuwait's oil infrastructure for demolition. In addition to preparing a defense of their newly acquired province, Iraqi forces conducted systematic, large-scale looting of Kuwait's state and private property. In the meantime, an American-led coalition of thirty-three nations poured land, sea, and air forces into the region. By the end of the year, a coalition ground force of 676,000 troops and 3,449 tanks faced an Iraqi military of 336,000 soldiers and an estimated 3,500 tanks.

---

[3] "Telephone Conversation with King Hussein of Jordan," 31 July 1990, Bush Library, National Security Council (NSC; Richard Haass Files), Working Files Iraq Pre-2/8/90 (4 of 6); Judith Miller, "Mideast Tensions; Egypt's President Calls for a Delay in Attacking Iraq," *New York Times*, 8 November 1990.

[4] Woods, *The Mother of All Battles*, 60–88.

Despite numerous last-minute attempts to resolve the standoff, Saddam rejected UNSC Resolution 678, which authorized member states to "use all necessary means" after 15 January to make Iraq restore Kuwait's sovereignty. Two days later, early on the morning of 17 January, coalition air and missile attacks swept over Iraq and began devastating its military and national infrastructure. Iraq's initial response was to hunker down in survivable positions, launch Scud missiles at military and civilian targets in Israel and Saudi Arabia, and fly the cream of its air force to Iran for safe keeping.

As the coalition's ground forces maneuvered to the west, beyond the far right flank of the Iraqi forces, Saddam shocked the world by launching a ground attack of his own on 29 January. In an initially successful but ultimately ill-fated multidivisional raid fifteen kilometers into Saudi Arabia, Iraq seized the nearly deserted town of al-Khafji and held it for a few days. By 1 February, however, the broken remnants of the attacking force slipped back into southern Kuwait, having accomplished little in the way of military objectives but having provided the regime (though not the military itself) with one of its few bright spots.

By the third week of February, Iraq's air force, navy, and much of its national command and control, as well as infrastructure, were devastated. Coalition air attacks on occupation forces in Kuwait had, after a month of both precision attacks and massive bombardment by B-52s, devastated morale and fatally weakened Iraq's position. As coalition air operations wore on, Iraq tried without success to use its relationship with the Soviet Union to arrange a face-saving cease-fire and preclude the threatened ground phase of the campaign.

The ground campaign began on 24 February with a maneuver that became known as the "left hook" far to the west of Iraq's primary defensive belts. Simultaneously, U.S. Marine and coalition forces assaulted directly into the teeth of Iraq's forces in Kuwait. The effect was nearly instantaneous. Iraqi forces disintegrated on contact. The combined maneuvers set the conditions for the U.S. Army's Seventh and Eighteenth Airborne Corps to drive into the exposed and increasingly chaotic rear of the Iraqi defense. The Iraqi retreat became a rout as Iraqi forces fled their newly acquired possessions helter-skelter. Coalition forces pushed quickly to recapture Kuwait City while the two corps swept through the Iraqi deserts to engage the trailing end of the Iraqi ground forces. After one hundred hours of ground operations, the coalition declared a unilateral cease-fire.

Despite the apparently obvious outcome of the war from the point of view of most Western observers, Saddam believed, and more important enforced, a view that Iraq won a political and military victory. At the political level, Saddam's hold on power beyond that of his nemesis, George H. W. Bush, was demonstrative proof of success. On a military level, "not losing" in the face of a thirty-three-nation coalition was the equivalent of a historic victory.[5]

RETURNING THE BRANCH TO THE TREE: REUNIFICATION AND PACIFICATION

In the run-up to the invasion, Saddam and his advisers tried to achieve tactical surprise while simultaneously placing the onus for the conflict on Kuwait. After the invasion, Saddam took steps to consolidate Iraqi control of Kuwait. He ordered Iraqi forces to construct defensive positions in Kuwait, augmented the Iraqi Army and Republican Guard, incorporated Kuwait as an integral part of Iraq, pressured foreign diplomats to leave the "province," and approved the use of brutal counterinsurgency methods. He even considered encouraging drug use among Kuwaiti youths. As diplomatic pressure on Iraq mounted in the fall of 1990, Saddam considered establishing a puppet regime and withdrawing from Kuwait, thereby extricating himself from his predicament while retaining control of the country.

Saddam and Members of the Ba'ath Party Discuss the Letter That Tariq Aziz Will Send to the Secretary of the Arab League Laying Out Iraq's Grievances toward Kuwait (shortly before 15 July 1990)[6]

Muhammad:[7] I am concerned that a number of Arab countries would unite and place their armies between us and Kuwait.

Saddam: So, what is the solution?

Muhammad: Our solution, I personally believe –

Tariq: Comrade Muhammad wants to take action before the memorandum.[8]

Muhammad: Yes.

Saddam: So you want to act before the memorandum, you want the element of surprise –

Muhammad: Yes.

---

[5] Kevin M. Woods and Mark E. Stout, "Saddam's Perceptions and Misperceptions: The Case of 'Desert Storm,'" *Journal of Strategic Studies* 33, no. 1 (February 2010), 12–13.

[6] SH-SHTP-A-000-894, "Saddam and Iraqi Officials Discussing the State of the Country and Sending a Diplomatic Letter to the League of Arab States," undated (circa 15 July 1990).

[7] This is most likely Muhammad Saeed al-Sahhaf, who became minister of foreign affairs in October 1990, or Muhammad Hamzah Al-Zubaydi, Regional Command member (1982–1991) and minister without portfolio.

[8] On 15 July, Aziz sent a memorandum to the secretary of the Arab League in which he laid out Iraq's grievances toward Kuwait. "Iraqi Letter to Arab League Threatening Kuwait," State 235637, 19 July 1990, FBIS; Caryle Murphy, "Iraq Accuses Kuwait of Plot to Steal Oil, Depress Prices," *Washington Post*, 19 July 1990.

Saddam: Fine. How are you going to use the element of surprise? What should we do to them?

Muhammad: Are you asking me?

Saddam: Yes.

Muhammad: I will examine my borders, take all my [oil] wells and tell them, "here!"

Male 1: The same havoc will be created –

Muhammad: No, once we do that, that will be the time to say, "Hey, here is what we have done, come on Arab countries, let us talk."

Saddam: Just now I understood Muhammad's goal; he wants to control the oil wells in depth in a surprise incursion instead of – In that case, there is no need to threaten them, even the Kuwaitis –

Male 1: Threatening is dangerous.

Muhammad: We directly [*inaudible.*]

Saddam: [*Laughing.*] Now the idea is clear, fine. Comrade Taha Ma'ruf, then Comrade Izzat and then Comrade Mizban.

Taha Ma'ruf: Your Excellency Mr. President, I think that we have a lot of debt internationally, regionally, and to the Arab countries, and we will be regarded as aggressors if we carry out such an action before we clarify it to the world. From what I heard on the news last week, there was a report that the next war within the Arab and Islamic World will be between Iraq and Kuwait. This news came from Reuters.

Saddam: One of the local Zionists.

Taha Ma'ruf: That was a week ago from Reuters.

Saddam: From Reuters or one of the locals?

Male 2: It's the same one, Your Excellency, that Zionist from Britain.

Taha Yasin Ramadan: [*Inaudible.*] The one that did it is Kuwaiti.

Taha Ma'ruf: Mr. President, it is important to involve the Arab League and the Arab countries in this case, because many Arab countries have asked for clarification [*inaudible*]. I recommend that we do not carry out this action before we give clarification and involve the Arab League. We have to reiterate that our debts have affected public expenditures; we have to provide clarification internationally.

––––––

Izzat: It [the memorandum] contains clarification to the Arab masses – first, to our kind Iraqi people who will confront this conspiracy, and it is these people who will endure the heaviest burden and serious and costly sacrifices. It also contains clarification to our Arab people. It is very important for the Arab people to understand that there is a conspiracy, a conspiracy led by Kuwait, and such conspiracy coincides with and complements the Zionist-led conspiracy to destroy Iraq. This memorandum has outlined these points accurately. So we want to inform our Arab people and our Iraqi people so that the world understands that the Iraqi leadership is aware of this Kuwaiti conspiracy, we are aware of this Zionist-Imperialist-Kuwaiti conspiracy against Iraq and against the Arab nations. After such clarification and explanation, Iraq will have a legitimate excuse to carry out its action, whether the action is that recommended by Comrade Muhammad or the one to approach the Arabs. I mean, Iraq will be excused and favorably looked upon for any actions it takes. Iraq will be excused for any actions it takes by the Arab nation, by the Arab regimes, by the whole world, and by the Arab masses. Not only excused; Iraq will be requested by the Arab masses and Iraqi masses to confront such a conspiracy with all means afforded to Iraq.

Also, it has what surprised me in the letter; it has flexibility, I mean we can also deduce from that letter that, I mean whoever reads it, whether he is Kuwaiti, Arab, Egyptian, Algerian, Saudi – he would see flexibility in it, in the sense that if the Arabs are upset about what Kuwait is doing, and if Kuwait and the Emirates are dissuaded from pursuing this policy, this problem would be over. This way they do not have to panic and bring Arab armies. This way we are not scaring them. The letter contains flexibility in that if we involve the Arab League and if they find a solution to the problem, then the problem will end. This letter states that if this impasse is resolved, then there is no problem between Kuwait and Iraq. Iraq is not bringing in a new problem with which to surprise the Arabs. This is an existing problem now, and Kuwait should take note of that because this is a conspiracy. So when the conspiracy stops, the problem is resolved. That is why I believe the letter is flexible. It aims that Iraq will act freely; this is juxtaposed to threats and the incursion because our relations and policies are clear.

Ali: Sir, we agreed in that meeting that this is our plan. The matter Comrade Muhammad proposed is to confirm what America has confirmed in this case – to make the Gulf [states] afraid of us before the war so that we will lose.[9] The other aspect, I mean the inclusive element in the letter, did not give any impression that we intend to swallow Kuwait.

Five Days after Invading Kuwait, the Revolutionary Command Council Votes on Unification with Kuwait and Whether to Demarcate Kuwait's Border with Saudi Arabia. Saddam Discusses the Need to Crush Kuwaiti Opposition (7 August 1990)[10]

Saddam: I need a solution to this problem. This is the situation in Kuwait now. I don't understand why you misinterpret it. I know the Kuwaiti society and I know what type of corruption and luxury this society lives in. We need to have a party

---

[9] Iraqi leaders complained on several occasions in 1989 and 1990 that the United States was trying to create an anti-Iraq coalition in the Gulf. See "Secretary's October 6 Meeting with Iraqi Foreign Minister Tariq Aziz," State 327801, 13 October 1989, accessed 3 April 2008 at http://foia.state.gov; "Wall Street Journal Interviews Saddam," FBIS-NES-90-128, 3 July 1990, JN0107095890, Baghdad INA (in Arabic), 1 July 1990, p. 25.

[10] *SH-SHTP-A-001-232, "Iraqi Officials Discussing the Occupation of Kuwait," 7 August 1990. For a recording in which Saddam's cabinet confirms the decision to incorporate Kuwait into Iraq and discusses various forms of unification, see SH-SHTP-A-000-632, "Saddam Meeting with Iraqi Ministers regarding the Advantages of Invading Kuwait," 4 August 1990.

to provide their youth with heroin; we should order a party to supply them with drugs.

Male 1: All Arabs did this, they all bring it [drugs] and they export it...

Saddam: Who do they think they are? They think they are better than any other Arab country and they look down at everybody else. They think that anyone who tries to get close to them and be friends with them is after their money. Comrade Ali?

Ali: Thank you, Sir. Everything has become clear regarding this issue. Neither the foreigners nor the Arabs before or now in Kuwait believed in integrated unity.

[Overlapping voices.]

Male 2: Yes, Sir, [inaudible] the Palestinian [inaudible].

Male 3: [Inaudible] would go to Kuwait, I mean would contribute –

Saddam: By God, he does not want to contribute; he wants to leave –

Male 3: [Inaudible.]

Saddam: ... We will wait for a period of time to take a breath. If we fail, we should immediately form a union. [Inaudible] whoever wants to leave let him leave; whoever dies let him die and whoever recovers let him recover. [Inaudible.] Dr. Sa'dun, this is the only solution.

Saddam: I am not surprised or touched, and even if I hear them [Iraqis who disagree with Saddam] screaming, it will not affect me.

Male 4: [Inaudible.]

Saddam: I defended the Iraqis when I invaded Kuwait. These are the [inaudible] Iraqis, but as far as these scraps taken from each army, about one quarter to a half of them are gypsies, I don't have much hope for them.

Male 4: I was talking based on [inaudible] 15 people. I mean all Kuwaitis are corrupt; their biggest crisis right now is moral perversion and so on. [Inaudible.] Each one has its own characteristic. We are not going to be able to control them. We just need to provide them with the main services.

Saddam: Could you, please, tell me what you have on the federal union?[11]

---

[11] The "federal union" refers to Iraq's relationship with Kuwait. In the first few days after the invasion the Iraqi media spoke of the need for a "provisional government" in Kuwait, which "may not exceed a few days or a few weeks" to establish. The Iraqis also announced a troop withdrawal from Kuwait. Although Saddam clearly aimed at a minimum to transform Iraq's neighbor into a client state, it is unclear exactly what type of relationship he foresaw and whether he originally planned to make it an Iraqi province. It is possible that he had planned to wait until international anger subsided before announcing an official annexation but came to believe that declaring an immediate union between the two was necessary to enervate the Kuwaiti insurgency, increase Iraqi morale, or deter foreign interventions. On 8 August 1990, the Revolutionary Command Council (RCC) announced Iraq's decision "to return the part and branch, Kuwait, to the whole and the root, Iraq, in a comprehensive,

Tariq: You mean the federal –

Saddam: Yeah.

Tariq: The army is one, the foreign policy is one, and of course, the government controls the economy and the country has a broad economy with a special department for the federal. Only the police – the public security, meaning the political security – only the local police, the municipalities, the education, the health, and the special councils. I mean now we have [*inaudible*] the Legislative Council. I mean they have a Legislative Council and an Executive Council, but it is not literally the government; the government is the federal government. The embassies are ones; the diplomatic corps is one, and one seat for the international institutions. One seat. And the regional territories are considered one, Sir, since the region is one and not divided in the united country.

Saddam: I need a good clarification of the situation of Kuwait. Let's start with Comrade Mizban. What is the future of the Iraqi-Kuwaiti relation now? Answer me in just one word.

Mizban: Union, Sir.

Saddam: What type of union? [*Overlapping voices as individuals in the room vote. Some of them vote for self rule.*]

Mizban: [*Inaudible.*]

Saddam: Dr. Sa'dun.

Sa'dun: [*Inaudible*] Self-ruling.

Saddam: Self-ruling. Comrade Taha?

[*Many people talk at the same time.*]

Saddam: How can you explain this? You are the Minister of Foreign Affairs; the government can control the situation for a period of time.

Tariq: My answer is a national union for one year until [*inaudible*]. I believe the ultimate and imminent goal in one year or one-and-a-half years is unity. But now [*inaudible*].

Saddam: Comrade Sa'id.

Sa'id:[12] I have a remark to add to what the comrades said. We expect the United Nations to make a move and try to liberate the Kuwaiti people. [*Inaudible.*] I believe this is what is going to happen. In my opinion, unity is the solution.

Saddam: Comrade Ali.

Ali: Sir, I had requested to speak a few times, but you did not give me the chance. Please, I would like to take two minutes of your time.

---

eternal, and inseparable unity." On 28 August, Iraq declared that Kuwait had become Iraq's nineteenth province. See Karsh and Rautsi, *Saddam Hussein*, 217–22; Marr, *The Modern History of Iraq*, 231–32.

[12] Probably Sa'id abd-al-Majid al-Faysal al-Tikriti, Ba'ath Party Regional Command chairman.

Saddam: No, no, with Comrade [*inaudible*]. We need to get going, because with every day that goes by we don't know what the next day is going to bring us!

Ali: Sir, if we establish an integrated union, anything else, you know we will not only lose Kuwait, but also our credibility with our people, our Party, our politics and the entire world! Besides, we would have to face the Arabs once again!

Saddam: Comrade Latif.

Latif: I believe this should not have [*inaudible*]; it could have been postponed to . . .

Saddam: Ahmed.[13]

Ahmed: [*Inaudible*.]

Saddam: Hussein.

Hussein Kamil: [*Inaudible*.]

Saddam: Muhammad.

Muhammad: Don't people know that Kuwait is a part of Iraq? I mean it is written in history. The Iraqis, the Kuwaitis, and the Saudis are supposed to know this fact! There is a part, Sir –

Saddam: [*Inaudible*.] Pass my regards to the provisional government. I need them to send a letter so that we can have an integrated union tomorrow.

Male:[14] At your order, Sir.

[*Inaudible background talk.*]

Saddam: With God's help [*all agree with Saddam*], and if I hear that you did not cut the tongue of anyone talking there deep from the esophagus, I will replace you all, including the Republican Guard Commander. You tell them, "You are Iraqis now," and if anyone opens his mouth or makes any noise, you need to empty all bullets in his throat.

Male: What if someone leaves outside the borders?

Saddam: We can open the borders if someone leaves, but we have to decide on the men we do not need, because once we open the borders they have to open [*inaudible*.]

[*Inaudible background talk.*]

Saddam: Do we need to define their borders?

[*Inaudible background talk.*]

Saddam: We need to start over there. Muhammad, do we need to demarcate the borders or is there no need to do so?

---

[13] Probably Ahmed Hussein Khudayr al-Samarra'i, chief of the president's office during the Mother of All Battles. In March 1991, he replaced Tariq Aziz as foreign minister.

[14] In several places in this recording, static prevented the translators from providing identifying information on the speaker beyond the fact that it was a male voice.

Muhammad: Yes, Sir, because Saudi Arabia controls a part of Kuwait! So, if we demarcate the borders to the part by Saudi Arabia, Kuwait has the biggest part and it is officially conferred at the Ministry of Foreign Affairs –

Saddam: Mizban.

Mizban: Sir, why should we demarcate the borders? Do we want to kick [inaudible] out of Kuwait?

Saddam: [Inaudible.]

Male: Sir, depending on the media, if they announce it immediately it would be difficult in this case.

Saddam Appraises American and International Reactions to the Invasion of Kuwait (7 August 1990)[15]

Saddam: But it was God who showed us the path. Our brain was worthless in this matter; it was God who guided us. We were heading in that direction and suddenly he turned us! We were not going to stay starving, God has blessed us. All that we wanted as a command was for the military operation to be carried out and then to prepare ourselves for a defensive posture under suitable circumstances. I say our timing was more than suitable. First, the operation went very quickly. Second, control of the situation was comprehensive. Third, we had ample time to prepare a defensive posture. And that was how it went. What else do we want? Do we want to take Kuwait in one day, and then [inaudible]?

Male 1: It would be shameful if they [the Kuwaitis] don't engage in a fight with us.

Saddam: I mean really, [laughing] can you imagine what would have happened whether they engage in a fight with us or not? Truly, none of us would like to be in the same situation as the American President and the West. Well, what is this? If they don't engage in a fight with us, there will be no one. The entire world would collapse! A loss, their money is a loss and their situation is a loss and they will even scare the rocks on which they are sitting. Okay, how about this Western prestige? Had they not threatened them – they did not threaten yet.[16] They are still preparing an international atmosphere. But this international atmosphere – we don't have atrocities that will evoke humanity as time passes by. On the other hand and as time passes, the human grasp languishes with regard to hostility. There is nothing left from Kuwait not to mention that the combat continues to force them to take a risk. Everything happened in 24 hours and now we sit and relax; everything was fine and everyone carried out his duties. Fine, and as time passes, how are they going to compensate for this five million [barrels] of oil? What would the impact be on the consumer, and on the international economy in general when the [price per] barrel fluctuates and registers $50? I really don't know what Bush plans to do in this regard!

Male 1: Even if they engage in a fight with us, so what?

---

[15] *SH-SHTP-A-001-233, "Saddam and Iraqi Officials Discussing Turkish, Russian and Chinese Perceptions of Iraq's Occupation of Kuwait," 7 August 1990.
[16] The identities of the subject and direct object in this sentence are unclear.

Saddam: I mean, what will they do if they engage in a fight? All they can do is bring their airplanes and start bombing: boom, boom, boom, boom, boom, boom. So what? Nothing will happen, we will give them hell. Give me one instance when an airplane has settled any situation. We are not like Panama, people to be scared by airplanes, okay, fine, what will they do here?[17] Their bombing will increase the number of refugees. The longer their aggression lasts, the more flags will be hoisted from the Arab Maghreb [Western Arab countries] to the Arab Mashreq [Eastern Arab countries]. [Inaudible] it started to feel the Arab spirit although it is very hard to accept the notion of an entire country immediately disappearing. I am saying this so you can understand the reactions of Sheikh Issa who is not, by God, a bad man.[18]

Male 1: No, the Arab stance has changed.

Saddam: But the others, I mean the popular stance remains noble and exceeds expectations. And the more time passes by – what the popular stance tries to do now is to watch us and see whether we are strong or weak.

Saddam Advocates Searching Foreign Embassies and Discusses the Creation of an Interim Government in Kuwait (circa 5–7 August 1990)[19]

Taha:[20] Mr. President, with regard to the case of the foreign embassies and the process of searching them, I believe this process might be harmful for some embassies since they have private guards. Any confrontation, killing and so forth, would give these foreign countries an excuse to interfere more, especially when talking about the large embassies.

Saddam: I mean, this is not urgent, but at the same time, if we were to be sure that . . . an important character such as Jabir Al-Ahmed, Saad, or Salah[21] were inside one of the embassies, we would raid it, even if they decide to host them and I do not care about the consequences.[22]

Taha: There are means, there are means to cut them off from the electricity, to disconnect their phones, I mean force them with other methods, other than [pauses] because –

---

[17] This appears to be a reference to the use of F-117A "Stealth fighters" during the 1989 U.S. invasion of Panama, which dropped two two-thousand-pound bombs near a barracks of the Panamanian Defense Force in an effort to induce the Panamanian troops not to fight.

[18] Issa bin Salman al-Khalifa, emir of Bahrain (1960–1999).

[19] *SH-SHTP-A-001-234, "Saddam and His Advisers Discussing Planned Actions in Kuwait following the Initial Invasion," undated (circa 5–7 August 1990).

[20] This may be either Taha Ma'ruf or Taha Yasin Ramadan.

[21] "Jabir al-Ahmed" is a reference to Jabir al-Ahmed al-Jabir al-Sabah, the emir of Kuwait. "Saad" probably refers to Kuwaiti Crown Prince Sheikh Saad Abdallah al-Sabah. "Salah" might refer to Salah Khalaf (Abu Iyyad), a very senior Palestinian Liberation Organization (PLO) and Fatah official who opposed the PLO decision to support Iraq's invasion of Kuwait. He was assassinated in Tunisia on 14 January 1991, possibly for his refusal to back Saddam.

[22] Saddam's disregard for the consequences of Iraqi brutality is further illustrated in his 20 September 1990 approval of beating up diplomats who left their embassies in Kuwait. SH-SHTP-A-000-654, "Saddam and Iraqi Officials Discussing How to Deal with Foreign Diplomats in Kuwait and International Perceptions of Iraq," 20 September 1990.

Saddam: It is a final option.

Taha: Final, yes.

Saddam: But if it has to be done, then it has to be done.

Taha: Okay.

Tariq: The political figure that supervises its structure –

Saddam: Yes, the political figure that supervises its structure. Do we need the interim government? Yes, Comrade Izzat?

Izzat: In my opinion, we truly need the interim government because there is a big difference between direct administration and the interim government in the first phase. We need to have a psychological and practical impact on the Kuwaiti people first, and then on the Arab and international milieu so that our earlier statements and decisions will take full effect, or have full impact on these milieus, because they asked for our help and we responded. But then the Kuwaiti people had a coup, which is according to the first statement, the Kuwaiti people voluntarily decided to change the traitor authority. It appears to me that Kuwaitis, I believe many Kuwaitis were fed up with the Kuwaiti government, but could not confront the Kuwaiti government in some circles that are extremely big.

Saddam: By the way, some citizens have started expressing their delight at having the troops around and so forth.

Male 1: In Kuwait?

Saddam: In Kuwait.

Izzat: So, Mr. President there would have been more boldness if there were an interim government.

Saddam: This is what the new Intelligence Director said.

Male 1: In what manner?

Saddam: Well, I did not ask him in which manner!

Male 1: Is it possible to [*inaudible*]?

Saddam: It is still early and I don't expect – [*voices overlap*].

Izzat: This way, Mr. President, once they see the soldiers, they will salute them, praise their action, and defame the government. Mr. President, the interim government is going to be very beneficial to us, especially in the first few days, and undermine many evil intentions or alleviate the danger of evil acts.

Saddam: This means you have to form it quickly.

Izzat: Yes, by God!

Saddam: And in this case, we have to consider figures that are not troublesome, I mean neither very weak nor troublesome. I mean you have to discuss it with Comrade Faisal Saneh, the ambassador, Hussein, and Sab'awi there.[23]

---

[23] Faisal Saneh was a leader of the Ba'ath Party in Kuwait. Sab'awi Ibrahim Hasan al-Tikriti was Saddam's half brother and head of Iraqi intelligence in Kuwait.

Izzat: [*Inaudible.*]

Saddam: They may want to understand it. From now on they need to keep in mind the relation between Kuwait and Iraq . . . and be convinced of this fact.

Tariq: [*Inaudible.*]

Saddam: They cannot bear it. We were able to tolerate it because – I don't mean by tolerate it that we only wanted a price for it. This matter was settled. I mean in the Command's mind, when it decided to intervene, it decided to adopt this plan, which includes acting on behalf of its territory and people. It should be this way and clear. Whoever wants to assume responsibility needs to know that, at the end, Iraq is a part of Kuwait and vice versa.

———

Saddam: I am thinking of defining the borders first and then working on establishing the union. When they go to Kuwait, strike the Iraqi Bubiyan and make all the land between Saudi Arabia and Kuwait collapse to become a part of Iraq, the old Iraq – before adding Kuwait to it – and then Kuwait will join.[24]

Tariq: [*Inaudible.*]

Saddam: It must be approved immediately.

———

Saddam: What did we agree on? Let Comrade Faisal be the head of the government. Comrade Faisal is old. He is my age, you know.

[*Inaudible background talk about Faisal.*]

Saddam: Write it down so you can notify Ayad Al-Duri, so he can save some time tonight until you guys get to him in the morning. You will need Al-Shu'ayba, the Arab League line and a few hours. You are going to need at least three hours. Number three is to be informed so there are no mistakes. Between two parentheses, Faisal is to prepare to take charge of the government. Government of what?

Male 1: The free provisional government.

Saddam: The free provisional government.

Izzat: The free provisional government of Kuwait.

Saddam: He will make contacts and prepare his mind for the rest of the ministers of the unified national elements until consulting with him at a different level and under the daily circumstances – just as an early reference to guide them until you arrive. Take a group of people you trust with you for protection purposes. Just like that. This is the way we have to be, soft and strong; soft with the soft and whoever steps out of line, just like Iraq at the beginning of the revolution.[25] We will kick and beat

---

[24] Bubiyan is an uninhabited island between Iran, Iraq, and Kuwait.

[25] It is unclear whether Saddam was referring to the Ba'ath revolution in Iraq (1968) or the revolution in Iran (1979). Following both regime changes, the Ba'ath regime brutally repressed Iraqi dissidents.

the one who gets out of line to the street and let him kick for two hours. This way everyone will know his limits.

Saddam Supports Brutal Counterinsurgency Methods and Pillaging Kuwait (third week of September 1990)[26]

Sab'awi: Comrade Ali [probably Chemical Ali] covered almost everything, except for a few details regarding the security aspect . . . Sir, I arrived in Kuwait on August 3 and I felt as if someone hit me on my head with a hammer. I was out of it and did not know what to do. But my action and tone changed in the second week and like comrade Ali said, even the Iraqis living in Kuwait had a different opinion than ours and some of them chose to work with the opposition. Things escalated in the third week until Your Excellency sent for us in the fourth week and gave us your directives in the presence of some comrades. The authorities you granted us were very helpful. As for the security aspect, and like comrade Ali has described, similar to weeks five and six and now being in the seventh week – for the past three weeks, we have treated them ruthlessly. Now, they are really desperate and frustrated and have started to change their methods – from someone on the street hitting the soldiers and running, or someone grabs him while he is driving. Now they have begun to lay mines in cars in a very primitive manner unlike what takes place in Lebanon or in Palestine, etc. This is according to primitive instructions they receive because they are not trained in that. These past weeks –

Saddam: You should destroy their bases before they learn any advanced techniques.

Sab'awi: Yes, Sir. In the past three weeks, any bullet shot from a neighborhood, that same neighborhood would be greatly harmed. To the extent that the others felt that when anyone committed such acts, he would harm people who did nothing. People were really coming to us with information and leading us, really.

Saddam: And this is what is required.

Sab'awi: Yes, during the past three weeks.

Saddam: [*Inaudible*] is a burden [*inaudible*].

Sab'awi: During the past three weeks, the security agencies obtained a good [data] base about agencies and other information. And the security agencies' work, now, during the past three weeks – I mean from the second day of the ninth month or the third day of the ninth month to the present – today I called, as I told Your Excellency, I called the brothers there in charge of the agencies and asked, "What is going on today?" They replied that there had not been one shot. I usually concentrate on police officers because they are the base that leads these activities, and the directive depends on them. And because Fahd al-Fahd is the [Kuwaiti] Director of State Security who is characterized by boastfulness to the extent that an organization called Al-Fuhud was formed after his name. We hit this organization and killed several officers who were majors and captains, police officers, I mean. We really destroyed them and destroyed

---

[26] *SH-SHTP-A-001-235, "Saddam and Iraqi Officials Discussing Plans for Kuwait after the Invasion," undated (circa third week of September 1990).

more than one cell that, through our security agencies, we were able to raid their headquarters.

Saddam: Yes.

Sab'awi: We slaughtered 28 people at one of the headquarters, 28 people who were officers at the State Security Department. What are their plans, and how do they receive their information? And after we completed the interrogation, we treated them harshly, really harshly, then killed and buried them. At eleven o'clock we took them to their places of residence in front of their homes. We brought the women out, killed them, and then burned the house. Sir, in fact we did not do that because we are criminals who like to kill. But this method is the best for those saboteurs who are exactly as Comrade Ali has described. It is very difficult for them to accept us because there is a huge difference between our ethics and theirs. For this reason we treated them ruthlessly so that they would lose hope and have one of two choices: either to leave or to abide by law.

––––––––

Saddam: What is keeping you, all the brothers here and who did not attend this session? What is keeping you busy here, in Baghdad? Your work is in Kuwait, I mean, you bring work, you bring the material there. Do you have anything you want to import from abroad?

Sab'awi: No, no.

Saddam: Huh? Anyone involved in importing and distribution should go and stay in Kuwait and not return to Baghdad until he finishes up the warehouses in Kuwait.

Sab'awi: Yes.

Saddam: What do you have to do here?!

Sab'awi: Sir, we only sent a small group.

Saddam: I mean should I be the one who goes there, by God, trade and siege, and so forth? And here we have warehouses right in front of us and we leave them to burn, everyday bursting into flames. Really this is blasphemy.[27]

PREPARING FOR AND ENDURING THE COALITION AIR CAMPAIGN

As the UN deadline for withdrawal approached in January 1991, Saddam sought ways to impede the coalition military action that he thought would soon come. He considered blowing up oil wells to create clouds of smoke that would hinder air strikes and planned to release mines into the Persian Gulf. At the same time, Saddam took measures to safeguard his diplomatic position and military capabilities. He declined to launch preemptive strikes

––––––––

[27] Saddam is referring to Kuwaitis burning their warehouses rather than letting Iraq take their goods.

against coalition air bases out of fear that this would simply provide a pretext for war against Iraq. He also resolved to keep the Iraqi navy out of combat to save it from certain destruction. Finally, the Iraqi military took a number of steps to disperse its Scud missiles and safeguard them from U.S. air strikes.

Iraq Considers How to Counteract the Coalition Air Assault (13 January 1991)[28]

Saddam: Hussein, what are your preparations, do you have any shortage or anything else?

Hussein Kamil: Good, good. As Your Excellency knows, the defense arrangements are never complete, but just [inaudible]. There is the system, the defense sites, the stockpiling, the soldiers' zeal, the spirit, all the precautionary measures, [a] clear picture for everyone and Tariq's project. Everything is complete.

Saddam: Tariq's project is the crude oil?

Hussein Kamil: Yes.

Male 1: Sir, concerning the oil installations being prepared to be destroyed, there is an order from Your Excellency to blow up these installations in case of a certain degree of danger, or we can wait for an order from Your Excellency. However, Sir, because Al-Wafra is near the [Kuwait/Saudi Arabian] borders, Your Excellency has given the local commander the authority to blow it up whenever he believes there is danger. Now Al-Burqan and the Navy remain. Would they be included according to the situation, or –

Saddam: According to the situation, according to the situation.

Male 1: That is to say, whenever we see it in danger –

Saddam: You could decide this according to the situation in the field of operations –

Male 1: That is to say, it should not be spared, blow it up whenever the situation becomes dangerous.

Saddam: God willing.

––––––

Male 2: Excuse me, Sir, if you allow me to say that if we spread these mines in the sea, we are going to shut off the navigation to ourselves, also, because the ebb and flow currents in the area do not even reach Iran. I mean there is no control.

Saddam: First of all, we are not using this sea, just release a number of these snakes and let them go wherever they go –

Male 3: [Inaudible.]

Saddam: What are we using the sea for?

[28] *SH-SHTP-A-001-236, "Iraqi Officials Discussing Al-Fao, Iran, and Saudi Arabia," 13 January 1991.

Male 2: No, we are not using it. We will release them during the ebb so that they would head south.

Saddam: Toward our brothers.[29]

Male 2: Yes.

Saddam: Toward our new Iranian brothers. That is it.

Saddam: Had we known that the people would understand us, we would have attacked them such that they would not have had a chance to lift a weapon against us, and captured all of these cursed enemies, because their computers are not yet programmed for this battle. They say there was a chance for peace, but the Iraqis blew it – as if everyone is working for peace while we are unaware of it! If conditions were otherwise, we would have captured even their aircraft since they don't know where to send them. Even when their aircraft fly they don't know a specific direction to follow. We would fire at them with your weapon. [*Laughter.*] Would the Americans be able to do anything if we captured 20,000 of them?

Iraqi Leaders Talk about Sending Their Air Force and Navy to Iran for Safekeeping (early January 1991)[30]

Hussein Kamil: We must change our navy so it will be more effective as a naval force and stay in places safe for it. Sir, the navy did take part in a defensive posture against Kuwait. However, they did not enter into a real battle with the Iranians. I mean we only lost one boat and so on!

Saddam: No, they did fight.

Hussein Kamil: Sir, they did fight, but not always when facing such a huge naval force –

Saddam: [*Interrupting.*] It is in our plan that our navy will not take part in the coming battle.

Hussein Kamil: Sir, we should not gather it but spread it out, and let the headquarters supervise it. We will let the Minister of Defense supervise it and monitor it. Otherwise, Sir, we will lose [it]. Not to mention, Sir, they brought a huge navy force. So, when our navy force goes out to sea to fight, every division that leaves, in my opinion, will not come back; it might do some harm, but it will not come back due to either an air or sea strike.

Saddam: We did not assign them to any interception duty. Hussein, do you remember the plan?

Hussein Kamil: Yes

Saddam: Our navy should not leave certain locations.

----

[29] Saddam seems to be speaking sarcastically.

[30] SH-SHTP-D-000-818, "Saddam and Iraqi Officials Preparing for the Commencement of US strikes on 15 January 1991," undated (circa early January 1991).

Saddam: I have one more thing that is more important that I want to be sure about. It is how we should spread out our units so that we do not get destroyed from the first naval bombardment.

Male 1: It is spread out all over and within a working plan that has been worked out so they are not all in one place.

Saddam: I had thought that some of them – we should have them cross over to Iran toward the Iranian sea ports so that, at least, the surprise attack will not take much from us.[31] Then, after sending them there, we can return them here so that they can act against the allied forces.

Male 2: Sir, this has been taken into consideration and was studied as far as the air force was concerned, as well as the naval force. As for the air force, they have eight airplanes. We told them we can send them away. As for the naval force, we do have a plan for it, and that is to spread them and not to have them moored in one place according to their assigned tasks. Those units not assigned to any task should leave the area. This is something within the planned activities. However, the matter of the eight airplanes –

Saddam: Don't they have shelters?

Male 2: Sir, these are Ilyushin-76s, and these airplanes are huge and are in their bases.[32]

Saddam: Does that mean they have no shelters?

Male 2: Sir, these planes are huge and we have distributed them over our bases. Each one on one base and that is the best we can do. We do not have hideouts or shelters for them as they say.

In a Retrospective Conversation, Saddam and His Advisers Discuss How Iraq Unleashed Scud Missiles while Protecting Their Launchers (circa 1993)[33]

Saddam: Explain to the leaders why the enemy failed to hit any of the [missile] launching bases until the last moment, until the combat stopped.[34]

Hazim Ayubi:[35] Sir –

---

[31] On 29 January, the remnants of the Iraqi navy made a run toward Iranian waters. They were set upon by U.S. naval aircraft in what has been described as the "Bubiyan turkey shoot." By 30 January, almost twenty vessels were sunk or heavily damaged.

[32] The Ilyushin-76 is a large, Soviet-built cargo plane.

[33] *SH-SHTP-V-001-237, "Saddam and Military Officials Discussing Lessons Learned in the Wake of the 1991 Gulf War," undated (circa 1993).

[34] Although the coalition made expansive claims during the conflict about its successes in "Scud-hunting," the official Gulf War Air Power Survey found afterward that "there is no indisputable proof that Scud mobile launchers – as opposed to high-fidelity decoys, trucks, or other objects with Scud-like signatures – were destroyed by fixed-wing aircraft." Thomas A. Keaney and Eliot A. Cohen, "Gulf War Air Power Survey Summary Report" (Washington, D.C.: Government Printing Office, 1993), 89–90.

[35] Lieutenant General Hazim Ayubi, commander of Iraqi Scud forces during the Gulf War.

Saddam: How we showed them to them [the coalition] in the Western area and how we withdrew them when it was time, how we dispersed them, and how later on they started to hit Israel, hit – [*Voices overlap.*]

Hazim: Sir, as a matter of fact, as far as the missiles – [*Voices overlap.*]

Saddam: So that they will have an idea – [*Voices overlap.*]

Hazim: Yes.

Saddam: And benefit from it in the future.

————

Hazim: The Western area was the theater of the Western operations that were mainly against Israel, and we were interested in getting it ready. Because it was wide open with no cover, we thought of many ways to carry out the duty with the minimum loss possible and minimum exposure possible. My talk about the unseen may not sound logical, but I believe in it. I mean believing in the unseen is true and it is mentioned at the beginning of *Surat Al-Baqara*.[36] The important thing in the camouflage operation was the prayer of Your Excellency for us; God responded to your prayer. You always pray to God to protect us without the practical guidance, without the clear combat instructions. You used to pray to God to grant us success and blind the sight of the enemy. I had this faith and so did my group, all of them. I used to spread it and talk about it because God responds to the prayer of the just commander.

The other point is the financial measures we took. Immediately after Al-Nidaa' Day, Your Excellency ordered us – I mean that was a big step in the war history – to empty the depots and not to keep shelters with missiles.[37] That operation was important and made us take advantage of the natural cover. The wars have proved that, as far as the missiles and maybe other sectors, taking advantage of the natural cover is better than any practical means because it is . . . I mean buildings, shelters or underground shelters . . . we take advantage of the ground [*inaudible*], the trees and small tricks with simple measures would be better since we are not going to rely on the establishment or the building we are going to use and is the only one we have. We are going to have many alternatives in natural cover. On July 31 – that came one day or two before Al-Nidaa' Day – the missile sectors moved to the Western area, moved to the Western area and were ready to fire at Israel. We reduced the firing time to four hours from the time we received the order. Operating missiles with liquid fuel takes a long time; 24 hours would hardly be enough for us to get it done, but we took certain measures so we could respond within four hours because Israel was threatening to strike Iraq at any time, and we had to respond immediately. So, the immediate response requires the time or battle procedure to be reduced to the least time possible. We did not stay in the same place for more than two or

---

36 "Surat Al-Baqara" is the second chapter in the Quran. Hazim appears to refer to Quran 2:2–3: "This is the Book; in it is guidance sure, without doubt, to those who fear Allah; who believe in the Unseen, are steadfast in prayer, and spend out of what We have provided for them." See Yusuf Ali translation, accessed 2 June 2009 at www.usc.edu/schools/college/crcc/engagement/resources/texts/muslim/quran/002.qmt.html.

37 Yum al-Nidaa', or "Day of the Great Call," was Saddam's term for 2 August 1990, the day Iraq invaded Kuwait.

three nights. Practically, we were supposed to change it every night, but that was impossible since all areas were going to be used. The Chief of Staff of the Army then, General Hussein Rashid, and the operations assistant Farid Sultan, he used to repeat Your Excellency's instructions in every meeting – used to emphasize, again, the fact not to stay even, when he was at the advanced command site in Basra. Your Excellency used to ask about this point in every meeting also; I mean it became a continuous re-enforcement or instructions for all groups and all officers.

Saddam: Stay about two days in the place before the combat starts.

Hazim: Yes. And then –

Saddam: I mean –

Hazim: And then in the period that followed, Your Excellency ordered to withdraw them towards Baghdad – all the equipment. Therefore, I inquired because it was going to take longer, I mean it was going to [inaudible] to the battle procedure during the move. So, I said the instant response is not the important thing, but to take revenge when we are prepared enough. I mean it is better, this way we don't destroy our launchers. Therefore, we withdrew them to places near Baghdad since it was safer and not empty, I mean the areas were occupied – [Voices overlap.]

Saddam: No, no, I wanted them to watch when we withdraw –

Hazim: Yes –

Saddam: They get the news and they would hit their traditional places –

Hazim: Yes –

Saddam: And that's what really happened.

Hazim: The place where they were.

Saddam: At the expected edge of firing, at the edge of the attack. We withdrew them, so for sure for the time they stayed – it was about –

Hazim: Almost four months.

Saddam: Four months. By that time they got the news. Once they heard they were withdrawn to Baghdad what would their expectation be? Towards their camps and that's why Al-Taji camp was hit badly.

Hazim: Yes.

Saddam: [Mumbling to someone.] But we left them in places – [Voices overlap.]

Hazim: Sir, also – [Voices overlap.]

Saddam: Known.

Hazim: The simple plans within our capabilities – [Voices overlap.]

Saddam: Besides, Baghdad has an air defense that is better and more important than our entire air defense wherever the missiles are.

Hazim: Sir, simple means – we were hoping for decoy launchers. We were not completely convinced they would serve the right purpose, because a big deception or extensive camouflage requires great capabilities while our army was not really dedicated to this because the Kuwait sector – as well as the other sectors – were important. Therefore, we built a brigade – decoy missile brigade very similar to the Russian launchers, which are the old System R-17 and not al-Nidaa',[38] and we opened them in places as if they were really in a camouflage situation. They were also hidden in a way that they didn't look inauthentic to the enemy.

Saddam: They give the sense of credibility; let's see [*inaudible*].

Hazim: I was not satisfied with this. I wanted to think, I mean to increase our equipment. So, we had those launchers I talked about called Luna, Arab and Luna's carriers that carry missiles only and don't launch; we have a lot of stock at the depot.[39] So, we prepared them and got them out also, in about – more than two brigades. They got mixed up and we created a group that we called "the First Special Decoy Group," but we did not call it – I mean we omitted the word "decoy" – and we called it "The Great Special Duty Group." We used it in the Western area and another one very similar to the first in Kuwait sector also. In addition to Luna's launchers, there was another brigade that moved amid the troops there and changed its location. Some of them could be real ones and could be launched. This took place in the Western area. I would like to give an idea about the enemy's capabilities. The capabilities of the enemy . . . if we were interested in al-Hussein [missile] launchers and the other Russian launchers – I mean the al-Hussein system also – it [the enemy] did not see them because we were concerned about hiding and moving quickly and not entering the sites until the last minute . . . So, I wonder how it did not see the First Special Decoy Group, which had more than 26 carriers and launchers, and they were also using similar tactics to the tactics of other missile groups but they were not launched. They used the natural cover.

We prohibited radio use. We prohibited using radio under any circumstances; we were using the land lines or liaison officers only. What arose in The Mother of All Battles [Um-al-Maarek] and even in the glorious Qadisiyyah Saddam [the Iran-Iraq War] was because there were no liaison officers or good liaison panels. But we formed a large group to help us handle communication between the Western and Southern areas of the country.

As far as electronic devices that help the enemy detect us, I prohibited their use, and that happened with God's guidance because we were supposed to comply with the instructions we received. But understanding the principles of war and the presence of Your Excellency, I mean we are honored to meet with you or when you called or sent one of the escorts, or gave direct instructions that concerned us, or supported us from the Presidential Council or the secretary with a clear instruction to us, or mobilized the capabilities of the country – such as the Ministry of Oil – with regard to choice of targets or the military intelligence or the air forces or others. This was, I mean, a great motif for us. So, at the last minute before heading to the battle on [January] the fifteenth, which was the warning given to Iraq, I prohibited opening the radar stations for the air types, because during launching operations we

---

[38] The R-17E was the Soviet designator for the Scud-B surface-to-surface missile. The al-Nidaa' was a Daimler-Benz launcher for the al-Hussein surface-to-surface missile. The al-Hussein had a longer range than the Scud-B, but was made primarily from Scud-B parts.

[39] *Luna* was the Soviet name for the Soviet-made, seventy-kilometer-range, rocket. It was designated the FROG-7 by NATO.

have to extract – I mean launch really high into the air, so that we can compensate for the difference in atmospheric conditions. So, I prohibited using them and some commanders said, "If it is okay, we will take the stations but we won't use them." I replied, "Don't take them, that way you cannot use them." This is also one of the war's secrets the inspection teams don't know.[40] They still don't know that we used air types.[41] We gave them the launching rates that took place while experimenting with the Military Industrialization Commission in the previous years... we were very concerned about protecting against land infiltration [e.g., by coalition special operations forces]. So, thank God, we did not face difficulties in this regard; thank God who granted us success.

Saddam: You had a company from the Special [Republican] Guard.[42]

Hazim: We had a company from the special guard and we also had a commando brigade from the 4th Corps, and we turned all that we could spare of the technical components to protection components – to protection components. So, they hit the missile shelters – they hit places we were not in, but they did not hit any places we were in during the war, or close to it or a land communication joint we were close to. They could not find themselves a place, either, during the inspections they performed since Security Council's Resolution was enforced or until this day. They could not find any place where we hid our equipment, because it is all [under] natural cover; they entered near them – they entered about 100 or 200 meters [away], not to mention we told them we complied with the plan since we could not act contrary to our opinions. But they did not go to where we hid [things] before or after the war – at all. This is regarding al-Hussein missiles.

Our troops were confident. And in the memoirs of De Pierre [British General Sir Peter de la Billière] distributed to us and in the memoirs we wrote during the years of war – he pretended we were scared and the shooting became inaccurate and without guidance.[43] The missile with all [of its] technical operations cannot be handled by one person. I mean an engineer, a technician or a military officer cannot operate the missile alone; it is a team work and the nice thing about it is that no one can master his work completely, even if he kept working for many years on one launcher, because the driver operates, the one running the engine operates, and the electrician operates; I mean many teams. Therefore, they can't spread the news that we were randomly aiming and launching. It is not a gun or a rifle that one person or two are going to use. Maybe they were scared and that's why they said the shooting became inaccurate in later phases, but I mean if we look at the facts, many targets were accurately hit at the end. I mean at the end of the battle, shortly before the cease-fire. I was, I mean, and I say it proudly, they were so confident to a point where my son, who was in fourth grade of elementary school at that time, I used to get him

---

[40] These were UN Special Commission (UNSCOM) inspection teams.

[41] This passage is obscure, but it may be a reference to the use of optically tracked meteorological balloons to gather atmospheric data necessary to adjust the missiles' flight path.

[42] The Special Republican Guard was responsible for the security of Baghdad and Saddam.

[43] Saddam had distributed de la Billiere's memoir to his officers, and a passage from this book seems to match Hazim's description. General Sir Peter de la Billière, *Storm Command: A Personal Account of the Gulf War* (London: HarperCollins, 1992), 226–27; SH-SHTP-A-000-830, "Saddam and Officials Discussing Ba'ath Party Support to Its Lebanese Branch, Ba'ath Ideology, and Other Party Affairs," undated (circa 1992).

involved with the troops. My son Mohamed who was in fourth grade launched two missiles himself. I mean he pressed [the button] himself and launched the missile. If our people were not confident as far as aircraft, I would have feared for my son.

THE GROUND WAR (24–28 FEBRUARY)

As the ground war commenced on 24 February 1991, Saddam often seemed more concerned with psychological and media aspects of the fighting than with the coalition forces streaming into Iraq and Kuwait. Accordingly, Iraqi officials looked to counter Western media portrayals of the war as a lopsided rout while relying on the Soviet Union to exert diplomatic pressure for an end to the conflict. As it became clear that the Soviet peace initiative would not succeed, Saddam had to grapple with a rapidly deteriorating military situation. He resolved to remain in Kuwait as long as there remained an even chance of success while simultaneously readying the Iraqi government to counter the invasion of Iraq proper. Saddam and his advisers prepared to arm the Iraqi people, to destroy installations that might be used to facilitate the coalition's advance, and finally to fight house to house in hopes of inflicting sufficient casualties to force Washington to quit the war.

Just before the Ground War Began, Saddam Discussed His Plans to Withdraw Iraqi Forces from Kuwait (23 February 1991)[44]

Saddam: I would like to make a clear statement: In the event America and its evil allies object to the Soviet Union's initiative, the Iraqi press agency has learned there will be cooperation with the political and religious tendencies in Kuwait to establish a national and democratic regime.[45]

Izzat: Sir, with this step, the world is going to look at us in a completely different way.

———

Male 1: Sir –

Saddam: Thank God for everything!

Male 1: What are your expectations toward the Americans' stance in the upcoming days? Do you believe they might try to – ?

Saddam: I do not believe the Americans will accept this project easily as it is. They might try during this period to twist another paragraph. This is the first point. The other point is that I am not comfortable with dashing out of Kuwait in the first four

---

44 SH-SHTP-A-000-633, "Saddam and His Political Advisers Discussing the Attack on Iraq and Reactions from Arab Countries," 23 February 1991.

45 Following the invasion of Kuwait, the Soviet Union proposed various initiatives for removing Iraqi troops from Kuwait in return for the end of economic sanctions and other UN resolutions against Iraq. For an account of the final Soviet mediation efforts and Iraqi responses before the onset of the ground campaign, see Woods, *The Mother of All Battles*, 212–19.

days, the city of Kuwait, Kazem city.[46] Here is the situation of our troops: Kuwait is by the ocean and if we withdraw in four days this will create a pocket within our troops where the governor of Kuwait or the American army might enter. Therefore, it is hard to tell what their next action will be, where they might use this pocket as a cover to hurt our troops while withdrawing.

Izzat: We should concentrate in these four days on withdrawing the soldiers in this direction.

Saddam: I gave instructions. I sent a letter this morning.[47]

Male 1: Mr. President, regarding the Iraqis over there, how many Iraqis do we have in Kuwait?

Saddam: Do we have anything else but the soldiers?

Male 1: No, I did not mean that. I meant the citizens.

Izzat: What are the citizens doing over there?

Male 1: Aren't they there?

Saddam: There are few Iraqi citizens over there; the offices and business are open and it is easy for them to conduct their affairs. Now what do you have?

Male 2: Sir, I have about 15 workers in Kuwait –

Saddam: No, no, we don't mean those. We are asking about the people living there.

Male 2: Oh, those living there. I have about 15.

Saddam: The remaining citizens are just a few.

Male 1: Sir, with regard to your pictures for the banners, would you like us to remove them before they would –

Saddam: Yes, I swear to God, from the first day, I thought it was inappropriate to –

Male 1: Yes, Sir, that is right, however, as soon as we hear anything regarding when they start –

Izzat: They can be removed in one day.

Male 1: What do you mean?

Izzat: They can be removed in one day.[48]

---

[46] On 22 February, Iraq agreed to completely withdraw from Kuwait City within four days and from the remainder of the country within twenty-one days. Robert Pape, *Bombing to Win: Air Power and Coercion in War* (Ithaca, NY: Cornell University Press, 1996), 217.

[47] For the letter, and the Soviet response, see section "As Coalition ground forces storm into Southern Iraq and Kuwait," in this Chapter.

[48] As one eyewitness recalled, the Iraqis had plastered pictures of Saddam "onto every round-about, wall, school, and lamppost" in Kuwait. The Kuwaiti resistance continued to post Kuwaiti flags and pictures of the royal family, and some Kuwaitis refused to display pictures of Saddam, even though such defiance reportedly led to severe punishment (including execution). Saddam probably wanted his troops to discreetly remove the pictures to prevent Kuwaiti resistance fighters from doing so more publicly. See Jehan S. Rajab, *Invasion*

Saddam: Even the buildings, have our people –

Male 1: They will get near the buildings. That's what I wanted to –

Saddam: Huh?

Male 3: What is going to happen at the end is that [*inaudible*]. After the army withdraws [*inaudible*].

Male 4: At night – at night –

Male 1: They will carry out the operation at night.

Saddam: It is better to withdraw the troops yourself, instead of the enemy doing it for you!

Male 1: I mean not at the beginning; if it is going to take two weeks it should start on the last day of the second week.

Saddam: Please record it! They specified the withdrawal should take four days!

Male 4: On the fourth day.

Saddam: From Kuwait City, four days.

Male 1: On the last day they should remove it at night. That's what I see –

Saddam: This is a good remark.

Male 1: Sir, could we assassinate the Prince of Kuwait upon his entrance to Kuwait? [*Laughter.*]

Male 3: I understand that it is a daring task; however, it is for a good cause. What are the Palestinians here for if they cannot arrange for something like this? They have not done anything during this period! We have not even heard of any courageous operation they carried out! Why? How could they call themselves Palestinians? They should call themselves Kuwaitis! They have not done anything.

Male 4: Abu-al-'Abbas has nothing, Mr. President.[49]

Saddam: They helped Iraqi intelligence in some operations [*inaudible*].

Male 2: None of these organizations did anything, including the Arab Liberation Front.

Male 3: They did not do anything.

Kuwait: An English Woman's Tale (New York: St. Martin's Press, 1996), 81; Sir E. Lauterpacht et al., eds., *The Kuwait Crisis: Basic Documents* (New York: Cambridge University Press, 1993), 271.

49 Abu Abbas was the leader of the terrorist group the Palestine Liberation Front. He is best known in the United States as responsible for the hijacking of the *Achille Lauro* and the murder of the wheelchair-bound Leon Klinghoffer. There is extensive documentation concerning the relationship between Iraqi intelligence and Abu Abbas. See Kevin M. Woods with James Lacey, *Iraqi Perspectives Project – Saddam and Terrorism: Emerging Insights from Captured Documents Volume 1* (Redacted), IDA Paper No. P-4287 (Alexandria, VA: Institute for Defense Analyses, November 2007), 27–29, accessed 24 March 2009 at www.jfcom.mil/newslink/storyarchive/2008/pa032008.html.

Male 1: Even when they carried out these operations for intelligence, they did it through the Front's fighters![50]

Izzat: It is documented.

Male 1: It is documented, Sir. Intelligence oversaw the operations, but the components who executed it were the Front's fighters. They carried out the operations in Lebanon.

Izzat: We saw it documented by intelligence; the intelligence official sent us a letter stating the Front carried out so and so and so [inaudible].

Male 1: There was such a good operation in France –

Sa'dun: Commander Taha's opinion is not 100 percent out of the question!

Saddam: Why should we not consider it?

Sa'dun: Demoralize them in such circumstances. We should not be surprised if they celebrate in Kuwait –

Male 1: The Americans are going to try to be in Kuwait on the 25th because it is their [the Kuwaitis'] National Day.[51]

Saddam Reacts to the Onset of the Ground War (24 February 1991)[52]

Saddam: Let us say their air superiority limits our movements a bit.

Male 1: In addition to this Sir, you know the situation of our units, thanks to Your Excellency. That is to say, it is a small possibility, but there are 30 kilometers between each brigade; it is a gap.

Male 2: The important thing is that our units' attack against that army be strong –

Saddam: By God, our units remain excellent.

Male 1: At six o'clock, they made an announcement saying, "Since our assault, five hundred have surrendered," [inaudible], just as I spoke with so and so, such as the Staff Brigadier General Abud from the force, he read me a correspondence, stating, "Until now," meaning eleven-thirty, saying, "Until now, the army corps has been hit with more than five hundred artillery shells."

Male 2: Now it is downgraded to a media and psychological war.

Male 1: In addition, they began saying, "Sections of Iraqis began surrendering by the thousands."

Male 3: Yes, the media is dirty –

---

[50] Probably a reference to Abu Abbas's Palestine Liberation Front. Alternately, this may be a reference to the Popular Front for the Liberation of Palestine.

[51] 25 February is National Day in Kuwait. It celebrates the date in 1950 when Sheikh Abdullah Al Salin Al Sabah came to power. Kuwaiti independence, however, came on 19 June 1961.

[52] SH-SHTP-A-000-666, "Saddam and Iraqi Officials Discussing a US-Led Attack on Faylakah Island and the Condition of the Iraqi Army," 24 February 1991. A full transcript and recording of this meeting are available on the Web site of the Conflict Records Research Center.

Saddam: What would they give – they would announce things they hope would occur or that they expect to occur.

Male 1: This thing boosts their morale. Therefore, to boost their morale, if they need a picture they will provide them with it, through those who surrender to them.

Saddam: I have said that before.

Tariq: Whoever goes to them is a coward.

Saddam: They must say the things others are expecting of them.

Male 3: We are waiting for the weather to get better.

Saddam: That is to say, their media's calculations are not correct.

Male 3: There are storms –

Tariq: Are there storms at the airport?

[*Overlapping talk, inaudible.*]

Tariq: Flights are not heavy over the airport.

Male 1: [*Inaudible.*]

Tariq: Sir, George Bush has rushed into the ground attack [*inaudible*].

Saddam: Because of the political position.

Tariq: They were in a rush. They did not expect us to agree [to the 22 February Soviet cease-fire proposal]. They thought we would put forth other conditions.[53] So, when they realized that –

Saddam: They expected us to disagree with the Soviets and it would then become a conflict between the Soviets and us, next, they would continue to—So that they could say, "Now you see the other side of them."

––––––––

Saddam: ... The most important thing to me is to make sure there would not be any confusion concerning the Soviets' initiative and our agreement on it.

[53] On 22 February, Tariq announced that Iraq agreed to a cease-fire and withdrawal from Kuwait over a three-week period if the international community would lift the sanctions within forty-eight hours. From Saddam's perspective, only "technical details" stood in the way of an agreement with the United States. President Bush, by contrast, expressed disbelief that Iraq would act in good faith, suggesting that it would take advantage of a lengthy withdrawal to further ravage Kuwait. He told Mitterrand, "If there ever was a reason not to have a delay or wonder if they are acting in good faith, this report [of Iraq's destruction of Kuwaiti oil facilities] is one ... I don't know how this man can continue to talk peace through the Soviets, and still be taking these kinds of actions." Bush wanted the Iraqis to withdraw within ninety-six hours; agree to an exchange of prisoners; and satisfy all UN Security Council resolutions, not merely those dealing with an Iraqi military withdrawal. See Woods, *Mother of All Battles*, 212–19; "George Bush Phone Call with French President (Mitterrand)," 22 February 1991, accessed 10 July 2009 at www.margaretthatcher.org; "POTUS to Mikhail Gorbachev, RE: [Comments on your letter reporting on your talks with Tariq Aziz]," Draft Letter, 19 February 1991, Bush Library, NSC (Richard Haass Files), Working Files Iraq – February 1991 (4 of 6).

Tariq: There is not any confusion.

Saddam: The last thing we did at eleven o'clock last night was issue a statement in the name of the representative of the Revolutionary Command Council Representative's Director, attacking Bush, his devious methods, his stand against the Soviets' initiative, and his persistence in the aggression. In addition, our units will not be deceived by, that is to say, by rhetorical games and with this method. Was the statement issued?

Male 1: Yes.

Tariq: Sir, I held a press conference –

Saddam: We emphasized in our statement our commitment to the, to the agreements of Tariq Aziz.

Tariq: At twelve o'clock, I [inaudible] I gave a very short statement,[54] [it] was very short to the international press and [inaudible], the Russian and Arab initiative will be approved [inaudible]. I also read to them its paragraphs and denied the allegations of bombing the oilfields and this, the Revolutionary [Command] Council has called for an investigating committee [inaudible].[55]

Saddam: We did not deny it in a way [inaudible].

Tariq: I denied it; I am the one who did it.

Saddam: That is to say, let an investigation committee come and examine the locations being struck in Iraq and anywhere else, including other locations in Iraq and Kuwait.

Tariq: I understood the intent of the statement; however, I was forced to –

Saddam: In order to oversee which of these strikes are military targets and which are not.

Tariq: However, I added by saying this was an American allegation and we are –

Saddam: [Interrupting.] They would not agree, because the committee would find out that all the targets struck in Iraq are not military targets. However, the oilfields we struck were legitimate military targets, in order to cause diversions.

Tariq: They came out to see and said that there are two hundred oil wells –

Saddam: We have commented on all of them.

[Overlapping talk, inaudible.]

Male 3: . . . their ground force relies on their air force.

Saddam: Generally, we rely on our fighters, because of our experience in the eight straight years of war.

---

[54] In Moscow as part of Iraq's diplomatic efforts, Tariq Aziz issued a statement discussing Iraqi views of the Soviet peace proposal and denying Iraqi complicity in the destruction of Kuwaiti oil wells. See Serge Schemann, "Moscow Hopes Iraqis Can Find 'Guts' to Retreat," New York Times, 24 February 1991.

[55] For the text of the RCC statement, see "War in the Gulf: Statement by Iraqi Revolutionary Council," New York Times, 23 February 1991.

Tariq: What we need to watch out for is the media.

Saddam: Yes.

———

Male 1: I want to suggest to Your Excellency to take a section of the units in Kuwait – that is to say, it would be better, so that we would not be affected by this gathering [coalition].

Saddam: No, if this happened we will increase it.

Male 1: [*Inaudible.*]

Saddam: Because whenever we reduce the force in our wing [i.e., flank], it would be weakened and leads to an imbalance in our positions.

Male 1: Excuse me, Sir, I did not mean from the wing, rather to increase the watch units in Kuwait to avoid being surrounded, to avoid being surrounded inside – I mean, at the last stage, Sir.

Saddam: That is to say, this subject is difficult for us, if you would stay firmly or withdraw completely. As long as it remains 50/50, we will stay there.

Male 1: Yes, we are –

Tariq: Thank God.

Iraqi Leaders Discuss Arming the People. The Leadership Expresses the Belief That America's Casualty Aversion Can Still Allow Iraq to Win (24 February 1991)[56]

Muhammad:[57] . . . in my opinion, we should take into consideration and examine the provinces by the Iraqi-Saudi borders, according to any order of Your Excellency. We should also fully prepare the fighters of the Popular Army in general.[58] As for the armament, it should be of the public, and not only the trained individuals, [but] for all the citizens and the party organizations that are trustworthy. And anyone capable of carrying a weapon, we should arm him. Let there be street warfare, each one from his house and even the woman who has the capability to meet the requirements to fight. I see that the comrades – just as a reminder – the comrades in charge of the organization, of course they took all these issues into consideration, each one in his sector.

---

56 SH-SHTP-A-000-931, "Saddam and His Advisers Discussing the US Ground Attack during the 1991 Gulf War, Garnering Arab and Iraqi Support, and a Letter to Gorbachev," 24 February 1991. A full transcript and recording of this meeting are available on the Web site of the Conflict Records Research Center.

57 Probably either Muhammad Hamzah al-Zubaydi, a Regional Command member (1982–2001) who became deputy prime minister in March 1991 and played a key role in suppressing the Shi'a uprising, or Muhammad Saeed al-Sahhaf, the minister of foreign affairs (1992–2001).

58 The Popular Army was a paramilitary militia affiliated with the Ba'ath Party. Initially constituted to "defend the revolution" in the early 1970s, by the Gulf War, it was a corrupt and ineffective shell of its former self.

Saddam: They have specific orders, in writing, on how to act, maneuver, and to attack in the countryside, in the city, weapon type, general public arming. Didn't you receive the instructions to the comrades from the rest of the command members?

Males 1, 2, 3, 4: Yes, Sir, all the instructions were received. The letter you sent, Sir, arrived – ways of arming and how to deal with border infiltration.

Muhammad: Sir, I'm sure of this. The picture in front of our people is clear and they want to fight America, and now the desire for them –

Saddam: In time it will clear up, in time America will stay with England and some of the oil states.

Muhammad: So we –

Saddam: I don't think this international coalition will continue to the end, and especially after the new political status that was stated.

Muhammad: I think that when the battle began, our people were united and I think with God's will, the victory is our ally, and with God's will, we will win, like the first blow, the flight that our people resisted on the sixteenth and seventeenth [of January when the air campaign began] now this first blow, I think our people will bear it and start – If we caused 5,000 American casualties in a period of time –

Saddam: Five hundred.

Sa'dun: Sir, we will win if we have one Iraqi casualty for one American casualty, two for two.

Saddam: I told the military four for one.

Sa'dun: I swear to God, Sir, he told him four for one.

Muhammad: Now we should try to cause casualties on their side as much as we can. For them, if you notice, Sir, and I am sure –

Saddam: Comrade Muhammad, whether it is our artillery or our direct fighters' fire, as long as they enter the battleground, they are going to bear casualties.

Sa'dun: It requires guts. It requires an action beyond the Staff Academy principles; it requires guts I mean, defeating numbers and technology by human courage.

As Coalition Ground Forces Storm into Southern Iraq and Kuwait, Iraqi Leaders Discuss Soviet Diplomacy. Saddam Proposes Destroying Naval Bases and Other Places Coalition Forces Might Capture and Says That Iraq Will Fight House to House (24 February 1991)[59]

Sa'dun: Practically speaking, the Soviet Union harmed us very greatly.

Saddam: Starting with the mobilization in one direction –

[59] SH-SHTP-A-000-630, "Saddam and His Advisers Discussing the Soviet Union and the State of the Iraqi Military," 24 February 1991. A full transcript and recording of this meeting are available on the Web site of the Conflict Records Research Center.

Sa'dun: From the beginning –

Saddam: – and finishing in such and such a situation ... as if they were going to play a role. They tricked us. It was a trick!

Sa'dun: [Soviet leader Mikhail] Gorbachev said in a meeting, "Please, I do not want you to think we are going to trick you, set a trap for you or anything." Anyway, the intentions are still [*inaudible*], but practically they are the same.

Saddam: Yeah, they led us to the same result; we mobilized our people and army in one direction, but then we changed direction and the [*inaudible*] happened in the midst of this change. Anyway, let us hope for the best![60]

———

Saddam: I believe that the people of this country will completely understand our situation. We accepted everything those who tried to mediate between us and the enemy wanted [*pause*] and even more.

Male 1: In order to avoid the last phase of the conspiracy, we need to withdraw from the borders.

Saddam: On their fathers'[*inaudible*] [*Arabic curse*], in the name of God we will fight them from house to house.

———

Saddam: As far as the amphibious landing, if they keep the same strategy, the one I gave them five days ago, to destroy all naval bases and all places that can be used for landing and are easy to reach.[61] All of it needs to be destroyed by fire, in order to make a dark cloud above the troops from the other side, like a natural shield, because I mentioned to them the possibility of an attack.

Males 1, 2, 3: [*A group of people are talking at the same time, saying that this operation will prevent aircraft from flying.*] Because of the dust they would not be able to see. Mr. President, why do you want to do this now? They have not announced anything! This is all deception, lies, and hypocrisy.

Saddam: They are going to attack by land. Good! They will get defeated.

———

Males 1, 2, 3: [*Talking about Tariq Aziz and the countries helping him.*] They announced that they will not participate. The one that made a move is the Soviet Union. He [Tariq] is coming back to Iraq through Amman. Our newspaper published that he is coming back from Jordan. This afternoon –

———

[60] Saddam blamed the Soviet Union for assuring him that if he removed his troops from Kuwait, no ground operations would ensue against his army. Yevgeny Primakov, *Russia and the Arabs: Behind the Scenes in the Middle East from the Cold War to the Present* (New York: Basic Books, 2009), 321.

[61] The coalition had gone to great lengths to create a deception that the U.S. Marines would mount an amphibious landing directly into Kuwait. See Gary P. Melton, "XVIII Airborne Corps Desert Deception," *Military Intelligence Professional Bulletin* 17, no. 4 (1991): 43–45.

Saddam: Check if the newspaper published when Tariq Aziz will arrive in Baghdad. [*Inaudible.*]

Hamid: Gorbachev may not have made a statement following the attack!

Saddam: The first letter I sent him is available; read it and also read our complete reply to him.

Hamid: To the Soviet Union, President Mr. Gorbachev:

We trusted you and we have placed Iraq's honor and the dignity of the Iraqi Armed Forces in this trust. Therefore, we have agreed on your peace proposal, which you had provided to us in spite of all [the] fiscal and mental severity facing the Iraqi fighter. This circumstance we are facing is not easy, especially when the other side did not respond either way. Even though we will keep our promise, Mr. President, we do know that the Americans, especially their president, have no honor and we do not trust them; therefore, we are working only with your peace proposal. We agreed to it because of our strong trust only in you and the Soviet Union.

The situation now is getting worse. The Americans send their threats and are planning to deceive Iraq. The way they presented their statement and threats, it seems they have no respect for the Soviet Union's position. We do not hear your specific, clear response countering their pathetic statements and threats. Our nation and army are confused. We are asking ourselves, "Which one is more significant: the Soviet Union's proposal or the Americans' threats?" Either way, we need to clear up this issue, in order to prevent the Americans from deceiving our armed forces and our people, by your reply to this letter. We thank you for your response.

Greetings to you and to the people of the Soviet Union,

Saddam Hussein

Saddam: What time did you receive it?

Hamid: I received it about six o'clock in the evening and sent it to the Soviet ambassador at ten pm.

Saddam: Now you can see why I was worried during the last two days. This is what happened.

Hamid: The Russian Ambassador –

Saddam: I made a statement in the name of Comrade Izzat in order to advise the naval forces. Since the communication means are [*inaudible*]. You made your call with [*pause*] the Russian Ambassador, what did you accomplish with him?

Hamid: I visited the Russian Ambassador at seven pm and I asked him to do his best to get us an answer through our Ministry of Foreign Affairs as soon as possible. The answer arrived at four-thirty am or around five o'clock.

Saddam: I received the answer at four-forty-five am. I did not know the answer. I mean, about the attack. Go ahead.

Hamid: Dear Mr. President, Saddam Hussein:

We thank you for your personal letter showing your concerns about the situation that is getting more complicated despite our joint efforts to implement the procedures for a peaceful solution for the dispute. I would like to point out [*inaudible*] your decisions to agree on a peaceful solution were an extraordinarily important step and changed the entire situation. After we received your letter indicating you have approved the [peace] project we had arranged with the Minister of Foreign Affairs, Tariq 'Aziz, here in Moscow, and that it will be approved by the Iraqi government, we quickly took the following steps to implement this project's terms: During the last 24 hours we made two long phone calls. The first one was with the American President, George Bush, followed by the leaders of Britain, Germany, Italy, France, and Japan. In fact, I was personally busy all day engaging in these discussions summarized in the following: [*inaudible*] postponed for a few months, created a new particular situation with exceptional [*inaudible*] as far as how important it is to find a peaceful solution for the problem. We called on the international coalition to use this opportunity to stop the bloodshed. For the sake of a fast solution for the mentioned peace proposal, we requested holding an exceptional session of the Security Council of the United Nations where the issues of the ceasefire supervision and monitoring and the forces' withdrawal will be discussed in the same manner as the other issues. At this time, the United Nations members are meeting in New York, discussing the situation. I should say that, in most cases, the reactions to this information are positive, and the efforts made to reach a peaceful solution to this situation are greatly appreciated.

At the same time, President Bush still insists on honoring the American party's request, and he is not willing to agree to our proposal. The American President claims he is doing this because he believes Iraq is carrying out environmental terrorism, blowing up the oil refining installations in Kuwait, as well as burning the oil fields. Tariq 'Aziz was clever in his statement at the press conference when he condemned the Americans' accusations against Iraq. He was prepared to clarify Iraq's position along with a meeting in the UN non-alignment committee.[62] This is what we are dealing with now. The United Sates can ignore what they don't like in a peaceful solution through the Security Council, and the Americans [can] begin land operations against Iraqi forces in the Gulf. We are taking the toughest procedures to avoid such a turning point of events, and it is still difficult to say whether these procedures are going to be successful.

I believe, under these circumstances, that it would be useful and important to announce, openly and clearly, your decision to withdraw all your forces from Kuwait to their locations on August 1, 1990 without delay or reservation. I also believe in this regard it is possible to address a letter to President Bush directly. It is very clear that, at this intense moment, we need a fast solution to end this important situation without argument. My suggestion is that it is very important for Iraq to withdraw its forces from the land. All of this will be discussed in the UN session. A number of nations are expecting that 21 days for the withdrawal of forces to be a long time. This is the timeframe we agreed on. These nations believe this delay is intentional. I suggest that you mention in your statements another timeframe for the withdrawal of forces of 9–10 days. Without doubt, this will create a different impression for Iraq and won't present any special difficulties. I replied to your letter promptly because I know how important this time is. We are following the situation carefully to avoid any other alternatives, because from the beginning our goal is to protect lives and the honor of the Iraqis and the other Arab nations in the Gulf region.

[62] Possibly a reference to the Non-Aligned Movement.

Greetings,

Mikhail Gorbachev

24/02/1991

Saddam: He still did not answer the question. It is nothing but talk!

Hamid: Mr. President sent a response to this letter and I gave it to the Russian Ambassador at 7:00 a.m.

Saddam: I wrote it at six-thirty. At this time I haven't received the news; therefore, you need to go to the Russian Ambassador and confirm with him the time and the date of my letter and when it was sent to Moscow, to prove to them that this letter was written before I received the news. [*Inaudible*] and this is what happened – so they would not say that this assurance came to us after the letter. Hope to God everything would go well. This is the letter in full.

Hamid: To Mr. President Gorbachev:

With respect, I received your response letter around 5:00, 6:00 a.m. Baghdad time on 02/24/91. I was very satisfied with its contents and I would like to offer my special thanks for all your hard work in this matter, because any help you offer us during this transition period would make the withdrawal faster, and we will use it to shorten the time, not lengthen it. Mr. President Gorbachev, we carry out our commitments if we make them, and the concern that President Bush and his allies express is nothing but a matter of not trusting us, they do not believe we will abide by what we say, and they are revealing their bad conscience, which is loaded with lies and deceptions. Bush's hands are loaded with bloodshed and the killing of innocent people... Now everything has become clear. Finally, I wish you all the luck with your agenda, because your agenda is to help peace, which is the opposite of what Bush, his mercenaries, or his friends are doing. Peace [be] upon you,

Saddam Hussein

6:30am, Baghdad time

———

Saddam: One of you needs to explain the situation [*One person agrees.*] Please read for us, bring the map – [*Tape stops.*] Is it marked?

Male 2: Yes, Mr. President, the 14th Infantry arrived at this holding line with the tank battalion. Also, here Sir, the 3rd Regiment of the 95th Brigade advanced and is currently in the direction of –

Saddam: That means that the 3rd Regiment is a part of the covering troops?

Male 2: Yes, Sir, one of these isolated ones. Here, Sir, the [*inaudible, possibly* enemy] force is estimated to be an armored brigade. Over there, Sir, they got three kilometers back by the covering troops the first time.

Saddam: They withdrew!

Male 2: Yes, Sir; this is Bubiyan and Failakah Islands [*sounds of pointing on a map*]. [*Inaudible.*] We had communication with them until eleven, but then we lost them.

Saddam: Communication stopped at eleven o'clock, but did they say anything before it got disconnected? It could be technical problems with their communication device.

Male 2: Yes, Mr. President, they were battered very hard until eleven o'clock.

THE PAGE OF TREASON AND TREACHERY: THE UPRISINGS

The tapes indicate that Saddam viewed the 1991 Shi'a uprising, which he labeled the "page of treason and treachery," as part of a grander plot against Iraq. From his perspective, the United States intended for its attacks to weaken Iraq's army, lower Iraqi morale, and thereby facilitate uprisings. Iran, for its part, trained the leaders of the Shi'a rebellion in Persia. In Saddam's accounting, the government lost control in seventeen of Iraq's eighteen provinces. Only al-Anbar Province in the west remained loyal.[63] When called to account for their loyalty, tribal leaders in Saddam City blamed local homosexuals and transvestites for their shortcomings. Saddam directed the sheikhs to "slaughter" or exile such sexual deviants.

Saddam and His Commanders Analyze the Causes of the Kurdish and Shi'a Uprisings, Attributing Them to a Cascade of Demoralization within the Army (3 April 1991)[64]

Saddam: Let him explain to you everything in brief, what happened in the north and in the south the way it occurred, I mean. Of course, it is clear that – I am not sure whether Sabir has this information or not. Timing was set for the action so that on the fourth day of the US land attack, the operation would begin in the south.

Sabir:[65] Excuse me, Sir. I don't have such information. But the information we are sure of is that they met –

Saddam: That's, that's what was confirmed in the investigation.

Sabir: Yes, Sir.

Saddam: Well, the investigation, I reviewed it briefly. Despite this detail, what happened, the preparation for what happened is according to the following. The Americans wanted to hurt Iraq by hurting its army. Its army would get destroyed. Such an opportunity was to be, eh, taken advantage of by all the greedy people or the hateful ones or those who had beforehand evil intentions against Iraq, whether they were from outside or inside Iraq. The entire siege, the air bombardment until the land attack began, they were all methods used to create the appropriate environment for the operation that took place. So, the appropriate environment was created.

---

[63] Woods, *The Mother of All Battles*, 9.

[64] SH-SHTP-A-000-739, "Saddam and Officials Discussing the State of the Iraqi Army, the 1991 Uprising, and the Withdrawal from Kuwait," 3 April 1991.

[65] Apparently Major General Sabir 'Abd al-'Aziz al-Duri, director of military intelligence during the Mother of All Battles who became director of general intelligence following the war.

The psychological aspect was the most important factor prepared, meaning the feeling of defeat that spread to the government offices first, before the defeat happened in fact and became a physical and effective condition, beginning by the change of all the headquarters. Well, if we had to change the location of a ministry because we were obliged to due to its specific location, if this happened, we had to accept it with the losses that accompanied it [*bangs the table*] and we even had to accept the loss of this ministry as one of the lessons to learn. Anyway! But this spread to the point where the governor would change the location of this ministry, and the security director would change its location, and the police director would change its location, and so on. And maybe their other secondary offices would change their location. What happened was that the government was nonexistent. Well, the government offices were nonexistent. In such a way that whoever would say he was a Sultan, it was possible for him to become Sultan. So, the traitors showed up in a certain situation supported by elements trained and specially prepared to play such a role in Iran. And they erupted in Basra and they erupted in other places you know and even in the north. The main elements that attacked us didn't come from Sulaimaniyah or from Irbil or from Dohuk.

Sabir: From outside.

Saddam: The main ones came from outside and the ones who moved with them, made their move after the outside action took place, meaning after the reaction came from outside. In other words, this applies to the south. Well, but not all the south. In the south, there were people who fought on the inside like those who came from outside. I mean, especially the organized ones of them, or those who were brainwashed with a series of life and religious norms to the point that they imagined that what they were doing was something they had to do regardless of all the other details. Other than certain exceptions that someone could notice, the majority of the people in the south played a role in preparing the requirement for the mutiny and the creation of a psychological condition, but they did not want the mutiny to happen the way it did. Imagine, it is not all the people of Missan, in the city of Amara, who wanted the rebellion the way it happened. But a large number of the people of Missan wanted the mutiny to happen as it did and wanted harsher results than those that occurred. In the north, things were different. In the north, and first of all those who carried out the insurgency in the north, eh, were experienced. It was a brigade that had a long practice with defeat.

Sabir: Yes, Sir.

Saddam: I mean, they have lived through generations of defeat and death. Well, a lot of them died and they were defeated a lot.

———

Saddam: In the north, our troops were not so weak. There were troops and the American bombardment did not initially take place near them, nor did they incur losses or sacrifices. That's why [*bangs the table*] this is what we should stop at and be a little harsher with our troops that were defeated in the north in a different manner than in the south. What do you see today? Your weapons are here, your properties are here, no one attacked you, you didn't lose anything. Why did you run away and declare defeat?

Hashim:[66] [*Addressing Sabir.*] Are part of them coming?

Saddam: The reason –

Sabir: [*Inaudible*] the fifth conflict.

Saddam: The reason is the psychological condition. The reason is the same issue we talked about. We said that the Kurds in Sulaimaniyah [in northeastern Iraq] felt the shock about Karbala [in central Iraq] in the same manner those who were in Zakho [in Northern Iraq] felt the shock of, eh –

Sabir: Kuwait.

Saddam: Kuwait. So, he [the Iraqi soldier in the north] was psychologically defeated. Well, he, I mean, when it comes to the material things, there was nothing to cause this defeat. When you come and you ask him, "Come and tell me why were you defeated?" There was no reason.

Hashim: He wouldn't be able to talk and wouldn't even be able to convince himself.

Saddam: Impossible. But the defeat was psychological. Well, he was defeated on the inside. When someone is defeated on the inside, all the external factors won't be able to stop him from being defeated.

———

Saddam: Let us please God and please our conscience. Let's go back to a medium-size and high-quality army. There are things I want to tell you. I made a decision about them and conveyed it to the command; namely, one of the reasons for what happened was this very large army. The details are the following. For a long time, we have been saying that we should get our army back to a reasonable size so we could focus on it. You remember when we were over with the [Iran-Iraq] war and we began, I mean, I began insisting on the necessity of being quick. Sorry, I mean on the necessity of a rapid demobilization. But we made mistakes when we took into consideration psychological and political factors we adopted militarily later on. When we entered Kuwait, to delay the attack, the, I mean the enemy's counterattack, we immediately declared the creation of a number of divisions at once. These divisions, the, the reason for announcing their creation was political and psychological. But we adopted them with the passing of time and they became a reality. We adopted them as divisions when in fact they were lacking equipment, preparation, and training and were imperfect from all viewpoints...

We want the best leader for the divisions. We select ten who are good. Then, when we come to select the next ten we find that they lack half the characteristics of the first ten. Then, when we come to select the ten next to reach 30, we find in them a quarter of the characteristics of the first ten. Then, when we go from 30 to 40, we find in them one eighth of the characteristics of the first ten, and so on until we reach the situation in which we were.

Hussein Kamil: This applied to the regiment and the commander of the division.

---

[66] Sultan Hashim Ahmed al-Jaburi al-Tai represented Iraq at the cease-fire negotiations with the coalition, played a key role in suppressing domestic uprisings, and served as minister of defense (1994–2003).

Saddam: So, the army is grouped and well-prepared, you choose its men correctly according to rules and the commanders based on a personal knowledge, not only rules. This one is the son of that individual and that one is the son of that other individual and so on. We should know his degree of loyalty, where he grew up when he was a child, the years he attended high school, what were his characteristics when he joined the military academy, and what's his goal. Without this, we cannot build a real army. A well-organized army composed of 15 divisions is better than an army of 45 divisions. Well! This is the basis. So, begin as of now and think accordingly. What's urgent, the matter I mentioned, which I need you to help me with.

The [uprising in the] north has destroyed the army. One of the reasons behind the army's ailment is the north. Even the riot that happened in Kuwait, one of its causes, one of its ailments – of course it did not begin on this scale. It began on a lesser scale and even the riot that happened in our country, the looting that took place in Iraq was perpetrated by the saboteurs, although some of them [*clears his throat*] had instructions to destroy only, meaning not to take hold of the power. It's impossible for the Iranians to take hold of the power. Just the infliction of destruction. And Iranians were primarily the ones who designed it. But part of the looting was caused by what happened in Kuwait. Well, in a way, people learned to extend their hands to the public's property. We did not tell people that Kuwait was not Iraqi and they could go and loot it, in order to make a difference between it and public property. Although Kuwait was Iraqi, looting continued in it. So, it created that kind of mixed understanding towards the public property.

Hussein Kamil Informs Saddam That His Inner Circle Was Too Scared to Tell Him about the Low Morale of Iraqi Soldiers during the Page of Treason and Treachery. The Leadership Also Discusses the Crucial Roles Played by the Air Force, Republican Guard, and Mujahadeen-e-Khalq (Spring 1991)[67]

Hussein Kamil: ... The points, which I would like to bring to your attention, Sir, because there is not enough time in this meeting to explain—

Saddam: The honorable people really show their true colors in these situations.

Hussein Kamil: Sir, we are used to talk – let us say on the armed forces level, although it is on a higher level than the armed forces – we did not provide you with the true picture of the situation, for a variety of reasons: fear or giving the impression that we had been shaken or because it is normal to be cautious. But from now on we are supposed to present you with the complete truth. Many times, either at the time of the disturbance or before, especially the Kuwait situation, which caused us suffering, Sir, for example, when we were in Kuwait, all the members in the supreme command – which you used to send someone to supervise them – morale reached a level, the lowest level anyone could ever reach. However, when we used to come and see you, Sir, we could not reveal it to you or inform you of the truth about our situation, as they say.[68]

---

[67] SH-SHTP-A-000-614, "Saddam and Officials Discussing the Uprising in the South," undated (circa March 1991).

[68] According to Mahdi Obeidi, one of Iraq's leading nuclear scientists, "Hussein Kamel was so afraid of Saddam that he feared bringing anything but good news." See Mahdi Obeidi and Kurt Pitzer, *The Bomb in My Garden: the Secrets of Saddam's Nuclear Mastermind* (Hoboken, NJ: John Wiley and Sons, 2004), 97.

Saddam: What you used to say, you used to express your dissatisfaction with the army's spirits at an early stage. However, I was very surprised to find out that you were the only one who felt that way about the army. I thought maybe the intelligence officers were not meticulous with you.

Hussein Kamil: If my colleagues will allow me, I would like to mention that many times I heard the same from others, including the commanders, Sir, the commanders noticed the same low morale among the army individuals, and they could not discuss it. I believe they were afraid, however, I noticed that all the people were –

Saddam: Were they afraid or shy?

Hussein Kamil: Well, it is both, I swear to God. I was the center for everyone to complain, everyone would stop by and complain to me. The governors would vanish, Sir, from their governorates, and the people heard that the management center was located at the reception; therefore, they would stop by and complain. I might have talked to you, Sir, regarding some of what I witnessed. One of the governors, Sir, from the Al-Mosul division, a division member and a chief of police, I believe from Al-Samawah, Sir, he walked all the way, from Samawah, he walked every district and county. He said, "I was hoping for just someone friendly to meet. I could not find anyone. I could not believe how we supported many people before, who are Sheikhs from tribes, some of them are close friends and party members' friends, and no one is willing to help us." I told him, "My friend, if we could not even find a friend to support us at this current time and to be friendly with you, what are we doing working for the governorate?" The governor of Al-Samawah, himself, said to me, "To be honest with you, we used to lie to the command and I believe if I mention this story to you, you might be convinced of it. And that is if I don't talk the same way others do, I would look to them as if I have not done anything. I might be replaced and people might feel sorry for me!" So, Sir, we don't have the time to list to the same old talk.

Saddam: Their official used to say to me, "The people and the party members are upset, with regard to your peace initiative decision, which will occur on 2/15." I said to him, "Why are the people and the party members upset?" He said, "You caused them to lose the chance to kill the Americans." That was a great concept. I explained the situation to him and I was very happy to hear that, if he indeed meant it! I had no doubts at all about what he stated. I thought he might be trying to make me feel better, since the withdrawal decision was not an easy issue.

———

Saddam: ... Lieutenant General Sabir ... was very confident. I allowed him to make important decisions, on all the issues. I used to avoid being with him in one location since I was also required to meet with Command and with members of the Revolutionary [Command] Council, who are some of our associates, and I was supposed to meet with 'Alaa. The Air Force played its part before this time; however, during the uprising of the east, what indeed benefited us was the pilots' expertise. The presence of Al-Hakam by Sabir made the latter operate the army's flight this way. Al-Hakam also had good and great energy. That was the whole picture of General Sabir, which I witnessed myself. I did not see Muhammad. Did I see you, Muhammad, during that time? Oh, yes, I did, for just one day. Muhammad's division was in high spirits, their belief in God was strong, and their belief in victory was serious ... As far as the military image, I have not seen that. When a negative issue accrues, the front must inform the rest.

Hussein Kamil: This way it will not accumulate on them.

Saddam: I used to call and sometimes Sultan, Hussein, or Saadi, would answer.[69] Did I talk to you on the phone Saadi? Yes, I believe once. The worst thing they used to tell me, in the worst times was, "It will get better, God willing." Their morale was excellent. The believer always retains his faith despite the difficult situations; however, we lost the middle situation, which is between the few believers and the few horrific ones. That was because of the massive pressure from the enemy, due to their strength and arrogance, some of them did not even remember the mercy of God, and that God is stronger than any other power. This shaking that occurred cracked the wall for those few horrific ones. Therefore, we lost, due to the shaking.

––––––

Hussein Kamil: Sir, when you used to call us, we would tell you, "God willing things will improve."

Saddam: Things did improve.

Hussein Kamil: You are right, Sir. It is not about defeat or – I swear to God, we made a promise with the sun, to shine again, and Sultan remembers it as if it were right now. After two hours, the situation improved by far – where in the next day – Sir, you remind me of a story that was best described by the Minister of Interior, whom you called in Basra and he said, "Sir, we achieved victories." So, when we realized what the situation was, which we did not expect, even when we responded to Your Excellency, we were astonished, not based on fear or non-belief.

Saddam: Fear is not in your nature, you are experienced. You were a brigade tank commander and you spread your blanket to sleep and you did not leave your tank in the Iranian's lands, so the Iranians would not steal it. You did not leave your tank until the last minute. All of you are very experienced.

Hussein Kamil: Sir, you got us used to victories and when we saw them [defeats] happening –

Izzat: It was a surprise to you.

Hussein Kamil: Withdrawal and anarchists on the inside.

Izzat: To be greeted this way by people upon returning from the battle is [inaudible].

Saddam: Yes.

Izzat: We can accept it

Saddam: Easily.

Izzat: But not the soldiers.

––––––

[69] Saddam might be referring to General Hussein Rashid, army chief of staff; Farid Sultan, operations assistant to Hussein Rashid; and Saadi Tuma Abbas, minister of defense.

Hussein Kamil: In fact, Sir, the Republican Guard achieved something, a glorious deed for Iraq that I, personally, can never forget – the Republican Guard's service for Iraq entirely. And General Sabir discussed this aspect, and although I was not in Basra and based on what we heard, the Republican Guard played a key role in Basra, and encouraged the rest of the army and expanded it [i.e., increased its size]. In fact, Sir, the Republican Guard's performance was superior, and this is something I can never forget – its role because it prevented Iraq from making any sacrifice because it could have cost us much more and still not achieved [*inaudible*], or a disaster could have happened in Iraq that would have been hard to deal with . . . I witnessed in the army, Sir, the appearance of some soldiers being slow on purpose and taking their own time, and I believe you are aware of this issue, Sir. We are working in every direction, in the meantime, calmly and optimistically, on forming an Iraqi army as it used to be. The last and long eight years [of the Iran-Iraq War] and the latest situation exhausted the army. Moreover, it did not allow the training establishments or establishments related to training the army to assign officers, meaning officers suitable for this position because we wanted good brigade commanders and good division commanders and forgot all about the training center, for instance, the military academy or the General Staff Academy. Or if we wanted to divide the good and existing number between either good leader, good commander, center commander or chief of military academy or general staff, we would realize that the good numbers of competent people were not enough. We need police officers to be good commanders and good leaders, trained through training establishments and special establishments, in preparing the army, which means, to be run by competent individuals . . .

To make the long story short, Sir, we need to prepare the army for six months, in order to improve it. Our army is a family and I do not have any negative incident to mention about them. Furthermore, and in order to be honest about the situation, I am not going to lie and say, "We do not need anything new for the army." Army is everything, we must choose the right candidates, choose the right centers, and concentrate on the training methods and on preparing the army and the people.

Saddam: Go ahead Lieutenant General Sabir.

Sabir: Sir, I forgot to mention two issues. If you allow me, I would like to mention gratitude to some individuals. The first issue, Sir, is the effort of the Mujahadeen-e-Khalq in repressing the uprising in some areas, to the degree that they saved Diyala Governorate. If Mujahadeen-e-Khalq were not in Jawwalah, we would have lost Jawwalah . . . The Iranians imposed on our land and attacked the Mujahadeen-e-Khalq and Diyala.

Saddam Meets with Tribal Leaders in Saddam City to Discuss the Tribes' Loyalties and the Appropriate Treatment of Rebels and Cross-Dressers (after 13 November 1991)[70]

Sheikh 1:[71] When the residents of the city noticed the increase in desertions, they approached the Minister of the Interior in this regard, Mr. Watban [Ibrahim

---

[70] SH-SHTP-A-000-891, "Saddam and Saddam City Tribal Leaders Talking in the Wake of Demonstrations and Riots in Saddam City," undated (circa late 1991 or 1992).

[71] As the sheikhs were not Iraqi government officials, the editors have removed their names to protect their identities.

al-Hasan], who issued an amnesty, by request of Your Excellency, of course, and handed over more than 60,000 [names]. [Sheikh 2] and I were awarded the first prize from the Ministry of the Interior for the largest number and ten [*inaudible*]. I also visited my province, Missan, and I met with the governor who gave us his instructions and then headed to the lakes [Al-Ahwar] according to his instructions.[72]

We came today, Mr. President, asking your forgiveness for the rabble-rousers' demonstration since none of the city residents were involved. Those people of the city are very faithful soldiers, who only wish to please you and to obey your orders. I would like to end my speech with a poem:[73]

You must be proud indeed, Mr. President of Iraq,
For as long as you wish, as high as the sky, no one ever was as proud as you are.
You are a very courageous president; courage itself fears someone eternally like
    yourself.
If crises occur, you take immediate action with your wisdom and bravery;
Therefore, do not pay attention to the dogs' howling.
You are magnificent and we are your soldiers who will never join someone else's
    leadership!
May peace be upon you! [*Applause.*]

Saddam: You may live long!

Male 1: Mr. President, [*inaudible*] that is how we knew you were angry in your heart with us. The etiquette is that the uncle visits his son and the uncle's father visits his father. Why is that? To clear his heart from any negativity towards him, therefore, we are just like [Shaykh 2] mentioned; we are asking you to remove any anger in your heart towards us. We are your soldiers along with our tribes and our children. Our battle, we stood in unity when you visited the such-and-such person, such-and-such city, such-and-such center, and such-and-such province, and you did not visit us. We knew then that you were angry in your heart at us; therefore, we beg you, we are your children and you are our father and whoever lies to you, we must kill him.

———

Saddam: The rabble-rousers do not know these notions. Those who dye their hair in green and red do not know these meanings, and it is a shame for you to let them live. You should slaughter them with your own hands. Those people who dye their

---

[72] The Missan governate, in southern Iraq, shares a lengthy border with Iran and was overrun by rebels during the Shi'a uprising. The mention of al-Ahwar is apparently a reference to Iraqi plans to drain the marshes.

[73] Flattering Saddam with poetry was commonplace in Iraq. Iraqi newspapers were replete with poems adulating him and his regime. At times, Iraqis appear to have avoided punishment by sycophantically praising Saddam with poetry. When a Military Industrial Commission director general was ordered to give Saddam a progress report on a missile project, he recited poetry he had written eulogizing Saddam. Saddam praised his poetry and "brushed aside" the details of the project. See Obeidi and Pitzer, *The Bomb in My Garden*, 181; Bengio, *Saddam's Word*, 9, 77–79, 84, 197.

hair and wear red lipstick like women, I say you must slaughter them and hold me responsible for it.

Male 2: We are afraid of the [inaudible].

Saddam: I take full responsibility for it!

Male 2: We are afraid that would be a crime.

Saddam: I take full responsibility for it and it is not a crime. Those people, I take full responsibility and it is not a crime.

All: You are right master.

Saddam: Whoever dyes his hair and wears makeup like women is effeminate. In my knowledge, the first *fatwa* of our Master Ali [ibn Abi Talib] was related to one case that happened to Muslims the first time where someone deviated. When asked about the solution – this might have happened during Umar's [ibn al-Khattab's] era – they asked Abu-Al-Hasan [Ali ibn Abi Talib], "What should we do with this man?" He replied, "We should climb to the highest point, throw him upside down and let him fall down head first." This was a big *fatwa*. What I mean here is that looking at the nitty-gritties in life will prevent you from looking at the big issues.[74]

––––––––

Saddam: I would like to answer your question about whether I am upset with you or not. I am not upset with you. If I were, I would have told you so and you know it. I am upset because of some of your children, but at the same time you covered up for them and forgot all about it.

We acknowledge the fact that out of 10,000 people we will find bad ones, maybe 20 bad ones, 30, 200, 300, and 400, why – and we should not become upset, but we should warn them and direct them to the right path. Whoever is following the wrong path, we say to him, "Listen son! This is the right path and you must follow it," because Muhammad Bin 'Abdallah, who is a prophet and we believe in him, he is a prophet right? And after Muhammad Bin 'Abdallah died and his tomb was still [inaudible]. But then Musaylama announced that he is a prophet and Sejah joined him. Is that not right? Is there any disagreeing on this? Isn't that recorded in the history? They did not bring those people to Islam, until they cut off 10,000 people's heads by swords. Can you imagine 10,000 heads by swords? They didn't follow the Quran when they beheaded those people. They committed their act regardless. They cut off lots of heads and got rid of many bad people, including those who treasured the Quran.[75]

––––––––

74 Ali ibn Abi Talib was caliph, the leader of the Islamic world, from 656 to 657. Umar was the second caliph, from 634 to 644. Abu-Al-Hasan refers back to Ali ibn Abi Talib. For Sunni Muslims, Ali was the fourth and last of the "rightly guided" caliphs, whereas Shi'a Muslims regard him as the first imam (leader of the Islamic community) and believe that his descendants are Muhammad's proper successors. The fatwa to which Saddam refers is unclear. See Karen Armstrong, *Islam: A Short History* (New York: Modern Library, 2002), xiv–xv.

75 Shortly after the death of Muhammad, Maslama (Musaylama) arose as a "false prophet" in eastern Arabia and Sejah as a "false prophetess" in northeastern Arabia. The new Islamic leaders compelled these apostates' followers to pay allegiance to Medina. See Hugh

Therefore, the Muslims were afraid that two or three more similar incidents would accrue, and they could not use the Quran as guidance for those people. They said, "Whoever memorized the Quran must put this in the Quran," and they put it in the Quran. Those people saw Muhammad Bin ʿAbdallah, God's Blessing and peace be upon him, and listened to his stories and he told them, "From Gabriel and God I brought you the Quran, if anyone believes of performing a better job, or a similar job, please do so." After he died, Musaylama said, "I am a prophet," Sejah said, "I will compete against you." Others who followed Muhammad before, said, "We will follow you." They returned to Islam because they were afraid of the swords. If the sword was neutral, of course God's will is the most important; however, if they did not enforce it, and the sword stayed neutral, we would not have been sure what our situation would look like now. We should not be surprised to find 100 or 300 [bad people]. I would not even be surprised to find 1,000 in Saddam City [today the Sadr City area of Baghdad, a predominantly Shiʾa area] because they will exist; however, I would be surprised if they existed while the rest remained neutral. But to watch the rest raising their swords to the thousand and ripping them apart, why would I be upset? I was upset at some officials in certain areas in Iraq or some Party members in certain areas in Iraq, because the good people adulated them since they [the good people] wanted to see them becoming prominent first.

—————

Saddam: May God bless you! I am just blaming you because, God forbid, if there was any defect and no men from the same place countered it, I must blame you.

Male 3: You should not be upset with us. We are your children.

Saddam: But for that small issue to happen in the midst of the big mess and to be tackled by people there, it will become a part of the past and the good people will remain in their places. We thank God.

Male 4: [*Inaudible.*]

Saddam: This subject never crossed my mind, and of course, Saddam City is your city just as it is my city, as well as the villages, farms, and the tribes. It is all for the good people and you all are good people. You must take care of it just as you care for Al-ʾUmara, Al-Diwania, and Salah Al-Din. Good people are strong willed.

Male 3: We shall protect our birthplaces, the revolution, and the party until death, God willing. We may not sleep and you may not see us in Al-ʾAmara, by the Westside, where my nephew was a victim of the rabble-rousers who struck his house and destroyed it. They did the same to my cousin's house. Can you believe that? However, his attitude was impressive, because he stood up to them and refused to escape, and whoever died in it, died. Thanks to God.

Saddam: We hope that this situation will never reoccur or affect Iraq at all.

Kennedy, *The Great Arab Conquests: How the Spread of Islam Changed the World We Live In* (Philadelphia: Da Capo Press, 2007), 55–56.

Male 5: We find the Sheikhs grouping together in fours and fives, before we know it. Even Mr. ʿAdel, who is in charge of the line, provided gas for us and we distributed it to other sources.

Saddam: I am seeking your help with the issue of those who dye their hair and wear women's clothes. This is shameful for Iraqis and against Islam. If a Syrian, Egyptian or Moroccan saw those people, he would laugh and say "What is that? Is that a man or a woman?" Iraqis are not like that, Iraqis are real men.

Male 5: Master, there is a more important issue than that, and it is hurting the citizens' feelings. There is someone from our citizens, a deserter soldier, I call them rabble-rousers. Why do I call them that? It is because he spends his day stealing from homes, and hurting people.

Saddam: Why did he escape and from what? We dismiss whomever comes back. So, what is he escaping from?

Male 5: This person is an escapee and commits all those horrific crimes. When we make a report at the center, they issue an inactive warrant for his arrest, then the case freezes and is forgotten.

Saddam: No, this is inappropriate and I say it to you and to everyone. Whoever tries to escape from it, we say to him, "Come here and face us. We heard this from Saddam Hussein."[76]

All: [*Applause.*]

Saddam: He needs to admit what he did. Enough hurt and pain. He must admit and if his group is dismissed, he can be dismissed along with his group, but if not, he may then return to his normal job. The taxi driver will go back to his old profession and the farmer –

Male 5: Master, if the soldier returns – if I were successful in convincing him of your order and he returns, to what authority should I –

Saddam: I was about to tell you right now. You need to submit forms to the Party organization in Saddam's City, explaining the situation and that is all. Captain ʿAbed, the secretary will listen, the attendant will listen, and the office chief will listen. They will all be aware of the situation. Help him pack his clothes, as the farmers say; however, you turn him over to the police officer and you say to him, "We have an order from Saddam Hussein that you must arrest this person, or we will report you." If you want to give them a chance the first time, talk to them first; tell them they should say to him, "You give the city and your family a bad name. If you do not wish to follow the correct path, you must leave the area." You are authorized to tell any rabble-rouser to leave his tribe if he does not follow the right path and our way. He must leave and take his family with him. Those are the most important issues for us.

---

[76] The regime punished deserters by cutting off their ears and branding them with a tattoo on their foreheads. *SH-SHTP-A-001-238, "Saddam and His Political Advisers Discussing International Interest in Iraqi Oil, Iraqi Army Deserters, and an Initiative to Settle Disputes with Saudi Arabia," 3 September 1994; Human Rights Watch, *Iraq's Brutal Decrees: Amputation, Branding and the Death Penalty*, 1 June 1995, accessed 8 July 2010 at www.unhcr.org/refworld/docid/3ae6a7f00.html.

IRAQ'S "VICTORY": SADDAM'S ASSESSMENTS OF THE WAR

The Iraqi leadership took steps to assess results from the Mother of All Battles, although Saddam frequently exerted pressure on his subordinates to reach specified conclusions. He disputed accounts that emphasized Western military prowess, and he explained to his subordinates that they must do likewise to protect Iraqi morale. Saddam expressed belief that Iraq's fighting spirit and other factors had forced President Bush to call a premature halt to the coalition's military aggression. He noted the devastation that a preemptive Iraqi strike would have wrought on gathering U.S. forces and promised retaliatory attacks on America. Rather than focusing on regrets, the tone of Saddam's comments is fatalistic: what occurred was nothing other than the will of God.

Saddam Suggests That Iraq's "Fighting Spirit" Led President Bush to Request a Cease-Fire (1 May 1991)[77]

Saddam: Describe what the state of the Republican Guard was before that. Before you were issued the order to withdraw, how strong were you when you clashed with the enemy?

Male 1: Sir, we fought the Iranian enemy, pardon me, Sir, the American enemy.

Saddam: Because I have an explanation that has one military aspect for Bush's action announcing a unilateral ceasefire.

Male 1: Sir, they were –

Saddam: After their armored ranks dashed and [they] talked dramatically, saying this was the first time such a big armored attack took place against the Iraqi forces since World War II and had a clash, after that they seemed as if they were preparing for something, for a military event. This image disappeared after that, to be replaced by a unilateral ceasefire statement. Of course, there is a political aspect that has to do with the Security Council meeting and other possibilities. Go ahead.

––––––

Male 1: At the same time, the commanders understood the situation and the combat, and we explained to them through the procedures we took during the meetings that our tanks had the ability and capability to fight the [*inaudible, possibly "American"*] tanks. This was a fact, Sir, and not just talk, where we had the technical ability and capability to fight the American tanks based on the information we were getting

---

[77] Audio recording of Iraqi officials briefing Saddam Hussein on the performance of Iraqi troops, particularly in Kuwait, 1 May 1991. *SH-SHTP-A-001-241, "Iraqi Officials Briefing Saddam on the Performance of Iraqi Troops in Kuwait," 1 May 1991. In other recordings, Saddam stated that Bush's fear of Iraqi armor and a destructive Iraqi Scud missile attack motivated Bush to call for the ceasefire. SH-SHTP-A-000-849, "Saddam and Military Officials Discussing the Condition of the Iraqi Army and its Possible Enlargement," 1 May 1991; and, *SH-SHTP-A-001-242, "Saddam and Military Officials Discussing Lessons Learned from the 1991 Gulf War," undated (circa 1993).

about their tanks and such through controlling the control panel [*inaudible*] on the tank, which was a part of a control panel that was on top of the tank, and any weather change or [*inaudible*] can affect the panel and prevent the soldier from fully using the tank or the gun or [*inaudible*] or his weapon in a fully functional manner. When they [the coalition forces] came, Sir, [*inaudible*] the tanks and realized the combat and resistance of our troops –

Saddam: That there was a fighting spirit.

Male 1: That there was a fighting spirit and they [the Americans] pulled their tanks. So, they pulled their tanks and emerged in their helicopters at a far distance that was out of range of the effective defense weapons, like the Apache, which the comrades and commanders know.

Saddam: It is known.

Male 1: Your Excellency is well aware of their ranges. I mean they came to fight us outside the range of the anti-aircraft weapons, where 10 or 20 helicopters would emerge at a time. So, during the battle, Sir, the ground battle, only the Tawakalna 'Alallah forces were seriously hurt in the first stages of the battle, after they clashed with the defensive site we had prepared and that we expected[78] –

Saddam: Was the entire defensive site within our land?

Male 1: Yes, Sir . . . The only thing that harmed us, Sir, was the attack that occurred in the first stages on the Tawakalna 'Alallah forces, which was outside of our intended defense area, hoping that we could withdraw it and [*inaudible*]. In fact, Sir, by the time we issued the withdrawal orders, before the division commander had a chance to issue his orders to his troops, we came in contact with the Americans. So when we came into the defensive site – or I can say that was one of the reasons that made them agree to the ceasefire [*inaudible*] without losses. Therefore, Sir, their rush in the first stages was not – Sir, after we came back and two days after our withdrawal, we were sending components to evacuate the weapons and vehicles to crossing point number six that the brothers know. It is sort of to the south of the ground control zone and they know it, Sir. They continued, Sir, they continued to withdraw gradually after we withdrew from [*inaudible*] areas. After that, Sir, we returned and some of our troops were distributed according to the plan that we got.

Saddam: You did not describe to me the impact following your withdrawal from the defense site.

Male 1: Sir, after we –

Saddam: The prepared one.

Male 1: Yes, Sir.

Saddam: I don't mean the first mobilization place for the troops, but the Basra defense site where the fighting occurred, as you described – from which you withdrew after that.

Male 1: We withdrew after that.

---

[78] The Tawakalna 'Alallah forces were a mechanized Republican Guard division.

Saddam: During this time after you withdrew from it, describe to me the state of the troops and the damages they sustained, I mean the damage that was done.

Male 1: Sir, as far as our withdrawal, we withdrew without giving the enemy the chance to affect us. I mean the land forces were not able to detect us or detect our withdrawal, because our withdrawal – our withdrawal orders came in at night [*inaudible*] in continuous contact with – I was able in the first stage to pull out the troops that were not close to the defense site, that were not in contact with the enemy. We pulled them to the back lines and after that we asked them, within the time frame we specified, to pull back the troops that were in contact with the enemy. So the troops were able to cut any contact with the enemy and pull back in an orderly controlled manner to the designated areas.

Saddam Discusses How Iraq Won the Gulf War and Whether It Should Have Engaged in Preemptive Attacks on Gathering Coalition Forces (circa March 1991)[79]

Saddam: Is it written in the books to have a preparatory bombardment for one month-and-a-half? Which book is it? Was it ever recorded in a war? Let's begin from the time they used the sword to the time they resorted to the attacks – to the atomic attacks during World War II. I mean the attack could not be measured . . . We could understand some of what happened. We could understand it, we could understand some of the negative aspects without giving it any legitimacy. We understand. We should show – We should show some understanding. But we should say decisively that the – the party that succeeded in a proportion of 50 percent is – is the master of the world when it comes to faith, eh – mental and nervous capabilities, and the – and human tenacity, because there has never been anything alike, neither in history nor in geography. I mean, the, eh, 30 countries unite against 17 or 18 million with the description that you have given. Well, even the 18 [*inaudible*].

After all that, some weak parties forget that – they are reminded every day [of] its [America's] power and because they are weak, some of them are still holding on to it. "See what America is going to do." The first country in the world which – which scares the most powerful countries just by what it publishes in the newspapers. Did they do something or didn't they? Did they do something? And they answer them, "At your orders." They celebrate and are busy with themselves. They want to celebrate the manner with which they defeated Iraq. How else could we explain it? Their celebration is an answer to their astonishment regarding how they defeated Iraq.

Male 1: But they were disgraced.

Saddam: Let's suppose that their military won . . . On the military level, Muhammad Bin 'Abdullah, who is the Prophet of God, was defeated in the military battle. It means that his army was defeated before the army of the infidels.[80] Why should it be a surprise when our army is defeated in the presence of the infidels' army in a way

---

[79] SH-SHTP-A-000-669, "Iraqi Officials Discussing the Retreat of Iraqi Troops from Kuwait and the Perceived Greediness of the United States of America," undated (circa March 1991).

[80] Saddam appears to be referring to the Battle of Uhud, which took place in the year 625 CE. The Quran attributes the defeat of the Muslims in this battle to the failure of some of them to follow Muhammad's orders on the battlefield.

beyond any measurement – beyond any measurement? There has been a reunion of the strongest powers existing in the world of the devils and infidels. The strongest scientific, technological, and military powers and the highest financial and economic potential existing in the region and the world without any exception. They all got together against us and they did not succeed despite what happened. They did not dare attack Baghdad. With the first bomb, their number increased and reached 30 countries. And they did not dare launch the first bomb to attack Baghdad but after six months elapsed, when the military siege was total so that no shot would be fired at them and not one bite of bread would reach us. Is that right or isn't it? That's the story of Iraq. Not to mention we are asking ourselves how to improve ourselves. But history has recorded that. It will tell the people that in fact this battle was the front fighting trench, with Baghdad and Amara in al-Madina. Iraqis came together and were united to the maximum. Women and men came together to face dangers to the maximum. The infant, the elderly, and the fighter came together to face dangers to the maximum. Such a condition never happened in all the wars of the world. But [*inaudible*] is better.

We thank God for what happened. We thank God for everything . . . The other thing I want to say to encourage you after giving you this fast introduction I found myself obliged to give you, is my assessment as a Chief of the General Command, and the regional command of the Revolution Command Council. The assessments of the Political Command as well as the General Command were similar to my assessment. I repeat, if we would have attacked them, after they launched the first bomb on Baghdad, if we would have attacked them immediately, we would have taken our revenge in a better way. Well, we would have taken our revenge in a better way. I cannot say that the picture would have changed. No. But we would have hurt them more. Before the combat we said they could demolish and destroy and so on, but we also said that we would be able to hurt them. We did not hurt them in a significant manner directly and – and physically. But be assured that we will and you will see it in your lifetime, God willing. America was over when the first bomb was launched on Baghdad. It came to an end spiritually and everything they are willing to do cannot protect them.

I know that they are the masters of the world; I am telling you that now. But they arrived to the summit in circumstances filled with, eh, despicable and corrupted interventions. I mean in – in circumstances – They arrived to the top, not with pride the way the cavalrymen would do so – they would remain in power for a long period of time. They reached the top by resorting to this corrupted way. Although America and the 30 countries want to celebrate their victory over Iraq, the latter will wear them away from the inside because of what they did to Iraq. And with each passing day more scandals are disclosed and more signs of weakness come to light. This will constitute the main and decisive basis. America will move fast away from the crown where it sat because all its cards were disclosed, as well as the way it deals with others. It lost morally because of its duplicity, which we confirmed before the beginning of the military operation. We had said that the Western world was embracing dual criteria. Immediately after the fight was over, the duplicity was exposed, dealing with the Palestinian issue.[81]

---

[81] This might refer to Kuwait's expulsion of four hundred thousand Palestinians from its territory immediately after its liberation in reaction to the PLO's support for Saddam.

We said immediately that America was lying about the issue of Kuwait. The issue of Kuwait was a kind of basis to the conspiracy. We have scratched its face and revealed all the historic background. It's natural and it's our right to approach the aspect of the historical background because it will score positively and in our favor and in the interest of our people. But this was not the issue. They have conspired against us. Why? To dominate the countries of the region from an oil viewpoint. Why? To control the world. These words, not everybody heard them. But they marked the beginning of an international educational operation, because the world at that time wanted to hear what we had to say. On the scene, there was America representing officially the world [other countries] and ourselves. And who was the enemy of the 33 countries? Iraq. And whatever Iraq was saying, they were listening to, the young and the old. An educational operation took place and nothing like it ever happened before. It took them a long time before having the courage to launch the first bomb to attack Baghdad. This education will not be worthless. This education will play a role in the observer's mind to pressure America and show it how to behave. Now, the entire world is convinced. France is convinced. China is convinced. Now, even France, China, and the Soviet Union are convinced that America came to dominate the world by attacking Iraq. It did not – it did not come to defend the values of the international law. This will begin corroding all their politics and everybody will begin fearing America. And the fear will begin.

Male 2: [*Inaudible.*]

Saddam: This fear will push toward the formation of a political coalition.

———

Saddam: I swear to God, if the Iraqi Army along with the Republican Guard would have gone to meet them accompanied by one or two regiments, they would have kicked them out and it would have been a large defeat. Well, it – it would have been over with. It would have been the end. It would have been the end. Thanks be to God for everything that happened. I forgot to tell you. [U.S. General Norman] Schwarzkopf, the one who led the operations against you – maybe you had the chance to read about it or [maybe] you didn't. Let me tell you about it. After the operations of Al-Khafji, some of the commanders came and said to me, "Sir, we think there has been a mistake.[82] It means that all our assessments about the American army were wrong." So, imagine if we would have attacked them before then and if we take into account the extent of the mistake, how the political situation would have changed. We will never know. [*Someone clears his throat in the background.*] But I am telling you what happened, that's what God wanted and it's okay.

Male 3: It's okay.

Saddam: That's it.

---

[82] Iraqi troops attacked and briefly took control of Al-Khafji, a town in Saudi Arabia, on 30 January 1990. For a discussion by Iraqi military leaders of the lessons Saddam learned from the attack, see *SH-SHTP-A-001-243, "Iraqi Military Officials Discussing the 1991 Gulf War," undated (circa 1993); Woods, *The Mother of All Battles*, 14–28.

Khalil [*unknown*]: Sir, if you would have come to us on the 31st, we had prepared and suspended the maps and we thought that you were going to give us the order to attack.

Saddam: No, it's wrong. It's wrong to attack before they launch the first bomb on Baghdad. But after the first bomb, everything is legitimate in the eyes of the entire world. Or on the contrary, the entire world will stop. They will all stop in fear, applauding us. Ha! The latter is better. What God wanted for us was okay. Thanks be to God.

Saddam Corrects His Staff's Analysis of American Air Power (27 November 1995)[83]

Saddam: It is not a subject of compliance that this booklet will affect the fighters with its wording now. Do we want to protect the fighters, or do we want to affect them in a negative way? We are to strengthen them. This is our duty. The fighter's rights are for us to protect him psychologically, and to increase his morale to confront the enemy. If we do not do this, then we are negligent. How can we do this and exaggerate? Some of the specifications that have nothing to do with the study are there. It has nothing to do with the study. It has no effect at all.

On the other hand, I did not see a presence or use of numbers, except for the numbers the enemy announced.[84] Where are our numbers? I will give you an example: the enemy said about the Apache [American AH-64 attack helicopter] that it conducted about 18,700 hours of operations. This is on page nine. Its number is 274 aircraft. Using simple calculations, if we take away 2,700 hours from these 18,700 hours and said that the remaining 16,000 hours are all fighting hours, and then we divide the 16,000 fighting hours over 274 aircrafts, the result is every two-and-a-half days, during these one-and-a-half months of bombardment, one fighting mission. Then the 270 aircraft every two days, I have your numbers, these are your numbers that you used, and I'm sure that they are American numbers, not Iraqi . . .

This is how you conduct a scientific study. It is based on numbers. Quote the Americans and say this is what the Americans said. This means this much. If it is supposed to be 16,000 fighting hours – why did I say 8,000? And you said why? Envision 16,000 fighting hours. Supposedly, the aircraft needs two hours to get from its place to reach the front. Then they recorded 8,000 mission hours times 16 Hellfire missiles, will equal to 128,000 missiles that they fired at us. If we calculate and say that the hit percentage is 72 percent, then they hit 100,000 of our weapons and vehicles. This is not me. Anyone that is interested in the scientific calculations can discuss this with you and tell you that this is in brief, that you did not spend any effort, that you opened the American booklets and records and gathered information from there. This is what happened. You are educating us according to the American booklets? Okay, all of you fought and suffered, why did you waste so

---

[83] *SH-SHTP-A-001-244, "Iraqi Military Officials Discussing Air Force and Army Performance during the 1991 Gulf War," 27 November 1995.

[84] It appears from the conversation that the Iraqis have drawn the U.S. data they are discussing from the following U.S. report: Department of Defense, *Conduct of the Persian Gulf War: Final Report to Congress* (April 1992), 664–70.

much blood? Another thing, the enemy used 136 A-10 [attack] aircraft. It conducted 8,077 missions.

———

Saddam: If we look at the 8,077 take-offs, each take-off is a plane, right?

Male 1: Yes, Sir.

Saddam: Okay, take 8,077 take-offs and multiply it by the load of all the kinds of airplanes. You will find how many hits you had and how many bombs and missiles they fired at you. Add all the airplanes and all the loads and all kinds of missiles and all kinds of bombs, and this way you can figure out the percentage of accuracy. This is a practical way. You are not talking about an army in Vietnam or an army in China. You are talking about your army. You know for sure how many vehicles, how many weapons, and how many tanks were hit. Take this into consideration along with the total airplanes and the payload, and then divide. For sure you will have the results. The result is, how accurate is the enemy? I do not want you to forge anything. Mention the truth as is. Why do give the enemy a free advertisement? Do we need this? We need to tell the fighter you were hit this much. These are your losses. And this case will not be repeated ever again. It will not be repeated. It happened one time and this is it. I'm not saying that the aggression will not be repeated. The aggression might be repeated. However, an aggression such as this one that they fabricated against Iraq with all of this mobilization, finances, and military means will never happen again. When the fighter knows that the accuracy rate was based on the fact that everything was in their favor, then what would be the rate if things were not in their favor? Isn't this our duty toward the Iraqi fighter? It is the truth. It is not forged. Truth as is. When you show the accuracy rate at 90 percent rate, then it is as if you wanted to harm your fighter psychologically. I'm sure that you do not mean this.

Correct this study based on this. Based on scientific numbers. How many hits the Iraqi army took? The answer would be this and that. How many missions for all kinds of aircraft? The answer would be this and that. Show the payload of every aircraft as is, as you had it in the book. Multiply and subtract, and you will have the rate of accuracy. If we take into account that the A-10 accomplished 8,077 missions, how many missions did each aircraft accomplish? The answer is about 30 missions. How many per day? The answer is 66 percent of a mission, which means it is less than one. They conducted less than one mission per day. From here you can calculate its capability, its management, and the technical support for the aircraft. Take as a guideline your airplanes in al-Qadisiyyah [the Iran-Iraq War]. How many take-offs would an airplane in al-Qadisiyyah fly when there is a battle? How many take-offs in one day?

Male 2: How many take-offs?

Saddam: The average is three. This is because we are a third-world country. This fact is controlling you even in your study. They conduct less than one take-off per day. This is America with all of its capabilities. It is not America alone. The whole world was here. We were conducting five take-offs per day, per airplane. This is per one airplane [inaudible]. From here we can calculate the preparedness and the readiness based on the administrative and technical services of the enemy pilots.

What is this scientific discussion? People are waiting on you. Who is more capable and listened to than you to write about the Americans now? Is this your writing about the Americans? The Vietnamese delegation is coming to sit with you. Did they come?

Male 1: They asked for permission, Sir. They will be here soon.

Saddam: They are going to be here to see the Iraqi experiment. Are you going to talk to them in this way? For God's sake are you going to show him this? . . . We should not blame the Iraqi fighter for any circumstances. This is good that a human is trained to fight the enemy, even if the same situation were to repeat itself. This is good. However, if we handle things in this manner, it is one thing, and if we handle it as was shown in the study, it is something else: the strength of the enemy regarding how it was depicted in the study, and regarding his helicopters and how they were effective, and his A-10 and how it is also effective. You depicted all of this as if it is a bogeyman. We should call it an armor-fighting fixed-wing airplane. We already talked about the A-10. Don't keep talking about it. This becomes an advertisement for the airplane. And this is what the Americans want. What time did these airplanes start to fly? We should not forget the facts. When did this airplane start to fly? It started to fly and work after the Iraqi fighter was exhausted. And as the Minister of Defense asked and said: "Was it flying missions when the fighters received their rations and they were in good spirits, etc?" When things for fighters started to become unbalanced, starting from the food rations to water, a new situation emerged. In these conditions – did you ever know that air support would last a whole month? And the ground offense would last only for three days? Where is this written? In what book? In what book? In what war? In what time period?

SIX

Special Munitions

You are Iraqis and you realize that even the special weapon that the brothers have, if they use it, it will lose its value... sometimes what you get out of a weapon is when you keep saying, "I will bomb you," [and] it is actually better than bombing him. It is possible that when you bomb him the material effect will be 40 percent, but if you stick it up to his face the material and the spiritual effect will be 60 percent, so why hit him? Keep getting 60 percent![1]

– Saddam Hussein, 7 July 1984

The captured Iraqi recordings provide valuable insight into Saddam's views on the utility of nuclear, biological, and chemical weapons. Scholars and policy makers have long debated the reasons Saddam used, and refrained from using, chemical and biological weapons. Whether Iraq (and states in general) sought weapons of mass destruction (WMD) for deterrence, compellence, prestige, or a combination of such factors has likewise been the subject of a great deal of analysis and speculation.[2] Behind these questions resided, for many, concern that the acquisition of nuclear weapons would lead Saddam to believe that he could engage in conventional aggression with less risk of U.S. military intervention or U.S.-Israeli nuclear intimidation.[3] Although Saddam and his advisers touched on some of these issues in

---

[1] SH-SHTP-A-001-035, "Saddam and Air Force Officers Discussing the Movements and Performance of the Iraqi Air Force during the Iran-Iraq War," 7 July 1984.

[2] For a succinct review of the literature on why states pursue nuclear weapons, see William C. Potter, "The Diffusion of Nuclear Weapons," in *The Diffusion of Military Technology and Ideas*, ed. Emily Goldman and Leslie Eliason (Stanford, CA: Stanford University Press, 2003), 148–49.

[3] According to Wafiq al-Samarrai, head of Iraqi military intelligence during the Gulf War, Saddam's plans for defending Iraqi gains in Kuwait centered on a desire "to stall for time, in order to produce nuclear weapons, so that he can have a deterrent power." PBS *Frontline* interview with Wafiq al-Samarrai on 2 May 2002, accessed 18 April 2006 at www.pbs.org/wgbh/pages/frontline/gulf/oral/samarrai/3.html.

Saddam, in Kurdish garb. The date of this photograph is unknown. (*Source*: *SH-MISC-D-001-245, "Pictures of Saddam and Izaat Ibrahim Al-Duri dated 2002 and Special Security Organization Administrative Correspondence dated 1999," 1999–2002)

public, analysts have received these public claims with healthy skepticism. This chapter presents transcripts of some of Saddam's private statements on the utility of WMD and the conditions for using them.

During Saddam's war with Iran, Iraq employed more than one hundred thousand chemical munitions against its Persian enemies and Iraqi Kurds. Iraq's use of the nerve agent Tabun in 1984 made it the first country to employ a nerve agent in war. Saddam and his advisers found chemical weapons useful for a variety of reasons, including softening enemy positions, creating disarray behind the opponent's front lines, and lowering Iranian morale. They concluded that chemical weapons had been particularly important in repelling Iran's human-wave attacks. According to Iraqi declarations, Baghdad used 1,800 tons of mustard gas, 140 tons of Tabun, and more than 600 tons of sarin from 1983 to 1988. It delivered these by means of 19,500 bombs, 54,000 artillery shells, and 27,000 short-range rockets. Roughly two-thirds of Iraq's chemical weapons were used in the final eighteen months of the conflict.[4]

By contrast, during the Mother of All Battles, Iraq appears not to have used chemical or biological weapons.[5] Scholars have posited several explanations for this. The most common is that intentionally ambiguous threats of U.S. nuclear retaliation deterred Saddam. When Secretary of State James Baker met with Tariq Aziz in Geneva on 9 January 1991, he shared a letter from President Bush that warned that "the American people would demand the strongest possible response" to a WMD attack. The letter continued, "You and your country will pay a terrible price if you order unconscionable acts of this sort." In 1995, Tariq told UN officials that Iraq had interpreted the letter from Baker as threatening nuclear retaliation and was consequently deterred from employing chemical and biological weapons.[6]

Several factors have prompted skepticism, however, as to whether Tariq's statement should be taken at face value. First, he had an incentive to present Iraq as easily deterrable to reduce Western concerns regarding remaining Iraqi WMD stocks and production capabilities. Second, the letter Baker gave Tariq threatened the same responses against Iraq-sponsored terrorist strikes and burning Kuwait's oil wells, yet Iraq did both.[7] Third, adverse wind conditions, the intensity of the U.S. campaign, coalition measures to protect its troops, and other factors might have hindered Iraq's ability to employ its special munitions or may have led Saddam to view his WMD options as insufficiently effective. Fourth, Baker also warned Tariq that the United States would seek regime change in response to Iraqi WMD use; Iraq's nonuse might be primarily attributable to fears of expanding U.S. objectives. Fifth, the United States was not the only country to warn Iraq.

---

[4] Central Intelligence Agency, "Transmittal Message," *Comprehensive Report of the Special Advisor to the DCI on Iraq's WMD* (hereafter, *Duelfer Report*), 23 September 2004, vol. 3, pp. 5, 10; Javed Ali, "Chemical Weapons and the Iran-Iraq War: A Case Study in Noncompliance," *Nonproliferation Review* (Spring 2001): 43–58.

[5] For a dissenting view, see Jonathan B. Tucker, "Evidence Iraq Used Chemical Weapons during the 1991 Persian Gulf War," *Nonproliferation Review* 4 (Spring–Summer 1997), 114–122.

[6] Victor A. Utgoff, "Nuclear Weapons and the Deterrence of Biological and Chemical Warfare," Occasional Paper No. 36 (Washington, D.C.: Henry L. Stimson Center, October 1997), 2n4.

[7] Saddam defends his decision to burn the oil wells in section "Saddam reacts to the onset of the ground war," a partial transcript of which is found in Chapter 5. Saddam also apparently sought opportunities to engage in terrorist attacks on coalition members. Woods, *The Mother of All Battles*, 215–18; section "Saddam and the Revolutionary Command Council discuss Libyan leader Mu'amar Qadafi's (and Iraq's) terrorist affiliations and potential operations," in Chapter 3.

Israel, France, Britain, and the Soviet Union likewise warned Iraq not to engage in chemical warfare. It is not entirely clear which, if any, of these factors mattered.[8]

Unfortunately, only a tiny fraction of the Ba'ath regime's WMD-related documents have survived the twelve years of Iraqi efforts to hide and destroy official records on the topic. In the late 1990s it was routine practice in Iraq to destroy even purely historic material on WMD for fear that UN inspectors might mistake such documents as contemporary records. Notwithstanding the limited number of records on the topic, the surviving documents and recordings present valuable insights. In the following transcripts Saddam and his advisers describe the conditions under which Iraq used and did not use chemical and biological weapons. They discuss, among other things, U.S. and Israeli military capabilities and intentions toward Iraq, Iraqi civil defense procedures, Iraq's need for nuclear weapons, and tactical and strategic uses of "special munitions."

EARLY THOUGHTS ON WMD

Saddam's private statements from the late 1970s and early 1980s indicate that he saw nuclear weapons as useful for both deterrence and compellence. He predicted that Israel would strike Baghdad with nuclear, biological, or chemical weapons or would provide Iran with biological or chemical weapons and encourage it to attack.[9] Saddam discussed Iraq's efforts to acquire a suitable deterrent and explained that extensive bomb shelters and civil defense procedures were necessary to protect Iraqi morale against Israeli nuclear blackmail.

Saddam foresaw that if Iraq possessed a nuclear weapon, it would be able to engage in conventional attrition warfare against Israel, the "Zionist Entity." Most important, he explained, such a war would excite the Arab masses and spark an uprising in Palestine. Saddam noted that American nuclear threats would deter Iraq from advancing beyond the Sea of Galilee, although they would not compel an Iraqi retreat or withdrawal.

---

[8] For leading studies on whether Saddam was deterred from using special munitions during the Gulf War, see Utgoff, "Nuclear Weapons," 2n4; Scott Sagan, "The Commitment Trap: Why the United States Should Not Use Nuclear Threats to Deter Biological and Chemical Weapons Attacks," *International Security* 24 (Spring 2000): 85–115; Norman Cigar, "Chemical Weapons and the Gulf War: The Dog That Did Not Bark," *Studies in Conflict and Terrorism* 15 (1992): 145–55.

[9] This is an interesting mirror of American concerns that Saddam might transfer WMD to Al Qaeda. For further discussions of the perceived Israeli-Iranian nexus, see Chapter 2.

Saddam Predicts the Effects Iraqi Nuclear Weapons Would Have on Conventional Warfare with Israel (27 March 1979)[10]

Saddam: This is what we envision: we envision a war with the enemy, either with the unity nation[11] or with the Iraqi-Syrian military effort, or with the Iraqi-Syrian-Jordanian military effort that should be designed based on long months and not just weeks... We have the capability to design it the way it should be designed.

Do we really want a war in which we gain miles quickly, but then step back and withdraw, or do we want the slow, step-by-step war, where every step we take becomes part of the land and we keep moving forward? The step itself is not the most important thing here; even more important is the widespread cheering from the masses that will accompany each step we take forward, which will reach every corner of the Arab world. This is more important than the meter, half-kilometer, and kilometer we will gain.[12] It may take a whole month to go three kilometers deep, but we cannot stop after one month. Of course, this has its requirements.

The most important requirement is that we be present in Iraq and Syria and will have planned ahead that the enemy, the air force, that the enemy will come and attack and destroy, etc. We should bear it and keep going – and go put pressure on our Soviet friends and make them understand our need for one weapon – we only want one weapon.[13] We want, when the Israeli enemy attacks our civilian establishments, to have weapons to attack the Israeli civilian establishments. We are willing to sit and refrain from using it, except when the enemy attacks civilian establishments in Iraq or Syria, so that we can guarantee the long war that is destructive to our enemy, and take at our leisure each meter of land and drown the enemy with rivers of blood. We have no vision for a war that is any less than this.

I mean, not this year, not this year and not in the next five years, as for the blitzkrieg and quick movements, as you know the situation in the Golan and how difficult it is.[14]

[10] SH-SHTP-A-000-553, "Saddam and Senior Advisers Meeting after the Baghdad Conference," 27 March 1979.

[11] Iraqi and Syrian officials had repeatedly professed desire to unify the two countries.

[12] Saddam does, in fact, switch from discussing miles to discussing kilometers. Whereas in this passage Saddam's focus is on how the push to liberate Israeli-occupied territories would excite and unify Arabs, on other occasions he emphasized the effect that a pan-Arab army would have on his ability to liberate these territories. In September 1980 he told his advisers, "If I had the Arab capabilities and abilities under my control, then I would sit with [Israeli Prime Minister Menachem] Begin. I would tell him this: 'Announce to the world that you are going to give me that land that you occupied on 5 June 1967, and then we will have a discussion.'" See SH-SHTP-A-000-835, "Saddam and Military Officials Discussing the Iran-Iraq War," 16 September 1980.

[13] In 1981, Saddam told his advisers, "It is inevitable that Israel will plan an attack against Iraq's vital facilities, an attack that will exceed conventional means... In the beginning of 1979, I think, we contacted some friendly countries [to acquire] a type of weapon that would make Israel hesitate if it decided to carry out such an attack against Iraq." See SH-SHTP-A-001-039, "Saddam and His Senior Advisers Discussing Israel's Attack on the Tamuz (Osirak) Reactor and Iraqi Civil Defenses," undated (circa mid- to late 1981).

[14] The following year, Saddam appears to have hinted that Iraq would obtain nuclear weapons around 1985. See section "Saddam claims that Iraq's history and scientific expertise uniquely qualify it to lead the Arab nation," in Chapter 3.

[*Banging on the table.*] If we go and give instructions to the Iraqi-Syrian armor to attack, we must expect that they will all be destroyed and retreat, if not to the same line, maybe beyond it. In a land this difficult, one must, primarily, work on it. We are in the process of exploring the movement that mobilization envisions, but the strategic vision is what is important, so that we won't give importance and mobilize us in the direction of planning a three-day war, in which we neither win nor lose and end there. That is what that is needed with the Zionist enemy.

What is required is a patient war, one where we fight for 12 continuous months. After 12 months, we take stock and figure out how much we have lost and how much we have gained. And we should consider losses in thousands, thousands, so that we plan to be prepared to lose in those 12 months 50,000 martyrs and keep going.

Saddam: But if we fight for 12 months in the Golan, and God willing the day will come when we fight, and when we overlook the Sea of Galilee we will hear the Americans threatening that if we don't stop our advance, they will throw an atomic bomb at us. Then we can tell them, "Yes, thank you, we will stop. What do you want?" "Stop and don't move, not even one meter, otherwise we will throw an atomic bomb on you," they reply. We will state that we have stopped, but we have not given up. We will stay and watch from the Sea of Galilee to see if there is any change in circumstances that will make us go forward further.

We don't want to risk the Ummah [the Islamic nation] to either win or get destroyed forever. No, we want it to advance. Advance even for a few meters according to political terms, and we want political progress, represented in an uprising process, that will accompany this military forward movement.

We have talked a lot in this meeting, but it's been a while since we have seen you like this.

Greetings to all of you.

[*End of recording.*]

Saddam and His Senior Advisers Discuss Iraq's Need for Civil Defenses and Efforts to Acquire a Suitable Deterrent against Israel and Iran (circa late 1981)[15]

Saddam: Yes, Mr. [*inaudible*].

Minister of Housing:[16] Your Excellency, we are dealing with the matter of building shelters, the modern large shelters that are chemical and nuclear-proof and that are under the responsibility of our ministry.

Saddam: Whose responsibility?

---

[15] SH-SHTP-A-001-039, "Saddam and His Senior Advisers Discussing Israel's Attack on the Tamuz (Osirak) Reactor and Iraqi Civil Defenses," undated (circa mid- to late 1981).

[16] The conversation earlier in the recording suggests that this is Muhammad Fadhil Hussein, minister of housing and construction (1979–1982).

Minister of Housing: Our ministry, we are tasked with executing [these projects]. Of course this is a new mission, but thank God we have made considerable progress now in that matter. We have completed 35 shelters, the capacity of each one is 1,500 [people], and there are 26 shelters under negotiation and 84 shelters will be announced within this year. God willing, we have also prepared ideal designs.

Saddam: This "underground" [*spoken in English*] will solve the problem.[17]

Minister of Housing: Excuse me, Sir.

Saddam: This "underground" [*spoken in English*] will solve the problem.

Minister of Housing: Yes, we have prepared ideal designs for nuclear-proof shelters with a capacity of 50–500 people. I mean if any institution wants any of these shelters with whatever capacity, we will be able to provide it, because we had a consultant who provided us with these designs.[18] Also with regard to the houses – and this is really an exciting matter – because the number of those who borrowed money to build shelters in their homes reached 25,000 people, and the process is ongoing.

Saddam: Explore the possibility of contracting with a company, enter into a contractual agreement with a company, and tell them to prepare a design, and even if we do not buy from them, we will pay for the design. Perhaps they will manufacture at our own expense. Perhaps they can produce one million cabins of this type, and it would probably be cheaper and feasible. I mean, if they produce it for us, if they provide us the factories, and the "know-how," as they say in English, we will produce it here in our country. I mean, we should not limit ourselves to only shelters. We should implement the simple projects that could protect the life of the Iraqi family, because the atomic attack on us is imminent. You see, I told you so about five years ago. Don't you remember at the command [offices], I said that Baghdad will be attacked with an atomic bomb? I mean, I was including the progress that Baghdad has reached in my calculations. For all the advancement that Baghdad has reached, people will not tolerate such advancement, and I am telling you now, Baghdad will be attacked by an atomic bomb one day. I mean, this is a strong possibility, I cannot say with absolute certainty, because this relies on the progress the world has achieved and relies on the deterrent capability the Arabs own [*Saddam knocks on the table*]. Baghdad will be attacked chemically, atomically, and by germs.

One day, Israel will provide the Iranians with the know-how to wage a germ and chemical attack. Israel will provide the Iranians – they will approach an Iranian official and tell him, "Why don't you attack them?" He will say: "I do not know how." Then they will tell him, "Come and we will teach you how to attack," and they will teach him how to attack us. One of Israel's objectives is not only as

---

[17] Iraq reportedly planned to build a subway system to protect the population from airstrikes and to provide transportation. Patrick Cockburn, "Baghdad suburb residents show war readiness," *Independent* (London), 22 December 1990.

[18] In 2003, a German engineer involved in the design and construction of some of these bunkers boasted that owing to the nine-foot-thick walls, whatever might happen in Baghdad in the course of a new war, "the bunker will live through it." Deirdre Tynan, "Hussein's Bunker 'Made in Germany': Boswau and Knauer Engineer Thinks Dictator Safe," accessed 22 May 2009 at www.pressetext.com/news/030328032/Husseins.bunker-made-in-germany.

[Israeli Prime Minister Menachem] Begin would say for the sole purpose of protecting the security of Israel from Iraqi scientific advancement, but also to prolong the war between Iraq and Iran, because the Israeli planners, their strategic brains, want Iraq to remain preoccupied with Iran. So when Iraq has a deterrent capability against Iran, this means that one day, Iraq will turn its back with ease against Iran, who will not be able to confront it. So when he [Begin] removes this part for a period of time, he will maintain continuously through his intelligence means, the political influence and other reasons as well, he will be able to keep Iraq busy through its confrontation with Iran.

So this is a second objective, it is point B after point A, which is concerned with the Zionist entity itself. And the security of the Zionist entity is not contingent on the Iraqi atomic bomb but Iraqi scientific and human advancements. Anyway, we will talk about this topic another day, God willing. So we have to have this protection for the Iraqi citizen so that he will not be disappointed and held hostage by the scientific advancement taking place in Iran or in the Zionist entity. The Iraqi citizen must have sufficient protection with simple means. In addition, the issue of the deterrent capability – this is a strategic matter that we should not forget. Even if the whole world is resisting such an endeavor, I mean the deterrent capability is not a provocative, hostile action, but it is a state that requires Iraqi protection as well as Arab protection. Without such deterrence, the Arab nation will continue to be threatened by the Zionist entity and Iraq will remain threatened by the Zionist entity.

Saddam: I have requested that it [the Ministry of Defense] import [gas masks], and to import in sufficient numbers the items that will be sold in stores. I mean, after we fulfill the army's requirement, we start to sell to the citizens in stores, where they will be showcased with awareness brochures, and the people will buy them.

Male 2: We have imported a very small amount.

Taha Yasin Ramadan: We have imported for the army, I mean.

Saddam: Consider the priority: The army is first, the citizens are second, because the army could be attacked, there are tactical bombs these days that are limited to the area of movement.

Minister of Housing: Area of movement.

Saddam: The area of movement and the area of operation, but the plan that we have laid out is that all Iraqis should have protective masks in addition to the other item. And after you are done with this task, we should commence awareness sessions in order to explain this matter. I mean, the Iraqi must understand that by adhering to the following precautions, dealing with the attack will become a regular matter. This way, the Iraqi citizen will not be scared from the process and be blackmailed, because there is a possibility that the nuclear threat will be used as a scheme to blackmail Arabs politically, and that this will impact the Arab psyche. And this is what they will do in the interval, before the Arabs possess the deterrent capability against such a situation.

––––––

Saddam: The Tammuz [Osiraq reactor attack of 7 June 1981] was not a surprise to us, not outside expectations. However, it is natural that whenever something like this happens, it is painful, because this is a dear fruit that we labored very hard to harvest. One of the fruits of the revolution and one for which we have exerted tremendous efforts politically, scientifically, economically for a long time. And before the war broke out, two years before the war broke out, or one year, I do not recall, we expected that after the year 1979, many superpowers would need to downsize this country [Iraq] or give it a lesson, or break it, break it psychologically, or actually. This is not because we are troublemakers as some superpowers are trying to portray us, as they are leery of our interest in nationalistic activities, but because we want Iraq to be actually prominent, prosperous, and an advanced country, not in words but in reality. In reality and not in just words, we want the Iraqi to live just like their people [the superpowers'] live...

We will become a burden on their minds, so that many will not be able to endure us, and the policies that they want for this region, and the conclusions of what they want – which is to totally subjugate the people of the region to meet their wishes and according to their choices – on this basis, we have stated that it is inevitable that Israel will plan an attack against Iraq's vital facilities, an attack that will exceed conventional means, and will target main rings that will stop development or will stop Iraqi prosperity in the programs of scientific and economic advancements, which are the main sources of Iraq's strength.

It is not a secret to say that based on our vision, and toward the end of the year, in the beginning of 1979, I think, we contacted some friendly countries [to acquire] a type of weapon that will make Israel hesitate if it decided to carry out such an attack against Iraq.[19] And we were very frank and clear in that regard, we said that we expect that Israel will exceed its limits, crossing the lines of Arab countries on its borders and will attack us in Iraq with its air force. That it will bomb our vital economic facilities, and will attack our petroleum facilities, and therefore, and in order that the Arab countries sharing borders with Israel will not be embarrassed politically and militarily, and in order to avoid being placed in a weak position in deterring Israeli actions, we reckoned that we have to have defensive means to carry out defensive actions. We have to be able to make Israel hesitate if it has contemplated such action. This took place in the year, in the early part of 1979,

[19] Iraq might have sought assistance in obtaining nuclear weapons from its allies, beyond help with the Osirak reactor, although this is unclear. In any case, Saddam was extremely wary of being caught clandestinely seeking enriched uranium. In public, he claimed that U.S., Israeli, and British intelligence agencies "offered us uranium before the war [with Iran], and asked us whether we wanted to purchase it...This is a policy of entrapment." Internal Iraqi documents confirm that Saddam feared entrapment. In March 1981, Saddam turned down an offer from unidentified individuals to provide Iraq with uranium for fear that the offer was part of an Israeli trap. The Iraqis, still fearing entrapment, were also very wary of offers of assistance from representatives of the A. Q. Khan network in late 1990. See Adrian Levy and Catherine Scott-Clark, *Deception: Pakistan, the United States, and the Secret Trade in Nuclear Weapons* (New York: Walker and Company, 2007), 220–21; "President Warns Israel, Criticizes U.S.," FBIS-NES-90-064, 3 April 1990, from Baghdad Domestic Service (in Arabic), 2 April 1990; see SH-PDWN-D-001-270, "Transcript of Saddam and Military Officials Discussing the Iran-Iraq War," 29 July 1993; see SH-MICN-D-000-741, "Correspondence between the Military Industrialization Commission and the Petro Chemical Group Regarding a Letter from A. Q. Khan Offering to Assist Iraq in Developing a Uranium Enrichment Program," October 1990.

therefore, we expected an Israeli attack against Iraq without an overt, announced war, and we expected this before the actual attack time frame...

And this indeed took place on the fourth of September 1980, when Iran attacked after it failed to achieve a full-scale military reaction from us, in relation to incidents at the border checkpoints. It waged war against us on the fourth of September when it attacked Iraqi cities: [*Saddam pounds on the table each time he mentions the name of cities that Iran attacked*] Khanaqin! Mandalin! Zurbatiyyah! And the oil area, Khanah![20] And after that, before the day, the 22nd, it attacked Shatt al-Arab and bombed Basra with its artillery.[21] All this was not because of Iraq, not because they were afraid of the Iraqi atomic bomb as the leader of the gang in Tel Aviv is stating, but this was mainly because they were afraid of the balanced and integrated Iraqi scientific, social, economic, and political advancements that are seriously heading toward their objectives for the purpose of building a new Iraq.

WMD USE AND NONUSE IN QADISIYYAH SADDAM

During the war with Iran, Saddam was deeply involved in strategic and even tactical decisions regarding chemical weapons. He recognized the limited physical effects that chemical weapons had on properly equipped and trained troops but stated that even unfulfilled threats to employ these weapons could possess a psychological value in excess of the material benefits of actually using them. Under such circumstances, he explained, Iraq should use only conventional weapons. However, Saddam noted, using chemical weapons at the front ensured that winds would return some of the chemicals to the Iraqi lines, thus leading Iraqi soldiers to believe they were under chemical attack and usefully preparing them to maintain high morale during future WMD combat. Iraq also used chemical weapons against its own troops in a training exercise to prepare the soldiers psychologically to face chemical weapon attacks.[22] Whether Saddam decided to employ chemical weapons, it seems, had much to do with how he thought such behavior would affect Iraqi and Iranian morale.

Saddam also claimed that chemical weapon attacks could provide non-psychological battlefield advantages for Iraq. Targeting Iranian command centers, he stated, would create logistical difficulties for the Iranians and force their troops to disperse; the dispersed forces, in turn, would prove easier prey for the Iraqis. Even if only one out of ten Iraqi chemical attacks were successful, he added, Iraq's enemies would still have to worry about the remaining nine. Chemical weapon strikes on Kurdish leadership targets,

---

[20] On 4 September 1980, Iran shelled Iraqi border towns.

[21] On 22 September 1980, Iraq launched a ground offensive, thus beginning the eight-year conflict with Iran.

[22] See *SH-IZAR-D-001-246, "Iraqi Military Correspondence regarding an Experimental Chemical Weapons Attack on 27 June 1985," July–August 1985.

he suggested, could soften the targets for attacks by Iraqi Special Forces. The international community would not condemn harsh measures against the Kurds as it would during times of peace, he predicted, because everyone viewed the rebellion as an attempt to weaken Iraq for the benefit of foreign powers.

Saddam Orders Exposing Iraqi Troops to a Chemical Attack for Training Purposes (27 March 1984)[23]

Saddam: I would like to [pause] – this is our chance to train our army on the use of masks and protection against chemical warfare. It is also an opportunity to remove any sense of intimidation in them in case they come under chemical attack, to minimize losses. I believe that we need to set a plan for chemical attacks that we will carry out, force our close formations to wear masks, and the strikes should be on the front line. I mean, whoever is not properly equipped at the front sites should be prepared to be affected, but not in a deadly way; he will be harmed. The reason for this is that first, they will be psychologically prepared, and second, they will be ready for this.

Male 1: They would launch the CS [tear gas], Sir; the CS is not [inaudible, but perhaps lethal], but you meant the training purpose.

Saddam: No, no, we will strike the enemy here; strike the enemy who will come to us, but in areas close to the front lines. That's why they need to wear the gear and be prepared, so the doctors can carry out their roles in treating cases that occur. We need to remove any intimidation that could occur to the Iraqi soldier should the enemy reach, someday, the [inaudible].

Male 1: As a matter of fact, Sir, I sent for the chemical corps director when I went to Basra and he gave me a tour of all main formations in order to make sure that all individuals truly have the protection gear and know how to use it. There were even some demonstrations because the chemical corps has [inaudible], Sir, and it has some of the gas. Carrying it out and wearing the mask is nothing but a procedure of checking the mask since some masks are not good as far as their charcoal and filtration. Sir, some of the formations are not equipped, in fact, they have two contracts. The cost is also low.

Saddam: German ones.

Male 1: Yes, Sir, and some of them are Bulgarian. So, we tried to distribute them with no exceptions inside the ministry council and they might have been provided now since it does not take long to supply them.

Saddam: We should supply some of the formations and apply accordingly since these formations are near Majnoun field.

Male 1: Yes, Sir.

Saddam: Why should we exclude South Majnoun field from the chemical attacks? We shall attack South Majnoun field.

---

[23] *SH-SHTP-A-001-247, "Saddam and High Ranking Officials Discussing Military Operations in the Iran-Iraq War," 27 March 1984.

Izzat: They do have these formations –

Saddam: We need to figure out from where –

Male 1: Where is the direction of the wind's impact?

Saddam: It is directed in a way that it will feel like our soldiers were attacked by the enemy's chemical weapons. I mean we will accept partial damages in order to prepare them psychologically and [*inaudible*], and also to accustom them to using the masks.

Male 1: Sir, we especially need to point out that the chemical reconnaissance units should normally deploy and give the troops an immediate warning. They call it a "show," Sir.

Saddam: Yes.

Male 1: It goes up high and [*inaudible*] –

Saddam: They will practice.

Male 1: Yes, Sir.

Saddam: They will truly practice in a way that will enable them to have the same combat capability as the army has in fighting with other weapons. We don't keep [*inaudible*] in the field, because their [*inaudible*] are going to develop scientifically and [*inaudible*] in the future and [*inaudible*].

Male 2: If they were really trained for these exercises before, Sir, they would have greatly focused on these issues.

Saddam: So we could benefit from the exercises by practicing.

Male 2: Yes, Sir.

Saddam: But we need to focus on practicing before training. On the one hand, we will strike. Why use the large prohibited area as a safety zone for our troops? We should reduce it, eliminate the enemy and train our troops!

Male 2: We also need to move part of the medical department's medicines there, Sir.

Saddam: Huh?

Male 2: The medical department related to treating the injuries needs to be moved there, too.

Saddam: Yes, anyone related to the chemical attack needs to practice this.

Saddam Tells Iraqi Air Force Officers of the Psychological Benefits of Threatening But Not Using Chemical Weapons (7 July 1984)[24]

Saddam: Once you use it [any weapon in Iraq's air force that has a "special status"] to destroy, you will lose its value. You are Iraqis and you realize that even the special

---

[24] SH-SHTP-A-001-035, "Saddam and Air Force Officers Discussing the Movements and Performance of the Iraqi Air Force during the Iran-Iraq War," 7 July 1984.

weapon that the brothers have, if they use it, it will lose its value.[25] The psychological effect will be lost, so what is the weapon? It is not all about material change. I mean, sometimes what you get out of a weapon is when you keep saying, "I will bomb you," it is better than bombing him actually. It is possible that when you bomb him the material effect will be 40 percent, but if you stick it up to his face the material and the spiritual effect will be 60 percent, so why hit him? Keep getting 60 percent!

Saddam and His Generals Discuss Attacks on Iraqi Kurds with Chemical Weapons and the Appropriate Circumstances for Such Strikes (1985)[26]

Saddam: . . . It has been five years since the war started; it probably will continue. I mean this is a known argument that the war will last for a long time. But none of us can determine exactly when it will end. Then the other issue that was pointed out by the comrade, the deputy,[27] while going up the stairs – that during the war and unlike in peaceful times, we need to hit hard. I mean, you can attribute the mutiny during peacetime to social reasons. However, during time of war, even the international arena views the mutiny as an attempt to weaken Iraq and to exploit the war to benefit forces, whether from outside or inside the region. This is true.

––––––––

Saddam: We are no longer the same as when we were inside the Iranian territories in the last few months, saying everything was fine, but it turned out to be the other way around in the morning. No, the battle should take place and continue from midnight to the morning, when they say such a company or regiment was destroyed at the most and over a period of time, and not an entire brigade in one day or in a short period of time in the most difficult circumstances, including those under which the battle of Banjwin took place.[28] Do you recall this battle? We mobilized two brigades and pulled them within 24 hours from the Iraqi army to join the other sectors. So why did we let them [the Kurds] off of the hook? I would like to add that their central commands are located within Iraqi territories. I mean they were not – the rebels' command centers – in Syria, Iran or Turkey. So, if their central command is located within our territories, why can't we execute the planned operations, drop operations, and operations where the air force and artillery take part, all under the control of the intelligence apparatus? Accordingly, it will be a [*inaudible*] surprise attack and an attack in sector [*inaudible*]. We mobilize – mobilize artillery – we mobilize in a way so that we are certain that our attacks, including the use of the special arsenal that will be used against a specific location that harbors the

[25] The Iraqis used the euphemisms "special weapons" and "special munitions" to refer to chemical or biological weapons.

[26] SH-SHTP-A-001-045, "Saddam and High Ranking Officers Discussing Plans to Attack Kurdish 'Saboteurs' in Northern Iraq and the Possibility of Using Special Ammunition (Weapons)," undated (circa 1985).

[27] Saddam frequently referred to Izzat Ibrahim al-Duri, the deputy chairman of the RCC, as "the deputy."

[28] In October 1983, Kurdish forces cooperated with the Iranian military to attack the city of Banjwin in northern Iraq. In retaliation, Saddam forcibly removed eight thousand Kurdish men from the area. Most were never heard from again. Phebe Marr, *The Modern History of Iraq*, 2nd ed. (Boulder, CO: Westview, 2003), 199.

leadership – we need to use the air force, which is equipped with the special arsenal, to attack leadership and command centers. Then we execute Special Forces assault operations by planes to destroy those who survived.

Izzat: We train –

Saddam: We train our troops so that they will accomplish a patriotic duty within this specific period. These are the ideas I wanted to discuss calmly in this limited range. Let's hear some of the comrades' comments. In the first phase, we excluded Jalal Talabani from this operation. There is a possibility that the attacks against the others will teach Jalal Talabani a lesson and intimidate the others to withdraw from the alliance with Jalal Talabani. On the other hand, if Jalal enters this phase directly and openly, we would have been ready along with others to face Jalal after gaining the experience. When Jalal starts, we would be in a position and completely ready to destroy him. Yes, Nizar.

––––––––

Nizar:[29] As for the special preparation, we have good results in that regard, even with regard to the chemical in case we strike a confined mountainous region, and [inaudible] to protect the target is right behind it. We need to take this into consideration, also, and train our soldiers, because [inaudible.] We need to make use of the strike. I think the bombing requires approximately eight hours. After we bomb the mountainous region, I suggest that we strike with this gas. That is why we need approximately eight hours, so that we can enter the area, so that we are not affected by the gas effects. This is important; gas effects last a long time. I personally, with regard to Special Forces troops [inaudible], I do not think too much of [inaudible]. There must be continuous action where we clean out the area and then launch the warheads. We have to continue our attacks against the enemy because even if we launch the warheads in the Northern Region and [inaudible] two warheads out of ten, we will still have eight moving warheads.

Saddam: Even if you launch one warhead, but we don't plan to launch, not even one warhead. If we launch one warhead we can grab four field commands – commanders only. I mean one should not think to acquire either everything or nothing; the entire sea starts with the relation between two atoms: the oxygen and nitrogen atoms that form the sea. Mao Zedong says every 1,000 kilometers starts with one step.[30] Is that not so? That is why, I mean, when we form a command post after removing four commanders from it, you know what will happen? First, they lost four commanders. Second, a psychological atmosphere is imposed on them that is not to their favor. Third, practical measures are imposed on them and also not to their favor.

Izzat: For all of their headquarters.

Saddam: All their headquarters will be forced to scatter, and when they scatter they will not be the same, as you are located in a centralized command when you are comfortable, and can make your decisions accordingly, since, I mean, they will carry out a series of steps that will force them to scatter their forces. This way they will

––––––

[29] Perhaps Nizar al-Khazraji, head of the Iraqi Army's First Corps (1984–1988) and later army chief of staff.

[30] Saddam is mistaken in several regards. Water is composed of hydrogen and oxygen, not nitrogen and oxygen. Additionally, Lao Tzu is widely recognized as the source of the quote "A journey of a thousand miles begins with a single step."

not be able to deploy their forces against you and attack you with three regiments against one company, because they are aware of the possibility of this type of attack if they mobilize their forces. So when you get rid of the mobilization element, it will be a matter of isolated companies, or even isolated units, or one of the light isolated regiments. They might adopt this method. You will also impose on them a heavy administrative burden during the winter. I mean, life is a series of steps. As the company location is important in war along the front where we fight and offer sacrifices, so is one successful planned assault out of ten. I mean this is not too bad, it is good. I say, by God, perhaps the other nine might still work, but they will remain threatened.

Nizar: [*Inaudible.*] There has to be enough time for training, because these formations and even Special Forces and the Army's air forces are not properly trained for a successful landing on rough terrain. [*Inaudible*] some of the sectors are well-trained.

Saddam: As far as these details, Nizar, let us keep our discussions around the essence of the idea. It goes without saying, naturally, the utilized sectors must, and I mean when we launch a chemical attack, they have to train on the use of, or to train to assault under the conditions of chemical attack. When we use them by air-dropping on mountainous regions, these forces must train by practicing air-drops on mountainous regions under realistic circumstances, and other matters as well.[31] But these are details, but we are discussing the essence of the idea, and notwithstanding all conditions, even if you take formations and train them at your area, you will have to take them for training and then return them to their original locations, and then after that you begin the assault. Do not mobilize them in your sector and train them while the rebels can see you doing it. No, to achieve the element of surprise, train them in your area under your command, but then send them back to be transported to you again in a way that the period between the mobilization and action should not exceed 72 hours, for instance. This will guarantee the element of surprise.

Nizar: Sir, as far as the transport ability, [*inaudible*].

Saddam: We will agree on that, perhaps Sinjar and Hamrayn can be suitable areas for training; it does not have to be in the north.[32] Yes, General Mahmud?

Mahmud:[33] Sir, the idea is very good and I think everyone who daydreamed about this idea now sees that it will be a reality. People used to dream about such wonderful ideas, now it is reality. But the issue at hand is that in order to carry it out we have to give some excuses. We have to make such excuses successful in order to do that. This is something that lies at the organizational and action level. It requires first that the plan will have to be highly mobile [and have] fire support, very useful information, as well as central command, and at the same time, it requires high quality information, dictating the necessity of the entire existing security systems being under the command of one person who will coordinate everything and will be directly responsible for all these forces, because their performance will be based on good information. I, of course, Your Excellency, support the idea of bombing,

---

[31] "Air-dropping" is the Iraqi term for a helicopter movement of infantry or special forces soldiers.

[32] Sahl Sinjar Airbase was approximately two hundred miles north of Baghdad. Jabal Hamrayn was a military base ninety miles north of Baghdad.

[33] Possibly General Mahmud Adham Bidaywi, Nebuchadnezzar Forces Commander, or Abid Hamid Mahmud al-Tikriti, Saddam's private secretary and WMD release authority.

in the same manner Israel used with the fedayeen. And the reason is that as you have stated, any [territory] holding operations will place large burdens upon us. The important point in this matter, Sir, is that our first strike must be very painful, and the reason, Sir, is that sometimes a person, when he does not know a certain matter you know, what he will do is that when he sees the helicopter roaming [*inaudible*]. But when the helicopter approaches and attacks with a weapon that does not affect the village, then he will start to be sarcastic and make fun of the helicopter.

––––––

Hamid Shaban:[34] [*Inaudible.*] And we have the weapons that we could strike heavily and with high accuracy any command or any location. We can direct the plane over a range of four kilometers; one plane can be equipped with 1,500 small bombs.[35] They will still cause damage even if they are not dropped accurately. A new method, as we say, you hit accurately as a mouse but you end as victorious as a bull. Later, we will photograph this area and let the pilots study them just like we did in Haj Omran where we had 33 fighter planes with a variety of bombs and their effects.[36] [*Pause.*] Well, the head of intelligence could tell us about it. If we had not been occupied with the mission, we would have shown you the results of these new bombs. You probably saw it once or twice. Many bombs, the 22, and they are big bombs.[37] We trained the pilots, but their accuracy was not that high. However, by using the new method, and the great number of bombs used will cover a great area that would come under attack; this, of course, after we glean accurate information and take good pictures of this area. Sir, even I do not think that we need the special arsenal [chemical weapons] if we were prepared with this new gear, Sir. I mean sometimes –

Saddam: I believe that we, as a command, we should be prepared to use even the special arsenal if there is a target worth doing that. It would be better, of course, to resort to the conventional weapons.

Saddam and Ba'ath Party Members Discuss Using Chemical Weapons against Iranian Soldiers and Civilians (6 March 1987)[38]

Abd al-Ghani:... The time we strike will definitely be left to the discretion of Your Excellency and the General Command of the Armed Forces. Sir, it is indicated to be

––––––

[34] Lieutenant General Hamid Shaban, head of Iraqi Air Force.
[35] Hamid is probably referring to Cardoen cluster bombs. Each bomb contains 240 "bomblets" that create a lethal zone of fifty thousand square meters. A quantity worth $200 million of these weapons were sold to Iraq between 1984 and 1988. These and other so-called bear spares were reportedly sold to Iraq with U.S. approval and assistance. See Howard Teicher, "Testimony before the United States District Court, Southern District of Florida," 31 January 1995, accessed 2 June 2009 at www.gwu.edu/~nsarchiv/NSAEBB/NSAEBB82/iraq61.pdf.
[36] A 1983 offensive by Iranian forces and their Kurdish allies.
[37] This is probably a reference to the Tu-22 BLINDER bomber. Iraq operated twelve of these.
[38] SH-SHTP-A-001-023, "Saddam and Ba'ath Party Members Discussing the Iran-Iraq War," 6 March 1987. This is the first session of the meeting recorded in *SH-SHTP-A-000-896, "Saddam and Other Government Officials Discussing the State of the Country during the Iran-Iraq War and the Use of Chemical Weapons," 6 March 1987. For a partial transcript of the second recording, see section "Saddam and military advisers debate the appropriate use of chemical weapons," in Chapter 4.

to the west of the cities since they are populated and have economic installations. Striking the cities is the psychological aspect that defeats the Persian enemy and indicates to them that al-Khomeini turned toward hating the Iranians themselves. It is true that the economic installation slows down the Persian economy, but at the same, striking the cities has economic and psychological results we need. The type of cities to strike must be, certainly, important cities with deeper impact, if possible, but at the same time this is an issue to be left to the General Command and to Your Excellency. But I have an opinion, Sir, regarding March 21.[39] On March 21, the situation will escalate inside Iran on a large scale and I believe if there is a possibility to strike them at that time inside the cities, any city, it could have a psychological effect as far as defeating the Persian enemy, as well as a higher positive psychological effect as far as the Iraqis. Thank you, Sir.

———

Sa'dun: I have a military question, Sir.

Saddam: Go ahead.

Sa'dun: Is the chemical weapon as effective as we think, I mean the way we think of it as civilians?

Saddam: Yes, effective on him who does not use the mask at that moment the way we think of it as civilians.

Sa'dun: You mean it exterminates by the thousands?

Saddam: Yes, it exterminates by the thousands [pause]. It exterminates by the thousands and restrains them from drinking or eating the food available, and [inaudible] from leaving the city for a period of time until it is fully decontaminated – nothing; he cannot sleep on a mattress, eat, drink or anything. They will leave [inaudible] naked.

Izzat: I have a comment on this.

Saddam: Yes?

Izzat: I agree on everything we discussed, but as far as the chemical weapons or the chemical weapon, I believe we should be as economical as possible when using it on the front since it is possible that some strikes on the front may not have the effective range of the weapon we envision, which Dr. Sa'dun Hammadi talked about due to the soldiers' position in the front. First, the Iranians almost started to use the masks now on the front, the front is open and the soldiers are spread out – an open brigade, an open division although their formations are not regular like the Khomeini Guard. But affecting them requires comprehensive circumstances, I mean technical and all aspects, such as no masks, they are more gathered with larger numbers, that's when the effective result would take place.

What I mean by economical use [is that] I don't know if we have a production capability that satisfies the strategic need specified in the speech of Mr. President; this would be another issue. We strike the troops with what we have whenever we have the chance and the circumstances, but if there is not enough production to have

[39] A temporary cease-fire was scheduled to end on this date.

a sufficient quantity for a strategic strike when needed, we should use this weapon economically until we have enough of what we need. I rely greatly on these strikes. I swear no one asks us why you struck.

Saddam: I am not sure, comrade Izzat, whether or not you know that the chemical weapon cannot be used unless I give an order to use it!

Izzat: Yes, I know.

Saddam: So, I have the entire picture before my eyes; the quantities and qualities will definitely be presented, their impact, the situation, etc.

WMD DETERRENCE AND COMPELLENCE IN THE MOTHER OF ALL BATTLES

In meetings with his generals and senior advisers in late 1990 and January 1991, Saddam commented on the conditions under which Iraq would use chemical and biological weapons. In late November, Izzat spoke of Iraq's "intention to use chemicals," and Saddam declared that Iraq would strike its enemies "with everything." On several occasions, Saddam indicated that he considered a U.S. nuclear strike entirely plausible and that Iraq, in preparation for such an eventuality, planned and executed massive evacuation drills in Baghdad and other Iraqi cities.

In late December, Ali Hassan al-Majid ("Chemical Ali") discussed with Saddam potential scenarios for Iraqi chemical attacks. Ali made a case against polluting Kuwait's sewers with chemicals because the chemicals would dissipate and be ineffective; would be difficult to neutralize; and after spreading to the sea, might harm Iraqis; concerns about U.S. retaliation were notably absent from the list. Ali also expressed concern that citizens fleeing south from Baghdad would be headed in the direction of the chemical warfare and would suffer greatly, thus indicating that he believed chemical warfare would likely ensue between Iraqi and Coalition forces. In mid-January, Saddam discussed the need to be ready to launch chemical and biological weapons at a moment's notice by both missiles and aircraft in case a "great necessity" arose. He explained to Tariq that although Iraq would launch conventional warheads at Israel, it would use nonconventional weapons only "in return for the warheads they use."

The editors found no evidence in the tapes indicating that Saddam believed American fear of Iraqi chemical or biological weapon attacks on Israel or the United States deterred an American push toward Baghdad; however, Saddam did claim that Iraq's armor, its fighting spirit, and a successful conventional Scud missile strike had caused Bush to order the unilateral cease-fire.[40] This is not to say that Saddam discounted the utility of

---

[40] See section "Saddam suggests that Iraq's 'fighting spirit' led President Bush to request a cease-fire," and note 76, in Chapter 5.

his chemical and biological weapons, or civil defenses, as useful deterrents. Saddam recalled that his threats to use binary chemical weapons in defense of the Arab nation had deterred Israel from attacking Libya. He also stated that U.S. leaders had postponed attacking Iraq because Iraq's civil defense preparations signaled to the Americans that they would suffer many casualties in the event of war.

Saddam and Palestine Liberation Organization Leader Yasser Arafat Discuss Israel's Nuclear Threat to Baghdad (19 April 1990)[41]

Saddam: . . . as for the American bases, which are all over the world, in Turkey, etc., we can sweep them. We have to be ready for that level, meaning we should not be happy with just the talk because talking is not just talking, it is a matter of decision and commitment. All the words that we said came through a series of meetings with the military officers. It didn't go like that – what the missiles can do, what the Air Force can do. We check our defenses and their requirements, we check our bases. What are the orders to be sent for these bases? When Baghdad is struck by atomic bombs, how we are going to react – we took all this into consideration. It is not our choice, I swear, but it is a must. When the enemy comes and there is no heavy foot that would stop it, the Palestinian issue and the Arab situation won't be any good; therefore, it is not our timing. If it were our choice we would have chosen different timing, but it is a matter of necessity, and we have to be obliged to the necessity that says we need a strong position now.

––––––

Saddam: Abu Ammar [Arafat nom de guerre], it is about the timing. If we had the right timing and the situation of Arab countries and Palestinians were fine, we would not have said what we are saying now and we would probably have been embarrassed by them. But as long as we are on this path, we will never make it and the enemy won't give us the chance for it. When the enemy saw a rocket, he said, "Iraq owns missiles that would reach Tel Aviv." Well, Tel Aviv has missiles that reach all Arab capitals. "Iraq has chemical weapons and successfully used them on the Iranians and therefore, Iraq won't think twice about striking Israel with chemical weapons." When you ask Tel Aviv, "Why would the Iraqis use the chemical weapon against you?" the answer is to restore Palestine for the Arabs, and do not assault the Arabs, and that is it! Therefore, you do not have to be afraid of the Iraqi chemical weapon anymore. But it is fine if Israel owns the atomic bomb; it has the right to do so!

Yasser: And the germ bomb. It is fine.

Saddam: It has the right!

Yasser: Also the atomic, chemical, and germ bomb. It has been confirmed. It [Israel] has 240 nuclear warheads: 12 nuclear warheads for every Arab capital. These things won't threaten Arab security!

---

[41] SH-SHTP-A-001-037, "Saddam Meeting with Iraqi officials, Yasser Arafat, and the Palestinian Delegation," 19 April 1990. A complete translation is available in Woods and Lacey, *Iraqi Perspectives Project – Primary Source Materials*, 19–24.

Saddam: So, I am saying these words and I am completely calm, wearing a civilian suit. [*Audience laughs.*][42]

Male 1: It is a matter of diplomacy.

Saddam: So, I say these words because we have to be ready for that level.

Saddam and His Inner Circle Discuss Iraq's WMD Capabilities and Deterrent Threats (circa mid-November 1990)[43]

Saddam: We have the ability to know that America can hurt us, but we have the ability to hurt America and the ability to block its advanced technological weapons, which it is going to use.[44] We have classified some, such as the Stealth aircraft, and we spoke at the strategic level.

Izzat: [*Inaudible.*]

Male 1: Hold Saudi Arabia liable, Sir.

Saddam: We talked and said we hold them liable [*overlapping voices*]. We had strong talk. I mean our line of talking was the same as you wanted it.

Male 2: That's it.

Saddam: But in a convincing way, since we have to control them before they can influence our people. I mean, we can still talk about what is going to happen, but without exaggeration. Make it look smaller, but with all the requirements so that our people will not be shocked.

Male 1: Sir, there is an indication in the draft resolution that was distributed to us yesterday [*inaudible*].[45] The topic is mostly related to the chemical issue where it says at the end that Iraq is not to strike with chemicals. So, psychologically, I believe with regard to our people – and a counter-psychological aspect inside Najd and Hejaz [regions of Saudi Arabia] and the existing American forces – I believe we should mention the same points Your Excellency mentioned on April 2:[46] that in case of aggression, we shall use all weapons we have, including the binary chemical weapon, as a requirement to have a positive impact on our people, and as a countermeasure against the American forces in Najd and Hejaz, since the resolution draft mentions the chemical in many places.

---

[42] Saddam and Arafat seem to be speaking sarcastically.

[43] SH-SHTP-A-000-848, "Saddam and His Advisers Discussing Potential War with United States," undated (circa mid-November 1990).

[44] Earlier in the transcript, Saddam noted that Iraqi experiments had demonstrated that the smoke from burning oil wells would create problems for coalition targeting. The burning oil in the experiment "formed a cloud with a height of 500 meters, where they [the experimenters] could not see the plane," he explained.

[45] UNSC Resolution 678, passed on 29 November 1990, authorized states to attack Iraq on or after 15 January 1991 if Iraq had not yet withdrawn from Kuwait.

[46] Saddam said in his 2 April 1990 speech, "If an aggression is committed against an Arab and that Arab seeks our assistance from afar, we will not fail to come to his assistance. [The United States and England] will be deluded if they imagine that they can give Israel a cover in order to come and strike at some industrial metalworks. By God, we will make fire eat up half of Israel if it tried against Iraq." "President Warns Israel, Criticizes U.S.," FBIS-NES-90-064, 3 April 1990, from Baghdad Domestic Service (in Arabic), 2 April 1990.

Tariq: There is no reference to it in the resolution draft.

Male 1: Yesterday –

Izzat: No, no, there is no reference.

Tariq: There is no reference in the draft resolution. This was just a talk between them!

Saddam: An American warning.

Male 3: An American statement. [*Overlapping voices.*]

Saddam: Either American or British –

Tariq: It is not there. This was their talk.[47]

Male 3: That Iraq used chemicals –

Tariq: The draft resolution states it is just chemicals.

Izzat: It is dangerous for us to reveal our intention to use chemicals; how do we do that?

Saddam: Huh?

Male 1: If it is in the resolution draft –

Tariq: We would give them an excuse for a nuclear attack.

Male 1: Yeah, and Israel also the same way, Sir. This is just an opinion.

Saddam: We will strike them with everything.

Male 1: With everything, with all our capabilities [*overlapping voices*].

Saddam: But we will not give Iraq [*overlapping voices*]. The Americans themselves asked me.[48] [*Inaudible*] They asked, "Do you [intend to] use the chemical, atomic, and I don't know what?" I said, "First of all, we don't have atomic [weapons] and if we did, we would have mentioned it without being embarrassed. But anyway, I want to tell you something and that is Iraq, no matter what, we will not give Iraq [to them]."[49] So, it became clear. Dealing with it requires certain circumstances and methods.

Male 2: Whether we need to approach the Russians or not, Sir, I believe approaching the Russians –

Saddam: But, if we want to use chemicals, we will exterminate them, you know. I mean they will not be able to get out of [*inaudible*].

[47] On 30 November, France and Britain made public a joint statement in which they warned Baghdad against "initiating the use of chemical or biological warfare." Soviet Foreign Minister Shevardnadze issued a similar warning shortly thereafter. Saddam's adviser (Male 1) appears to have conflated these statements and UNSC Resolution 678. W. Andrew Terrill, "Chemical Warfare and 'Desert Storm': The Disaster That Never Came," *Small Wars and Insurgencies* 4, no. 2 (Autumn 1993): 270.

[48] Saddam might be referring to the 31 August 1990 interview with CBS newsman Dan Rather in which Rather pointedly asked about Iraq's WMD policy. See "Excerpts from Interview with Hussein on Crisis in Gulf," *New York Times*, 31 August 1990.

[49] This section was difficult for the translators to make sense of, as speakers' voices overlapped, and it is unclear where exactly Saddam's quotations of American statements begin and end.

Male 2: God willing!

Saddam: Because we discovered a way with destructive power that is 200 times more than the destructive power of the same type of chemical we used on Iran. I mean the destructive power is 200 times more than what we used to use.

Male 3: But they will ask, "Do you have the [*inaudible*] bomb?"

Tariq: No, they are going to talk about the thermal bomb.[50]

Saddam: No, they will talk about the nuclear bomb.

Male 2: The nuclear bomb, yes.

Izzat: And the thermal bomb.

Tariq: No, no, the thermal one. The nuclear bomb falls under a different chapter.

Saddam: An old thermal one.

Izzat: They talked about it yesterday.

Tariq: It creates explosion and gases.

Male 4: The Jordanians say the Iraqis made a bomb that when they launch it, all people become crazy. [*Laughter.*] Everyone becomes crazy, and therefore the Saudis are going to [*inaudible*].[51]

Saddam: Only few in the world come to our level as far as the chemical and germ weapons superiority, maybe two, one or maybe none as far as quantity and quality. I mean we have germ weapons 40 years, and anyone who steps on it would die, would burn.[52]

[*Inaudible background talk followed by laughter and jokes about Arabs.*]

Male 3: Let us relieve the Ummah [Islamic nation] of Israel.

In a Meeting with the National Command, Saddam Discusses the Need for an Iraqi Deterrent and Reminisces about Iraq's Missile Strikes on Israel during the Mother of All Battles (25 January 1995)[53]

Male 1: Mr. President... based on your speech on April 2... if Israel attacks any Arab country, we will use the binary chemical weapon to attack.[54] Therefore, they planned according to this...

---

[50] Possibly "thermobaric" or "incendiary" bomb.

[51] This comment might refer to Iraq's use of nerve gas against Iranian troops. During a 1984 attack to retake the Majnoun Islands, for instance, the Iraqis launched Tabun at their Iranian foes. Male 4's comment about people going crazy may have been a play on words, as *Majnoun* in Arabic means "crazy." See Joost R. Hiltermann, *A Poisonous Affair: America, Iraq, and the Gassing of Halabja* (New York: Cambridge University Press, 2007), 32–35.

[52] Saddam probably means that the germ weapons Iraq has are so powerful that their effects can last forty years.

[53] SH-SHTP-A-000-716, "Saddam and Top Political Advisers Discussing Hostilities with Israel," 25 January 1995.

[54] See *supra* note 46.

Saddam: And we built a defensive, defensive umbrella from Libya to Syria so that we are certain that no one would get the impression that an attack could take place on even one Arab regime friendly to us.[55]

Male 1: Yeah, yeah.

Saddam: It was not Libya that struck Baghdad with missiles, or Syria whose regime we have a clear position on.

Male 1: Yes.

Saddam: Indeed, Israel was unable to attack any Arab then!

Male 1: That's true.

Saddam: Although the entire scenario had indications that there was planning to strike the Libyan nuclear reactors.

Male 1: Yes.

Saddam: That's why I said "not Libya," since I was certain the international media was paving the way for a strike on Libya.

Male 1: Yes.

Saddam: Launched by Israel.

Male 1: Yes.

Saddam: But, since this was the way they were talking, that's it, Israel was no longer capable of making predictions.

Elias:[56] You can sense in their talk their hidden desire to use atomic power to destroy Iraq, but they are unable to use it.

Male 1: [*Inaudible*] the Americans, but they are annoyed.

Saddam: Yes, it is in their planning, I mean by analyzing their planning, any war that is inconvenient to them and where Iraq constitutes a vital part of it, they will strike Baghdad since striking Damascus or Amman would affect them. Therefore, the ultimate point that can hurt the Arabs or that they ultimately want to hurt is Iraq because mostly they fear Iraq and not the –

Male 1: Without getting affected by the strike's impacts.

Saddam: Therefore, they will strike Iraq, strike Baghdad, but once Iraq has a deterrent force their weapon will become neutralized.

Male 1: Of course!

Saddam: It will not be possible.

Elias: And during the battle [Israel will] fear for the Americans because if the weapon were used it would affect the American soldiers.

Saddam: What weapon?

[55] Saddam is apparently referring to Iraq's extended security guarantees to protect the Arab nation from Israeli aggression.
[56] Dr. Elias Farah, a Ba'athist intellectual.

Elias: The atomic! [*One person after another repeats:* "The atomic."]

Male 2: The atomic, not to hit Baghdad –

Male 4: Should Iraq get struck in the same battle –

Elias: During the battle –

Saddam: Yes, of course since this atomic dust spreads.

Elias: Because they hovered several times over the area where the –

Male 1: The Western region.

Elias: Where the missile platforms are, but they did not act independently from the instruction and agreement with –

Saddam: They want to say that their capability is more precise than that of the allies, but neither they nor the others – [they] failed tremendously in being able to follow the maneuver because of the missiles that were hitting them.[57]

Male 1: It crippled them.

Saddam: They regarded [it] as too much for the Arab mind, of course, for the third-world countries in general and the Arab mind in particular. Yet they instilled in the mind of the entire world that the Arab mind is underdeveloped as far as a confrontation capability! I mean the Arab mind is undeveloped and not the Arab capability.

Male 1: Hmm.

Saddam: So, this scared them all, of course, I mean the Arab mind is not underdeveloped!

Elias: What made them bear the missiles was that they were thinking of something else; when Yitzhak Shamir[58] was asked whether he used this chemical –

Saddam: Yeah, he did; he had no other choice.

Elias: [*Laughing.*]

Saddam: You can see him and his folks in the meeting wearing [masks].

Elias: They were scared of the chemical.

Saddam: Because the first missile instilled fear in them that faded after they tested it and realized it did not have any chemical effect. Some of them choked in their masks and when this happened, they thought it was the chemical and they died before they even died.[59] [*Laughter.*]

---

57 Translator comment: This is, in fact, what Saddam says in Arabic.

58 Shamir was Israeli prime minister during the 1991 Gulf War.

59 This might be a reference to the three Israeli citizens who died of heart attacks when an Iraqi al-Hussein missile struck an apartment complex in Tel Aviv on January 22. See William C. Yengst, Stephen J. Lukasik, and Mark A. Jensen, "Nuclear Weapons That Went to War," DNA-TR-96-25, draft final report sponsored by the U.S. Defense Special Weapons Agency and Science Applications International Corporation, October 1996, 373, accessed 8 January 2009 at www.npec-web.org.

The Revolutionary Command Council Discusses Civil Defense Measures and Iraqi Morale in the Face of Potential Nuclear Strikes on Iraqi Cities (29 December 1990)[60]

Ali: Some have suggested that we pollute it [the Kuwaiti sewer system] with chemical material. I, frankly, did not agree to that, because as you know, such pollution requires a great deal to prepare for how we will sanitize, how we will clean, and then I do not know when [*inaudible, possibly* "the rain"] will come down, and the possibility that it will wash it down, and thus its efficacy will almost be nil. Consequently, this will hurt us at sea, especially if it is used in larger quantities than what was previously determined, or more than expected. We will start dry runs and efficient and swift practices from the 10th, Your Excellency Mr. President, until the 14th. We did not start with the citizens as they are scared from the beginning. We do not want to scare the citizens, as I fear that this will negatively affect the fighters' morale when they see the fear and reaction of citizens. So we decided to wait a period of two weeks. I mean, this period is for us, for the fighters, so we can begin the first dry run or the first practice to vaccinate our comrades and our troops. And then the following days, oh, frankly, the other four days, we decided to give the last two days as a rest for the soldiers, I mean for the fighters. This way they are prepared for the night of the 15th.

———

Ali: The other comment, Your Excellency, is what is happening in Baghdad with regard to civil defense awareness. There is an explanation about the effects of atomic, nuclear bombs, its efficacy, what does it do, how many people will it kill and how many people will it decimate. All of this awareness is frightening the people and instilling fear. The professors who come and lecture at the ministries, at the schools, at other places, they present details of this war or this bomb. We do not have to do that; we only have to provide awareness about preventive measures of such bombs. But when we keep discussing the effects of these bombs [*speaker laughs*]. Honestly, Sir, we drive them crazy.

The other comment, perhaps our brothers at civil defense are not paying sufficient attention to it, and this is that the evacuation usually takes place to the north and not to the south. I am sure they know, but as you know, north Baghdad is hindered by the Dijla River, those who come from al-Tharthar.[61] And we only have one bridge; if that bridge is hit, all of Baghdad will be at a standstill. We have to acquire a group of bridges and we have to quickly mount bridge heads now, so that whenever the need exists to erect them, we could do so. This matter worries me a lot. I am concerned with the right side of the Dijla River, not its left. I fear that it will be completely severed, then the exodus will take place toward the south and heading to the south, if it is in the direction of chemical attack and I mean, the contamination, this is a dangerous state.

---

[60] SH-SHTP-A-001-042, "Saddam and the Revolutionary Command Council Discussing the Iraqi Invasion of Kuwait and the Expected US Attack," 29 December 1990. For more information on Iraq's plans and exercises to evacuate Baghdad in the event of coalition WMD strikes, see *SH-PDWN-D-001-248, "Correspondence between Presidential Diwan and Other Iraqi Authorities Discussing Emergency Evacuation Plans for Iraqi Cities in the Event of an Attack Using Weapons of Mass Destruction," 29 December 1990.

[61] The Dijla River is a tributary to the Tigris.

But this, this fear factor, I urge you to stop it. I wonder why were we educated, all of this hoopla about the effects of nuclear and atomic attack. These are scare tactics. It frightens the children, it frightens their parents, it frightens the fighter...

––––––

Izzat: Your Excellency Mr. President, what Comrade Ali has stated regarding the timing of the mass attack is correct. It is true that it has caused a state of fear in society. I mean, this could create such a state. Even now, such a state of fear exists among some troops. Some of the troops are suffering from an unbalanced state with regard to their thinking about how to deal with the war. We cannot segregate the society from the soldiers in the war front. If the society is in a state of fear, it will affect the fighters, and I agree with what Comrade Ali has stated, they go to their –

Saddam: Families.

Izzat: Families, so worried about this state and they hear that their families will be in this miserable state, being subjected to bombing, high temperature, poisoning, and other effects. They will be demoralized. So I suggest, and I support Comrade Ali, that explanation shall be limited to prevention only.

––––––

Saddam: Comrade [Izzat], give me leeway to speak frankly with you, at this moment of ours. He who does not want to contribute in raising the morale, I urge him not to contribute in the lowering of morale. It is not right that I speak in this manner at the Command level, but let me be frank with you. What are we, a bunch of kids?...

The civil defense has brought us back, at least in Baghdad, to a period when public opinion was agitated, like when we were engaged with Iran. Why did this happen? I have said from the beginning, Comrade Izzat, I swear on your moustache to pay attention to civil defense.[62] Isn't that so?[63] I had a hunch that civil defense would not be up to par. So why, why is this happening? Our people are united. Excellent. Its morale is high, and if you spoil the population, you might as well throw it away in the garbage. Is this the way to preserve our people's morale? What is wrong with you? Don't you listen to the people? What is this? Are the people considered a burden on us? Should we treat the people like robots? I have only scared you once throughout my entire life before a war and I have rectified my action in the manner of which you already know, when I scared you and told you that we will be hit by atomic bombs.

One time you say we want Kuwait, and after that if something happens like this rumor, then you adopt another opinion. I asked you, "Are you ready?" And you

[62] Swearing on someone's moustache is a traditional Arab way of swearing on his honor.
[63] Iraq apparently began evacuating key cities very shortly after invading Kuwait. According to an Iraqi transcript of a 6 October meeting between Saddam and Soviet envoy Yevgeny Primakov, Saddam expressed concern to the Soviet envoy that it would be problematic for Iraq to withdraw from Kuwait under U.S. pressure. He argued that Iraq's leaders could not claim that they were surprised by the strong U.S. reaction, as the Iraqi people "will say no; your assessment was correct, because we know you evacuated the cities of Baghdad, al-Basra, and Salah ad Din [the Iraqi governorate containing Tikrit] in anticipation of an American nuclear attack; your assessment was for a situation that is more difficult than war." Saddam added, "What would be our answer then?" See SH-PDWN-D-000-533, "Saddam Meeting with a Soviet Delegation," 6 October 1990.

responded, "Yes we are ready," and then I rectified my [scare tactic] action, and I told you to erase all that I had said... We did not agree, Comrade Izzat, that this is the correct approach for evacuation. Comrade Izzat, you supervise evacuation. I told you that evacuation, we are not the ones who will evacuate people. I said that at the Command meeting.

Izzat: The written plan –

Saddam: But – no problem – after the plan, I told you, Comrade Izzat, that evacuation should be carried out by citizens acquainting themselves with the countryside. And you told me that this will facilitate many things for us, and will make evacuation very smooth. And Comrade Sa'd, you also spoke.

Sa'd:[64] [*Inaudible voices in the background*] You informed me and told me do not [*inaudible*] but do not inform them.

Saddam: But tell them –

Sa'd: And we applied this to a section of Baghdad.

Saddam: And this will make me comfortable, those who want to go can go, and those who do not want to go, do not have to go. Fine. With regard to evacuation, this war is not with Iran, not even with Israel, because Israel relies on American satellites for the purposes of photographing us, and sometimes the Americans cooperate with them, and other times they do not. This is based on existing policies. Right now, when we have identified six areas designated for evacuation, are these areas known or not known? Well, which one is better for these human masses: to be bombed in tents, or to be bombed while they are in their houses?

Male 5: If they intend to attack them?

Saddam: If they intend to attack them directly, they will bomb them while they are in their tents.

Male 5: Easier –

Saddam: ...Is transferring [evacuating] two million people our goal? The mission is preserving the morale of those two million people after we have completed the evacuation. I place emphasis on having the Iraqi remain in his home to maintain his high morale. This will be better than moving him through a practice [evacuation]. If the Iraqi loses his morale, he is defeated. Perhaps I may not venture into war, but it is possible that I will win the war without fighting; this is possible, even if you give it one percent, one per thousand, and this is still a valid possibility. However, if the Iraqi loses his morale, I lose the war before fighting.

Now do you see how this phenomenon yields opposite results? So now I am not satisfied with the morale of the citizens of Baghdad. Namely, I am not satisfied with civil defense measures that contribute to such low morale.

Izzat: [*Inaudible.*]

Saddam: Why, Comrade Izzat, what is happening with us? Didn't we say when we were discussing the evacuation plan, that every citizen should befriend a rural citizen,

---

[64] Possibly Sa'd Abd al-Majid al-Faysal al-Tikriti, Ba'ath Party Regional Command chairman.

just in case the war expands and we are forced to evacuate? We should not explain to the citizen what the atomic bomb will do. I mean, I do not know what is happening. This talk about the atomic bomb is futile, [*inaudible*] and the talk by Iraqi scientists. No scientist has ever fought throughout the entire globe. Why has America not ventured to a war for a long time? Because it is watching our preparation. It realizes that it will suffer from great human casualties.

Saddam Discusses with Senior Officials the Circumstances under Which Iraq Will Use Chemical and Biological Weapons (circa second week of January 1991)[65]

Male 2: Sir, the design of the suit is with a white shirt and a collar [neckline] like a dishdasha.[66]

Saddam: Then my design is right.

Hussein Kamil: Absolutely right, Sir.

Saddam: Then work on it and make the corrections to the sizes.

Male 2: Sir, we will amend it to be exactly with the neck line.

Saddam: Even if it appears a little bit. Now when someone wears a suit, of course the shirt line will appear a little bit, but here I prefer not to have it obvious.

Male 2: Sir, you can see that nobody is wearing it.

Saddam: It's forgotten, but now I will ask Abu Muthanna,[67] because he is the best at remembering. [*Shackling noise.*] Since 1958 the Iraqi army has been using these kinds of suits [*People talking in the background.*]

Saddam: I want to make sure that – close the door please [*door slams*] – the germ and chemical warheads, as well as the chemical and germ bombs, are available to the "concerned people," so that in case we order an attack, they can do it without missing any of their targets.

Hussein Kamil: Sir, if you'll allow me. Some of the chemicals now are distributed; this is according to the last report from the Minister of Defense, which was submitted to you, Sir. Chemical warheads are stored and are ready at air bases, and they know how and when to deal with, as well as arm, these heads. Also, some other artillery machines and rockets are available from the army. While some of the empty "stuff" is available for us, our position is very good, and we don't have any operational problems. Moreover, in the past, many substantial items and materials were imported. Now, we were able to establish a local project, which was established to comply with daily production. Also, another bigger project will be finalized within a month, as well as a third project in the coming two to three months that will keep us on the safe side, in terms of supply. We, Sir, only deal in common materials like phosphorus, ethyl alcohol and methyl –

---

[65] Unlike other captured recordings cited in this study, the editors have not had access to this recording. The transcript is taken from the *Duelfer Report*, vol. 1, "Regime Strategic Intent," 97–100.

[66] The dishdasha is the long, generally white tunic traditionally worn by Arab men.

[67] Reference unclear.

Saddam: [*Interrupting.*] Etcetera – this is not important to me.

Hussein Kamil: So, Sir, regarding the germs and [*pauses*] –

Saddam: And the chemicals.

Hussein Kamil: No, we have some of the chemicals available –

Saddam: [*Interrupting.*] So, we qualify that the missiles, by tomorrow, will be ready on the 15th.

Hussein Kamil: Sir, we don't have the germs.

Saddam: Then, where are they?

Hussein Kamil: It's with us.

Saddam: What is it doing with you? I need these germs to be fixed on the missiles, and tell him to hit, because starting the 15th,[68] everyone should be ready for action to happen at anytime, and I consider Riyadh as a target.

Hussein Kamil: Sir, let me explain to you. What we produced now are the rocket heads and the containers, and we distributed them underground in three different locations. We considered these locations the best places we have, and that if we had a chance to scatter and to find more locations, then we would have done it. These locations are far away from Baghdad; this is problematic because of transportation which will take seven days to commute, but we minimized all the transportation procedures in a way. However, when we want to transport it, we cannot do it within one day, Sir, and if we want to do it by plane, then, Sir, we have to go for the method [*pause*] –

Saddam: Let's talk about it later. [*Waiters enter the room, sound of plates banging and side conversations with the waiters. Door slams.*]

Hussein Kamil: Sir, we have three types of germ weapons, but we have to decide which one we should use, some types stay capable for many years – [69]

Saddam: [*Interrupting*] We want the long term, the many years kind.[70]

Hussein Kamil: Sir, this option is available and all other options are available as well.

Saddam: You mean at which time we use it and at which moment!

Hussein Kamil: Yes, Sir. That is why there has to be a decision about which method of attack we use: a missile, a fighter bomb or a fighter plane.

Saddam: With them all, all the methods.[71]

---

[68] Saddam is referring to the 15 January 1991 deadline for Iraq to withdraw from Kuwait or be forced to comply with UNSC Resolution 678 through "all necessary means."

[69] Hussein is apparently referring to Iraq's possession of botulinum toxin, *Bacillus anthracis* (anthrax) spores, and aflatoxin.

[70] Dried anthrax can remain potent for hundreds of years, whereas liquid anthrax can stay good for up to twenty years. Rod Barton, *The Weapons Detective: The Inside Story of Australia's Top Weapons Inspector* (Melbourne: Griffin Press, 2006), 154–55.

[71] Iraqi officials later told UN inspectors that they had prepared delivery via all three methods. Iraq reportedly filled sixteen Al Hussein warheads with botulinum toxin, five with anthrax,

Hussein Kamil: Sir, we have to calculate now –

Saddam: [*Interrupting*] Hussein knows about those.

Hussein Kamil: Sir, there are some calculations we have to do, since we have modified fighters.[72] The bombs or the warheads are all available, but the moment for using them at zero hour is something we should indicate, Sir. We will say that this will be launched –

Saddam: [*Interrupting*] At the moment of use, you should launch them all against their targets.

Hussein Kamil: All of the methods are available, Sir.

Saddam: We don't want to depend on one option. The missiles will be intercepted and the planes, at least one will crash, but whenever the missiles or planes fall down over the enemy land, then I consider the goal is achieved and the mission fulfilled.

Hussein Kamil: Sir, it is available and stored "somewhere," but if you, Sir, order us to transfer it, we are a bit worried it will cause contamination. It has been stored for 45–47 years, and yet has not been certified as being safe.[73] Sir, it had been experimented on only once and some of the employees, Sir, were contaminated.

Saddam: I want – as soon as possible – if we are not transferring the weapons, to issue a clear order to the "concerned people" that the weapon should be in their hands ASAP. I might even give them a "non-return access." I will give them an order stating that at "one moment," if I'm not there and you don't hear my voice, you will hear somebody else's voice, so you can receive the order from him, and then you can go attack your targets. I want the weapons to be distributed to targets; I want Riyadh and Jeddah, which are the biggest Saudi cities with all the decision makers, and the Saudi rulers live there. This is for the germ and chemical weapons.

---

and four with aflatoxin. It filled 100 R-400 or R-400A bombs with botulinum toxin, fifty with anthrax spores, and another seven with aflatoxin. It also attempted to modify MiG-21s into remotely piloted vehicles (RPVs) and to equip them with spray tanks. *Duelfer Report*, vol. 3, "Biological Warfare," 48, 59.

72 On 10 January 1991, Iraq conducted a flight test to see how well a modified MiG-21 fighter operated as an RPV. Other flight tests might also have taken place. *Duelfer Report*, vol. 2, "Delivery Systems," 42.

73 R. L. Vollum, an Oxford bacteriologist, isolated bovine anthrax during the 1930s. The British used Vollum's strain in biological weapon tests in 1942 and transferred it to the United States. In 1986, Iraq received a sample of this strain from the American Type Culture Collection (ATCC), a nonprofit biological resource center. U.S. Customs approved the export, and the U.S. Centers for Disease Control and Prevention sent Iraq strains of additional viruses for public health purposes. At the time, anthrax was readily available: of the 450 repositories listed in the World Directory of Collections of Cultures of Microorganisms, more than 50 openly sold anthrax. The *Duelfer Report* states that Iraq researched different anthrax strains but settled on the ATCC variant "as the exclusive strain for use as a BW." Hussein Kamil's comment that the pathogen "has been stored for 45–47 years" indicates that he might be referring to Iraq's possession of this strain. See *Duelfer Report*, vol. 3, "Biological Warfare," 9, 21; Dominic Kennedy, "Saddam's Germ War Plot Is Traced Back to One Oxford Cow," *The [London] Times*, 9 August 2005; Barry E. Zimmerman and David J. Zimmerman, *Killer Germs: Microbes and Diseases That Threaten Humanity* (New York: McGraw Hill, 2003), 217; "Report: U.S. Supplied the Kinds of Germs Iraq Later Used for Biological Weapons," *USA Today*, 30 September 2002.

Hussein Kamil: In terms of chemical weapons, we have an excellent situation and a good grip on them.

Saddam: Only in case we are obliged and there is a great necessity to put them into action. Also, all the Israeli cities, all of them. Of course you should concentrate on Tel Aviv, since it is their center.

Hussein Kamil: Sir, the best way to transport this weapon and achieve the most harmful effects would come by using planes, like a crop plane, to scatter it. This is, Sir, a thousand times more harmful. This is according to the analyses of the technicians –

Saddam: [*Interrupting*] We should consider alternatives Hussein. Meaning that if the planes don't arrive, then the missile will, and if the missile is intercepted, the plane will arrive.

Hussein Kamil: Sir, it is rare that the missiles are intercepted.

Saddam: Anyways, it is our duty to think of all the bad scenarios of this mission. Then Israel first, and if the Americans attack us with unconventional, harmful types of weapons, or at the moment we see it feasible to attack. But as for now, put Riyadh and Jeddah as targets.

Saddam: Air Force Commander [Muzahim Sa'b Hasan Muhammad al-Nasiri], you should coordinate with the minister of industry to get access to the weapons in the shortest time possible, of course with a lot of consideration for technical and safety factors. Also, I want to give a written authorization to the "concerned people" that is signed by me, in case something happens to me. You know this is a life and death issue, all the orders about targets are sealed in writing and authenticated. Furthermore, for the officials from the missile authority, you should coordinate with them so that they take the missiles to locations. They are to inform the chief of staff, or operations commander deputy, to go to Hussein, Minister of Industry, and go with the same necessary procedures. Regarding the chemical weapon –

Hussein Kamil: [*Interrupting*] We are really in good control of it, Sir.

Saddam: No, I mean it should be with the "taking action" people.

Hussein Kamil: Sir, the chemical is available and our establishment is the one responsible for transporting the weapon and supervising how it is used.

Saddam: Excellent. Do you have anything stocked in the establishment stores?

Hussein Kamil: We have [empty] heads but we also have production all over.[74] Not only in the factories; it is scattered.

Saddam: I want you to keep in mind that by the 15th nothing should be stored in your factories that the "enemy" can have access to.

---

[74] It is unclear to the editors why the translation in the *Duelfer Report* describes the heads [apparently warheads] as empty, as Hussein Kamil does not appear to have explicitly said this. According to an Iraqi defense ministry memorandum dated 31 December 1990, Iraq prepared twenty-five missiles with "special warheads." See *SH-MICN-D-001-249, "Reports and Correspondence between the Military Industrialization Commission and the Ministry of Defense regarding Chemical Weapons Production," 31 December 1990. See also *Duelfer Report*, vol. 3, "Biological Warfare," 48, 59.

Hussein Kamil: Sir, the Ministry of Defense should pull that "stuff" out. The Ministry of Defense already ordered 25 percent of that stuff. When and if they ask us for the rest, we will have no problem supplying it. Sir, we are in an excellent and prepared situation regarding the missile warheads and fighters' bombs. They are all modified and ready for launching any time, the chemical and the germ.

[Sound of plates banging.]

Saddam: Where are most American forces and troops gathered and concentrated?

Speaker 2: Sir, it is in [King] Khalid Military City, "Madinat Khalid," located 60 kilometers past Hafr al-Baten in Saudi [Arabia], where the front General Command and Air Force Command are located. Most of the American army sectors, Sir, are by the coastal side in Al-Dammam, where most of the camp complexes exist.

Saddam: I want these big gatherings and complexes to be allocated properly and given to the Air Force commander to be added to the above targets of the germ weapons. This should be done by an order to Muzahim.[75] This is by a direct order and it has the green light from me, since this mission doesn't fall into daily regular operations. I will issue a letter, signed by me, listing the commands and the alternative plans and probabilities of this mission, which should be followed literally.

Male 2: Sir, economically important targets such as refineries, power plants, and water reservoirs – should we include them in the mission?

Saddam: These locations should be put under the regular Air Force operations, and included in attacks not on this particular mission.

Hussein Kamil: Sir, these vital locations must be added to the mission and become priority targets of the biological and chemical weapons, because this will end all sorts of life. People are drinking water from these desalination plants and getting their fuel from refineries, thus ending the mission –

Saddam: Muzahim has already written these locations down and will take care of it, refineries and –

Muzahim: [Interrupting] The refineries and desalination plants, Sir.

Saddam: May God help us do it.

[Lull in conversation.]

Saddam: We will never lower our heads as long as we are alive, even if we have to destroy everybody.

Saddam and His Advisers Discuss Iraqi Missile Attacks on Targets in Israel and Saudi Arabia (circa 17–18 January 1991)[76]

Saddam: Just as we have agreed before, we have to be cool and calm, we have to maintain our vital assets and demonstrate how to use such vital assets to mount a

---

75 Muzahim Sa'b Hasan Muhammad al-Nasiri, air force commander, former head of the Fedayeen Saddam and one of Saddam's bodyguards, and future deputy director of the Military Industrial Commission.

76 SH-SHTP-A-001-043, "Senior Iraqi Officials Discussing Coalition Operations against Iraq," undated (circa 17–18 January 1991).

severe blow against them. And for your knowledge, we will launch missile attacks against Tel Aviv and the main cities of Israel today. We will attack them all.[77]

Tariq: Conventional missiles?

Saddam: Yes, conventional missiles. I mean we will use the other warheads, you know, in return for the warheads they use.

Male 1: Yes.

Saddam: So that the battle gets more exciting. It is time. We do not care about two hundred aircraft plus or two hundred aircraft minus, and then why would Israel maintain its strength? Let us involve Israel in the fight. Let us see if they are up to it.

Tariq: Your Excellency, we have attacked targets in Saudi Arabia and – [78]

Saddam: Some of the Saudi refineries after that, we will attack the Saudi cities.

Male 1: And why after that?

Saddam: Let us concentrate on Israel. Let us break the bone of America's daughter, let all the West witness, let them relay the deaths that will occur.

Male 1: Yes, yes.

Saddam: And after that, we will alternate our attacks. We will mount attacks against Israel, then mount attacks against Saudi Arabia, is that not so, or not?

Male 2: Oh yes. [*Overlapping voices.*]

Saddam: Riyadh, Jeddah, I mean we will strike all the cities within our missiles' range, with the exception of Holy Mecca and Medina the Luminous [*al-Medina al-Munawara*]. We do not want to launch any missiles at these sites.

Izzat: [*Inaudible*] the other day there was a program on the Israeli TV where they asked a woman, "What do you think of the aggression?" She said, "We do not want to fight with Iraq."

Saddam: The Saudi?

Izzat: Yes, the Saudi.

Tariq: Our missile bases are safe, God willing, Sir.

Saddam: Yes, all of them are safe.

Male 2: But Israel, how many times have they announced that they have attacked the bases?[79]

---

[77] Iraq first launched Scuds at Israel on 18 January 1990.

[78] This might refer to Iraq's 17 January artillery barrage on targets in the Saudi town of Khafji. Rick Atkinson, *Crusade: The Untold Story of the Persian Gulf War* (New York: Houghton Mifflin, 1993), 66.

[79] It is unclear why this adviser believes that Israel attacked Iraqi missile bases. Publicly available sources record no instances in which Israeli leaders claim to have attacked Iraq during the Mother of All Battles, although it was common in both public and private discussions for Saddam's inner circle to assume Israeli involvement in U.S. actions, and vice versa.

Saddam: Is it not the long-range missiles?

Male 3: Yes, yes.

Saddam: These long range missiles, we have exposed them for their viewing for an entire month, so that they can see it – photograph it. And when I guessed that the war was inevitable, I summoned the father of missiles and told him, "I do not want anyone to know the location of even one single missile," and I agreed with him how he will distribute the missiles throughout, and where he will store them.[80] And consequently, not even one single missile was hit during all these raids.[81]

Tariq: [*Inaudible.*]

Saddam: Just now we will start using missiles, and in full force, tomorrow morning. If I know [tomorrow] you are strong enough and you have the nerve, I will wait two, three, four days before launching them.

[*All speak at the same time.*]

Saddam: So, we will attack them tonight, God willing.

Izzat: Military targets?

Saddam: By God, you know, I regard all Israeli cities to be targets. They have fixed, main targets, government headquarters, main factories, etc., but this will take place.

Izzat: We will say they are main targets.

Saddam: We will also say [*inaudible*].

Tariq: We will announce official targets, Your Excellency, and if they fall on residential areas, it will be [looked at as] conventional afterwards.

Saddam: It will be conventional, they will also reciprocate by attacking us with missiles. They have missiles.

Izzat: I wonder whether they have cruise missiles.

Male 3: No, they have a different kind.

Saddam: They [the Israelis] have Pershing missiles.[82]

---

[80] Saddam appears to be referring to a 12 January 1991 meeting with Lieutenant General Hazim Abd al-Razzaq al-Ayyubi, the commander of Iraq's surface-to-surface missile (SSM) corps. See Hazim Abd al-Razzaq al-Ayyubi, "Forty-Three Missiles on the Zionist Entity," *Al-Arab al-Yawm* (in Arabic, Amman), 27 October 1998, 31–32.

[81] The U.S.-led coalition raided fixed Iraqi positions, yet Iraq had deployed its missiles with its mobile units.

[82] The development of the conversation makes clear that Saddam is referring to Pershing I or Pershing IA missiles, not the longer range Pershing II. In any event, Israel did not have Pershing missiles of any kind. The Ford administration considered selling Pershings to Israel but ultimately decided against it. Kamil Mansur and James Cohen, *Beyond Alliance: Israel in U.S. Foreign Policy* (New York: Columbia University Press, 1994), 120–21. The commander of Iraq's Republican Guard, Lieutenant General Ayad Futayih al-Rawi, commented in a captured recording that Iraq dispersed its forces because it believed the United States had transferred Pershing missiles with nuclear warheads to Saudi Arabia. See *SH-SHTP-V-001-250, "High Ranking Officers Discussing US and Coalition Aggression towards Iraq and Military Preparations for Expected Attacks," 1993. In fact, by the time of this meeting,

Male 3: They don't have Pershing.

Many speakers at the same time: Jericho, Jericho [missiles].[83]

Saddam: Pershing. They have Pershing. They have had Pershing for a long time!

Tariq: For a long time.

Izzat: For a long time, the American Pershing.

Tariq: I do not think the Pershing has the range for Baghdad.

Izzat: The Pershing has a range of 520.

Saddam: The Pershing can reach al-Habbaniyah.[84]

Tariq: Yes, Fallujah and al-Habbaniyah, yes.

Saddam: But perhaps the Jericho could have that range. They [America] must have given them [Israel] some missiles at that time –

---

the United States had destroyed most, but not all, of its Pershing missiles in accordance with the Intermediate-Range Nuclear Forces Treaty provisions. Woods, *The Mother of All Battles*, 169–70, n112.

[83] After Iraq first attacked Tel Aviv with Scud missiles, U.S. Deputy Secretary of State Lawrence Eagleburger predicted that Israel would respond by launching Jericho surface-to-surface missiles at Iraq. As part of its policy of ambiguity regarding whether it has nuclear weapons, Israel has neither confirmed nor denied possession of Jericho missiles. See Avigdor Haselkorn, *The Continuing Storm: Iraq, Poisonous Weapons and Deterrence* (New Haven, CT: Yale University Press, 1999), 130; Dan Williams, "Israel Could Use Ballistic Missiles against Iran," *Washington Times*, 19 March 2009.

[84] An Iraqi air base in the western desert of Iraq.

SEVEN

The Embargo and the Special Commission

> I have given them [the Americans] everything. I mean, I have given them everything: the missiles, and the chemical, biological and nuclear weapons. They didn't give you anything in exchange, not even a piece of bread. They didn't give us anything in exchange, well, they have become worse...It means that they will bring the regime they want and will give it to the person they want.
>
> – Saddam Hussein, circa 19–21 August 1991[1]

The U.S.-led coalition in 1991 demanded that Iraq verifiably divest itself of weapons of mass destruction (WMD) and long-range rockets as the price of peace. Twelve years later, a different U.S.-led "coalition of the willing" justified its invasion of Iraq based primarily on allegations of Iraq's noncompliance with its disarmament obligations. To understand Saddam's views and behavior regarding the UN sanctions and inspections, one must comprehend why one war ended, why another began, and what happened in the intervening years, best characterized as neither war nor peace.

Iraq's experience with sanctions, according to Saddam, preceded its invasion of Kuwait. In the year before the invasion, Saddam accused the United States of establishing an embargo by refusing to extend further agricultural export credits to Iraq.[2] The UN Security Council (UNSC) attempted to reverse the occupation with sanctions under UNSC Resolution 661. UNSC Resolution 661 paved the way for UNSC Resolution 687, which the Security Council passed on 3 April 1991, a month after the cessation of hostilities.

UNSC Resolution 687 provided for continuing sanctions to compel Iraq to verifiably divest itself of WMD-related programs and long-range missiles, and to dissuade it from further acquisition activities. Permanent members

---

[1] *SH-SHTP-A-001-210, "Saddam and His Inner Circle Discussing Upheaval and the Communist Coup Attempt in the Soviet Union," undated (circa 19–21 August 1991).

[2] SH-SHTP-A-000-671, "Saddam and Senior Advisers Discussing the Iraqi Invasion of Kuwait," 30 September 1990; see SH-PDWN-D-000-533, "Saddam Meeting with a Soviet Delegation," 6 October 1990.

Tariq Aziz salutes on the left, and Abd al-Tawab Mullah Huwaysh, the deputy prime minister and minister of military industrialization (2001–03), salutes on the right. The photograph is dated 29 April 2001. (*Source:* *SH-MISC-D-001-276, "Photos of Iraqi Officials on Various Occasions," April 2001)

of the UNSC, however, differed in their interpretation of paragraph 22 of the resolution. Whereas the United States and United Kingdom interpreted it to mean that Iraq had to completely disarm before the United Nations would lift any of the sanctions, France and Russia called for sanctions to be lifted in piecemeal fashion to reward Iraq for significant, yet incomplete, compliance with its disarmament obligations.[3]

---

[3] In paragraph 22, the Security Council, "Decides also that upon the approval by the Council of the programme called for in paragraph 19 and upon Council agreement that Iraq has completed all actions contemplated in paragraphs 8 to 13, the prohibitions against the import of commodities and products originating in Iraq and the prohibitions against financial transactions related thereto contained in resolution 661 (1990) shall have no further force or effect." For Resolution 687 and a discussion of the different interpretations of paragraph 22, see "Security Council Resolutions – 1991," accessed 2 December 2008 at www.un.org/Docs/scres/1991/scres91.htm; George A. Lopez and David Cortright, "Containing Iraq: Sanctions Worked," *Foreign Affairs* 83 (July–August 2004).

Saddam apparently decided to destroy Iraq's WMD stockpiles during the summer of 1991, although he refused to admit that his regime had weaponized biological agents and sought to retain dual-use production capabilities.[4] Despite Iraq's destruction of its WMD stockpiles, its fierce resistance to certain inspections, intimidation of inspectors, refusal to name former suppliers, and inability or unwillingness to provide complete and accurate disarmament declarations all undermined the verifiability and credibility of its disarmament.

Both publicly and privately, Saddam and his subordinates expressed the belief that the United States and the UN Special Commission for Iraq (UNSCOM) wished to prolong the sanctions and inspections regardless of Iraqi compliance.[5] They alleged that the United States bribed inspectors, that UNSCOM was collecting targeting information for the United States, and that inspectors might plant evidence with which to accuse Iraq. Saddam, for his part, attempted to politicize the inspection process. He bribed senior UN officials and foreign leaders, linked oil contracts with states' behavior toward Iraq in the United Nations, and provoked crises as a means of creating circumstances that he believed would lead to favorable compromises for Iraq.

Throughout his reign, Saddam instructed his subordinates to neither completely accept nor completely reject Iraq's disarmament obligations; rather, he pursued a path of partial compliance. Saddam repeatedly, between 1991 and 2003, told his senior subordinates that "Iraq did not have anything hidden" or that "they destroyed everything." Although given the nature of the regime, it is not clear that he was universally believed.[6] Saddam and Chemical Ali, while in coalition custody after the U.S.-led invasion, indicated that Saddam had pursued ambiguous disarmament to satisfy international disarmament demands without signaling weakness that might encourage an Iranian or Israeli attack.[7] Such a course of deliberate ambiguity seems likely to have influenced Iraq's behavior, although the ambiguity certainly had other sources also. Poor Iraqi record keeping made verification difficult and may have contributed to Iraq's confusing and contradictory signals.

---

[4] *Duelfer Report*, vol. 1, "Transmittal Message," 9.

[5] UNSC Resolution 687, the 3 April 1991 cease-fire resolution to the Gulf War, established UNSCOM to oversee Iraq's compliance with its new disarmament obligations. UNSCOM took the lead on the non-nuclear provisions, while sharing responsibilities with the International Atomic Energy Agency (IAEA) for overseeing Iraq's compliance in the nuclear-related area.

[6] In addition to the reference cited beginning on page 345, see SH-SHTP-A-000-990, "Meeting between Saddam Hussein and Senior Advisors," 1995 and SH-SHTP-A-001-198, "Saddam and His Advisors Discuss the Rules of the UN Security Council," undated.

[7] Woods et al., *Iraqi Perspectives Project: A View Of* (2006), 91–92; Piro casual conversation with Saddam, Session Number 23, 13 May 2004; Piro casual conversation with Saddam, Session Number 24, 11 June 2004.

Iraq's unwillingness to allow more intrusive inspections, for fear that they would enable the United States to collect targeting information on the Ba'ath leadership, also prevented greater transparency. Additionally, eliminating technical uncertainty over the existence of clandestine biological weapon programs is extremely difficult in industrialized societies. In short, a certain degree of ambiguity was probably inevitable. In the end, Iraq's incomplete compliance failed to satisfy American disarmament demands or stave off the U.S.-led invasion.

THE EARLY YEARS (1991–1993)

In the early years of sanctions and UNSCOM inspections, Iraq engaged in a variety of confrontations and disputes with the international community. Saddam complained as early as autumn 1991 that complying with inspectors' demands only worsened Iraq's position and that UNSCOM was collecting data that could be used to target the Iraqi leadership. Saddam ordered his subordinates to resist and intimidate the inspectors, and discussed Iraqi efforts to foster division among permanent UNSC members.

Saddam Laments to Senior Advisers That Complying with Inspectors Hardens Sentiment against Iraq (circa 19–21 August 1991)[8]

Saddam: One of the mistakes some people make is that when the enemy has decided to hurt you, you believe there is a chance to decrease the harm by acting in a certain way, but it won't. The harm won't be less.

Male 1: The enemy is determined; he has a plan he is following.

Saddam: And he is determined to follow his plan, but you don't try to get a new friend to face his hostility. This matter is important, it is not insignificant. Well, what is animosity? What did the Americans show us as a possible sign for partially decreasing their harm? We didn't see anything coming from them. I have given them everything. I mean, I have given them everything: the missiles, and the chemical, biological and nuclear weapons. They didn't give you anything in exchange, not even a piece of bread. They didn't give us anything in exchange, well, they have become worse. The last three resolutions are not relevant. There is no connection. Well, immediately, tac, tac, tac, they made decisions. A little bit more, they wanted to bring their armies to let them stand up at the entrance of the oil wells and to tell us, "We are the ones to give you the oil. We are the ones to decide whether to give it to you or not to give it to you. We are the ones to decide how much to take from the oil." Well, that's it. It means that they will bring the regime they want and will give it to the person they want.

Male 1: And now an expert is supposed to come and inspect.

---

[8] *SH-SHTP-A-001-210, "Saddam and His Inner Circle Discussing Upheaval and the Communist Coup Attempt in the Soviet Union," undated (circa 19–21 August 1991).

Saddam: Why should we be courteous with him? Nothing in the situation requires us to be courteous.

Saddam and His Inner Circle Discuss Iraq's Intelligence on Future UN Inspections (circa September–October 1991)[9]

Tariq: They were afraid of a surprise raid, because we know the inspection team schedule, so we prepare for these teams.[10] We sit down, we analyze all the possibilities, etc. We present them with the political picture as we read it. And I myself have earlier stated that Comrade Abd was attending these meetings.[11] I told them, "Do not tell me about a military attack. Do not include it in your calculations. You are not to deduce, we only have our own conclusions. You provide us with your work, let us understand and we will tell you what you should be doing." So despite our listening to their comments, but the matter of –

Saddam: We did not keep them busy.

Tariq: Politics is our specialty . . . There are other aspects about this aircraft, there are political and security considerations to look at, etc., just as the comrade has stated. But from the technical aspect, it is possible that this aircraft will use thermal photography. I mean they have already photographed the sites, but they did not photograph the bottom. They say they want to photograph some areas, the areas where they think there is something in them, so we have to prepare for that.[12]

[*Recording stops for about twenty seconds.*]

Saddam: Yes, Comrade Muhammad.

Muhammad:[13] Your Excellency, in reality, it is evident that through these events –

Saddam: Did they specify a timeframe for such a survey?

Dr. Sa'dun: No. No, Your Excellency.

Muhammad: But they have specified when they want to begin.

Saddam: Huh?

Muhammad: The beginning, I mean.

Male 1: The middle of the month.

---

[9] *SH-SHTP-A-001-251, "Saddam and Top Political Advisers Discussing a United Nations Air Survey Request," undated (circa September–October 1991).

[10] Information from earlier in the recording indicates that "they" apparently refers to General Amir al-Saadi, Hussein Kamil, and a group of Iraqi technicians. Amir was Saddam's presidential science adviser and liaison with the UNSCOM inspectors. Charles Duelfer, the deputy chairman of UNSCOM, later assessed that only 1 percent of what UNSCOM intended as surprise inspections actually surprised the Iraqis. Duelfer, *Hide and Seek*, 93.

[11] Likely Abd al-Ghani al-Ghafur, cabinet minister without portfolio.

[12] This appears to be either a reference to UNSCOM's initial use of American U-2 high-altitude reconnaissance planes or foreign helicopters during inspections. Iraq agreed to re-accept UNSCOM helicopter flights on 4 October 1991. "U.N. Starts Helicopter Flights to Find Missile Sites in Iraq," *New York Times*, 4 October 1991.

[13] Possibly Muhammad Hamzah al-Zubaydi, whom Saddam promoted from deputy prime minister to prime minister on 13 September 1991.

Muhammad: They specified the beginning but not the duration. Following through the events and observing the behavior and actions of the American president, his announcements, the main objective now that they aspire to achieve is to target Mr. President [Saddam] in person. And all that the comrades have stated, and the manner in which they [the Americans] are acting, I believe that all of this is like looking for excuses. And they want to execute a certain counteraction by any means. Bush's announcements are indicative of that. So, Your Excellency, what I wish is that we should be patient and courageous and that we should be flexible in order to get past this critical phase, because almost the whole world is greedy in an unusual manner. And there is Arab and non-Arab assessment against you and against the regime in general, but the main aim is to target Mr. President himself. Your Excellency, I support what Dr. Sa'dun has stated, and in reality, for the purpose of not giving them any excuse, in addition to that, we should cooperate.

For the sake of the future, we have to get past this phase that we are going through right now. We have to be really flexible and in the future, God willing, everything will be fine.

———

Saddam: What I want is this: First, our objection should remain firm. I mean our disapproval should remain firm, and we have to present it in a way that it is against our will. And at the same time, because what they can execute today, on another day they will not be able to carry out. Because every state has its own timing in light of its general capability. Even their military presence in the region, and our nature, and the nature of the neighbors, all these elements will be considered at the moment. There is a difference between our approval and our disapproval. This is the first point.

The second point: We should force them to specify a timeframe . . . Because if they do not determine the timeframe, it is possible that this will continue for ten years. They will be coming every time, and the security threat will remain.

Male 2: Of course.

Saddam: I mean, because when they started their aggression they had little information about us.

Sa'dun: Yes.

Saddam: And I have proof, I mean this is not just casual talk, I know, there are certain matters that I know, that their information about us is very little. But now, their information about us has increased, that is in the security aspect. One person escapes from the special sites, they ask him for example, who comes to the site? Who sleeps here and who does not sleep here? I mean this is new information. They base their assessment on such information, and compare them with other sites, who sleeps here and who does not sleep here? And consequently, they base their assessment on such information.

They take it for granted, they want to photograph the areas that will differ from their expectations. Perhaps their satellites have not paid sufficient attention to these sites. Therefore, this state of affairs will continue and it will continue to be a dangerous state unless our memorandum is clear in requesting a timeframe for this matter.

Tariq: But the duration of its presence in Iraqi airspace will be known because it is part of the notification process.

Saddam: Regardless of that, regardless of that, I mean we know about their presence, but we need to know the time it will take to complete its mission, from the beginning, from the first day until the last day.

Tariq: Yes.

Saddam: We have to know that.

Tariq: Yes.

Saddam: [*Inaudible.*] It will not be an indefinite process. An open ended –

Male 2: Correct.

Saddam: This is one aspect. It might be more suitable to say why does it have to be an American aircraft? Why can't we use a Soviet aircraft? For example, the five countries[14] should agree on the manner of operation, and the type of equipment used in the aircraft. I mean we should instigate, instigate problems, we should give others excuses, the others are on the sidelines, I mean, they are saying, "Why should we immerse ourselves in this matter? We will not get anything out of it." I mean why does Iraq have to feed them bread? And Iraq should not be at their mercy, asking whether they will approve or disapprove. Approve or disapprove, Iraq should have readily available texts that it will be able to utilize during its maneuvers with the concerned parties.

Male 2: True.

Saddam: I mean, in general, I see our policies are leaning toward the direction of blindness. I want to bring in other parties to the problem. We are saying, here is the country that is leading the aggression against us, we want to know the type of equipment that the United Nations needs to complete its mission. First, there are the five countries, they have to study the needs and requirements of the United Nations. Do they need these types of equipment? Do they need this type of aircraft? Does this operation have to be supervised by this entity? For example, is India part of the Security Council? Let us involve others. Well, okay, perhaps they do not have to hear that, but at least we have instigated some issues.

Male 2: Yes.

Saddam: The text is important. We should say, anyway, despite our conviction with our position, and the correctness of our position, etc., we will not hamstring aviation of this type if it is forced upon us. We should emphasize the words "if it is forced upon us," this way it is not considered approval, but we say, "If it is forced upon us and adopted by the United Nations." Let them respond to this. We are saying the United Nations has adopted this, and this is required and is needed, and we do not buy your suggestions. The participation of the Soviets and India, the participation of a monitoring entity over the type of equipment really needed for that purpose. At least by doing that we have preempted and weakened the conspiratorial aspect of this matter.

14 This is a reference to the five permanent members of the UN Security Council.

If the conspiratorial aspect is weakened or removed, then we could say that we have achieved something. I mean, because a single person is not the same as three. I mean when three technicians see the aircraft flying, inspect the type of equipment used, etc. Let them [*inaudible*.]

We should not go to war because of this, because we are not at a stage to enter a war, but at least let us harass our enemy. Why, why are we – we should not harass them with our refusal, nor harass them with our acceptance, but we should always place lines for them to cross, lines between refusal and acceptance. I mean, we should involve others, involve them in a manner that different opinions will emerge.

Saddam Orders Iraqis to Resist and Intimidate UN Inspectors (July 1992)[15]

Saddam: The helicopters: Break the propellers on the countries present when they take off and do not leave anything that says United Nations to remain in Iraq. I mean, whatever happened, happened. This is reasonable. Does it not occur to them that it is reasonable to put matters in context? Perhaps they have taken this into consideration, and perhaps not! Therefore, but I would say, no one could say that a military operation will not take place, I mean against Iraq. There is no one.

Also, and likewise, no one could say with certainty that there will be a military operation if we say that no one will be allowed to enter the Ministry of Agriculture. They mixed up all the papers, they formulated a memorandum from the United Nations, but I did not confirm.

My observation is simple, not a grand one. My observation is that their matter, I feel that they got tangled with regard to the Ministry of Agriculture, I mean this is my general analysis, and they intended military action and that is why they fabricated the Ministry of Agriculture matter.[16]

This high probability analysis is founded on observations that we witnessed. The Iraqi solution was presented to the Security Council, and after he visited us, [Rolf] Ekeus, not when he was there, he came and visited us and the comrades have discussed with him and he realized how solid our position was.[17] And we were very flexible, and the comrade told him our suggestion, and he presented our suggestion and has presented all matters that he believes that we carried out to hinder their mission.

---

[15] *SH-SHTP-A-001-252, "Saddam and the Council of Ministers Discussing UN Sanctions and Possible US Invasion," undated (circa July 1992). In early July, Iraq refused UNSCOM inspectors access to the Ministry of Agriculture, where there were thought to be documents pertaining to Saddam's missile programs. The UNSC subsequently declared Iraq to be in violation of UNSC Resolution 687. After the United States began preparing to renew the air war against Iraq, UNSCOM inspectors were allowed access to the building, though it was widely believed that Iraqi officials had removed the incriminating documents in the interim. See "Iraq Rebuffs UN Inspection Order," *Washington Times*, 8 July 1992; Jeffrey Smith and Ann Devroy, "US, Allies Plan Ultimatum to Iraq," *Washington Post*, 24 July 1992.

[16] Tariq made a similar allegation in November 1995. See section "Saddam and his inner circle question whether U.S. presidential candidates seek war," in Chapter 1.

[17] Rolf Ekeus was the director of UNSCOM (1991–1997).

The Security Council has adopted its decision, but rejected our suggestion. However, the manner of this rejection was different than before, where in the past they used to pay us a visit every time and be on our case. This time, they left the door ajar, and said that Iraq must cooperate with the Special Commission's suggestions.

Tariq: The Special Commission.

Saddam: As a politician, I understand this as if the Security Council has not made a decision yet about the attack. I mean, I also understand that America is behind such a decision, because America – you know, I do not place any hope in the Security Council as to when it will agree. I believe it all depends on what America wants and the Security Council will follow suit and comply with America's [wishes], including the attack [against Iraq].

But can America withstand the repercussions of the aggression? And can the President [George H. W. Bush], in light of the competitive race [election], make such a decision alone, without consulting other institutions? Because in the past he has sought consultation from those institutions; how would he be able to handle matters now without seeking their consultation? Perhaps he could, and perhaps he could not. It goes both ways.

This war, let us say, it will be a trial war, even though it is a big war. The manner in which it was presented, are they tangled in this matter? Did they evaluate all the facts? I mean they have inspected all ministries; there aren't any ministries left that they did not inspect. That is why this is not a small matter: it calls for a war, it calls for a war, Comrade Tariq.

However, can we maintain our solid, core position? And to maintain technical cooperation, perhaps we can avoid these matters and we have an exit out of this. It is true that we have now reached what we call the middle ground; however, on the surface, we are winners.

Tariq: Yes

Saddam: They have not been dealing with us before on level ground; this is the first time we are dealing with them on equal footing, and perhaps we can reach a middle ground with a meaningful advantage for us. They have just about agreed to half of it. To half of it they have agreed. So this suggestion of yours can achieve the core of this matter.

This will be a much-needed experience for the masses. I, as an Iraqi citizen, and as a responsible official, I regard this as a gift that has fallen from the sky. I do not believe this, even the Ministry of Agriculture? Oh, do not say Ministry of Industry or the Military Industrialization Commission. Good. Say Ministry of Agriculture. Our people don't have to plunge into battle all at once. Perhaps our people can go through a series of battles that will give experience, that is to say prepare them, and so on. This is one of the battles that I say our people must appreciate.

Regardless what is said, that these demonstrations were pre-orchestrated, well, let me say, there is not any demonstration throughout the world that is not orchestrated.[18]

---

[18] At the time, the Iraqi media dishonestly reported that UNSCOM had taken 250 Iraqi employees hostage at the Department of Agriculture building. The Iraqi government

I mean, even demonstrations in England are orchestrated. Is there any party or union out there that does not orchestrate a demonstration? Any society, I mean we have the unions, the parties, [and] party branches, but the most certain thing that they were convinced of and that really scared them is the masses' fury and anger. The masses hate them to death, the masses have scared them. By God, we have not scared them [the UN inspectors] as much as our masses did, those dogs.

Male 1: [*Inaudible.*]

Saddam: The masses have scared them, let them see the situation we are in . . . our people express their allegiance emotionally, to a scary level. Frankly, they [the UN inspectors] are scared. This is not acting. [*Other people talking in the background.*]

I mean, let us say, everything has its own timing. Let us say, we, the Iraqi policy, the policy of being too accommodating, is a wrong one. Because such an accommodating policy has made them feel comfortable, especially the bad ones among them, as they have manifested their arrogance and have exhibited their ugly side. They act worse than an occupier when they walk through a directorate, and last night's movie exposed that and there will be more movies coming up.[19]

They complained about the minister of media, and they complained about this and that. All right, let us unleash the Iraqi masses so that they realize what they are up against. So from now on, Comrade, I want you to clearly inform your people, and tell them that this war is yours, but we want you to deny them food, do not serve them, this applies to any entity that says United Nations. I mean, do not give them food, do not sell them anything, do not offer them drinks, do not cooperate with them, period. They have to feel that when they come to Iraq, it is as if they're going inside an oven. Finish their work as quickly as possible, hurry them up with their reports.

———

Saddam: The Iraqis are positive. But when it comes to foreigners, there is something that you and I know about them: the Iraqis are very hospitable with foreigners; they invite them to their houses.

They serve them, and the foreigner feels that he is in paradise. [But now] do not even greet them, do not give them any facilities, period. I am talking from the people's perspective, as citizens: do not sell them anything, do not buy anything for them. I mean they have to feel that they are going inside an oven. They should bring their sandwiches with them, so that they can finish their work quickly and go back to their country.

Oh, talking about this subject, I forgot to say, an Israeli attack is not in the formula, it is highly unlikely. But how can I describe to you the situation right now? Now,

reportedly transferred several busloads of women to the scene, along with a truck of government-supplied fruit, vegetables, and eggs for the women to launch in the direction of the inspectors. Once the cameras quit rolling, the "hostile" crowd and "worried-looking government officials" reportedly relaxed immediately and became jovial. Tim Trevan, *Saddam's Secrets: The Hunt for Iraq's Hidden Weapons* (London: HarperCollins, 1999), 184.

[19] Saddam is speaking metaphorically.

Bush is saying you should not criticize my new policy because it contributes to peace and benefits for Israel as well as regional stability. He got rid of his secretary of state, he got rid of those losers, some of them were weak and incapable, some were unlucky, some were helpless.[20]

Such a move at this time is not easy, it is not easy. I mean, it is not easy for planes to fly from Saudi Arabia and to strike Baghdad. Before, Kuwait told them it is easy, oh Comrade Hosni [Mubarak], to put an army or planes in Saudi Arabia to come to strike Baghdad. The situation is now different than before. I mean before, they would use Kuwait as an excuse, but what about now, what is the excuse? They hate Fahd [bin Abdul Aziz al-Saud], then use demonstrations to send a message, to place a message on the wall. Perhaps before, they did not give consideration because of Kuwait, their neighbors, etc. Their disloyal agent, the ruler of Kuwait, perhaps he will convince them that Iraq refused an inspection of the Ministry of Agriculture, so he will tell them to bring their planes and bomb Iraq. I mean, this is not easy, this is not like before, the easiest ring they have now is Turkey and Kuwait, I mean, the location of Kuwait and Turkey. I mean, this is the easiest ring for them, to carry out an action of this type. That is, if they want, these are just points and will not change our decision.

However, we have conducted our analysis, and I see that these are some of my observations with regard to this matter. So, yes, the statement made by Comrade Mizban is correct, learning is very important, and it is important to learn in any subject. This even applies in the concept of give and take; however, we should not deviate from the core of our subject. Our core subject here is the breach of Iraqi sovereignty in the manner they came with. This is dangerous, and I would say very dangerous. It is dangerous and very dangerous, and retreating from our decision will make us incapable of confronting them in all the battles that we plan to fight with them.

Comrade Tariq, this is the tasking, work on it. Our core demand is that we want neutral people whom we will agree upon. We nominate India and China. If they have other nominees, we will hear what they have to say. The ones we approve will be the only ones to enter the Ministry [of Agriculture]. We will submit to them a report from the committee. We should tell them, "Listen people, the thing that we suspect, like existing traces, you may find it in some locations or you may realize that it was transferred to another location, we want you to search for it." We must tell them, "Is there anything you want us to look for?" Or boxes, perhaps we want to take some swipes, so only those people will go to the Ministry. They should be afforded cordial treatment from us; however, they are not allowed to enter the office of the Minister or the office of under-secretaries, the offices of under-secretaries. Also, do not allow them in the Human Resources Archives offices, I mean the personnel records area, what do you call it? The personal data of employees, there is no need to enter this area. And what did we say?

[20] By mid-July 1992, it was widely rumored that James Baker would resign as Bush's secretary of state to run the president's reelection campaign. The announcement was made in late July, and Baker resigned on 23 August. See Michael Wines, "Looking to Baker to Save Bush Anew," *New York Times*, 15 July 1992; Barbara Crossette, "Eagleburger Is Viewed as the Likely Successor," *New York Times*, 22 July 1992.

Tariq: Agriculture.

Saddam: Agriculture, the farming areas, all the statistics, we regard all of these to be national secrets. How will we be able to protect our people's confidentiality? Because our people will say, "Look at those arrogant folks, they come to prey on us." Perhaps this will be the solution, perhaps not. However, this is within our control [*inaudible*]. If they suspect anything, tell them we suspect it too, but we need the technical assistance of those attendees, but not from this group, the people that they brought.

No problem, tell them this is the brief, take a look at it, but outside the Ministry. I mean, there are ancient Chinese proverbs. Muhammad bin al-Qasim al-Thaqafi, they told him, "Man, you made up your mind to visit China and here we brought you its soil so that you can step on it." I mean, they achieve their purpose, that is if their purpose is really what is needed. However, our goal will also be accomplished; we have protected our sovereignty to a great level. As a first trial, this is fine, as a first trial, this is fine. I am confident that this is very good practice for the command, the people, the party. I mean, this is good practice. Good, anyway, if they do not agree. Then let them do what they want; we did our part. We know our people: it is not easy for us to be flexible, because when we are flexible, but at the same time maintain our core, the people will be angry at them.

Tariq: Yes.

Saddam: Those who preserve the core, those who preserve the core do not feel that we have cut them off.

THE MID-1990S: EXPECTATIONS OF A "CROSSING" (1994–1996)

Saddam predicted that Iraq would escape international sanctions in the mid-1990s. He explained that his deployment of Republican Guard divisions to the border with Kuwait would create an international crisis that, in turn, would lead to negotiations, compromises, and concessions for Iraq. He called the encounter "the crossing to the other bank," thus indicating belief that the crisis would facilitate the end of the sanctions.[21] He declared 1995 to be the year of the crossing, though the defection of Hussein Kamil ensured that Iraq's attempts to escape sanctions would prove no more successful in 1995 than they had the previous year.[22] In the following tapes, Saddam and his advisers discuss the 1994 Republican Guard deployment and how alleged U.S. politicization of the inspection regime, Iraq's unauthorized procurement of gyroscopes, and American enmity hindered Iraq from coming clean.

[21] Ofra Bengio, ed., *Middle East Contemporary Survey: Iraq 1976–1999* (Tel Aviv: Moshe Dayan Center for Middle Eastern and African Studies, Shiloah Institute, Tel Aviv University), CD-ROM version, vol. 18/1994, 350.

[22] Ibid., vol. 19/1995, 310. For information on the defection, see Chapter 8.

Saddam Says That He Had Deployed Republican Guard Divisions to the South with the Hope of Creating a Crisis (circa 9–10 October 1994)[23]

Male 1: They are tasking a Republican to be an intermediary with Iraq, indicating George Shultz, the previous American Secretary of State, because we have dealt with him.[24]

Saddam: Is that who was assigned to Bosnia-Herzegovina?[25]

Male 1: No.

Tariq: No, this is the Republican who was US Secretary of State during the Reagan administration. At that time the American-Iraqi relations were good and consequently [inaudible].

Taha Yasin Ramadan: [Inaudible] other agreements.

Saddam: Go ahead, Comrade Muhammad. Proceed, Comrade Muhammad.

Muhammad:[26] Yes, Your Excellency.

Saddam: Let him read it, I have a comment to make, and then you read to us after that.

Muhammad: Yes, Your Excellency, as per your order.

Saddam: Just as we said, we have convened a series of meetings about this matter, especially during the last couple of months. And we have also convened a series of meetings in the past according to the situation. And we have reached the conclusion that if the sanctions are not lifted in the upcoming round, I think the last one, or on the tenth round, I mean on the tenth [of October], if they are not lifted, then we have to proceed to a crisis.[27] And this crisis might create new horizons where

---

[23] *SH-SHTP-A-001-253, "Saddam and Top Political Advisers Discussing Relations with Saudi Arabia and Other Neighbors," undated (circa 9–10 October 1994). Saddam and his advisers discussed the 1994 Republican Guard deployment to southern Iraq in a number of other recordings also, including SH-SHTP-A-000-989, "Saddam Meeting with Council of Ministers," 15 April 1995; SH-SHTP-A-000-991, "Saddam and Senior Political Advisers Discussing UN Resolutions and Possible Iraqi Withdrawal from Kuwait," undated (circa October 1994); SH-SHTP-D-000-759, "Saddam Meeting with Members of Al-'Ubur Conference, National Command, Iraqi Regional Command and Revolutionary Command Council," undated (circa 1994); SH-SHTP-A-000-565, "Saddam and High Ranking Officials Discussing US Plans to Attack Iraq, Irrigation Projects, and other Military Issues," undated (circa 1995).

[24] There is nothing publicly available indicating that the Clinton administration engaged Shultz as a special envoy to Iraq in 1994.

[25] Saddam is apparently referring to Richard Holbrooke, who served as assistant secretary of state for European and Canadian affairs (1994–1996) and was the primary architect of the Dayton Peace Agreement (1995) that ended the war in Bosnia.

[26] Possibly Muhammad Saeed al-Sahhaf, minister of foreign affairs, or Muhammad Nuri al-Shammari, head of the Civil Defense Department.

[27] UNSC Resolution 715 (1991) called on the UN secretary-general and the director-general of the IAEA to submit semiannual reports on Iraq's compliance with its disarmament obligations. The Iraqis sometimes referred to the periods between the reports as rounds. See Resolution 715 (1991), accessed 19 December 2008 at www.un.org/Depts/unmovic/documents/715.pdf. Some news reports indicated that Ekeus would submit his semiannual

the political environment will be more conducive. It might lead to much stronger capabilities and stronger proof to develop the situation with those concerned with international politics.

In the previous meeting we also said that diplomacy has some limits, such that every factor and capability that is present cannot work as deeply in the country according to exigencies, reaching a stage where foreign policy cannot be carried out in the country. Diplomacy will reach a point that it will fail to implement the country's policies in a balanced way. That is why other factors have to be considered, subject to availability, to evaluate the possibility of activating this front. And we also stated in that meeting that in all circumstances, we do not accept dying of hunger. In other words, we do not accept that our people will die of hunger and we are just sitting idle watching it become like Somalia, or like Haiti, or the other countries whose people were dying of hunger, and watch our people receive leftovers thrown in by the Westerners in a humiliating manner, without affording our people an actual rescue.

We have stated overtly to the Iraqis that if you lose your patience, before you lose your patience, just say that your patience is running out, and it has reached the edge, and we as responsible officials, when we view this, we tell you that these are the statements of righteousness and logic, and if we discovered that our capabilities have reached the point that you will starve and die of hunger, if that is the case, we will open the vaults of the universe to you. You may conclude what you conclude. This was clear, I mean, this message was clear to the Iraqis, I mean the basics of the current Iraqi situation.

We have moved two divisions. One of them is a Republican Guard division to Basra, and we have followed that with a third division. This third division we have moved is what has made the Americans place its army on alert, because this means there are four Republican Guard divisions close to each other.[28]

One is an old one; it is part of the emergency plan of Salih Fort, and the fourth division is the 30th. Together with the presence of army capabilities in depth, it became apparent to them [the Americans] that such a capability can carry out a serious action, I mean, this action will move the situation, in the same manner that you are following through.

We are always concerned that our people will have [the] strong conviction that there are no alternatives – there is no idea that could serve the action of lifting the sanctions that the mind could come up with, without placing it in its correct context. A crisis like this one requires, I mean it requires give and take, as the political literature states, that will produce results that are differentiated into a single result that is responsible for the others and the situation is dealt with in a manner that will not make the other differentiated results the main result.

---

report on 10 October 1994. Robert Block, "Desperate Saddam Takes On the World," *Independent* (London), 10 October 1994.

[28] Iraq's deployment of Republican Guard forces toward Kuwait precipitated a U.S. military response. Operation Vigilant Warrior began on 7 October 1994 and eventually involved the emergency deployment of ground, air, and naval forces to Kuwait and the region. See W. Eric Herr, "Operation Vigilant Warrior: Conventional Deterrence Theory, Doctrine, and Practice" (Maxwell Air Force Base: Air University Press, 1996).

I have spoken about mobilization and I believe that mobilization must continue because the sanctions continue, and because the alternatives we could choose if we found out that the mean – or the other means – are incapable of achieving the objective, our clear objective in this phase, which is the lifting of the sanction phase. And in order that our friends will not use that as an excuse for inaction or evading the positions we have built through one year or more, with them, I say that we inform the French, the Chinese, the Russians, I mean immediately after this meeting. We inform them and tell them that we noticed their concerns with regard to the presence of a part of the Republican Guards Forces in Basra.

Male 3: The Army.

Saddam: No, no, I mean the Army, I mean it, I mean it, I mean that the Army is present in its indisputable regular locations, and this is a gain for us. They have tried that in the past and they have failed. The Army is in the area, for the purpose of any possible action from Iran, for any other possibility, but the new element here is the Republican Guard, its presence in the Basra region. This augments the possibility that the Army may carry out an action against Kuwait. I mean this is what gave way to the thunderstorm.

Male 1: They know that the Republican Guard is [*inaudible*].

Saddam: [*Inaudible*] you know that this is our natural right, [and] that we are free to carry out an action as long as we are in our territory. We are free to move our forces according to established plans to confront any possibility, or for the purpose of training we carry out. Despite that, we want to give you an opportunity to double your efforts, an opportunity to strengthen your efforts, so that we see the outcome of your efforts, and we hope that your effort will yield the favorable and specific result of lifting the sanctions off the Iraqi people. Confronting such facts, the command has decided on the withdrawal of these forces and completing their training in another governorate, and not Basra Governorate, and stop right there.

Male 2: [*Inaudible.*]

Saddam: I mean Basra.

Izzat: Not north of Basra, outside Basra, outside the governorate.

Saddam: I prefer that we say outside Basra Governorate.

Izzat: [*Inaudible.*]

Saddam: Anyway, we tell them that this matter [*inaudible*], as if we are not allowed to reinforce our existing sectors, or substitute them, or conduct exercises in Basra Governorate, we categorically reject that. However, in this situation, this is our decision.

Izzat: [*Inaudible.*]

Saddam: Anyway, outside the area that [*inaudible*] in this instance, we give them leeway, when the orders are given, I mean after you notify them, you are to proceed with the implementation of this plan. By doing this, we will deny the Americans any legitimacy they have to continue pursuing negative outcomes that nullify the already achieved objectives, and this will expose them in the next Security Council meeting, that is in light of our friends' attacks, logic and objections, and in front of our logic and our position. [*Inaudible*] our sectors are here, [*inaudible*] at any time we can move them and return them back to the area of our choosing [*inaudible*].

Saddam and His Advisers Analyze How Great Power Politics and Personal Ambitions Will Affect an Upcoming UN Special Commission Report (circa March 1995)[29]

Tariq: When Ekeus finished his trip to Moscow, our ambassador met with the Russians and he sent us a report, which I have seen. But the Russian Ambassador in Baghdad brought in a specific report, more specific and much clearer, and he has handed it over to Amir.[30] It relates to the outcome of the Ekeus discussions. We have not submitted it to Your Excellency yet, so it would be beneficial if Your Excellency would review it.

Saddam: What are its conclusions?

Tariq: Its conclusions are that with regard to the subject of the four files [nuclear, biological, chemical, and rockets], he is willing to submit a positive report to the United Nations and that he believes that Iraq has accomplished a lot, I mean with regard to its obligations. And that the American position is not legally sound, I mean with regard to paragraph 22.[31] He requested assistance and he told them, "But I have a problem with the Iraqis regarding the biological issue. If the Iraqis would just help me in this issue, I would not complicate matters for them. I am willing to propose closing the file, meaning, without any additional complications." And he requests the Russians to pressure the Americans.

Saddam: If there are unbroken pieces of iron in this period, Ekeus will try to break them. The result will be that he won't present a report, meaning with the description that you presented very well. The description that you presented is very good, a cover for the Americans to continue their attempts, but this process leads to something like a middle solution, not a decisive one.

Tariq: Yes.

Saddam: This is my analysis.

Tariq: Yes, I mean, his main short-term objective is that there will be a midway solution for this current situation.

Male 1: Not to lose the Americans.

---

[29] *SH-SHTP-A-001-254, "Saddam and Top Political Advisers Discussing Diplomacy with the United States and Russia," undated (circa March 1995) .

[30] This is apparently a reference to General Amir al-Saadi.

[31] Tariq's comment that the U.S. position was "not legally sound" might refer to U.S.-U.K. insistence that paragraph 22 of UNSC Resolution 687 (the cease-fire resolution to the Mother of All Battles) required Iraq to completely disarm before the United Nations would lift any of the sanctions. France and Russia, however, called for sanctions to be lifted in piecemeal fashion to reward incomplete Iraqi compliance. See Lopez and Cortright, "Containing Iraq."

Saddam: He [Ekeus] wants to take the position of that Egyptian.[32]

Tariq: Yes, but Your Excellency, he will not be able, even if he wants to be the Secretary-General of the United Nations.

Saddam: I mean he will continue to extend his term until he merges with the Secretary-General.

Tariq: But Your Excellency, he will not be able to become the Secretary-General, as there are two superpowers who are permanent members who suspect his intent.

Saddam: That is why he is cajoling the Russians and the French after the Russians and the French exhibited their detailed, specific interests.

Tariq: Yes, yes, he was forced to cajole them, because if there is one veto against him, he will lose that opportunity. And if he wants to look for a job, European of course, the French will have a role, so he cannot play the American game with all its ramifications. He has to observe, he has to adopt a middle ground approach between the American position and the opposing one. That is why His Excellency Mr. President's assessment is correct, that Ekeus will work toward a midway solution, or that he will present elements that support a middle ground solution, or that contribute to a break-through.

———

Saddam: In this period, Ekeus is also interested in sending messages that would make us comfortable with his intentions, because when he speaks with non-aligned nations, he knows that these words will reach us.

Tariq: Oh yes, absolutely.

Saddam: When he speaks with the Russians, he knows that these words will reach us one way or another.[33]

Tariq: Yes.

Saddam: He is afraid that April will come and Iraq still will not have given him anything, and at that time, Iraqis will stand up and say, look we have accomplished all these achievements, but we did not receive anything in return, we do not have anything.[34] Then we will review all of our previous positions.

---

[32] Saddam and Tariq are apparently referring to Boutros Boutros-Ghali, the Egyptian secretary-general of the United Nations at the time.

[33] Richard Butler notes that Russian and French officials attached to UNSCOM regularly compromised sensitive information. Duelfer also cites evidence that Russia and France shared intelligence on UNSCOM with Iraq. See Duelfer, *Hide and Seek*, 102, 121; Butler, *The Greatest Threat: Iraq, Weapons of Mass Destruction, and the Growing Crisis of Global Security* (New York: Public Affairs, 2000), 132.

[34] As previously noted, UNSCR 715 (1991) called on the UN secretary-general and director-general of the IAEA to submit semiannual reports on Iraq's compliance with its disarmament obligations. The reports came out each fall during October or November, and each spring in April. Saddam is referring to the upcoming 10 April 1995 report (S/1995/284). A copy of this report was accessed 16 December 2008 at www.un.org/Depts/unscom/Semiannual/srep95-284.htm.

Saddam and His Advisers Discuss Iraq's Compliance with Inspections and Their Perceptions of U.S. Politicization of the Inspection Process (circa January–February 1995)[35]

Saddam: [Let us discuss] Ekeus's politics.

Male 1: With regard to Ekeus's last tour, Mr. Vice President [Taha Yasin Ramadan] has met with him.

Tariq: Your Excellency, General Amir [al-Saadi] has travelled today. He has the technical details, but I have reviewed all their preparations and I have convened two meetings with Ekeus. The first meeting, I requested him – I was briefed on the technical discussions he carried out with General Amir and his assistants. I told him [apparently Ekeus] to tell me, "I want you to give me your assessment as to what has been achieved and whatever issues remain."

He [Ekeus] talked in four areas. The first area concerns the monitoring. He said that "the monitoring is complete and I will inform the Security Council in my upcoming April report, and will say that the monitoring system is working, and is operational." Then I asked him, I said to him, "Aren't you going to insert words like 'provisional,' 'temporary' and 'testing' and so forth?" He said, "No. The testing has been completed in October and this is what is happening." The monitoring system is considered working, that is, according to Resolution 715 . . . So with regard to the monitoring, there is no problem.

With regard to the missiles, we agreed with the Special Commission that this missile field has been closed since the end of 1992 or the early part of '93. They started questioning the lower ranks, and inquired about deals that were forged with smaller countries and inquired about some purchases . . .

Saddam: Here we go again, we are going back to the missile issue?

Tariq: [*Inaudible.*] No, Your Excellency.

Saddam: So what is it then? When we close this file, then start looking for its key, then this means that it was not closed!

Tariq: No, the matters are starting to be much clearer . . . approximately 95 percent has been resolved; there are only a few small remaining matters yet to be resolved. They will work on such matters during the upcoming period, as, according to their own admission, it does not affect the monitoring system. Likewise, with regard to the chemical [issue], in brief, I mean frankly, we have prepared a comprehensive report for Your Excellency's viewing . . .

The problem is in the biological matter, I mean the problem that they [apparently the UNSCOM inspectors] raised is the biological factor. They are emphasizing on their part that Iraq is striving to produce germ weapons, striving, saying,

Yes, we do not have any evidence, and we do not have any conclusion that points to the fact that you have produced biological weapons in quantities, I mean significant

[35] *SH-SHTP-A-001-255, "Saddam and Top Political Advisers Discussing the Agricultural Situation in Iraq and UN Inspection Teams," undated (circa January–February 1995).

quantities. However, you are not telling the truth. You have pursued them; however, you did not reach the level of production, I mean in serious quantities. But you are denying what you have done, and this is raising our concern.

So with regard to this subject matter, I mean –

Saddam: What is the significance of the assumption that Iraq has pursued [biological weapons]? This will not change the situation. As they say, the monitoring system is working, they have destroyed everything, [and] they're looking for more equipment to destroy.

Tariq: Not necessarily equipment, Your Excellency. We have studied this matter in depth, and Comrade Muhammad knows its details.[36] I mean, suppose we tell them [UNSCOM inspectors], okay, let us assume that we have produced. They will tell us, fine, come and narrate the whole story from its beginning, so they want to review, I mean [inaudible].

Saddam: Meaning, he [Ekeus] says which of the facts changed, but he only –

Tariq: No, he does not change.

Saddam: [Inaudible.] I am concerned that all of this is nothing but excuses.

Tariq: He [Ekeus] is not changing the facts. However, the Americans, the Americans are saying, "Look, Iraq has admitted that it has a biological weapon program," and that Iraq will secretly produce such weapons for the purpose of terrorism; this is what is happening.

Saddam: Okay, fine, and if Iraq confesses that it aims to produce it secretly, and that it has the capability, that is according to the American statement, what will we get for doing that?

Tariq: Yeah, what Ekeus is saying –

Saddam: What?

Male 2: Destroying the factories, al-Hakam, this is the point that it –[37]

Saddam: I agree that this is the case but [inaudible] the factory.

Tariq: No, no, it is al-Hakam, their eyes are on al-Hakam.

––––––––

Tariq: I mean, they [UNSCOM inspectors] expect that as they come, we will tell them, "Please come in, here are five kilograms or ten kilograms of germ weapons that we have produced, and please receive them," and it will be over. He [apparently Ekeus] said, "The international experts," according to his allegations, "are not convinced with your responses and you have purchased materials." I mean it seems that we purchased in 1989 – the Ministry of Health purchased 18 tons of dual-use material in this field. They purchased 18 tons. So he [Ekeus] asked me, "Why did you purchase such a quantity?" I told him, "Welcome to the third world."

36 This is likely a reference to Muhammad Saeed al-Sahhaf, Iraq's foreign minister (1992–2001).
37 Biological weapons facility, southwest of Baghdad.

I told him that I have written a paper which will be published in Harvard University Magazine.[38]

———

Tariq: Perhaps a technical staff member said we needed it. Perhaps he [apparently the staff member] told him [Iraq's Minister of Health], "I need one ton," and he answered him, "Just one ton?[39] Why don't you purchase 20 tons, just like what we do when we purchase trucks, sometimes we buy 5,000 trucks?" So General Amir told him that sometimes we have too much stock that is piled up without ever having a need for it. So I told him, "If you really want to be fair, and objective, you have to take matters from this angle.[40] However, if you want to search for excuses to continue the sanctions, then this is another matter."

This matter, Your Excellency, is the only remaining matter . . . They [Amir and Riyadh al Qaisi, deputy foreign minister of Iraq] met with the Russian ambassador and the Russian ambassador came and briefed Amir. I mean, the conclusions of their meetings reveal that he [the Russian ambassador] is under great pressure from the Americans and that the Americans are pressuring him, pressuring the experts and adopting scare tactics with them. And some experts are afraid, and consequently they are forced to exaggerate. And he told him [Amir] that the Americans want, I mean they want to instigate any incident for the sake of prolonging the sanctions until October. And in October, they will also rebuff any calls to lift Iraqi sanctions, until Iraq gets frustrated, I mean until Iraq gets angry and expels the experts. And consequently they will take this as an excuse to come in and bomb Iraq and bomb factories like al-Hakam and others.

Saddam: [*Inaudible.*] After April, October, it will [*inaudible*].

Tariq: This is what has been narrated. I mean, he told the Russian ambassador, and the Russian ambassador, no, it is clear.

Saddam: He [apparently the Russian ambassador] told him [apparently Amir], do not be frustrated in April, but you may be frustrated in October. In other words, they are giving us six months.

———

[38] Tariq Aziz, "Law of the Jungle," *Harvard International Review* 17 (Summer 1995): 30–33. In this article, Tariq Aziz maintained that international law is primarily a product of Western European "political, economic, and cultural heritage." In particular, he argued that international law should not be used to infringe upon national sovereignty and he called for reforming the United Nations in such a way as to reduce the power of the permanent members of the Security Council and increase the power of the "developing world."

[39] Although Tariq identifies Iraq's Minister of Health in 1989 as Samir al-Shaykh, Edmund A. Ghareeb lists Abd al-Salem Muhammad Saeed as Iraq's minister of health at the time. Ghareeb, with Beth K. Dougherty, *Historical Dictionary of Iraq* (Lanham, MD: Scarecrow Press, 2004), 376.

[40] Charles Duelfer labeled this line of argument the "progressive idiocy theory." Duelfer's skepticism proved justified when on 1 July 1995 Iraq admitted that it used some of this material between 1988 and 1991 to produce botulinum toxin and *Bacillus anthracis* spores. See Duelfer, *Hide and Seek*, 98–100, and *Duelfer Report*, vol. 3, "Biological Warfare," 15.

Tariq: Ekeus, just as I have described to Your Excellency, Ekeus works to benefit the Americans, but Ekeus is not American, I mean he is not an American citizen. Ekeus is Swedish, and he is keen not to reveal his true motives in front of his people and his country, and in front of the Europeans, that he is a cheap American agent in a way that he serves them with unacceptable services. That is according to the view of the entire world. Ekeus has used up all the excuses he can think of. He interfered in the minutest details, those that are justified, and those that aren't justified. This game should have an end, the game is going to end, so, when April comes and he tells them, "No, this is not right, and I suspect Iraq and that Iraq is hiding information," this time, the French will simply announce that Ekeus is an American agent...

The French ambassador has stated that it is impossible to acquire 100 percent of the information Ekeus wants. This is impossible; the main issue is that Iraq does not own weaponry that will threaten the security and stability of the region. And this is achieved, according to the reports Ekeus submitted, but we are waiting for his April report to tell us about the status of the monitoring. So they, I mean these technical and detail-oriented games that Ekeus plays, are no longer the main element.

Now, the matter is more political in nature. With whom has America entered the battle? I mean, just as we previously expected, when the technical and legal excuses are removed from America, then America will play a political role and say, "I will not suggest lifting the sanctions against Iraq for political reasons," ha, for reasons neither related to Ekeus nor to [inaudible]. This is just so that we have a clear vision for the upcoming period and decide how we will confront it...

Where do you think she [Madeleine Albright] is going, Your Excellency? America has excluded five countries, it has excluded three permanent members: France, China and Russia. She decided not to visit them, and she excluded Indonesia and Nigeria. She will go to London, as she coordinates with them. She is going to London for coordination. She will visit Oman, the Czech [Republic], Honduras, and will meet with Botswana's foreign minister. All of these countries are tiny. What will Madeleine Albright discuss with them? Will she discuss Ekeus's file or will she threaten them? These are small countries, she will threaten them...

So the Americans are confronting a battle in the event that the Russian and French proposal is presented, that it will not gather nine votes,[41] this way they are not forced to use their veto power and be perceived as the one blocking the proposal. So they will connive with these small countries. This is the game, and it is an overt game. I mean it is an overt political game just like what occurred with [UN] Resolution 687, if Your Excellency recalls, in November 1990 when [U.S. Secretary of State James] Baker was harassing Yemen, and went to Malaysia and invited the Malaysian foreign minister to San Francisco, and cajoled all these countries until a favorable vote was passed to that resolution they proposed. So, now this is the situation. The battle became overtly political, more so than technical or legal.

---

[41] Nine votes are needed to pass a UNSC resolution, assuming no vetoes by any permanent members.

Three Months before Hussein Kamil Defected to Jordan, Saddam and His Senior Leadership Discuss the Advantages and Disadvantages of Cooperating with Inspectors (2 May 1995)[42]

Saddam: [*Recording begins midsentence.*] How can you be sure that the information about the chemical program, which is to be delivered to the Security Council by the Iraqis, is credible? If there were a problem with the chemical program, Ekeus would have grounds to say it was true about the biological program in 1993. Again, when the Iraqis are pressured, they present new information; therefore, it would not be believable. I mean, that is a foundation, which would be easy for the listener to believe when Ekeus has new issues about any of the programs. He will use it when he becomes cornered in the battle of discussion. Now let us hear from Comrade Amir.

Amir: Sir, truthfully now [*inaudible*] we have put a defense plan in place and Your Excellency was aware of the full picture, where the confidence of success is 70 percent and 50 percent, depending on the UN paragraphs. Truthfully, we have worked on it, but now, Sir, our effort is solely focused on the subject of the biological program. In addition, there is a special team of inspectors in which all of their efforts are now concentrated on the biological program and the passing time during these few weeks has given them the chance to collect and examine the information. I mean, are we neglecting here –

Saddam: Are you talking about the biological program or are you talking about another subject?

Amir: No, Sir. Sorry, it is not that, if I may say?

Saddam: Yes.

Amir: There are grounds for that, but there are no credible grounds left for the chemical program and missiles. However, there are grounds for the biological program. Sir, one could be suspicious of it [the biological program] if we concentrate on it [*inaudible*] and the trafficking effort and dodging everything in regard to it. Therefore, if one does not have anything or have anything left, for example, one should concentrate on their efforts to achieve results.

Now, there is a strong ground for achievement on the subject of the biological program. Now, Sir, the subject of the biological program has become a subject with a strong foundation against us that was adopted by the Security Council's members. I mean I am sorry to say that we are responsible for this subject, I mean, we wanted to succeed and we have succeeded in a few paragraphs, and when we went to Russia we convinced the Russians with creative manners about the reasons why [*voices overlap*]

Saddam: [*Interrupting.*] [*Inaudible*] when the Russians asked about bringing up new information?

Amir: Yes, Sir, I will answer that now, Sir. God bless you and keep you. There is no hope for us now in extracting the technical, for implementing paragraph 22 [of UNSC Resolution 687].

---

[42] SH-SHTP-A-001-011, "Saddam and High Ranking Officials Discussing Iraqi Biological and Nuclear Weapons Programs," 2 May 1995.

Sir, getting back to the subject of the difficulties that Your Excellency has mentioned, I mean, without exaggeration it is consuming us day and night. I mean, it is choking and disturbing us and if we are late for our main work, it could be, Sir, this subject, has a cost and an effect [*inaudible*] a loss, a loss. There is a good likelihood that we can achieve a positive outcome without a downside, going beyond 70 or 80 percent.

Sir, we must sit down with Your Excellency and maybe we will be able to calculate and organize this effort. However, Sir, without doing this, the possibility to succeed in UN paragraph 22 will be zero and this is what they would like to see happen.

Saddam: Yes, Comrade Tariq?

Tariq: Sir, even though comrade Lieutenant General Amir raised a point during the discussion about the 10th of April in the Security Council in addition to the questions we submitted to the members of the Council, but they did not address them. If we assume, for the sake of argument, that there is no biological file in the entire story – I mean according to Ekeus there is no biological file, and Ekeus presented his report on the chemical, missiles, and the monitoring, while the International Atomic Energy Agency presented its report on the nuclear aspect – for the second time I say that I seldom use the words "I am sure," but I am 99.9 percent sure in this report that the French and the Russians did present their project in terms of why Ekeus's report was not carefully discussed and why the questions were not put forth. It was for two reasons. The first is bad luck. On both days, the 10th and the 11th, the Security Council had a very busy schedule at the time of their meeting in the morning to hear Ekeus's report –

Saddam: [*Interrupting.*] What do you mean?

Tariq: No, Sir. I told you last time, that a lot of work in the Security Council has been neglected. Whereas sometimes they would not give sufficient time for some files, if there would be more persistent pressure on them to give sufficient time, if the French, the Russians, and the Chinese would tell them next week, then they would have no choice. When Ekeus presented his report, they said that we would meet tomorrow to discuss it. From what I have seen, the discussion was brief.

The other aspect that made Ekeus's report confusing is the draft resolution discussed at the same time. The third is frustration, which is the most important, the most important. Yesterday's file frustrated Russia and France because they saw a large gap they could not fight, which is why they did not put forward any questions. If Comrade Amir can remember, similar questions were presented to them [Russia and France] in the past and they have been put forth to the Security Council, I mean, in this past January and March. In the past, we briefed them and told them not to only ask Ekeus questions, but they must rather request an answer – ask and surround Ekeus with questions and allow silence afterwards.

–––––––

Tariq: Therefore, I have stated that if we solve the biological program problem... the French and the Russians will lay their plans on the table, and the Americans would discuss their plans, of course. They would then say, "There is a point here and a point there," at which time the serious discussions would start. Comrade Amir and I do not agree on these serious discussions. He says France is Ekeus. Fine, in biological, France is Ekeus. However, let us look again at [*inaudible*] the speech of the ambassador of France in January in the Security Council [*inaudible.*] He said, "The search for perfection is not a reality, you cannot achieve a point of 100 percent in every field. The fundamental mission of Ekeus for the Special Commission is that Iraq not have any weapons that can pose a threat to security and stability in the region."

Sir, this is a plan, an opinion. [*Inaudible.*] Ekeus's opinion differs from this. Ekeus wants to achieve 100 percent. His desire, with the United States' support, his personal cowardly behavior – because he is a coward – Who would say, from the representatives of countries, "Stand by me, I am convinced?" For that reason, when I asked him the question, instead of answering, he tried to dodge the question [*inaudible*]. That is why from the Russian and French perspective, there is the possibility of embarrassment in the big picture.

I, uh, I mean, uh, I agreed with the Comrade Foreign Minister when he said, "We have paid for the games that we played." I mean, we have paid the price for it. We paid in 1991 when our weapons were destroyed. They and we have destroyed the entire nuclear program and the missiles. The main plants were destroyed also. I mean, there are only a few things left of the game. It is not in our interest to remove ourselves from the game, because getting out of the game should have happened at the time when we did not present sacrifices.

———

Saddam: General Hussein.

Hussein Kamil: Thank you, Sir. Sir, I did not want to talk and be this open if it were not for Your Excellency's initiation and clarification and Mr. Tariq's words that we have produced biological weapons. We have not clarified everything that we have and they can raise now or one year or two later, three issues with regard to the subject of missiles. These issues have not been announced. The first one is the location and the second one is their lack of knowledge about our work regarding the missile issue. Sir, this is my job and I have known it for a long time. It is not an easy position and it is critical according to what they know. If God is willing, I will explain it to Your Excellency.

Sir, are we thinking that they are not raising the issue of the chemical program? In addition, are we thinking that the biological program is the only problem? No, Sir. I think they have detailed information about the missiles. If they want to raise this issue, let them, because as I mentioned, we did not complete it. They have a bigger problem with the chemical program than the biological program, a lot bigger than the biological program.

It is not the weapons, the size of the imported material, the size of materials produced that we presented to them or the size of the materials used. They knew that not all of this was true. We have not told them that we used it on Iran, nor have we told them about the size or kind of chemical weapons that we produced, and we have not told them the truth about the imported material. Therefore, Sir, if they want to raise an issue, I mean, they will see that our argument is the issue of the biological program.

I disagree. I must be truthful before you, Your Excellency. Your Excellency, I stand before you and openly disagree with this subject. What they want is paragraph after paragraph. For the time being, we do not want them to say that we were not forthcoming. Now, Sir, I will repeat, is it better for us to announce it or stay secretive? Again, Sir, about the biological and the chemical programs, we disagree with them, but not about the 17 tons. No, our substantial disagreement is known.

Sir, this is the big issue. Some of our teams are working in one direction, where another team does not know that they are working above in the same direction. Therefore, they could find it out if they wanted to. The, the reason they know about it is, that we imported a quantity from America and we imported a quantity from Europe. However, we did not come forth with the quantities...

Sir, about the nuclear program, we say that we have revealed everything. In addition, we have an unannounced problem with the nuclear program, and I think they know about it because there are working teams that are working and some of these teams are not known to anyone. This team is a group and the other is – I am sorry, Sir, but I must talk clearly, even though everything is done and we are through with it, but if you wonder whether they knew or not, I can tell you they did not: not all methods, not all means, not all scientists and not all locations. I say this frankly.

Yes, there are unrevealed activities, so Your Excellency and we will understand that if they would come and say that the biological program is still the same – no, Sir, the biological program is the least of our issues and – I mean that I am sorry to say that it is the most insignificant problem, because the 17 tons are not a problem compared to the thousands of tons here and there, and where did they go, how were they manufactured and how were they used? Truthfully, Sir, we have to be honest so that when the Resolution is issued, it will not only be based on the biological program because if it were, it would [include] the missiles tomorrow, and the nuclear program would be the day after, and so on.

Sir, it was true when the French said that this is the way; however, there is more to it than that. They have debated the issues with Ekeus [inaudible], they asked him, why are you talking about the Iraqis without knowing, and why are you not telling them, that they have not done this or that? That is what the French ambassador said in the Security Council. Sir, [inaudible] the French are playing games, true games. Sir, getting back to the subject, are we revealing everything?

If we continue to be silent about the issue at hand, I must say that it is in our best interest not to reveal it, not only in fear of exposing the technology that we have or that we possess or to hide it for future agendas. Sir, the game has advanced and it has now become clear to most of the representatives of the nations who are compelled to cooperate with America. Now they are siding with Iraq...

Sir, we have discussed with Dr. Amir how to take great precautions and how to get out of this problem. We believed that we were finished after Iraq's confession, which is already done. He himself [apparently Ekeus] inspected the biological program and the al-Hakam plant; they [UNSCOM inspectors] inspected all of it. We met them there and told them, "Here it is." They inspected all the air vents, water pipes, even the air, they inspected everything, and he [apparently Ekeus] created the file, as you know. He has raised and renewed it a great deal. Sir, where were the nuclear materials transported to? A number of them fled outside of Iraq, while another number knew some details about the nature of our work. I mean, in the past they left for the north, I mean, they got out.[43] Therefore, Sir, to solve this issue, we must stand firm.

Why should we stand firm? We should stand firm because of the time that will allow us to confess all that we have. Sir, this estimate could take up to five years while they [apparently UN inspectors] are trying to solve it. He [Ekeus] spent five years to inspect, confirm and compare, and check how much we took for such and such a company, where we used it and when, and then got to Iran's issue and said that we used nuclear weapons, which, in my opinion, is another story that he [Ekeus] will bring against us if Ekeus and the American position stay strong.[44] However, Sir, if they weaken, they will vanish, even if we manufactured missiles or something that is not permitted. This is what I believe would happen if the position of the countries were to change. Moreover, Sir, my personal belief is that the top countries want to move forward, except France. France is very behind, I mean, Lieutenant General Amir told me that the Russian position is much more compassionate with us. Comrade Amir said that the French companies, which we are negotiating with on very valuable contracts, are not responding now [inaudible]. Anyway, we are not happy, we are upset... Instead of us admitting to the biological program, Sir, we should ask the specialists: "How can we close the 17 tons? We do this and that and these are all the details that we have. How can we know when this file will be closed?"

Saddam's Inner Circle Discusses Transshipment of Prohibited Gyroscopes through Jordan and Joint Efforts with Members of the UNSC to End the Sanctions (circa November 1995)[45]

Tariq: ...concerning the biological weapons, it has been proven that we produced 200 bombs, and we must prove that they have been destroyed. When he [Ekeus] came in the beginning of August, we gave him a document explaining the destruction of 175 of them. Therefore, he will send this document to a lab to be examined by a method they call forensic analysis. This type of test proves the authenticity of the date of the document. He is mentioning that this document has been presented to him, but he would not mention to the Security Council that he is sure of the destruction of 175. Therefore, it is clear, from our perspective, that we provided this document. However, the last chapter of this issue will take possibly one to two weeks or up to a month. Therefore, because we have accomplished this much so far, we are confident in accomplishing what is left, compared to other issues, issues related to the chemical [program], like VX [a nerve agent], for example. We are on the verge of proving that this is a failed program, and was not used in the Iraqi armament. The failure of this program has been proven in some of these documents, and the other part will require a scientific analysis.

---

[43] Kamil appears to be referring to defectors who knew of Iraq's WMD programs. Two such individuals, Wafiq al-Samarrai and Khidhir Hamza, escaped for the West via Iraq's Kurdish north in 1994.

[44] Kamil apparently meant to say "chemical," not "nuclear," weapons. It was well established that Iraq had used chemical weapons in its war with Iran, although the Iraqis continued to deny it. Nobody accused Iraq of using nuclear weapons.

[45] *SH-SHTP-A-001-256, "Saddam and Top Political Advisers Discussing a Visit by Prime Minister Tariq Aziz to the United Nations Delegates," undated (circa November 1995).

Concerning the skepticism of other members, our known friends, excluding France, which is a special case, I will take care of it personally. They started to listen to us, that is to say, they started to listen and pay attention to this information. If I may say, they began to have some resuscitation, if I am correct, after their frustration. It could be the result of the foreign minister's effort during the session of the [UN] General Assembly meeting. He came back again, concerned. He had truthfully done some work. Of course, every one told him to take care of [*inaudible*] the issue that affected us, and we are on the way to [*inaudible*].

The news that emerged concerning the equipment being sent to Iraq from Jordan created confusion and instability. That is to say, how can you provide a document proving the destruction, on one hand, while you are bringing back the equipment components to build missiles, on the other hand, which are banned by the UN resolutions?[46] Even though these manufactured missiles are within the permitted range.

Saddam: Even if they were within the range?

Tariq: Yes, there are two types, Sir: one where they banned importing anything that is for military use and it is continuous, while the other one is [a] production sanction. I mean, if we have this material and we used it in a 120-kilometer range missile, we would not be held accountable for it. Is that true, Comrade Amir?

Amir: That is not the issue. The issue is the ban and the monitoring. Even if the permissible missiles exceed the range, we should inform them of it.[47]

Tariq: That we are going to produce it.

Amir: If we did not inform them it will consider –

Tariq: Importing anything from the outside is definitely prohibited, I mean, at this time and until the ban is lifted, which will have special guidelines. Of course, this is clear with respect to the violation [of the ban]. We gave them some clarifications that we discovered afterwards that we had really obtained equipment of this type inside Iraq. The employee in charge of it did not inform his superiors, Comrade Amir Rashid, what these materials were because he did not think that they were important. Issues like this are silly and insignificant, in which it fell through the cracks. I mean, this should have been –

Saddam: [*Interrupting.*] What is the truth? Where is the truth in this?

---

[46] In November 1995, Jordanian officials seized more than US$25 million of advanced missile parts, including gyroscopes and accelerometers, in Amman. The equipment came from Russia and was en route to Iraq. R. Jeffrey Smith, "U.N. Is Said to Find Russian Markings on Iraq-Bound Military Equipment," *Washington Post*, 15 December 1995.

[47] The meaning here is unclear. By definition, missiles exceeding the 150-kilometer range limit imposed on Iraq after the 1991 Gulf War would be impermissible. Amir likely meant to say, "Even if the permissible missiles *don't* exceed the range, we should inform them of it." The UNSCOM inspectors insisted in a meeting with Amir a few months earlier that they needed to monitor Iraq's research and development plans for short-range (permitted) missiles to ensure the Iraqis were not extending the ranges to prohibited levels. See Tim Trevan, *Saddam's Secrets*, 242.

Amir: Sir, I was supposed to investigate this evening so I would know where we stand. However, the preliminary information concerning the issue is as follows: As far as they know, some of the specialists or others think that we are strict on them, especially Husam and I, concerning the issue of freezing the activity, and that is causing us a problem with the Special Commission. Namely, they have drawn up a contract of conventional material not specified as part of [*inaudible*], which is a very sensitive issue to the secretary of control and guidance.[48] They have set their own price in the contract. Sir, I have not yet seen the results of the investigation. That is to say, they have inflated the price of the contract many times on the conventional electronic equipment, which is permitted and is not part of the issue. The quantities are not consistent, that is to say, the banned quantities, as you know.

In astonishment, I asked, "What is going on with this issue?" Moreover, I asked him when he came back today, if they were under your command, and in addition, if you were aware of this issue. He said, "I do not remember this issue, possibly [*inaudible*] informed them of this issue." After this issue –

Tariq: [*Interrupting.*] Whom did you tell? What is his name?

Amir: Sir, the material is coming to Amman – conventional and banned material, prohibited, if I am correct. The details about this material that – That is to say, even though they investigated this person, this person talks clearly about this issue. He said, "I have an agreement with so-and-so," with – all the names that you are hearing about, Sir. [*Whispering.*] They have agreed with so-and-so, for him to obtain gyroscopes. This issue is clear, this contract is sold at the location, and the second party has raised its price. For example, our dollar being raised to five dollars. That is to say, one would know the difference, dollar for dollar. [*Inaudible*] to cover the banned material.

Of course, they mentioned it to our people that they know about it, the investigation and the problem and so on. Therefore, they were caught in lies, so it could be contract issues or – that is to say, the truth appears that one of the containers was coming to Baghdad, through that entrance [*inaudible*]. Thereafter, I was informed about everything – meaning, everything and so on. Therefore, a situation developed with them, that is to say, we were very worried, and we have not slept a wink. Thereafter, they made up a story because they did not have the facts about the issue. We said, can any of you tell us about this issue, or do any of the comrades have any information or know of someone who has any information or document? Please, this is the last chance. Of course, I do not want to exaggerate these words, but I have repeated them ten times in various meetings [*inaudible*].

However, Sir, the vice chairman of the Council of Ministers said the same thing. It could have been the fifth or sixth time before they took their words seriously. Therefore, they told them about Husam, because he was asking for this information for Comrade Amir. They did not tell them that it was an issue about gyroscopes. How could they tell them? [*Laughing.*] They told him, it was insignificant official material that has been secretly shipped. We were worried that it would create a problem, so we sent it east. It appears that Husam said that there is no need to tell Comrade Amir about the issue. Through various meetings, about seven or eight,

---

[48] This reference is unclear.

they said, "In order to serve our intelligence, you must be involved so that we can be heading in the right direction. [*Inaudible*] we are the command that is concerned about this issue – it is your duty to tell us."

Therefore, this person has started something big, and he told me that he is worried that Husam will be upset with him. He is your comrade. Therefore, I told him [*inaudible*] the Special Commission, as long as there is an inspection team present. Husam told this person, "Inform the Special Commission, just as General Amir told you." Imran did not say that it was gyroscopes, instead he said, simple electronic equipment and it came by mistake.[49] Therefore, after the results of the investigation, it is now clear that it was this type of flaw. Sir, that is to say, what is important now is the results from the Special Commission. If this flaw did not occur, the Special Commission would not be called. According to the timing, they knew that this was going to happen, because it happened in June. Therefore, they were waiting for the right time. They have numerous teams that know what we are going to say; therefore, they know the timing and you know the rest of the details, Your Excellency.

Tariq: Sir, this incident has overshadowed our conversations, but –

Saddam: [*Interrupting.*] This little uproar is like the time a bear, in a story whose origin I can't remember, was trying to swat a fly off of his dear friend's face. He picked up a rock and hit the fly and knocked his friend's head off.

Tariq: Yes, exactly. Disregard the French position that Your Excellency wants to deal with in a special manner. The Russian position remains the same, it is a generous position.

———

Tariq: They [apparently the Russians] said, "Our position has not changed, but we were disturbed by this issue that happened. This story about the gyroscopes has been tampered with." He [apparently a Russian envoy] said, "We are paying attention and will investigate this issue, in which I have sent for Moscow to investigate how it was sent because there are other issues of smuggling, mafia and –" but the man was very clear and they have dealt with Comrade Amir and Husam where they listened to their facts with a great deal of importance. They were giving and taking and they said that they would follow up, just as they were working with us in the past.[50] China remains in the same position ... We concentrated on the new ones, the new members of the Security Council.

---

[49] This individual is not further identified.

[50] In later meetings, senior Russian officials reportedly complained that information Iraq shared with UNSCOM about the gyroscope imports had portrayed Russia in an unfavorable light. In a 27 March 1996 meeting, the director of Russia's Department of International Organizations told the Iraqis, "If Iraq provided the Committee [UNSCOM] with new documents, this would increase the suspicion against it." Lieutenant General Amir Hamudi Hassan noted that this constituted a request "not to elaborate in giving details about receiving supplies from Russia." In a 28 March 1996 meeting with Russian Deputy Foreign Minister Victor Posuvalyuk, Posuvalyuk complained that Iraq's "cooperation ... and sincerity with the Special Commission [UNSCOM] ... has damaged Russia's position." See SH-MISC-D-000-203, "Report on an Iraqi Delegation Visit to Russia and France," 6 April 1996.

Saddam: One after another.

Tariq: One after another. We had a very good meeting with the Egyptians and a good meeting with Chile and [*inaudible*] delegation and Dr. Amir al-Saadi has met with you. The meetings were good in general.

Tariq Aziz Informs Saddam That UN Secretary-General Boutros Boutros-Ghali Told Him That the "Entire World" Bribes UN Inspectors. The Iraqi Leadership Also Discusses How to Benefit from France's Economic Difficulties (January 1996)[51]

Tariq: It is possible that if we agreed with the Secretary-General, we started pumping oil and the political situation improved in our interest, and like the French minister[52] said it would be a pledge to implement the 22nd article [paragraph 22 of UNSC Resolution 687]. The other possibility, in which the Russians and the French themselves might participate, is that they will say, "Since, brothers, you are doing fine and everything is going well, why would you let us clash with the Americans while we have our point of view? We can give you another break and make it half, increasing it by 50 percent along with the alleviation of some restrictions and finding out the reasons that disturbed the Secretary-General and what you have done to bother him."

They promised us to [*inaudible*] the American [*inaudible*]. Nobody was clear and honest with us in this regard because of what we were facing [*inaudible*] and we wanted to avoid any clash with the United States, but we heard from the people close around us about this definite possibility.

Izzat: And therefore, it is stronger.

Tariq: Yes, this possibility is present. However, Sir, from what I read and based on my experience with the Security Council resolutions, these resolutions are like a piece of elastic; you can make it longer or shorter. I mean this resolution could have a very bad implementation that can either truly result in exacerbating the abnormal situation in Northern Iraq, or not, if the Secretary-General is not pushed in this direction.

Regardless of his personality, the Secretary-General mocks the United Nations' issues and interference; he would laugh when someone mentions the rules of the United Nations. He told me, "Assign ten intelligence people for every one I appoint and pay them. Buy them like others do; why don't you do the same?"[53]

---

[51] SH-SHTP-A-001-143, "Saddam and Top Political Advisers Discussing Relations with the UN Security Council," 1 January 1996.

[52] This is likely a reference to France's foreign minister at the time, Hervé de Charette.

[53] The Arabic word used here for "buy" is *ishtarouhem*, meaning to bribe. Saddam, for his part, had Tariq offer Ekeus several million dollars to favorably close UNSCOM investigations into Iraq's missile, chemical, and biological weapon programs. Ekeus reportedly responded, "That is not the way we do business in Sweden." Francis Harris, "Saddam's $2m offer to WMD Inspector," *Daily Telegraph* (London), 12 March 2005; *SH-SHTP-A-001-255, "Saddam and Top Political Advisers Discussing the Agricultural Situation in Iraq and UN Inspection Teams," undated (circa January–February 1995). The chief of Iraqi intelligence's counter-UNSCOM unit reportedly told Scott Ritter that, by the end of 1997, Iraq had almost

Saddam: For your information, this way is [*inaudible*.]

Izzat: He would say, "Give me [*inaudible*]."

Tariq: No, no, but how [*inaudible*]; that is to say, I have nothing to do with him [a UN official appointed by the UN secretary-general], not even anything to discuss with him under the table.[54]

Saddam: Anyone can deal with this.

Tariq: With this, Sir, but this is a war! The folks are ready [*inaudible*] you remember Oscar,[55] Samir Vincent[56] and [*inaudible*] when they came to Geneva this year; they were ready and they are still ready. He is just waiting for our okay and says, "Sending someone requires spending some money, but we should be able to manage." He [apparently the secretary-general] says it: "I will appoint one for you, but you need to hire ten intelligence people. Buy them, man. Buy them and pay them: the entire world does it. Why can't you do it?"

Izzat: [*Inaudible*.]

Saddam: Comrade Ali, do you have any comment?

Ali: Thank you, Sir. In fact, the deputy, Mr. Izzat, reported a lot. But if we don't lay a strong foundation for the negotiations, to be the basis for our negotiations, we would lose all the mobilization we have made against this resolution. We clarified the reasons for our refusal and we were convinced of these reasons, which we spread to our people and the entire world. The Russians and the French said, "We are not going to reject this resolution; we are going to keep [*inaudible*]," but now, the French are so enthusiastic to implement this resolution. The Secretary-General has his circumstances, etc. Based on the interpretation presented by comrade Tariq a few minutes ago, which for sure is his own conviction, through the papers, his work, his practice and his experience, we should go to the Secretary-General and explain what we really need from him: what are the points on which it would be impossible to agree on and what are the points that can be negotiable.

completely penetrated UNSCOM operations in New York and Baghdad and could monitor inspections' developments from beginning to end. One source of frustration for Duelfer was that selling UNSCOM secrets to the Iraqis was not, within the UN context, considered spying. "It was breaking rules, but not laws," he explained. Moreover, UNSCOM could not arrest an employee for working for the Iraqis or having a romantic relationship with an Iraqi intelligence officer, nor could it fire the offender. Ritter, *Iraq Confidential*, 265; Duelfer, *Hide and Seek*, 114.

54 This reference is unclear.

55 Oscar Wyatt, the founder of Houston's Coastal Corporation, paid illegal kickbacks to Saddam's government for oil sales through the UN Oil-for-Food program. He pleaded guilty to conspiracy charges in 2007. See Press Release, U.S. Attorney, Southern District of New York "Texas Oilman Enters Mid-Trial Guilty Plea to Charges of Conspiring to Make Illegal Payments to the Former Government of Iraq," 1 October 2007, accessed 23 March 2009 at http://newyork.fbi.gov/dojpressrel/pressrel07/illegal%20payment100107.htm.

56 Samir Vincent, the president of Phoenix International LLC and a former consultant for Coastal Corporation, was convicted in 2008 of providing Baghdad with illegal lobbying services. See Department of State, Bureau of International Information Programs, "Justice Department Secures Guilty Plea in Oil for Food Scandal," 19 January 2005.

If they want to know our intentions and when we might reject, let them know because we are going to tell all our friends. We are going to tell them, so, let them know our intentions! But if he already coordinated and was seeking a personal interest, we will expose him, also, and look after ourselves.

In fact, Mr. President, our [*inaudible*] depends on our original rejection, we [*inaudible*] entirely because we had great mobilization for the first one and we succeeded, thank God; it was a serious mobilization. But whether the Parliament and the National Council agree or disagree now, we are not consistent to agree. Accepting [this resolution], Mr. President, will take us into a dark valley from which we can never get out unless we give up everything, the Great Qadisiyyah [Iran-Iraq War] and Um al-Maarek [Mother of All Battles, i.e., the 1991 Gulf War]; everything will be gone! How can this be possible and after all, is this colonialism?

It is simple and I am convinced of Comrade Tariq's recent explanation. We need to send a very clear letter stating that we cannot agree on it, but tell him, "It is possible to negotiate should we receive a letter from you. We are ready and so are our papers once you tell us when and where. Whether you come to negotiate with us or you prefer that we come to you, either way is fine, we will go for it and rely on God!" If this explanation were useful to us we would have done something since April and would not have postponed it until now. It will still not be [*inaudible*], God willing. It is still the beginning, thank God. But, Mr. President, to negotiate without any solid ground, the prices will be sky high and the trust will be lost. Every resolution we rejected before, we used to reconsider and negotiate, and then approve. This is what is going to happen with this resolution now.

Sir, I did not have the hunch that the French were so enthusiastic about issuing the resolution the way comrade Abu Ziyad [Tariq Aziz] explained when he said, "They promised me they were not going to reject it, use the veto or have a conflict with the Americans, but we are going to [*inaudible*] until it sinks." This was their statement. I remember Comrade Tariq talked with the French one when he left and asked, "Huh, what did you do?" "We did something you will be pleased with. I mean, we agreed on something you like," the French one replied. I believe they said this so that we can either accept this explanation or not. These are the points they brought up. But for us to say now that we came to the conclusion that this explanation is right and it is based on a new foundation, what will happen to what we said before then?

Saddam: Comrade the Minister of Foreign Affairs?

Muhammad Saeed al-Sahhaf: President Leader, as far as the French, there is a technical observation that I believe is very useful. When Boucher, head of the Middle East Bureau, visited Baghdad, I met with him before Comrade Tariq got the chance to do so and asked him specific questions. One of my questions was why do French companies procrastinate, extend and not settle? "Yes, we instructed the French companies to engage in a maximum amount of negotiations, talk with the Iraqi side and find out where the interests of companies are, but we restrained them from signing for political reasons," he replied, referring to the sanctions imposed on Iraq.

So, when they raised the debt issue that is related directly to the companies with the Deputy Prime Minister [Tariq Aziz], I believe, President Leader, that due to their economic situation in France now, they made heavy commitments that caused their problems. They receive [$]12 billion a year as support from the government for their social and health insurance systems' funds. As a result of this support and the lavish expenditures on health and social insurance, they now have a $46 billion deficit. Forty-six billion dollars plus twice over 12, this will make it $24 billion, which will require them two years to pay it off in order for the French economic situation to survive after two years without the government support and other issues, in a way it will be qualified to be implemented, to be signed and ratified as the final and legal ratification according to the European Monetary Union and the Treaty of Maastricht. They have a true economic problem, President Leader.

If the insinuation given to the deputy prime minister was right, I believe it is time now to tell them there must be serious work and signing; meaning they need to commit, President Leader, with regard to the debt issue. That has two benefits. First, they will be committed, and the Russian example as far as [Yevgeny] Primakov may be useful here.[57] Second, it is very useful to us, President Leader, where the European companies started to go register in the compensation fund in order to collect on their debts. So, it would be better to invite them to the bilateral negotiation; the French have achieved something very useful with them. This is the only point I would like to see on our agenda with the French side in order to reach an agreement with them to sign.

President Leader, I have some technical remarks regarding [UN] Resolution 986. I had a long meeting with Boutros-Ghali on October 5. It was a Friday, President Leader, where the meeting lasted about two hours with the presence of other counselors and the atmosphere was dusty [troubled] for us because of what had happened.[58] I interrupted him and threw in a detailed sentence. He said, "Your situation is bad and I am not willing to make any commitment to you for anything. Accept the resolution because the fact that you accept is going to do you a favor where it is going to shake some dust off you." Time went by and they realized this was not going as they expected and they showed some flexibility with the deputy prime minister.

So, I think the point, President Leader, is the political tactics for the purpose the deputy prime minister mentioned. They believe that once they see us contained we will have no other choice but to accept this resolution, but once they do not see us under the hammer they would grant us one concession after the other. If they see us in control and able to escape from this trick by not accepting this article, if they

---

[57] Primakov served as Russia's foreign minister from January 1996 through September 1998, at which point he became prime minister. According to Butler, Primakov told him, "Without being asked... that Iraq owed some US$8 billion to Russia for military equipment. For this reason, Russia wanted the disarmament phase ended and the oil embargo lifted. Russia needed that money badly, and it would not be paid unless Iraq was able to sell oil freely." It appears that the Iraqi foreign minister is telling Saddam that French economic difficulties might lead France to allow its oil companies to sign contracts with Iraq in exchange for Iraqi repayment of its loans. Primakov reportedly accepted Iraqi bribes, which might have whetted the Russian foreign minister's desire to end the sanctions. Butler, *The Greatest Threat*, 106–7; Duelfer, *Hide and Seek*, 102.

[58] The two men met to discuss implementation of Resolution 986 on October 6, 1995, a Friday. "Monday Highlights," *Federal News Service*, 10 October 1995.

do not see us under the hammer, then they would feed us, then they would give us flexibility.[59]

THE DEMISE OF UNSCOM (1998)

By the late 1990s, the sanctions regime was coming apart. French and Russian enthusiasm for maintaining the sanctions was fast waning, and, much to the chagrin of Richard Butler, Ekeus's successor as head of UNSCOM, UN Secretary-General Kofi Annan had begun to undermine UNSCOM by making deals directly with the Iraqis on their disarmament obligations.[60] In these recordings, Saddam and his advisers discuss ways to exploit this situation. In a recording from February 1998, they discuss the advantages of working with Annan rather than the UN Security Council, a compensation agreement with Benon Sevan, the UN official in charge of the Oil-for-Food Program, and the possibility that inspectors would plant evidence. In a recording made several months later, they resolve to resist inspections even though Iraq had essentially dismantled its WMD capabilities. Saddam's obstructionism precipitated Operation Desert Fox, a series of U.S. and British air strikes in December 1998.[61]

The Iraqi Leadership Discusses the Memorandum of Understanding with Kofi Annan to Allow Inspections of Iraq's Presidential Sites. Taha Mentions Iraq's Agreement on Compensations with Benon Sevan and Predicts That Iraqi Bribery Will Lead to Increased Support from Russia, France, and China (circa 23 February 1998)[62]

Saddam: He [Kofi Annan] asked for a direct meeting with me.[63] And he wanted to – he took out a paper and he told me that these were the two issues. I told him that, God willing, we will solve them right away. The first issue, instead of [*pause*] we should not [*pause*] we should not call it "inspection" or "visit." Let's call it "entrance" and it will be accepted. Well, in fact, it's like you are entering the country and the issue is solved. So, we solved it. I told him that with regard to the recurrence

---

[59] The article that Muhammad refers to, presumably in Resolution 986, is unclear. For the text of Resolution 986, see www.un.org/Docs/scres/1995/scres95.htm (accessed 4 February 2010).

[60] Butler, *The Greatest Threat*, 127–54; Trevan, *Saddam's Secrets*, 361–67.

[61] Julian Borger and Ewen MacAskill, "Missile Blitz on Iraq," *Guardian*, 17 December 1998.

[62] SH-SHTP-A-000-785, "Saddam and Advisers Discussing the Economic Sanctions Imposed on Iraq in 1998 and Possible UN Inspections," undated (circa 23 February 1998). For an additional recording in which Saddam and his advisers discuss the Memorandum of Understanding with Annan, see *SH-SHTP-A-001-257, "Saddam and Iraqi Officials Discussing Conditions for a UN Security Council Visit," undated (circa 1998).

[63] For the perspectives of UNSCOM's chairman and deputy chairman on the issues discussed in this meeting, see Butler, *The Greatest Threat*, 127–54; Duelfer, *Hide and Seek*, 140–50.

of the visit, if two months were not enough for him, we will make them four months. And during these four months he could solve all the matters he wished.

Male 1: The whole issue will be solved.

Saddam: The issue was solved in this manner. Of course, in the meeting, I told him because I spoke about [*pause*] I told him, "Look, you come and you outline previous resolutions and specific matters. You should also put the emphasis on the other rights of Iraq in accordance with the resolutions and they should get the attention they deserve, among which the embargo is not mentioned. This should be mentioned" . . .

So, we solved this issue. During the briefing, the comrades asked him if this [the time issue] would be included in the statement. He answered them that it wouldn't and it should be kept aside . . . Comrade Tariq said, he said, he told him, "Well, is this a gentlemen's agreement?" He answered him, "Yes, it is a gentlemen's agreement." I reiterated that yes, it was okay and we trusted Annan and his brothers. They were all witnesses and well-informed, and Annan himself was a witness. Let's rely on God and the [religious] leaders of Karbala.[64] In the text, there was no separate mention in a sentence of [*pause*], well, of the recurrence [of the visit], but there was mention of the expression [*pause*] "for this time and the [*pause*] the next times." Well, according to the gentlemen's agreement they should meet within four months and –

Male 1: It means that the recurrence is mentioned from the beginning.

Saddam: And – and that's it. That's what Comrade Muhammad mentioned. Well, I should tell you that they got something out of this agreement. They got something technical. It means something technical and legal. It means that Iraq came back, seven years later, to confirm its compliance with the resolutions. It's true: We legally overstepped the proper bounds of authority, but they had historical and legal meanings. Yes. And the agreement was passed –

Male 1: [*Inaudible.*]

Saddam: Of course, its meanings are different than [*pause*] – Of course, they continuously say that, but this time it is in the form of a document bearing a signature. But it has other important meanings. It is the first time that a negotiation is made with Iraq. It's the first time that –

Male 1: There is a supported agreement.

Saddam: They listen to the viewpoint of Iraq. It's the first time the military squadrons are replaced [*pause*] by negotiations allowed by the Security Council and negotiations based on the Security Council's resolutions.[65] Well, it's not, it's not a negotiation about something new, I mean. The outcomes reached are issued in the form of resolutions. Just the [*pause*] the signature. Now, with the signature, the world will understand that Iraq is more sincere. Once they submit the first report about the

---

[64] Karbala, Iraq, is one of the holiest of cities for Shi'a Muslims. Saddam, though Sunni, used Shi'a symbolism on occasion. For many years he and his advisers had refrained from using Karbala as a symbol, however, since the Iranians had made use of it as a Persian Shi'a symbol during the Iran-Iraq War. See Bengio, *Saddam's Word*, 176–91.

[65] The Arabic word here, *asatil*, can mean either "squadrons" or "fleets."

sites and they say that there is nothing implicating in them, the US and British lies will come to light and this is very meaningful.

―――――

Muhammad:[66] For the first time also the Secretary-General plays a role by creating a special team pertaining to the issue of the Security Council's resolutions with which they consecrated the Special Commission, an issue related to the Special Commission they created with more power than the Security Council. Now, from a practical viewpoint, the Special Commission constitutes the support on which Americans rely for almost everything. This agreement has hurt this issue and pushed the Secretary-General to create a special team. And the Secretary-General is the one to pick out the experts from the, the Special Commission, and from the International [Atomic Energy] Agency, on an individual basis and not in accordance with the rules of these two institutions...

We are giving success to what the Russians, French, and Chinese will do in adding experts, and this for the balance of power we have been asking for – and confirmed in the agreement with the Russians, Mr. President, which strongly opposes – a considerable gap has been created before this agreement so it would be approved with a docum[ent] – with the help of a second document now –

Saddam: We asked for a balance of power and he promised –

Muhammad: Yes.

Saddam: That he will form a team –

Muhammad: Yes.

Saddam: On a balanced basis.

Muhammad: And he committed himself before Your Excellency, that he will work accordingly. Not for the special team which will be formed, but for, well, in the meaning that he will help the Russians and others by appointing the experts, the way he appointed Bakar, and the way Boutros-Ghali appointed Ekeus.[67]

Now the current Secretary-General has become involved in the matter and this thanks to this agreement, Mr. President. Even from the technical viewpoint, from the technical viewpoint of the work, this aspect is beneficial to us and God willing, it will bring a noticeable benefit.[68]

The – Mr. President, it has been ordered that procedures should be set for this special team when it comes to work on the investigation. Special procedures should be set for its activities and not in accordance with what is being accomplished by those

[66] This is probably Muhammad Saeed al-Sahhaf, foreign minister of Iraq (1992–2001).

[67] This might be a reference to Malaysian Lieutenant General Aboo Samah Bin Aboo Bakar, who was appointed force commander of the UN Operation in Somalia (UNOSOM II) in January 1994. At the time, Annan was undersecretary-general of the United Nations.

[68] This preference for working with the secretary-general rather than UNSCOM is evident in additional recordings from this period as well; see, for instance, *SH-SHTP-A-001-257, "Saddam and Iraqi Officials Discussing Conditions for a UN Security Council Visit," undated (circa 1998).

jerks working in the Special Commission. Comrade Tariq Aziz and the Secretary-General of the United Nations agree on the type of procedures according to which their work is implemented in the presidential locations. Comrade Tariq, pursuant to Mr. President's orders, has prepared a letter which has been signed today prior to the signature of the agreement. He confirmed the following points in the letter ordered by Mr. President.

First, to forbid the request of any documents because seven of the presidential sites have no documents in them, and the essential one contains the government documents. So, this location has nothing to do with what they are doing. So, he [Kofi Annan] told him [Tariq Aziz], "Yes."

Second, the samples that could be taken, in case they need water samples, soil samples, grass samples to be analyzed in the laboratory located in Baghdad, the samples [pause] well, let's say the water samples, the same quantity of water should be divided. We get a part, they get a part and the others get another part. So they don't cheat . . .

Saddam: This is in the [pause] we have to say it, to the [pause] it just happened the day before yesterday –

Muhammad: Yes.

Saddam: To say it to the comrades.

Muhammad: Mr. President, this has been ordered in details, well, for – if ten individuals enter [a facility to be inspected], they will be accompanied by at least ten Iraqis. Each individual will be accompanied by another individual. Each one is accompanied by another one, if not more.

Saddam: One of them could throw an object and another individual of them would say that he found it.

Muhammad: Yes.

Saddam: It could be a chemical or nuclear object or –

Muhammad: Yes, Mr. President. We prepare for them a way for reaching the facilities –

Saddam: [Apparently speaking with Male 3.] This is Kozyrev.[69]

Male 3: There is no one.

Saddam: Yes.

Muhammad: We provide them with means of transportation, Iraqi means of transportation, so that their means of transportation and the UN and I don't know what could enter our locations. We supply them with cars and we supply them with escorts –

Saddam: That's the effort we will make, comrades.

Muhammad: We will also keep this –

[69] This is an apparent reference to Andrei Kozyrev, Russian foreign minister (1990–1996).

Saddam: It should be in harmony with the –

Muhammad: With the rank of the –

Saddam: [*Inaudible.*]

Muhammad: Yes.

Male 3: It will make a difference.

Muhammad: The, this is not, this is not a sudden visit. This is an agreed upon visit. Therefore, the issue of the sensitive locations does not apply to it or to what would explain it. We won't let these arrangements go further because the visit of the sensitive locations, the way it is understood, means an attack with choppers. This is forbidden.

———

Taha: Mr. President, the importance of this decision has come. I mean, if it would have come after the attack, its importance would not have been like prior to the attack. If it would have come two weeks earlier, it's not like now when we are at the edge and they want to smash us. This is a service, do you understand me, it has been proved without a doubt that Iraq is accepting its agreement not out of fear. And in fact, in the press conference, Comrade Tariq paid attention to this point and spoke about it in – in an excellent manner – besides, we have gone through trials, but people repeat this and – the location of the squadrons which are present.

The, honestly, what worries me in that is how to consolidate the trust of the, those who are in doubt, I mean. The percentage of those in doubt is still elevated, in Iraq and in the Arab political arena. As much as we could consolidate [*pause*], I mean, not those who trust us, but those who are in doubt. Well, not now. We have passed now to this phase in a satisfactory manner. Mr. President, I believe that in the next four months, additional factors will come forward to consolidate Iraq's power to influence the countries. I believe that the position of Russia, France and China will be stronger in a second confrontation. First because of personal interests which will get materialized and because of, because, of what they will get out of this issue for the benefit of their existence and their role.

———

Taha: The president of the committee was present. [Benon] Sevan was present.[70] He was present at the [*pause*] – He [*apparently Sevan*] came with him [*apparently Annan*]. "If you have remarks for us, we are ready. Tomorrow, we will send you a letter including the points we spoke about regarding the plan" –

Saddam: He wants to work on finalizing the compensations.

[70] Benon Sevan was the executive director of the UN's Office of the Iraq Program. For an investigation into the UN role in the oil-for-food scandal, see Paul A. Volcker, Richard J. Goldstone, and Mark Pieth, Independent Inquiry Committee, *Report on the Management of the Oil-for-Food Programme*, 7 September 2005, accessed 22 September 2008 at www .iic-offp.org/Mgmt_Report.htm.

Taha: Yes. We included them. I asked him about the compensation money. He said, "I understand them." Mr. President, if they deduct 1 percent – [*inaudible discussion between Saddam and others*]. We have succeeded with regard to the expenses –

[*End of recording.*]

Saddam Discusses Areas in Which Iraq Should Continue Refusing UN Disarmament Demands and the Possibility of War with the United States. Only Weeks Afterward, Saddam Forced UNSCOM Inspectors Out of Iraq, Which Led the United States and Britain to Bomb Iraq during Operation Desert Fox (circa late November 1998)[71]

Saddam: Abu Ahmad [Izzat Ibrahim al-Duri], at the Council of Ministers and the General Command – I mean after I asked Lieutenant General Amir to say to them, "Is there anything else left that they have not destroyed or inspected?" because maybe some – [*inaudible*] someone quoted what one of the escorts said, that one comrade named so and so said, "I wish we launched a few missiles on the Kuwaitis!" they might be thinking we still secured missiles and so forth.

Izzat: We just [recently] struck them with six.

Saddam: Tell them, brother. Tell them at the Council of Ministers how much they have destroyed and how much is left. He did not say. I said, "Do we have anything? Do we have missiles, biological research, chemical weapons, or what is called enriched uranium production and armament?" He said, they have destroyed everything! So, what is left? He said that they kept saying, "You need to give us the names of individuals, companies and countries you used to deal with," although they can find a way to know, especially the countries.

Tariq: Now they know that 85 percent of them because they [*inaudible*].

Saddam: But we – you as command members, you must always remember some actual facts, while there are other things that we are not required to disclose to the public opinion. So far it is the public opinion and the other factor. The other factor is that they want to destroy the moral basis for our relations with the other nations, countries and individuals. For example, any two friends will differ in opinions, and it is not nice to talk behind your friend's back, telling some stories your friend said while they were both on good terms.

Izzat: [*Inaudible.*]

Saddam: Or they used to be friends, but once their friendship is over and one of them says something against the other one, the latter would say he did not say that. But when you start quoting things, you will be forcing me to justify. Therefore, the first one should not say anything! Aren't these the Iraqi traditions for people who have traditions and understand? Unless you come and say who deals with you, that is when they will go and get them, and that is when we will be forced to tell people the story of the other party, which we did not have to. Or even if we did, I am afraid that someone would pass by and say, "Hello, brother. How do you expect me to

---

[71] SH-SHTP-A-001-198, "Saddam and His Advisers Discussing United Nations Rules and the UN Security Council," undated (circa late November 1998).

stop by while you did this to me and ruined my future, or you did this to so and so?" You see, you do not have to say the other one [unspecified]; you do not have to.

When I say you do not have to, this does not mean do not say it. You do not have to say it – when they come and we give them names, but then they come back and say, "Didn't you give us the names of people yourselves?" this becomes something established, established against us. Then someone would go and tell them something and they will come and tell us, "We heard so and so from such a country." We can contest this before the law and say, "If you want to believe that country it is up to you, but we did not deal with it." We will give them the liberty to believe what they want to believe, but we cannot tell them, "Okay, this becomes something against us." And they will reply, "Well, you launched this many bombs, this many missiles, this many chemical containers or gun related things, this many tube [launchers] and they were reinforced. We reinforced them with real chemicals and they knew it and destroyed them. This makes this many tons and the raw materials you bought from these parties make this many tons, so come on, tell us where the difference went." We have to tell them in this case where the difference is: On such a day, we distributed such and such, and so forth. We will find ourselves facing the international law, talking about one thing after the other. They are going to try everything, not to mention the fact that they destroyed everything they wanted to destroy and said Iraq implemented 95 percent of the resolutions. Isn't that what Ekeus said? As for the five percent, it might take another ten years without getting results. We hardly accomplished 95 percent in three years. So, where are we going to end up if we pursue the five percent? So, we are implementing the substance of this resolution. But to give them names for all the reasons we mentioned, they will be dreaming to get even one name from us for moral, ethical and humanitarian reasons!

I am afraid, comrades, after all I said that you might think we still have hidden chemical weapons, missiles and so forth. We have nothing; not even one screw.

Izzat: None of our enemies even need [inaudible, presumably chemical weapons and missiles].

Saddam: Why wouldn't they? Had they struck Baghdad and I were to have 100 missiles, wouldn't I launch them at Israel? Do I need them or not?[72]

Izzat: [*Inaudible.*]

Tariq: Yes, but almost – Your Excellency sees [*inaudible*] in the future as a result of what has been implemented before.

---

[72] Charles Duelfer provides the following partial translation of this recording, which in significant ways differs from the past few lines of our translation:

Saddam: We do not have WMD.
Unidentified Male: We don't need it.
Saddam: Why don't we? If they would have come and attacked Baghdad, don't you think we would have needed it to send to Israel?

The preceding few lines of dialogue also resemble, but are not identical to, the description that Chemical Ali, from coalition captivity, gave of an earlier RCC meeting. Ali reportedly claimed that Saddam informed his advisors that Iraq lacked WMD, but rejected a suggestion to remove ambiguity over the matter since the uncertainty served to discourage an Israeli attack. Duelfer, *Hide and Seek*, 408; Woods et al., *Iraqi Perspectives Project* (2006), 91–92.

Saddam: This is in case there is still a future and that is why they try to –

Izzat: [*Inaudible.*]

Tariq: If they are afraid [*inaudible.*]

Saddam: Comrade Taha Maruf?

Taha: Mr. President –

Saddam: What they fear the most is your intelligence, they see that the Command remained tight together and honest to its principles, logos, goals, programs and people, and day after day, it becomes more convinced, more loyal and determined.

Taha: Regarding his arrival here, it looks like his task was more political than technical. Therefore, I suggest that before he meets with the technicians to meet with the minister of foreign affairs or Mr. Tariq in order to understand his main lines of approach.[73]

In his previous visits and at a certain phase, it appeared to me he wanted certain types of solutions regarding the resolution then. But now many events and statements that were discouraging preceded his arrival, including the speech of the American president in Korea, delivered to soldiers, where he started the speech by saying, "Do you remember a week ago when I ordered the armed forces to bomb Baghdad and [*inaudible*] to all American soldiers [*inaudible*]."[74] Also, the statements of the American vice president – statements that were really impudent and strong compared with [what normally appears in] the American press, I mean the comment on these statements and the comment's conditions.[75] But at the same time, we do not know whether or not they can engage in a comprehensive war with Iraq.

Saddam: No, a comprehensive war the way [*voices overlap*] –

Taha: The same way as –

Saddam: [*Inaudible.*]

Taha: . . . the American reputation is fading now in Somalia and other places. The last attack on Iraq raised a torrent of criticism even by their close allies.[76]

––––––––

[73] Taha might be referring to the anticipated arrival of Roger Hill, whom Butler sent to Iraq in early December 1998 to lead UNSCOM teams. See Butler, *The Greatest Threat*, 200.

[74] This is apparently a reference to President Clinton's speech at the U.S. Air Force base in Osan, South Korea, on 22 November 1998. The president promised "to contain the weapons of mass destruction threat of Saddam Hussein" and warned that he would order airstrikes, if necessary, to force Iraq to more fully cooperate with the UN inspectors. Bill Sammon, "Clinton Targets Weapons Threats: Pledges to Contain Iraq, North Korea," *Washington Times*, 23 November 1998; Bob Deans, "After Asian Trip Clinton Faces Rocky Fall," *Cox News Service*, 22 November 1998.

[75] The editors were unable to locate such a statement by U.S. Vice President Al Gore.

[76] This might be a reference to U.S. cruise missile strikes in September 1996 to punish Iraq for attacking the Kurdish city of Irbil. For international criticisms of the U.S. actions, see David M. Malone, *The International Struggle over Iraq: Politics in the UN Security Council, 1980–2005* (New York: Oxford University Press, 2006), 93–95.

Saddam: It is [going to be] one of two things: either negotiation and agreement or [*inaudible*]. We decided this time that in case of negotiation after we maintained our position to the point where the council had met and we did not tell them our position had changed – if they negotiate and we reach any agreement, they should not repeat the attack. And if we have an argument, but they will not achieve their goal with the help of God, they will also not repeat the attack. I mean whether we argue or not, a new door will open up. And whichever of the two doors or other doors God wants is fine. We will leave the choice to God.

Izzat: [*Inaudible.*]

Saddam: As for the Council of Ministers, I explained to them and based on our experience, I would say the worst possibility is more likely to happen and therefore, you have to be prepared for the worst possibility.

[*End of recording.*]

EIGHT

Hussein Kamil

We have cut off the treacherous branch from our noble family tree.
— Ali Hassan al-Majid ("Chemical Ali"), 23 February 1996[1]

Sometime during the night of 7 August 1995, a line of cars slipped across the Iraq-Jordan border and drove to Amman. When Saddam Hussein awoke, he learned that his son-in-law Hussein Kamil had defected to Jordan along with Kamil's brother and the two men's wives, both of whom were Saddam's daughters. Raad Hamdani, the commander of the Republican Guard II Corps, recalled that when Saddam telephoned him around noon to inform him of the defection:

All I heard was screaming, cursing, and insults... Then Qusay [Hussein] came to the phone with a hoarse voice; he said, "If Hussein Kamil gets near you, he should be killed immediately." I could hear Saddam Hussein in the background cussing and screaming: "That dog! That villain!" It was horrible.[2]

The "deviation" was a blow to the regime, not only because part of Saddam's immediate family had abandoned him but also because Kamil, having headed Iraq's Special Security Organization, Republican Guard, and Military Industrialization Commission (MIC), possessed valuable information about Saddam's personal security procedures and weapons programs.

The defection came at a particularly inopportune time for Saddam, and despite Iraqi efforts to discredit Kamil, it had serious consequences for Saddam's regime.[3] Believing the end of UN sanctions to be at hand, Saddam had recently rejected the Oil-for-Food Program under which

---

[1] This quote is taken from a letter from Chemical Ali to Saddam, in which the former explains his rationale for ignoring Saddam's presidential pardon and killing Hussein Kamil. See Dilip Hiro, *Neighbours, Not Friends: Iraq and Iran after the Gulf Wars* (London: Routledge, 2001), 100.

[2] Woods interview of Lieutenant General Ra'ad Hamdani, Aqaba, Jordan, 15–17 May 2007.

[3] In the wake of the defection, the regime blamed Kamil for concealing hundreds of thousands of pages of WMD-related documents at his chicken farm, which it then turned over to

Saddam takes a tour of a Military Industrialization Commission facility. Hussein Kamil, with his hand pointing toward the artillery piece, appears to be giving the tour. This picture comes from a video recording of the tour, dated 27 April 1992. (*Source*: *SH-MICN-D-001-277, "Saddam Visiting a Military Industrialization Commission Facility," 27 April 1992.)

Iraq would be allowed to sell limited quantities of oil to purchase food and medicine for the Iraqi people. Kamil's defection changed this situation dramatically. Revelations of a more comprehensive weapons-of-mass-destruction (WMD) program than Saddam had previously disclosed reinforced suspicions of Saddam's every move, derailed Iraqi efforts to end the sanctions, and forced Saddam to accept the Oil-for-Food Program he had just spurned.

Kamil's defection also led Saddam – temporarily, as it turned out – to change course in his dealings with UN Special Commission (UNSCOM) inspectors. Having earlier threatened to throw the inspectors out of Iraq, Saddam became far more forthcoming in the months following the defection. After conducting an internal review that established the information Kamil had access to but which Baghdad had withheld from UN inspectors, Iraqi officials disclosed the existence of a biological weapons program, invited the

UN inspectors. Avigdor Haselkorn, *The Continuing Storm: Iraq, Poisonous Weapons and Deterrence* (New Haven, CT: Yale University Press, 1999), 113.

inspectors to visit new sites, and turned over new documents pertaining to Iraq's weapons programs.[4]

The internal fallout from this episode was also significant. As the transcripts in the second part of this chapter demonstrate, Kamil's defection reverberated within the upper levels of the Iraqi leadership. The incident fostered fears in Baghdad that Jordan and the United States might be plotting an attack on Iraq that Kamil could aid with his detailed knowledge of the country's industry, infrastructure, and security apparatuses. Accusations and mistrust increased among Saddam's inner circle.[5] Saddam relieved his son Uday, whose drunken violence and long-standing rivalry with Hussein Kamil might have helped precipitate the defection, from most of his positions. He also publicly announced a "disowning" (tabaru') of his relatives.[6]

After a few months in Jordan, once the political and media firestorm subsided and he was no longer a celebrity, and facing a lawsuit for threatening a Jordanian journalist, Kamil quietly asked Saddam for forgiveness and an opportunity to return home.[7] Saddam pardoned his son-in-law and let him return in February 1996. It should have been clear to Kamil that Saddam's pardon would not protect him from murderous revenge. Kamil's apparent faith in Saddam's pardon was so misplaced that some analysts came to believe that the reason he trusted Saddam and was returning was that he had never really defected in the first place; rather, they suggested, Saddam

---

[4] On 14 August 1995 Saddam received a report by Husam Muhammad Amin al-Yasin, the director of Iraq's National Monitoring Directorate, listing prohibited Iraqi weapon programs with which Kamil was familiar, but that Iraq had not declared to UN inspectors. These included Iraq's crash-course program in fall 1990 to create a nuclear weapon using fuel from the Osiraq reactor, weaponization of biological agents in Scud missiles in 1990, and destruction of these biological agents in mid-1991 rather than late 1990, as Iraq had previously declared. See SH-INMD-D-000-657, "Report from Husam Mohammad Amin, Director of the National Monitoring Directorate, on Hussein Kamil," 14 August 1995; Duelfer Report, vol. 3, "Biological Warfare," 53. For a lengthy list of revelations about Iraqi WMD programs, all stemming from Kamil's defection and the regime's reaction, see UN Special Commission on Iraq, Report to the UN Security Council, S/1995/864, 11 October 1995, accessed 2 June 2009 at www.un.org/Depts/unscom/sres95-864.htm.

[5] Saddam expressed concern that treason of the type perpetrated by Kamil "might recur." Abd al-Tawab Mullah Huwaysh, Kamil's replacement as director of the MIC, reported that the defection exacerbated Saddam's paranoia and sense of insecurity. SH-SHTP-A-000-837, "Saddam and Senior Political Advisers Discussing the Treason of Hussein Kamil," undated (circa late 1995–early 1996); Duelfer Report, vol. 1, "Regime Strategic Intent," 21.

[6] In December 1992, Kamil complained in a letter to Saddam about Uday's attacks on him in the Babel newspaper, offered his resignation, and warned, "If a nation cannot protect or show appreciation for its responsible people, the people will not be loyal to it. That is why I am completely quitting my government job . . . before things become worse for the promise I made to keep, since it was connected to you, Sir." See SH-SPPC-D-000-235, "Letter to Saddam from Hussein Kamil Tendering his Resignation," 27 December 1992; Aburish, The Politics of Revenge, 338.

[7] Nigel Ashton, King Hussein of Jordan: A Political Life (New Haven, CT: Yale University Press, 2008), 343.

had sent him to Jordan disguised as a defector to spy on Iraqi opposition groups, to provide inspectors with misinformation, or for other purposes.[8] Neither Kamil's killing nor any material in the recordings, however, lends credence to such theories.

Once Kamil was back on Iraqi soil, Ali Hassan al-Majid ("Chemical Ali"), who was Saddam's cousin and Kamil's uncle, led Saddam's sons Uday and Qusay and other men in restoring their family's honor by killing Kamil and much of his extended family in a thirteen-hour fire fight.[9] Chemical Ali wrote to Saddam, explaining his rationale for ignoring the pardon: "We have cut off the treacherous branch from our noble family tree. Your amnesty does not obliterate the right of our family to impose the necessary punishment."[10] The official General Security Directorate (GSD) incident report showed that government officials were on the scene when the killings occurred but were ordered not to intervene. In his written statement, the GSD's Brigadier General Ajil Hazza' Salim stated:

Major Ra'id from the Bayya Directorate called me and said he went with a force to the accident location and saw a house surrounded by civilians exchanging fire with people inside the house . . . he noticed the presence of Mr. Ali Hassan al-Majid, Uday and Qusay [Saddam's sons], and Rukan [director of the Office of Tribal Affairs] and others. And that he was informed by Mr. Zuhayr from the Special Security Organization to withdraw, for it was a tribal matter involving the traitor Hussein Kamil, and they excluded the official authorities from interfering.[11]

It is unlikely that these events occurred without Saddam's authorization, and it is clear from the record that he approved of them. "Death is God's act, and treason is the Devil's act," he said. "It would be a better honor for him and less harm to the Iraqi people, if God would have taken his soul."[12]

---

[8] Richard Butler, "Why Saddam Husayn Loves the Bomb," *Middle East Quarterly* (March 2000), accessed 6 June 2009 at www.meforum.org/article/33; Peter F. Sisler, "Kuwaiti Calls Iraqi Defection Theatre," *United Press International*, 21 February 1996; Ben Barber and Bill Gertz, "Iraqi Defectors Return to Baghdad with Pardons: Move Taints Data from Saddam's Kin," *Washington Times*, 21 February 1996.

[9] Sandra Mackey, *The Reckoning: Iraq and the Legacy of Saddam Hussein* (New York: W. W. Norton & Company, 2002), 325.

[10] Hiro, *Neighbours, Not Friends*, 100. On 23 February 1996, the Al-Majid clan wrote a letter to Saddam in which they explained why they killed Kamil despite the president's pardon, and requested forgiveness for breaking the law. See Letter from Al-Majid clan to Saddam Hussein explaining why they killed Hussein Kamil despite government pardon, 23 February 1996.

[11] See General Security Directorate statements regarding the killing of Hussein Kamil, 27 February 1996, in SH-IDGS-D-000-383, "General Security Directorate Records Regarding the Killing of Hussein Kamil," February 1996.

[12] SH-SHTP-A-000-833, "Saddam and Officials Discussing the Treason of Hussein Kamil and Developments in Iraq," undated (circa mid- to late August 1995).

Finally, Kamil's defection contrasts interestingly with other instances of dissent in Saddam's government. In October 1995, for example, Iraqi ambassador to the United Nations Nizar Hamdun sent Saddam a long letter containing wide-ranging criticisms of the regime and temporarily refused to return to Baghdad. Saddam replied in a pointed (and even longer) letter that accused Nizar of disloyalty and rebutted many of his assertions, but he also distributed Nizar's missive for discussion among the Iraqi leadership. When Nizar eventually returned to Iraq in 1998, he was not subjected to the sort of exemplary punishment inflicted on Kamil. Nizar's private criticism did not have the same potentially devastating consequences for Saddam as had Kamil's very public defection. Nor did it have the family implications. Thus, the dictator took a more circumspect approach when dealing with this internal discontent.[13]

THE TRAITOR: WHY DID HE DEFECT?

Kamil's defection led to a great deal of speculation in Saddam's inner circle as to why he had left. The discussions tended to focus on three non-mutually-exclusive hypotheses. The first was that Kamil was mentally ill. The second was that he had fled to avoid repercussions for illicit activities. The third was that he had frustrated political ambitions.

Saddam and Senior Officials Discuss Hussein Kamil's Behavior after Brain Surgery (17 August 1995)[14]

Saddam: The foreign doctor that did the surgery for him explained to the – there also was a Jordanian doctor overseeing the surgery.[15] He told them to be wary of him. This man is not normal and his situation could lead to suicide.

Male 1: This means that he could kill someone else or himself.

---

[13] See SH-SPPC-D-000-498, "Letter and Memo Responding to Ambassador Nizar Hamdun's Criticisms of the Iraqi Regime," November 1995; Daniel Pipes, "Obituary for Nizar Hamdoon (1944–2003)," *Middle East Quarterly*, Fall 2003, accessed 28 September 2008 at www.danielpipes.org/article/1310. Saddam's reaction to defiant behavior on the part of the dictator's half-brother, Barzan Ibrahim al-Tikriti, also provides interesting comparisons. Shortly after Kamil's defection, Barzan, who was serving in Geneva as Iraq's representative to the United Nations, publicly criticized Uday Hussein and disobeyed Saddam's orders to return to Iraq. "Saddam Hussein's Half Brother Criticizes Heir," *New York Times*, 31 August 1995.

[14] *SH-SHTP-A-001-259, "Saddam and Top Political Advisers Discussing Hussein Kamil's Mental Health and Problems with King Hussein of Jordan," 17 August 1995.

[15] Although the identity of the "foreign doctor" is unclear, Dr. Ashraf al-Kurdi, a Jordanian who was Arafat's personal physician, provided the Iraqis with details of Hussein Kamil's surgery in Amman. See SH-SHTP-A-000-837, "Saddam and Senior Political Advisers Discussing the Treason of Hussein Kamil," undated (circa late 1995–early 1996).

Saddam: We never heard this before.

Male 2: Behind the ear – my impression is that operation was behind the ear.

Saddam: No, they dug in here, this area[;] therefore his eye is gone, if you notice. They performed the operation through the nose.

Male 1: They also removed some cancerous cells and growths. It was benign.

Male 3: His injury affects his behavior and makes his behavior aggressive and the tendency to change from one mood to another. This could lead to a kind of depression that can lead to suicide.

Saddam: The Jordanian doctor asked Dr. Umid [*inaudible*]. He said, "Lord have mercy." He said that because through the operation this [the changes in Hussein Kamil's personality] will increase.

Male 1: [*Inaudible.*]

Saddam: [*Inaudible.*] He also said that he was asking Dr. Umid for pills. I do not know what kind of pills, sedative pills. I noticed before he went to surgery. I noticed because of the way he was speaking to me, it did not flow. I noticed that twice. One time he came to me up in the Buhayrat.[16] He came to me driving a car, so I called his brother and told him to follow him in a car and take him home, because I was worried about his situation, and come to me when you get back because I want to talk to you. I asked, "Do you notice anything with him?" They did not realize it yet. He said, "No, Sir, I did not notice anything." But sometimes he gets a headache. I said this is his situation that I saw. I was afraid that while driving the car he could get in that situation and commit suicide. So, you should pay attention to him until we see his health condition.

———

Male 2: There was an Iraqi doctor.

Saddam: An Iraqi specialist also talked to Dr. Umid. [*Inaudible*]. He reached the same conclusion that the foreigner and Jordanian have reached. It is better for him to go crazy than – we described him that way and we will not back away from this description.

Male 2: Why did they not tell [*inaudible*] before [*inaudible*] the Minister of Health [*inaudible*]?

Saddam: This is the situation in Third World countries. He was embarrassed to tell us. At the Military Industries [Military Industrial Commission], they have noticed all of these conditions. Sometimes he is depressed and very angry and sometimes he is transformed into something else. The contradictions – he had these contradictions in him, originally, but they have increased lately.

Male 2: It increased because of the disease.

---

16 Buhayrat ath Tharthar is a lake about seventy-five miles north of Baghdad, between the Tigris and the Euphrates rivers. Saddam might be referring to a palace near the lake.

Saddam Tells the Revolutionary Command Council That He Warned Hussein Kamil about Being Too Politically Ambitious (15 August 1995)[17]

Saddam: The last treasonous act of Hussein Kamil has two factors. The first factor is ambition: love of accomplishment. But he realized that this accomplishment could not be achieved by this March and with the image that he drew for himself. Hussein Kamil wanted to become the deputy prime minister, and the next step, during the stage of Saddam Hussein, or after Saddam Hussein, is to reach the whole authority. I explained to you how his brain is working. I did not reach this conclusion just now; I made this conclusion much earlier. Some of you may be wondering, why did Hussein Kamil not become the deputy prime minister? Although, based on the general context where he was standing, this was not so odd. But Saddam Hussein did not want to make him the deputy prime minister. His sickness makes him close to the position that he aimed at, which is the deputy prime minister and later on, the prime minister. Of course he could not explain all his desires in front of Saddam Hussein, so he avoided these matters for his appointment. But the whole picture was presented in front of me, and it was clear that he was going to request from the others to deliver his opinion, shamelessly, to escalate to this degree or that degree or this position or that position. I listened. Sometimes I made a comment, which was not understood – how do I see the disease of this man? And sometimes I explained things briefly. Then how do we not –

I will say the other factor to finish. The other factor is the feeling that Saddam Hussein will find out about all his [Hussein Kamil's] illegal behavior, his exploitation, and his deviation. That is why he ran away. He ran away under the feeling that the ideas he had on his mind would not be possible to achieve with Saddam Hussein. So he stopped and did not cross the limits. He stopped as a minister in the Iraqi government. And as a minister in the Iraqi government, his works were approaching Saddam Hussein's microscope to view whether he was doing it the right way or in another way that includes a deviation and therefore, he packed and left, thinking to himself, "Let me go with my dignity before he [Saddam] takes away that title from me, and let me go in a different situation." And as I stated in my letter, any headline with "why" may not suffice for us to make a conclusion and be able to answer it. Because the one who wants to betray, does not explain, and does not say why I want to betray. I mean, when he explains to us why he wants to betray, then we would say, "one, two and that's it." But he is sick of the prestige and the authority in both of them . . . so he deviates.

Before this time, of course, I told him about his disease. Not this year, but a long time ago. I told him: "Hussein, you." He said: "Yes." I told him: "You are sick to the point that you do not see any limit except the position of Saddam Hussein." I told him: "I am warning you, this is dangerous, dangerous for you, and it is dangerous to have such an imagination, because this is the Ba'ath Arab Socialist Party, and maybe there is no such leader in the world who talks to his family as clearly as Saddam Hussein talks." All my family now understands, but the oldest ones and

[17] SH-SHTP-A-000-837, "Saddam and Senior Political Advisers Discussing the Treason of Hussein Kamil," undated (circa late 1995–early 1996).

Hussein, among them, and maybe others still do not understand what Saddam Hussein means.

————

Humam:[18] My Master, colleagues, you have talked and covered all matters, but I still have one observation. Your Sovereignty inquired about the surgical procedure that he [Hussein Kamil] had. Maybe there will be benefits from explaining this information. We had in our family the same case of disease similar to his case – an educated, cultured and qualified patient with a higher degree than his degree – and a change started to appear in his behavior in the past few years. A strange, aggressive behavior and his unnatural desire to quarrel, before we discovered the disease. And a surgery was done to remove the entire tumor, which is similar to the state of Hussein. And when I asked the doctor about the change in his behavior and the aggressive desire and the quarrel and the quarreling with people, he told me this is an effect from the tumor and it is expected that it influences his behavior even after completing the surgery.

Saddam: What is the name of the doctor?

Humam: Dr. Abdul Hadi Al-Khalili, Sir.[19] He is a distinguished scientist but he is not approved by us in Ebin Sina,[20] because he is of Iranian descent, but he is one of the brightest scientists in his specialty. Sir, this is a fact and we have to accept it. And Your Sovereignty can ask specialized physicians, him or others, from the brain specialists who know about the symptoms with patients before and after the surgery with this disease.

Saddam: He quarrels with people for any reason.

Humam: He is sick, my master, this is the truth and I believe that this disease might lead him one day to commit suicide and I expect this to be soon because of his disease. This is what I wanted to explain because that talk about him may last for good.

Saddam: Yes, Doctor [*inaudible*].

The Cabinet Doctor [unknown]: Thank you my Master, the Leader President. The truth is that I do not want to downplay the reality and the treacherous accident, but we should be fair with ourselves. We were confronted with the reality and what Dr. Humam said is a real medical condition in medicine and it is known especially when the tumors are located in the frontal lobe of the brain, which affects the memory and the behavior.

Saddam: The memory and what?

The Cabinet Doctor: The memory and the behavior and the manners.

Saddam: Behavior!

[18] Humam Abd al-Khaliq Abd al-Ghafur, minister of higher education and scientific research (1980s–2003).
[19] Abdul Hadi Al-Khalili was the chair of the neurosurgery department at the University of Baghdad (1988–2005).
[20] A prestigious hospital in Iraq.

The Cabinet Doctor: Behavior, manners. Patients with this disease before the invention of the CT scan and the MRI used to be treated as crazy under the supervision of wise elderly people and psychiatrists. Immediately the behavior changes: if she is a woman or a religious man they may become the opposite or totally aggressive... The doctor told me that this condition will continue even if the tumor were not big, and even in its smallest size, the brain electricity has changed and the incidence of migraines will continue and he has to take his medications all his life. In addition to that, he has to watch for any state of depression, or the opposite, for any unusual arousal and happiness, because they are the first symptoms. The doctor asked me if he has any symptoms like megalomania or something like that.

Saddam and His Advisers Discuss Hussein Kamil's Embezzlement of State Funds (mid- to late August 1995)[21]

Male 1: I believe, Sir, if you allow me to interpret here, I feel that corruption started at the end of 1993 when you appointed him as the Minister of Industry and Minerals... He worked freely, and he wanted to hire other ministers. Unfortunately, the people close to him used to encourage him and give him what he needed. Sir, I expected him to become a command member or deputy prime minister. Frankly, I was one of those people who used to pray for him to become a command member and not deputy prime minister; truly, so that we would not have a problem. He did it, indeed, and I was right in my expectations. If he had not become deputy prime minister and a command member, he would have caused us problems,[22] and I was afraid, but I did not expect him to go to Jordan. It did not occur to me, but I was sure he was going to cause a problem in Iraq should he not get these posts. So, Sir, this is one point. At the end of 1993 and in 1994, he started to deal with the financial aspect alone in such an incredible way! We used to hear about it, but it was hard for us to believe it. But what he used to do when he heard someone talking about him was to [inaudible] him and tell the [inaudible] around him – but thank God, I could not be like them in this regard and I would not be able to do it for him. He would tell his people to [inaudible] to such and such minister. Sir, I sent some documents where some of them state [inaudible], once the companies are registered in the Ministry of Trade, he would have a sensitive position in it. And as you know, Sir, every company has tens of thousands of shareholders. He would look for one official of his relatives and do an inventory of the shares he has in the company. This is something hard to do in the computer, Sir. But he did it so that he could have it ready for Your Excellency so that he could torture that person. So, it was such a sly way to punish people and get rid of them.

————

Male 1: The Minister of Education asked him to do something, but he did not do it. You know that Hamid[23] used to tell me everything, but I used to stay away because

[21] SH-SHTP-A-000-762, "Saddam and Iraqi Ministers Discussing the Treason of Hussein Kamil," undated (circa mid- to late August 1995).

[22] Kamil became neither deputy prime minister nor a member of the Revolutionary Command Council.

[23] Possibly Hamid Abu al-Shalabi, an individual mentioned later in the conversation but not further identified. Alternatively, it could have been Hamid Hammadi, Saddam's secretary and office director during the 1980s and minister of information during the 1990s.

he was a problem. I asked him to give the Ministry of Education some allocations, but he would not listen to me, and I asked him why he would not give some allocations to the Ministry of Education. He did not answer.

Saddam: You mean that he did not give them the allocations that they needed?

Male 1: Yes, Mr. President, when he became a minister he did not like me to sit behind the ministers, and he asked Mr. Hamid Abu al-Shalabi to stop doing these things. This man, when he became a minister, we started to have problems. He would change the ministers as he saw fit. I mean, Mr. President, that you had given him strong support. This non-stop support started four years ago. Especially after the end of 1993, when he became the Minister of Industry, everything he said, would go. And he started to do things as he saw fit, and he spent money as he liked, built fantastic homes and allocated project money of 158 million [*unspecified currency, presumably U.S. dollars*] and started to win over trivial people. It is really shameful to say it, Sir, but he is such an utterly dirty and corrupt man! Let me explain to you where 1 million became 20 million. In 1993, 19 million disappeared and no one recorded this amount, then I discovered [*inaudible*] in this bank. I found out this information, this information, I received it from Ahmad Ismail.[24]

Saddam: This man has authority and you should follow his orders.

Male 1: Mr. President, this is right, as of this time we are still afraid of him, some of us are afraid that he would come back into authority. About the road that he opened, he spends 158 million on these roads, and some of them are still not done.

———

Hazim:[25] After all this happened, he had a nervous breakdown, Mr. President, and he became fiery.

Saddam: This is some of the work that made him walk out; this is the truth. He wants to use his own special way in all of his work, especially the hidden [weapons] storage, and to enhance industrial production. Yes I do know he is horrible and we need to get rid of him.

———

Hikmat:[26] Mr. President, when he found out that you trusted him, he started to include patriotism in his work, and made me feel that he was a man of high authority. He said to me, "I have trust in you to execute the operation in full. I do not have to be involved with you; prepare everything for me." He was ordering me to do this work. At this time I needed to regain respect for myself [*inaudible*] – military production and all money decisions, the secret was I do not know how to pressure them, and made them withdraw the money gradually. [Hussein Kamil said] "I do not want the Americans or anyone to know about this plan. You will receive the money and organize a committee and the money would be under your name. Then you will bring it to me without anyone knowing about it. You will place it in my bedroom in a safe, then you will keep the key and you will protect it, and another key should be in my [Hussein Kamil's] office." In his office! He can get to his office

24 Unknown individual.
25 Probably Hazim Ali, a senior official in Iraq's biological weapons program.
26 Hikmat Mizban Ibrahim al-Azzawi, minister of finance (1995–2003).

but it would be impossible for other people to get into his office in the middle of the night to get the money. He gathered $9 million, which I explained to him that 35 percent of this money is for contracts. "How we are going to withdraw it?" He said, "Something is going to happen before the 15th of this month. We should withdraw it. You do not have to comply with anything in order to withdraw it. You decide and use your usual way, so [*inaudible*]." The problem was that he was working on planning a mass betrayal, this is what he was doing.

———

Hikmat: Mr. President, he made those companies donate to the Military Industrialization Commission in order to cover their needs. I am not sure exactly what the number was, but one of them was 250,000 [*unspecified currency, presumably U.S. dollars*] while the other one was 150,000. For a private sector company to donate 250,000 to the Military Industrialization Commission in times like this we should raise a statue for the owner of this company. He also said not to worry about paying it back for six months to a year depending on the progress of our matters. So, he created such dramatic atmospheres around these four individuals in terms of patriotism, generosity and loyalty. Once we got the money, we bought some commodities and enjoyed the money.

After a few months, one of the ministry officials asked, "How are we going to pay the money back to these people? What do you think of selling them cigarettes in dollars?" the other one replied. "How are you going to give it to them in dollars, we are supposed to bring commodities according to a barter?" But the first one said, "Let us give it to them exclusively for a period and see how the issue goes." Then he asked, "For how much should we give it to them, Nizar?"[27] Nizar replied, "Give it to them for 65 dollars since the carton is sold for 65 dollars in the market."

Male 2: Someone said a different price.

Hikmat: I am sure this was the price, and then he said, "I sell it for 45 a carton since the ration card was stopped!" Mr. President, imagine how this money would be distributed. Each person would get a quarter of a million dollars if the carton sells for 45 dollars, which is a monopoly. Now the price of a carton of cigarettes went up to 85 dollars in the market. Every day he distributed 3,000 cartons – 3,000 times 40 dollars, divided by four – each one will get a 120,000 [dollar] profit monthly, then they will gain a third of a million dollars each month. I was surprised when some dealers came to me and asked me why we are giving the carton of cigarettes for 45 dollars to these people and they are willing to buy it for 65 dollars a carton. So, I presented this offer to him, but he said no, we already agreed on this price, and this is none of my business, they will keep doing this until the market price is reduced. Mr. President, they will keep on robbing the country at $100,000–120,000 daily. This amount is the profit, not sale, and this is only the cigarette case and the way the prices in the market worked.

There are other immoral activities in the market, and we have proof about it in his telephone book, which includes females' names and phone numbers. Okay, a person can go out with one or two, ten, but with 150 girls! This is strange, Mr. President, which will prove his dishonesty. What I mean is that he was an authorized official

———

[27] Unknown individual.

and he should be very responsible. He should not steal. How can a political man steal? He said this is the time for the Weapons of Mass Destruction group, and he asked for information [*inaudible*].

Tariq: I said this is the President's order. He said, "This is not important; when you see him just let him know that Hussein Kamil requested this information." Then after he provided us with moral support and information about Russia selling Iran reactors, we gave him the information he needed. Then he started to talk. Then we found out that he was a traitor, Mr. President. This is my opinion.

Saddam and Various Officials Discuss Hussein Kamil's Corruption and Interest in Nuclear Weapons (mid- to late August 1995)[28]

Saddam: I give you a formal apology on behalf of the country and the relation that we had with Hussein Kamil before he committed treason. In addition, I want to thank the ones who accepted the work, especially when it was unwillingly. In spite of that, they continued to go forth because the one who introduced Hussein Kamil to them is Saddam Hussein. Now I would like to hear from each one of you, not a very long paragraph but a very short one, about your new achievements, starting with a line filled with energy, liveliness, and great thinking as a living part of your great Iraqi nation. If any of you has a comment, let him tell us. This new problem regarding Ukraine, let's see if we – because we are able to contact Lieutenant General Amir[29] both ways. I told him to contact him to see if there are any new developments today, because some issues cannot be delayed; they require an immediate solution. He told me [*laughing*] that the new bomb, so to say, is legal or rather insignificant. Therefore, he instructed a group that went to Ukraine to discuss the issue.[30] What can we say? We say, may God leave him behind.

––––––

Saddam: Whatever happened, not to worry. I told them yesterday at the Council of Ministers I would not change my nature. Meaning, are we going to change the unlimited trust for people that we have? I told them, we are not going to change it. Trust is the major thing . . . Because of this principle, we have suffered because of some people. Whenever we praise them unfortunately, they would not understand it, rather, they would say, "They glorify themselves. They would say, "We are much greater than what Saddam thinks of us," not to say that you would be like them. However, I would not change my nature. We must reward the philanthropist for his work. We must reward the good work, and at the same time, we must urge balance. Any difficulties or successes should not create an imbalance in the human being.

Mahmud: Thank you very much, Sir, for letting me speak first. If you allow me to say to you I am nervous, because I will be in –

[28] SH-SHTP-A-000-833, "Saddam and Officials Discussing the Treason of Hussein Kamil and Developments in Iraq," undated (circa mid- to late August 1995).

[29] Amir Muhammad Rashid al-Ubaydi, minister of oil (1996–2003).

[30] Iraq had a nuclear scientific relationship with Ukraine dating to the 1970s. In the mid-1990s, UN inspectors uncovered evidence of illegal weapons trafficking. See Joby Warrick, "Iraq Opened Consular Office in Kharkiv in December 2002," *Washington Post*, 28 November 2002.

Saddam: Take your time, talk just as though you were sitting between your brothers.

Mahmud: Thank you, Sir.

Saddam: That is to say, do not even worry about the grammar. Even though I emphasized this issue to the ministers when they write, however, we are not here to write, we are just talking just like you would talk normally, and take your time.

Mahmud: Sir, my name is Doctor Mahmud Muhammad Husan Muzaffar, director-general of the main plant for planning productivity operations, one of the installations of the MIC [Military Industrialization Commission].[31] Sir, in regard to what Your Excellency has stated so kindly, I have noticed a very deep meaning to your words that is very moving. I would like to assure you, we are among those who joined the MIC in its journey, and it has been an honor to receive instructions and work closely with the Lieutenant General Amir Muhammad Rashid.

The MIC in every aspect represents Saddam Hussein. It is true that Hussein Kamil, whom Your Excellency, as you stated, introduced to the MIC, and we see your great modesty in repeating your apology three or four times. Therefore, Hussein Kamil used to represent Saddam Hussein and his words, and Saddam Hussein is always a symbol of our work, and to all the comrades, researchers, and scholars present here. Concerning the issue of the two bombs, which Your Excellency wanted us to talk about, in fact it was during the period of the Greater Bairam Holiday.[32] I think we went exactly during the Greater Bairam Holiday, we went at that time to congratulate Hussein Kamil. Some of our comrades were there before us, and then I went in with the Comrade Brigadier General Abd al-Hasan, the director of the al-'Iz Installation. I have relations with Ukraine related to our research and activities there. He was talking with Brigadier General Na'im, who is in charge of one of the companies with the Ukrainians. So, when I went in they stoked the subject and he told me, "I have some interests now related to weapons issues." So, this issue really emerged. He said, "Make sure before I forget to try to convince them, concerning the two nuclear bombs, the two small bombs."

Saddam: [Inaudible.]

Mahmud: Yes, he revived the issue. The instructions are always from the director of the [Military Industrial] Commission.

Saddam: Therefore, you did not happen to speak with them?

Mahmud: Of course not!

Saddam: You did not talk to them?

Mahmud: Impossible.

Saddam: Thank God, then. [Laughing.]

All: [Laughing.]

---

[31] Mahmud went on to head MIC's Yugoslav procurement connection while working as a scientific adviser in the Iraqi embassy in Belgrade. See *Duelfer Report*, vol. 1, "Regime Finance and Procurement," 112.

[32] The Eid Al-Adh'ha (Greater Bairam) is an annual Muslim festival associated with the Al-Hajj pilgrimage.

Saddam and His Senior Advisers Discuss the Timing of Hussein Kamil's Defection (mid- to late August 1995)[33]

Saddam: Yes, interior conspiracies.[34] This proves their inability to make the journey reconcile with corruption. And when it was getting close to exposing the conspiracies in the world around Iraq and the key players of these conspiracies before the international public opinion, and the possibility of getting close to having the sanctions lifted, making clear enough that this regime would not conclude a truce, negotiate or [accept] intervention in serious matters, he exploded. Otherwise, had Hussein Kamil known we could bargain with matters of principle, he would not have exploded. Had he known he could become the prime minister and the next step head of state according to a context prepared by Saddam Hussein, he would not have exploded.

———

Saddam: At one time he and Ali [Hassan al-Majid] had a disagreement at the cabinet meeting so I yelled at them and told them that I could not accept the creation of empires under the Ba'ath Socialist Party regime. Taha was there, Tariq was there. The Deputy [Izzat Ibrahim al-Duri] was not there. I told them that the country is the country of Ba'ath and the ministry is for the people. I cannot accept the creation of empires or closing a ministry. A minister is a representative of the people. I cannot accept empires. At the same time I talked clearly to them and I told them that it is best if my relatives are not in power and when I am forced to put them in the service of the Ba'ath it should be temporary. He interpreted these principles and the letter at the Conference of Iraq[35] as though he were the one being targeted. He even told his secretaries that on that subject I was talking about him and that I was talking in general but I meant him.

Male 1: [*Inaudible.*]

Saddam: He saw that Ali was dismissed from the Ministry of Defense after he was elected to be in the leadership of the country. He got the feeling that he had to escape.[36]

---

[33] *SH-SHTP-A-001-260, "Saddam Discussing the Details of Hussein Kamil's Escape," undated (circa mid- to late August 1995).

[34] Saddam and Tariq had been discussing earlier conspiracies against Iraq in response to the Ba'ath regime's efforts to transform Iraq and its refusal to compromise its principles.

[35] The eleventh congress of Iraq's Ba'ath Party was held 8–9 July 1995. "Ba'th Party Conference: Ba'th Party elects new command, Saddam declines post of secretary for life," *BBC Summary of World Broadcasts*, 11 July 1995. Originally published by Iraqi News Agency (in Arabic), 9 July 1995.

[36] Saddam's reference to an individual's election to a leadership position is unclear. In the year leading up to the defection, Saddam's sons had steadily risen in power at the expense of the al-Majid wing of the family (Chemical Ali, Hussein Kamil, and Saddam Kamil). In 1994, Hussein Kamil lost control of smuggling operations through Turkey to Uday. In 1995, Uday began targeting Hussein Kamil's commissions for various purchases and imports, and Qusay took Saddam Kamil's position over Saddam's personal security detail. On 16 July 1995, Saddam replaced Chemical Ali as defense minister and made him party head of the Baghdad-al Karakh region. The demotion came, reportedly, as a result of Ali's illegal smuggling activities. As Mackey writes, "Uday and Qusay circled their brothers-in-law like vultures waiting to devour the carcasses of their rivals." See Marr, *The Modern History of Iraq*, 272; Mackey, *The Reckoning*, 323–24.

Male 1: It was not part of his original plan.

Saddam: I believe he arranged it with King Hussein, I mean he told King Hussein in order to give the impression that he was in disagreement with the country [Iraq], with the leadership. I am sure of this, except for the timing. Perhaps he could have chosen a different timing and different steps, but I believe he was forced into this timing and steps. With the arrival of our timing, in terms of the end of August, either you give us our rights or take your stuff and leave.[37] It seems that the Americans are not bidding on entering a battle without a front, so they told him, "Come on, we will make you a front."[38]

Tariq: I believe this is most likely what happened because there are supporting facts, Sir, such as his meeting with King Hussein in July[39] – and the American military preparations are not new, Sir, these preparations we are going to see and that are continuous.[40]

Saddam: Yes, continuous but they were aborted – aborted so far.

Tariq: Yes, their substantial aspect was aborted, but they are still going on. Besides, Sir, if you also notice something important about Hussein's behavior – Hussein [Kamil] is a minister, a state official, and directed wide external communications related to his work, but he did not travel.

Saddam: Yes, he did not travel.

Tariq: This year in July and August he decided to travel. You know this best. Did you ask him to travel or did he plan for it and ask for your permission?

Saddam: No, he told me that he was invited by the Russians and by the Bulgarians. I told him go ahead, travel, but be aware of the security side.

Tariq: Fine, in this case he was the initiator?

Saddam: He was the initiator.

---

[37] In his 17 July 1995 National Day speech, Saddam warned that if the Security Council did not end the sanctions, Iraq would quit cooperating with UN weapon inspectors. Several days later, Iraq's foreign minister announced a deadline of 31 August 1995. See Duelfer, *Hide and Seek*, 106.

[38] Saddam appears to mean that the Clinton Administration believed that Kamil might emerge as the head of an anti-Saddam clique within the Iraqi leadership. After Kamil's defection, Secretary of Defense William Perry said that the possibility of a "pro-Western team" taking power in Iraq was "a question which we have thought about very, very seriously... and we are working on." Bill Gertz and Rowan Scarborough, "Perry Warns Iraq to Back Off," *Washington Times*, 15 August 1995.

[39] King Hussein reported that he discussed with Kamil, roughly four weeks before Kamil's defection, the need for changes in Iraq. See Ofra Bengio, ed., *Middle East Contemporary Survey: Iraq 1976–1999* (Tel Aviv: Moshe Dayan Center for Middle Eastern and African Studies, Shiloah Institute, Tel Aviv University), CD-ROM version, vol. 19/1995, 318.

[40] The United States had previously scheduled a military exercise with Jordan in October, but because of the defection and subsequent Iraqi troop movements, it was pushed up to late August. Eric Schmitt, "U.S. Action in Persian Gulf Is Said to Seek Iraqi's Ouster," *New York Times*, 19 August 1995.

Tariq: Before then he did not travel. In my estimation, it seems that – based on the facts and not just a guess, because we should look at the facts and link them together – he, if you remember, Sir, the issue of August and the issue of entering a battle was a decision made in June. We started talking about it in April,[41] if you remember, Sir, after we rejected Resolution 986,[42] and following Ekeus's report in June, we said we would get to the biological issue.[43] We decided on August, if you remember, Sir. We met with the leadership and the council and we decided that we would get to the biological issue and that we would give Ekeus two months and that this is sufficient for giving him everything, and after the two months that is it, because he would not need more.[44] This was in June. The committee was formed and headed by the Deputy[45] in order to prepare the country and the strategic reserve and it was clear that we were going to battle.

Saddam: It was clear for him that we were going to engage in a battle.[46]

Tariq: … He knew that there was a time when our relations with the Special Commission [UNSCOM] and the [UN] Security Council would explode. The first trip was in July and he met with King Hussein and perhaps he communicated with him, because he was there for several days.

Saddam: It was enough for him to tell King Hussein, and King Hussein would do all the communication that he wants.

Tariq: Yes, Sir.

Saddam: With Israel and with America.

Tariq: You can verify – King Hussein –

---

[41] In April 1995, Ekeus issued a report concluding that Iraq might have concealed a biological weapons program from UN inspectors, which prompted another of the periodic confrontations between Saddam and the UNSC. Barbara Crossette, "Iraq Hides Biological Warfare Effort, Report Says," *New York Times*, 12 April 1995.

[42] UNSCR 986 was a so-called Oil-for-Food resolution, allowing Iraq to sell a limited amount of oil to pay for food, medicine, and other essentials. See UN Security Council Resolution 986, 14 April 1995, accessed 23 July 2008 at www.casi.org.uk/info/undocs/scres/1995/9510988e.htm.

[43] On 20 June 1995, Ekeus reported to the UN Security Council that "Iraq obtained or sought to obtain all the items and materials required to produce biological warfare agents in Iraq. With Iraq's failure to account for all those items and material for legitimate purposes, the only conclusion that can be drawn is that there is a high risk that Iraq purchased them and used them at least in part for proscribed purposes – the production of agents for biological weapons." S/1995/494, accessed 4 March 2009 at http://documents.un.org/mother.asp.

[44] See *supra* note 37.

[45] Saddam and his advisers frequently referred to Izzat Ibrahim al-Duri, the deputy chairman of the Revolutionary Command Council (RCC), as "the deputy."

[46] According to Kamil, Saddam had planned to attack Kuwait and eastern Saudi Arabia in August 1995 but called the invasion off after the defection. It is unclear whether the "battle" Saddam and his advisers are discussing refers to a planned invasion, an Iraqi refusal to continue cooperating with UN inspectors, or something else. See Jamal Halaby, "Defector Says Iraq Was Set to Invade; the Reported Targets: Kuwait, Saudi Arabia," *Chicago Sun-Times*, 21 August 1995.

Saddam: But we have to verify his relationship with the Russian deputy [Foreign] minister [Viktor Posuvalyuk], the Jewish guy who visited us several times and who made sure to visit Iraq lately to meet with him.[47]

Tariq: But during his last visit he [Posuvalyuk] said that he wanted to meet with the president and with Tariq [Aziz] and Hussein Kamil. Meeting Hussein Kamil was very important. I even told the foreign minister to let the President know so that he could wash his hands of it, but he said that it was important to meet Hussein Kamil.

Saddam: Hussein Kamil brought us news saying that the Kuwaitis [were] asking for a relationship through a Kuwaiti businessman. I told you about this.

Tariq: Yes, Sir.

Saddam: He discussed this with him and when he did so, I told him, "Once you go to Moscow, meet with him."

Tariq: He saw him. The delegation told us that he disappeared for six hours, I mean for a few hours, but nobody knew where he was. Anyway, Sir, in July – King Hussein revealed this, King Hussein is going to help us a lot in shedding light on the situation – King Hussein said he came and explained the situation. King Hussein said, "Of course, I sent a message with him." But it is obvious that he told King Hussein that the situation was not good and that it should change, and perhaps he told him that I [Hussein Kamil] have agreed with the Americans or I am ready for this change. His latest travel was planned. On the 27th of July, he requested reports from Husam Muhammad Amin and from Dr. Mahdi [Obeidi] about the latest development in relations between the Special Commission and Iraq from Husam, and he requested a report from Mahdi since he was working on a program that was obsolete, dead, and nobody has been asking about for the last four years. He took it. He asked him to tell him about it and then he wrote about it to me.[48] Therefore, on the 27th of July he had in mind –

Saddam: He already decided.

Izzat: Even before the 27th –

Saddam: In the last ten days, I saw on the faces of three of them something wrong, but did not think it was conspiracy.

Tariq: Because he was getting close to the timing!

Saddam: I interpreted it that something was bothering them. His brother, my escort, was complaining about a migraine, etc. I even agreed with one of them, their younger

---

[47] Posuvalyuk reportedly met with Kamil on 8 July 1995 in the Russian republic of Kalmykia. One week after Kamil returned from this trip, the two met alone for an hour in Baghdad. These and a handful of other events led Iraqi officials to question whether Russia had played a hidden role in the defection. See SH-IISX-D-000-768, "Reports Concerning Hussein Kamil's Treason and Escape with Reference to a Uranium Enrichment Program," June 1995–July 1997.

[48] Kamil met with Mahdi Obeidi, who had headed Iraq's centrifuge program, the night before the defection. Obeidi wrote that Kamil had asked him questions about the centrifuge program during this meeting, but Obeidi's account says nothing about Kamil requesting a written report on 27 July. See Obeidi, *The Bomb in My Garden: The Secrets of Saddam's Nuclear Mastermind* (Hoboken, NJ: John Wiley and Sons, 2004), 162–65.

brother. I said to him, "Where have you been? I haven't seen you for a while?" His face did not look relaxed to me. He said, "Sir, I was sick" or something. During the last 10 to 20 days his decision was final.

Tariq: It seems that they started making arrangements since July.

Tariq: Sir, he had to get out before the end of August even if it was a week before. Why? Because he needed time to prepare the information for the Americans and the Americans needed to classify this information and enter it into the computer so that at the end of August they could give to the president of the Special Commission or present it at the Security Council. He needed to be outside of Iraq before August 30th.[49]

Saddam: The timing was appropriate for planning.

Tariq: But he rushed by ten days or a week for other reasons. It is possible. This is the political aspect that provides evidence. Otherwise what are these joint maneuvers between Jordan and America?

THE DEVIATION: EFFECTS OF THE DEFECTION ON THE REGIME

In addition to implications for the sanctions regime, Hussein Kamil's defection had potentially dire implications for Saddam and his former comrades. First, Saddam and his inner circle were afraid that Hussein Kamil was plotting with the Americans and Jordanians to overthrow Saddam. A memo written by the Iraqi intelligence service several days after Hussein's defection observed that the escape coincided with the following:

1. America's pressure to reach an agreement among Kurds, to stop intransigence among themselves, and to coordinate with them to attack Iraqi military formations[50]
2. American military exercises with Jordan near the Iraqi border
3. American military exercises in Kuwait
4. Deployment of American forces in the region[51]

---

[49] In July 1995, Iraq had threatened to cease all cooperation with UNSCOM and the International Atomic Energy Agency (IAEA) if the United Nations did not move to end the sanctions by the close of August. "UNSCOM: Chronology of Main Events," accessed 5 November 2008 at www.un.org/Depts/unscom/Chronology/chronologyframe.htm.

[50] Mustafa-al-Barzani's Kurdish Democratic Party and Jalal Talabani's Patriotic Union of Kurdistan (PUK) fought a civil war for control of the Kurdish north in the mid-1990s. By August 1994, the fighting had killed one thousand Kurds and displaced more than seventy thousand. Phebe Marr, *The Modern History of Iraq*, 2nd ed. (Boulder, CO: Westview Press, 2004), 280.

[51] See SH-IISX-D-000-407, "Report by the Director of Iraq's Intelligence Service on the Defection of Hussein Kamil," 29 August 1995.

The memo went on to declare, "At the early part of 1995, American intelligence and the U.S. Congress received information that Mr. President the Commander [Saddam] would remain in power for [only] six–eight months if economic sanctions remained." Last, the intelligence memo noted:

Following the criminal escape of Hussein Kamil, the Secretary of Defense William Perry announced on 15/8/1995 that he invites the Iraqi opposition to stand behind Hussein Kamil as he represents an alternative to Mr. President, the Commander, God forbid, as he is a strong Sunni man and is capable of maintaining order.[52]

Second, the incident raised the ugly question of trust. Might there be additional traitors in their midst? Saddam did not look kindly on treason and reportedly once commented that he knew who would betray him even before they themselves knew.[53]

Saddam and His Senior Advisers Speculate That Hussein Kamil May Be Conspiring with Jordan and the United States to Provoke Iraq (mid- to late August 1995)[54]

Male 3: Sir, the [military] maneuvers between Jordan and America – what is their goal? Israel?

Saddam: The American president is threatening that if Iraq tries to interfere –

Male 3: The maneuvers, Sir, are preplanned, but they are maneuvers between Jordan and America and they are the first in the history of the relationship between Jordan and the US. Preparing the Jordanian army for what? What is the Jordanian army? It is only protection for the regime. The Jordanian army is prepared for a war. The military support is a cover.

Saddam: Conspiring support.

Male 3: A cover. Second, King Hussein called [U.S. president Bill] Clinton to tell him that they [Hussein Kamil's party] had arrived.

Saddam: On the same night at four o'clock.[55]

Male 3: They knew that people were coming and he wanted to tell him that they arrived. And Clinton announced it. Yes, they were exposed. That gave us a clear indication that this has a political aspect to it. There is a political and conspiratorial political aspect related to the fate of the regime and related to the timings that we have determined for the prospects of battle. Then he [Hussein Kamil] revealed himself in

---

52 See SH-IISX-D-000-407, "Report by the Director of Iraq's Intelligence Service on the Defection of Hussein Kamil," 29 August 1995.

53 Woods et al., *Iraqi Perspectives Project: A View Of* (2005), 7n35.

54 *SH-SHTP-A-001-260, "Saddam Discussing the Details of Hussein Kamil's Escape," undated (circa mid- to late August 1995).

55 It is unclear how the Iraqis came to this conclusion. President Clinton does not mention this in his recounting of the episode in William Jefferson Clinton, *My Life* (New York: Random House, 2004).

the press conference by saying that he is working against the regime.[56] When we return to the scenario of his behavior, according to King Hussein's claims, he was recommending moderation in dealing with countries and he was recommending resolving problems in order to lift the sanctions fast. That is not true, Sir. Everyone knows that Hussein was promoting tension in relations. In one meeting, if you remember, in April, May, or June, he expressed deep doubt in France and Russia. He was saying: "Why do we depend on France? And who said that France is faithful to us? And how do we know that Russia, France, and America are not swapping roles?" Do you understand, Sir?

Saddam: Yes, I do.

Male 3: I even answered him, and I told him that these are countries that have interests [in Iraq]. He wanted us to doubt. He wanted us to reach a point of absolute discouragement.

Saddam: So we do not make the decision.[57]

Male 3: To the contrary, he wanted us to make a decision while we are feeling discouraged and feel that we have no option but getting into a battle, because there is no other option. Because there is no political alternative and there is nobody who will help us in lifting the sanctions [inaudible]. The issue of the [inaudible], you see what role it has in the embargo. Especially in the last three months, it became clear that once you compare between this and that, there is a clear chain for a plan that aims at sending a military attack against us. He knows the areas that can hurt us in economics and security. He knows them well. His information will be exact: "Hit this electricity station."

Saddam: No one has better information than he has.

Male 3: Yes, this refinery, this site. He will paralyze the economic and security situation. He knows then that he is the alternative. He will announce before then, but this is when he will come to take control. Also, we should ask the intelligence to find out what American individuals and land forces are in the maneuvers [with Jordan], because sea maneuvers include Marines. Among the issues we should also consider is the possibility for a plan to create a tense situation on the Iraqi-Jordanian border, in order to justify bringing in a land force. They will blame Iraq to justify the action. They will bring an Iraqi general to say – who sees the people that come in if the Americans do not film it. Those who will enter will say that the Iraqi army joined Hussein Kamil, and they are forming a revolution against the regime. They will come close to the borders of Baghdad within a confusing situation and lack of communications and electricity. I think that this issue was planned a long time ago.

I am starting to doubt this guy who came to us. Perhaps he does not know, but perhaps Clinton sent him to us to deceive us into thinking that we might start

---

[56] See "Iraqi Defector's News Conference: Husayn Kamil Hasan says he will work for the Overthrow of the Iraqi Government," Jordanian TV, Amman (in Arabic), 12 August 1995, in BBC Summary of World Broadcasts, 14 August 1995.

[57] From the context, this appears to be a reference to Saddam's threat to cease cooperating with UNSCOM if the sanctions were not lifted.

negotiating with them, in order to facilitate things.[58] The other forces [*inaudible*] the French. Sir, let us review the reports. The French, during his meeting with Barzan[59] said you should not behave the way America wants you to behave. Go back to the report, Sir. Do not keep pushing the Special Commission, because this is what America wants. The Russians – regardless of the possibilities that Dr. [Viktor] Posuvalyuk might be collaborating and has something. They gave us the same advice. Ivanov[60] –

Saddam: – was clear.

Male 3: Was clear. The two sides that helped us and who have intelligence informa-tion have greatly warned against rushing to the end of August. Not to support the [UN] Special Commission, but because they feel that something is being arranged. We should keep in mind this political aspect while we analyze the situation.

Male 2: Mr. President, during the press conference he presented himself [*inaudible*] in the best interest of the Iraqi people, and that he has old disagreements [*inaudible*].

Male 3: This is contrary to his behavior over the last five years since we entered the escalation with Kuwait.

Saddam and the National Command Speculate That King Hussein Is Using Hussein Kamil to Provoke a Confrontation with Iraq (17 August 1995)[61]

Male 4: Some of the comrades from Iraq are wondering if the [*inaudible*] will be held, because they are in the national office and they do not know and are not enlightened. I think the faster we are, the more dangerous it is, because the Party needs to issue something. In addition to what the comrades have said, there is one more possibility with all the other options: thinking about using Hussein Kamil in confrontation with Iraq. In my estimation, after reading King Hussein's interview with the Zionist newspaper, King Hussein believes he has a larger role than he actu-ally does and perhaps he used Hussein Kamil. But the impression is that the goal is to apply pressure more than change. The goal is pressure: pressuring the leadership and the party in Iraq, more than change. In spite of denying that he is communi-cating with leaders, Saddam Hussein and the leadership in Iraq, in the last meeting between him and Hussein Kamil, he said I gave him a verbal message to the Presi-dent telling him there needs to be change in the understandings that you presented earlier.

Saddam: The same message that Hussein – Qasim brought. He wants us to have relations with Israel to end the embargo with America. Hussein Kamil brought me the message and I told him this is a silly message, because he sent me Marwan

---

[58] This is a possible reference to U.S. Representative Bill Richardson's meeting with Saddam in July 1995 to negotiate the release of two U.S. prisoners. See section "Iraqis discuss communications with the Clinton Administration," in Chapter 1.

[59] Barzan Ibrahim al-Tikriti, Iraq's ambassador to the United Nations in Geneva.

[60] Probably Igor Ivanov, Russian first deputy minister of foreign affairs.

[61] *SH-SHTP-A-001-259, "Saddam and Top Political Advisers Discussing Hussein Kamil's Mental Health and Problems with King Hussein of Jordan," 17 August 1995.

al-Qasim.[62] I explained to Marwan al-Qasim that if you want the bilateral relations to stay normal, do not bring in Israel and please end this subject.[63] He tried again and I told him, "I told you to end this subject. Our position is clear."[64] I told Hussein Kamil that those defeatists need people to be defeated with them in order to see that they are not alone in that defeat. For Iraq this is impossible. Before he walked in, he shut his mouth. This is the message.

Male 4: This is the talk: changing the understanding and joining the peace process.

Saddam: We will not change our understanding and we will not join the peace process. That is our answer. Because our understandings are right, our understandings are right, unless they can install people like Hussein Kamil, who would change the understandings and the direction of Iraq. This will never happen.

Male 4: We are sure of this.

Iraq's Minister of Finance Worries That the Defection Will Destroy Trust within Saddam's Inner Circle (mid- to late August 1995)[65]

Hikmat: As for my second observation, it seems to me that the trust we place in each other is exaggerated and needs to be evaluated, and this traitor was trusted by all of us. He claimed that some of what he did was on your orders. In addition, you personally were aware of his activities . . . I was confused about how to handle the situation. If we had reported all of his activities to the President [Saddam], this might not have happened, but this is not a realistic way to handle the situation, because the President has no time for small things like this. Then I started thinking about how the President trusts us after all this. He [Kamil] was shameless. Any person who has honor needs to review his personal [conduct] and his family conduct. After all, this person [Kamil] was shameless and the problem is, do we have to convey small and big issues to the president? This would be unreasonable. One

---

[62] Marwan Qasim was the chief of the Royal Court in Jordan and a former Jordanian foreign minister (1988–1991).

[63] Jordan had signed a peace treaty and established diplomatic relations with Israel in 1994.

[64] Nigel Ashton, who had access to King Hussein's private archives, wrote that in early summer 1995, Israeli Prime Minister Yitzhak Rabin asked King Hussein to arrange an invitation for him to meet with Saddam in Baghdad. In June, the king sent Marwan Qasim to Saddam with a letter requesting such an invitation. "Saddam did not rule out direct contacts with Rabin," Ashton wrote but also did not want "to work through lower-level intermediaries." Jordan's acceptance and protection of Kamil caused relations between Iraq and Jordan to plummet, which ended the effort to arrange a high-level meeting. See Ashton, *King Hussein of Jordan*, 337–38. According to an internal Iraqi report dated 18 July 2001, Saddam told Nikolai Kartuzov, Russia's ambassador-at-large and former ambassador to Baghdad, that Marwan had proposed to King Hussein that improving relations between Baghdad and Tel Aviv would improve conditions for Iraq. Saddam claimed he told Marwan that he was uninterested, as his regime was not the bargaining type. The Iraqi leader also stated that the United States was behind Marwan's effort, as well as a similar message from the Vatican. See SH-SPPC-D-000-334, "Transcript of a Meeting between Saddam and a Russian Delegation," 18 July 2001.

[65] SH-SHTP-A-000-762, "Saddam and Iraqi Ministers Discussing the Treason of Hussein Kamil," undated (circa mid- to late August 1995).

of the small issues, for example, is the shameless Abd al-Jalil case.[66] One word please, Mr. President. I believe that every person who has honor and nationalism, that nothing would change him unless something from deep in his mind shocked him, and we need to review our character and examine ourselves and our family behavior. I do not know how our President will trust us? The first thing I thought about was how this mountain of Iraq [Saddam] did not tremble. I do not understand, Mr. President!

Saddam Thanks Revolutionary Command Council Members for Their Loyalty and Notes That Treason Is Not Unique to Iraq (15 August 1995)[67]

Saddam: I hate to interrupt Mr. Adnan.[68] My friends, I hope that you hear each other, because the topic needs all these stories, so all of us can learn lessons. Your respect for Hussein Kamil was not for his personality, even when he crossed his limits. And I want to thank you because you were respecting him or – let me phrase it more accurately – you were tolerating him and tolerating his disadvantages just for this reason, which is Saddam Hussein. Therefore, I thank you very much. Because the principle in my assumption is that you respect Saddam Hussein, and you have such a large amount of love for him on a national basis and not on a personal basis. So you tolerated the person who insulted you very much and insulted the country and insulted the course with its great meanings, because it seemed that he had the trust of Saddam Hussein, and because you value Saddam Hussein in your hearts. And you tolerated what you suffered because of him, and I do understand that. But so that the deviation and the treason do not recur, which might recur . . . Is the treason, which we have in Iraq, exclusive?

Male 2: Of course not.

Saddam: The answer on the general international level is "no."

THE RECKONING: THE DEATH OF HUSSEIN KAMIL

On 17 February, Hussein Kamil wrote a letter to Saddam in which he begged for forgiveness and permission to return to Iraq. Taped telephone conversations between Kamil and a reporter indicate that the defector expected a positive response and was "excited, expectant, constantly expressing his admiration for Iraq and its President, at times bursting into laughter." Kamil expressed trust in Saddam's generosity based on family relationships: "He was my uncle before he was my father-in-law. We are one

---

[66] This appears to refer to Ghanem Abd al-Jalil Saudi, a former member of the RCC, whom Saddam had executed for treason in 1979. See Karsh and Rautsi, *Saddam Hussein*, 115.

[67] SH-SHTP-A-000-837, "Saddam and Senior Political Advisers Discussing the Treason of Hussein Kamil," undated (circa late 1995–early 1996).

[68] From the context, this appears to be Adnan 'Abd al-Majid Jasim al-'Ani, who replaced Kamil as minister of industry and minerals.

family."[69] Kamil's faith in his family ties is ironic, given that he met his end in a shootout with tribal members on his return. On behalf of his tribe, Chemical Ali condemned Kamil's betrayal in the starkest of terms:

This small family [of al-Majids] in Iraq denounces Hussein Kamil's cowardly act and strongly rejects the treason which he has committed and which can only be cleansed by inflicting punishment on him in accordance with the Law of God... His family has unanimously decided to permit with impunity the spilling of [his] blood.[70]

In the following recording, Tariq reads Saddam a letter in which Kamil requests a pardon and permission to return. Izzat advises Saddam to allow the return, on condition that it be handled in a way that will not harm the regime. Perhaps foreshadowing the regime's differentiation between a state pardon and a tribal pardon, Izzat comments, "We do not want to take revenge, the revenge is the revenge of the Iraqi people..."

Saddam, Tariq, and Izzat Read a Letter from Hussein Kamil and Discuss Conditions for the Defector's Return (17–19 February 1996)[71]

Tariq: This is a letter from Hussein Kamil to Mr. President:

God's fiduciary and his Prophet, in the name of God, the most merciful, the Compassionate. Mr. President, the Commander, may God protect you, and make you glorious, as God is the one who listens and he is the one who fulfills. Dear Sir, first, I would like to extend my complete apology for what has happened despite its dangerous nature. And I hope that you accept my apology for this, and I know how compassionate you are.[72] I know your generosity and know very well your ability to overcome all crises no matter how complex they become, and I am confident of your firmness and history will vouch for Your Excellency. Mr. Commander, I never intended at any given day to leave my country and stay far away from it, and it never crossed my mind to hurt Your Excellency and I have never fathomed to live anywhere except in my country.[73] I am among those who criticize anyone who wishes

---

[69] Robert Fisk, "Tapes Reveal Why Iraqi Traitor Went Back to Die: Robert Fisk Hears the Last Testament of the Man Who Betrayed Saddam," *Independent* (London), 28 February 1996.

[70] Hiro, *Neighbours, Not Friends*, 95.

[71] *SH-SHTP-A-001-205, "Saddam and His Inner Circle Discussing a Letter from Hussein Kamil," 19 February 1996. It appears that Hussein Kamil dictated the letter to his brother, Saddam Kamil.

[72] In an interview with *Time* magazine on 18 September 1995, Kamil offered a less favorable (but more accurate) assessment of Saddam's compassion: "If there is a conversation between two people in which one of them criticizes any subject related to the regime, the fate of both of them is execution. Anybody who criticizes the regime, even in the slightest way, faces execution." Moreover, "I know the regime in Iraq. I knew even before my departure that they would be ready to set aside the entire Iraqi budget to eliminate Hussein Kamil." See Dean Fischer, "Inside Saddam's Brutal Regime," *Time*, 18 September 1995.

[73] Saddam was certainly aware of Kamil's public efforts "to topple the regime" in Iraq. See "Iraqi Defector's News Conference: Husayn Kamil Hasan says he will work for the Overthrow of the Iraqi Government," Jordanian TV, Amman, 12 August 1995, in *BBC Summary of World Broadcasts*, 14 August 1995.

to reside away from his country, and I consider this to be a strange and unbeneficial event.

As for the reason why I left my country and stay away from it, Mr. Commander, and God is my witness, we were subjected to grave and unexpected circumstances. This unfortunate event has forced me to leave quickly against my will, leaving behind my country, family, relatives and everything. However, I was forced to do that and I did not know where I would settle, and I did not even know my fate, and I hope that you forgive me for not explaining in sufficient detail here, for fear that someone will read my letter and know its details. And this is a personal matter, and I hope that no one will read this except Your Excellency. This way you can evaluate the circumstance and know exactly what has happened. Anyway, the matter is left for Your Excellency's assessment.

Your Excellency, Mr. Commander, following my departure, it never crossed my mind at all to hurt anyone from near or far. However, what has frustrated me are these allegations that were issued against me from some officials in Baghdad, as they claim that I am an agent for the American intelligence.[74] And this is insane, and this is an allegation that will not be accepted to be issued by anyone. Why am I accused of espionage against my country and for whose benefit? Even though I have dedicated my life for the sake of my country, serving it in construction, serving it by fighting for its defense, and my life was subjected to destruction a thousand times without any fear from me and without retreat. All that I wanted was to uphold the name of my country in pride and in the name of Mr. President, the Commander. And consequently, I was accused by those who knew me very well. They allege that I am a hostile spy, working against my country, and this is an unfathomable injustice. Your Excellency appreciates that very well and knows that we were raised hating the Americans. So why am I accused of being a spy for America against Iraq, which is in our blood, and we do not breathe anything except Iraq's air, and without Iraq, there is no life for us?

Anyway, the important matter, Your Excellency, Mr. President, is that we thank God for your safety and your health, and we hope that God will always be on your side to protect our glorious leader Saddam Hussein. May God protect him and defend him and lengthen his life. I want Your Excellency to know that your photo and the photo of all your kind family is hanging in every angle of the house, and from day one of our arrival, and every time we receive new photos, their numbers accumulate, and this is a known fact, Your Excellency. Our children did not know

---

[74] Tariq, for one, publicly accused Kamil of working for the CIA. The day before he returned to Iraq, Kamil insisted that he had not revealed any sensitive information "because Iraq, while I was there, had already completed the elimination of all weapons of mass destruction." He continued, "Nothing was left...It was not me who disclosed this but Baghdad which has uncovered all its cards. I did not reveal more than Baghdad did." Ekeus confirmed, "He was always quite cautious in his conversations with us," and "He told the U.N. 'I will not give you anything which I consider undermining or would put in doubt the security of Iraq.' So, he was not spilling everything he knew in these talks..." See "Former Defector Denies Giving Away Iraq's Secrets," *Agence France-Presse*, 22 February 1996; Ben Barber and Bill Gertz, "Iraqi Defectors Return to Baghdad with Pardons: Move Taints Data from Saddam's Kin," *Washington Times*, 21 February 1996; "US Forces in Show of Strength," [Melbourne] *Sunday Herald Sun*, 20 August 1995.

until today the reason for our departure and leaving Baghdad... they always recall Papa Saddam and Mama Sajidah,[75] also, their brothers Uday and Qusay and their aunty and maternal cousins. This is their daily topic. They keep reminding us. They keep dreaming their vision, their dreams of viewing Your Excellency and the kind family. They compete with each other to describe stories of those dreams, and even the young one, he started to imagine many stories with different variations.

I repeat my sincere apology to Mr. President for what I have done, and the rest is reserved for Your Excellency. And I say to Your Excellency that I am loyal to you and the defense of our country Iraq, and this is a fact, and I hope that God Almighty protects you. And I cannot read what he is writing, not I nor anyone else, and God is my witness, I will be closer than anyone for the purpose of serving Your Excellency. And I promise that I will personally learn from this lesson, for the sake and service of my country, and I will avoid as much as possible all mistakes, and [accept] whatever fate has for me. I hope that Mr. President, the Commander, will forgive us and permit us to return to our country Iraq so that we can live under your umbrella and your large tent, and may God bless you.[76] My warmest greetings to Your Excellency and to the entire family, with all respect and salutations. Written by Saddam Kamil, date 17 February.

Saddam: Comrade, the Deputy.

Izzat: Your Excellency, I hope that this matter will be discussed in a deep, scientific, political, and preliminary manner. I mean it is not as simple as the comrades made it appear. This is not a case of one of us becoming angry and leaving for a few days, and wanting to make up with him. Or a case in which he wants to make up with us, and we will save face and tell him to come. It is not that simple. Principally, the question should be, is it better for Hussein [Kamil] to remain outside [Iraq]? Or is it better for him to return? I believe his return is better, even if he used up all his tricks, and it appears that this is the case. He does not have anything else to give, that is why he felt that, not only that he has ruined his life, but he also has ruined his family's life as well. He felt that if he continued to commit such stupidity, the shame would follow him wherever he went and would follow our circles as well. He has committed grave errors, errors that are rarely committed, in terms of details and as a matter of principle.

But we have to discuss how he will be coming back. This way we have carried out our duties toward our people. We have educated our people, we have educated our party. Our party has criticized us a lot, and our people have criticized us a lot. The fifth columns and our enemies have instigated such criticism; they started to spread hostile propaganda against us. So many stories were written about the betrayal of Hussein Kamil. So is it just like that and with such ease that we issue forgiveness and tell our people, "No big deal"? Or do we just tell the people that Hussein Kamil has apologized and then we will allow him to return?

First, my opinion is – this way I am not wasting your time – I believe that [*inaudible*] it is not our objective to take revenge against Hussein [Kamil] and it is not our

----

[75] Saddam's wife, the mother-in-law of Hussein Kamil.
[76] Living under Saddam's umbrella and tent indicates being under his protection and care.

objective to take revenge against Hussein, in terms of our maternal relationship, but we have to account for his behavior. However, all Iraqis – we do not want to take revenge, the revenge is the revenge of the Iraqi people – not from the South, not from the North, not from the Dawa [P]arty,[77] not from the Communist [P]arty, not from such and such party, [*inaudible*] from any Iraqi element, from any of these directions. So, on principle, if his return is better than his stay overseas, then we have to formulate his return in a manner that will not harm us, or harm our party or harm our people.

We should dispatch one representative and tell him to write a letter in which he should criticize his actions. He has to confess that he has committed criminal actions first against the person who created him, the person who took him when he was a child from his mother and created him, and then he betrayed him. This should be the first confession he should state in that letter. And then he should state that it was through his betrayal [that] he has betrayed his doctrine, his principles, his path, and that he will return without any condition or stipulations and he is ready to be hanged in the biggest public square in Baghdad as a sacrifice to the Commander's principles and the Commander's image.[78] But you and we should give him the message that there will be a pardon granted to him. I believe this is the way for his return, [the letter] should include this sharp text. If it is not sharp enough, then his arrival will harm us, then it would be better for him not to return.

---

[77] The Dawa Party was a Shiite opposition group. Membership in the party was punishable by death.

[78] On 20 February 1996, Iraqi television reported that Saddam presented a combined meeting of the RCC and State Command with a letter in which Hussein Kamil requested a pardon and permission to return to Iraq. The RCC and State Command approved the request. For copies of what appear to be the two letters in which Kamil asked Saddam for forgiveness, see SH-SPPC-D-000-915, "Letters to Saddam from Hussein Kamil Requesting Forgiveness," February 1996. See also "Return of Husayn Kamil: Iraqi TV Reports Return of Husayn Kamil," BBC *Summary of World Broadcasts*, 22 February 1996.

Epilogue

The editors of this volume have worked intimately with Saddam's legacy for several years. We believe that the contents of this study well reflect the Saddam we know. This, of course, is an utterly subjective judgment. Furthermore, some recordings capture only part of what are clearly longer-running conversations on the same topic, or they capture narrow aspects of wider-ranging conversations. For these reasons, we do not believe that readers should consider our conclusions here, such as they are, definitive. Years of work will be required before an ecological understanding of Saddam emerges.[1] As U.S. Secretary of Defense Robert Gates has argued, important insights and lessons will remain hidden until the Iraqi records are publicly available to the academic community.[2] Because the purpose of this study is more to invite future research than to present a definitive analysis of authoritarian decision making, we have left detailed analyses of Saddam's psyche and the role of bureaucratic politics in Iraq to others.

This study will have succeeded if it encourages scholars to use the Conflict Records Research Center (CRRC) to study the collection of recordings and supporting materials. After all, there is no shortage of work to do. Although this study focuses on Saddam Hussein, it is also about the United States. Saddam's regime is gone forever, yet the need remains for U.S. policy makers to accurately assess which policies toward Iraq worked and which did not. Then they must wrestle with the more complicated issue of why a given policy succeeded or failed if the lessons are to help shape options for situations unrelated to events in Iraq.

---

[1] An ecological approach to history considers "how components interact to become systems whose nature can't be defined merely by calculating the sum of their parts." John Lewis Gaddis, *The Landscape of History: How Historians Map the Past* (New York: Oxford University Press, 2004), 55.

[2] Robert M. Gates's speech to the Association of American Universities, Washington, D.C., 14 April 2008, accessed 9 June 2009 at www.defenselink.mil/speeches/speech.aspx?speechid= 1228.

From left to right, Taha Ramadan, an unknown brigadier general (in the background), Izzat al-Duri, and Saddam. The date is unknown. (*Source:* *SH-MISC-D-001-278, "Taha Yasin Ramadan's Photo Album," April 2000).

The editors have not settled on a set of discrete conclusions, yet certain predominant patterns have surfaced as a result of our efforts. Saddam emerges from the manuscript as a highly competent, intelligent, but intellectually undisciplined decision maker – a lively, quick-witted, and fickle man given to restless digressions on a surprising range of topics, many of which he appeared to understand poorly or in decidedly unique ways. At times, his worldview, borrowing a British diplomat's description of Stalin, consisted of a "curious mix of shrewdness and nonsense."[3] Men like Hitler, Stalin, and, we believe, Saddam, were deluded about a great deal; nevertheless, they were unquestionably masters of their particular craft: gaining, maintaining, and exercising power. Although this work does not directly address Saddam's efforts to gain or maintain power, these areas are well covered in existing literature; it does offer insights into the object of his quest – the exercise of power. The captured Iraqi tapes, and the CRRC more generally, provide

[3] Christopher Andrew and Julie Elkner, "Stalin and Foreign Intelligence," *Totalitarian Movements and Political Religions* 4, no. 1 (2003): 77.

Saddam and Taha Ramadan enjoy a lighter moment. The date is unknown. (*Source:* *SH-MISC-D-001-278, "Taha Yasin Ramadan's Photo Album," April 2000).

rich ground for understanding this historically recurring mix of competence and incompetence.

The tapes provide abundant evidence of Saddam's brutality. This is important, particularly regarding the occupation of Kuwait, as popular histories of the Gulf War often focus far more on coalition military history or critiques of policy and style than on portraying the overall barbarism of the occupation.[4] This focus has led too many observers to underestimate the depravity of official Iraqi behavior.[5] The captured tapes, by contrast, reveal that Saddam heard reports, and in many cases explicitly approved, of his lieutenants treating Kuwaitis "harshly, really harshly." Harsh behavior included cutting off tongues; summarily executing those who voiced opposition; collectively punishing communities for harboring resistors; and to discourage others, "slaughtering" resistors in front of their wives before burning down their homes.[6]

[4] For instance, see John R. MacArthur, "Remember Nayirah, Witness for Kuwait?" in *The Iraq War Reader: History, Documents, Opinions*, ed. Micah L. Sifry and Christopher Cerf (New York: Simon and Schuster, 2003), 135–37.

[5] For a reaction by one such observer, see Tom Regan, "When Contemplating War, Beware of Babies in Incubators," *Christian Science Monitor*, 6 September 2002.

[6] See Chapter 5.

In certain areas, though, information in the tapes is more exculpatory. For instance, the recordings from the 1990s are consistent with the conclusion that Iraq no longer had weapons of mass destruction (WMD). Saddam explained to his advisers that Iraq lacked WMD, yet at times needed to withhold cooperation from UN inspectors to prevent Iraq's enemies from collecting intelligence and to preserve Iraq's honor and dignity.[7] Moreover, he said, he had concluded that the United States would pursue regime change regardless of Iraqi compliance with UN inspectors' demands.[8] Many analysts, in the United States and elsewhere, saw things similarly.[9] How U.S. policy might have differed had the United States had access to and understood the kind of information presented in this study will likely remain an argument without end.[10]

The tapes leave us uncertain, at times, how to apportion responsibility for Iraqi policies. The aphorism "Saddam is Iraq; Iraq is Saddam" provides a useful starting point, yet obfuscates even as it enlightens. Although there is certainly a great deal of truth behind allegations that fear of Saddam prevented Iraqi leaders from offering candid advice or opposing foreign adventurism or human rights abuses, Iraqi decision making was never completely reducible to one man. Saddam's advisers' accounts are often far too self-serving. According to an FBI report, Ahmed Hussein Khudayr al-Samarrai, who had served under Saddam as prime minister and foreign minister, told his interrogators it "simply was not true" that Revolutionary Command Council (RCC) decisions emerged "after debate and consultation":

[Saddam] Hussein made nearly all RCC decisions unilaterally without RCC input or debate. If meetings occurred at all, only Hussein's closest two or three advisors would have been involved. Khudayr generally learned of the RCC's "decisions" via a telephone from Saddam Hussein or from Presidential Secretary Abid Hamid Mahmud al-Tikriti.[11]

By contrast, the captured recordings suggest that responsibility for Iraqi policies was more diffuse. The range of opinions expressed in meetings with Saddam is at times striking – even on such vital questions as how to prepare the diplomatic ground for the invasion of Kuwait and what to do with

---

[7] See Chapter 7.

[8] See section "Saddam laments to senior advisers" in Chapter 7.

[9] Robert S. Litwak, *Regime Change: U.S. Strategy through the Prism of 9/11* (Washington, D.C.: Woodrow Wilson Center Press, 2007), 136–37; Malone, *The International Struggle over Iraq*, 157.

[10] The phrase "argument without end" is taken from the Dutch historian Pieter Geyl's famous definition of history. Pieter Geyl, *Use and Abuse of History* (New Haven, CT: Yale University Press, 1955), 47.

[11] Federal Bureau of Investigation, "Prosecutive Report of Investigation Concerning Saddam Hussein," 10 March 2005 (declassified 11 May 2009), 3.

Kuwait once invaded.[12] On a handful of occasions, Saddam even put issues to (nonunanimous) votes.[13] Saddam clearly found a few positions unacceptable, such as suggestions that he step down from power or that Iraq seek rapprochement with Israel, yet he appears to have generally encouraged discussion and even allowed debate.[14] Advisers advocated policies Saddam was likely to detest, such as withdrawing troops from Kuwait before the ground war began and cooperating fully with UN inspectors, by arguing that doing so would strengthen Saddam's hold on power or enable Iraq to escape a conspiracy.[15] When Nizar Hamdun sent Saddam a lengthy letter criticizing his policies and calling on the dictator to initiate democratic reforms, Saddam accused Nizar of disloyalty and attacked many of his assertions, yet distributed Nizar's missive for discussion among the Iraqi leadership.[16] Senior ministers such as Chemical Ali and Hussein Kamil, moreover, were able to disregard Saddam's directives in implementing policies.[17] Even in Saddam's Iraq, a degree of volition remained inviolate.

Scholars and analysts have largely discounted Iraqi defectors' WMD-related reports, yet self-serving defector claims from the 1980s continue to exert a tremendous, and largely unquestioned, influence on interpretations of Saddam's role in earlier Iraqi history. Recordings from the Iran-Iraq War, many of which were translated too late to be included in this study, indicate that Saddam's wartime behavior may have been less inept than observers have previously assessed. Whereas high-level defectors from Iraq's military and intelligence apparatuses cast blame for Iraq's military misfortunes squarely on Saddam's micromanagement of their work, and his misguided directives, the tapes suggest that Saddam was only partly to blame. Saddam clearly misunderstood much about warfare, foolishly invaded his

---

[12] See sections "Saddam and members of the Ba'ath Party" and "Five days after invading Kuwait," in Chapter 5.

[13] SH-SHTP-A-001-226, "Saddam and His Advisers Discussing Pan-Arab Security Issues," undated (circa January 1989); sections "Saddam and members of the Ba'ath Party" and "Five days after invading Kuwait" in Chapter 5.

[14] During the Iran-Iraq War, Saddam executed his health minister for suggesting that Saddam end the war by temporarily stepping down as president of Iraq. In 1984, Tariq Aziz told Rumsfeld that if Tariq encouraged Saddam to improve relations with Israel, Saddam would have him executed. See Woods et al., *Iraqi Perspectives Project: A View Of* (2006), 7–10; Howard Teicher, "Testimony before the United States District Court, Southern District of Florida," 31 January 1995, accessed 2 June 2009 at www.gwu.edu/~nsarchiv/NSAEBB/NSAEBB82/iraq61.pdf.

[15] Section "As coalition ground forces storm into Southern Iraq and Kuwait," in Chapter 5; section "Saddam and his inner circle discuss Iraq's intelligence on future UN inspection," in Chapter 7.

[16] See SH-SPPC-D-000-498, "Letter and Memo Responding to Ambassador Nizar Hamdun's Criticisms of the Iraqi Regime," November 1995; Pipes, "Obituary for Nizar Hamdoon (1944–2003)."

[17] Federal Bureau of Investigation, "Prosecutive Report of Investigation Concerning Saddam Hussein," 43; Chapter 8.

much larger neighbor, and too frequently micromanaged affairs about which he knew little, yet his generals were also "'winging it' and filling body bags" as they "sort[ed] out what work[ed]."[18] The tapes indicate that Saddam came to realize months into the war, before his generals, that Iraq would never be able to force Iran to make peace by attacking solely military targets. He pushed his generals to expand the war by going after Iranian economic targets, which, it seemed to him, benefited Iraq.[19] According to Lieutenant General Ra'ad Hamdani, a Republican Guard commander, Saddam's decisions during the war helped his military deal with loss of control in the field and, in at least one key instance, kept a defeat from turning into a disaster.[20] As in the case of the Iran-Iraq War, ongoing translation efforts and interviews with former officials will continue to enhance our understanding of the topics presented in this study.

Whether and how Saddam's statements vary in different settings promises to reveal much about his thinking and beliefs. For instance, one interesting insight from the Iraqi recordings and documents is the consistency between Saddam's public speeches and his private conversations. Saddam's conspiratorial, anti-Semitic worldview provides an excellent case in point. In public, Saddam and his subordinates blasted Israel and Jews for pushing Iran to initiate hostilities with Iraq, perpetuating the war by supplying Iran with weapons, persuading the United States to clandestinely arm Iran, encouraging Kuwait to undermine Iraq's economy by overproducing oil, and so forth.[21] Although Saddam might have publicly expressed opposition to Israel as a tactic to increase his following in the Arab world, the frequency with which he articulated anti-Jewish and/or anti-Israel sentiments and these same conspiracy theories in private suggests that such expressions were genuine. Comparative content analyses of Saddam's private and public language will enable more authoritative conclusions. In the meantime, as Woods and Stout wrote about the lessons Saddam took from the Gulf War, his record appears to show "that, by and large, Saddam repeatedly laid out his views in public ... Saddam, it turns out, was quite sincere in this way."[22]

---

[18] General James N. Mattis, commander of U.S. Joint Forces Command, wrote, "'Winging it' and filling body bags as we sort out what works reminds us of the moral dictates and the cost of competence in our profession." Williamson Murray and Richard Hart Sinnreich, eds., *The Past as Prologue: The Importance of History to the Military Profession* (New York: Cambridge University Press, 2006), 7.

[19] Kevin Woods and Williamson Murray are currently writing a book on the war that will discuss this in greater detail.

[20] Ra'ad Hamdani, *Qabl an Yugadiruna al-Tarikh* (Beirut: Arab Scientific Publishers, 2007), 82. The editors are grateful to Joseph Sassoon for bringing this point to our attention.

[21] Bengio, *Saddam's Word*, 134–39; Marr, *The Modern History of Iraq*, 224; FBIS, "Turkish Paper *Hurriyet* Interviews Saddam: Third Installment," *Hurriyet* (in Turkish), 13 February 1992.

[22] Woods and Stout, "Saddam's Perceptions and Misperceptions," 27.

Perhaps this sincerity should not be surprising.[23] Saddam wrote his own speeches: few advisers had the temerity to propose revisions, and even they knew that at times they must keep quiet.[24] The dictator also seemed to take pride in speaking his mind in public. "We speak freely against America without paying much attention to be careful in phrasing our statements," he boasted, unlike the Russians, who, he said, "are very meticulous in their choice of words to the extent of choosing every letter."[25] A more comprehensive treatment of Saddam would rest on detailed comparisons of information in his public speeches, his private conversations, FBI interrogation reports of the dictator and his subordinates, memoirs of key participants, and careful analyses of his behavior, many of which are only now beginning to enter the public sphere.[26]

The FBI's May 2009 declassification of many of Saddam's interrogation reports came as this book was nearing completion, thereby preventing the editors from thoroughly comparing information in the recordings with Saddam's claims to his interrogator. However, even a simple comparison of the two reveals stark differences. Saddam frequently denied decisions caught on tape and otherwise tried to avoid providing information to Special Agent George Piro, his interrogator, that he thought might be used to build a legal case against him. For instance, he told Piro that he had never ordered his military to remove equipment or other items from Kuwait, yet in a contemporary recording he angrily ordered his subordinates to intensify the looting.[27] He denied having discussed the possibility of using chemical weapons during the Mother of All Battles, claiming that such an idea did not even "cross our mind," yet several recordings belie this

---

[23] Bruce Jentleson notes that Saddam did not necessarily express his "true beliefs" in his public rhetoric; rather, he suggests, Saddam often spoke instrumentally to arouse "the Iraqi people to distract them from their own domestic plight and xenophobically legitimize his own brutal rule, and/or another effort at Nasserite casting of himself as the defender of the Arab world, and/or as a tacit bargaining strategy to intimidate an American administration." See Jentleson, *With Friends Like These*, 203–6.

[24] According to one of Saddam's interpreters, Saddam sent his most important speeches to the main leaders of the Ba'ath Party for vetting, but only Tariq and Houda Ammash dared to offer suggestions. See Saman Abdul Majid, *Les années Saddam: Révélations exclusives* (Paris: Fayard, 2003), 91–93.

[25] *SH-SHTP-A-001-262, "Saddam and Top Political Advisers Discussing the Iraqi Invasion of Kuwait and International Positions on Iraq," undated (circa late 1994). As Woods observes, "Saddam took great pride in saying in public what he intended and using subsequent events to validate his historic role." See Woods, *The Mother of all Battles*, 309.

[26] For instance, see Majid, *Les années Saddam*; "Saddam Hussein Talks to the FBI: Twenty Interviews and Five Conversations with 'High Value Detainee # 1' in 2004," accessed 5 September 2009 at www.gwu.edu/~nsarchiv/NSAEBB/NSAEBB279/index.htm; sources in note 7 of this study's Introduction.

[27] Piro interview of Saddam, Session Number 11, 3 March, 4; see also section "Saddam supports brutal counterinsurgency methods and pillaging Kuwait," in Chapter 5.

assertion.[28] Saddam said he knew nothing of Iraqi atrocities in Kuwait during Iraq's occupation, but this was far from true.[29] Other instances in which his claims in the interrogation reports clearly contradict information in captured recordings include whether Iraq had burned Kuwaiti oil fields, whether Saddam was aware of the 1991 Shi'a and Kurdish uprisings, if Iraq "abided totally" with UN decisions, and whether he had ordered his soldiers to respect the Geneva conventions.[30]

Saddam's claim that if sanctions ended he would have sought a U.S. security guarantee to protect Iraq from Iran is also suspect given that Saddam, as the tapes reveal, had deeply distrusted the United States for decades.[31] While in captivity, Saddam might have thought that emphasizing amity toward the United States, but enmity toward Iran, would benefit him in his upcoming trial. Then again, his pragmatic pursuit of rapprochement with long-standing adversaries (most notably Iran in late 1990) leaves one wondering whether his professed desire for an alliance of sorts with the United States might have been genuine.[32] Saddam reportedly thought the United States needed him. When Iraqi prosecutors announced that they sought his execution, he reportedly told his lawyer that this was merely a U.S. attempt to put greater pressure on him to secure his cooperation against Iran.[33]

Saddam's perception of his interrogator as the stenographer of his dictated memoirs is also worth considering. Piro, cognizant that Saddam would talk only if he felt that he stood to gain by doing so, encouraged his prisoner to answer questions "for the sake of history."[34] When Saddam spoke, he spoke with his legacy in mind. This was inevitable for someone as obsessed

---

[28] Piro interview of Saddam, Session Number 13, 11 March 2004, 4; see also sections "Saddam and his inner circle discuss Iraq's WMD capabilities and deterrent threats," "Saddam discusses with senior officials the circumstances under which Iraq will use chemical and biological weapons," and "Saddam and his advisers discuss Iraqi missile attacks on targets in Israel and Saudi Arabia," all in Chapter 6.

[29] Piro interview of Saddam, Session Number 10, 27 February 2004, 2; see also section "Saddam supports brutal counterinsurgency methods and pillaging Kuwait," in Chapter 5.

[30] Piro interview of Saddam, Session Number 10, 27 February 2004, 3–4; Piro interview of Saddam, Session Number 14, 13 March 2004, 3, 5; Piro interview of Saddam, Session Number 4, 13 February 2004, 5; Federal Bureau of Investigation, "Prosecutive Report of Investigation Concerning Saddam Hussein," 73; see also sections "Saddam reacts to the onset of the ground war," "Saddam and his commanders analyze the causes of the Kurdish and Shi'a uprisings," and "Saddam supports brutal counterinsurgency methods and pillaging Kuwait," all in Chapter 5; section "The Iraqi leadership discusses the memorandum of understanding," in Chapter 7.

[31] Piro casual conversation with Saddam, 11 June 2004, 3.

[32] For instances of Saddam's "revolutionary pragmatism," see Jerrold M. Post, *Leaders and Their Followers in a Dangerous World: The Psychology of Political Behavior* (Ithaca, NY: Cornell University Press, 2004), 215, 230–31.

[33] Yevgeny Primakov, *Russia and the Arabs: Behind the Scenes in the Middle East from the Cold War to the Present* (New York: Basic Books, 2009), 322.

[34] Piro interview of Saddam, Session Number 6, 16 February 2004, 5.

with his role in history as was Saddam. In the first interview, the former dictator commented that it was important to him what people would think of him five hundred or one thousand years in the future.[35] In later visits, he repeatedly expressed interest in having the interviews published.[36]

Above all, Saddam wished to be known as bold, daring, and noble. Much of his public language, Jerrold Post observed, is "designed to demonstrate his courage and resolve to the Iraqi people and the Arab world."[37] Americans were hostile and conspiratorial enemies, Saddam told his advisers toward the end of the Iran-Iraq War, yet Iraqi bravery and honor demanded even their respect.[38] "We [Iraqis] are among the few remaining cavaliers," he explained to Piro.[39] Although Saddam certainly believed much of what he told Piro, and many of his statements are correct (and even insightful), analysts should treat his claims from captivity with caution.

Memoirs and public statements are valuable but in many cases far less reliable than a state's internal records. In a contest between a contemporary recording, a public statement, and a memoir (including a dictated memoir), the recording is virtually always most reliable.[40] Hence the value of these particular captured records.

Writing about recordings, however, poses its own problems. The preface to the most recent edition of the State Department's Foreign Relations of the United States (FRUS) series mentions inaccuracies in earlier FRUS transcripts and notes:

Readers are advised that the tape recording is the official document, while the transcript represents solely an interpretation of that document... The most accurate transcripts possible... cannot substitute for listening to the recordings. Readers are urged to consult the recordings themselves for a full appreciation of those aspects of the conversations that cannot be captured in a transcript, such as the speakers' inflections and emphases that may convey nuances of meaning, as well as the larger context of the discussion.[41]

---

[35] Piro interview of Saddam, Session Number 1, 7 February 2004, 2.

[36] Piro interview of Saddam, Session Number 4, 13 February 2004, 1.

[37] Post, *Leaders and Their Followers*, 212, 224.

[38] He explained, "They [Americans] might not like you, they might conspire against you, but they respect you. If one of you went to them they would listen to you and respect you. It would be different if someone else went to them." *SH-SHTP-A-001-263, "Saddam Discussing US Policy in the Gulf," undated (circa 1988).

[39] Piro interview of Saddam, Session Number 4, 13 February 2004, 5.

[40] Although Marc Trachtenberg persuasively argues that documents (and especially recordings) are generally superior to memoirs and public statements, Duelfer notes an instance in which an Iraqi leader usefully identified a document as a forgery. See Marc Trachtenberg, *The Craft of International History: A Guide to Method* (Princeton, NJ: Princeton University Press, 2006), 151–54; Marc Trachtenberg, "Documentation: White House Tapes and Minutes of the Cuban Missile Crisis," *International Security*, 10 (Summer 1985): 164–203; Duelfer, *Hide and Seek*, 375–76.

[41] U.S. Department of State, *Foreign Relations of the United States, 1969–1976. Vol. E-10: Preface to Documents on American Republics* (Washington, D.C.: Government Printing

Transcribing is "treacherous" and mishearing "inevitable," writes David Greenberg, as a result of background noises, faint speech, overlapping conversations, and unfamiliarity with speakers' voices.[42] These warnings are even more appropriate for the transcripts in this volume, given the added difficulties associated with translating Arabic to English. As linguists visit the CRRC, they will uncover shortcomings in our work. Such lurking shortcomings notwithstanding, the captured recordings provide unparalleled insights to the inner workings of an authoritarian regime.

Office, July 2009), accessed 4 August 2009 at http://history.state.gov/historicaldocuments/frus1969-76ve10/preface.

[42] David Greenberg, "The Cuban Missile Tape Crisis: Just How Helpful Are the White House Recordings?" *Slate*, 22 July 2003 accessed 18 June 2011 at http://www.slate.com/id/2085761/.

Appendix: Timeline

Year	Date	Event
1932	3 October	Iraq achieves independence from Great Britain.
1941	2 May	Britain invades Iraq, overthrows the pro-Axis government, and installs Faisal II as king.
1958	14 July	General Abd al-Qasim takes control of Iraq following a successful coup.
1963	8 February	Iraqi Prime Minister Qasim is ousted in a coup led by the Arab Ba'ath Socialist Party.
	18 November	A group of military officers overthrows the Ba'ath government.
1968	17 July	A Ba'ath-led coup ousts Prime Minister Arif. General Ahmad Hasan al-Bakr becomes president. Saddam Hussein, relative of Bakr, becomes vice president.
1975	6 March	Iraq and Iran sign the Algiers Accord, in which they agreed to share the Shatt al-Arab waterway.
1978	17 September	The Camp David peace accords are signed between Israel and Egypt.
	5 November	Arab League meeting in Baghdad ("Baghdad Summit") condemns the Camp David accords.
	7 November	Iraq and Syria announce their plans to form a unified state.

(continued)

This timeline borrows from the following sources: David M. Malone, *The International Struggle over Iraq: Politics in the UN Security Council, 1980–2005* (New York: Oxford University Press, 2006), 321–37; Tim Trevan, *Saddam's Secrets: The Hunt for Iraq's Hidden Weapons* (London: HarperCollins, 1999), 393–416; Edmund A. Ghareeb with Beth Dougherty, *Historical Dictionary of Iraq: Historical Dictionaries of Asia, Oceania, and the Middle East, No. 44* (Lanham, MD: Scarecrow Press, Inc., 2004), xvii–xxxvii.

Year	Date	Event
1979	16 January	Islamic Revolution ousts the Shah of Iran.
	February	Ayatollah Khomeini arrives in Tehran in February.
	16 July	President al-Bakr resigns and is succeeded by Vice President Saddam Hussein. Within days, Saddam executes at least twenty potential rivals, members of the Ba'ath Party, and military.
	4 November	Iranians seize U.S. diplomats in the U.S. embassy in Tehran as hostages.
	27 December	Soviet Union invades Afghanistan.
1980	1 March	United States forms the Rapid Deployment Joint Task Force (RDJTF).
	4 September	Iran shells Iraqi border towns.
	17 September	Iraq abrogates its 1975 treaty with Iran.
	23 September	Iraq launches a ground offensive, beginning the eight-year conflict with Iran.
	4 November	In U.S. presidential election, Ronald Reagan defeats Jimmy Carter.
1981	7 June	Israel attacks an Iraqi nuclear research center at Tuwaythah (Osirak reactor) near Baghdad.
	29 November	Iran begins a major assault against Iraq.
1982	10 June	Iraq declares a unilateral cease-fire.
1983	1 January	U.S. Central Command (CENTCOM) is established.
	26 November	U.S. National Security Directive 114 says that the United States will do what it takes, within the law, to prevent Iraq from losing to Iran.
	20 December	U.S. Secretary of Defense Donald Rumsfeld meets with Saddam in Baghdad.
1984	27 March	Iraq begins a tanker war by attacking shipping near the coast with Iran.
	July	The Central Intelligence Agency begins delivering intelligence to Iraq.
	11 November	United States and Iraq resume diplomatic relations.
1985	May–June	Iraq and Iran bomb each other's population centers in the Battle of the Cities.
1986	9 February	Iran captures the Al-Fao Peninsula, which surprises and deals a major blow to Iraq.
	2 August	Saddam offers peace to Iran in an open letter.
	13 November	President Reagan addresses the nation on why his administration provided Iran with arms.
1987	17 May	Saddam officially apologizes after an Iraqi missile hit the USS *Stark*, killing thirty-seven Americans.
	7 July	UN Security Council Resolution (UNSCR) 598 calls for a cease-fire, troop withdrawal, and commission to determine responsibility for the conflict. Iraq accepts, and Iran rejects, the provisions.

Year	Date	Event
	22 September	The United States attacks an Iranian ship that was placing mines in the Persian Gulf.
	December	Beginning of the First Intifada (Palestinian uprising).
1988	16 March	Iraq attacks the Kurdish town of Halabjah with a mix of poison gas and nerve agents, killing five thousand people.
	29 April	The United States announces that it will protect all shipping in the Gulf.
	15 May	Soviets begin withdrawal from Afghanistan.
	April–August	Iraq achieves a number of battlefield victories, including recapturing the Fao peninsula and Majnoun islands.
	20 August	The Iran-Iraq War ends; 1 million soldiers are estimated to have been killed during the eight years of fighting.
	8 November	George H. W. Bush defeats Michael Dukakis in U.S. presidential election.
1989	15 February	Last Soviet troops leave Afghanistan.
	May	Egypt is readmitted to the Arab League.
	2 October	U.S. National Security Directive 26 states that U.S. policy is to engage Saddam's regime with the hope of improving Iraq's behavior.
	9 November	The Berlin Wall falls.
1990	19 February	Saddam Hussein demands that U.S. warships depart the Gulf.
	2 April	Saddam says Iraq has binary weapons and will "make fire eat half of Israel if it tries anything against Iraq."
	30 May	At an Arab League summit, Saddam calls for Arabs to liberate Jerusalem and demands $27 billion from Kuwait for its oil overproduction.
	15 July	Tariq Aziz, Iraq's foreign minister, accuses Kuwait of stealing Iraqi oil from the Rumaila oil field.
	17 July	Saddam threatens action if Kuwait and the United Arab Emirates fail to comply with new oil quotas designed to raise oil prices.
	24 July	Iraqi troops deploy to the Kuwaiti border. The United States begins a naval exercise with the United Arab Emirates.
	25 July	April Glaspie, U.S. ambassador to Iraq, meets with Saddam and reports that Saddam desires to resolve the crisis peacefully.
	1 August	Iraq walks out on talks with Kuwait held in Jeddah, Saudi Arabia.
	2 August	Iraq invades Kuwait. UNSCR 660 calls for a full withdrawal of Iraqi troops from Kuwait.

(continued)

Year	Date	Event
	3 August	The United States and Soviet Union issue a joint statement condemning the invasion and calling for an immediate withdrawal.
	6 August	UNSCR 661 imposes economic sanctions on Iraq.
		Saudi King Fahd agrees to permit U.S. troops on Saudi soil.
	7 August	Fifteen thousand U.S. troops begin moving into Saudi Arabia.
1990	8 August	President Bush declares that "a line has been drawn in the sand."
		Iraq announces the formal annexation of Kuwait.
	10 September	Iran and Iraq renew full diplomatic relations.
	29 November	UNSCR 678 gives Iraq until 15 January to comply with all previous resolutions. After that date, coalition forces are authorized "to use all necessary means" to force compliance.
	29 December	U.S. congressional Democrats threaten to cut off funds for Operation Desert Shield unless the president seeks congressional approval before attacking Iraq.
1991	7 January	Gulf War begins with coalition forces aerial bombing Iraq – Operation Desert Storm.
	9 January	U.S. Secretary of State James Baker meets with Tariq Aziz in Geneva. Iraq vows to attack Israel if war begins. Aziz refuses to accept a letter from President Bush to Saddam Hussein.
	12 January	U.S. Congress authorizes the use of forces necessary to fulfill UN commitments.
	15 January	UN deadline for withdrawal passes.
	17 January	Operation Desert Storm begins at 2:30 a.m. in Baghdad with air and missile attacks.
		Iraq launches Scud missiles at Israel and Saudi Arabia.
	28 January	Iraq launches a multidivision operation into Saudi Arabia to seize al-Khafji and disrupt coalition operations.
	13 February	Coalition ground operation begins.
	24 February	Kuwait is liberated by Coalition forces.
	27 February	Iraq accepts the terms of a cease-fire. The primary cease-fire resolution is UNSCR 687 (April 3) requiring Iraq to end its weapons-of-mass-destruction programs, recognize Kuwait, account for missing Kuwaitis, return Kuwaiti property, and stop supporting international terrorism. Iraq is required to stop repressing its citizens.
	March	Shi'a and Kurds rise up in rebellion.
	3 April	UNSCR 687 provides cease-fire terms. Iraq's parliament accepted the terms 6 April.
	18 April	Iraq submits first semiannual disarmament declaration, as required by UNSCR 687.

Year	Date	Event
	15–21 May	The International Atomic Energy Agency (IAEA) conducts first inspection of Iraq's nuclear facilities.
	9 June	The UN Special Commission (UNSCOM) conducts its first chemical weapons inspection.
	June	The coalition imposes a no-fly zone that bars Iraq from flying military aircraft over territory north of the thirty-sixth parallel in Iraq.
	23–28 June	Iraqis fire on UNSCOM and IAEA inspectors trying to intercept calutrons (related to nuclear weapons).
	18–20 July	Inspectors uncover Iraqi efforts to conceal ballistic missiles, destroy the missiles, and launch support equipment.
	11 October	Iraq rejects UNSCR 715, which approved of a plan for ongoing monitoring and verification of Iraq's disarmament obligations.
	25 December	Dissolution of Soviet Union.
1992	May–June	Iraq delivers the first of many full, final, and complete disclosures regarding its prohibited weapon programs.
	6–29 July	Iraq refuses UNSCOM access to the Ministry of Agriculture, leading to a crisis.
	26 August	The United States, United Kingdom, and France establish a no-fly zone to protect the Shi'a in southern Iraq.
	3 November	William Jefferson Clinton defeats George H. W. Bush in U.S. presidential election.
1993	13 April	The United States attacks Iraq in response to evidence that Iraq attempted to assassinate former President Bush while he visited Kuwait.
	26 November	Iraq accepts the monitoring and verification provisions in UNSCR 715.
1994	6–8 October	Iraq deploys troops near its border with Kuwait and threatens to quit cooperating with IAEA and UNSCOM inspectors. The United States responds by sending additional troops to Kuwait.
1994	15 October	Iraq redeploys its troops away from the border following the U.S. troop deployment; Russian diplomacy; and UNSCR 949, which demanded that the troops withdraw.
	10 November	Iraq confirms its recognition of Kuwait and its boundary with Kuwait.
1995	10 April	UNSCOM announces that its ongoing monitoring and verification plan has become operational.

(*continued*)

Year	Date	Event
	June	Marwan Qasim, chief of the Royal Court in Jordan, meets with Saddam in an attempt to arrange a meeting between Saddam and Israeli Prime Minister Yitzhak Rabin.
	July	Iraq announces that unless considerable progress has been made toward ending sanctions by the end of August, it will cease cooperating with UN inspectors.
	1 July	Iraq concedes that it had an offensive biological weapons program but denies that weaponization occurred.
	16 July	Congressman Bill Richardson (D-NM) meets with Saddam to seek the release of two American aerospace workers who crossed the border into Iraq. The meeting leads to the prisoners' release.
	8 August	Hussein Kamil, the director of Iraq's Military Industrialization Commission and son-in-law of Saddam, defects to Jordan. Iraqi officials assert that Hussein had concealed from them, and from inspectors, important information about prohibited Iraqi weapons programs. Iraq admits that it had weaponized biological agents.
	November	Jordanian officials seize more than US$25 million of advanced missile parts, including gyroscopes and accelerometers, in Amman. The equipment came from Russia and was en route to Iraq.
1996	May–June	UNSCOM oversees destruction of al-Hakam, Iraqi's primary plant producing biological warfare agents.
	12 June	UNSCR 1060 finds Iraq in violation of its obligations to provide access to UNSCOM teams.
	19–22 June	Iraqi and UNSCOM officials agree on procedures for inspecting Iraq's "sensitive sites."
	8 August	The UN approves Iraqi plan for distributing oil-for-food proceeds.
	31 August	Iraqi military enters Iraq's Kurdish north, occupying Irbil.
	2 September	The United States responds to Iraq's incursion into the north by launching cruise missiles and extending the no-fly zone in the south to the thirty-third parallel.
	5 November	Bill Clinton defeats Bob Dole in U.S. presidential election.
	10 December	The Oil-for-Food Program begins.
1997	13 November	Iraq expels American UNSCOM inspectors.
	20 November	UNSCOM inspections resume, with Americans, thanks to a Russian-brokered agreement.
	17 December	Iraq bars UNSCOM from "presidential and sovereign" sites.
1998	13 January	Iraq stops cooperating with UNSCOM, allegedly because it contains too many U.S. and U.K. inspectors.

Year	Date	Event
	20–23 February	UN Secretary-General Kofi Annan meets with Saddam and signs a memorandum of understanding for inspection of presidential sites.
1998	5 August	Iraq quits cooperating with UNSCOM.
	29 September	Congress makes replacing Iraq's regime official U.S. policy by passing the Iraq Liberation Act.
	31 October	Iraq ends all interactions with UNSCOM.
	16–19 December	Following UNSCOM's withdrawal from Iraq, the United States and United Kingdom bomb Baghdad in Operation Desert Fox.
	21 December	Russia, France, and Germany advocate ending sanctions against Iraq.
2000	27 January	Hans Blix becomes the chairman of the UN Monitoring, Verification, and Inspection Commission (UNMOVIC), the successor organization to UNSCOM.
	7 November	George W. Bush defeats Al Gore in U.S. presidential election.
2001	11 September	Al Qaeda terrorists attack the World Trade Center and Pentagon.
	7 October	The United States invades Afghanistan.
	27 November	Saddam rejects President Bush's call for the return of weapon inspectors.
2002	16 September	Iraq allows weapon inspectors to return.
	2 October	U.S. Congress passes a resolution that authorizes the president to use force, as he deems necessary, against Iraq.
	8 November	UN Security Council adopts Resolution 1441, which gives inspectors the right to search anywhere in Iraq for prohibited weapons.
	13 November	Iraq accepts UNSCR 1441.
	27 November	UNMOVIC begins inspections in Iraq.
	7 December	Iraq provides a lengthy disarmament declaration.
	19 December	U.S. Secretary of State Colin Powell says Iraq is in "material breach" of its disarmament obligations.
2003	19 March	The United States begins its attack on Iraq.
	9 April	United States takes control of Baghdad.
	13 December	U.S. troops capture Saddam.

References

Published Sources

"25 Aug Solarz Interview with Saddam Husayn," JN021914 Baghdad INA (in Arabic), 25 August 1982, Digital National Security Archive IG00075.

"Bush State of the Union Address," *Cable News Network*, 29 January 2002.

"Bush's State of the Union Speech," *Cable News Network*, 29 January 2003.

"Clinton Has 'No Difference' with Bush on Iraq Policy," *United Press International*, 14 January 1993.

"Egypt President Mubarak Comments on Gulf Crisis," *BBC Summary of World Broadcasts*, 10 August 1990.

"Europe's Muslims More Moderate: The Great Divide: How Westerners and Muslims View Each Other," Pew Global Attitudes Project, 22 June 2006 (http://pewglobal.org/category/survey-reports/2006/).

"Excerpts from Interview with Hussein on Crisis in Gulf," *New York Times*, 31 August 1990.

"Former Defector Denies Giving Away Iraq's Secrets," *Agence France-Presse*, 22 February 1996.

"Full Text: Saddam Hussein's Speech," *Guardian*, 17 January 2003.

"Gaafar Numeiri: Sudan Leader Backed Camp David Accord," *Boston Globe*, 31 May 2009.

"Gadhafi Expected in Cairo to Restore Egypt-Sudan Links," *United Press International*, 1 July 1991.

"General Assembly Renews Call for free Puerto Rico," *United Press International*, 4 August 1982.

"George Bush Phone Call with French President (Mitterrand)," 22 February 1991.

"Hussein Must Not Be Allowed to Provoke Future Crises: Christopher," *Agence France-Presse*, 12 October 1994.

"International Projects: Iraqi Secret Police Files Seized by the Kurds during the 1991 Gulf War," http://ucblibraries.colorado.edu/archives/collections/international.htm.

"Iraq and Kuwait: Iraqi Foreign Minister's Letter to President of UN Security Council," *BBC Summary of World Broadcasts*, 14 January 1993.

"Iraq Balks at Border," *Newsday*, 2 June 1992.

"Iraq Rebuffs UN Inspection Order," *Washington Times*, 8 July 1992.

"Iraqi Cease-Fire Offer and Comment: RCC Declares Unilateral Cease-Fire, Calls for 'Constructive Dialogue' with US," *BBC Summary of World Broadcasts*, 21 January 1993.

"Iraqi Defector's News Conference: Husayn Kamil Hasan Says He Will Work for the Overthrow of the Iraqi Government," Jordanian TV, Amman (in Arabic), 12 August 1995, in *BBC Summary of World Broadcasts*, 14 August 1995.

"Iraqi Letter to Arab League Threatening Kuwait," declassified cable (formerly confidential), State 235637, 19 July 1990, Digital National Security Archive IG01465.

"Iraqi President Addresses ACC Summit Issue of Soviet Jews and US Presence in Gulf," *BBC Summary of World Broadcasts*, 26 February 1990.

"King of Morocco Receives Iraqi Deputy Prime Minister," *BBC Summary of World Broadcasts: The Monitoring Report*, 6 May 1992.

"Meeting with Israeli Defense Minister Ariel Sharon, 4:00–5:00 p.m., Tuesday, May 25" (pages 1–2, 8, 11 Only), declassified (formerly secret), 21 May 1982, Digital National Security Archive IG00071, Origin: United States, Department of State, Bureau of Near Eastern and South Asian Affairs; United States, Department of State, Bureau of Politico-Military Affairs.

"Memorandum from the President's Assistant for National Security Affairs," National Archives, Nixon Presidential Materials, National Security Council Files, box 138, Kissinger Office Files, Kissinger Country Files, Middle East, Kurdish Problem vol. 1, June '72–October '73, formerly classified "Secret; Sensitive; Exclusively Eyes Only."

"POTUS to Mikhail Gorbachev, RE: [Comments on your letter reporting on your talks with Tariq Aziz]," Draft Letter, 19 February 1991, Bush Library, National Security Council (Richard Haass Files), Working Files Iraq – February 1991 (4 of 6).

"President Warns Israel, Criticizes U.S.," FBIS-NES-90-064, 3 April 1990, from Baghdad Domestic Service (in Arabic), 2 April 1990.

"Reaction to King Husayn's Speech: Husayn Kamil Says Atmosphere in Saddam Husayn's Family Is 'Troubled,'" Radio Monte Carlo – Middle East, Paris (in Arabic), 25 August 1995, in *BBC Summary of World Broadcasts*, 28 August 1995.

"Report: U.S. Supplied the Kinds of Germs Iraq Later Used for Biological Weapons," *USA Today*, 30 September 2002.

"Return of Husayn Kamil: Iraqi TV Reports Return of Husayn Kamil," *BBC Summary of World Broadcasts*, 22 February 1996.

"Rumsfeld Mission: December 20 Meeting with Iraqi President Saddam Hussein," London 27572 (http://library.rumsfeld.com/doclib/sp/38/12-21-1983.%20Cable.%20Rumsfeld%20Mission%20-%20Dec%2020%20Meeting%20with%20 Iraqi%20President%20Saddam%20Hussein.pdf).

"Saddam Husayn's Interview for Spanish Television," *BBC Summary of World Broadcasts*, 29 December 1990.

"Saddam Hussein Talks to the FBI: Twenty Interviews and Five Conversations with 'High Value Detainee # 1' in 2004."

"Saddam Hussein's Half Brother Criticizes Heir," *New York Times*, 31 August 1995.

"Secretary's October 6 Meeting with Iraqi Foreign Minister Tariq Aziz," State 327801, 13 October 1989.

"Tareq Aziz Seeks Arab Support to End Sanctions on Iraq," *Agence France-Presse*, 4 May 1992.

"Telephone Conversation with King Hussein of Jordan," 31 July 1990, Bush Library, National Security Council (Richard Haass Files), Working Files Iraq Pre-2/8/90 (4 of 6).

"Texas Oilman Enters Mid-Trial Guilty Plea to Charges of Conspiring to Make Illegal Payments to the Former Government of Iraq," press release, U.S. Attorney, Southern District of New York, 1 October 2007.

"The New Presidency: Excerpts from an Interview with Clinton after the Air Strikes," *New York Times*, 14 January 1993.

"Towards an International History of the Iran-Iraq War, 1980–1988," conference transcript, *A Critical Oral History Workshop*, Washington DC: Woodrow Wilson Center, 25–26 July 2005.

"U.N. Committee Reaffirms Right of Puerto Ricans to Independence," *Associated Press*, 15 August 1985.

"U.N. Starts Helicopter Flights to Find Missile Sites in Iraq," *New York Times*, 4 October 1991.

"UCLA: Gov Richardson Recounts His Deals with Hussein, Castro," 11 March 2008, www.youtube.com/watch?v=trqEqll6-iE.

"UNSCOM: Chronology of Main Events," www.un.org/Depts/unscom/Chronology/chronologyframe.htm.

"US Forces in Show of Strength," Melbourne: *Sunday Herald Sun*, 20 August 1995.

"Wall Street Journal Interviews Saddam," FBIS-NES-90-128, 3 July 1990, JN0107095890, Baghdad INA (in Arabic), 1 July 1990.

"War in the Gulf: Statement by Iraqi Revolutionary Council," *New York Times*, 23 February 1991.

"When the Shah Needed the Best in Care," *U.S. News and World Report*, 5 November 1979.

Aburish, Saïd K., *Saddam Hussein: The Politics of Revenge* (London: Bloomsbury, 2000).

Aftandilian, Gregory L., *Egypt's Bid for Arab Leadership: Implications for U.S. Policy* (New York: Council on Foreign Relations, 1993).

Alem, Abdolrahman, "War Responsibility: Governments or Individuals?" in *The Iran-Iraq War: The Politics of Aggression*, ed. Farhang Rajaee (Gainesville: University Press of Florida, 1993) pp. 55–68.

Ali, Javed, "Chemical Weapons and the Iran-Iraq War: A Case Study in Noncompliance," *Nonproliferation Review* (Spring 2001) pp. 43–58.

Amuzegar, Jahangir, *The Dynamics of the Iranian Revolution: The Pahlavis' Triumph and Tragedy* (Albany: State University of New York Press, 1991).

Andrew, Christopher, and Julie Elkner, "Stalin and Foreign Intelligence," *Totalitarian Movements and Political Religions* 4, no. 1 (2003).

Ashton, Nigel, *King Hussein of Jordan: A Political Life* (New Haven, CT: Yale University Press, 2008).

Atkinson, Rick, *Crusade: The Untold Story of the Persian Gulf War* (New York: Houghton Mifflin, 1993).

Aziz, Tariq, "Law of the Jungle," *Harvard International Review* 17 (Summer 1995).

Aziz, Tariq, PBS *Frontline* interview, original broadcast 25 January 2000.

Baghdad 02186, "Codel Dole: Meeting with Saddam Hussein," 12 April 1990, available through the Declassified Documents Reference System.

Bakhtiar, Shahpur, and Fred Halliday, "Shahpur Bakhtiar: 'The Americans Played a Disgusting Role,'" *Middle East Research and Information Project Report*, no. 104, (March–April 1982).

Baktiari, Bahman, "International Law: Observations and Violations," in *The Iran-Iraq War: The Politics of Aggression*, ed. Farhang Rajaee (Gainesville: University Press of Florida, 1993).

Baram, Amatzia, "Mesopotamian Identity in Ba'thi Iraq," *Middle Eastern Studies* 19, no. 4 (October 1983).

Barber, Ben, and Bill Gertz, "Iraqi Defectors Return to Baghdad with Pardons: Move Taints Data from Saddam's Kin," *Washington Times*, 21 February 1996.

Barton, Rod, *The Weapons Detective: The Inside Story of Australia's Top Weapons Inspector* (Melbourne: Griffin Press, 2006).

BBC News, "Timeline: Arab League," 17 September 2008.

Be'eri, Eliezer, *Army Officers in Arab Politics and Society* (Jerusalem: Israel Universities Press, 1969).

Benard, Cheryl, and Zalmay Khalilzad, *The Government of God: Iran's Islamic Republic* (New York: Columbia University Press, 1984).

Bengio, Ofra, "Saddam Husayn's Novel of Fear," *Middle East Quarterly* 9 (Winter 2002).

Bengio, Ofra, ed., *Middle East Contemporary Survey: Iraq 1976–1999* (Tel Aviv: Moshe Dayan Center for Middle Eastern and African Studies, Shiloah Institute, Tel Aviv University), CD-ROM.

Bengio, Ofra, *Saddam's Word: Political Discourse in Iraq* (New York: Oxford University Press, 1998).

Beschloss, Michael R., ed., *Taking Charge: The Johnson White House Tapes, 1963–1964* (New York: Touchstone, 1997).

Block, Robert, "Desperate Saddam Takes on the world," *Independent* (London), 10 October 1994.

Borger, Julian, and Ewen MacAskill, "Missile Blitz on Iraq," *Guardian*, 17 December 1998.

Bose, Tarun Chandra, *The Super Powers and the Middle East* (New York: Asia Publishing House, 1972).

Brands, Hal, "Inside the Iraqi State Records: Saddam Hussein, 'Irangate,' and the United States," *Journal of Strategic Studies* 34 (February 2011).

Brands, Hal, and David Palkki, "'Conspiring Bastards': Saddam Hussein's Strategic View of the United States," *Diplomatic History*, forthcoming.

Broughton, Philip Delves, "The Nice Side of Saddam," *Spectator*, London, 6 December 2003.

Butler, Richard, "Why Saddam Husayn Loves the Bomb," *Middle East Quarterly* (March 2000).

Butler, Richard, and James Charles Roy, *The Greatest Threat: Iraq, Weapons of Mass Destruction, and the Crisis of Global Security* (Cambridge, MA: Public Affairs, 2000).

Case Western Reserve University School of Law, "Iraqi High Tribunal Trials," *Grotian Moment: The International War Crimes Trial Blog*, http://law.case.edu/saddamtrial/index.asp?t=1.

Central Intelligence Agency, *Comprehensive Report of the Special Advisor to the DCI on Iraq's WMD*, vols. 1–3, 30 September 2004.

Chutkow, Paul, *Associated Press*, 3 August 1978.

Cigar, Norman, "Chemical Weapons and the Gulf War: The Dog That Did Not Bark," *Studies in Conflict and Terrorism* 15 (1992).

Claire, Rodger, *Raid on the Sun: Inside Israel's Secret Campaign That Denied Saddam the Bomb* (New York: Broadway Books, 2004).

Clark, Sir Terence, interview with Charles Cullimore, 8 November 2002, British Diplomatic Oral History Programme.

Clarke, Duncan L., "Israel's Economic Espionage in the United States," *Journal of Palestinian Studies* 27 (Summer 1998).

Clinton, William Jefferson, *My Life* (New York: Random House, 2004).

Cockburn, Patrick, "Baghdad Suburb Residents Show War Readiness," *Independent* (London), 22 December 1990.

Cohn, Victor, and Susan Okie, "Doctors Say Shah Could Leave U.S. in 4 Weeks," *Washington Post*, 15 November 1979.

Cordesman, Anthony H., *Iraq and the War of Sanctions: Conventional Threats and Weapons of Mass Destruction* (Westport, CT: Praeger, 1999).

Cordingley, Patrick, *In the Eye of the Storm: Commanding the Desert Rats in the Gulf War* (London: Hodder and Stoughton, 1996).

Crossette, Barbara, "Eagleburger Is Viewed as the Likely Successor," *New York Times*, 22 July 1992.

Crossette, Barbara, "Iraq Hides Biological Warfare Effort, Report Says," *New York Times*, 12 April 1995.

Davis, Eric, *Memories of State: Politics, History, and Collective Identity in Modern Iraq* (Berkeley: University of California Press, 2005).

de la Billiere, General Sir Peter, *Storm Command: A Personal Account of the Gulf War* (London: HarperCollins, 1992).

Deans, Bob, "After Asian Trip Clinton Faces Rocky Fall," *Cox News Service*, 22 November 1998.

Dekker, Ige F., and H. H. G. Post, eds., *The Gulf War of 1980–1988: The Iran-Iraq War in International Legal Perspective* (Boston: Martinus Nijhoff, 1992).

Duelfer, Charles, *Hide and Seek: The Search for Truth in Iraq* (New York: Public Affairs, 2009).

Fineman, Mark, "Iraq Frees American Jailed for 205 Days," *Houston Chronicle*, 16 November 1993.

Fischer, Dean, "Inside Saddam's Brutal Regime," *Time*, 18 September 1995.

Fisk, Robert, "Tapes Reveal Why Iraqi Traitor Went Back to Die: Robert Fisk Hears the Last Testament of the Man Who Betrayed Saddam," *Independent* (London), 28 February 1996.

Fisk, Robert, "Vain Leader Playing a Dangerous Game That He Can't Afford to Lose," *Independent* (London), 14 October 2000.

Foreign Broadcast Information Service, "Saddam Husayn Addresses Visiting U.S. Senators," Baghdad Domestic Service (in Arabic), 17 April 1990.

Foreign Broadcast Information Service, "Text of President's Speech to National Assembly," Baghdad Domestic Service (in Arabic), 18 September 1980.

Foreign Broadcast Information Service, "Turkish Paper *Hurriyet* Interviews Saddam: Third Installment," *Hurriyet* (in Turkish), 13 February 1992.

Foreign Broadcast Information Service-NES-90-074, 17 April 1990, "Saddam Husayn Addresses Visiting Senators," Baghdad Domestic Service (in Arabic), 16 April 1990.

Francona, Rick, *Ally to Adversary: An Eyewitness Account of Iraq's Fall from Grace* (Annapolis, MD: Naval Institute Press, 1999).

Freedman, Lawrence, *A Choice of Enemies: America Confronts the Middle East* (New York: Public Affairs, 2008).

Freitag, Ulrike, "Writing Arab History: The Search for the Nation," *British Journal of Middle Eastern Studies* 21, no. 1 (1994).

Friedman, Thomas L., "Clinton Affirms U.S. Policy on Iraq," *New York Times*, 15 January 1993.

Gaddis, John Lewis, *The Landscape of History: How Historians Map the Past* (New York: Oxford University Press, 2004).

Gates, Robert M., speech to the Association of American Universities, Washington, D.C., 14 April 2008.

Gertz, Bill, and Rowan Scarborough, "Perry Warns Iraq to Back Off," *Washington Times*, 15 August 1995.

Geyl, Pieter, *Use and Abuse of History* (New Haven, CT: Yale University Press, 1955).

Ghadban, Najib, "Some Remarks on the Distorting Literature about Saddam Hussein," letter to the editor, *Political Psychology*, 13 (December 1992).

Ghareeb, Edmund A., with Beth Dougherty, *Historical Dictionary of Iraq: Historical Dictionaries of Asia, Oceania, and the Middle East*, no. 44 (Lanham, MD: Scarecrow Press, 2004).

Gieling, Saskia, *Religion and War in Revolutionary Iran* (London: I. B. Taurus, 1999).

Goldstein, Donald M., and Katherine V. Dillon, *The Pacific War Papers: Japanese Documents of World War II* (Washington, D.C.: Potomac Books, 2006).

Gordon, Michael, "US Decides to Add as Many as 100,000 to Its Gulf Forces," *New York Times*, 26 October 1990.

Grier, Peter, "Iraq's Hussein Raises Eyebrows by Freeing American Hostages," *Christian Science Monitor*, 17 July 1995.

Halaby, Jamal, "Defector Says Iraq Was Set to Invade; the Reported Targets: Kuwait, Saudi Arabia," *Chicago Sun-Times*, 21 August 1995.

Halloran, Richard, "U.S. Has Acquired Soviet T-72 Tanks," *New York Times*, 13 March 1987.

Hamdani, Ra'ad, *Qabl an Yugadiruna al-Tarikh* (Beirut: Arab Scientific Publishers, 2007).

Harris, Francis, "Saddam's $2m Offer to WMD Inspector," *Daily Telegraph* (London), 12 March 2005.

Haselkorn, Avigdor, *The Continuing Storm: Iraq, Poisonous Weapons and Deterrence* (New Haven, CT: Yale University Press, 1999).

Herr, W. Eric, "Operation Vigilant Warrior: Conventional Deterrence Theory, Doctrine, and Practice," (Maxwell Air Force Base: Air University Press, 1996).

Hiltermann, Joost R., *A Poisonous Affair: America, Iraq, and the Gassing of Halabja* (New York: Cambridge University Press, 2007).

Hiro, Dilip, *Neighbours, Not Friends: Iraq and Iran after the Gulf Wars* (London: Routledge, 2001).

Hiro, Dilip, *The Essential Middle East: A Comprehensive Guide* (London: Carroll and Graf, 2003).

Hiro, Dilip, *The Longest War: The Iran-Iraq Military Conflict* (New York: Routledge, 1991).

Howard, Michael, "The Lessons of History," *History Teacher*, 15 August 1982.

Human Rights Watch, *Iraq's Brutal Decrees: Amputation, Branding and the Death Penalty*, 1 June 1995, www.unhcr.org/refworld/docid/3ae6a7foo.html.

Ivanovich, David, "Defense for Iraqi Notes Emerges; Wyatt's Lawyers Say Oilman Relayed Messages in Bid to Avert War," *Houston Chronicle*, 7 September 2007.

Jennings, Peter, and Forrest Sawyer, "Showdown with Saddam," *ABC News Saturday Night: Peter Jennings Reporting*, 7 February 1998.

Jentleson, Bruce W., *With Friends Like These: Reagan, Bush, and Saddam, 1982–1990* (New York: W. W. Norton, 1994).

Jervis, Robert, "Bridges, Barriers, and Gaps: Research and Policy," *Political Psychology* 29, no. 4 (2008).

Karsh, Efraim, and Inari Rautsi, *Saddam Hussein: A Political Biography* (New York: Grove Press, 1991).

Keaney, Thomas A., and Eliot A. Cohen, "Gulf War Air Power Survey Summary Report," (Washington, D.C.: Government Printing Office, 1993).

Kennedy, Dominic, "Saddam's Germ War Plot Is Traced Back to One Oxford Cow," *Times*, London, 9 August 2005.

Kennedy, Hugh, *The Great Arab Conquests: How the Spread of Islam Changed the World We Live In* (Philadelphia: Da Capo Press, 2007).

Kifner, John, "Confrontation in the Gulf; Arab Vote to Send Troops to Help Saudis; Boycott of Iraqi Oil Is Reported Near 100%," *New York Times*, 11 August 1990.

King, John, "Cheney: Administration Plans to Continue Gulf Buildup," *Associated Press*, 25 October 1990.

Kramer, Gudrun, "Anti-Semitism in the Muslim World. A Critical Review," *Die Welt des Islam*, 46 (November 2006).

Kutler, Stanley I., *Abuse of Power: The Nixon Tapes* (New York: Free Press, 1997).

Kuziemko, Ilyana, and Eric Werker, "How Much Is a Seat on the Security Council Worth? Foreign Aid and Bribery at the United Nations," *Journal of Political Economy* 114, no. 5 (2006).

Lathrop, Charles E., *The Literary Spy: The Ultimate Source for Quotations on Espionage and Intelligence* (New Haven, CT: Yale University Press, 2004).

Lauterpacht, Sir E., C. J. Greenwood, and Marc Weller, eds., *The Kuwait Crisis: Basic Documents* (New York: Cambridge University Press, 1993).

Levy, Adrian, and Catherine Scott-Clark, *Deception: Pakistan, the United States, and the Secret Trade in Nuclear Weapons* (New York: Walker and Company, 2007).

Lewis, Paul, "Confrontation in the Gulf: Mitterrand Says Iraqi Withdrawal Could Help End Mideast Disputes," *New York Times*, 25 September 1990.

Lieberthal, Kenneth, "The U.S. Intelligence Community and Foreign Policy: Getting Analysis Right," Brookings Institution Foreign Policy Paper Series, no. 17, September 2009.

Lippman, Thomas W., "Arab Plan Moves to Counter Treaty: Arab Foreign Ministers Meet to Plan Retaliation for Pact," *Washington Post*, 27 March 1979.

Lippman, Thomas W., "Iraq and Syria: Two Old Foes Move to End Their Hostility," *Washington Post*, 17 May 1979.

Litwak, Robert S., *Regime Change: U.S. Strategy through the Prism of 9/11* (Washington, D.C.: Woodrow Wilson Center Press, 2007).

Long, Jerry M., *Saddam's War of Words: Politics, Religion, and the Iraqi Invasion of Kuwait* (Austin: University of Texas Press, 2004).

Lopez, George A., and David Cortright, "Containing Iraq: Sanctions Worked," *Foreign Affairs* 83 (July–August 2004).

Lowther, William, *Arms and the Man*, (New York: Ivy Books, 1991).

MacArthur, John R., "Remember Nayirah, Witness for Kuwait?" in *The Iraq War Reader: History, Documents, Opinions*, ed. Micah L. Sifry and Christopher Cerf (New York: Simon and Schuster, 2003).

Mackey, Sandra, *The Reckoning: Iraq and the Legacy of Saddam Hussein* (New York: W. W. Norton, 2002).

Majid, Saman Abdul, *Les années Saddam: Révélations exclusives* (Paris: Fayard, 2003).

Malone, David M., *The International Struggle over Iraq: Politics in the UN Security Council, 1980–2005* (New York: Oxford University Press, 2006).

Mansur, Kamil, and James Cohen, *Beyond Alliance: Israel in U.S. Foreign Policy* (New York: Columbia University Press, 1994).

Marr, Phebe, *The Modern History of Iraq*, 2nd ed. (Boulder, CO: Westview Press, 2004).

Mathews, Tom, "The Road to War," *Newsweek* (28 January 1991).

May, Ernest R., and Philip D. Zelikow, "White House Tapes: Extraordinary Treasures for Historical Research," *Chronicle of Higher Education*, 28 November 1997.

May, Ernest R., and Philip D. Zelikow, *The Kennedy Tapes: Inside the White House during the Cuban Missile Crisis* (New York: Harvard University Press, 1997).

McGeary, Johanna, George Russell, and William Stewart, "Failure in Fez," *Time*, 7 December 1981.

Megally, Naguib, "Mubarak Firmly Backing Coalition," *United Press International*, 22 January 1991.

Meisler, Stanley, *United Nations: The First Fifty Years* (New York: Atlantic Monthly Press, 1997).

Melton, Gary P., "XVIII Airborne Corps Desert Deception," *Military Intelligence Professional Bulletin* 17, no. 4 (1991).

Miller, Judith, "Mideast Tensions; Egypt's President Calls for a Delay in Attacking Iraq," *New York Times*, 8 November 1990.

Mneimneh, Hassan, untitled oral presentation at "Working With and on Memory in Iraq," sponsored by George Washington University's Institute for European, Russian, and Eurasian Studies, Washington, D.C., 15 January 2009.

Mufti, Malik, *Sovereign Creations: Pan-Arabism and Political Order in Syria and Iraq* (Ithaca, NY: Cornell University Press, 1996).

Murphy, Caryle, "Iraq Accuses Kuwait of Plot to Steal Oil, Depress Prices," *Washington Post*, 19 July 1990.

Murray, Williamson, and Richard Hart Sinnreich, eds., *The Past as Prologue: The Importance of History to the Military Profession* (New York: Cambridge University Press, 2006).

Myers, Steven Lee, "Standoff with Iraq: The Overview; The President and the G.O.P. Diverge on Iraq," *New York Times*, 5 February 1998.

Nasrawi, Salah, "Leader of Radical PLO Unit Confirms Libya Closed His Camps," *Associated Press*, 5 November 1990.

National Security Directive NSD-26, "US Policy Toward the Persian Gulf," 2 October 1989.

Newton, Ambassador David, telephone interview with David Palkki, 25 March 2008.

Obeidi, Mahdi, and Kurt Pitzer, *The Bomb in My Garden: The Secrets of Saddam's Nuclear Mastermind* (Hoboken, NJ: John Wiley and Sons, 2004).

Oberdorfer, Donald, "Missed Signals in the Middle East," *Washington Post*, 17 March 1991.

Omestad, Thomas, "Psychology and the CIA: Leaders on the Couch," *Foreign Policy* 95 (Summer 1994).

Packer, George, "The Next Iraqi War: What Kirkuk's Struggle to Reverse Saddam's Ethnic Cleansing Signals for the Future of Iraq," *New Yorker*, 4 October 2004.

Pape, Robert, *Bombing to Win: Air Power and Coercion in War* (Ithaca, NY: Cornell University Press, 1996).

Peterson, Trudy, "Archives in Service to the State: The Law of War and Records Seizure," in *Political Pressure and the Archival Record*, ed. Margaret Procter, Michael Cook, and Caroline Williams (Chicago: Society of American Archivists, 2006).

Pipes, Daniel, "Obituary for Nizar Hamdoon (1944–2003)," *Middle East Quarterly* (Fall 2003).

Pipes, Daniel, *The Hidden Hand: Middle East Fears of Conspiracy* (New York: St. Martin's Press, 1998).

Piro, George, casual conversation with Saddam, session number 23, 13 May 2004.

Piro, George, casual conversation with Saddam, session number 24, 11 June 2004.

Piro, George, interview of Saddam, session number 1, 7 February 2004.

Piro, George, interview of Saddam, session number 3, 10 February 2004.

Pollack, Kenneth M., *Arabs at War: Military Effectiveness, 1948–1991* (Lincoln: University of Nebraska Press, 2002).

Pollack, Kenneth M., *The Persian Puzzle: The Conflict between Iran and America* (New York: Random House, 2005).

Post, Jerrold M., "Explaining Saddam Hussein: A Psychological Profile," presented to the House Armed Services Committee, December 1990.

Post, Jerrold M., *Leaders and Their Followers in a Dangerous World: The Psychology of Political Behavior* (Ithaca, NY: Cornell University Press, 2004).

Potter, William C., "The Diffusion of Nuclear Weapons," in *The Diffusion of Military Technology and Ideas*, ed. Emily Goldman and Leslie Eliason (Stanford, CA: Stanford University Press, 2003).

Primakov, Yevgeny, *Russia and the Arabs: Behind the Scenes in the Middle East from the Cold War to the Present* (New York: Basic Books, 2009).

Rajab, Jehan S., *Invasion Kuwait: An English Woman's Tale* (New York: St. Martin's Press, 1996).

Reagan, Ronald, "Address to the Nation on the Iran Arms and Contra Aid Controversy," 13 November 1986.

Regan, Tom, "When Contemplating War, Beware of Babies in Incubators," *Christian Science Monitor*, 6 September 2002.

Ritter, Scott, *Iraq Confidential: The Untold Story of the Intelligence Conspiracy to Undermine the UN and Overthrow Saddam Hussein* (New York: Nation Books, 2005).

Rustmann, F. W., Jr., *CIA Inc.: Espionage and the Craft of Business Intelligence* (Washington, D.C.: Brassey's, 2002).

Sagan, Scott, "The Commitment Trap: Why the United States Should Not Use Nuclear Threats to Deter Biological and Chemical Weapons Attacks," *International Security* 24 (Spring 2000).

Sammon, Bill, "Clinton Targets Weapons Threats: Pledges to Contain Iraq, North Korea," *Washington Times*, 23 November 1998.

Schafer, Susanne M., "Cohen Dampens Expectations about Military Strike Capabilities," *Associated Press*, 1 February 1998.

Schemann, Serge, "Moscow Hopes Iraqis Can Find 'Guts' to Retreat," *New York Times*, 24 February 1991.

Schlesinger, Arthur M., Jr., Diary entry for 25 March 1964, cited on the Miller Center's Presidential Recordings Program Web site, http://tapes.millercenter.virginia.edu/.

Schmitt, Eric, "U.S. Action in Persian Gulf is Said to Seek Iraqi's Ouster," *New York Times*, 19 August 1995.

Shaw, Eric D., "Saddam Hussein: Political Psychological Profiling Results Relevant to His Possession, Use, and Possible Transfer of Weapons of Mass Destruction (WMD) to Terrorist Groups," *Studies in Conflict and Terrorism* 26 (2003).

Sick, Gary, "The United States in the Persian Gulf," in *The Middle East and the United States: A Historical and Political Reassessment*, ed. David W. Lesch (Boulder, CO: Westview Press, 2003).

Sisler, Peter F., "Kuwaiti Calls Iraqi Defection Theatre," *United Press International*, 21 February 1996.

Smith, Jeffrey, and Ann Devroy, "US, Allies Plan Ultimatum to Iraq," *Washington Post*, 24 July 1992.

Smith, R. Jeffrey, "U.N. Is Said to Find Russian Markings on Iraq-Bound Military Equipment," *Washington Post*, 15 December 1995.

Smolansky, Oles M. and Bettie M. Smolansky, *The USSR and Iraq: The Soviet Quest for Influence* (Durham, NC: Duke University Press, 1991).

Smucker, Philip, "Iraq Builds 'Mother of All Battles' Mosque in Praise of Saddam," *Daily Telegraph*, 29 July 2001.

State 046070, "Reaffirmation of Persian Gulf Policy," 02/11/90, Bush Presidential Records, National Security Council, Richard N. Haass Files, Iraq Pre-8/2/90 [1].

Stewart, Cameron, "Butler Smeared in Iraqi Talks Video," *Weekend Australian*, 15 August 1998.

Sykes-Picot Agreement, 15 and 16 May 1916, www.lib.byu.edu.

Tatchell, Jo, "Saddam the Romancier," *Prospect Magazine* 100 (July 2004).

Teicher, Howard, "Testimony before the United States District Court, Southern District of Florida," 31 January 1995.

Terock, Adam, *The Superpowers' Involvement in the Iran-Iraq War* (Commack, NY: Nova Science Publishers, 1998).

Terrill, Andrew, "Chemical Warfare and 'Desert Storm': The Disaster That Never Came," *Small Wars and Insurgencies* 4, no. 2 (Autumn 1993).

Trachtenberg, Marc, "Documentation: White House Tapes and Minutes of the Cuban Missile Crisis," *International Security* 10 (Summer 1985).

Trachtenberg, Marc, *The Craft of International History: A Guide to Method* (Princeton, NJ: Princeton University Press, 2006).

Trevan, Tim, *Saddam's Secrets: The Hunt for Iraq's Hidden Weapons* (London: HarperCollins, 1999).

Trevor-Roper, H. R., *Hitler's Table Talk 1941-1944: Secret Conversations* (New York: Enigma Books, 2007).

Tucker, Jonathan B., "Evidence Iraq Used Chemical Weapons during the 1991 Persian Gulf War," *Nonproliferation Review* 4 (Spring-Summer, 1997).

Tyler, Patrick E., "US Finds Persian Gulf Threat Ebbs; a 'Strategic Shift' over Iran's Oil," *Washington Post*, 7 February 1990.

Tynan, Deirdre, "Hussein's Bunker 'Made in Germany': Boswau and Knauer Engineer Thinks Dictator Safe," www.pressetext.com/news/030328032/Husseins .bunker-made-in-germany.

UN Security Council, "Resolution 715," 1991.

UN Security Council, "Resolution 986," 14 April 1995.

UN Special Commission on Iraq, Report to the UN Security Council, S/1995/864, 11 October 1995.

United Kingdom, House of Commons, Committee on Standards and Privileges, Annex of the Sixth Report, "Combined Media Processing Centre-Qatar/UK CI Report: Authenticity of Harmony File ISGP-2003-00014623," 17 July 2007.

U.S. Department of Defense, *Conduct of the Persian Gulf War: Final Report to Congress*, April 1992.

U.S. Department of State, Bureau of International Information Programs, "Justice Department Secures Guilty Plea in Oil for Food Scandal" (19 January 2005).

U.S. Department of State, *Foreign Relations of the United States, 1969–1976. Vol. E-10: Preface to Documents on American Republics* (Washington, D.C.: Government Printing Office, July 2009).

U.S. Federal Bureau of Investigation, "Prosecutive Report of Investigation Concerning Saddam Hussein," 10 March 2005 (declassified 11 May 2009).

U.S. Senate Select Committee on Intelligence, "Nomination of Robert M. Gates to be Director of Central Intelligence," report together with Additional Reviews, 102nd Congress, 1st sess., 1992, Exec. Rept.

U.S. State Department Memorandum, Richard W. Murphy to Undersecretary Armacost, "U.S.-Iraqi Relations: Picking Up the Pieces," declassified (formerly secret), 5 December 1986.

Utgoff, Victor A., "Nuclear Weapons and the Deterrence of Biological and Chemical Warfare," Occasional Paper No. 36 (Washington, D.C.: Henry L. Stimson Center, October 1997).

Volcker, Paul A., Richard J. Goldstone, and Mark Pieth, *Independent Inquiry into the United Nations Oil-for-Food Programme* (New York: United Nations, 2005).

Von Drehle, David, and R. Jeffrey Smith, "U.S. Strikes Iraq for Plot to Kill Bush," *Washington Post*, 27 June 1993.

Wafiq al-Samarrai, PBS *Frontline* interview, 2 May 2002.

Wallis, David, "The Way We Live Now: 1-26-03: Questions for Bill Richardson; Negotiator at Large," *New York Times*, 26 January 2003.

Warrick, Joby, "Iraq Opened Consular Office in Kharkiv in December 2002," *Washington Post*, 28 November 2002.

Webster, Richard, "Saddam, Arafat and the Saudis Hate the Jews and Want to See Them Destroyed," *New Statesman*, 2 December 2002.

Williams, Dan, "Israel Could Use Ballistic Missiles Against Iran," *Washington Times*, 19 March 2009.

Wines, Michael, "Looking to Baker to Save Bush Anew," *New York Times*, 15 July 1992.

Wines, Michael, and Richard E. Meyer, "North Apparently Tried a Swap for Soviet Tank: Deal with Iran for Captured Vehicle Failed," *Washington Post*, 22 January 1987.

Wolfe, Robert, ed., *Captured German and Related Records: A National Archives Conference* (Athens: Ohio University Press, 1974).

Woods, Kevin M., and Mark E. Stout, "Saddam's Perceptions and Misperceptions: The Case of 'Desert Storm,'" *Journal of Strategic Studies* 33, no. 1 (February 2010).

Woods, Kevin M., with James Lacey, "Iraqi Perspectives Project – Saddam and Terrorism: Emerging Insights from Captured Documents, Volume 1 (Redacted)," IDA Paper P-4287 (Alexandria, VA: Institute for Defense Analyses, November 2007).

Woods, Kevin M., with James Lacey, *Iraqi Perspectives Project – Primary Source Materials for Saddam and Terrorism: Emerging Insights from Captured Iraqi Documents*, vol. 1–5.

Woods, Kevin M., "Captured Records – Lessons from the Civil War through World War II," presented at International Studies Association annual convention, San Francisco, 29 March 2008.

Woods, Kevin M., interview of Lieutenant General Ra'ad Hamdani, Aqaba, Jordan, 15–17 May 2007.

Woods, Kevin M., Michael R. Pease, Mark E. Stout, Williamson Murray, and James G. Lacey *Iraqi Perspectives Project: A View of Operation Iraqi Freedom from Saddam's Senior Leadership* (Washington, D.C.: Joint Center for Operational Analyses, 2006)

Woods, Kevin M., et al., *Iraqi Perspectives Project: Toward an Operational-Level Understanding of Operation Iraqi Freedom (U)*, IDA Paper P-4022 (Alexandria, VA: Institute for Defense Analyses, 2005).

Woods, Kevin M., et al., *Saddam's War: An Iraqi Military Perspective of the Iran-Iraq War*, McNair Paper No. 70 (Washington, D.C.: National Defense University Press, 2009).

Woods, Kevin M., *Iraqi Perspectives Project Phase II – Um Al-Ma'arik (The Mother of All Battles): Operational and Strategic Insights from an Iraqi Perspective*, IDA Paper P-4217 (Alexandria, VA: Institute for Defense Analyses, 2007).

Woods, Kevin M., *The Mother of All Battles: Saddam Hussein's Strategic Plan for the Persian Gulf War* (Annapolis, MD: Naval Institute Press, 2008).

Woodward, Peter, *The Horn of Africa: Politics and International Relations* (London: I. B. Tauris, 1996).

Wright, John, "Iraq Told to Allow U.N. Flights to Resume . . . or Else," *Associated Press*, 15 January 1993.

Wright, Robin, "News Analysis; Pressure to Remove Saddam Hussein Builds; Persian Gulf: Calls to Eliminate Iraqi Leader Come from Many Corners. All Strategies Are Fraught with Difficulties," *Los Angeles Times*, 6 February 1998.

Yengst, William C., Stephen J. Lukasik, and Mark A. Jensen, "Nuclear Weapons That Went to War," DNA-TR-96-25, draft final report sponsored by the U.S. Defense Special Weapons Agency and Science Applications International Corporation, October 1996.

Zimmerman, Barry E., and David J. Zimmerman, *Killer Germs: Microbes and Diseases That Threaten Humanity* (New York: McGraw Hill, 2003).

Zverina, Ivan, "U.N. Committee Votes to 'Decolonize' Puerto Rico," *United Press International*, 14 August 1986.

Captured Iraqi Sources

Audio Files

SH-SHTP-A-000-553, "Saddam and Senior Advisers Meeting after the Baghdad Conference," 27 March 1979.

SH-SHTP-A-000-555, "Saddam and His Revolutionary Command Council Discussing Reagan's Speech to the Nation on Iran-Contra Revelations (part 2)," 15 November 1986.

SH-SHTP-A-000-556, "Saddam and His Inner Circle Discussing Iran-Contra Revelations," 15 November 1986.

SH-SHTP-A-000-561, "Saddam and His Inner Circle Discussing the Iran-Iraq War and UN Security Council Resolutions Related to the War," undated (circa 1981).

SH-SHTP-A-000-565, "Saddam and High Ranking Officials Discussing US Plans to Attack Iraq, Irrigation Projects, and Other Military Issues," undated (circa 1995).

SH-SHTP-A-000-567, "Saddam and Yasser Arafat Discussing the Israeli Attack on the Palestinian Liberation Organization's Headquarters," 5 October 1985.

SH-SHTP-A-000-571, "Saddam and His Inner Circle Discussing Israel's Attack on the Tamuz (Osirak) Reactor," undated (circa mid-June 1981).

SH-SHTP-A-000-614, "Saddam and Officials Discussing the Uprising in the South," undated (circa March 1991).

SH-SHTP-A-000-619, "Culture and Information Office Meeting in Which Saddam Talks about the Palestinian Issue and Yasser Arafat," 8 September 1978.

SH-SHTP-A-000-626, "Saddam Discussing Neighboring Countries and Their Regimes," undated (circa 1980–1981).

SH-SHTP-A-000-627, "Saddam and Senior Military Officials Discussing Arms Imports and Other Issues Related to the Iran-Iraq War," undated (circa late 1983–early 1984).

SH-SHTP-A-000-630, "Saddam and His Advisers Discussing the Soviet Union and the State of the Iraqi Military," 24 February 1991.

SH-SHTP-A-000-631, "Saddam Discussing General Issues and Iraqi Military History," undated (circa 1988).

SH-SHTP-A-000-632, "Saddam Meeting with Iraqi Ministers regarding the Advantages of Invading Kuwait," 4 August 1990.

SH-SHTP-A-000-633, "Saddam and His Political Advisers Discussing the Attack on Iraq and Reactions from Arab Countries," 23 February 1991.

SH-SHTP-A-000-654, "Saddam and Iraqi Officials Discussing How to Deal with Foreign Diplomats in Kuwait and International Perceptions of Iraq," 20 September 1990.

SH-SHTP-A-000-666, "Saddam and Iraqi Officials Discussing a US-led Attack on Faylakah Island and the Condition of the Iraqi Army," 24 February 1991.

SH-SHTP-A-000-669, "Iraqi Officials Discussing the Retreat of Iraqi Troops from Kuwait and the Perceived Greediness of the United States of America," undated (circa March 1991).

SH-SHTP-A-000-670, "Saddam and His Senior Advisers Discussing Iraq's Foreign Relations and the Policies of Various Countries," 11 October 1990.

SH-SHTP-A-000-671, "Saddam and Senior Advisers Discussing the Iraqi Invasion of Kuwait," 30 September 1990.

SH-SHTP-A-000-674, "Saddam and His Inner Circle Discussing the United States, Leaders of Gulf States, the 1991 Gulf War, and other Issues," undated (circa February–March 1991).

SH-SHTP-A-000-711, "Saddam and Iraqi Officials Discussing the King Fahad Initiative, Relations with the USSR, and Perceptions of other Middle Eastern Countries," 3 October 1981.

SH-SHTP-A-000-716, "Saddam and Top Political Advisers Discussing Hostilities with Israel," 25 January 1995.

SH-SHTP-A-000-733, "Saddam and His Advisers Discussing UN Security Council Resolutions and a Possible Ceasefire during the Iran-Iraq War," 19 July 1987.

SH-SHTP-A-000-739, "Saddam and Officials Discussing the State of the Iraqi Army, the 1991 Uprising, and the Withdrawal from Kuwait," 3 April 1991.

SH-SHTP-A-000-753, "Saddam and Senior Advisers Discussing Bill Clinton's Administration and Its Attitudes toward Iraq," undated (circa 14 January 1993).

SH-SHTP-A-000-756, "Saddam and Senior Advisers Discussing a Potential Military Conflict with the United States," 9 February 1998.

SH-SHTP-A-000-762, "Saddam and Iraqi Ministers Discussing the Treason of Hussein Kamil undated (circa mid- to late August 1995).

SH-SHTP-A-000-785, "Saddam and Advisers Discussing the Economic Sanctions Imposed on Iraq in 1998 and Possible UN Inspections," undated (circa 23 February 1998).

SH-SHTP-A-000-813, "Saddam and Senior Military Officials Discussing Various Military Operations, Including Re-capturing the al-Fao Peninsula," undated (circa 1992).

SH-SHTP-A-000-830, "Saddam and Officials Discussing Ba'ath Party Support to Its Lebanese Branch, Ba'ath Ideology, and Other Party Affairs," 1992.

SH-SHTP-A-000-833, "Saddam and Officials Discussing the Treason of Hussein Kamil and Developments in Iraq," undated (circa mid- to late August 1995).

SH-SHTP-A-000-834, "Saddam and Political Officials Discussing How to Deal with the Republican Guard and Other Issues following the 1991 Gulf War," undated (circa 1992).

SH-SHTP-A-000-835, "Saddam and Military Officials Discussing the Iran-Iraq War," 16 September 1980.

SH-SHTP-A-000-837, "Saddam and Senior Political Advisers Discussing the Treason of Hussein Kamil," undated (circa late 1995–early 1996).

SH-SHTP-A-000-838, "Saddam and Senior Ba'ath Party Members Discussing the Transition from Bush to Clinton," undated (circa 4 November 1992).

SH-SHTP-A-000-848, "Saddam and His Advisers Discussing Potential War with United States," undated (circa mid-November 1990).

SH-SHTP-A-000-849, "Saddam and Military Officials Discussing the Condition of the Iraqi Army and Its Possible Enlargement," 1 May 1991.

SH-SHTP-A-000-857, "Saddam and Iraqi Officials Discussing the Liberation of Al-Fao and Its Broader Implications," 18 April 1988.

SH-SHTP-A-000-872, "Saddam and Advisers Discussing the US Airstrikes on Iraq, the Election of Clinton, and Sanctions on Iraq," 13 January 1993.

SH-SHTP-A-000-891, "Saddam and Saddam City Tribal Leaders Talking in the Wake of Demonstrations and Riots in Saddam City," undated (circa late 1991 or 1992).

SH-SHTP-A-000-894, "Saddam and Iraqi Officials Discussing the State of the Country and Sending a Diplomatic Letter to the League of Arab States," undated (circa 15 July 1990).

*SH-SHTP-A-000-896, "Saddam and Other Government Officials Discussing the State of the Country during the Iran-Iraq War and the Use of Chemical Weapons," 6 March 1987.

SH-SHTP-A-000-931, "Saddam and His Advisers Discussing the US Ground Attack during the 1991 Gulf War, Garnering Arab and Iraqi Support, and a Letter to Gorbachev," 24 February 1991.

SH-SHTP-A-000-989, "Saddam Meeting with Council of Ministers," 15 April 1995.

SH-SHTP-A-001-990, "Meeting between Saddam Hussein and Senior Advisers," 1995.

SH-SHTP-A-000-991, "Saddam and Senior Political Advisers Discussing UN resolutions and Possible Iraqi Withdrawal from Kuwait," undated (circa October 1994).

SH-SHTP-A-001-010, "Saddam and Senior Ba'ath Party Officials Discussing UN Sanctions on Iraq," 15 April 1995.

SH-SHTP-A-001-011, "Saddam and High Ranking Officials Discussing Iraqi Biological and Nuclear Weapons Programs," 2 May 1995.

SH-SHTP-A-001-023, "Saddam and Ba'ath Party Members Discussing the Iran-Iraq War," 6 March 1987.

SH-SHTP-A-001-035, "Saddam and Air Force Officers Discussing the Movements and Performance of the Iraqi Air Force during the Iran-Iraq War," 7 July 1984.

SH-SHTP-A-001-037, "Saddam Meeting with Iraqi officials, Yasser Arafat, and the Palestinian Delegation," 19 April 1990.

SH-SHTP-A-001-039, "Saddam and His Senior Advisers Discussing Israel's Attack on the Tamuz (Osirak) Reactor and Iraqi Civil Defenses," undated (circa mid- to late 1981).

SH-SHTP-A-001-041, "Saddam and His Cabinet Discussing Sanctions, the United States, Egypt, Turkey, and other Issues," 6 October 1996.

SH-SHTP-A-001-042, "Saddam and the Revolutionary Command Council Discussing the Iraqi Invasion of Kuwait and the Expected US Attack," 29 December 1990.

SH-SHTP-A-001-043, "Senior Iraqi Officials Discussing Coalition Operations against Iraq," undated (circa 17–18 January 1991).

SH-SHTP-A-001-045, "Saddam and High Ranking Officers Discussing Plans to Attack Kurdish 'Saboteurs' in Northern Iraq and the Possibility of Using Special Ammunition (Weapons)," undated (circa 1985).

SH-SHTP-A-001-143, "Saddam and Top Political Advisers Discussing Relations with the UN Security Council," 1 January 1996.

SH-SHTP-A-001-167, "Saddam and Ba'ath Party Members Discussing the Status of the Party in the Arab World and the Exploitation of the Muslim Brotherhood as an Ally," 24 July 1986.

SH-SHTP-A-001-197, "Saddam and Senior Advisers Discussing Ties between a Variety of Countries, Including Iraq-Egypt and Iraq-US Relations," undated (between 29 December 2000 and 6 January 2001).

SH-SHTP-A-001-198, "Saddam and His Advisers Discuss the Rules of the UN Security Council," undated (circa late November 1998).

*SH-SHTP-A-001-203, "Saddam and His Senior Advisers Discussing UN Security Council Efforts to Create a Ceasefire in the Iran-Iraq War" (1987).

*SH-SHTP-A-001-205, "Saddam and His Inner Circle Discussing a Letter from Hussein Kamil," 19 February 1996.

*SH-SHTP-A-001-206, "Saddam and His Inner Circle Discussing UN Inspections, Elections in the United States and Russia, and Other Issues," 22 November 1995.

SH-SHTP-A-001-207, "Saddam and Senior Ba'ath Party Members Discussing Iraqi laws, Pardons, and Various Other Issues," 22 July 1995.

*SH-SHTP-A-001-209, "Saddam and Senior Ba'ath Party Officials Discussing Iraq's Occupation of Kuwait," September 1990.

*SH-SHTP-A-001-210, "Saddam and His Inner Circle Discussing Upheaval and the Communist Coup Attempt in the Soviet Union," undated (circa 19–21 August 1991).

*SH-SHTP-A-001-211, "Saddam and Ba'ath Party Members Discussing Issues Involving Oil, the United States, Terrorism, and Other Topics," 1 March 2001.

*SH-SHTP-A-001-212, "Saddam and Ba'ath Party Members Discussing a Variety of Issues, Including the Overthrow of Qassem and 'The Protocols of the Elders of Zion,'" undated.

*SH-SHTP-A-001-215, "Saddam and His Inner Circle Discuss Zionism and 'The Protocols of the Elders of Zion,'" undated (circa mid-1990s).

*SH-SHTP-A-001-216, "Saddam and His Inner Circle Discussing Various Intelligence Services, Hamas, and Other Issues," 30 December 1996.

*SH-SHTP-A-001-217, "Saddam and His Inner Circle Discussing the Iraqi Army's Performance in Northern Iraq, Relations with the United States and Russia, and UN Security Council Resolution 598," undated (circa 21 January 1988).

SH-SHTP-A-001-218, "Saddam and His Senior Advisers Discussing Relations with Jordan and Changes in Clinton's National Security Team," undated (circa late 1996 or early 1997).

*SH-SHTP-A-001-219, "Saddam and Military Officials Discussing Reorganizing the Intelligence Service," 14 January 2001.

SH-SHTP-A-001-220, "Saddam Meeting with a Foreign Official," undated (circa 19 August 1987).

*SH-SHTP-A-001-222, "Saddam and His Senior Advisers Discussing the Second Palestinian Intifada," 6 December 2000.

*SH-SHTP-A-001-223, "Saddam and Government Officials Discussing Ba'ath Party Issues, International Sanctions, and Other Political Concerns," 9 May 1992.

*SH-SHTP-A-001-224, "Saddam and His Political Advisers Discussing the Possibility of a US Attack and Perceptions of other Arab Countries," undated (circa 1990–1991).

*SH-SHTP-A-001-225, "Saddam and His Political Advisers Discussing Iraq's Foreign Policy, Security Council Decisions, and the Possibility of War with the United States," 1 November 1990.

SH-SHTP-A-001-226, "Saddam and His Advisers Discussing Pan-Arab Security Issues," undated (circa January 1989).

SH-SHTP-A-001-228, "Saddam Discussing Ba'ath Party Principles and History, Military Strategy, and General Administrative Issues," undated (circa February 1982).

*SH-SHTP-A-001-229, "Saddam and Military Officials Discussing the Iran-Iraq War and Iraqi Military Capabilities," 30 October 1980.

*SH-SHTP-A-001-231, "Iraqi Officials Discussing the Iran-Iraq War and the Al-Fao Battle," 18 April 1988.

*SH-SHTP-A-001-232, "Iraqi Officials Discussing the Occupation of Kuwait," 7 August 1990.

*SH-SHTP-A-001-233, "Saddam and Iraqi Officials Discussing Turkish, Russian and Chinese Perceptions of Iraq's Occupation of Kuwait," 7 August 1990.

*SH-SHTP-A-001-234, "Saddam and His Advisers Discussing Planned Actions in Kuwait following the Initial Invasion," undated (circa 5–7 August 1990).

*SH-SHTP-A-001-235, "Saddam and Iraqi Officials Discussing Plans for Kuwait after the Invasion," undated (circa third week of September 1990).

*SH-SHTP-A-001-236, "Iraqi Officials Discussing Al-Fao, Iran, and Saudi Arabia," 13 January 1991.

*SH-SHTP-A-001-238, "Saddam and His Political Advisers Discussing International Interest in Iraqi Oil, Iraqi Army Deserters, and an Initiative to Settle Disputes with Saudi Arabia," 3 September 1994.

*SH-SHTP-A-001-241, "Iraqi Officials Briefing Saddam on the Performance of Iraqi Troops in Kuwait," 1 May 1991.

*SH-SHTP-A-001-242, "Saddam and Military Officials Discussing Lessons Learned from the 1991 Gulf War," undated (circa 1993).

*SH-SHTP-A-001-243, "Iraqi Military Officials Discussing the 1991 Gulf War," undated (circa 1993).

*SH-SHTP-A-001-244, "Iraqi Military Officials Discussing Air Force and Army Performance during the 1991 Gulf War," 27 November 1995.

*SH-SHTP-A-001-247, "Saddam and High Ranking Officials Discussing Military Operations in the Iran-Iraq War," 27 March 1984.

*SH-SHTP-A-001-251, "Saddam and Top Political Advisers Discussing a United Nations Air Survey Request," undated (circa September–October 1991).

*SH-SHTP-A-001-252, "Saddam and the Council of Ministers Discussing UN Sanctions and Possible US Invasion," undated (circa July 1992).

*SH-SHTP-A-001-253, "Saddam and Top Political Advisers Discussing Relations with Saudi Arabia and Other Neighbors," undated (circa 9–10 October 1994).

*SH-SHTP-A-001-254, "Saddam and Top Political Advisers Discussing Diplomacy with the United States and Russia," undated (circa March 1995).

*SH-SHTP-A-001-255, "Saddam and Top Political Advisers Discussing the Agricultural Situation in Iraq and UN Inspection Teams," undated (circa January–February 1995).

*SH-SHTP-A-001-256, "Saddam and Top Political Advisers Discussing a Visit by Prime Minister Tariq Aziz to the United Nations Delegates," undated (circa November 1995).

*SH-SHTP-A-001-257, "Saddam and Iraqi Officials Discussing Conditions for a UN Security Council Visit," undated (circa 1998).

*SH-SHTP-A-001-259, "Saddam and Top Political Advisers Discussing Hussein Kamil's Mental Health and Problems with King Hussein of Jordan," 17 August 1995.

*SH-SHTP-A-001-260, "Saddam Discussing the Details of Hussein Kamil's Escape," undated (circa mid- to late August 1995).

*SH-SHTP-A-001-262, "Saddam and Top Political Advisers Discussing the Iraqi Invasion of Kuwait and International Positions on Iraq," undated (circa late 1994).

*SH-SHTP-A-001-263, "Saddam Discussing US Policy in the Gulf," undated (circa 1988).

*SH-SHTP-A-001-269, "Saddam and His Advisers Discuss Iraq's Compliance with UN Inspectors, UN Sanctions on Iraq, Iraqi Tribes, and Other Issues," undated (circa 1991–1992).

Video Files

SH-SHTP-V-000-589, "Saddam and Military Officials Discussing the Iran-Iraq War and the Al-Qadisiyyah Battle," undated (circa July–August 1988).

SH-SHTP-V-000-612, "Saddam and Senior Military Officials Discussing Efforts to Retake the Majnun Area," undated (circa summer 1988).

*SH-SHTP-V-001-237, "Saddam and Military Officials Discussing Lessons Learned in the Wake of the 1991 Gulf War," undated (circa 1993).

*SH-SHTP-V-001-250, "High Ranking Officers Discussing US and Coalition Aggression towards Iraq and Military Preparations for Expected Attacks" (1993).

Document Files

SH-AFGC-D-000-393, "Transcript of a Meeting of the General Command of the Armed Forces during the Iran-Iraq War and Telephone Conversations," (January 1981–October 1994).

SH-GMID-D-000-842, "General Military Intelligence Directorate (GMID) Intelligence Reports on Iran," (January 1980–July 1980).

SH-GMID-D-000-898, "General Military Intelligence Directorate (GMID) Memos Discussing Iranian Chemical Weapons Capability," (October 1987–September 1988).

SH-GMID-D-001-227, "Intelligence Reports on Iranian Military Capabilities Including Artillery, Air Power, Ammunitions, and Bases," 29 July 1980.

SH-IDGS-D-000-383, "General Security Directorate Records regarding the Killing of Hussein Kamil," February 1996.

*SH-IDGS-D-001-213, "General Security Directorate Memorandum on the Dangers of the Cartoon Character Pokemon," 2001.

SH-IISX-D-000-407, "Report by the Director of Iraq's Intelligence Service on the Defection of Hussein Kamil," 29 August 1995.

SH-IISX-D-000-768, "Reports Concerning Hussein Kamil's Treason and Escape with Reference to a Uranium Enrichment Program," (June 1995–July 1997).

SH-INMD-D-000-657, "Report from Husam Mohammad Amin, Director of the National Monitoring Directorate, on Hussein Kamil," 14 August 1995.

*SH-IZAR-D-001-246, "Iraqi Military Correspondence Regarding an Experimental Chemical Weapons Attack on 27 June 1985," (July–August 1985).

SH-MICN-D-000-741, "Correspondence between the Military Industrialization Commission and the Petro Chemical Group regarding a Letter from A. Q. Khan Offering to Assist Iraq in Developing a Uranium Enrichment Program," October 1990.

*SH-MICN-D-001-249, "Reports and Correspondence between the Military Industrialization Commission and the Ministry of Defense regarding Chemical Weapons Production," 31 December 1990.

*SH-MICN-D-001-277, "Saddam Visiting a Military Industrialization Commission Facility," 27 April 1992.

SH-MISC-D-000-203, "Report on an Iraqi Delegation Visit to Russia and France," 6 April 1996.

SH-MISC-D-000-903, "Book on the Events of the 1991 Gulf War," 25 September 1992.

*SH-MISC-D-001-204, "Diary of Barzan al-Tikriti," undated (circa 2000).

*SH-MISC-D-001-245, "Pictures of Saddam and Izaat Ibrahim Al-Duri dated 2002 and Special Security Organization Administrative Correspondence dated 1999," (1999–2002).

*SH-MISC-D-001-271, "Collection of Saddam's Personal and Family Pictures Including Uday's Wedding," undated.

*SH-MISC-D-001-272, "Photos of Saddam on Different Occasions," November 2002.

*SH-MISC-D-001-273, "Photos of Saddam with High Ranking Military Officers and Government Officials," (May 2002–February 2003).

*SH-MISC-D-001-275, "Pictures of Saddam and an Identity Card," undated.

*SH-MISC-D-001-276, "Photos of Iraqi Officials on Various Occasions," April 2001.

*SH-MISC-D-001-278, "Taha Yasin Ramadan's Photo Album," April 2000.

SH-PDWN-D-000-240, "Letters Authorizing the Execution of an Air Force Warrant Officer for Sabotaging a Plane Engine," (April–May 1986).

SH-PDWN-D-000-499, "Order from Saddam to Give $25,000 to the Families of Palestinian Suicide Bombers," 4 March 2002.

SH-PDWN-D-000-533, "Saddam Meeting with a Soviet Delegation," 6 October 1990.

SH-PDWN-D-000-546, "General Military Intelligence Directorate Assessment of Israeli Intentions toward Iraq," 22 May 1990.

SH-PDWN-D-000-607, "Transcript of Meetings between Saddam and Senior Advisers," (25 February 1985–31 July 1986).

SH-PDWN-D-000-730, "Transcript of an Armed Forces General Command Meeting," 26 May 1988.

*SH-PDWN-D-001-221, "Minutes of the Meeting between Saddam and As'ad Bayud Al-Tamimi, the Chief of the Islamic Jihad Movement (Bait Al-Maqdis)," 30 September 1990.

*SH-PDWN-D-001-248, "Correspondence between Presidential Diwan and other Iraqi Authorities Discussing Emergency Evacuation Plans for Iraqi Cities in the Event of an Attack Using Weapons of Mass Destruction," 29 December 1990.

SH-PDWN-D-001-270, "Transcript of Saddam and Military Officials Discussing the Iran-Iraq War," 29 July 1993.

SH-SHTP-D-000-557, "Saddam and His Senior Advisers Discussing Iraq's Historical Rights to Kuwait and the US Position," 15 December 1990.

SH-SHTP-D-000-559, "Saddam and His Inner Circle Discussing Relations with Various Arab States, Russia, China, and the United States," undated (circa 4–20 November 1979).

SH-SHTP-D-000-609, "Saddam and His Inner Circle Discussing the Iran-Contra Affair," undated (circa late 1986 or early 1987).

SH-SHTP-D-000-759, "Saddam Meeting with Members of Al-'Ubur Conference, National Command, Iraqi Regional Command and Revolutionary Command Council," undated (circa 1994).

SH-SHTP-D-000-760, "Saddam and Political Advisers Discussing the Production of Biological Materials in Iraq, the Iran-Iraq War, UN Inspections, and the Arab-Israeli Conflict," undated (circa 1996).

SH-SHTP-D-000-797, "Saddam and Iraqi Commanders Discussing Weapons Inspections and how the United States intends to continue the Sanctions on Iraq," undated (circa June 1996).

SH-SHTP-D-000-818, "Saddam and Iraqi Officials Preparing for the Commencement of US strikes on 15 January 1991," undated (circa early January 1991).

SH-SPPC-D-000-235, "Letter to Saddam from Hussein Kamil Tendering his Resignation," 27 December 1992.

SH-SPPC-D-000-334, "Transcript of a Meeting between Saddam and a Russian Delegation," 18 July 2001.

SH-SPPC-D-000-498, "Letter and Memo Responding to Ambassador Nizar Hamdun's Criticisms of the Iraqi Regime," November 1995.

SH-SPPC-D-000-915, "Letters to Saddam from Hussein Kamil Requesting Forgiveness," February 1996.

*SH-SPPC-D-001-258, "Letter from Al-Majid Clan to Saddam Explaining Why They Killed Hussein Kamil Despite a Government Pardon," 23 February 1996.

*SH-SSOX-D-001-214, "Lecture by the Director of the Special Security Institute on Zionist Intelligence Guidelines and Duties," 11 September 2002.

Index